Christ Child

Synkrisis: Comparative Approaches to Early Christianity in Greco-Roman Culture

SERIES EDITORS:

Dale B. Martin (Yale University) and L. L. Welborn (Fordham University)

Synkrisis is a project that invites scholars of early Christianity and the Greco-Roman world to collaborate toward the goal of rigorous comparison. Each volume in the series provides immersion in an aspect of Greco-Roman culture, so as to make possible a comparison of the controlling logics that emerge from the discourses of Greco-Roman and early Christian writers. In contrast to older "history of religions" approaches, which looked for similarities between religions in order to posit relations of influence and dependency, Synkrisis embraces a fuller conception of the complexities of culture, viewing Greco-Roman religions and early Christianity as members of a comparative class. The differential comparisons promoted by Synkrisis may serve to refine and correct the theoretical and historical models employed by scholars who seek to understand and interpret the Greco-Roman world. With its allusion to the rhetorical exercises of the Greco-Roman world, the series title recognizes that the comparative enterprise is a construction of the scholar's mind and serves the scholar's theoretical interests.

Stephen J. Davis

Christ Child

CULTURAL MEMORIES OF A YOUNG JESUS

Yale UNIVERSITY PRESS
New Haven &
London

Published with assistance from the Louis Stern Memorial Fund and the Frederick W. Hilles Publication Fund of Yale University.

Yale University Press books may be purchased in quantity for educational, business, or promotional use. For information, please e-mail sales.press@yale.edu (U.S. office) or sales@yaleup.co.uk (U.K. office).

Set in Sabon Roman type by Westchester Book Group.
Printed in the United States of America.

Library of Congress Cataloging-in-Publication Data

Davis, Stephen J.
Christ Child : cultural memories of a young Jesus / Stephen J. Davis.
pages cm.—(Synkrisis: comparative approaches to early Christianity in Greco-Roman culture)
Includes bibliographical references and index.

ISBN 978-0-300-14945-6 (cloth : alk. paper) 1. Jesus Christ—Childhood.
I. Title.
BT320.D38 2014
232.92—dc23

2013035683

A catalogue record for this book is available from the British Library.

This paper meets the requirements of ANSI/NISO Z39.48-1992 (Permanence of Paper).

10 9 8 7 6 5 4 3 2 1

Contents

Acknowledgments

This book has taken shape over the past half decade, and to paraphrase President Barack Obama, I did not build it alone. Before me, other scholars did foundational work that made my own research possible. Above all, I must acknowledge my indebtedness to the text critical work of Tony Burke, whose CCSA volume, *De infantia Iesu evangelium Thomae graece* (2010), is an indispensible resource for people working on early Christian infancy traditions. I also stand on the shoulders of other recent scholars whose research has proven invaluable in a variety of different ways: among them, Reidar Aasgaard, Chris Frilingos, Stephen Gero, Cornelia Horn, Lucas van Rompay, and Sever Voicu on sources related to Jesus' childhood; Jan and Aleida Assman, Paul Connerton, Astrid Erll, and Maurice Halwachs on the sociology of cultural memory; and Wolfgang Iser, Hans Robert Jauss, Stanley Fish, William A. Johnson, and Peter Kivy on reading and (oral) performance. I hope that my approach to this material contributes meaningfully to the ongoing conversation about the readerly uses to which Jesus' childhood has been put, from antiquity to the present day.

Several trips to visit European churches, libraries, and museum archives have helped facilitate my research and writing. In December 2009, I made a brief visit to St. Martin's Church in the village of Zillis, Switzerland, with funds from my Yale research account, to examine the painted panel ceiling that is the subject of Appendix C. I am also grateful to the Whitney Humanities Center at Yale University for three separate A. Whitney Griswold Faculty Research Grants.

The first Griswold grant funded a weeklong visit to Oxfordshire, England, in June 2009, where I examined a copy of the *Arabic Gospel of the Infancy* (Oxon. Bodl. Or. 350), housed in the Bodleian Library at Oxford University, and visited medieval chapels featuring wall paintings related to Jesus' childhood.

The second Griswold grant sponsored a trip to Athens, Greece, in June 2010, where I conducted research into the representation of children in funerary reliefs at the National Archaeological Museum and paid a visit to the Department of Childhood, Toys, and Games at the Benaki Museum. I am very grateful to the department director, Maria Argyriadi, for giving me special access to the Benaki collection and for a stimulating conversation during my visit.

The third Griswold grant helped cover travel and incidental expenses related to a three-week stay in June 2011 at the Institutum Judaicum Delitzschianum at the Westfälische Wilhelms-Universität Münster, where I researched ancient and medieval Jewish traditions related to Jesus' childhood. My deepest thanks go to the institute director, Prof. Dr. Folker Siegert (now emeritus), who served as my official Gastgeber for that fortnight and who (along with his wife, Inge) showed me warm and generous hospitality.

My research stay in Münster was also supported by a renewal of my Humboldt Fellowship, and I want to express my gratitude to the Alexander von Humboldt Foundation and to the Humboldt Haus for making that research possible. Thanks are also due to Stephen Emmel, who had originally served as my Humboldt Gastgeber during my initial fellowship year in 2006–7. Our conversations over coffees and dinners are fond memories from my return visit in 2011. Finally, I would be remiss if I did not mention my dear friends Wolfgang and Heidi Zierau, who (along with their daughter, Nicole) hosted me for dinner one evening during the late stages of Heidi's battle with cancer. That battle ended in January 2012, and I hope that this book does its small part to honor her memory.

My preparation of this book for publication also benefited from opportunities to present the results of my research at different workshops and conference venues. I presented material from chapter 7 to members of the Late Antiquity Research Group of Central New York (LARCNY) in Syracuse, N.Y. (March 2010), and to participants at the Conference on Asceticism and Exegesis in Early Christianity in Siegen, Germany (October 2011). From 2009 to 2012, at four successive annual meetings of the Society of Biblical Literature (SBL), I presented papers with material drawn from chapters 3, 4, and 6 and Appendix C. Finally, in the summer of 2013, I was also invited to share my work from chapter 7 with the members of the Association pour l'étude de la littérature apocryphe chrétienne (AELAC) in Dole, France.

An earlier version of chapter 3 appeared under the title "Bird Watching in the Infancy Gospel of Thomas: From Child's Play to Rituals of Divine Discernment," in a Festschrift for my Yale colleague Harold Attridge, entitled *Portraits of Jesus: Essays in Christology*, ed. S. E. Myers (Tübingen: Mohr Siebeck, 2012), 125–53. I want to thank the editor of that volume, Susan E. Myers, and the editors at Mohr Siebeck for permission to include a revised version of that piece in this book.

As I indicate at the beginning of chapter 1, this book has also been substantially shaped by my teaching experiences at Yale. In particular, I would like to thank Ludger Viefhues-Bailey, with whom I co-taught the undergraduate course "Memory, Culture, and Religion" in the spring of 2008, and Hindy Najman, with whom I co-taught the graduate seminar "Reading Practices in Antiquity" in the spring of 2012. My thanks also extend to the students in these two classes, as well as in my solo-taught courses "Patristic Greek" (spring 2010), "Christians and Muslims in the Arab World" (2010 and 2012), and "Arabic Christian Literature and Theology" (spring 2012), where some of the relevant primary source material was vetted.

Several scholars have been generous with their time and energies in reading either all or part of this book and in offering critical feedback. On this score, I especially want to thank Tony Burke, Andrew Jacobs, Rebecca Krawiec, Dale Martin, Hindy Najman, and the two outside reviewers, Chris Frilingos and Annette Yoshiko Reed, for their exceedingly helpful comments and critiques. I also express my deep gratitude to Yale University Press editor Jennifer Banks, who has been a guiding hand and a valuable conversation partner throughout the process of writing this book, and to Otto Bohlmann and Rona Johnston Gordon, for their meticulous work of copyediting, proofreading, and indexing.

In a book about the child Jesus and social memory, it should not be surprising that my work has given me ample occasion to reflect on my own youth, and in chapters 3, 4, and 5 I use vignettes from my own past interactions with parents, friends, and teachers as a (playful) device for thinking about how Jesus' childhood was remembered. Making cameo appearances in these vignettes are my father (Donald E. Davis), two of my childhood friends (Mark Ashley and Mike McMinn), and my elementary school principal (Mr. Kiscaden). I extend my thanks to them and to their past selves for unwittingly indulging me as I conscripted them for this purpose.

Finally, let me turn to immediate family. I reached the final stage of completing this manuscript as my elder daughter was just starting college, as my son was just starting eleventh grade, and as my younger daughter was just starting high school. In this context, it should also not be surprising that the writing of this book has given me many occasions to reflect back on my own experience as a parent and on how my own children's younger years have retreated all too quickly into a partially remembered past. It is only appropriate, then, that I dedicate this book to them—to Evanleigh, Harrison, and Rowyn, who find themselves now on the cusp of adulthood—and (as always and as promised) to my wife, Jenny, with whom I share cherished and constantly evolving memories of a life spent together.

PART I

Methods and Approaches

1

Cultural Memories of a Young Jesus

"The past is never dead. It's not even past."

—William Faulkner,
Requiem for a Nun (1951), act 1, scene 3

In a Yale University course I taught entitled "Memory, Culture, and Religion," I opened the class by asking students to identify their very first memories from childhood. The response was overwhelming: some shared memories of a favorite toy or keepsake; others an early image of their mother or a sibling; still others a landmark event in the life of their family. As the students reminisced, what was striking was the way that their memories of childhood almost invariably turned out to have been mediated and determinatively shaped by subsequent circumstances, relationships, and activities, and especially by different kinds of communal acts—telling and retelling stories in family circles; or viewing photo albums and slide shows with other family members.

If we were able to transport ourselves back in time, we would discover, I suspect, that most of the events being "recalled" did not take place exactly in the way that they were later remembered: certain details would be added or left out for reasons ranging from the strategic to the innocuous. And occasionally we would find that the events in question never took place at all—created out of the shared muse of family memory lore.

These observations from my class are, in fact, consistent with recent findings in the sociological study of human memory. Beginning with Maurice Halbwachs's work in the first half of the twentieth century, there has been a burgeoning appreciation among sociologists for how human remembrance of the past is constructed in the present and framed by the dynamics of social groups, especially by their practices and physical environment. More recently, scholars such as Pierre Nora, Jan Assmann, Paul Connerton, Aleida Assmann, and Astrid Erll have shed more light on the role that physical and practical "sites"—including texts, bodies, landscapes, and rituals—play in the cultivation of social memory. Nora adopted the phrase "sites of memory" (*lieux de mémoire*) to refer to material artifacts (including texts, images, and physical spaces) that serve to re-present the past in symbolic and/or functional ways.

In this book, *Christ Child: Cultural Memories of a Young Jesus,* I try to translate these insights to ancient Christian recollections of Jesus' childhood. As we shall see, such recollections were shaped by repeated acts of storytelling, and by a range of cultural and religious "sites"—from household, funerary, and divinatory practices to athletic and educational settings in the Graeco-Roman world; and from pilgrimage and polemics to science and asceticism in early medieval Jewish-Christian and Christian-Muslim encounters. In the process we shall see that such cultural memories of a young Jesus were mediated not only through the reading of texts but also through the hearing of stories and the viewing of images. The product of this work, I hope, will be a richer, more textured account of the way that histories of interpretation happen, and a more flexible and expansive sense of how stories and texts about Jesus were read, retold, transmitted, and transformed in and through a wide array of late ancient and early medieval *lieux de mémoire*.

The centerpiece of this study is a collection of stories most commonly known as the *Infancy Gospel of Thomas*. But this is a modern title: in earlier times it was known in Greek as the *Paidika*, the "Childhood Deeds" of Jesus, and that is how I refer to it throughout this book. Preserved in Greek, Latin, Syriac, Arabic, Slavonic, Georgian, and Ethiopic, the contents and order of the *Paidika* vary (sometimes quite significantly) from manuscript to manuscript. Such variations reflect changes brought about by the activity of storytellers, scribes, and translators across the centuries. But when one compares the different versions, it is possible to identify something of a "core content"—a set of stories shared by the majority of early textual witnesses.[1] Especially prominent among them are tales involving miracles, cursing, and classrooms.

Most of the manuscripts begin with the story of a five-year-old Jesus playing by a rushing stream, forming pools and purifying them, and then forming clay birds out of the mud at the bottom of the pools. When accused of performing these actions on the Sabbath, he claps his hands and brings the birds to life (ch. 2). Two cursing stories follow. When his accuser (the son of the high priest Annas) harasses him by trying to destroy the pools that he had formed, the young Jesus causes him to wither away and die (ch. 3). Immediately after this, Jesus curses to death a boy who runs into his shoulder on the street (ch. 4). Both of these incidents draw a rebuke from his father, Joseph (ch. 5).

The next sequence of stories involves Jesus' encounters in the classroom with a teacher named Zacchaeus (chs. 6–8). The teacher tries to instruct the child in the alphabet, beginning with the letter *alpha.* Jesus first refuses to respond, and his irritated teacher strikes him on the head. Then after an angry outburst, Jesus recites all the letters from alpha to omega, accuses his teacher of not really understanding their true nature, and proceeds to interpret the form of the alpha in cryptic terms. Zacchaeus is left baffled by the child's wisdom and returns him to Joseph unsure of whether he is a god or an angel, and with a word Jesus lifts the curses that he had previously leveled against his antagonists.

The rest of the *Paidika* consists of a mélange of other miracle stories and school scenes. While Jesus is playing in an upstairs room with other children, a boy accidently falls to his death. Accused of pushing him, Jesus immediately raises the boy, who testifies to Jesus' innocence (ch. 9). When a seven-year-old Jesus is sent to fetch water for his mother and the pitcher he is carrying breaks, he collects the spilt water in his cloak and returns home with it (ch. 10). When sowing seeds in the field with his father, Joseph, Jesus reaps one hundred measures from just one measure of grain (ch. 11). At the age of eight, he is an apprentice in his father's carpentry shop and miraculously stretches a beam of wood that had been cut too short (ch. 12). Two more school episodes that follow seem to recapitulate elements of the first. Just like his predecessor, Jesus' second teacher tries to teach him the letters and ends up striking him when the boy challenges his authority. This time, however, Jesus responds with a curse, and the teacher falls down and dies (ch. 13). Next, a third teacher brings Jesus into his classroom, and the child utters awe-inspiring words from the lectern, which prompts his instructor to return him to Joseph as not in need of teaching. Pleased by these words, Jesus proclaims that his former teacher would be saved and released from his curse (ch. 14). These school scenes are followed by another miracle account in which Jesus heals his brother James, who has been bitten on the hand by a snake (ch. 15).[2] Finally, the sequence of stories concludes with a retelling of Jesus' encounter at the age of twelve with the teachers in the Temple from the Gospel of Luke 2:41–52 (ch. 17).

Unfortunately, this rather quick-and-dirty plot summary belies a much more complex situation. Historically and textually speaking, the story presented by the *Paidika* is far from seamless. It is known for its controversial contents and reputation: in chapter 1, I discuss the turbulent treatment of the *Paidika* in modern scholarship and contested evaluations of Jesus' childhood, and in light of these debates I propose a new (more constructive) approach—one grounded in the study of cultural memory. The ancient history of the *Paidika* is just as vexing as its modern legacy: in chapter 2, I explore the difficulties faced in reconstructing the early history and form of the text and in assessing how late ancient and early medieval audiences would have encountered such stories. In the end, the goal of these first two chapters is to present something of a primer for the rest of the book, in which I trace the idiosyncratic pathways that these stories traveled in their history of interpretation.

A Brief History of Scholarly Disrespect

The modern scholarly "rediscovery" of the *Paidika* took place in 1675, when the German historian Peter Lambeck (Petrus Lambecius) quoted several lines from a Greek manuscript of the text in his catalogue of library holdings at Vienna. In the same catalogue, he also cited another copy of the work he had come across in Paris.[3] Within thirty years, a partial edition of the Vienna manuscript and a complete one of the Parisian text would be published.[4] In the nineteenth century, new editions of the text incorporated evidence from additional manuscripts written in Greek and Latin (as well as Syriac and other languages).[5]

As the contents of the *Paidika* came to light, it quickly became clear that the text was not to most early modern scholars' tastes, and they had no hesitation in voicing their decided displeasure. In the eighteenth and nineteenth centuries, several scholars who commented on the text made a point of lambasting its literary and ethical character. On stylistic grounds, the text was likened to a cheap novel and judged to be "barbarous," "gross," and full of "miracle-mongering."[6] Its contents were seen to imply "a very low state of intellect and morals" on the part of its author and readers, who were assumed to have been associated with the "popular" masses (certainly not the Greek literary and cultural elite).[7] The young Jesus portrayed in its pages was likewise spared no invective: his actions were alternatively castigated as "violent and vindictive," "bizarre and completely spiteful," or "offensive and repulsive."[8]

These kinds of disapproving characterizations were often linked with efforts to paint these stories as "heretical" in their theology and outlook. For quite a long time, the *Paidika* was assumed to have had its origins in early Christian Gnostic circles.[9] Known to modern scholars as the *Infancy Gospel of Thomas*, the work was frequently confused with the *Gospel of Thomas* (which prior to its 1945 discovery at Nag Hammadi in Egypt was known only from hostile secondhand reports by early Christian heresiologists). Even after it became clear that the *Gospel of Thomas* found in that cache of documents was a completely different work, assumptions about the *Paidika*'s allegedly Gnostic origins lingered in the face of evidence to the contrary.[10]

Indeed, derisive attitudes toward the *Paidika* have persisted into the late twentieth and early twenty-first centuries. In recent years, the tales about Jesus' childhood have still been considered by some to be "altogether beyond the bounds of common sense"[11] and "lacking in good taste."[12] The child Jesus has been derogated as an "*enfant terrible*,"[13] a mischief-maker who was guilty of "ridiculous and shabby pranks,"[14] and an "incorrigible," "cruel," and "awful" boy whose "menacing recalcitrance" quickly earns him "a very bad reputation."[15] Indeed, as recently as 2011, the author of a monograph dedicated to reconstructing the *Paidika*'s social setting and audience could write, "It is no wonder that this infancy gospel has . . . caused bewilderment and even disgust among present day readers. With its mixture of ingratiating and unsavory elements, particularly in its depiction of Jesus, . . . [the *Paidika*] has become an object that scholarship has had great problems addressing."[16] Such unrelentingly pejorative descriptions need to be unmasked for what they are—perspectives too often still shaped by inherited Victorian-era assumptions about what constitutes good literature (or proper ethical behavior), and by unacknowledged canonical biases that judge "apocryphal" literature by standards different from those applied to the "scriptural" books of the New Testament.[17]

In this book, I push back against this tendency to read the *Paidika* as a particularly "strange" piece of ancient literature.[18] Just because a story appears peculiar to our eyes does not mean that it would have been equally out of sync with the (diverse and often fractious) sensibilities and expectations of ancient readers.[19] To overemphasize the shock value of these infancy stories, I think, is to risk missing the ways in which those tales in fact played off late ancient perceptions about the figure of Jesus and about childhood as a life stage. As we shall see, in the hands of such early Christian storytellers, the young Jesus proved to be eminently malleable: almost like Silly Putty, he took on the unmistakable imprint of any cultural object or data with which he came into contact.

Ancient Childhood and the Paidika*'s Portrait of Jesus*

Fortunately, in the past two decades, a handful of scholars have begun making more of a concerted effort to situate the *Paidika* in relation to everyday Graeco-Roman and early Christian social settings and expectations about childhood. Rather than dismissing the stories out of hand as absurd or laughable, historians of the late ancient world have started taking the

Paidika seriously as a source of cultural data—as a text that supplies us with important information about what was considered typical, and what was considered atypical, in the literary representation of children as social actors in the late ancient Mediterranean world.

This recent trend in *Paidika* research has coincided with the emergence of childhood studies in the late 1980s and early 1990s as a thriving, interdisciplinary field of sociological research. The impact that this field has on the study of children in late antiquity may be measured in the number of publications produced over the past twenty-plus years. In addition to historical surveys and summaries, critical assessments of the state of the field, and bibliographical essays,[20] there has been a plethora of books and articles published on the specific topics of birth and nursing,[21] childrearing and discipline,[22] orphanhood and adoption,[23] early education,[24] illness, death, and burial,[25] and a range of other subjects, including evidence for disabilities among the young and problems associated with physical and sexual abuse in ancient and medieval societies.[26]

One important line of inquiry has homed in on the question of whether ancient Greeks and Romans would even have defined "childhood" as a distinctive life stage. In his landmark 1960 book, *L'enfant et la vie familiale sous l'Ancien Régime* (translated into English two years later under the quite different title *Centuries of Childhood: A Social History of Family Life*),[27] Philippe Ariès put forward the revolutionary thesis that "childhood"—both as a concept and as a discrete social life stage—was in fact a modern invention that did not apply as such to premodern societies. Ariès's work has since been critiqued: while he helpfully deconstructed certain unexamined modern conceptions about childhood as a static, universal life stage, he failed to account for evidence regarding the role that conceptions of childhood played in shaping social identities in premodern cultures, even if those conceptions were not always as clearly and consistently demarcated as we would like.[28]

The study of children in early Christianity has proven to be equally robust, as increased attention has focused on the role of the young in both theological discourse and social practice—from the use of children as ready-made metaphors and examples (alternatively valorized or problematized) in sermons and treatises, to the donation and induction of children into monasteries as novices.[29] This body of work has had a leavening effect on recent *Paidika* research.

Several scholars have, to varying degrees, made observations about late ancient childhood as a pertinent social historical context for reading the stories of Jesus in the *Paidika*. Let me start with a brief mention of Ronald Hock, who touched on the sociological dimensions of the *Paidika* in discussing the tales about Jesus at school in his 1995 book, *The Infancy Gospels of James and Thomas*. Under the heading "Cultural Backgrounds," Hock noted how "the educational conventions of the elementary school classroom" informed the stories' details about what Jesus did when he was at school: from his oral recitation of the alphabet, to his receiving of corporal punishment administered by the teacher.[30] While Hock's treatment of such social data related to Graeco-Roman childhood was rather perfunctory, his observations would set the stage for more thorough and sustained investigations into how the portrayal of Jesus' childhood in the *Paidika* related to the lives and activities of children in late Roman society.

One scholar in particular was instrumental in advancing this line of inquiry. In 2001, Tony Burke completed a doctoral dissertation on the *Paidika* at the University of Toronto, and after almost another decade of research, he published the results of this work in a significantly revised and expanded form, under the title *De infantia Iesu evangelium Thomae graece* (2010).[31] While Burke's primary purpose was to publish critical editions of the four different Greek recensions of the *Paidika*, he also devoted considerable attention to the question of how Jesus' representation in the work might be linked to literary and material evidence from antiquity, especially pertaining to late Roman idealizations of childhood.[32]

In addition to his text critical work, one of Burke's landmark advances was in his nuanced reading of the role that Jesus' "idealized childhood" played in the *Paidika*. He notes parallels between the *Paidika* and other tales about the childhoods of extraordinary people—from immortals and gods, to cultural heroes such as emperors and philosophers.[33] Intriguing examples of such thematic correspondence include stories about the child Heracles killing snakes and killing a tutor for chastising him,[34] and about the Egyptian god Si-Osiri and the prophet Moses outwitting their teachers as children.[35] Why were ancient authors especially concerned with telling stories about how these figures manifested extraordinary virtue and uncanny wisdom already in their early years?[36] In such tales about heroic childhoods, Burke detected evidence for a more widespread "push toward adulthood" in late Roman society.[37] This "push" found literary expression in the biographical motif of the *puer senex* (the "old child"),[38] but it also came to visual expression in funerary epigraphs and images in which deceased children were portrayed in idealized, adult-like poses.[39] In this context, he asked the question, "What was it about the experience of childhood in antiquity that led the adults who created this material to strip away childhood qualities from their subjects?"[40]

With this question in his sights, he drew a sharp contrast between the Romans' adult memories of their childhoods (which, according to him, were characterized by a general disregard, anxiety, disinterest, and desire to forget that period of life) and their corresponding eagerness to imagine and idealize the childhoods of their gods and heroes. Borrowing a concept from the art historian Janet Huskinson, Burke labeled the resulting "tendency to portray the child as older than her or his years" as a kind of "social viewing" whereby such age discrepancies were rendered invisible to the reader/viewer, and whereby certain strongly marked cultural expectations regarding children's passage to adulthood came to the surface in both literature and art.[41] In this way, Burke analyzed the stories about Jesus in the *Paidika* in terms of the discursive uses that adults made of children in ancient Roman society—or, to adapt a turn of phrase by Claude Lévi-Strauss, how adults used children as objects "to think with."[42]

Burke's pioneering work in this area had the effect of opening the door wide for further investigations of the *Paidika*'s use of childhood, and a handful of scholars stepped across this threshold with diverging aims and results. Some, not content with Burke's reading of "idealized childhood," on the contrary searched for traces of verisimilitude and correspondence in the text—narrative details that may reflect actual social expectations related to children in the early centuries CE.

Thus, Cornelia Horn and John Martens, in their 2009 book *"Let the Little Children Come to Me": Childhood and Children in Early Christianity,* asked whether and to what extent the *Paidika* can serve as a helpful source for reconstructing the everyday lives of ancient Roman and Jewish children. To this question, the two authors offered a somewhat ambivalent answer. On the one hand, they acknowledged Burke's point: that the *Paidika*'s stories of Jesus as a child depict him "transcend(ing) the common norms," and thus do not give direct access to actual children's lives. On the other hand, they still affirmed that "common cultural understandings of childhood and family life often underlie such stereotypical portrayals."[43] In their view, stories in which Jesus learns a trade from his father or does chores for his mother provide us with "a rather authentic picture of a child's work in the service of an ordinary family in the ancient world," and "allow us to examine what second- and third-century Christians deemed reasonable to expect for a boy growing up in a Galilean village."[44] Other scenes—in which his teachers take Jesus into their homes as their pupil, instruct him in the alphabet as a first stage of education, and administer corporal punishment as a form of discipline—likewise suggested to them possible correspondences with Jewish and/or Graeco-Roman educational conventions.[45] In the end, while Horn and Martens nominally acknowledged the difficulties of working with "idealized" literary portrayals, they nonetheless maintained that these stories must reveal something about "the mundane reality of a child's life in the second century."[46]

Reidar Aasgaard, in his book *The Childhood of Jesus: Decoding the Apocryphal Infancy Gospel of Thomas* (2009), also showed considerable confidence that the *Paidika*'s "narrative world"—and especially its depictions of Jesus as a child—can serve as "a window into the world of its author and audience, or at least into a world generally recognizable to them."[47] While Aasgaard also acknowledged the particular challenges involved in trying to trace direct lines of connections between the *Paidika* tales and the "real world," he nonetheless insisted that the text may indeed "have a close affinity to some specific reality," and thus reflect "the setting(s) in which it originated and was retold."[48]

On the basis of such assumptions, Aasgaard went about the task of cataloguing textual elements that evoke details of "daily life and social relations," especially life in rural and village settings in the eastern Mediterranean.[49] These descriptive details include story settings (houses, workshops, schoolrooms, streets and gathering places, streams and wells, farmland and forests), as well as objects and foodstuffs tied to daily activities (pitchers used to fetch water, grain used to make bread, clothing, playthings, beds, yokes and plows, books and lecterns). In addition, Aasgaard itemized the social values evidenced in the stories (such as respect for peers, reverence and obedience toward parents and teachers, erudition) and noted the curious ways that the *Paidika*'s Jesus seems to challenge and disrupt those ideals.[50] Aasgaard's conclusion was that Jesus' rebelliousness may represent traces of a kind of social protest or resistance associated with "middle, or lower middle, class strata" in "the eastern Mediterranean countryside."[51]

According to Aasgaard's reconstruction, then, the *Paidika* was "a popular tale from early rural Christianity," rooted in the oral culture of "a middle/lower class stratum,"[52] designed especially for the purposes of information, entertainment, and edification.[53] It should be noted that Aasgaard's use of the category "popular" in his analysis is out of step with the work of recent historians of late antiquity who have critiqued "two-tiered" models that posit a sharp dichotomy between "popular" versus "elite" religiosity.[54] Yet, it was on the basis of these assumptions about the edifying and entertaining purposes of "popular literature" that Aasgaard went on to make his boldest claim yet—namely, that the main target audience of the *Paidika* was in fact not adults but *early Christian children*. For him, the *Paidika* therefore constituted "Christianity's first children's story."[55] Aasgaard's "child perspective" approach, which drew on "modern psychological insights on children,"[56] subsequently met with considerable skepticism. Burke, for instance, criticized Aasgaard in particular for failing "to present any comparative literature from antiquity written for such an audience."[57]

Such critiques of Aasgaard's conclusions have not stopped other scholars from revisiting questions about childhood and narrative verisimilitude in the *Paidika.* One example of this continued interest was Ursula Ulrike Kaiser's recent article "Jesus als Kind" ("Jesus as Child").[58] While she, like Burke, rejected Aasgaard's argument that the *Paidika* was intended for children,[59] Kaiser nonetheless shared with Aasgaard a tendency (1) to read it as a useful source on the lives of ancient children, and (2) to draw on contemporary psychological categories in trying to reconstruct the profile of the work's early audience. First, on the question of the social realism of Jesus' childhood, Kaiser was especially troubled by how to account for scenes showing Jesus cursing others to death—a data set that seemingly did not suggest a readily apparent link to everyday children's activities. To resolve this question, she drew comparisons to the mischievous children of the gods in other religious traditions and suggested that such actions might have had particular associations with the kinds of tricks that Graeco-Roman children actually played on each other.[60] Second, on the question of audience, she argued that the *Paidika* was intended not for children but rather for the *parents of children.* In making this argument, she appealed to her own life experience "as the mother of a six-year-old and a seven-year-old son," conjecturing that ancient parents must have been just as stressed out and doubtful about their success as their modern counterparts. Accordingly, she imagined that such stories would have brought a certain "relief" (*Entlastung*) to parents since it would have been clear to them from these stories that the child Jesus "had violent conflict with other children, broke dishes, and behaved impudently and in a know-it-all way over against his parents and teachers," just like the readers' own children.[61] It was in this context that Kaiser suggested that the *Paidika* be seen as "a children's book for adults."[62] Kaiser's use of contemporary parental psychology as a basis for historical reconstruction, however, proved just as problematic as Aasgaard's assumptions about a correspondence between modern children's reading practices and what children did in ancient households.

In any case, Horn and Martens, Aasgaard, and Kaiser all rest uneasy with the emphasis Burke placed on the *Paidika*'s Jesus as an adult in a child's guise and with the strong dichotomy Burke set up between "the harsh everyday reality of children and adult idealization of them."[63] In their eyes, Burke's conclusions failed to appreciate fully the ways in which the Jesus of the *Paidika* was represented as a "realistic" child in his physical appearance, personality, activities, interaction with others, and gender socialization.[64] In response, each of these scholars tried to narrow the gap between the social world and the text by stressing corresponding (rather than contrasting) elements.

While these considerations of the *Paidika*'s Jesus as a true-to-life child represented a pendulum swing away from Burke's emphasis, there has been at least one scholar who has recognized the virtues of Burke's more discursive approach: Chris Frilingos, whose article "No Child Left Behind: Knowledge and Violence in the *Infancy Gospel of Thomas*" was published in the same year as Aasgaard's monograph.[65] Frilingos's primary concern in that article was to relate the stories about Jesus in school to Graeco-Roman *paideia,* the standards and practices associated with the instruction of children in the ancient Mediterranean world. Yet, Frilingos was not satisfied with drawing simple lines of connection between the stories and the social world that engendered them. Instead, his goal was "to put the gospel in relation to important cultural problems of the day," by considering the stories as crucibles for cultural negotiation in matters pertaining to childhood.[66] In reading the schoolroom scenes in the *Paidika,* Frilingos trained his eye on Jesus' ability in the stories to "play Greek as well as any native Greek," and on how Joseph's and his teachers' acts of corporal punishment are revealed as impotent. For Frilingos, children's education in the *Paidika* is a "contact zone," and the classroom is "a space in which tradition could be explored and challenged . . . a plausible setting for thinking about legitimated violence."[67] In this way, Frilingos followed Burke by recognizing that "the childhood stories about Jesus addressed 'grown-up' questions of power and authority" and by returning the focus to the *Paidika* as "an instance of (adults) 'thinking with children.' "[68]

This selective summary of recent scholarship reveals the contours of important ongoing debates related to childhood in the *Paidika.* While all have agreed that the work scrutinizes the subject of childhood in and through the figure of Jesus, there is lingering disagreement on two main issues. The first is related to whether and to what extent the *Paidika* was representing Jesus primarily in terms of adult or childhood attributes. Thus, while Burke analyzes Jesus as a *puer senex* whose childlike qualities have been "strip[ped] away" (in line with a larger cultural trend toward suppressing childhood memories and associations),[69] Horn and Martens, Aasgaard, and Kaiser have argued for verisimilitude between the activities of Jesus in the *Paidika* and the everyday experience of children in late Roman and/or Jewish societies. The second issue relates to questions of audience and agency. While Aasgaard has argued that the primary target audience of the *Paidika* was children, Burke, Kaiser, and Frilingos have rejected this thesis and pressed for various understandings of how an adult audience would have used the category of children (and more specifically, the child Jesus) "to think with"—whether for the valorization of adulthood, the assuaging of parental anxiety, or the renegotiation of cultural values related to ancient education.

In this book, I self-consciously situate my work in relation to each of these debates. On the one hand, with regard to questions of audience and agency, I stand firmly with the latter camp (Burke and company) in rejecting Aasgaard's notion that the *Paidika* gives special access to a "child perspective,"[70] and instead I direct my attention to the particular kinds of cultural work that ancient and medieval adults performed in and through their telling of stories about children. On the other hand, with regard to the representation of Jesus in the *Paidika,* I think it is important to recognize and give account for how this Jesus conforms to stereotypes of Graeco-Roman childhood in his activities and social environs, and yet also diverges from them in his expressions of power and authority.

The result is a hybrid figure: a heterogeneous subject or "contact zone."[71] To borrow the rhetorical language of Homi Bhabha, this Jesus is a "contradictory utterance," a figure "split in enunciation."[72] Or, to opt for a manuscript metaphor, the Jesus of the *Paidika* is a palimpsest on which the scripts of childhood, adulthood, and divinity are successively and simultaneously inscribed.[73] Part of my analysis of this palimpsestic Jesus is the identification of an emerging but still somewhat embryonic "christology" in which a range of human (both childlike and adult), superhuman, and divine characteristics intersect in a tenuous balance.[74]

The Christ Child in Cultural Memory: A New Sociological Approach to a History of Interpretation

One of the primary questions I ask in this book is how the hybridity and multiplexity of this young Jesus would have been mediated for and by late ancient and early medieval readers and audiences. To put it another way, what cultural resources did Graeco-Roman and medieval readers have at hand to help them make sense of Jesus' childhood, and what role did perceptions of the past play in this process? To address such questions, I utilize methods grounded in the sociology of cultural memory, a field that provides descriptive language well suited for the analysis of the *Paidika* and its history of interpretation.[75] My task in the remainder of the chapter is to make clear how my investigation of stories about Jesus as a child benefits from insights drawn from the field of memory studies.

The study of memory as a social phenomenon finds its roots in the work of Maurice Halbwachs (1877–1945).[76] In the 1920s, Halbwachs coined the phrases "collective memory" (*mémoire collective*) and "social frameworks of memory" (*cadres sociaux de la mémoire*) to describe the way people's perceptions of the past are crucially shaped and conditioned by their life experiences within social groups.[77] Three fundamental insights from Halbwachs's research would have a lasting impact on subsequent scholarship.

The first is the observation that human beings' memories of the past are determinatively shaped *by present-day concerns.*[78] In his book *Les Cadres sociaux de la mémoire* (1925), Halbwachs addressed the "reshaping operation" performed in and through the memory, noting that "even at the moment of reproducing the past our imagination remains under the influence of the present social milieu."[79] Later, in his posthumously published *La Mémoire collective* (1950), he reasserted that "a remembrance is in very large measure a reconstruction of the past achieved with data borrowed from the present, a reconstruction prepared, furthermore, by reconstructions of earlier periods wherein past images had already been altered."[80] The implications of these statements were profound. Halbwachs was saying that memories get built up across time by a process of accretion, insofar as they are inextricably framed by a succession of present-day concerns. This meant that human memory does not provide direct access to what happened in the past: instead, such access is inevitably mediated (and therefore affected to varying degrees) by present circumstances.[81]

Halbwachs's second fundamental insight was that memories of the past are also mediated through the dynamics of group interactions: in other words, they are framed, constituted, and constructed *in and through the interactions of specific communities.* In his early work Halbwachs asserted, "It is in society that people normally acquire their memories. It is also in society that they recall, recognize, and localize their memories."[82] Toward the end of his career, he would reassert this point even more strongly. "A remembrance . . . must start from shared data or conceptions. These are present in our mind as well as theirs, because they are continually being passed back and forth. This process occurs only because all have been and still are members of the same group. This is the only way to understand how a remembrance is at once recognized and reconstructed."[83] While Halbwachs recognized a range of relevant social contexts, he focused especially on the role of families in shaping remembrances of past events "from a common domain."[84] In his eyes, human access to the past was mediated through the complex dynamics of social interactions in the home, and thereby subject to alteration and embellishment.[85]

The third fundamental insight credited to Halbwachs is that memories of the past are framed *by the physical spaces in which acts of remembrance take place.* In this vein, Halbwachs wrote about "the localization of memory."[86] In his book on the topography of the Holy Land, he argued for instance that early memories of Jesus' life had become inextricably linked with "points in the terrain."[87] Halbwachs also wrote about the way that collective memory can be "based on spatial images" and tied to "habits related to a specific physical setting," from family homes, to the layout of city streets, to the contours of countrysides and landscapes:[88] "Thus, every collective memory unfolds within a spatial framework . . . (and) we recapture the past only by understanding how it is, in effect, preserved by our physical surroundings."[89] Here too the implications of Halbwachs's findings quickly became evident. Memories can be invented, contested, reappropriated, transformed, and consolidated in and through the administration of spaces and the performance of rites within those spaces. In this way, they are recognized to be just as malleable—just as susceptible to renovation and recontouring—as the buildings and landscapes to which they are tied.

Since his death in 1945, Halbwachs's work has been sifted and critiqued in good measure—and, in the process, refined and developed—by subsequent sociologists who have followed in his footsteps. Some have charged that Halbwachs's language of "collective memory" is inadequate to the task, just a cipher for vague and/or outmoded concepts such as "myth" and "tradition."[90] Others have proposed alternative terms such as "social memory" and "cultural memory" to describe how perceptions of the past are mediated through communal processes across time.[91] Over the past three decades, researchers have paid more careful attention to the "two levels on which culture and memory intersect"—the cognitive and the social-medial.[92]

Five scholars since Halbwachs have left an especially deep imprint on the social and medial dimensions of memory, and have accordingly played a prominent role in shaping my own approach to the topic: Pierre Nora, Jan Assmann, Paul Connerton, Aleida Assmann, and Astrid Erll. Each of these scholars has advanced our understanding of how *places, practices, texts, images, and other material media* contribute to the formation of "memory cultures."

Pierre Nora introduced the term "sites of memory" (*lieux de mémoire*) to designate cultural loci in which memories of the past become crystallized or incarnated, and through which the collective identities (especially of nation states) are reoriented and recentered.[93] Such sites of memory can be associated with everything from geographical locations, buildings, monuments, and public images to historical and mythical figures, commemorative events, and written texts. Nora's usage of the term *lieux* ("sites") helpfully highlights the localized (and multiply distributed) character of memory practices, whether tied to a physical landscape or to a mythic motif replicated in literature and art. In this book, I seek to describe how certain cultural sites functioned as privileged lenses through which ancient readers viewed the childhood of Jesus.

Paul Connerton and Jan Assmann have used the terms "social memory" and "cultural memory" to describe societal mechanisms for remembering the past. Connerton was especially interested in how human perceptions of the past become habituated and "sedimented in the body" in and through various kinds of "incorporating" and "inscribing" practices.[94] By "incorporating practices," he meant a range of unobserved (and yet thoroughly ingrained) mnemonic actions performed in the body, from the repertoire of gestures connected with standards of etiquette to ritual postures and performances within liturgical settings.[95] By "inscribing practices," he meant actions that store or encode information for later retrieval: the most prominent example is the use of the alphabet in writing, which transfers the properties of speech to replicable written forms.[96] Jan Assmann's analogous term, "cultural memory," also refers to traditionary processes mediated across time through different formalized modes of communication such as writing and ritual practice.[97] In this book, I use the terms "social memory" and "cultural memory" as synonyms. As terms of analysis, they help focus my attention on the way stories about an infant Jesus would have been informed by the cultural uses made of children (including children's bodies), and by ritualized practices ranging from oral performances to disciplines of writing.

Aleida Assmann and Astrid Erll have highlighted the role that material media play in such memory processes. In her book on *Erinnerungsräume* ("memory spaces," or "realms of remembrance"), Aleida Assmann examined the "close reciprocal relationships between various media and the metaphors of memory," focusing especially on four types of material media: script, image, bodies, and places.[98] With respect to "script" or "writing" (*Schrift*), she did important work on the afterlife of texts, which pass through different stages of use, disuse, and reuse: as actively read documents ("texts"), as preserved objects bearing a heightened cultural value ("relics"), as historical artifacts used to reconstruct the past ("traces"), as unused or discarded objects no longer deemed to have value ("trash"), and as objects of renewed cultural interest ("information").[99] The close attention she paid to different stages or phases of use has proven illuminating for my investigation of the *Paidika* and its history of reception (that is, the various cultural uses to which the stories were put).

Aleida Assmann's treatment of "image" (*Bild*) and "places" (*Orte*) is also helpful for framing my study of the *Paidika*. In the case of images, she emphasized their immediacy and power in shaping the cultural memory of viewers:

"Images adapt in a different way than texts do to the landscape of the unconscious: there is a fluid boundary between image and dream, through which the image is raised up to (the level of) vision and is granted a life of its own."[100] Places embody for participants an apparent "continuity of permanence" (*Kontinuität der Dauer*). Thus, for example, even as sites such as ruins, commemorative monuments, and cemeteries "mark a past life that is dead and forgotten, estranged and lost," they also "mark the possibility of a remembrance that is . . . reawakened and brought back to life."[101] As I reconstruct the way that early readers would have encountered stories from the *Paidika,* I also pay close attention to the mediating role that cultural markers—visual images, physical spaces, and the practices associated with them—would have played as *Erinnerungsräume,* "memory spaces" that helped such readers connect Jesus' childhood to their own social world and life experience.[102]

For Astrid Erll, such "memory spaces" function as cultural "cues," prompting viewers, participants, and readers to constructive acts of recollection or "recall" (*Abruf*).[103] In this context, Erll's work on cultural memory may be fruitfully applied to the problems raised by the so-called linguistic turn for the historical study of late ancient narratives. This "turn" has called into question scholars' use of stories found in early Christian gospels and lives of saints as reliable sources for reconstructing events as they actually happened in history.[104] Attempts to make one-to-one correspondences between the narrative world of the text and the "real world" behind the text have become increasingly problematized.

Erll addresses the epistemological chasm (*Kluft*) between these two worlds in her treatment of narrative literature as one medium of cultural memory. She suggests that certain connections between the two worlds (narrative and "real") may be made by investigating the "strategies of reception" and common "cultures of memory" shared by interpretive communities.[105] That is to say, Erll would have us focus on the role of readers and on "contexts of enculturation" (schools, places of religious instruction, and other social locations) that serve as vehicles for the circulation and reception of narrative tales.[106] In so doing, she sees new potential for giving account of the way that readers' "relation to reality" (*Wirklichkeitsbezug*) frames their reading practices and helps them contextualize the narrative world they encounter in the text.

This is exactly what I hope to accomplish in my study of the *Paidika* and its "readerly" reception. My goal is to analyze the *Paidika*'s early history of transmission in terms of "contexts of enculturation" related to children in the late ancient world, and what Erll calls "intermediality" (*Intermedialität*)—the intersection of readers with images, places, and practices that stamped their engagement with the text and thereby shaped their memories of the young Jesus.[107] Throughout this book, I use the terms "social memory" and "cultural memory" to talk about the kinds of constructive and creative work performed by late ancient and medieval authors, readers, and communities upon the "past"—in this case, a particular set of stories related to Jesus' childhood—in and through sites of memory encountered in their respective present-day environments.[108]

2

Texts and Readers

In his study of the relationship between texts and readers, Stanley Fish famously posed the question, "Is there a text in this class?"[1] For my purposes in this second chapter, I might rephrase the question slightly: Is there in fact a "text" in this book, and if so, what is it? In putting it in these terms (scare quotes and all), I mean to query our everyday conceptions of "texts" as singular, stable, clearly bounded pieces of writing, held together in our minds by the ascription of identifiable titles and genres, as well as by our strongly held notions of originating authors and/or authorial figures.[2] These issues are particularly relevant for early Christian stories about Jesus as a child, where the manuscript record is notoriously inconsistent and hard to decipher.

What exactly is it that we are studying when we speak about the *Paidika*? In my first chapter, for the purposes of simplification and introduction, I spoke about the collection of stories as if its contents, structure, and literary character were prepackaged for modern readers, neatly wrapped in a pristinely preserved, gift-wrapped box. But what happens when we open the package, ripping away the wrapping paper like a child opening a long-awaited present under a Christmas tree? What do we find inside? What happens when we dig a little deeper, when we try to trace back the *Paidika*'s textual history to its early roots? What kind of text are we left with, and how should this affect our interpretive approach? In this chapter, I address these questions and especially their implications for how we imagine the *Paidika* stories to have been read, heard, and disseminated in late antiquity and beyond.

Crucial to my approach here is a shift of focus away from authors and unitary texts and toward disparate groups of readers and audiences. My analysis proceeds in three steps. First, I discuss certain problematic assumptions about the textual character of the *Paidika,* including its modern identification as a "gospel." Second, I turn my attention to questions of literacy and orality, exploring how and in what settings infancy stories would have been read and/or heard in late antiquity. Third, I trace the evidence for ancient readers' citations of *Paidika* traditions and note the implications for how we document and date written collections of such tales. On this basis, I explain the reasons for my decision to focus on individual story units as a way into the history of the text and its interpretation.

The Trouble with Texts, Titles, and Genres

Nearly every modern scholar who has studied the *Paidika* has identified it as an "infancy gospel" and has expended a fair amount of energy discussing its relationship to the New Testament Gospels. There are good justifications for this, the most prominent of which rests on similar content and themes.[3] In the *Paidika,* as in the four canonical Gospels, Jesus clashes with Jewish leaders regarding actions he performs on the Sabbath. As an infant, the young Jesus performs signs and wonders just as he would as an adult: raising the dead, healing the physically afflicted, sowing seeds, and reaping an unexpectedly large harvest.[4] Some of his teachings and the words of those around him—his utterance about seeking and finding (5.3), and his first teacher's words about his origins (7.2)—find loose parallels in the synoptic Gospels.[5] Furthermore, his issuing of verbal curses that cause people to "wither" or "dry up" is reminiscent of scenes like the story of the fig tree preserved in Matthew and Mark.[6] It is with the Gospel of Luke, however, that the *Paidika* seems to have the closest connections.[7] This link with Luke is most notable in the final episode: the story of Jesus' encounter with the teachers in the Temple in *Paidika* 17 closely follows Luke 2:41–52.[8]

In light of these thematic and verbal connections, scholars have argued that, at the time of its composition, the *Paidika* must have been designed to supplement or even improve upon the New Testament gospel accounts by way of "filling gaps" in the biography of Jesus.[9] According to this line of interpretation, the absence of any information about Jesus' childhood from his infancy to the age of twelve in the earlier gospel record served as something of an irritant and catalyst, prompting production of new stories designed to fill in these lost years of Jesus' life. Accordingly, modern academic readers have tended to see in the *Paidika* a "kinship" of form and content that would have even been quickly recognized by readers familiar with the canonical Gospels.[10]

This theory that the *Paidika* was quite literally a stopgap measure—that it was intended to plug a childhood-shaped hole in earlier Christian traditions—is partially explanatory, but it also remains problematic on more than one level.[11] First of all, it tends to treat the *Paidika* not as a collection of stories worthy of study in their own right but as a derivative product, a footnote or appendix to the New Testament Gospels and other earlier Christian literature. Second, in at least some of its iterations, this theory relies on static, anachronistic assumptions about the circulation, accessibility, standardization, and canonization of the New Testament Gospels during the first three centuries CE.[12] Recent scholarship has repeatedly underscored the fact that in early Christian communities (just as in the wider Roman society) the number of people boasting functional literacy would have been woefully small, most certainly less than 15 percent.[13] Among this number, even fewer would have owned or had regular access to books. Individual churches (especially outside cities) rarely would have had access to a full complement of scriptural writings, and this situation did not change significantly until into the fourth century when matters of canonization came to a head and when mechanisms for the production and distribution of bibles began to evolve due to imperial patronage (and even then things remained in flux depending on one's geographical and social location).[14] These demographics should give us pause about placing undue emphasis on the *Paidika*'s intertextual relationships to a corpus of New Testament Gospels that may not have been readily available to readers and hearers for the purpose of close exegesis and comparison.[15]

A third danger associated with this view of the *Paidika* as a historical "appendage" to the New Testament Gospels has to do with its modern identification as a "gospel," which has had misleading implications related to assumptions about genre and readership. As I mentioned in chapter 1, the commonly used title *Infancy Gospel of Thomas* is a modern scholarly invention, and its use as a label has had unintended (and unfruitful) consequences for our understanding of the work.

The *Paidika* was initially assigned the title *Gospel of Thomas* in the late eighteenth and early nineteenth centuries.[16] Debate arose about whether it corresponded to the "Gnostic" gospel of the same name mentioned by early Christian heresiologists but still undiscovered at the time.[17] After the real *Gospel of Thomas* was discovered at Nag Hammadi, Egypt, in 1945, scholars renamed it the *Infancy Gospel of Thomas* to distinguish it from its supposed namesake.

The problem is that in our earliest manuscript evidence this so-called *Infancy Gospel of Thomas* was never given the title of gospel, nor was it originally associated with Thomas. The attribution to Thomas appears in medieval Greek recensions but is absent from earlier manuscripts.[18] The title "gospel" cannot even claim a medieval legacy. Early modern scholars chose this title as a way of trying to link the collection of childhood stories to ancient Christian gospel literature about Jesus. The designation has stuck: scholars continue to refer to it as the *Infancy Gospel of Thomas*, even while (occasionally) acknowledging it as anachronistic.[19] What is not acknowledged is how this designation (with its strongly marked assumptions regarding literary genre and social reception) has effectively constrained the historical imaginations of scholars when it comes to envisioning the ways that these stories were both read and heard among late ancient audiences. This is where I think a reconsideration of the relationship between title, genre, and readership is in order.

As best we can determine, the original title for the collection of stories about Jesus' childhood was *Paidika tou Iēsou*—"Childhood Deeds of Jesus."[20] The title *Paidika*, a plural adjective meaning "related to childhood," is well attested in the Greek manuscript evidence.[21] The Latin and Syriac versions witness the same core title: in both, the "Childhood Deeds of Jesus" is the common way of designating the collection of stories.[22]

The title *Paidika* is also corroborated in patristic citations. Two fourth-century authors use this term in referring to the infancy stories. Epiphanius of Salamis (writing ca. 376) mentions Jesus' "divine signs . . . [which] he is said to have performed in play as a child" (*theosēmeia . . . ha legetai peri autou en paigniōͅ hote paidion ēn pepoiēkenai*) and designates them as his "childhood miracles" (*paidika sēmeia*). While it is unclear whether Epiphanius had access to the stories in oral or written form, he saw them as beneficial for combating the teachings of certain "other sects."[23] A decade or two later, the bishop of Antioch, John Chrysostom, took a less favorable view of these miracle stories, calling them false inventions. Yet he too refers to them as "Christ's childhood deeds" (*paidika . . . tou Christou*),[24] and thereby provides further evidence that the title *Paidika* was already fairly standardized as a label for this collection of tales in the fourth century.

Later Latin and Greek sources tell the same story. In the Roman West, the *Decretum Gelasianum* (ca. sixth century) lists a "Book of the Infancy of the Savior" (*Liber de infantia salvatoris*) in an accounting of apocryphal works, differentiating it clearly from a certain "Gospel of Thomas" (*Evangelium nomine Thomae*) used by the Manichaeans.[25] Similar references by later writers such as Maximus the Confessor (ca. 580–662),[26] Anastasius of Sinai (seventh century),[27] George Syncellus (d. after 810),[28] and Euthymius Zigabenus

(d. after 1118)[29] make it clear that the title *Paidika* remained in currency into the middle Byzantine period and beyond.

This preponderance of evidence is the reason I have chosen to eschew the modern title *Infancy Gospel of Thomas* in favor of the more historical title *Paidika.* It is my hope that this shift in terminology will free us up to consider the different ways these stories may have been perceived among different sets of readers.

It should be noted, for example, that in antiquity the Greek word *paidika* had a mixed resonance. A neuter plural form, it was frequently employed as if it were a singular noun by Plato, Xenophon, and other classical authors to mean something like "darling boy," in reference to a male child or adolescent with whom an adult male had become sexually intimate (equivalent to the Latin *deliciae*).[30] This usage of *paidika* to denote a boy lover remained widespread among late ancient Greek and Roman authors such as Dio Chrysostom,[31] Plutarch,[32] Aelius Aristides,[33] Lucian,[34] Dio Cassius,[35] Herodian,[36] Flavius Philostratus,[37] and Diogenes Laertius.[38] A number of ancient Jewish and Christian authors also knew and used the term in speaking about Greek and Roman sexual practices: among them, Philo of Alexandria,[39] Josephus,[40] Clement of Alexandria,[41] Hippolytus,[42] Origen of Alexandria,[43] Eusebius of Caesarea,[44] and John Chrysostom.[45] Even though it is clearly not the primary or intended sense of the Greek title, this more salacious connotation of the term *paidika* may have given these stories of the child Jesus a provocative air among some prospective readers, akin to the effect of racy headlines in a modern gossip magazine.

However, the word *paidika* of course was also employed commonly in a more general (and less scandalous) sense, as a true plural form that neutrally described objects or actions pertaining to childhood. Within certain literary circles, this common use came to have a more technical application as a marker of genre. In relation to literary narratives, especially the *Lives* of heroic figures—known in Greek as *bioi* and in Latin as *vitae*—the word *paidika* became particularly associated with stories, songs, or sayings about the extraordinary deeds such famous figures were supposed to have performed during their youth, long before they had gained their public, adult reputation. For two relevant examples, we may turn to the early second-century Greek author Plutarch and his writings on the emperors Alexander and Pompey.

First, in his treatise *On the Fortune of Alexander,* Plutarch writes: "But of the genuine sayings of Alexander we might first review those of his youth [*ta paidika*]. Since he was the swiftest of foot of all the young men of his age, his comrades urged him to enter the Olympic games. He asked if the competitors were kings, and when his friends replied that they were not, he said that the contest was unfair, for it was one in which a victory would be over commoners, but a defeat would be the defeat of a king."[46] Here, the term *paidika* is invoked in reference to "the genuine sayings of Alexander": most probably, a collection of stories and teachings with a section devoted to his early life. Second, in his treatise on Pompey the Great, Plutarch seems to have in mind a similar literary collection of laudable tales about the childhood of a famous figure. He begins by comparing the emperor to an accomplished athlete whose early victories have been virtually washed away by the rising tide of later triumphs: "Just as athletes who have won the primacy among men and borne away glorious prizes everywhere make no account of their boyish victories [*tas paidikas . . . nikas*] and even leave them unrecorded, so it is with the deeds which Pompey performed at this time; they were extraordinary in themselves, but were buried away by the multitude and magnitude of his later wars and contests, and I am afraid to revive them, lest by lingering too long upon his first essays, I should leave myself no room for those achievements and experiences of the man which were greatest, and most illustrative of his character."[47] What is most notable about this account is the literary and archival detail supplied by the analogy that Plutarch draws. He alludes to the practices of recording (*anagraphein*) and making an account of (*logon . . . tithenthai*) victories won in childhood (*tas paidikas nikas*), as well as other extraordinary deeds (*praxeis*) accomplished at a young age. He also alludes to the stacks of papers in which such early biographical accounts tend to become buried (*katakechōsmenas*). Plutarch leaves us with the image of a library or collection in which the greatest "achievements and experiences" (*erga kai pathēmata*) of such famous men are preserved.

Plutarch was writing these words in the early second century, not too long before the *Paidika*—the *Childhood Deeds of Jesus*—began to circulate, whether in oral or written form. In this context, the identification of this collection of stories as *Paidika* would have marked them as a particular kind of cultural product for both hearers and readers—for hearers, as a specific form of "storytelling"; for readers, as a specific type of literary genre. In either case, the stories told about the young Jesus conformed to established features of Graeco-Roman biographies, in which backstories of accomplishments in childhood served to presage greatness in adulthood.[48]

On this subject, Burke has contributed a sustained and nuanced discussion. The impressive range of ancient literary examples he cites—including Quintilian's and Menander's rhetorical instructions on the praise of prominent figures in panegyrics, Apollodorus's accounts of the wonders performed by heroes and gods in their infancy, the miscellaneous biographies of Alexander the Great and other emperors, the lives of philosophers and sophists by Philostratus,

Porphyry, and Iamblichus, and Jewish and Christian tales of biblical and patristic exemplars—shows how the *Paidika* exhibited the standard content of the *bios* genre.[49] For Burke, the *Paidika* conforms to the conventions of ancient biography, but "the biographies of child emperors who perished before they reached adulthood," are distinguished by the fact that their protagonists' childhood activities "cannot anticipate future accomplishments."[50]

This statement by Burke hinges in part on his insistence that "the overall text was a self-contained narrative."[51] The problem I have with Burke's argument at this point is his unduly rigid conception of genre, which relies too heavily on notions of stable ("self-contained") texts and of fixed features that determine the classification of text types. What is lost in this picture is how both texts and genres are malleable creatures in the hands of readers. Thus, when speaking about the *function* of the text, Burke focuses almost exclusively on different rhetorical characteristics and possible authorial motives—praise, burlesque, satire, polemics—so as to underscore the way that "meaning is genre-bound."[52] Missing is a deeper investigation of the way genre conceptions in antiquity were under constant negotiation—formed, de-formed, and re-formed through the mixing and matching of key elements, constituted and reconstituted through authorial and readerly acts of notation and selection.[53] Hindy Najman has helpfully proposed that genres be understood in terms of "constellations," the lines and features of which might look quite different in the eyes of different observers (you say Orion, I say a lion) but were in any configuration only visible to those who were trained to see them as such.[54]

With this comes a set of vital questions related to texts and ancient practices of reading. Who was reading (or listening to) these kinds of *bioi* in Greek and Roman society? What physical and social settings facilitated interaction with stories such as the *Paidika?* What different kinds of "training" equipped readers and listeners to discern the lines of their literary constellations? In what follows, I want to cast my net as wide as possible in order to consider the diversity of settings in which the *Paidika* may have been encountered. In the end, however, I shall be focusing especially on Graeco-Roman households as privileged venues for reimagining and reconstructing the stories' early reception.

From Written Texts to Oral Performance

When we try to imagine how people would have encountered the *Paidika* in late antiquity, it is vital that we recognize the diversity of activities, locations, and communities involved, and how each of those specific "reading cultures" (or, more broadly, sets of "communication practices") would have produced different constructions of meaning for the interpretation of the stories.[55] As William A. Johnson puts it: "The meanings that readers construct differ . . . largely in dependence on the (sub)culture in which the reading occurs."[56]

Evidence from the Greek and Roman worlds amply demonstrates that texts were read alone and in groups (in the company of friends, family members, and domestic servants),[57] in public settings, private homes, and spaces in between (for example, worship spaces converted from domestic architecture, family cemetery plots, and so on),[58] for purposes of study, entertainment, contemplation, and/or intellectual debate. We may picture a Roman matron at breakfast reading and responding to a letter from her brother regarding the economic management of the family's landholdings and agricultural produce,[59] an adolescent struggling through a few lines of Homer or Plato as part of an afternoon school lesson,[60] a dinner party host and his guests enjoying the spectacle of a trained servant or professional lector dramatically reciting a heroic tale from a deluxe literary scroll before they debate its moral implications over wine,[61] a solitary scholar digesting a scientific treatise at night in a cramped study lit by a flickering oil lamp,[62] or an illiterate apprentice hearing biblical texts read three times a day and learning them by heart so as to gain admission into an Egyptian monastery.[63] In each of these settings, the act of reading had a different social valence, and the text being read accordingly held a different semantic value. In short, it makes a big difference where and when texts were read, what kind of texts they were, and who was reading them. In the words of Hans Robert Jauss: "The social function of literature manifests itself in its genuine possibility only *where the literary experience of the reader enters into the horizon of expectations of his (or her) lived praxis.*"[64]

Unfortunately, treatments of early Christian literacy and reading practices have too often been hamstrung by excessively rigid dichotomies (public versus private, elite versus popular, spoken versus silent, oral versus written, and so forth), as well as by canonical and (more broadly) "religious" biases regarding usage patterns.[65] Harry Gamble's chapter "The Use of Early Christian Books" is a prime example. He divides the subject into three main categories. The first is "public reading," which for him is associated almost exclusively with "assemblies for worship," with "scripture" as the conveyed content.[66] His second category is "private use." Here again, Gamble's historical imagination mostly extends only to questions related to "the availability of scriptural texts" and to the use of texts for devotional exercises and "spiritual development" (he draws a sharp contrast with non-Christian literature that was thought in some quarters "to endanger spiritual health").[67] Gamble's third category is "magical use," which comprises charms and amulets, fortune telling, and bibliomancy. Once again, all the examples he cites pertain only to the use of "scripture," but in this case the patterns of use are characterized not as spiritually edifying but as "trivialized" and "perverse": in Gamble's eyes, "there was nothing especially Christian in this practice."[68] This theological judgment aside, what is missing in all of this is a recognition of how early Christian reading practices extended far and wide, to texts that fell outside the (still not fully defined) category of "scripture,"[69] and to settings and interpretations that did not conform to what certain New Testament and patristic scholars have deemed as sufficiently "religious" or "Christian" in character.[70]

When it comes to narrative prose works (Christian or otherwise), we have relatively little direct evidence for what ancient readers did with them, but it would seem that Christian reading practices fell largely in line with broader Graeco-Roman trends.[71] We know that those who read ancient romances and narratives of apostolic acts were sometimes inspired to write new stories in imitation of earlier models (a basic skill developed in oratorical-literary education),[72] or to edit the original versions for new communities of readers.[73] As we shall see, the same holds true for our collection of "Childhood Deeds": the *Paidika* sponsored a variety of new tales about Jesus' early escapades, which were eventually incorporated into expanded editions.[74] In these cases, acts of reading went hand in hand with acts of writing.

But ancient readers' engagement with the *Paidika* was by no means restricted to literary activities such as editing and composition. There are also indications that the infancy tales may have been shaped in the context of oral storytelling. This was not unusual. A good number of ancient prose works contain elements that suggest they were conceived, at least in part, to be performed in group settings.

Often cited as possible evidence for oral performativity are scenes in which characters in the narratives tell each other their life stories. Occasionally, such scenes incorporate "individuals and crowds who listen and react to—and thus guide audience response to—the tales they hear."[75] One potential example of such anticipatory "reader" response is the eavesdropping that takes place in the novella *Apollonius, King of Tyre,* where we find a noble young man Athenagoras and a companion secretly listening in as his beloved—the virtuous princess Tarsia, who is unwillingly indentured to a brothel—tells her life story to an interested client. The story she tells is in fact the story of the novella itself.[76] Hints of a similar vicarious, voyeuristic dynamic may also be operative in the *Paidika,* where the adult crowds stand at the margins and listen in on the young Jesus' words and actions, alternatively expressing dismay or marveling in wonderment.[77] These scenes, with their elements of "self-referentiality" and "inscribed doubleness," may give hints about social expectations attending the readerly performance and audience reception of such literary narratives.[78]

In this context, it is significant that the eighth and final book of the second-century romance *Leucippe and Clitophon* has the protagonists recounting their autobiographical tales at a sequence of dinner parties, or *symposia*.[79] For some readers, such scenes may have had the effect of cultivating a mimetic relationship between text and audience, especially in cases where the reading of the novel itself was also taking place over a meal among a gathering of feasting friends. Such domestic meal gatherings would have been prime settings not only for the reading of philosophical texts but also for the oral interpretation of heroic *bioi* and other prose works—stories that would have provided occasion for skilled readers to perform character dialogues as "speech in character" (*prosōpopoiia*) and for listeners to engage in dialogue and debate over the contents of the narratives. There is even evidence from the late second or early third century that the reading of literary prose in private homes sometimes may have also been coordinated with the visual decoration of the rooms in which such readings took place.[80]

The shift of focus to questions of audience reminds us that when thinking about the *Paidika* and its early history of interpretation, we must be prepared to imagine a range of social settings in which (and in relation to which) they were written and read, told and heard. This is the reason I cast my net quite wide in parts 2 and 3 of this book, looking for potential "sites of memory" in a variety of places and practices, in order to identify the cultural lenses through which readers and hearers would have sought to bring the stories into particular focus. These contexts for reception provide a "depth of field" for locating the *Paidika* within a panorama of Graeco-Roman and (later) early medieval milieus.

I think it safe to assume, however, that at least during the early stages of the tales' transmission the Graeco-Roman household would have been a primary location for individual and group reading practices, especially over meal gatherings.[81] In *The Earliest History of the Christian Gathering*, Valeriy Alikin has noted that "what first-century Christians did during the symposium part of their gathering conformed by and large to what happened during symposia in the Graeco-Roman world in general," and that it was also "the social context in which the words of Jesus were passed on and stories about him were told."[82] The reading or telling of such stories in early Christian "symposia" also sponsored conversations, lessons, and interpretations among participants, focusing on matters of everyday life, on ethical implications, or on theological and philosophical questions.[83]

Two early Christian works give us tantalizing glimpses of how activities of reading, interpretation, and philosophical debate were envisioned as taking place in household settings. The *Apostolic Tradition,* edited in the fourth century but containing earlier traditions from the second and third centuries, preserves valuable information about what happened at noneucharistic Christian symposia where conversations over meals were spurred on by the drinking of wine and by the occasional argument or debate. The text mentions a meal with bread and wine that is "not the eucharist" at which guests should eat "in silence, without arguing," following the lead of the bishop (or presbyter or deacon), who functioned as the host of the gathering.[84] The fact that there was a need for such behavioral prescriptions suggests that less regimented symposia practices were common (or at least common enough to elicit commentary and attempts at "correction"). While the *Apostolic Tradition* does not specifically mention readings taking place at these evening gatherings, it is clear that certain members were expected to be functionally literate and to be engaged in the practice of reading for edification. In cases where no teacher was present at the common "assembly" (*ekklēsia*), the text exhorts each one to "take a holy book and read enough of it to gain an advantage from it" at home.[85]

Another possible source of information on such meal gatherings is Methodius of Olympus's *Symposium* (ca. 300 CE). Modeled after Plato's work by the same name, the text presents a scenario in which a group of ten virgins are invited to a meal in a paradisiacal garden, hosted by Virtue (*Aretē*), the daughter of Philosophy (*Philosophia*). After all the food and feasting is done, each one in turn gets up to give a discourse in praise of virginity. Each speech functions as a commentary on a series of excerpted texts, read or quoted for the occasion, followed by the presentation of arguments, dialogical exchanges, and songs. And interestingly enough, the subject of childhood is deemed worthy of being included as a subject for discussion. Thus, the fifth presenter, Thallousa, commenting on Lamentations 3:27 ("It is good for a man that he bear the yoke in his youth"), makes a point of arguing that "it is good, indeed, from childhood [*ek paidōn*], to submit the neck to the divine hand," and "to keep the flesh undefiled from childhood [*ek paidōn*]" as well.[86] This theme is reiterated in the final speech by Domnina when she concludes that "the exercise which prepares the soul from childhood [*ek paidōn*] for desirable and delectable glory . . . is chastity."[87] Here, Methodius presents an idealized vision of a meal gathering in which the participants cite, interpret, discuss, and debate the proper understanding of a biblical text, with its implications for understanding childhood as the training ground for virtue.

What are the implications of privileging the household as a primary setting for the reception of narrative works such as the *Paidika?* What implications does this have for our understanding of *who* the "readers" were, and *how* the "reading" took place? Let me begin with the first question.

It is commonly recognized that the core constituency for any literary work in antiquity necessarily would have consisted of an elite, literate class within the larger Graeco-Roman population. Yet, in his discussion of the Greek novel, Tomas Hägg has rightly sought to free us from an unduly rigid "literacy/illiteracy dichotomy," pointing out that "illiterate" people could also have been "part of the audience of the novel, namely, as listeners."[88] His insight into the demographics of such potential audiences is true whether we imagine the setting for such readings to be Graeco-Roman households in general or Christian house churches in particular. Such microcommunities would have included not only the "intellectual elite" (that is, those who were "truly literate and capable of reading also for their pleasure") but also a spectrum of "quasi-literates," "semi-literatures," and "illiterates" who might have had occasion to hear the stories read aloud, at evening dinner gatherings or at other assemblies where narrative prose functioned as aural "reading-matter."[89]

Nonetheless, it was a very small cadre of highly educated readers who would have been indispensible social agents in dissemination of stories like the *Paidika.*[90] Richard Hunter writes, "The patterns of circulation and reception of the ancient literature about which we know most were largely determined by the partly complementary phenomena of elite taste and scholarly choice, the inherent conservatism of school curricula, and the market-forces of the book-trade."[91] Plainly put, when it comes to narrative literary forms such as the ancient novellae and heroic *bioi* (and yes, the *Paidika* as well), all the available evidence we have—from the styles of handwriting on papyrus copies, to perspectives on family, education, and sexual desire in the stories themselves, to the sociological implications of citation patterns (that is, who was quoting such texts and to what purpose)—leads us to the unavoidable conclusion that this literature "is most easily understood precisely within elite circles of the Hellenised empire during the second and third centuries CE."[92]

This turn toward the role of audience also helps us address the question of how acts of reading took place. Textuality and orality were intimately intertwined in antiquity,[93] and here again, analogies to late ancient novels will prove instructive in our study of the *Paidika.* Some scholars have traced the historical roots of both novels and *bioi* (including the "Childhood Deeds") to practices of oral storytelling,[94] but I am especially interested in how processes of oral transmission *continued concurrently* with the reading of written texts.

In a world where groups, large and small, heard texts read to them by trained lectors, where even solitary acts of reading were often voiced, audience and readers would have become habituated to hearing stories with minds and bodies trained to the task.[95] In such a world, the categories of "oral" and "written" would not have been kept in separate, hermetically sealed boxes, and for us to try to quarantine them would be artificial and ultimately misleading.[96]

Even in their written form, the ancient novels and the *Paidika* bear traces of orality. Such traces do not simply signal processes of oral transmission prior to the production of written copies; they also would have facilitated the ongoing oral interpretation of such texts. In the case of the Greek novel, Hägg has highlighted in particular stereotyped conjunctive phrases linking episodes (such as the *men . . . de* clause), the recapitulation of details previously covered, the foretelling or foreshadowing of future events, and direct address on the part of the narrator—all of these were elements that would have resonated with oral contexts of performance.[97]

When it comes to the *Paidika,* there are several formal or structural elements that may be tied to oral-aural settings of transmission and performance.[98] The first is the division of the stories into clearly marked episodes not closely tied to the larger narrative context, with frequent use of stereotypical conjunctions to mark transitions both within and between episodes.[99] István Czachesz has recently observed how the episodic character of early Christian gospels and acts literature would have been especially conducive to oral-aural group reading practices, where listeners would have had to rely upon their "short-term" or "working memory" to process details of stories on the fly and to return (by way of "serial recall") to noteworthy details for later review and discussion.[100] Indeed, in the case of the *Paidika,* apart from a couple of rather superficial narrative linking devices,[101] each story could readily stand on its own as an easily digested independent unit.

Second, the story variants attested in the different Greek recensions of the *Paidika* exhibit both "stability in core" and "flexibility in detail"—dual characteristics of oral traditions.[102] Here, the inclusion of three teacher episodes is indicative. Alex Olrik in his typology of folkloric principles identifies triple occurrences of narrative material as markers of oral composition ("The Law of Three").[103] In the *Paidika,* threefold repetitions appear not only at the macrolevel of episodes but also at the microlevel of phrases and keywords. In the first school scene, there is a hitch in the narrative when Jesus' entrance into the school or classroom is repeated three times. First, Zacchaeus implores Joseph to "bring him into the school" (*agage auto eis to paideutērion*); second, the narrator describes how Joseph actually "led him into the school" (*apēgagen auton eis to paideutērion*); third, we are told that the schoolmaster himself "led him into the school/classroom" (*ēgagen auton eis to didaskaleion*).[104] Such hitches are generally thought to be characteristic of oral performances, instances of where storytellers repeat or reiterate details to emphasize a point or to refocus their listeners' attention.

Later in the same teacher episode, another triple repetition occurs when Jesus describes the lines of the letter *alpha* as "of the same form, of the same thickness, of the same family" (*homoschēmous, homopacheis, homogeneis*), a phonetic play that would have rhythmically resonated in the ears of story listeners.[105] In the Syriac, Slavic, and later Greek recensions, Jesus' verbal commands to the sparrows,[106] and to the young man splitting wood,[107] are uttered in tripartite form, signs that the *Paidika* may have continued to be transmitted orally in some settings for an extended period of time.[108] Other possible structural indications of orality include repeated phrases to signal the openings and endings of passages,[109] and (as in the case of Greek novels) the use of flashbacks and/or foretellings as markers of story development.[110]

In addition to such structural features, the *Paidika* contains verbal cues for performativity. While the first-person role of the narrator is a secondary element and thus not strongly foregrounded,[111] the stories themselves contain dialogical elements and performative prompts that hint at opportunities for a lector to dramatize scenes and thereby elicit the response of his or her audience. Two-person (and occasionally three-person) dialogue permeates the text, with verbal exchanges between Joseph, Jesus, and the sparrows (2.4), the high priest's son and Jesus (3.1–2), Jesus and Joseph (5.1–3), the teacher Zacchaeus, Joseph, and Jesus (6.1–2b), Jesus and the crowd (6.2c–e), Jesus and Zacchaeus (6.2f–4), Zacchaeus and Joseph (7.1–4), Jesus and the parents of the dead child Zeno (9.2), Jesus and Zeno himself (9.3), Jesus and Joseph (12.1–2), Jesus and the second teacher (13.1–3), Joseph and the third teacher (14.1–3), Mary and Jesus (17.3), and Mary and the scribes and Pharisees (17.4), all presented in rather close succession.[112]

The performative potential of these scripted conversations becomes most clear, however, in chapter 2, where Joseph interrogates Jesus by asking him, "Why are you doing these things on the Sabbath?" Jesus responds simply by "clap[ping] his hands together with a shout" and commanding the birds to fly away. In the context of a society where "oral performance of narrative was in semi-dramatic style," where "dialogue was spoken in character" and "inflected to indicate emotional meanings," and where "recitation was accompanied by nearly constant gesturing,"[113] one can imagine a reader verbally inhabiting Joseph's tone of indignation and then physically mimicking Jesus' gesture of clapping. The same holds true for other scenes where Jesus skips about playfully (6.2e), laughs (8.1), or even blows on the hand of his snake-bitten brother (15.2).

Finally, interspersed throughout the dialogical texture of the stories, one also finds "words belonging to the semantic domain of oral communication and aural reception,"[114] such as verbs of speaking, saying, telling, hearing, and listening. Two examples occur in chapters 6 and 17, where the audiences hearing the *Paidika* read aloud would have found themselves aligned with anonymous crowds of people in the narrative, "listening" (*akouontes*) to the words of Jesus and responding with either stunned silence or curious surprise.[115]

Taken individually, each of these narrative elements might be seen as innocuous. But taken together, they constitute rather pervasive and persuasive evidence for what Reidar Aasgaard has described as "oral coloring."[116] These features are also consistent with what we know about the performative adaptation of *prosōpopoiia*—the mimetic creation of dramatic characters—in ancient narrative contexts.[117] Scholars have documented this method of representing *personae* and dialogical situations in a range of first- and early second-century novellae and *bioi*.[118] Alicia D. Myers has also convincingly argued that prosopopoetic speech attributed to Jesus in the Gospel of John—words that "startle or even anger other characters within the text"—would have been, at least in part, calibrated for performance and audience effect.[119] Faced with the judgments of others that Jesus was the author of "inappropriate speech" (an inappropriateness partially "occasioned by perceptions of his youth"),[120] actual readers and hearers of these Johannine dialogues would have been prompted to respond with their own emotional and rational judgments about Jesus' words. In this way, "the reader who reproduced the sounds of speech and the audience who heard the words" would have been challenged to "make sense of the thoughts"—that is, to try to construe the words spoken as somehow "appropriate" to both the character and the context of the story.[121]

I would argue that similar processes would have been at work for readers and hearers of the *Paidika* stories at different stages of their history of transmission, and that an appreciation for such interactions of text and oral performance in late antiquity should inform our understanding of the way that late ancient audiences sought to align these tales about a young Jesus with their own privileged sites of cultural memory. As I turn now to the evidence for early Christian citations of the *Paidika,* questions about *who* was reading the stories, *in what settings* those acts of reading took place, and *in what form* the stories were encountered should remain at the forefront of our minds.

Tracking a Readerly History of the Paidika: *From Manuscripts to Early Christian Citation*

In this final section of chapter 2, I need to acquaint my readers with the textual history of the *Paidika,* including both manuscript evidence and external citations by late ancient interpreters. In the context of tracing this history, I shall identify certain vexing problems related to textual origins and the dating of these infancy tale traditions. How do we come by the form of the text often translated today under the (problematic) title *Infancy Gospel of Thomas?* How does that form relate to the form of the stories originally circulating in late antiquity? The answers to these questions will help explain how early readers and hearers would have engaged with the text, and why I have chosen in this book to focus on selected story units as entry points into its history of interpretation.

The traditional second-century dating of the *Paidika*[122] has been based not on surviving manuscripts but on "external witnesses"—early Christian authors who make reference to the stories of Jesus' childhood in their own writings. But as it turns out, both kinds of evidence prove problematic for reconstructing the earliest form of the narrative. The earliest manuscripts of the *Paidika* date from the fifth and sixth centuries. A fragmentary fifth-century Latin palimpsest (a manuscript in which the earlier writing has been mostly erased and replaced with a later text) is our earliest documented copy. Preserved at the national library in Vienna, the reconstructed sections include parts of the following stories: Jesus' miracle involving the sparrows (2.2–4), his cursing of the boy who runs into Jesus' shoulder (4.2–5.1), Jesus' encounter with the first teacher Zacchaeus (8.1–2), his (temporary) raising of the boy named Zeno who fell off a building to his death (9.1), the third teacher story (14.1–3), and Jesus' conversation with the teachers in the Temple (17.1–2).[123] Our other earliest witnesses are two Syriac manuscripts, both also incomplete: one is a sixth-century copy in the British Library;[124] the other is a fifth- or sixth-century copy at the university library in Göttingen, Germany.[125] These early Latin and Syriac copies do not get us all the way back to the period of the text's origins, but they have proven invaluable for reconstructing what has been referred to as the "short form" or "short recension" of the *Paidika.*[126]

For a time it was proposed that the *Paidika* might have been composed in Syriac, but there is now a clear consensus that the original language was Greek.[127] Unfortunately, the Greek manuscript evidence is complicated.[128] None of the extant copies dates to before the eleventh century, and all contain later, expanded collections of stories. These augmented compilations are characterized not only by extra tales but also by more subtle internal changes designed to "soften the image of Jesus" and to bring the text into conformity with the New Testament Gospels.[129]

Despite this fact, the earliest Greek manuscript—an eleventh-century manuscript from Jerusalem called Codex Sabaiticus 259 (= Gs)—nonetheless still proves quite useful for reconstructing what the "short recension" of the Greek *Paidika* would have looked like.[130] It represents an "intermediary text," which when stripped of two chapters (*Paidika* 1 and 16) and of other minor editorial additions allows us to line up its contents quite closely with the early Syriac and Latin witnesses.[131] I provide a critical translation of this text in Appendix A and cite it throughout this book. When used carefully, and when collated with the other early Syriac and Latin versions, this Greek text from Jerusalem is currently our best resource for studying the *Paidika* stories in their original language.

But the manuscript record still leaves us with a gaping lacuna when it comes to understanding the shape of the *Paidika* collection prior to the fifth century, and this is why the traditional second-century dating must be taken with a grain of salt. What form did the collection take during the second, third, and fourth centuries? Where and how did these stories circulate? Orally, in written form, or via some combination of these two modes of transmission? Independently, collectively, or again in some combination of the two? When exactly were the stories grouped into relatively standardized narrative frameworks? The manuscript record discussed above really shows us the end point (or various end points) of a complex historical process that had its roots in the earlier centuries of the Common Era. For a glimpse at how these stories were received by earlier readers and hearers, we can turn to a scattering of secondary witnesses—ancient Christian authors who mention *Paidika* traditions and thus provide us with valuable external evidence as to when, where, and in what form the stories were being transmitted and interpreted.

Our earliest external witnesses come from the second century, which is the main reason most scholars have dated the *Paidika* to this period. But here is the rub: in none of these second-century witnesses do we find evidence for a fully developed narrative with multiple and diverse tales in sequence. Rather, the pattern of citations suggests that these tales were recounted and interpreted *in the form of individual story units,* or at most in mini-groupings of *story types*.

There are four potential witnesses to the *Paidika* stories from the second century CE. One of these is Justin Martyr (ca. 150 CE, Rome), who mentions in his *Dialogue with Trypho* that Jesus was "the son of Joseph the carpenter" and was "considered to be a carpenter" himself.[132] He then goes on: "For, when (Jesus) was among men, these are the carpenter's works he used to make, ploughs and yokes, by which he was teaching both the symbols of righteousness and an active life."[133] Some have argued that Justin's reference to "ploughs and yokes" is in fact an allusion to *Paidika* 12, where Joseph, "a carpenter" engaged in "making ploughs and yokes," was miraculously assisted by Jesus in the matter of expanding a bed to its proper size.[134] However, there are at least two reasons to question whether Justin was actually familiar with this particular infancy account. First, the phrase "ploughs and yokes" was stereotypically associated with the trade of carpentry in ancient sources. A telling source is the third-century *Acts of Thomas,* which narrates the story of that apostle's mission to India: on two separate occasions in the work he is referred to as a "carpenter" (*tektōn*) whose craftsmanship consists of being able to make "ploughs" (*arotra*) and "yokes" (*zugoi*), as well as a number of other wooden items, including augurs, goads, pulleys, boats, oars, and masts.[135] Second, Jesus is referred to as "the carpenter" and "the son of the carpenter" in the Gospel of Mark (6:3, *ho tektōn*) and the Gospel of Matthew (13:55, *ho tou tektonos huios*), respectively.[136] And in Matthew 11:29–30, the image of the yoke is used by the writer to talk about the burdens and easiness of the life of discipleship. Therefore, Justin probably was drawing on a combination of these gospel sources, as well as on the common perceptions of the carpentry trade in his *Dialogue,* rather than on an early *Paidika* tradition.[137]

We are on somewhat firmer ground with the three other potential witnesses from the second century—the *Epistle of the Apostles,* the Valentinian *Gospel of Truth,* and Irenaeus of Lyons's treatise *Against Heresies*—all of which associate Jesus with classroom environments. A passage from the *Epistle of the Apostles* gives an account that closely resembles the second teacher story from the *Paidika* collection: "This is what our Lord Jesus Christ did, who was delivered by Joseph and Mary his mother to where he might learn letters. And he who taught him said to him as he taught him, 'Say Alpha.' He answered and said to him, 'First you tell me what Beta is.' And truly [it was] a real thing which was done."[138] The details given here are reminiscent of *Paidika* 13, where the teacher likewise instructs Jesus to "Say Alpha," and Jesus responds by saying, "First tell me what Beta is. . . ."[139]

The immediate context for this citation in the *Epistle of the Apostles* is the anonymous writer's concern to combat docetic views of Jesus—views that saw his humanity as only an appearance or a façade. Thus, the author of the *Epistle* uses the childhood of Jesus as a tool with which to think theologically. For his apologetic purposes, this story about Jesus at school serves as concrete evidence that Jesus came in the flesh—that "[it was] a real thing that was done."[140] Whether it was a "real text" that the author of the *Epistle* had access to is another question, of course. There is no hard-and-fast evidence here that he was working with a fully elaborated narrative: he may very well have learned of this teacher story through an independently transmitted written text, or through an oral telling of the tale (or both).[141] Nonetheless, the *Epistle of the Apostles* does tell us that one of the teacher stories was already circulating in the second century and that it had gained an interested audience in the person of this author, and perhaps among his opponents as well.[142]

The Valentinian *Gospel of Truth* and the early Christian heresiologist Irenaeus provide further evidence that stories about a young Jesus at school were known—and sometimes hotly contested—among different Christian groups vying for interpretive authority in the second century. The author of the *Gospel of Truth* (ca. 140–180), in an effort to explain how the divine Father manifested himself to humanity in Jesus Christ, writes the following: "He became a pedagogue [Coptic, *jaumaït*], at peace and occupied for a time with places of instruction [*m-ma n-ji sbō*]. He came forward and uttered the word [*sheje*] as [if he were] a teacher [*sah*]. People who thought themselves wise in their hearts [*nsophos nhrēï hm-pouhēt*] came up to him, testing him, but he upbraided them, for they were foolish [*hnpetshoueit*]. . . ."[143] This portrayal of Jesus as fulfilling the role of teacher in the *Gospel of Truth* is consistent with both the Valentinians' intellectual emphasis on knowledge (*gnōsis,* that is, "acquaintance" with the divine) and their valorization of philosophical teaching as a social practice.[144]

But the details of this account also seem to suggest a possible allusion to one or more of the *Paidika* teacher stories, in which Jesus is brought into classrooms (*paideutēria/didaskaleia*) and assumes the role of a teacher (*didaskalon*) who speaks "awe-inspiring words" (*rhēmata phobera*), while his supposedly wise instructors—identified by Jesus as "the foolish in heart" (*hoi asophoi* $t\bar{e}_i$ $kardia_i$)—are left alternatively dumbfounded, baffled, and stupefied, their lack of insight exposed by a child.[145] The connections are closest with the Zacchaeus episode (*Paidika* 6–8), but it is possible that other schoolroom scenes (attested or unattested) may have served as inspiration for the author's presentation of Jesus as a divine pedagogue.[146] In this context, it is interesting that Valentinus elsewhere claimed to have had a vision of the Word in the form of an "infant child" (*pais nēpios*) who spoke to him and answered his questions.[147] Whether or not this visionary experience might have inspired a broader Valentinian interest in Jesus' childhood, we simply do not know.

In the end, this account in the *Gospel of Truth* certainly does not provide secure grounds for imagining that the author had a full written narrative of the *Paidika* in his hands. What it does provide is possible evidence for the author's awareness of one or more teacher stories as a narrative "type" (*tupos*) that could readily be applied to the Valentinian understandings of divine knowledge (*gnōsis*).[148] The first teacher episode featuring Zacchaeus supplies the closest content match, but the plural reference to "places of instruction" of course raises the question of whether already in the second century a small collection of classroom episodes might have begun to circulate together, either orally or in a short, written mini-collection. It is also possible that if the author knew only some version of the Zacchaeus tale, the triple narration of Jesus' entry into Zacchaeus's classroom (mentioned earlier) could also account for the plural reference to "places of instruction." In any case, the *Gospel of Truth* provides helpful corroborating evidence on one point: that by the middle of the second century, infancy tales about Jesus and the teacher(s) were available to readers as independent story units (or as grouped story types).

Our next valuable piece of evidence comes from Irenaeus of Lyons, who wrote a treatise *Against Heresies* around the year 180 CE. In a section written against the Marcosians, a sect associated with Valentinus's disciple Marcus,[149] Irenaeus accuses them of having "written" (*graphein*) and "fabricated" (*plassein*) a great number of "apocryphal and spurious writings" to confuse people who do not understand the "letters of truth" (*ta tēs alētheias . . . grammata*).[150] Here, Irenaeus counterposes the category of "apocryphal" (*apokrupha*) or "spurious" (*notha*) writings to the category of scriptural books, which he refers to as "the letters of truth."[151] At the same time, the phrase "letters of truth" is meant to play off and parody what he viewed as the misguided Marcosian use of texts and letters. Earlier in the treatise, he had described and derided Marcosian speculation about "the nine mute letters" (*ta aphona grammata ennea*) in the Greek alphabet, which they interpreted as being in the image of the "Father" and of "truth" (*alētheia*).[152]

As an illustration of their alleged inventiveness, Irenaeus goes on to report on a particular "reckless act" or "crime" (*rhaͅdiourgēma*) propagated by Marcus's followers—the dissemination of a story about when "the Lord was a child and learning the letters."[153] "His teacher said to him, as is customary: 'Say Alpha.' He answered: 'Alpha.' Again, the teacher commanded him to say 'Beta,' but the Lord answered, 'First you tell me what alpha is, and then I shall tell you what Beta is.' "[154] Summarizing the story, Irenaeus makes a point of highlighting the quotidian nature of its details: the teacher's practice of putting a student through drills to memorize the alphabet is seen as "customary" (*kathōs ethos*)—a scene taken from a typical ancient classroom. According to Irenaeus, however, the Marcosians interpreted this story in an esoteric way, as an allegory on "the unknown, which Jesus revealed in the type [*tupos*] of the alpha."[155]

In Irenaeus's late second-century account of Marcosian letter speculation, we have our first compelling evidence for a written version of a story about Jesus attending school. Even if we dismiss the animus-driven claim that Marcus and his followers must have been the inventors of this tale (which I think we should, given its ubiquity as a heresiological trope), it is apparent that Irenaeus (and presumably the Marcosians themselves) were indeed familiar with a written text containing the story. Thus, Irenaeus classifies the tale in the category of "apocryphal and spurious *writings* [*grapha*]."[156] Once again, however, we lack definitive evidence for a larger narrative context or an assembled written collection. What Irenaeus describes simply matches "the classical form of an apophthegm: quick introduction, query, concise dominical saying,"[157] perhaps a variant form of the first or second teacher episode. The narrative details of Irenaeus's account match up especially well with the early Syriac version of Jesus' second classroom encounter, but it diverges in certain details from the contents of the Greek *Paidika*.[158]

Therefore, the text known by Irenaeus and his Marcosian opponents seems to have been one of perhaps several variant stories about Jesus' encounters with schoolteachers that began to circulate in the second century. As we saw in the case of the *Gospel of Truth,* such tales may occasionally have been transmitted as part of small clusters of story units linked by theme. In this context, it is notable that Irenaeus, immediately after discussing the Marcosian use of this infancy tale, cites a passage from Luke 2:49, the story of the twelve-year-old Jesus speaking with the teachers in the Temple. Some scholars have argued that this Lukan account may have prompted early Christian speculation on how Jesus' preternatural wisdom manifested itself before this event during his childhood years, and may have served as a catalyst for efforts to fill in a narrative gap: it is possible that the juxtaposition of teacher and temple stories in Irenaeus's pattern of citations hints at their early association in the transmission history of the *Paidika* and in the Marcosians' reading practices.[159] Unfortunately, the nature of the surviving evidence makes this reconstruction far from certain. What is beyond dispute, however, is the absence of solid evidence in the second century for a more fully fleshed-out *Paidika* narrative featuring a chronological framework and a variety of episodes.

For such evidence, we must wait until the fourth century.[160] In his *Panarion* (or *Medicine Chest*), a work written against heresies between 374 and 377 CE, Epiphanius, the bishop of Salamis, Cyprus, refers to the "divine signs" (*theosēmeia*) that Christ was said to have performed "in play when he was a child" (*en paigniō$_i$ hote paidion ēn*).[161] For Epiphanius, these "childhood signs" (*paidika . . . sēmeia*) have a positive function—namely, "to deprive the other sects of an excuse" for claiming that Jesus had only enjoyed the miracle-working gifts of the Holy Spirit after his adult baptism, when the dove descended upon him from heaven.[162] As in the case of Irenaeus (and perhaps the *Epistle of the Apostles*) two centuries earlier, we get a glimpse again of how stories about Jesus' childhood became fodder for theological debate and polemics. But a crucial difference here is that the stories are cited in the plural: the consistency with which this fourth-century author refers to these "signs" and the use of the adjective *paidika* suggest that he may have known these stories as part of a larger narrative collection of infancy stories, transmitted under an increasingly standardized heading or title.

This is confirmed by a near contemporaneous source, a sermon written by John Chrysostom between 386 and 398 when he was bishop of Antioch. In his homily, Chrysostom likewise refers to "those signs [*sēmeia*], which they say are Christ's childhood deeds [*paidika*]," but in his case, he has a markedly negative attitude toward them.[163] To him, they are patently "false" (*pseudē*), "fabrications" (*plasmata*) introduced by others with uncertain motives: if Jesus had in fact been known for working miracles "from his early age" (*ek prōtēs . . . hēlikias*), we should expect that the writer of the Gospel of John would have known this fact and that there would have been no need for John the Baptist to pave his way in adulthood.[164] Chrysostom's use of the same terms—*sēmeia* ("signs") and *paidika* ("childhood deeds")—as found in Epiphanius's account suggests that they both were probably familiar with a collection containing multiple miracle stories connected with Jesus' childhood.[165] While Epiphanius and Chrysostom give no clues about the contents of such a collection at this stage, the fact that fifth- and sixth-century manuscripts of the *Paidika* survive in Latin and Syriac makes it more likely that these two authors knew of a written source in Greek with a similar narrative scope.[166]

Two other late ancient witnesses to the *Paidika* remind us, however, that, even in the fourth century and later, the pathways for the transmission of such infancy stories could prove to be far from regular or predictable. The first is a work called the *Questions of Bartholomew* (ca. fourth century), which contains a saying attributed to Mary that seems to allude to Jesus' miracle with the birds in chapter 2 of the *Paidika:* "Mary said to them [the apostles]: 'In your likeness God formed the sparrows and sent them to the four corners of the world.' "[167] The second is the *History of Joseph the Carpenter* (fourth to seventh century), in which Joseph briefly recounts how Jesus healed a boy bitten by a snake (cf. *Paidika* 15), how the parents of the boy came to Jesus with angry accusations and were pacified only when the boy was saved (cf. *Paidika* 9), and how Joseph himself had occasion to lay hold of Jesus' ear while admonishing him with instructions about his behavior (cf. *Paidika* 5.2).[168]

In each of these two cases, the connections with known *Paidika* tales are convincing but rather loosely framed. Thus, *Questions of Bartholomew* provides us with our first external witness to the iconic story of Jesus and the sparrows; however, the detail about the birds' flight to "the four corners of the world" (along with its interpretation as a symbol of the apostles) is not attested in the early versions of the *Paidika* collection.[169] In the case of the *History of Joseph the Carpenter,* the links to three different infancy episodes (from *Paidika* 5, 9, and 15) would seem to suggest knowledge of a fuller narrative version, but there are notable details in the snake story that diverge. While the anonymous boy in Joseph's account is bitten on the hand, in the *Paidika* it is Jesus' brother James who is bitten in the foot. It is unclear whether these divergences are the result of oral fluidity, textual variants, or slipshod citation (that is, the author's proclivity to mix and match, and to change and conflate, different episodes from his source material).

In the end, after surveying all this evidence, we are left with a picture of an early transmission history that was far from simple or straightforward, and as a result the textual origins of the *Paidika* remain elusive. What we can say, with a fairly high degree of confidence, is that stories about Jesus' actions as a child—particularly scenes of him in school—began circulating in both oral and written form during the second century, and that over the next two or three hundred years, an extended written collection, with multiple episodes stitched together in a loose narrative framework, was edited and distributed, even as individual pericopes also continued to be passed around by word of mouth, written down, cited, read, heard, edited, and recombined in various new forms and configurations.[170]

What is especially striking to me, and what has not always received enough appreciation from historians, is the predominance of the *pericope* as the primary datum for the early reception and interpretation of the text—that is, the extent to which the *Paidika* stories were experienced by readers and hearers principally *at the level of the story unit.*[171] From the *Epistle of the Apostles,* the *Gospel of Truth,* Irenaeus, and the Marcosians on the episode(s) about Jesus at school to the *Questions of Bartholomew* on the miracle involving the sparrows—early Christian readers and hearers seem to have engaged with these infancy traditions not so much in terms of an extended narrative sequence (a particularly modern preoccupation perhaps), but with eyes and ears trained to scope out individual tales, or tale types, as illustrative or instructive vignettes. In particular, we see how stories about Jesus as a child found two very different, but not incompatible, applications in the hands of recipients.

On the one hand, they were seen as realistic or recognizable scenes from everyday life in Greek and Roman society. Thus, when the author of the *Epistle of the Apostles,* in recalling the story about Jesus learning letters, insists that "truly (it was) a real thing which was done," he understood the "realness" of the scene as not only laden with important theological implications but also (and most crucially) grounded in a familiar set of actual practices and settings associated with childhood. Similarly, in arguing against Marcosian letter speculation, Irenaeus feels it important to note in an aside that the schoolteacher's instructions to Jesus are "customary" (*kathōs ethos*)—that is, typical of what one would encounter in an ancient classroom.

On the other hand, these individual stories were taken up as tools in the sometimes contentious negotiation of religious and social difference. Early Christian readers of different stripes used Jesus' childhood "to think with" and to mark themselves off from other groups with whom they found themselves in disagreement. Whether between the author of the *Epistle of the Apostles* and his anonymous docetic opponents or between Irenaeus and the Valentinian followers of Marcus, the *Paidika* traditions became fodder for controversy over the identity of Jesus and over the shape of Christian identity.

These insights have been crucial to my decision to focus on the reception history of particular infancy stories, and to read these stories—first—in relation to Graeco-Roman social *realia* (including both objects and practices), and—second—in relation to aspects of intra- and interreligious encounter in late antiquity and the early medieval period.

In part 2 of this book, I focus on three different story units or tale types: in chapter 3, the miracle story of Jesus and the birds (*Paidika* 2–3); in chapter 4, accounts of Jesus' fatal curses leveled at his antagonists (*Paidika* 3, 4, 13); and in chapter 5, the scenes of Jesus' encounters with teachers in school and in the Temple (*Paidika* 6–8, 13, 14, 17). In each of these case studies, I explore how the narrative details characteristic of these story types would have prompted connections with cultural "sites of memory"—places, practices, and visual artifacts—drawn from the life setting (*Sitz im Leben*) of their readers and hearers.[172]

Then, in part 3 of the book, I turn my attention to evidence for how the stories from the *Paidika* got caught up in the midst of interreligious controversy and encounter. Chapter 6 examines Jewish and Christian intersections, beginning with a pilgrimage site commemorating the reputed location of Jesus' school in sixth-century Nazareth and ending with medieval Jewish-Christian polemics. One example of such polemics is found in the *Toledot Yeshu,* a Jewish "counter-gospel" about Jesus' youth that incorporates the miracle of the sparrows from the *Paidika* and plays off his reputation as one who possessed the power to curse. Another is found in the work of Christian scribes who altered manuscripts of the *Paidika* to accentuate and enflame Jesus' childhood opposition to his Jewish antagonists. Finally, in chapter 7, I explore evidence for Muslim and Arab Christian interest in these infancy stories—especially the bird and teacher tales—found in the Qur'ān, an *Arabic Gospel of the Infancy,* Ṣūfī "science of the letters," and Muslim Indian hagiography. The result, in the end, is an idiosyncratic, but I hope useful and interesting book—one that traces, in fits and starts, the complex process whereby the figure of a young Jesus came to occupy a unique but ever-shifting place in late ancient and early medieval cultural memory.

PART II

Graeco-Roman Sites of Memory

3

Bird-Watching

When I was a child I thought my father possessed some kind of secret wisdom about the ways of birds. In southeastern Pennsylvania, we would often hear sparrows, robins, blue jays, cardinals, and the occasional oriole, but what got him most excited were the varied vocalizations of the mockingbirds. Before I knew it, he would be tweeting or warbling out a response that mimicked (albeit with a marked human accent) the fluctuating tones and rhythms of their jesting calls. On other occasions, Dad would look up at the sky to spy a solitary hawk floating on an air current high above, or (just as mesmerizing) a flock of geese in their distinctive V-formation. The flock's shared natural instinct to organize themselves in the form of this alphabetic sign was a testimony to the mystery of creation, and Dad's ability to decipher the meaning of their movement—north in advance of summer, south in anticipation of winter—seemed almost divinely inspired to my young, unpracticed eye. In my childhood memories, I recall my father as a mystical adept in the ways of amateur ornithology and myself as his not-so-skilled young apprentice.

The five-year-old Jesus whom we meet at the beginning of the *Paidika* is a bird-watcher, an observer of avian sounds and flight. In our early written versions of the *Paidika*—in Greek, in Latin, and in Syriac—the story of a five-year-old

Jesus playing in pools of water, making sparrows out of clay, and bringing those birds to life is consistently featured as the first episode in the narrative.

When we first encounter Jesus, he is five years old and "playing at the crossing of a stream."[1] First, he gathers the flowing water into ponds and purifies it. Second, with other boys gathered around at play on the Sabbath day, he takes "soft clay from the mixture" and shapes it into the form of twelve sparrows.[2] The story then concludes with an accusation and a miracle. A Jew notices what Jesus is doing and informs Jesus' father, Joseph, that the boy is violating the Sabbath through his actions.[3] When Joseph comes to ask Jesus why he is doing this on the Sabbath, Jesus does not respond; instead he simply "clapped his hands together" and commanded the birds to "go and fly like living things."[4] We are told that, in response to his words, the sparrows immediately took flight and "went away twittering."[5]

In later literature and art, the image of Jesus animating the clay sparrows takes on a life of its own, as an iconic witness to the Christ child's wonder-working powers. The tale became one of the most popular stories about Jesus' childhood in late antiquity and the Middle Ages. Variations on the story appear not only in Greek, Latin, and Syriac but in Slavonic, Georgian, Armenian, Irish, Ethiopic, and Arabic traditions as well.[6] In the previous chapter, I mentioned how the early Christian *Questions of Bartholomew* interpreted the tale, likening the flight of the birds to the apostles' mission to the four corners of the world.[7] It is also recollected in two different verses in the Qur'ān, where 'Īsa (Jesus) tells the Children of Israel, "I fashion for you out of clay the likeness of a bird, and I breathe into it and it is a bird, by Allah's leave" (Sura 3:49), and later Allah asks him to recall that act, saying: "Remember . . . how you created from clay a likeness of a bird with my permission, and how you breathed upon it and it became a bird with my permission" (Sura 5:110).[8] By the medieval period in the Latin West, this miracle of Jesus bringing clay birds to life would find its way into the iconography of churches and chapels, such as St. Martin's in Zillis, Switzerland, where a painted ceiling panel depicts Jesus releasing one of the sparrows as two other boys look on (see Appendix C).[9] But before I get to the "afterlives" of this story,[10] it is important for us to reimagine how it would have struck its early readers and hearers.

Almost all scholars who have examined this story have sought to unlock its meaning with a biblical key: specifically by trying to ferret out possible scriptural allusions and track down sources of inspiration from the Old or New Testament. As I pointed out in the last chapter, this turn to texts—particularly, *canonical* texts—as privileged aids for mining the *Paidika* for meaning can carry with it unwarranted assumptions about ancient readers' access to such sources and their modes of engagement with them. In this chapter, I mark the limitations of this approach and instead read the tale from a new vantage point—one specifically informed by the study of social memory, lived praxis, and *lieux de mémoire.*

As employed by Pierre Nora, the phrase "sites of memory" (*lieux de mémoire*) refers to the objects and bodies, places and practices, that function to re-present the past in functional or symbolic ways for particular communities.[11] One of the motivating questions of this book as a whole is how the *Paidika* itself would have functioned as a site of memory for reimagining the contours of Jesus' childhood in late antiquity. But another question, inextricably related to the first, concerns how this text and its stories would have sponsored cognitive links with other cultural sites of memory as part of the process of reception. In the case of the story about the sparrows, what social *realia* would have been most relevant to ancient readers and hearers as they sought to make sense of the young, wonder-working Jesus portrayed in the *Paidika?*[12] What would Jesus' interaction with birds—both clay and live—have signified to ancient recipients of this work? How did the setting of the story—"at the crossing of a stream"—relate to the actions performed by this child savior? Where might we turn to find cultural "sites" that would have informed ancient understandings of Jesus' actions?

In seeking out sites of memory as crucial points of reference for the text's interpretation, I have two operating assumptions. The first is that any such sites must be readily accessible, embedded in everyday locations and activities that would have seemed almost second nature to denizens of the late ancient Mediterranean world. The second is that these sites must somehow be connected with the status and role of children in Graeco-Roman society.

For those interested in mining the cultural context of ancient texts, these questions and assumptions may seem commonsensical. What distinguishes my "social memory" approach from traditional sociohistorical criticism? The answer lies in the emphasis I place on *the work that ancient readers performed upon the past, using data (sites of memory) from their present-day society as tools for interpretation.* The implications for my study of the *Paidika* are twofold. On the one hand, I contend that Jesus' childhood would have been "remembered" in and through commonly shared, socially produced presuppositions about what a prototypical childhood looked like in the Graeco-Roman world. On the other hand, I suggest that Jesus' prodigious demonstrations of power and insight would have been read through another set of contemporary coordinates—images and objects, practices and rituals understood to provide human beings (children included) with special access to divine power. The end result of such cultural memory work was a young Jesus whose childhood would have been marked as simultaneously conventional and extraordinary in the eyes and ears of those who encountered these stories.

Bird-Watching in the Bible

In seeking to contextualize the story of Jesus and the birds, scholars often have resorted—almost by default—to searches for possible scriptural allusions and antecedents. Arguments for biblical allusions in the story have hinged in part on the use of specific vocabulary. In the *Paidika,* the Greek word *strouthia* is used to refer to the birds that Jesus brings to life. This term can refer generally to "small birds," but it can also refer more specifically to "sparrows" as a species.[13] Notably, the same Greek word appears in Matthew 10:29–31 and Luke 12:6–7 where Jesus compares the value of human beings favorably to that of sparrows. In Matthew, we are told that the price of sparrows is two for a penny and that "not one of them will fall to the ground" without the Father's knowledge (10:29). In Luke, their price on the street has gone down slightly (two pennies will get you five), but their divine valuation remains the same: "Not one of them is forgotten in God's sight" (12:6). Some scholars have tried to press for a connection between the *Paidika* account and these particular verses from the synoptic Gospels, but there is little else in the story to develop such a connection.[14]

In their search for biblical antecedents, scholars have relied not only on terminological interconnections but also on broader thematic and narratological parallels. One example of this is a recurrent effort to interpret Jesus' act of bringing the birds to life as a recapitulation of the creation story in Genesis 1–2.[15] According to this reading, Jesus' act of gathering the water (*hudata*) into pools and purifying it by means of a word (*logos*) echoes God's ordering of the waters (*hudata*) by means of a verbal command in Genesis 1:6–10 (especially as read through the lens of John 1:1–3).[16] As in the creation of humankind out of the earth (*gē*) in Genesis 2:7, Jesus forms the birds out of "soft clay from the mud" (*ek tēs huleōs pēlon*) and gives them life in chapter 2 of the Greek *Paidika.*[17] The placement of the story about the pools and the sparrows at the beginning of the collection is cited as further evidence that it presented a "creation narrative" in miniature, modeled after God's creation of the world in Genesis.[18]

Matthew 10:29–31, Luke 12:6–7, and Genesis 1–2 may (or may not) have served as specific biblical touchstones—scriptural sites of memory—among some early Christian readers trying to make sense of the story.[19] Given the multireferential and intermedial nature of reading practices in antiquity, however, these texts alone are not sufficient for elucidating the full range of associations involving birds, children, and divine power in early Christian cultural memory. To track down such associations requires us to use a wider-angle lens for our task of bird-watching in the Graeco-Roman world.

Birds and Children in Graeco-Roman Culture

In ancient literature and art, birds find frequent association with children. They are mentioned together in poems and letters, and visually linked in paintings and sculptured reliefs. We also discover connections between children and birds reinforced in social practices performed both inside and outside ancient households. Greek and Roman children played with toys modeled after birds and kept birds as pets, while birds (and children) were also used as technological props for negotiating encounters with the divine in magical spells and in oracular settings.

The young Jesus' actions with inanimate and live sparrows bear a striking resemblance to certain aspects of these social practices. This raises a pair of important questions. How might such seemingly disparate objects and activities have served as practical sites of memory for early recipients of the Greek *Paidika?* How might readers and hearers have utilized these images from everyday life as a lens through which they "remembered" Jesus' childhood? To answer these questions requires historical imagination, grounded in a careful examination of relevant sources and concrete settings. On the basis of such evidence I argue that for many ancient readers and hearers Jesus' childlike play and wonder-working in the story of the sparrows would have simultaneously signaled two things: his experience of a typical human childhood, and his embodiment of divine potency.

CHILD'S PLAY (1): BIRDS AS TOYS

Let me begin with some observations about how birds, as a narrative device, would have helped mark the young Jesus as a typical child for Graeco-Roman readers. After diverting the water into pools, Jesus' first act is to shape the moist clay into the form of birds. In this context, it is important to note that there is widespread evidence in classical and late antiquity for the use of terracotta animal figurines—including lions, bears, crocodiles, rams, camels, horses, pigs, dogs, cats, and birds—as children's toys.[20] Indeed, actual examples of such toys have been found across a broad geographical range in Greek, Roman, and Egyptian cultural settings.[21]

A brief survey of the archaeological record will serve to illustrate how common animal toys would have been in households from classical to late antiquity, and how readily accessible such toys would have been to the retrospective manipulations of adult social memory. With regard to this material data, I start with two initial observations. First, a good number of the ancient toys now preserved in museum collections were originally recovered from children's graves. Second, clay figurines of birds feature prominently in this corpus of evidence.[22]

One of the earliest examples comes from the fourth century BCE: a group of objects recovered from a child's tomb includes a number of earthenware toys, most notably two animal statuettes of a rooster and a horse.[23] Clay forms of roosters, hens, ducks, and pigeons from the Roman period survive as part of the collections of antiquities housed in Oxford, Mainz, Heidelberg, and Cologne.[24] In London, the British Museum collection includes one ancient toy consisting of two clay birds mounted on a wooden stick: children could make the birds "fly" by rotating the figures on its axis.[25]

The use of such clay figures as children's toys is in fact attested all across the Roman Empire, from Britain in the west to Palestine in the east.[26] Excavations of the Agora in Athens have turned up numerous clay toys and rattles shaped in the form of domesticated animals, including birds.[27] Similar examples of rattles and wheeled toys have been found in late antique Egypt.[28] In the Fayum Oasis, the figure of a clay hen was found alongside camels, cattle, pigs, and horses made of the same material.[29] While many of these clay toys would have been manufactured for children by adults, there is also literary and archaeological evidence for children's involvement in "the shaping of clay or mud into various playthings and toys" extending into the medieval and Byzantine periods.[30] Jesus' act of fashioning birds from the wet clay of a streambed in the *Paidika* closely resembles this kind of creative activity, and in this context the story would have probably recalled for readers real-life examples of children's play with clay models.

The fact that most of the terracotta toys in the archaeological record were originally deposited in children's graves suggests that death and burial served as a common setting for the shaping of such social memories. For parents forced to bury their sons and daughters prematurely, the deposition of such objects in their graves was a physical act through which they sought to remember their sons and daughters at play. When it came to the young Jesus (whose life also would meet a premature end), the image of him shaping birds out of clay as a child would have performed similar cultural work in the minds and memories of readers.

Apart from such funerary contexts of remembrance, children's play with bird toys also shaped adult social memories of childhood more regularly in everyday household encounters. As Johan Huizenga has noted, the temporal and spatially delimited character of play—that is, its particular association with household times and spaces—effectively marked it off from other cultural activities and caused it to assume a "fixed form" in the cultural consciousness of Graeco-Roman grown-ups.[31] As a ritualized set of actions, play is eminently repeatable (both in actual practice and in the halls of memory) and therefore transmittable from one generation to the next as a shared *lieu de mémoire*.[32] In this context, the story of Jesus playing with clay birds would have served as a medium—a literary "realm of remembrance" (*Erinnerungsraum*)—for reinforcing adult perceptions of what children typically do, and for marking Jesus (at least on one level) as a typical child.

CHILD'S PLAY (2): CARING FOR PETS

After shaping the sparrows out of clay, Jesus' second action is to bring those birds to life and command them to fly into the air. The image of a young boy interacting with live birds that follow his commands would have had another ready-made association in Graeco-Roman social memory: the keeping of birds as pets. This association is illustrated by the later reception of the tale in the *Arabic Gospel of the Infancy,* where a variant version of the story has Jesus take the birds he has fashioned out of clay and make them walk, leap, stand still, fly, perch, eat, and drink at his command—actions that correspond to the way a pet bird is trained to heed its young owner's wishes.[33]

If the ancient material record for terracotta bird toys was abundant, the evidence for children's interest in and care for live birds as playthings is even more plentiful.[34] In her study of childhood in ancient Greece and Italy, Ada Cohen has identified birds as "ubiquitous live toys" for the younger set.[35] Indeed, both literary and material evidence attest to the popularity of domestic bird care in the ancient world: numerous authors mention cases of children keeping birds, and birds are frequently depicted in the company of children on both painted pottery and sculpted stone monuments.[36]

From the third century BCE to the second century CE, a whole series of ancient authors make passing reference to the practice of keeping birds as pets among both elite and nonelite Romans.[37] The list of domesticated bird species is long. Plautus refers to jackdaws, ducks, quails, and crows as common presents for children.[38] Ovid and Columella both remark on the raising of doves as a commonplace in Roman society.[39] Pliny the Elder reports on how the emperor Nero and Britannicus (the son of the emperor Claudius) kept nightingales and a starling as pets during their boyhood years.[40] Pliny the Younger relates how the son of the Roman senator M. Aquilius Regulus owned nightingales, parrots, and blackbirds.[41]

Sparrows are featured prominently among the literary sources. In the first century BCE, Catullus composed his famous pair of poems about his lady Lesbia's pet sparrow (*passer*), in which he describes how it would allow itself to be held by its mistress and would peck at her finger, how it would hop in her lap and chirp only for her.[42] While scholars have often emphasized the erotic subtext of the lady's relationship to the sparrow,[43] the poet's depiction of the bird's interactions with its owner draws on common social images associated with the domestication of winged creatures as pets. Further evidence comes from the Roman rhetorician Marcus Cornelius Fronto, active during the middle of the second century CE. He tells of how his grandson kept sparrows (along with chickens and pigeons) as pets, and shares how he himself was also said to have had a passion for these same kinds of birds during his own childhood ("from my earliest infancy").[44] This common practice of keeping sparrows as pets continued in later centuries. Writing around 398 CE, Augustine of Hippo in his *Confessions* recalls his own childhood, associating it with playthings like nuts, balls, and pet sparrows (*passeres*).[45]

In addition to these written sources, there is abundant material evidence for domesticated birds and their close association with children from classical antiquity to the early Christian period. Domestic vessels and decorative items provided one social context for the visual representation of this motif. Ceramic bowls (*choes*) from Athens and other places in classical Greece depict small children with their winged pets. On a late fifth-century BCE red-figure example discovered in the Athenian Agora, for example, a nude boy holds a small bird at arm's length in his left hand while reaching out to it with his right.[46] During the Hellenistic period, artisans produced terracotta figurines with tender scenes of children cradling and kissing birds in their hands,[47] as well as less tender ones of children watching a cockfight.[48]

Evidence from the late Roman period includes wall paintings, sculptures, and mosaics recovered in situ from private homes and public worship spaces. A wall painting of an infant boy with two birds (one a dove and the other a duck) was found in a first-century CE house at Pompeii.[49] The child, identified in the painting as "the boy Successus" (*puer Successus*), may also have been the subject of a stone sculpture discovered in the garden area of the same residence, which likewise depicts a boy holding a dove.[50] Later mosaics discovered at early Christian sites in Palestine provide additional useful information about the domestic care of winged creatures as pets: in selected examples, birds are depicted in cages or with tethers around their necks to prevent them from flying away, sometimes in the company of human handlers.[51]

The vast majority of material artifacts, however, once again come from cemeteries—especially grave stelae, sarcophagi, and the occasional wall painting—evidence spanning an enormously broad temporal and spatial horizon from Attic Greece, to Roman Britain, to late ancient Egypt.[52] Recently, some historians have argued that the representation of birds in Graeco-Roman funerary art had specific symbolic functions. Ada Cohen sees birds, due to their timelessness and lack of individuating features, as alluding to the "tenuous contact between the world of the dead and the world of the living."[53] Janet Huskinson, observing that birds convey "a whole range of ideas—innocence, tenderness, naturalness, and elusiveness," proposes that they also may represent "the soul or life-force" of the child.[54] Indeed, Plutarch compares the soul to a "captive bird" in his *Consolation to His Wife,* a work written after the death of their infant daughter,[55] and on contemporaneous Roman reliefs on children's sarcophagi the personified female Psyche (Soul) is shown in the company of birds.[56] In these cases, there is a frequent association of birds with the souls of prematurely deceased children.

These possible symbolic connections notwithstanding, it is important to recognize the shared cultural memory captured in the pervasive representation of birds and children on ancient tombs—namely, that pet keeping was recognized as a common activity among young boys and girls in antiquity. Four scene types in funerary sculptures and paintings underscore the variety of activities typically associated with children's care of birds in the home:

1. child standing in the company of a bird;[57]
2. child holding a bird in hand;[58]
3. child offering/receiving a bird to/from someone else;[59]
4. child feeding, petting, or playing with a bird.[60]

Types 1 and 2, which present scenes of the deceased child simply standing or holding/petting the bird, constitute the vast majority of the extant examples. While the figure of the child in these images appears rather stylized and static, the artists nonetheless highlight the quotidian nature of the scenes, often depicting the deceased child in the company of parents, toys, and other pets.[61] The other two types accentuate various bodily movements associated with the practice of caring for pets. Type 3 (scenes of children offering a bird to or receiving a bird from another child or a parent) seems to be a special feature of Attic grave stelae. The evidence for type 4 ranges later, extending into the Hellenistic, early Roman, and late antique periods: these scenes typically represent children in more dynamic, playful interaction with birds, including petting, feeding, and assorted acts of mischief. Such actions may be likened to Paul Connerton's "incorporating practices," insofar as the representation of children's bodies in motion "stylistically re-enact[ed] an image of the past," commemorating a set of gestural performances that signaled childhood play to the viewer.[62]

The act of petting birds in particular may have been designed to evoke a tender, emotional response from viewers in the context of memorial graveside practices, but it also would have evoked specific household memories of children at play. Two examples show how artists used contextual images to underscore the playful association of this act. First, a Hellenistic funerary relief preserved in the J. Paul Getty Museum in Los Angeles shows the placid figure of a twelve- or thirteen-year-old girl named Apollonia: she stands and reaches up to pet a dove that is perched on top of a short pillar, while in her left hand she holds a ball.[63] Second, a Roman sarcophagus carved during Trajan's reign (98–117 CE) depicts a young boy (the deceased) reaching out to touch the head of his pet goose; the playfulness of his gesture is reinforced by the smaller figure of a boy to his right, perhaps his younger brother, who grasps the handle of what looks like a scooter.[64]

The function of such stelae as markers of memory connected with children's play becomes even more explicit in scenes depicting more vigorous physical interaction with birds. On some funerary reliefs, children are captured in the act of feeding birds, or mischievously trying to keep food away from their pets.[65] In the Catacomb of Domitilla in Rome, one artist has etched the figure of a boy chasing a peacock: he holds a stick with a string at the end, perhaps a kind of makeshift whip; the peacock seems intent on keeping a healthy distance.[66] While this scene is unique to Roman funerary art, other scenes of children at play with birds are preserved in sculpted miniatures from domestic contexts, including a number of variations on a boy wrestling with a goose.[67]

I have surveyed a healthy cross-section of this ancient material evidence. How is this evidence relevant for a contextualized reading of the *Paidika?* What does it tell us about how ancient readers and auditors would have encountered this story of Jesus and the birds? And what kind of cultural memory work was at stake in such images and stories?

One thing is clear: at home, at cemeteries, and at shops that sold ceramic bowls and children's toys,[68] denizens of the ancient Mediterranean world—pet owners and non–pet owners alike—would have encountered visual stimuli that reinforced the association of children with the practice of keeping birds (and other domestic animals) as pets. In some cases, men and women would have been reminded of their own childhood interactions with roosters and geese, nightingales and peacocks, pigeons and sparrows.

What I would like to suggest is that the image of a young Jesus at play, interacting with clay models and live birds, would have served a social function similar to the ornithological sites of memory reviewed above. From the get-go, this *Paidika* story would have marked Jesus' human childhood as one that conformed to certain familiar patterns and practices among children in the Graeco-Roman world. As such, it would have served as a site of memory for recipients of the Greek *Paidika* in at least two ways. For a select few, it would have allowed them to draw cogent connections between Jesus' actions and their own childhood experiences. For a broader audience, the *Paidika* would have worked to reinforce and shape a shared cultural perception—a collective memory, if you will—of bird figurines and bird keeping as connected with typical child's play, and Jesus as having experienced a typical childhood.

Divine Signs: Birds in Ancient Cultic Worship, Magical Practices, and Augury

Having underscored how the story of Jesus and the birds would have evoked commonly shared images of Graeco-Roman childhood, grounded in a range of material culture from toys to graveside images, I also want to argue that this same scene would have simultaneously elicited a competing set of cultural memories—memories drawn from other spheres of ancient society that would have destabilized Jesus' representation as a typical child and that would have cast him in a very different light in the eyes of readers. Thus, even as the image of Jesus forming clay figures of birds and releasing live birds into the air would have prompted specific associations with common forms of childhood play, these same actions would also have had other, very different cultural resonances among the same communities of reception. In what follows, I explore how these actions would have recalled for readers certain conventional ritual actions associated with votive dedications, magic, and divination, in which birds (or bird figurines) served as key technological props.

Dating back to the Minoan and Mycenaean periods in Greece, the use of terracotta bird figurines as votive offerings and as signs for the epiphany of a god are attested in house sanctuaries.[69] In fifth- and fourth-century BCE Greece, clay birds were also found in public sanctuaries like that of Demeter in Acrocorinth. Excavations at Corinth have also yielded figurines of boys carrying grapes, toys, and animals (including birds), usually interpreted as scenes of cultic offering—as idealized depictions of ritual practices in which children may have actually participated.[70] Various other ceramic statuettes connected with a possible cultic (and/or domestic) provenance have been uncovered during excavations at the Arabian sites of ed-Dur and Thaj, as well as at Babylon, Seleucia on the Tigris, and Dura Europos.[71]

During the classical period, live birds came to be closely linked with the worship of Kore and Aphrodite,[72] and sparrows in particular benefited from the god Apollo's special protection at Branchidae in Anatolia.[73] Such cultic associations survived in some areas into Roman late antiquity: according to Claudius Aelianus (ca. 175–ca. 235 CE), in his day the killing of a sparrow dedicated to Asclepius in Athens still brought a penalty of death to the transgressor.[74] The presence of birds would also later become closely associated with dedicatory offerings and healing practices at the pilgrimage shrines of Christian saints.[75]

In ancient Egyptian magical practice, birds—both inanimate and live—were frequently incorporated into spell prescriptions, and sometimes the rites intentionally seemed to blur the lines between the role played by molded animal figurines on the one hand and living, breathing specimens on the other. Thus, the early and quite fragmentary *Papyrus Westcar* (18–16th century BCE) preserves the story of a chief temple priest named Webaoner who magically transforms the wax figure of a crocodile into an actual reptile by throwing it into a lake. (The crocodile then performs the useful service of devouring his wife's illicit lover.)[76] In another story, an Egyptian high priest named Neneferkaptah animates clay figurines through verbal incantations.[77]

In the late ancient Greek magical papyri (*Papyri Graecae Magicae*) much attention has been given to the way ritual practitioners manipulated human-shaped clay figurines in order to exert control over the minds and bodies of eroticized female targets in certain binding spells.[78] Much less attention has been given to a similar theory of correspondence at work in the use of bird statuettes and mummies by the same guild of specialists. One papyrus dated to the fourth or fifth century CE instructs the spell giver first to "take a Circaean falcon and deify it," setting its corpse up "as a statue in a shrine made of juniper wood."[79] The practitioner is then supposed to dedicate a sacrifice and "speak directly to the bird itself," for the purpose of summoning Orion and "[coming] face to face as companion [to the god]."[80] The next entry in the same papyrus tells the one performing the rite to "grasp a falcon's head" and shake it in his right hand before dedicating it as a sacrifice.[81] This series of actions is designed to elicit a divine sign—the appearance of another (live) falcon that flies down, flaps its wings, lands in front of the spell agent, and then takes flight again, only to disappear into the heavens—a sign linked to the epiphany of the god described as "an aerial spirit."[82] A similar connection between the flight of birds and divine epiphanies may be found in other spells, including an amulet with a Coptic invocation offered up to "the Father Pantokrator" (identified with the god Atikhis), who "must fly like the birds of heaven" to save the petitioner.[83]

Live birds in the Greek magical papyri are not only sacrificed in petition to the gods. Ritual practitioners—not unlike Jesus in the *Paidika*—also hold and release live birds, observe their flight, and even speak to them directly and give them commands. In one charm to induce insomnia or wakefulness, the release of a bat or a bird (*ornufin*) with the name of the god and an incantation written on its wing is thought to bring about the charm's intended effect.[84] Another spell designed to revitalize a sun scarab is accomplished "through the twenty-five living birds." This is perhaps an allusion to the release of one bird per hour over the course of a whole day, with the rebirth of the scarab taking place after the first hour of the new dawn (the first day of the month).[85]

In other rites, spell givers address birds directly with spoken commands designed to control—either to suppress or to motivate—their vocalization and flight. Such actions rested on the premise that those reciting the spells were empowered to communicate with birds in their own language, and that this language was one shared by the gods themselves. Thus, in one rather lengthy magical rite, the one reciting the spell calls on the creator god in several sacred tongues, including "birdglyphic" (*orneoglufisti*) and "falconic" (*hierakisti*), and then claps (*krotein*) three times.[86] These greetings are later echoed by an angel and a falcon (probably understood as the instantiation of the god Horus).[87] Further on, "the practical uses of this sacred book" are finally disclosed to the spell owner, who is notably addressed as a "child"—someone who at one time made an oath in the "temple of Jerusalem" and who will be "filled with divine wisdom."[88] The book's practical uses include (among other things) the power to resurrect dead bodies, to kill snakes, and to determine the life or death of a bird by reciting the words of the spell into its ear.[89]

The cluster of themes laid out here bears an intriguing resemblance to details found in early Christian traditions about the young Jesus' precocity. In the *Paidika,* the Christ child indeed engages in debate with Jewish legal experts in the Jerusalem temple, resurrects a dead boy named Zeno, kills a serpent who had unwisely bitten his brother James, and also claps and speaks words in a way that holds power over the life of birds.[90] It would certainly be too much of a stretch to try to argue that this particular spell was crafted with such infancy stories in mind. It is not unreasonable, however, to raise questions about how such kinds of ritual language and practice might have informed the worldview of the *Paidika*'s early audience. Indeed, the repeated recitation of such rites in the Greek-speaking Mediterranean world would have helped cultivate in its population a close association between efficacious speech (as a manifestation of heavenly wisdom) and the instrumentality of birds in ritualized performances of divine power. Thus, even for those predisposed against anything that smacked of so-called magic, these rites would have provided a practical reference point for making (an alternative) sense of Jesus' actions in the *Paidika.*

As further evidence for the dissemination of such cultural assumptions, I turn finally to one last spell from the Greek magical papyri and thence to the wider ancient practice of divination. The spell in question is an invocation to the sun god Helios in which the one reciting the prayer assumes a position of sovereignty over the cosmos. Specifically, the spell giver first commands the "circling birds of air" to "keep quiet" and orders the "rivers, streams, and fountain (flows)" to stand still.[91] Then, he tells the "birds of augury" to "stop everything beneath the sky" and warns snakes hiding in their dens to "attend the cry and be afraid."[92] As before, one notes that Jesus performs a similar set of actions in the *Paidika,* where he directs the flowing waters of a "rushing stream" into standing pools, commands the flight (and vocalization) of birds, and later seeks out and destroys the "miscreant snake" that had bitten his brother James (cf. *Paidika* 15).[93] In these scripted actions, the child Jesus manifests a recognizable kind of physical control over the natural realm that would have tallied rather neatly with ancient readers' expectations regarding the divine efficacy of spells and other ritual forms of power in the Graeco-Roman world.

The Graeco-Roman divinatory practice of taking the *auspices*—alluded to quite plainly in the Helios prayer when the spell giver appeals to "birds of augury" for aid—constituted another highly visible ritual setting involving live birds, and it provides a final case study for gauging the cultural import of Jesus' actions in the *Paidika.* In the larger ancient corpus of magical papyri, divination spells frequently feature children as privileged mediums who exhibit a particular aptitude for prophetic insight—for gazing at and seeing the gods ("those who fly through the air"), and for communicating information from the divine realm in a straightforward and truthful manner.[94] As a species of divination, augury therefore would have served as yet another practical site of memory for readers trying to "discern the signs" related to the young Jesus' activity of bird-watching.

Augury—referred to in Greek linguistic settings as ornithomancy—involved a set of ritual methods used for discerning the will of a god. What distinguished augury from other divinatory methods was its practitioners' studied focus on the flight of *birds* as a sign of divine favor (or disfavor). On "auspicious" occasions, augurs would release birds into the air and observe their direction of flight and listen to the sounds they made, interpreting those movements and noises as portents of future events. In ancient Greece, the practice of "bird interpretation" (Gk. *oiōnoskopeia*) was sometimes linked with oracular practice, as at Delphi, where, "beside the stream and shrine of Earth," birds were seen to be "messengers and heralds" whose presence pleased the gods and who conveyed indications of the divine will to supplicants through their sounds and calls.[95] More frequently, Greek "bird interpreters" (Gk. *ornithoskopoi, ornithokriteis, oiōnoskopoi*) probably would have been encountered as members of local familial guilds or as freelance itinerants.[96]

Under the Roman Republic, the public role of *augures* was increasingly formalized through the formation of a college of priestly magistrates (*pontifices*) who oversaw and regulated the taking of the *auspices* on various occasions—especially at elections and inaugurations, and at the crossing of territorial boundaries.[97] As such, augury was widely viewed as "a scientific art of public utility."[98]

A special class of rites called *peremnia* involved taking auspices beside a stream or river before one made a crossing.[99] In Roman culture, rivers and streams were regarded as "ominous barriers . . . separating the living from the dead," and *peremnia* were acts of augury designed to counteract the potential for ritual violation (*vitium;* pl. *vitia*) or unfavorable omens associated with those locations.[100] Cicero (106–46 BCE) explicitly refers to the custom of taking auspices beside rivers in his treatise *On Divination* while comparing the different ways augury was performed at Rome and in foreign lands. By the first century BCE, such acts of *peremnia* were no longer consistently practiced by Roman legions on the march, but cultural memories of this military practice would have been reinforced in educational settings through readings of Virgil's *Aeneid* (book 9), where the king Turnus pauses by a brook and makes a vow to heaven to pursue war.[101] In late ancient commentary, this action was explicitly read as a rite of augury.[102]

By Cicero's day, however, the actual practice of augury had been relocated to "city locations" (*ad urbanas*),[103] and during the reign of Augustus (27 BCE–14 CE) the constitutional "right of augury" (*ius augurium*) came to be formally invested in the emperor himself, who accordingly took on the title of *pontifex maximus.* In this context, Livy (59 BCE–17 CE) ties the practice of bird interpretation to the "peace of the gods" (*pax deorum*), which was understood to prevail over the destruction caused by war and natural disasters."[104] A century later, the historian Suetonius (d. after 130) uses wordplay to connect Octavius's official augural role as emperor with his decision to take the name Augustus: "He preferred to be called Augustus . . . because religious places which are consecrated by an 'augur's' ritual [*in quibus augurato*] are called 'august' [*augusta dicantur*]," and because "Rome had been founded by an august augury [*augusto augurio*]."[105] Here, Suetonius makes allusion to the widely known tradition that Romulus had founded Rome after seeing "twelve sacred birds" fly down from heaven, an event interpreted as a sign of divine favor for the "throne" he established there.[106] A similar link between augury and the establishment of ancient cities may be noted in early Greek traditions,[107] but in the case of Rome, the retelling of this foundation legend came to serve an important purpose within an emerging imperial cult—namely, to give a historical warrant for the emperor's public role as high priest and divinely ordained king.[108]

In his recent book *The Son of God in the Roman World,* Michael Peppard has similarly interpreted the dove's appearance at Jesus' baptism in Mark 1:9–11 in relation to ancient Roman practices of augury, especially insofar as such practices marked the gods' endorsement of imperial power.[109] In addition to citing sources such as Suetonius, he also draws cogent comparisons to the early Christian *Protevangelium of James* where, prior to Jesus' birth, a dove flies down and alights on Joseph's head at the Temple.[110] In both Mark and the *Protevangelium,* Peppard sees the appearance of birds as "an omen indicating divine election," and as "a Christian counterpoint to the . . . imagery of imperial lore."[111]

My survey of the role augury played in Greek and Roman societies likewise provides cultural coordinates for understanding how Jesus' miracle with birds might have been read and contextualized by early recipients of the *Paidika.* In a world where the act of releasing birds into the air and observing their flight was associated with the ritual discernment of divine favor and the inauguration of newly ordained leaders—where the release of birds by the banks of streams was understood to absolve a person of possible ritual transgressions; where the vision of twelve birds in the heavens would have recalled stories endorsing the establishment of a new reign of peace, a new kingdom ruled by a priest-king—Jesus' actions at the beginning of the *Paidika* would have taken on an added significance. They would have been perceived as gestures that effectively countered, co-opted, and Christianized the ritual repertoire of magic and divination so ubiquitous in ancient society.[112]

From children's play with birds as toys and pets to the use of birds and bird figurines as votive offerings and as ritual accoutrements in magical practice and augury, the identification of these diverse sites of memory has allowed me to begin to test out my audience-oriented approach to the Greek *Paidika.*

This approach carves out an imaginative space for discerning the social coordinates for early audiences' reception of these stories. In the case of the story of Jesus and the birds, I have suggested that these coordinates may be found in a set of shared cultural associations related to birds, childhood, and ritual acts of power. For Graeco-Roman readers—Christian and non-Christian alike—such social memories were sedimented in readily recognizable practices and material artifacts.[113] The final product of such memory work would have been a multilayered reading of the young Jesus both as a typical, recognizable child and as a divinely endowed prodigy whose actions portend the later, adult fulfillment of his miracle-working potency.[114] As we shall see in the next chapter, the prodigious skills of this young Jesus extended not only to the utterance and ritual performance of life-giving words but also to acts of cursing and dealings with death.

4

Cursing

Some of my own most vivid memories from childhood include conflicts on the playground. I remember wrestling on the ground with my best friend, Mark Ashley, after a hotly contested tetherball match. I remember punching another friend, Mike McMinn, in the stomach after he had gotten up in my face, gloating after his team scored a touchdown in touch football. Then I recall running away as fast as I could, with Mike chasing me around the swing, hurling a string of curses in my direction. Fortunately, I outran him—and the dire effects of his words—until he and I were both gasping and out of breath.[1]

In chapter 2 of the Greek *Paidika,* the young Jesus forms sparrows out of clay and then brings them to life while playing by a rushing stream. In chapter 3, on the heels of this life-giving miracle, his power takes an unexpected turn when, with a word, he suddenly deals out death to one of his fellow playmates. The playmate in question was one of the children who had observed the result of his interaction with the birds. Identified as "the son of Annas the high priest," the boy approaches Jesus and asks him, "Why are you doing such a thing on the Sabbath?" In indignation, he then takes a willow bough and with it destroys the pools that Jesus earlier had gathered together and purified by means of a word. The boy's hostile action makes all the water drain away, and as a result the pools dry up (*xērainein*).[2] Jesus' response is unhesitating and unforgiving: he turns to the boy and says, "May your fruit be rootless and may your shoot be dried up like a young branch charred by a violent wind!" His words have an instantaneous effect. "Immediately," we are told, "that child dried up [*xērainein*]" as well.[3]

This story of Jesus' encounter with the son of the high priest is just one of three stories that end with a lethal utterance by the Christ child. Throughout the rest of the *Paidika,* these utterances are pointedly identified as "curses" (*katarai*). In the next episode (chapter 4), Jesus is walking down the street with Joseph when a child runs and crashes into his shoulder. Jesus turns and says to him, "Cursed be your guide" (*epikataratos soi ho hēgemōn sou*), and the child dies on the spot. After marveling at how Jesus' "word becomes a deed," the parents of the child beg Joseph to "teach him to bless and not to curse [*eulogein kai mē katarasthai*]."[4] Later, in chapter 14, when his second teacher strikes him in frustration, Jesus responds by cursing him, and the teacher falls down and dies straightaway.[5]

Taken together, these stories in which Jesus curses others to death serve as a second case study for my method of reading the *Paidika* as a (textual) "site of memory"—one that would have prompted readers and hearers to make meaningful links to other social and material sites of memory in the Graeco-Roman world. Indeed, these curse episodes raise a pair of important questions. First, how would early recipients of the *Paidika* have made sense of Jesus' fatal speech in relation to their own awareness of cursing as a cultural practice in antiquity? Second, how would such stories about Jesus as a curser and about other children (and adults) as cursing victims have conditioned readers' understanding of Jesus as a divinely endowed prodigy?

By way of addressing these questions, I highlight "three C's"—childhood, cursing, and competition—as closely interrelated cultural points of reference that help explain why the *Paidika* depicts Jesus as a child embroiled in interpersonal conflict and engaged in verbal acts of deadly power and how this depiction would have intersected with the expectations of ancient Graeco-Roman audiences. I begin with an investigation of the nearly ubiquitous role that social conflict and competition played in the lives of ancient children and youth. Then I turn my attention back to the *Paidika* stories (and especially Jesus' curse of the anonymous boy in chapter 4), reading then as instances of childhood conflict and suggesting how forms of social competition and cursing would have inflected Graeco-Roman memories of Jesus' experiences as a child.

Children and the "Agony" of Competition

CONTESTS OF BODIES: SPORTS AND GAMES

In antiquity, competitive games and sports were an integral part of young children's (especially boys') social interactions. Some of these activities were relatively sedentary, such as games analogous to modern jacks or dice,[6] or board games using pebbles or nuts as the moving pieces.[7] Others required more strenuous physical interaction, from skimming stones, shells, or potsherds over the surface of bodies of water to tug-of-war and sports involving the use of balls and/or sticks.[8] Not surprisingly, such testosterone-fueled activities sometimes could lead to fights. A wrestling match between two young boys, complete with hair pulling, has been vividly captured in stone by the sculptor of a sarcophagus relief preserved in the Museo Chiaramonti at the Vatican.[9] In their competitions on the "playground"—on the street or in an open field—ancient children sometimes also mimicked the kinds of athletic events featured at regularly celebrated public games and festivals. Certain forms of imitative play served to prepare children for assuming adult roles later in life.[10]

Thomas Wiedemann classifies different types of play (Greek, *paigma;* Latin, *ludus*) according to stages of childhood development, highlighting a transition to "collective" or "sociodramatic" play from the ages of four to seven, a period in which the child begins to act out adult roles. In the case of boys, playacting often established and reinforced differentiations of status, with leaders among the group impersonating the role of kings, judges, or generals. In everyday Graeco-Roman life, this kind of collective play sometimes modeled itself after popular competitions in the arena, including chariot racing and gladiatorial contests. The imagined realism of such childhood games was enhanced through the wearing of specially marked costumes, such as toy armor and uniforms. Finally, from the ages of seven to twelve, children took part in games with more complex rules, sometimes involving elements of risk or chance, or contests of strength. Ball sports—interactive, competitive games in which the young participants adhered to a system of rules and exerted themselves physically—were especially common among male children of this age as well as among those in their teens.[11] Surviving literary and material sources provide us with vivid images of boys wrestling over the possession of balls, or tossing them to each other.[12] Just as in the case of athletic games and competitions today, sometimes such activities resulted in collisions and injuries: a Roman legal *Digest* from late antiquity reports one incident where a ballplayer accidently ran into a slave boy, knocking him down and breaking his leg.[13]

It was also probably during these younger developmental years that children began being trained in local gymnasia in preparation for competitions at the classical Greek games, where formal athletic events for older boys (from around the age of twelve and up) were instituted early on at places like Olympia, Corinth, Nemea, Delphi, and Epidaurus, as well as at regional and local venues.[14] In addition to athletic contests, such festival games featured poetry readings, dramatic performances, and musical recitals, with competitions for children and youth scheduled at times separate from the adult events. This varied program was designed to celebrate *agōn*—the spirit of contest or competition, embodied in the struggle to attain supremacy in virtue.[15]

Such agonistic events for children and youth continued to be observed on a regular basis into the Roman imperial era in both the Greek East and the Latin West. At major and minor festival venues, the organization of boys' events became increasingly elaborate, with multiple age divisions to accommodate children and youth of different developmental stages.[16] The athletic events held at such games ranged from footraces of different lengths (such as the *stadion*) and charioteering competitions (including races that combined running with horse riding and handling), to combat sports such as wrestling, boxing, and the virtually no-holds-barred *pankration*.[17] The multidisciplinary *pentathlon* was an event that combined different sporting events and involved competitions in discus, javelin, jumping, running, and wrestling.

Prepubescent boys competed and sometimes achieved victory in such competitions. In the fifth century BCE, Pindar reports that Pytheas of Aegina "won the crown for the pancratium [*pankration*] in Nemea's games," despite the fact that he had not yet begun to show any signs of facial hair.[18] In the fourth century BCE, a twelve-year-old boy named Damiscus of Messene prevailed in a sprint race (the boys' *stadion*) at the Olympian games: his age was recorded on an inscription in the district of Elis in the Peloponnesos. The same inscription was still on public display (and still legible) six centuries later when the second-century CE traveler Pausanias wrote down its contents for posterity in his *Description of Greece*.[19]

Damiscus is our youngest attested victor from Greek antiquity, and it is on the basis of Pausanias's report on Damiscus's inscription that historians have used twelve years old as a presumed lower cutoff age for entry into official boys' competitions. But it is very possible that younger athletes participated in such games without achieving a victory worthy of commemoration in stone. The standards applied in determining whether a young boy could compete may not even have been based solely on a determination of age but rather on more subjective assessments of the child's physical readiness.[20] Pausanias reports on the case of a certain Pherias of Aegina, who was deemed too young to compete at Olympia: "Being judged to be as yet unfit to wrestle, [he] was debarred from the contest."[21] This is often cited as evidence for the establishment of a minimum-age standard at the Olympic games by the middle of the fifth century BCE.[22] If this is so, however, it also serves as corroborating evidence that children younger than the minimum age were engaged in training for such competition.[23]

What did such training look like, and where did it take place? Although there were specific precincts and periods of time set aside for the purpose of training before the start of competition at the various pan-Hellenic festival games, the physical education of young boys in fact began much earlier, in places closer to home. In the hometowns of aspiring young athletes, sons would accompany their fathers to publicly administered gymnasia, or would be sent to local *palaistrai* (smaller public or private buildings used for training, sometimes incorporated into the larger gymnasia, and sometimes established as independent facilities).[24] At such institutions, fathers would place their sons under the care of trainers—*gymnastai* and *paidotribai*—who would monitor their physical condition and exercise regimen.[25] In cities such as Ephesus, an athletic supervisor called an *epistatēs* was assigned to oversee the training of boys in the local gymnasium, a civic service that "afforded non-wealthy boys the chance to train and show promise."[26]

This guild of athletic trainers continued to offer services to families with aspiring children in the second and third centuries CE. Lucian of Samosata (ca. 125–180 CE) reports on the kinds of exercises overseen in such programs:

> Next we have thought up different kinds of athletics and have appointed coaches for each type. We teach one how to box, another how to compete in the pankration, so that they can become used to hard work, to stand up to blows face to face, and not to yield through fear of injury. This creates two valuable traits in our young men: it makes them brave in the face of danger and unsparing of their bodies, and it also makes them strong and vigorous. Those who wrestle and push against each other learn how to fall safely and spring up nimbly, to endure pushing, grappling, twisting, and choking, and to be able to lift their opponent off the ground. . . . From this training they acquire skills which they may need some day in war. For it is clear that if a man so trained grapples with an enemy, he will trip and throw him more quickly.[27]

The Christian moral philosopher Clement of Alexandria, a contemporary of Lucian, promotes "such athletic contests" as a suitable preparation for manhood among young boys: for him, "a stand-up wrestling bout" (*orthē palē*) was "a struggle with graceful strength" especially conducive to maintaining their health during years of growth.[28]

There were differing opinions on the value of such training. In the first half of the third century CE, Flavius Philostratus of Athens (ca. 170–247 CE) comments critically on how overzealous trainers (*gymnastai*) "take a boy athlete, make him strip, and then exercise him as if he were a mature man."[29] By contrast, the anonymous author of a treatise entitled *The Education of Children* (*De liberis educandis*), probably also active in the third century, held a view closer to that of Clement: for him, the training offered by *paidotribēs* ("the exercise of bodies," *tōn sōmatōn agōnia*)—was crucial preparation and practice for "the contests of war" (*hoi stratiōtikoi agōnes*) men would face in adulthood.[30] The author's use of the word *agōnia*—a derivation from the Greek noun *agōn* ("contest, competition")—closely links the physical education of children "with the agonistic festival culture" for which such training was preparation.[31] This high valuation of *agōn* therefore infused not only the periodic contests held at Olympia and other festival games but also children's everyday physical interactions with each other in the gymnasium and on the playground—formal and informal training grounds for the expression (and resolution) of conflict and competition in ancient Graeco-Roman society.

CONTESTS OF WORDS: PERFORMANCE, DECLAMATION, AND DEBATE

Graeco-Roman cultural memories of agonistic competition were by no means restricted to the sphere of athletics. To be sure, in the minds of both children and adults the "agony" of victory would most often have been associated with superior physical prowess in running races and wrestling matches. However, the word *agōn* had other associations as well. For one, this ethos of competition also came to expression in musical recitals, poetry readings, and dramatic performances—events which typically preceded the athletics at festival games and in which children often participated for prizes.[32]

There is evidence for such nonathletic contests in both Greek and Roman festival settings. At the Greek Pythian games, held at Delphi every four years, the final two days of the five-day festival featured the athletic and equestrian events, but day three was dedicated to the performative and verbal arts. Competitions in music and dance had long been a part of the agonistic program; by the first century CE, contests in poetry recitation and tragic acting were added as integral parts of the proceedings.[33] Public declamations were likewise incorporated into late Roman agonistic festivals held in Italy and Sicily, where the emperor sometimes presided over the conferring of prizes.[34] The prestige of such competitions did not deter young children from participating: the epitaph of a twelve-year-old boy named Q. Sulpicius Maximus reveals that he had entered one of these contests with a Greek poem organized in forty-three hexameters.[35] Finally, ancient dramatic performances at such festivals were another important ritualized setting for the cultural expression of *agōn*. In the theater, this Greek term was often used to denote a verbal dispute between two persons in which the second person to speak inevitably prevailed over his opponent.[36]

Outside the games, the ethos of *agōn* also informed the ancient practice of law and the field of jurisprudence, where debate before a judge took on the character of a contest between two disputants at court.[37] In the classical Athenian legal system, there was such an emphasis on oral argumentation that written documents were viewed as "a late and dubious entry into a well-established agonistic arena."[38] Aristotle himself compares the process of litigation to athletic or poetic competition: each is, in its own way, a kind of *agōn*.[39] Recent study of Cicero's legal speeches has confirmed that such an ethos of competition continued to flourish in Roman lawcourts.[40]

While children obviously were not employed as professional lawyers, they were trained for legal forms of debate from a young age in their school lessons on the art of public declamation. Teachers of rhetoric—from the Greek sophists to Latin orators such as Gaius Albucius Silus (fl. Augustus's reign) and Quintilian (ca. 35–100 CE)—also sometimes pleaded cases in court.[41] Thus, Michael Winterbottom writes, "It was not only that the schools influenced the courts by training future lawyers; Albucius, like other declaimers, led a double life between lecture hall and courtroom."[42] Schoolroom declamations therefore were often designed to emulate arguments presented by lawyers and judges. Furthermore, debates between teachers and pupils were often cast as "mock battles": the position advocated by the orator was called his "stance" (*stasis*), not unlike that of a wrestler at the beginning of a bout, and the "plea" (*antilēpsis*) and "counterplea" (*metalēpsis*) were likened to the "clutch" or "hold" by which each wrestler gripped his opponent.[43] The agonistic context of such rhetorical training—and in particular, this cultural connection between forensic debate and athletic competition—perhaps comes to fullest expression in Quintilian, who counsels each student to "be present at as many trials as possible and be a frequent spectator of the battle in which he is destined to take part," and to prepare and argue speeches based on actual cases, "training himself, as we see gladiators do, with real weapons."[44]

Thus, in Greek and Roman societies, public declamation and debate served as important nonathletic contexts for the cultivation and expression of an agonistic social ethic among both children and adults. Whether it was through rhetorical exercises in school as a preparation for legal careers or through dramatized debate at festival performances where the last word held sway, these practices produced in both participants and observers "durable, transposable dispositions" toward competition as a mode of cultural encounter.[45]

Agonistic Encounters in the Paidika

Having assembled and surveyed this evidence for conflict and competition in the lives of ancient children, I shall now return to my main concern: how exactly did the curse stories in the *Paidika* interact with such social performances of *agōn?* In short, I would suggest that the picture of a young Jesus engaged in a series of (sometimes violent) interpersonal conflicts in the *Paidika* would have been read in agonistic terms by early recipients of the work. Far from being mystifyingly obscure to ancient readers, these stories would have engaged with ancient readers' specific expectations about agonistic encounter as a primary social context both for the formation of a child's identity and for the practice of cursing in the Graeco-Roman world.

Indeed, as we have seen, in the Greek *Paidika,* the conflicts and curses come fast and furious. In chapter 2, Jesus is playing with other children when "a certain Jew" goes to Joseph and accuses Jesus of violating the law of the Sabbath by his actions. When Joseph rebukes his son, Jesus commands the birds to take flight, in a gesture that flaunts his creative power in the face of the charge before him.[46] Immediately after this, in chapter 3, tensions rise further when the son of the high priest Annas follows up this accusation of Sabbath activity with a series of bullying actions. Taking a willow bough, the boy "upset the pools and caused the water that Jesus had collected together to drain out; and he dried up the places where the water had collected." Jesus, however, gets the last word in the encounter, leveling a curse that causes the child himself to "dry up."[47] In chapter 4, another boy collides with force into Jesus, and Jesus again responds with a verbal curse that is immediately efficacious.[48] Later, after the child's parents complain to Joseph, Jesus blinds their eyes, and then when Joseph tries to scold his son by grabbing hold of his ear, Jesus again has the last word by proclaiming his father's "natural ignorance."[49] Finally, in chapters 6 through 8, Jesus has an (ant)agonistic encounter with a teacher at school, in which he endures physical violence in the schoolroom when he is hit in the head as punishment for his perceived intransigence.[50] Later, this classroom scenario is reprised two more times with a second and third teacher (chs. 13–14).[51] In each case, Jesus prevails over his instructor through a verbal display of his knowledge—or, in the case of the second teacher, a well-timed curse. While the episode with the second teacher introduces a renewed element of contestation to the narrative (culminating in another of

Jesus' fatal curses), the final schoolroom scene effectively resumes and resolves the conflict through another virtuoso rhetorical performance on the part of the child savior. After the third teacher takes him to the classroom "with fear and much struggle [*agōn*]" (14.1),[52] Jesus turns the tables and offers the class an oral declamation. When his instructor acknowledges the "grace and wisdom" of his student's inspiring "words" (*rhēmata*), Jesus pronounces that "the one struck down [i.e., teacher no. 2] shall also be saved" (14.3–4).[53]

These three schoolroom scenes pit Jesus against instructors whom he bests through the persuasive or maledictory force of his words. The agonistic nature of these encounters, however, is most strongly marked in his dialogue with the first teacher (chapters 6–8). Jesus utters a "word" or "speech" (*logos*) to the teacher (6.2b), and a crowd of unidentified Jewish onlookers marvel at his "words" (*rhēmata; logoi*) (6.2c).[54] Later, in answer to the crowd's comments, he first responds with an "exhortation" (*paraklēsis*) that silences his listeners (6.2f).[55] Then, in the company of his teacher he makes an "exposition" (*prosēgoria*) of the lines of the first letter, an exposition that is also described as a "teaching" (*didaskalia*) and a "defense" (*apologia*) (7.1).[56] In the end, the "clarity of his word" (*to tranon tou logou autou*) is identified as a source of shame (*aischunē*) to the teacher, who laments the fact that he has been "mastered [*nikēthēnai*] by an exceedingly small child" (7.2–3).[57]

Each of the episodes detailed here—from the accusation of Sabbath violation and Jesus' curse of the child who destroys his water channels to his conflicts with teachers at school—features an agonistic encounter involving Jesus and other characters in the narrative, including children his age, the parents of those children, and even his father, Joseph. In every instance, the encounter involves a verbal exchange in which Jesus prevails by means of a powerful word. How, then, do Jesus' repeated acts of cursing fit into this picture? What cultural memories would his curses—set amid such conflicts and struggles for preeminence—have prompted in the minds of early readers and hearers of these tales?

To answer this question, I want to examine more closely the story in chapter 4 about Jesus' cursing of the boy who hit his shoulder.[58] Commentators have variously described this boy's action as "accidental" or "careless,"[59] and have insisted on observing that Jesus' curse "ill-fits the offense which occasions the punishment."[60] Over against such readings—which typically emphasize the surprising and seemingly random nature of their encounter—I argue that the details of the story quite specifically evoke agonistic language associated with Greek gymnasia and athletic contests, where, as we shall see, curses were often part of the competitive terrain negotiated by participants.

In *Paidika* 4, the Greek verb used to describe what the anonymous child does to Jesus' shoulder has especially caused interpreters consternation. *Erragē* is the aorist past tense of *rēgnunai,* a verb that conveys different kinds of violent or destructive actions: to break asunder, to shatter, to rend or tear (as in clothing or skin), to wreck (or be wrecked). And yet, the child's action against Jesus' shoulder seems to have had little physical effect on Jesus. For this reason, modern translators have often chosen more muted terms to convey the force of this action: thus, the child must have "bumped" into Jesus' shoulder,[61] or perhaps accidentally "collided" (Fr. *s'heurter*) into him.[62] However, no comparative linguistic evidence has yet been cited to support these interpretations of the term. In what follows, I seek to address this problem.

A passage from the writings of the second-century emperor Marcus Aurelius (121–180 CE) helps elucidate an important cultural resonance of the verb *rēgnunai.* In his second-century work, *Meditations* (ca. 170–180 CE), a self-help manual and ethical guide inspired by Stoic philosophy, Marcus Aurelius reflects on the proper response one should have if inadvertently hurt during a wrestling competition. He describes the scenario as follows: "In the gymnastic exercises [*en tois gumnasiois*] suppose that a man has torn you with his nails, and by giving you a blow on your head [*tē$_i$ kefalē$_i$ errageis*] has inflicted a wound."[63] In this instance, Marcus Aurelius uses the verb *rēgnunai* (in its participial form *errageis*) to describe something like a wrestling tackle that has had the effect of injuring its recipient.

Would ancient readers and hearers of *Paidika* 4 have understood the anonymous boy as making such a maneuver on Jesus? The fact that the boy aimed his blow at Jesus' shoulder—and not some other part of his body—probably would have reinforced the association with wrestling. Graeco-Roman wrestlers often used moves that specifically targeted their opponents' shoulders.[64] One such move, mentioned by a late ancient scholiast commenting on Homer's *Iliad,* involved a hold in which the attacker attempted to hook his arm under the opponent's shoulder to gain control over him.[65] Other common moves involved exerting pressure on one or both shoulders in order to perform a hip throw or waist lock. Such maneuvers are visually represented in a variety of settings, from large-scale paintings on the walls of Egyptian tombs to smaller-scale paintings on Greek ceramic vases.[66] Among the corpus of ceramic evidence, one cup from Tarquinia shows various exercises in the *palaistra,* including that of a young man aiming a downward blow at the shoulder of another young man, who blocks the attack with an upraised arm.[67] Other pieces of Greek painted pottery feature images of wrestlers grabbing or hooking the shoulders of their opponents, or using shoulders as leverage to execute a throw.[68]

These same tactics were still being taught to young, aspiring athletes in the second and third centuries CE when the stories of the *Paidika* began to circulate. One wrestling manual from this period, preserved on papyrus, gives instructions on how to perform a shoulder throw: "You underhook with your right arm. You wrap your arm around his, where he has taken the underhook, and attack the side with your left foot. You push away with your left hand. You force the hold and fight it out.—You turn around. You fight it out with a grip on both sides."[69] The quality of the handwriting on the document indicates that manuals like this one would have been produced for sale and widespread distribution, most likely for use by trainers and students at local *gymnasia* and *palaistrai*. In this context, it would not be surprising if such moves were regularly imitated by children not only in their supervised training but also in their unsupervised play.[70] Indeed, in late Roman Italy, mosaics and paintings adorning public and private baths frequently featured wrestlers in an array of offensive and defensive postures, scenes that conflated "images of physical activity in the baths or gymnasium with scenes of athletic victory in public competitions," and that invited bathers "to identify themselves with the figures represented there."[71]

One other piece of evidence is helpful for understanding the actions of the anonymous boy in chapter 4 of the *Paidika*. A few decades after Marcus Aurelius, Flavius Philostratus, the Greek sophist with ties to the Roman imperial court of Septimius Severus, wrote a treatise called *De gymnastica* on the Olympic games and other athletic contests. In that work, he addresses the training of children for those competitions, and at one point he underscores the importance for young girls to "be trained in athletics and . . . undergo exercise to run [*trechein*] in public, for the sake, I presume, of [producing] a goodly race of children and [for the sake] of their more effectively bringing forth offspring on account of the fact that their body has been broken in [*hupo tou errōsthai to sōma*]."[72] Once again, as in the case of Marcus Aurelius, the social context for Philostratus's use of the verb *rēgnunai* is athletic training in the public arena: Philostratus employs it in the passive voice (*errōsthai*) to refer to the way that the body is "broken in" and prepared for competition through the arduous physical exercise of running.

Given the language used in this athletic handbook, it is significant, then, that the boy who struck (*erragē*) Jesus' shoulder in the *Paidika* did so while running (*trechein*) in a public venue. In light of the fact that the verbs *rēgnunai* and *trechein* were linked with the physical activities of wrestling and running in the contemporaneous Greek writings of Marcus Aurelius and Flavius Philostratus, the use of these same verbs to describe the actions of this anonymous boy probably would have prompted the early readers and hearers of the *Paidika* to associate such actions with the familiar sight of children training for athletic competition. That is to say, for Graeco-Roman readers, the physical contact between the boy and Jesus may have been seen not as a chance collision but rather as a typical feature of the contests of strength and speed regularly witnessed in the gymnasia and at the Greek games. Does this mean that Jesus himself was implicitly being portrayed as a competitor in the arena? If so, what were the implications for his power and status in the story?

With these questions in mind, I turn my attention back to Jesus' act of cursing itself. For ancient recipients well acquainted with the customs surrounding Graeco-Roman athletes' training for competition, the curse Jesus directed against the running boy would have been understood not as a strange or unexplainable response but as an expression of agonistic social practice (something akin to modern trash talk with teeth). In other words, Jesus' cursing in the *Paidika* would have been understood not simply as the volatile actions of an unpredictable child (as so often depicted in modern scholarship) but as a recognizable ritual action performed by someone with access to divine power and wisdom.

Far from a rare occurrence, cursing was a nearly ubiquitous feature of ancient Mediterranean subcultures. Curses could be brought into effect through the utterance of oral incantations, the writing of texts, and/or the performance of scripted actions, and they sometimes involved "technological props" (such as totemic figurines or a piece of the victim's hair or clothing) produced and manipulated by a ritual agent.[73] The texts of curses and imprecations were written or inscribed on a variety of surfaces, from public monuments and gravestones to more portable media (such as papyri, ostraca, and the like).[74] Curses inscribed on lead tablets were by far the most common. They are often referred to as "binding spells"—*katadesmoi* in Greek, *defixiones* in Latin—because they were designed to immobilize and incapacitate their targets, rendering them completely subject to the control of the spell agent.[75]

While these *defixiones* were sometimes produced in private by nonspecialists, more often they seem to have been manufactured by professional magicians (*magoi*) or scribes who adapted standardized curse formulae to the specifications of the individual commissioning the work for his or her private usage.[76] After reciting the prescribed words and performing the requisite actions, the spell owner would finally deposit the text of the *defixio* and any accompanying items in an undisclosed, usually subterranean location, such as a well, river, or tomb.[77] Especially favored spots were the burial places of children and those who had died in an "untimely" fashion, since they were thought to remain in their graves restless and ready to inflict harm against those who deserved to be cursed. Indeed, the archaeological record confirms that the practice of depositing *defixiones* with children's corpses continued for centuries and spanned different geographical regions—from a child's grave in Athens dated to the late fifth-century BCE to the burial place of a young person who lived in Nubia during the fourth or fifth century CE.[78]

The controlling uses to which such curses were put also varied widely, from capturing the gaze and erotic desire of a prospective lover[79] to inflicting psychic or bodily harm (including mental suffering, physical illness, or even death) upon a rival or an enemy.[80] Bringing about the demise of the spell victim was the desired goal in traditional Greek curses such as funerary imprecations, which often featured language of death and destruction. One grave inscription from northwestern Asia Minor simply pronounces, "May he die, dead and gone" (*ōlēs exōlēs apoloito*).[81] While such language is relatively rare in early Greek *defixiones* prior to the fourth-century BCE,[82] it becomes more common by the Roman imperial period when binding spells seem to have become more "lethal" in purpose. Thus, the owner of a lead tablet deposited in an Athenian well during the first century CE beseeches the goddess Hekate to visit "utter destruction" upon the anonymous thieves who broke into his house.[83] Another first-century CE tablet discovered in a Sicilian tomb seeks revenge against a certain Eleutheros, requesting the goddess to "eliminate him from the human race."[84] Along the same lines, a fourth-century Greek tablet found in Rome calls for its victim (a man named Cardelus) "to be punished and to die an evil death."[85]

Such practices of cursing were not the exclusive preserve of adults. There is evidence to suggest that in antiquity children sometimes served as the agents, mediums, or victims of such spells. In Lucian of Samosata's second-century essay on the traveling wonder-worker and healer Alexander of Abunoteichos, the protagonist is described as having apprenticed himself as a prepubescent boy to a doctor who taught him the craft of "magic and divinely uttered spells."[86] While Lucian's work is unreliable for reconstructing the biography of the historical Alexander of Abunoteichos, it does present a characteristic profile of what such training might have looked like in ancient Graeco-Roman society—"the picture of a certain kind of career" that apparently sometimes had its start at a very young age.[87]

In other circumstances, children were employed as mediums in rites of divination. Apuleius (ca. 125–180 CE), in defending himself against charges of magic, refers to a false rumor that he had bewitched a boy. Notably, even as he denies the charge, he acknowledges that this rumor fell "within the limits of popular credence," and goes on to cite other reports about boys who were inspired by incantations to foretell the future or to divine the location of lost coins.[88] Elsewhere, he observes that the boys chosen for this service were supposed to be bodily pure (that is, inexperienced sexually) and dressed in pure linen garments.[89] A generation or two later, the early Christian writer Hippolytus (ca. 170–236 CE) also makes reference to the role that young boys played as mediums.[90]

The papyrological record confirms this literary witness: at least ten examples of spells featuring children as mediums and/or magicians' helpers have been documented.[91] In most of these rites, the boys conscripted for this purpose are possessed by the god (or gods) and, as a consequence, experience visions of future events. Thus, one "vessel divination" from the third century CE describes how the boy assistant is to gaze into a vessel filled with light and summon the gods until he confirms that they have entered him, saying, "They have already come." At this, the magician recites formulae and invocations that prompt the gods to action at his bidding.[92]

Sarah Iles Johnston has perceptively noted the spell's operating assumption that the child medium possesses a penetrating, divinatory gaze.[93] In this context, it is interesting that in the *Paidika* the power of Jesus' gaze is highlighted on more than one occasion. In the story of his encounter with the first teacher, we are told that he looked at (*emblepein,* lit. "gazed into") his father and the teacher Zacchaeus before speaking cryptically about his identity.[94] Then, later, after Jesus has exposited upon the nature of the first letter of the alphabet, Zacchaeus speaks to Joseph in awe and wonderment: "Take this child away from me, brother! For I can't bear his severe look [*blemma*] or clear speech [*logos*]."[95]

Finally, children also sometimes found themselves the unwitting victims of curses, most often as what we might call "collateral damage" in spells targeting parents or other family members. Thus, a fourth-century BCE lead tablet from Greece (Attika) names a number of people—including a carpenter named Oineus—and consigns them and all their children and wives to "their graves."[96] While some of these ancient curse tablets seek to "bind" (*katadein*), "convey" (*komizein*), or "register" (*katagraphein*) children,[97] others have a more deadly aim. One example is a tablet dated to the third century BCE deposited in a grave at Charsonesos, on the northern shore of the Black Sea. The spell, after naming the names of the designated targets, calls upon Fate and levies the following curse: "Do not let there be any profit for these men, but may they and their children perish [*apolluo[i]nto kai paides autois*]."[98]

This widespread evidence for children's social roles as spell agents, as mediums in rites of divination, and as the targets of curses suggests that ancient Greeks and Romans would have had their social memories shaped in some measure by such practices. Indeed, the image of children as both potential practitioners and victims of curses provides a context for understanding how Jesus' acts of cursing other children (as well as adults) in the *Paidika* would have been received as culturally plausible scenarios—scenarios that in turn helped shape readers' perceptions of who this young Jesus was.

So how, then, did cursing relate to competition? How would the agonistic language in the story of Jesus' encounter with the anonymous boy in *Paidika* 4 have evoked readily recognizable social "sites of memory" for readers? To locate such sites, we can turn again to competitive venues like festival games and courts of justice, both of which were known to be especially conducive to practices of cursing. A well-placed curse served as a means by which athletes and advocates sought to gain an advantage over one another and to minimize the risks associated with injury and/or loss of face.[99]

Christopher Faraone has observed that both judicial curses and curses against athletes and other kinds of public performers were conditioned by "agonistic relationships."[100] While most judicial curses date primarily to the classical and Hellenistic periods, the evidence for spells related to athletics and other forms of public competition notably extends into the second and third centuries CE, the period during which the *Paidika* stories began to circulate.[101] Several surviving spells target actors, theatrical teachers, and choral directors who participated in festal competitions for awards and prizes. One early Sicilian curse consigns "all leaders of choruses [*chorēgoi*]," along with "their children and fathers . . . to defeat both in the contests and outside the contests."[102] A later Syrian spell from the third century CE binds a choral leader (*ho mesō chōrō*) and his entire chorus, as well as a certain Huperechios who is identified as a dancer and pantomime actor: the curse agent aims to "destroy (and) cancel all assistance" available to Huperechios, including that of his divine protector, "the bewigged pantomime *daimon*."[103]

Curses related to athletic training and competition were perhaps even more ubiquitous in late antiquity. To wit, a cache of five leaden curse tablets against wrestlers has been discovered in a well in the Athenian agora, each dated to the third century CE and each commissioned for a different match. Three of the five spells target the same unfortunate wrestler, a man named Eutychianos.[104] One of them seeks to "bind him in the unlit realm of oblivion," and to "chill and destroy the wrestling which he is about to do." If Eutychianos were to manage to attend the competition, the spell agent calls upon the daemons to intervene "in order that he may fall down and make a fool of himself."[105] Another of the five curses uses similar language against a Macedonian wrestler named Petres, who is to "fall down and disgrace himself" if he chooses to compete in his scheduled match.[106]

Other extant curses were written specifically with runners in mind. A spell found in the same Athenian well where the five curses against wrestlers were discovered invokes the daemons to prevent a certain Alkidamos from "getting past the starting lines of the Athenaia," and (if he does manage to start) make him "veer off course and disgrace himself."[107] This spell was by no means an isolated case: similar late Roman *defixiones* connected with footraces have been found at Corinth and Isthmia in Greece and at Oxyrhynchus in Egypt.[108] The intended effects of such curses—to incapacitate their victims, to deprive one's opponents of bodily strength, to prevent them from running swiftly and/or from colliding violently with their competitors—is echoed many times over in the expansive corpus of late antique curses against horse racers and charioteers as well.[109]

Once again, this range of cursing practices—a visible and widely acknowledged feature of Graeco-Roman society—would have served as "realms of remembrance" (*Erinnerungsräume*) for readers of the *Paidika*. The marked language and tone used in the story of the boy who bumps into Jesus' shoulder—the boy's physical aggression and Jesus' targeted verbal response—recall the kinds of agonistic social arenas where competitors regularly made recourse to proactive means to gain advantage and protect themselves through the enactment of maledictory charms. Indeed, the context of competitive cursing is confirmed in an oft-overlooked detail at the end of another story, in *Paidika* 10—the one in which Jesus accidently breaks his mother's pitcher and then miraculously retrieves the spilt water in his cloak. After Mary blesses her child, the narrator adds the comment, "For they were afraid lest someone cast a spell [*baskainein*] on him."[110] This explanation makes sense in an agonistic world where blessings and preemptive cursing were understood to be effective means of countering the ever-present threat of an anonymously placed spell.

"Cursed be your hēgemōn*!": From Athletic Trainers to the Ruling Faculty of the Soul*

In this context, let us now examine the words of Jesus' curse itself in *Paidika* 4. After the anonymous boy launches into his shoulder, Jesus turns to him and says, "As for you, cursed be your *hēgemōn!*"[111] The vocabulary employed here is significant: it clarifies not only how this story would have prompted cultural memories of agonistic cursing practices in the Graeco-Roman world but also how, by extension, the story would have evoked certain philosophical (and biblical) assumptions about divine reason, judgment, and power.[112]

The word *hēgemōn* would have held several resonances for late ancient Greek readers. While often used to refer generally to someone who takes on the role of a "leader" or authoritative "guide," such as a commander or captain in an army, the term also had more specialized applications.[113] Here, I focus on two different ways that this term might have been interpreted by early readers of the *Paidika*—first, in the context of Graeco-Roman agonistic practices; and second, in the context of Hellenistic philosophy and its influence over ancient Jewish and Christian understandings of human virtue and its relation to the nature of God.

First, documentary and literary sources ranging from the third century BCE to the second century CE show how the word *hēgemōn* was used in agonistic social contexts to refer to athletic trainers and choral directors whose job was to prepare their charges for competition. One late first- or early second-century inscription even refers to the president or head of a gymnasium as a hēgemōn.[114] Other Greek examples use the term to designate leaders of boys' choruses, including one mentioning local "leaders of boys" (*hēgemones paidiōn*) who serve at the festival games or "contest" (*agōn*) dedicated to Zeus Homolōios in Boeotia.[115] In the second century CE, the Greek grammarian Julius Pollux offers further confirmation of this usage: in his *Onomasticon,* he associates the phrase *hēgemōn chorou* ("leader of the chorus") with a number of other Greek terms connected with musical performance and leadership.[116] The inclusion of the term *hēgemōn* in Pollux's thesaurus suggests that it retained a similar semantic association around the time that the stories of the *Paidika* began to circulate and be recorded in writing.

How does this evidence for the use of the term *hēgemōn* as a title for both heads of gymnasia and choral leaders inform my study of the story? It means that its early readers and hearers may have been inclined to interpret Jesus' maledictory words in this sense, linking it to an agonistic social milieu in which curses functioned as a means of "managing potential risks" posed by adversaries, including rival young competitors and their trainers.[117]

For the more philosophically inclined, however, the word *hēgemōn* would have carried other important associations as well. In Stoic philosophical circles, a derivative form of this Greek noun—the substantive adjective, *to hēgemonikon*—was used to refer to the mind or rational faculty as the "ruling element" or "guiding principle" of the soul and as the source of "power" (*dunamis*) and "movement" (*kinēsis*) in the body, governing everything from the subtle transmission of sensory perceptions to the control of larger motor skills such as walking or running.[118] This "hegemonic" core of the human person was understood to reflect, relate to, and indeed represent an extension of the universal Reason (*Logos*), the divine Word who served as an intermediary and cosmic link between the godhead and creation. By the first century CE, this notion of the *hēgemonikon* had become thoroughly integrated into the popular and eclectic Platonic philosophy of the day, the intellectual milieu of many ancient Jewish and early Christian authors. Thus, views of *to hēgemonikon* as the seat of human reason and as an attribute derived from the divine Mind came to be shared not only by Stoic thinkers of the period such as Epictetus and Marcus Aurelius (121–180 CE)[119] but also by Hellenistic Jewish writers such as Philo of Alexandria and the author of 4 Maccabees,[120] by the Middle Platonic philosopher Plutarch,[121] and by the Christian moral theologian Clement of Alexandria.[122]

In their writings, these authors sometimes use the word *hēgemōn* as a synonym for *to hēgemonikon,* in reference to the human rational faculty or to divine Reason. Thus, in Philo, the mind is "the ruler [*hēgemōn*] of the entire soul," and the aim of philosophy is to "improve the soul and its ruler [*hēgemōn*] the mind."[123] Commenting on the creation account in Genesis, Philo elaborates on the fundamental connection between the mind and its Creator: "It is in respect of the Mind, the sovereign element [*hēgemōn*] of the soul, that the word image is used; for after the pattern of a single Mind, even the Mind of the Universe as an archetype, the mind in each of those who successively came into being was molded. It is in a fashion a god to him who carries and enshrines it as an object of reverence; for the human mind evidently occupies a position in men precisely answering to that which the great Ruler [*hēgemōn*] occupies in all the world."[124] Here, just as God is the Mind of the universe (and indeed due to this fact), the human mind serves as the "god" (*theos*) and "ruler" (*hēgemōn*) of the person engaged in reverent contemplation of divine things. Similarly, the anonymous author of 4 Maccabees identifies reason (*ho logismos*) as "the ruler of the virtues" (*tōn aretōn hēgemōn*) (1:30) and as "the ruler of the emotions" (*hēgemōn tōn pathōn*) (7:16).[125]

Philo and the author of 4 Maccabees were not the only ancient authors to make this connection, seeing the governing capacity of human reason as an anthropological extension of the divine prerogative. In the second century, Plutarch accordingly identifies Zeus as "a god who is first ruler [*archōn prōtos*] and governor [*hēgemōn*] of the universe, possessing mind [*nous*] and reason [*logos*],"[126] and affirms that "the soul, which partakes of mind, reason, and harmony, was not only the work of God, but part of him; not only made by him, but begot by him."[127] His near contemporary the late second-century emperor Marcus Aurelius touches on the practical implications of this hegemonic theology when he instructs the reader of his *Meditations* to "run [*treche*] to your own governing self [*to seautou hēgemonikon*] and . . . to the governing self of the universe, that you may remind yourself [*summnēmoneuein*] of that of which you are a part."[128] In this context, the philosophical life itself was framed as a kind of memory practice. In order to keep the governing principle of one's soul "intact" and "under control," in order to allow it to direct the body and the senses in a proper fashion,[129] one needed to "remind oneself" (*mnēmoneuesthai*) and "remember" (*mimnēskein*) the archetypal, creative cause of the *hēgemonikon* in the divine Mind.[130] In Philo's terms, only if one adopts God as one's "leader" (*hēgemōn*) can one truly hope to free one's mind from the passions.[131]

The same logic applied to philosophical devotees of the Greek gods. Thus, Epictetus addresses those who "have such a leader [*hēgemōn*] as Zeus" and urges them to give their concerns over to his control so that they might abandon fear and not be troubled anymore.[132] Elsewhere, in speaking of the supreme God's governance of the world's affairs, Epictetus offers his own personal testimony as an example of how to "discipline" (*gumnazein*) oneself against fear: "I obey, I follow, lauding my commander [*hēgemōn*] and singing hymns of praise about His deeds."[133]

Note that both Marcus Aurelius and Epictetus speak about this process of aligning one's *hēgemonikon* with the divine mind in terms of an athletic struggle: one must "run" (*trechein*) to attend to one's *hēgemonikon,* and one must endeavor to "discipline" (*gumnazein*) it against fear and the passions. The same kind of agonistic language is found in Philo as well. In his treatise *On the Creation of the World,* he compares "those who provide gymnastic and scenic contests" (*hoi tous gumnikous agōnas kai skēnikous tithentes*) to God in his role as "the Ruler [*hēgemōn*] of all things: "Just as givers of a banquet, then, do not send out the summonses to supper till they have put everything in readiness for the feast; and those who provide gymnastic and scenic contests [*hoi tous gumnikous agōnas kai skēnikous tithentes*], before they gather the spectators into the theatre or the stadium, have in readiness a number of combatants and performers to charm both eye and ear; exactly in the same way the Ruler [*hēgemōn*] of all things, like some provider of contests or of a banquet, when about to invite man to the enjoyment of a feast and a great spectacle, made ready beforehand the material for both."[134] In another treatise, Philo reads the story of Joseph in Genesis 46 as an allegory regarding "the soul that is shepherded by God" and the soul's role of shepherding in turn the "irrational nature" of the body, comparing the actions of Joseph and his brothers to a "contest" (*agōn*)—one which they "engage [*diagōnesthai*] with all their might" and in which they continually seek to disclose "the free, noble, and ruling [*hēgemonikon*] character of their nature."[135] He also compares the human mind to a chariot racer who steers the soul on a straight course and "rules the whole living being as a governor [*hēgemōn*] does a city."[136]

Indeed, in ancient Greek literature—from biographies, to letters, to topical treatises—one finds examples of the mind's agonistic struggle to control and subdue the passions likened to a wrestling match or to the rigorous training a wrestler undergoes in preparation for such competition. Thus, it is not a coincidence that biographical tales about Plato make a point of portraying him in his youth as a champion wrestler.[137] During the first three centuries CE, the philosophical metaphor of a wrestling match is almost ubiquitous, appearing in the writings of Philo and Epictetus and also early Christian authors such as Paul the apostle, the later pseudo-Pauline author of the Letter to the Ephesians, and the third-century theologian Origen of Alexandria.

In his treatise *Every Good Man Is Free,* Philo tells a story about the Greek flute player and poet Antigenidas's encounter with "a certain rival professional" (*tis tōn antitechnōn*) who comes to him one day "in anger." Imagining that their conflict might end up in blows or threats of death, Antigenidas calmly responds: "Frightful things do not scare me; I am not inferior to boxers or pancratiasts, who though they see but dim shadows of true excellence, since they only cultivate robustness of body, yet endure both bravely. For the mind within me which rules the body [*ho hēgemōn sōmatos*] is by courage so well-braced and nerved, that it can stand superior to any kind of pain."[138] For Philo, the well-trained mind rules over the body in such a way that it conditions itself to be impervious to pain, just as a boxer or wrestler through strenuous physical exercise builds up his bodily strength and forges within himself an unyielding spirit of courage.

Epictetus casts the philosopher's training of mind over body as a similar form of gymnastic training. Counseling would-be philosophers among his readers to "digest" the principles that he has laid out, he urges them to "show us some change in your governing principle [*hēgemonikon*] . . . just as the athletes show their shoulders [*ōmoi*], on account of which they exercised [*gumnazesthai*] and ate."[139] He goes on to emphasize that, in order to pursue such a philosophical program, a person "ought to be of a certain age, and lead a certain kind of life, and have God as his guide [*hēgemōn*]."[140] Here, Epictetus draws on his readers' cultural familiarity with the image of young wrestlers training for the festival games and their distinctive physique—especially the musculature of their shoulders, developed under the guidance of a trainer—in order to draw an analogy to the philosopher's cultivation of the mind as the governing principle of both soul and body.

The wrestling motif is found in early Christian literature as well. Throughout his letters, the apostle Paul presents his mission as a kind of *agōn*—as an extended struggle in the face of strong opposition.[141] Thus, he urges the church in Rome "to struggle together" (*sunagōnizesthai*) with him in prayer and exhorts the church in Philippi to "stand firm" (*stēkein*), to "participate in the contest together with one soul" (*mia*$_i$ *psuchē*$_i$ *sunathlein*), and not to be intimidated by their "opponents" (*antikeimenoi*).[142] In so doing they enter into the same "struggle" or "competition" (*agōn*) that Paul himself was engaged in. Paul often speaks of this *agōn* in terms of a footrace: hoping not to "run" (*trechein*) in vain, he "presses on" (*diōkein*) and "strains forward" (*epekteinesthai*) toward the "goal" in order to obtain the "prize" (*brabeion*).[143] At other times, however, Paul also paints his struggle in terms of the harsh training a pancratiast undergoes in preparation for his pugilistic wrestling matches. Thus, in his First Letter to the Corinthians, he first describes the life of the gospel in terms of a *stadion* (a race in the pentathlon just under two hundred meters in length) in which "the runners all compete, but only one receives the prize" (*hoi . . . trechontes pantes men trechousin, heis de lambanei to brabeion*). Then he goes on to emphasize how each athletic contender (*agōnizomenos*) learns to exercise self-control (*enkrateuesthai*) through disciplined training. Paul concludes by pointing to himself as a metaphorical example: "So I do not run aimlessly, nor do I practice boxing [*pukteuein*] as though beating the air; but I beat my body and master it [*hupōpiazō mou to soma kai doulagōgō*]."[144]

In the late first and early second century, other early Christian authors writing in the name of Paul adopted this agonistic language for similar ends. The author of 1 Timothy makes repeated references to "fighting the good fight" (*strateuein tēn kalēn strateian*),[145] and the readers of 2 Timothy are told that, just as in the case of someone who "competes in athletic competition" (*athlein*), they too will not be able to "receive the crown" (*stephanesthai*) unless they "compete" (*athlein*) according to the rules.[146] This language also pervades the Letter to the Colossians, where the writer (1:29–31) speaks about "struggling" (*agōnizesthai*) with all the "energy" (*energeia*) he could muster in such a great "contest" (*agōn*), and urges the recipients of his letter not to allow themselves to be "disqualified" on account of following false teachers.[147] At the end of the letter, he holds up a certain Epaphras as an example of someone who is constantly "contending for a prize" (*agōnizesthai*) in his prayers.[148] This agonistic language is echoed in the Letter to the Ephesians, where the author (6:12) imagines (in quite elaborate terms) a gladiatorial contest in the arena and describes the Christian's struggle against the devil as "our wrestling match [*hēmin hē palē*] . . . [which is] not against flesh and blood, but against the rulers, against the authorities, against the cosmic powers of this darkness, against the spiritual forces of wickedness in the heavenly places."[149]

In early Christian biblical interpretation, this verse from Ephesians in particular became a favored exegetical proof text for talking about the soul's struggle against lust and other temptations associated with bodily passions. Thus, in the second century, Clement of Alexandria, in commenting on passions and spiritual powers against which we contend in "our wrestling match" (*hē pale hēmin*), observes how they have the power to leave "impressions on the soft and yielding soul," and yet they readily surrender the crown of victory to "those who engage in the contest with more athletic energy" (*hosoi de athlētikōteron ton agōna metacheirizontai*).[150]

Finally, about a half century later, Origen of Alexandria interprets Ephesians 6:12 along similar lines in his treatise *On Prayer,* although he goes further in connecting the Pauline metaphor with the concept of the mind or soul as the *hēgemonikon* of the body. Toward the end of the work, as part of an extended commentary on the Lord's Prayer, Origen discusses the phrase "Lead us not into temptation, but deliver us from evil." After associating temptation with "the flesh that wars against the spirit" and conceding that "all human life on earth is a trial," he nonetheless offers his readers encouragement by quoting Paul's words in 1 Corinthians 10:13: "God will not let you be tested beyond your strength, but with the testing he will also provide the way out so that you may be able to endure it." Then, expanding on this point, Origen makes reference to the "wrestling match" of Ephesians 6:12:

> Whether the "wrestling match" [*palē*] is against the flesh that lusts or wars against the spirit, or whether this match is against the soul of all flesh (that is, the faculty that rules [*to hēgemonikon*] over the body in which it resides, also called the heart)—and such is the case with the "wrestling match" of those who are tempted with human temptations, or (alternatively) with more mature, advanced athletes [*athlētai*] who no longer wrestle with "flesh and blood" and are no longer tested by the human temptations that they have already trampled down—our struggles [*agōnismata*] are "against the rulers, against the authorities, against the cosmic powers of this darkness and spiritual forces of wickedness."[151]

What is even more interesting is that in the very next chapter of his treatise, Origen returns to his theme of wrestling against temptation and applies it to the life of Christ as told in the Gospels. He does so by way of a comparison between Christ and Job (whom he calls "the athlete of virtue"). According to Origen, "while Job wrestled two falls [*duo palaismata palaisas*] and prevailed, he did not contend for a prize in a third such contest [*triton ouk agōnizetai tēlikouton agōna*], for it was necessary that the three-round wrestling match [*hē peri tōn triōn palē*] be reserved for the Savior, as it is recorded in the three gospels, when the Savior who was known in human form won his three bouts over the enemy."[152]

Taken altogether, the language and imagery in Origen's treatise *On Prayer* suggest a compelling context for understanding the cultural resonance of Jesus' encounter and curse in *Paidika* 4. Here one can begin to see how ancient readers, armed with memories of athletic and agonistic practices from Graeco-Roman society, would have made sense of Jesus' encounter with the boy who strikes his shoulder and Jesus' ensuing curse against the boy's *hēgemōn*. For such readers, the story would have functioned on another level as a parable or allegory in which Jesus—the self-trained *hēgemōn* of his own soul—fends off a bodily trial like a well-trained wrestler who subdues an opponent. Indeed, we find a similar agonistic application in John Chrysostom's treatise *On Vainglory and the Right Way for Parents to Bring Up Their Children*, where he likens the struggle for virtue to the exercises a boy undergoes in a wrestling school among his peers:

> And let there be many on all sides to spur the boy on, so that he may be exercised and practiced in controlling his passions among the members of the household. And just as athletes in the wrestling school train with their friends before the contest, so that when they have succeeded against these they may be invincible against their opponents, even so the boy must be trained in the home. Let his father or brother oftentimes play the chief part in treating him with spite. And let them all strive their hardest to overcome him. Or let someone in wrestling stand up to him and defend himself so that the boy may try his strength against him. So, too, let the slaves provoke him often rightly or wrongly, so that he may learn on every occasion to control his passion. If his father provoke him, it is no great test; for the name of father, taking first possession of his soul, does not permit him to rebel. But let his companions in age, whether slave or free, do this, that he may learn equability amongst them.[153]

Similarly, the Jesus of the *Paidika* would have been understood to embody divine Reason (*Logos*) in such a way that it allows him to discipline a wayward young soul whose *hēgemōn* has led him astray.

Both Philo and Epictetus remark often about the way bodily pleasure can steer a person's rational faculty along the wrong path. Once removed from its position as the rightly oriented "ruler" or "guide" for the soul, it quickly becomes subject to "blind guides" (*hēgemones tuphloi*) and falls prey "now to one external impression and now to another."[154] When one reads the story of Jesus' cursing of the boy in the *Paidika* in terms of these cultural assumptions, it is interesting to note that the parents and backers of the cursed child (Jesus' "accusers") are described as incapable of raising up "wise words" (*phronima rhēmata*) for themselves, and therefore they are deemed deserving of their own punishment, which takes the form of blindness (*etuflōthēsan*).[155] It is also noteworthy that, when speaking about souls preoccupied with external things and tempted by pleasure, Philo and Epictetus choose examples from agonistic social settings and make observations about the special predilections of children. Philo compares pleasure to the "leader of a chorus" (*hēgemōn chorou*) at a festival competition who addresses a seductive song "to the mind."[156] Epictetus talks about people who eschew the hard work necessary for improving one's "governing principle" (*to hēgemonikon*) and who instead focus on "externals" (*to ektos*) and "outside things" (*ta eksō*). He compares them to playacting children who, emulating professional dramatists, divide up their personae by taking on different roles, "now a philosopher, later on a tax-gatherer, then a rhetorician, then a procurator of Caesar." In this way, he counsels those who want to be governed by a unified rational faculty not to act "like children do" (*hōs ta paidia*), but to hold fast to the disposition of a philosopher.[157]

Septuagintal Language and the Power of Jesus' Performative Speech

If the story of the boy cursed by Jesus in chapter 4 of the *Paidika* is to be read as an agonistic scene—one that dramatizes the fate of a young soul whose *hēgemōn* failed to provide sound guidance and who therefore had become a threat to others—how then are we to understand the force of Jesus' curse against the boy's *hēgemōn*? As mentioned above, it is first of all a curse that would have underscored the Christ child's identity as one who, even while engaged in activities typical of childhood, had already attained a measured, hegemonic control over his body and soul, and thus had already graduated to an advanced level as a philosopher-athlete engaged in an agonistic contest with temptation. In its immediate textual or narrative context, the story of Jesus' curse subtly anticipates his subsequent displays of divine wisdom in his encounters with his teachers later in the *Paidika* (the topic of my next chapter). At the same time, among readers whose eyes and ears were trained to find intertextual connections, the story may have been seen as proleptically anticipating Jesus' later success as an adult in resisting and repelling the assaults of Satan's three temptations in the desert.[158]

And yet, the specific language of the young Jesus' curse in chapter 4 would also have marked his identity as one who possesses the power of divine speech in another way. The Greek word that he uses to effect his curse—*epikataratos* ("cursed")—originated as a term in the Septuagint (the Greek Old Testament), and during the first three centuries of the Common Era is picked up almost exclusively by Jewish and Christian authors commenting upon the Greek Bible, including Philo, the author of 4 Maccabees, Paul, Justin Martyr, Theophilus of Antioch, and Clement and Origen of Alexandria. In the *Paidika,* when the parents of the cursed child appeal to Joseph to "teach him to bless and not to curse" (*didaxon auton eulogein kai mē katarasthai*), their words invoke the language and structure of Deuteronomy 27–28, which lists the "blessings" (*eulogiai*) that will accrue to those who obey God,[159] alongside two catalogues of "curses" (*katarai*) that will fall upon those who disobey until they are "destroyed" (*exolethreuesthai*) and "come to sudden ruin" (*apolesthai en tachei*).[160] In this catalogue of curses, the adjective *epikataratos* is used repeatedly to enact judgment against various species of wrongdoers (including "the one who misleads a blind person on the road" in 27:18). Paul cites this set of divinely mandated curses in Galatians 3:10: "Cursed [*epikataratos*] is everyone who does not observe and obey all the things written in the book of the law."[161] This same set of curses would likely have resonated in the minds of early Christians reading or hearing this story in the *Paidika* for the first time.

For early recipients of this story, the placement of the term *epikataratos* in Jesus' mouth would have further reinforced their understanding of the young Jesus as the human embodiment of divine Reason, as the *Logos* incarnate. First, there is contemporaneous literary evidence that Jesus' pronouncement of the curse would have been seen as a sign of his rational control over the passions, rather than as a random or capricious act as it has been interpreted in modern scholarship. In 4 Maccabees, edited around the first or second century CE, this same Septuagintal language of cursing was picked up and applied specifically to a critique of the passions very similar to the one that informs the story of Jesus' encounter with the boy in the *Paidika.* In chapter 2, the anonymous author of 4 Maccabees alludes to the story in Genesis 34 about the rape of Dinah—especially the revenge her brothers Simeon and Levi took by slaughtering the Shechemites, and their father Jacob's subsequent censuring of their violent act.[162] Later in Genesis (49:7), the story is revisited when Jacob gives his last words to his sons and declares a curse upon their rash act of vengeance, saying, "Cursed [*epikataratos*] be their anger." Steeped in Hellenistic philosophical conventions, the author of 4 Maccabees offers commentary on the words of Jacob's curse, and reads the patriarch allegorically as "reason" personified: "Why else did Jacob, our most wise father, censure the households of Simeon and Levi for their irrational slaughter of the entire tribe of the Shechemites, saying, 'Cursed [*epikataratos*] be their anger'? For if reason could not control anger, he would not have spoken thus. Now when God fashioned human beings, he planted in them emotions and inclinations, but at the same time he enthroned the mind among the senses as a sacred governor [*hēgemōn*] over them all."[163] Jacob's curse, pronounced against a violent action bred out of anger, is interpreted by the author of 4 Maccabees as an example of the rational, hegemonic control Jacob's mind exerted over his senses. In this first- or second-century Hellenistic Jewish writer, one finds a ready-made model for the kind of reading strategies that, I submit, would have been applied to Jesus' curse against the violent boy's *hēgemōn* in the *Paidika*.[164]

Second, the specific curse language used in the Septuagint and echoed in the *Paidika* also found its way into rites of cursing employed among Jewish diaspora communities in the Graeco-Roman world. Thus, in a second-century CE inscription from Chalcis, Greece, one finds a curse written by a certain Amphicles, a "Judaizing" Gentile (perhaps someone acquainted with the early Christian movement in Greece), who liberally incorporates biblical vocabulary and phrases into his text. For anyone who "injures or breaks" or otherwise "dishonors" the statue on which the curse is written, the writer promises a series of misfortunes taken directly from Deuteronomy 28: "May [the] god strike this person with trouble and fever and chills and itch and drought and insanity and blindness and mental fits" (cf. vv. 22 and 28). He goes on to declare that any perpetrator of such untoward acts will not be able to "walk on land," but speaks a Deuteronomic blessing upon anyone who cares for or protects the monument: "May grace and health watch over him."[165]

This is not an isolated case: similar examples have been discovered across the eastern Mediterranean. An inscription erected for public viewing in a cemetery on the island of Rheneia—perhaps connected with a Jewish or Samaritan community residing there during the second century BCE—utilizes Septuagintal language in several places and alludes to a range of Greek biblical texts, including Exodus, Leviticus, Numbers, Deuteronomy, Job, Jeremiah, Sirach, and 2 Maccabees.[166] A number of mid-third-century burial inscriptions from Phrygia, probably connected with a local Jewish community, threaten anyone who disturbs the graves in the area with "the curses written in Deuteronomy."[167] These examples, grounded as they are in shared assumptions about the privileged power of biblical language, provide a context for understanding how Jesus' verbal curses in the *Paidika* would have fitted certain readers' *a priori* assumptions about the efficacy of maledictory speech.

In particular, they would have supplied eminently adaptable cultural reference points for understanding the potency of Jesus' words in these stories, even in the absence of the elaborate ritual technologies often associated with Graeco-Roman *defixiones*.

The text of the *Paidika* anticipates such questions by emphasizing how Jesus' words immediately brought about their intended results without any other action on his part. Such efficacy of speech is vividly demonstrated in chapter three with Jesus' curse of Annas's son. After Annas's son has "dried up" (*exēranthē*) Jesus' pools, the latter turns the tables on him by declaring, "May your fruit [*karpos*] be rootless and may your shoot be dried up [*xēros*] like a young branch charred [*ekkaiomenos*] by a violent wind."[168] The immediate (and ironic) result of Jesus' words is that the child himself "dried up" (*exēranthē*).[169]

For audiences familiar with the Gospels of Matthew and Mark, this play on the Greek verb *xērainein* ("to dry up") would have evoked and presaged Jesus' curse of the fig tree as an adult.[170] In Matthew, the language is almost identical: after Jesus pronounces his curse forbidding the tree from ever giving "fruit" (*karpos*), we are told that the fig tree "dried up at once" (*exēranthē parachrēma*).[171] In the Markan version of this story, the effect of Jesus' curse is delayed until the following morning when the disciples see the fig tree "dried up to its roots" (*exērammenē ek rhizōn*), a fact that Peter reiterates when he remarks to Jesus, "Rabbi, look! The fig tree that you cursed has dried up" (*rabbi, ide hē sukē hēn katērasō exērantai*).[172] While borrowing language from both these stories, Jesus' curse of the high priest's son in the *Paidika* especially follows Matthew in underscoring the instantaneous effect of Jesus' words.

This emphasis on the efficacy of Jesus' words also applies to other episodes in the *Paidika,* and to the work's history of redaction. In chapter 4, after Jesus curses the boy, who immediately dies, the parents of the child question where he is from with trepidation, since "his word [*rhēma*] becomes a deed [*ergon*]."[173] Later scribes also added material to accentuate this same theme. In chapter 2, a redactor added the comment that Jesus' action of purifying the water in the pools was accomplished "by the administration of his word alone and not by any deed" (*katastasei logou monon kai ouk ergō$_i$*).[174] Similarly, in chapter 7, after Jesus' first lesson in school in which he ends up mastering his teacher, a later scribe embellishes the teacher's lament over the fact that he cannot bear "the clarity of his word."[175]

In these stories—whether considered individually as story units or collectively as part of a sustained narrative motif—the words of Jesus' fatal curses and his life-restoring blessings function linguistically in a way analogous to

J. L. Austin's concept of "performative utterances." In his book *How to Do Things with Words,* Austin defined such utterances in terms of their effective force—that is, in terms of the speaker's ability to accomplish certain ends through a verbal gesture alone. To utter certain phrases such as "I do" or "You are now husband and wife" in appropriate social circumstances (a marriage ceremony) is both to perform and to effect specific results in and through the act of speaking itself.[176] Expanding on Austin, Paul Connerton has recognized how blessings and curses, as performative speech acts, presuppose a range of shared social memories related to issues of power and submission, trust and vulnerability. Such speech acts not only reinforce prior assumptions and attitudes; they also "effectively bring those attitudes into existence" time and time again through mnemonic repetition and through the way they become encoded bodily "in set postures, gestures and movements."[177] Austin's and Connerton's insights about how language works can be profitably applied to Jesus' acts of cursing in the *Paidika.* Within ancient Greek societies, where the vast majority shared assumptions about the efficacy of beneficent or maledictory speech, the act of speaking the words of a blessing or curse was tantamount to bringing about the effects of that blessing or curse in the life of its recipient or victim. In other words, the act of saying a blessing or curse made it so.

The young Jesus encountered in the *Paidika* not only speaks a word and makes it so; as the *Logos*-endowed ensoulment of a rightly ordered *hēgemōn,* he himself is cast as the utterance of God, personified and performed.[178] For the one whose "word [*rhēma*] becomes a deed [*ergon*],"[179] the scenario turns out to be not simply that of a physical contest or encounter. It is in fact also a contest of rhetoric and reason—a *logikos agōn,* to borrow the language of an inscription from Roman Egypt—where the power of the word prevails and the performance of philosophical *paideia* becomes a spectator sport.[180] As I have argued, the early recipients of the infancy stories would have been equipped to read the signs and script of this performance through engagement with sites of memory associated with children, cursing, and competition in the ancient Mediterranean world—through cultural contact with images of young athletes in training, of ritual practitioners performing curses, and of philosophers and teachers championing the life of the mind. In the end, the product of such social memory work was a Christ child—a cursing Jesus—whose identity was indelibly stamped by the distinctive and familiar contours of agonistic relationships in Graeco-Roman society.

5

Learning Letters

When I think back to my own early school days, there are certain images that immediately come to mind—the physical spaces and paraphernalia, interactions with teachers and landmark lessons, and of course traumatic events involving conflict or discipline. I remember hard wooden desks and chairs, dusty blackboards, and no. 2 pencils that constantly needed sharpening. In kindergarten, I recall struggling in vain to write my letters neatly on the page. Those penmanship lessons never took: I still cannot hold a ballpoint correctly, and my handwriting is terrible. In first grade, I recall feeling a sense of triumph after I had memorized my multiplication tables up to twelve. On the wall, a paper cutout of a hot-air balloon rising into the air marked my progress as I moved upward through the numbered levels. At 12 × 12 = 144, I had reached the stratosphere. I remember getting in trouble for the first time: at the age of five I was sent to stand in the corner after accidently stepping on the heels of the girl in front of me as we practiced walking in a circle (apparently a valuable skill). And I remember my constant fear of the principal Mr. Kiscaden and his wooden paddle, used on naughty children who misbehaved. Such were the life lessons learned in Rohrerstown Elementary School.

The *Paidika* contains three different episodes in which Jesus enters classrooms and interacts with teachers. The first—by far the longest, spanning three chapters (*Paidika* 6–8)—dramatizes an extended contest of wills between Jesus and a teacher named Zacchaeus.[1] The story begins with an initial interchange in which Zacchaeus proposes a curriculum based on the learning of letters and good behavior, and Jesus responds by marking the source of his own knowledge as outside his listeners' experience and even prior to the creation of the world. Jesus then follows Zacchaeus to the school, where the teacher writes out and recites the letters of the alphabet, repeating the name of each letter over and over again in the expectation that Jesus will respond in kind. When Jesus intentionally remains silent, Zacchaeus becomes angry and strikes the child on the head. After Jesus' anger abates, he proceeds to recite the entire alphabet, before speaking cryptically about the shape of the letter *alpha*. In the end, Zacchaeus—shamed and silenced by "an exceedingly small child" (*paidiou panu mikrou*) who must be "either a god or an angel"—begs Joseph to take Jesus away.

The second school episode (*Paidika* 13) takes place three years later.[2] Jesus is now eight years old, and Joseph decides to hand him over to another master. The second teacher does not waste time in conversation: he writes down the alphabet straightaway and orders the boy, "Say alpha." As with the first teacher, Jesus does not comply but instead issues his own demand: "You tell me first what beta is and I shall tell you what alpha is." And again, his teacher becomes angry and strikes him. This time, Jesus reacts very differently: he responds not with words of wisdom but with a swift curse that causes the man to fall down and die.

The third episode (*Paidika* 14) takes place only a few days later.[3] A third teacher intrepidly approaches Joseph and asks for the chance to teach his child the alphabet. After he has received Joseph's permission, he leads Jesus to the classroom. Upon entering, Jesus walks directly to the lectern, where he finds a book. But instead of reading from it, he opens his mouth and begins speaking "awe-inspiring" and "divinely approved" words that amaze both the teacher and the rest of the children. When Joseph runs to the school to make sure everything is fine, he finds the teacher alive and well, testifying to Jesus' "grace and wisdom."

Early in the *Paidika*'s history of transmission, these three story units may have constituted something of a mini-collection of tales, grouped together by common theme.[4] As a tale type, they were probably modeled in part on Luke 2:41–52, the story of the twelve-year-old Jesus in the Temple, which would come to be included (in a very slightly expanded form) as the concluding chapter of the *Paidika*.[5] As such, these teacher episodes reimagine Jesus at earlier stages of learning: they are retrospective attempts to recollect what it would have looked like for such a precocious, wonder-working child to undergo elementary education as a rite of passage. In the *Paidika,* however, this rite of passage is envisioned not as a smooth and uncontested coronation in the classroom but as a contest involving conflict and competition over the nature of true knowledge.

Throughout this chapter, I explore how Jesus the schoolboy performs a dual role: on the one hand, his experience conforms to certain standard conventions of Graeco-Roman education; on the other, his encounters with teachers reveal wisdom, maturity, and power far beyond that of his adult mentors. Once again, sociologies of memory serve as my conceptual framework. What I want to examine in more depth is how this balance and tension in Jesus' characterization would have been grounded in specific "sites of memory" familiar to readers and hearers of the stories. What shared recollections related to childhood and elementary schooling would have been prompted by these stories? How did Jesus' schools function as "memory spaces" for readers to "think with," as they recalled their own local educational settings? What kind of cultural work did Jesus perform for the *Paidika*'s early audience in his demonstration of mastery over the ABCs?

In his book *Das Alphabet in Mystik und Magie* (1925), Franz Dornseiff writes, "An occupational concern with the letters of the alphabet was something that marked the essential character of childhood, and it is known that remembrances of childhood, by way of association, could become factors in the religious lives of adults."[6] Dornseiff was on to something here, and throughout the rest of this chapter, I follow his lead by focusing my attention on Graeco-Roman elementary education as fertile ground for the kind of social memory work I am describing. As it turns out, in antiquity, to remember one's letters was not only a practical pathway toward understanding words and texts; it also could serve as a mystical means to understanding the cosmos and its creator (or creators).

School Days and School Ways: Social Memories of the Graeco-Roman Classroom

In the ancient world, adults who had experienced a modicum of education would have had their own reservoir of scholastic memories from which to draw. Educational levels of course varied widely according to differences in class, geography, and gender, but even those who never set foot in a classroom would also have had vicarious but tactile access to classroom spaces through a range of social and material media—from storytelling and drama to art, artifacts, and architecture. In the following sections, I cast my net wide for relevant sites of memory, examining the role that texts and books, stories and images, classroom spaces, and teaching practices all played in shaping the educational "imaginarium" of the *Paidika*'s audience.

BOOKS: EDUCATIONAL MANUALS AS SITES OF MEMORY

Some adult memories of the classroom came to be written down and canonized, as it were, in multigenerational manuals or handbooks called *Hermeneumata*—edited collections of texts composed by different schoolteachers in Latin and Greek over the course of six or seven centuries (from around the third century BCE to the late third or fourth century CE) and designed for the purpose of elementary instruction.[7] Originally used as part of a bilingual curriculum in the late ancient Latin West (probably Gaul), these "glossaries" survive in various versions but typically contain four common elements: (1) an alphabetical dictionary, (2) a dictionary organized according to topic, (3) a section of so-called colloquia, and (4) texts for reading practice.[8]

It is the third element—the colloquia—that especially served as textual repositories for Graeco-Roman social memory related to children's education. These colloquia were not formal dialogues but rather more like "little scenes from everyday life in dramatized form,"[9] ancient renditions of a typical child's "Day in the Life." Beginning with the young student's hygienic routine after getting out of bed, the colloquium follows him as he attends school in the morning, returns home for lunch, and then spends time at the baths and the forum in the afternoon and evening.[10]

While certainly idealized for the purposes of moral formation, the school scenes in the *Hermeneumata* present what are generally regarded as "largely plausible" vignettes that realistically depict the ins and outs of a well-to-do Roman child's elementary education.[11] From these sources, we glean information about the child's preparations for and arrival at school, about his interactions with teachers and fellow students in the classroom, and about the nature of the lessons that would take place there.

An account from one of these colloquia (found in the *Hermeneumata Stephani*) describes how the student, after collecting his writing kit and exercise book, goes to school accompanied by his tutor (*paedagogus*).[12] The young boy reaches the school by proceeding through a portico, walking up a flight of stairs to the second floor, and then lifting or pulling aside a curtain that allows access to the classroom space. Immediately upon arrival, while still on the ground level, he exchanges greetings with his fellow students; then, after ascending, he greets the assistant teacher and next the schoolmaster, who welcomes him with a kiss.

Elsewhere in the same manual, student readers are supplied with helpful phrases to use as they try to find a place to sit in class: "Let me have my place." "[This is] my bench/footstool/stool." "Squeeze in a bit." "Go over there." "This is my place." "I was here first."[13] One observes a similar concern with seating arrangements in another handbook, called *Hermeneumata Celtes:* "Then I sit in my place, on a bench, or a stool, or a step, or a footstool, or a chair."[14] Apparently, in this particular Roman classroom, when it came to finding a suitable seat, any horizontal surface would do!

The colloquia also give us glimpses of students at work. In urban as well as rural settings, classrooms often functioned like one-room schoolhouses where different age groups performed a range of separate tasks simultaneously. Older students might be found erasing their previous day's work from their wax tablets and then copying a new text on the basis of a teacher's model. After completing the writing assignment, they would hand it over to their instructor for correction.[15] Others might be heard reading aloud, reciting colloquia from memory, doing a dictation exercise, or reviewing grammar.[16]

At the same time, the youngest students would be tasked with learning their ABCs. The *Hermeneumata Einsidlensia* describes how, "when the teacher bids them, the little ones engage in letters and syllables, and one of the older students pronounces them aloud for them."[17] And in the *Hermeneumata Celtes,* we learn that "the smallest ones get up to [recite] syllables" while the more advanced present oral declamations, read, or go through their commentaries and rules of grammar.[18] Those who performed such tasks well were praised; those who performed them badly received a flogging.[19]

These colloquia should certainly not be mistaken for historical accounts of actual student experiences. But they do give us valuable information about what went on in ancient schools, insofar as they were probably based on teachers' cross-generational observations about educational customs and procedures, leavened with a healthy dose of idealized memories related to their own childhood instruction.

Here I might draw instructive analogies to the way Cicero, Marcus Aurelius, and Augustine of Hippo recollected their own schooldays as adults. In the first century BCE, Cicero viscerally recalls the anxiety brought about by the sudden and unexpected arrival of the master into the classroom: "Look out! Get your hands off the writing tablet! Here's teacher, sooner than we had hoped! There'll be a beating for Cato's team."[20] But he also carries with him the warm memory of reading a favorite line from Homer's *Iliad* that he had loved "from childhood" (*a puero*).[21]

Marcus Aurelius calls to mind how one of his private teachers—a man named Rusticus—had taught him "to write letters in the simple style" and "to read books carefully."[22] He also recollects, with a hint of pride, his prudent self-control in moments of conflict or disagreement with his tutor:

"Though I was often angry at Rusticus I never went to extremes for which I should have been sorry."[23]

Finally, Augustine (354–430 CE), much like Cicero before him, remembers the threat of beatings and how he and his fellow students had begged his teachers to spare them when they were caught in the midst of mischief.[24] Such traumatic memories of his elementary school days come to expression especially in book 1 of his *Confessions:* "If I was slow to learn, I was flogged," and "[if] my mind was absorbed only in play, . . . I was punished."[25] And all the while, he suspected that his parents remained "amused at the torments" inflicted by his instructors upon him and his classmates.[26] While the discursive style of the *Hermeneumata* is not framed in such autobiographical terms, the colloquia, with their vivid vignettes of everyday life in a Graeco-Roman classroom, would nonetheless have performed a similar kind of memory work for ancient readers.

STORIES AND ART: MYTHIC AND MUNDANE IMAGES AS SITES OF MEMORY

Admittedly, the company who read such handbooks—and indeed, the number of adults with even a basic level of schooling—would have constituted a rather small percentage of the total population. Greek and Roman education was largely the preserve of the wealthy and those of independent means. The overwhelming majority of elementary instruction took place in the homes of those who had the wherewithal to hire personal tutors.[27] By comparison, the evidence for the establishment of self-standing schools in Mediterranean towns and cities seems fairly scattered.[28] Probably funded by wealthy private donors, these schools may have served a certain small percentage of students drawn from outside the upper class as well.[29]

Despite these rather narrow educational demographics, however, the "catchment area"[30] for the dissemination of social memories related to school life would in fact have been somewhat wider than simply the literate and landed aristocracy and those who had direct experience of the classroom. Popular stories of famous teachers, along with visual images of children at school on display in public and private settings, disseminated certain common perceptions of educational conventions to a wider audience.

One source of images about teachers was ancient mythology. Stories about the centaur Chiron (tutor of Achilles, Apollo, and Asclepius) and about Linus (teacher of Mousaios, Iphicles, and Heracles) circulated widely in oral and written form, as well as in a range of visual media. On ceramic vessels, reliefs, and wall paintings, Chiron and Achilles were presented, respectively, as "the ideal schoolmaster" and "the typical Athenian schoolboy."[31] Versions of the

Chiron story still remained part of folkloric parlance into the second century CE when the tale was recorded in Ps.-Apollodorus's *Bibliotheca,* a "library" of Greek myths and legends.[32] Early Christian writers from the second to the fourth century—including Justin Martyr, Lactantius, and Gregory of Nazianzus—also demonstrate a familiarity with Chiron's reputation as the tutor of gods and heroes.[33]

The teacher and poet Linus was also popular among Greeks and Romans, and on a number of ancient ceramic vessels one finds him depicted as "a typically Athenian schoolmaster in a typical schoolroom."[34] One cup from ancient Caere near Rome has a painted scene of him engaged in a recitation lesson with the boy Mousaios: the teacher sits and unrolls a scroll ready to dictate, while the student stands with a tablet and writing utensil in hand.[35] On a *skyphos* (a type of jug with handles) from the same region, Linus teaches the diligent Iphicles how to play the lyre, while Heracles (not the model student) is shown being led reluctantly to Linus's school.[36] Heracles's tutelage under Linus famously did not end well: the two quarreled and fought, and other painted cups and jars from antiquity show the ill-tempered Heracles viciously attacking and killing his teacher with a stool.[37] Despite his conspicuous failure to bring Heracles to heel, Linus retained the reputation as the teacher of letters par excellence into the late Roman period: the Latin writer Tacitus (56–117 CE) even attests to a tradition that Linus was the one "who invented the shapes of sixteen letters" of the Greek alphabet.[38] In the second and third centuries, Linus's standing as a learned man and teacher was discussed and debated by Christian apologists such as Tatian (ca. 120–180 CE) and Origen (ca. 185–254 CE).[39]

Such retellings of Greek mythology were certainly not the only way—or even the primary means—by which images of the classroom came to be disseminated and planted in Greek and Roman cultural memory. More pervasive were visual images depicting children engaged in everyday school activities. In classical Greece, scenes showing students interacting with teachers were painted on hundreds of cups and vases available for sale in ceramic shops and visible to the general public on the street where vendors plied their trade. Such ceramic vessels, as well as terracotta figurines depicting school scenes, are preserved in museum collections across the globe, in Athens, Berlin, Brussels, Florence, Istanbul, London, Madrid, New York, Paris, Washington, and Würzburg.[40] Surviving scene types include images of children walking on their way to school or sitting in the classroom engaged in reading, writing, and recitation exercises. One painted vase even shows children playacting a school scene: a boy sits in the master's chair holding a staff, while two others approach him with book rolls in hand.[41] This artistic repertoire reveals a range of cultural associations that ancient Greeks would have brought to mind when they thought about the education of their children.

During the late Roman period, images of teachers interacting with students were painted on the walls of rooms in posh private homes and carved into stone reliefs that adorned funerary spaces. Wall paintings with school scenes have been found at Pompeii and Herculaneum, buried in ash after the catastrophic eruption of Mount Vesuvius in 79 CE. One such painting at Pompeii depicted a small child in the midst of his lessons; his teacher sits in a chair holding a roll, with a box containing more papyrus rolls on the floor near his feet.[42] Another example—contemporaneous in date, but much less sanguine in theme—survives at nearby Herculaneum.[43] In the painting, a student is held down by two of his peers while the schoolmaster flogs his back with reeds. In the background a teacher stands holding another set of reeds, ready for a second round of punishment. To the left, students try in vain to concentrate on their lessons: one of them can't help peeking out of the corner of his eye at his unfortunate classmate.

Finally, a late second- or third-century CE Roman funerary relief from Germany—the so-called Neumagen School Relief—shows a more tranquil scene of teacher-student interaction.[44] The bearded schoolmaster sits in a chair with his hand upraised as if to emphasize an important point. Two students are seated on either side, holding their scrolls open and concentrating on their reading. To the right, a third student arrives carrying a satchel in his left hand and raises his right hand up in a form of greeting.[45]

Such imagery of ancient educational practice would have served as ready-made sites of memory—cultural markers and signposts—for recipients of the *Paidika*. Indeed, the details of Jesus' encounters with his teachers correlate in significant ways to what we know about teaching and learning at the elementary level in Graeco-Roman society. In what follows, I show how the *Paidika* stories intersected with the spaces and practices of late ancient education, and thereby served as a catalyst for memory work related to childhood performed by readers and hearers.

CLASSROOMS: PHYSICAL SPACES AS SITES OF MEMORY

The *Paidika* stories provide only very sparse details about the imagined physical space of the classrooms where Jesus was taken for his lessons, but what little we can glean from the narrative matches the data we have from antiquity. In Greek and Roman societies, a wide variety of locations were used as "schoolrooms"—open-air arcades or porticos partitioned off by a curtain, dimly lit apartments rented at a bargain rate, halls (*exedrae*) furnished for the purpose in private homes, or (only for a select number of advanced students attending well-funded city academies) purpose-built auditoriums equipped with daises and tiered seating.[46] How do Jesus' classrooms in the *Paidika* correlate with this range of possibilities?

There is not much to go on, but the first and third teacher episodes (*Paidika* 6–8 and 14) make it clear that Jesus attends class not at home but at a separate location called a *paideutērion.*[47] In late antiquity, the word *paideutērion* seems to have had rather generic connotations as a place dedicated for the purpose of instruction where students of different levels learn side by side. Thus, the Christian writer Clement of Alexandria likens the church to a "common school" (*to koinon touto paideutērion*) that welcomes people in without regard to socio-economic station.[48]

In chapter 6 of the *Paidika,* we are told that, after first leading Jesus "into the *paideutērion,*" the first teacher, Zacchaeus, then leads him "into the *didaskaleion.*"[49] In both literary and documentary sources, the word *didaskaleion* ("place of teaching") is the most common term used to designate a school or classroom for children, with the more specific word *grammatodidaskaleion* ("elementary school or classroom") also occurring frequently. In her studies of papyri from Hellenistic and Roman Egypt, Raffaella Cribiore has cited specific examples of *didaskaleia,* including schools for first-level instruction in second-century BCE Memphis, first-century CE Fayum, and fourth-century CE Oxyrhynchus.[50] In the case of the first teacher episode in the *Paidika,* what seems to be envisioned is a primary school classroom (*didaskaleion*) located within, and only accessed through, a building or complex of rooms called a *paideutērion.* Jesus gains access to the former after entering the latter.

The spatial relationship between the *didaskaleion* and the *paideutērion* is an oft-overlooked detail in the story, but it is an interesting one worthy of a brief digression. What evidence do we have related to the location and configuration of schoolrooms in Graeco-Roman society? Some of the best architectural evidence comes from Pompeii, where first-century graffiti and inscriptions provide clues about teaching activity in the city. One example is a grafitto scratched on the wall of "a school run by a certain C. Iulius Helenus" that "makes it clear that students who neglected their lessons could expect a flogging from the master."[51] A second example is an inscription written by a certain schoolmaster named Potitus: found on a pilaster beside an entrance into a building, the text mentions "young boys" (*pueri* and *poveri*) and "pupils" (*discentes*).[52] Laurentino García y García has surmised that the building on which this inscription was recorded belonged to Potitus and functioned as some kind of school.[53] Other inscriptions on the ground floor appear to confirm this hypothesis. In addition to recording three male names, Marcus,

Festus, and Proculus (perhaps the names of students?), they contain the fragmentary traces of the words "beaten" (*vapula*) and "beaten three times" (*III vapulo*). Despite their partial preservation, these phrases suggest that the ground floor may have been used for punishing students who misbehaved.[54]

Given the layout of the building and the location of this inscriptional evidence, García conjectures that "wooden stocks, *compedes* . . . used to punish younger pupils at the pillory" may have been "placed near the western pilaster, where everybody, even passers-by, could easily see them."[55] He goes on to draw conclusions about where the primary activities of instruction took place: "It seems, then, considering the recurring evidence, that the prevailing intent of the teachers was to keep the *discentes* (pupils) fenced in by a *pergula* (enclosed classroom), placed in the upper and more secluded storey of a building, for the evident purpose of keeping the pupils as far as possible from the street, with its clamour and distractions. Apparently, for this reason, a *hortulus* (garden) was usually interposed between the *pergula* (classroom) and the street and served as a boundary, materially separating the two conflicting scenes."[56] García's reconstruction may go slightly beyond what the evidence will bear in this particular case, but there is at least one other important ancient source that alludes to the use of second-story rooms as classroom space: the corpus of *Hermeneumata* mentioned earlier. In the *Hermeneumata Stephani,* the model student negotiates an architectural landscape not unlike the one reconstructed by García at first-century Pompeii. Upon the student's arrival at his destination, he first makes his way "through the portico which leads to school," then comes to "the staircase" and quietly goes "up the stairs," and finally draws open a curtain to gain access to the classroom itself.[57]

This archaeological and literary evidence from the first three centuries CE indicates that Greeks and Romans would have been accustomed to finding elementary school classrooms on the second floors of buildings (as well as in assorted other places). The reason this is significant for our interpretation of the *Paidika* relates not only to the story of Jesus' encounter with Zacchaeus but also to the story that immediately follows in chapter 9.

Chapter 9 of the *Paidika* tells a tragic tale.[58] A child named Zeno falls out of a "certain upstairs room" and dies.[59] The bereaved parents accuse Jesus of pushing the child and causing his death. Jesus denies the charge, and then to prove his innocence he raises the child from the dead to give his testimony. When the child confirms that Jesus is not guilty, Jesus instructs him to "fall asleep" again. At the end of the story, the child is dead, but the parents nonetheless praise God and worship Jesus.[60]

This story about Zeno's death seemingly bears no relation to the three chapters that immediately precede it. Or at least, that is what scholars have generally assumed.[61] While it is likely that Zeno's story originally circulated independently, certain important details may give us a hint as to why it was placed immediately after the episode at Zacchaeus's school in the earliest narrative versions of the *Paidika.* These details include the temporal markers at the beginning of the story, the description of the children's actions, and the spatial setting for the events described.

First, the story of Zeno opens with a temporal transition ("Again, after many days. . . .").[62] This opening phrase does two things at once. Even as it establishes a distinct time frame for the action that follows, it links the Zeno episode with the foregoing chapters through the initial placement of the adverb "again" (*palin*). This word is used to introduce a section of text only one other time in the *Paidika,* and in that instance it ties together two consecutive miracle stories (*Paidika* 15–16) that involve markedly similar thematic elements (the collection and splitting of wood, and Jesus' healing of injuries sustained to hands and feet).[63]

Second, the initial sentence in *Paidika* 9 sets the stage for what is to ensue by introducing a vignette of Jesus "playing with other children."[64] His activity of "playing" (*paizein*) with his peers verbally recalls earlier episodes in *Paidika* 2 and 6 when he was "playing" (*paizein*) by the stream and when he was "playing with" (*paizein pros;* that is, "teasing" or "mocking") onlookers before agreeing to enter Zacchaeus's school.[65] But this scene, as a literary *lieu de mémoire,* also implicitly calls to mind the kind of recreational group interaction that schoolmates would have engaged in during their times of recess from lessons. In their study of childhood in early Christianity, Cornelia Horn and John Martens have noted how in late ancient classrooms "playing and studying competed with one another for children's attention."[66] As a case in point they cite Jerome, who remembers the way he, as a young boy, used to fill his breaks from school with games and other recreational pursuits.[67] The scene of Jesus playing with his friends in *Paidika* 9 may have prompted analogous childhood memories for early readers and hearers of the text. Earlier, in *Paidika* 6, Zacchaeus had identified "learn[ing] to love those [one's] own age" as a key learning objective for primary education, equal in importance to the learning of letters. It is not inconceivable that this scene of Jesus playing nicely with others also was meant to be taken as a sign of the way that he had mastered this "core curriculum."

Third and finally, in light of the archaeological and literary evidence cited earlier, the specific location where Jesus and the other children are at play in chapter 9 would have strengthened the narrative connection between the Zacchaeus and Zeno episodes. The description of children congregating "in an upstairs room" is reminiscent of the kind of architectural layout of schools witnessed at Potitus's place in Pompeii and in standard educational handbooks like the *Hermeneumata*. Here, I envision Graeco-Roman schools, with their sometimes particular and recognizable configuration of rooms, as key interpretive coordinates—as easily accessed social sites of memory—for educationally informed recipients of the *Paidika* stories. This new reading of the Zeno story admittedly remains speculative, but it may provide new insight into the rationale for its editorial placement immediately following the scenes of Jesus in the classroom.

TEACHERS AND STUDENTS: EDUCATIONAL PRACTICES AS SITES OF MEMORY

I now turn back to examining the *didaskaleia* of Zacchaeus and his unnamed counterparts in *Paidika* 6–8 and 13–14. As I mentioned before, in Greek literary and documentary sources, the term *didaskaleia* frequently designates schools or classrooms that offered instruction at the primary level to younger children (mostly between the ages of seven and fourteen).[68] But the papyrological record also attests a wider application: in some cases, it also was used to refer to educational establishments offering more advanced instruction to older students (and even in some cases adults).[69] Thus early readers of the *Paidika* would have probably imagined the *didaskaleia* of Zacchaeus and his unnamed counterparts as encompassing a range of grades, beginning with the youngest children.

Social historians have often analyzed ancient Greek and Roman education according to three tiers or levels, corresponding very roughly to the categories of primary, middle school, and secondary education.[70] At the first level, beginning students would learn letters—reading, writing, and some basic arithmetic—under the guidance of a *didaskalos* ("teacher"), a *grammatodidaskalos* ("teacher of letters"), or a *grammatistēs* ("elementary schoolmaster").[71] At the second (higher primary) level, students received instruction in language, literature, and grammar from a *grammatikos* ("grammarian"). At the third and most advanced level, experienced students learned the subtleties of rhetoric and speech from a *sophistēs* ("master educator, professor") or *rhētōr* ("rhetorician").[72] These levels were by no means fixed in stone: student placement and advancement was determined not by age but by stages of learning development; and there were significant local and regional variations from place to place and from period to period. In addition, Greek and Roman society supported other teacher roles that did not fit so neatly into this three-tiered schema—roles that would have complemented, and in some cases competed with, these institutionalized positions. One such role was that of the *paidagōgos*, a private tutor who offered elementary instruction in the home, sometimes a household servant who was available to chaperone the children as they attended school outside the home.[73] Another was that of the *kathēgētēs,* a jack-of-all-trades instructor who offered lessons to students across a wide range of learning levels. *Kathēgētai* often moved from place to place to find employment, setting up shop as local teachers for periods of time in towns where demand for their versatile services was greater.[74]

In the *Paidika,* Jesus' teachers are described as both *kathēgētāi* and *didaskaloi.*[75] The details of their representation correspond to what is known about the social role and status of freelance instructors who traveled around seeking employment and trying to establish themselves in particular locales by contracting with families to take on their young sons as prized pupils.[76] In *Paidika* 6.2b, one enigmatic statement placed in the mouth of the young Jesus may be read as underscoring the itinerant (and therefore rather tenuous) social status of such *kathēgētai* in Graeco-Roman society. After Zacchaeus requests to take Jesus under his wing, Jesus turns to him and says: "Being a teacher [*kathēgētēs*] you were brought forth with good natural disposition. But as for the name [*onoma*] with which you are named, you are a stranger [*allotrios*]."[77] Here, I think what is at issue is not Zacchaeus's given name but rather his title as a *kathēgētēs.* In this context, readers would have understood Jesus' words as underscoring the fact that Zacchaeus fits the profile of a teacher who has come from elsewhere seeking employment and has found it in a local school.

In the *Paidika,* the vulnerable social status of Zacchaeus and the other two teachers is conveyed in different ways: in their interaction with Jesus' father, Joseph; in their changing demeanor toward Jesus as their student (from flattery to violence to lament); and in Jesus' responses to them as figures who lack true authority. In all three teacher episodes, the responsibility for Jesus' educational upbringing falls to Joseph in his role as *paterfamilias.* This would have conformed to prevailing Graeco-Roman expectations related to fathers' involvement in their sons' schooling.[78] Thus, it is Joseph who is approached by teachers seeking to take Jesus on as their pupil (*Paidika* 6.2, 6.2f, and 14.1), who vets the instructors to determine their suitability (6.2a, 13.1, and 14.1), who physically accompanies Jesus to the classroom (6.2f, 7.2–4) or closely monitors his progress while there (14.3), and who administers discipline after school (13.3). By comparison, the teachers in these stories are represented as subordinated caretakers, as surrogates subject to both the family's and the child's authority. In order to recruit and then win over Jesus, two of them resort to sycophancy. Zacchaeus takes Jesus into the classroom, all the while "flattering [*kolakeuein*] him," and the third teacher, speaking with Joseph, makes no bones about the fact that he plans to use "flattery" (*kolakeia*) to teach Jesus letters.[79]

In antiquity, flattery marked the subordinate role in a patron-client relationship, and was often criticized by moral philosophers as a vice that betrayed false friendship and monetary self-interest.[80] Over time, it especially came to be associated with the subservience of teachers and scholars who tried to ingratiate themselves with the wealthy and influential. The Epicurean philosopher Philodemus, writing in Herculaneum during the first century BCE, produced three books entitled *On Flattery* in which he dispensed "practical advice on how to treat students of high station."[81] Plutarch (ca. 46–120 CE) compares flatterers to parasites that leech off of those with "renown and power," noting that teachers of young and wealthy students typically lavish them with flattery and praise.[82] Lucian of Samosata (ca. 120–after 180 CE) offers a similar social critique in his treatise *On Salaried Posts in Great Houses* (also known as *The Dependent Scholar*): there, he satirizes the life of Greek instructors "who attached themselves to the households of great Roman lords and ladies" and humiliatingly plied their patrons with blandishments in order to secure a wage.[83] The portrayal of Jesus' instructors as flatterers in the *Paidika* reveals how the infancy stories would have served as other venues for this widespread social critique of the teaching profession in antiquity.

In the case of Zacchaeus, it is also noteworthy that when flattery has no discernible effect over his young charge, the older man resorts to another recognizable pedagogical method—physical violence—as a means of asserting his (tenuous) authority in the classroom.[84] The second teacher does the same, striking Jesus when he proves incompliant, with unfortunate results.[85] As we have already seen in paintings and graffiti from Herculaneum and Pompeii, and in the autobiographical reflections of Cicero and Augustine, the schoolmaster's harsh physical discipline of students was a mainstay of Roman social memory related to school life. Thus, the Roman poet Juvenal (late first or early second century CE) employs the phrase "to subject your hand to the rod" (*manum ferulae subduximus*) as synonymous with the verb "to learn."[86] Horace even nicknames one of his teachers "Rod" (*Plagosus*).[87] The same associations held true for the Greek-speaking world. In the second century CE, Lucian of Samosata speaks with intimate familiarity about the practice of disciplining students by hitting them with a stick.[88] Such memories of pedagogical intimidation were reinforced through classroom exercises. A case in point is a wax tablet from Roman Egypt, now preserved in Berlin. It contains a maxim written once by the teacher and copied four times by a beginning-level student: it reads, "Work hard, boy, lest you be thrashed."[89] To be thrashed was to submit to a kind of moral formation—the blows were understood to form the student into an educated and ethical subject, like malleable metal shaped by the blows of a coppersmith's hammer. Such was the steep price paid for trying to follow the path of Greek paideia.[90]

The beatings administered by ancient teachers are usually taken as a sign of the publicly sanctioned, almost tyrannical authority they wielded over their students: "an institutionalized symbol of (their) unequal relationship."[91] This conclusion is most certainly correct: along with slaves, children occupied the lowest rung of the social ladder. At the same time, however, the social standing of many primary educators was far from secure in the ancient world. I have already touched on the itinerant and financially dependent status of *kathēgētai* such as Zacchaeus and his compatriots. There were other systemic hardships to be endured as well. Elementary-level instructors were not only sometimes ill educated and subject to "the contempt of the upper class";[92] they were also often denied legal and financial benefits that other, more advanced-level educators enjoyed.[93] Commenting on "the precariousness of the teacher's position" in the Graeco-Roman world, Cribiore aptly notes that while "pupils were slaves of their teachers," at the same time "a teacher was a slave of many masters," answerable to the diverse displeasures of parents, grandparents, guardians, and their own students.[94]

In the *Paidika,* the first two teachers' violent efforts to make Jesus compliant only reveal the rather fragile nature of their control over the classroom. In each case, there is kickback from the Christ child, whether in angry words of one-upmanship ("I want to instruct you rather than being instructed by you, since I know the letters you are teaching more accurately and much better than you") or more drastically in the utterance of a deadly curse.[95]

We have several other examples of situations in ancient literature where a teacher's supposedly unassailable authority suddenly was shown to come undone. In his Latin play *Bacchides,* the playwright Plautus (ca. 254–184 BCE) scripts a scene that provides a comedic commentary on the lack of discipline demonstrated by students in his era. He laments the fact that "nowadays, before a youngster is seven years old, if you lay a finger on him, he promptly takes his writing tablet and smashes his tutor's head with it."[96] These words are placed in the mouth of a tutor named Lydus, who goes on to ask, "Can a teacher exert authority here under such conditions, if he is beaten first himself?"[97] In the late first or early second century CE, the satirist Juvenal paints a similar picture of a classroom disrupted by student revolt. Even though "the teacher should hold the place of a revered parent," Juvenal knows of several instructors who were "cudgelled each by his own pupils."[98] Two fourth-century writers likewise describe scenarios of student-on-teacher violence. The Greek rhetorician Libanius composed one of his orations "to reproach some students who had treated a pedagogue roughly, tossing him up and down on a rug," and the Christian writer Prudentius describes how the martyr Cassian was murdered by a group of angry students who broke their writing tablets against his face.[99]

Granted, given the literary genres of these various accounts, one cannot guarantee that the incidents referred to by Plautus, Juvenal, Libanius, and Prudentius were actual, historical cases of students rebelling or teachers getting their comeuppance. They may very well have been invented for the purpose of social critique or for an object lesson. But even if this is the case, such stories tapped into a vein of uncertainty, and even outright scorn, regarding elementary teachers and their methods in Graeco-Roman society. The retelling of such tales reinforced the social perception that—far from being masters of their own domain—instructors of children were, in Plautus's words, "worthless old baggage."[100]

The *Paidika*'s portrayal of Jesus' teachers as unqualified hacks contributes to this wider cultural discourse. Indeed, like the stories of students turning the tables and beating their teachers, the *Paidika* dramatizes a role reversal in which Jesus takes on the role of the master and his instructors assume the role of bewildered students. In chapter 7, Zacchaeus is left "baffled" by Jesus' teaching and offers up a lament over his shame at being "mastered by an exceedingly small child."[101] Speaking to Joseph, he says, "Woe is me, brother! He dumbfounds me. I cannot follow [him] in my mind. I have tricked myself—I, the thrice-wretched one. I thought that I would have him as a student, but I have been found to have him as a teacher."[102]

The unabashed teaching posture of Jesus himself was what elicited this melancholy response, and it strongly underscores the role reversal dramatized in the story. His *parrhēsia* ("bold speech") stands in especially sharp contrast to Zacchaeus's earlier obsequiousness. In this context, it is worth noting the observations of the first-century BCE authors Horace and Philodemus. Horace compares the behavior of a flatterer to that of "a schoolboy . . . repeating his lessons to a stern master," while Philodemus likens harsh or frank criticism to a beating administered by a teacher.[103] In the *Paidika,* Jesus' bold speech marks him out as the true "master" who delivers verbal beatings to his instructors and unmasks them as neophytes in the ways of wisdom.

So far, in my examination of the teacher episodes in the *Paidika,* I have highlighted elements that would have contributed to an aura of verisimilitude in these stories—elements that would have helped reinforce connections between the narrative representation of Jesus' teachers and readers' cultural memories about the reputation of elementary instructors and the schooling of young students in the Graeco-Roman world. This aura of verisimilitude is constructed through details related to the use of classroom space, the educational responsibilities of parents, the social status and disciplinary methods of teachers, and the behavior of students who sometimes worked to undermine their teachers' authority.

There is one element, however, that I have not yet discussed: the content of the teaching itself. In the *Paidika,* the young Jesus is brought to school to learn his ABCs. In the next section of this chapter, I discuss how this curricular detail would have reinforced early readers' perception of Jesus as a typical student undergoing a readily recognizable elementary course of study. But I also explore how this narrative detail would have sponsored other kinds of cultural memories—memories about the way letters were manipulated for more mystical ends, and about Jesus as an alphabetical adept possessing powers far beyond the grasp of his instructors.

Letter Lore: The ABCs and All Their Tricks[104]

FIRST LESSONS

In the *Paidika,* the crux of Jesus' encounter with each of his three teachers is alphabetic instruction.[105] In chapter 6, Zacchaeus asks Joseph for permission to take on the five-year-old boy as his student "so that he may be instructed in letters [*grammata*]." Once in the classroom, Zacchaeus writes out the alphabet (*alphabēton*) and then orally repeats each letter over and over again to Jesus in the hope that the knowledge will sink in. After Jesus is stubborn and Zacchaeus disciplines him with a smack to the head, the Christ child proves he has already mastered this lesson by reciting aloud "all the letters from alpha to omega." Then, he challenges his schoolmaster. Accusing him of being ignorant of "the alpha, which is in accordance with nature," Jesus commands him, "First teach me the alpha and then I shall trust you to speak the beta."[106]

In chapter 13, Joseph hands Jesus over to a second teacher because "he wanted him not to be at a loss when it came to letters." When the teacher writes out the alphabet for his new student and instructs Jesus to "Say alpha," Jesus responds with a different challenge: "You tell me first what beta is and I shall tell you what alpha is."[107] Finally, in chapter 14, the third teacher takes Jesus into the classroom, again intending "to teach [Jesus] letters." There, Jesus makes a beeline for the lectern and demonstrates his more advanced wisdom by speaking "awe-inspiring" and "divinely approved" words.[108]

This repeated focus on learning letters conforms to what we know about the elementary-level curriculum in ancient Greek and Roman schools. We have already seen how the *Hermeneumata* envisioned the youngest students ("the little ones") doing exercises involving "letters and syllables" as the first assignment in class each morning.[109] On the reported testimony of Greek writers such as Hippocrates and Aristotle, most scholars take seven as the typical age at which families would have sent their sons to school for their first instruction outside the home.[110] Juvenal also cites seven as the appropriate age for placing children under the tutelage of "bearded preceptors."[111] There was no hard-and-fast rule, however, and indeed, as Cribiore notes, "age limits could vary widely, and age did not determine precise educational thresholds."[112] Thus, while the first-century Latin author Quintilian counseled that boys should not be "taught to read" before the age of seven, he also reluctantly admitted that some children were introduced to the classroom prior to that, regardless of "however small" (*quantulumcumque*) their initial advances in learning might be.[113] Accordingly, Wiedemann reports that in the Roman world "schoolmasters began by teaching five- or six-year-olds the Greek alphabet," before moving on to Latin letters and more advanced grammatical instruction.[114] In this context, the fact that Joseph first takes Jesus to school at the age of five would, in and of itself, not necessarily have marked the boy off as a prodigy. This may have been viewed as a premature start in certain quarters, but it would not have been completely out of the ordinary for students to get their first taste of lessons at that age.

In antiquity, education was all about repetition and memorization, and the scenes of Jesus' teachers drilling him on the names of the letters would have looked very familiar to the early recipients of the *Paidika*. In Greek and Roman literature, one finds this method of instruction in both its oral and its written expressions. An example of repetition in oral instruction comes from the Alexandrian poet Herodas (third century BCE): in one of his *Mimes,* he imagines a dramatic scene involving a schoolmaster named Lampriskos and a remedial student named Kottalos. The boy's mother laments the fact that her son "does not even know the letter alpha, unless someone shouts it at him five times."[115]

For repetition in writing exercises, we may turn to Quintilian, who refers to "examples" used in the classroom—teachers' models that students were supposed to copy over and over again until they got them right.[116] In some cases, teachers would physically guide their students' writing hands until the forms of the letters became part of their muscle memory; at other times, teachers would incise the letters onto the surface of a waxed wooden tablet and ask students to trace the pattern by allowing the stylus to be "guided by the grooves."[117] Quite a few ancient examples of such teachers' models and students' exercises have survived, not only on waxed (and unwaxed) wooden tablets but on papyri and ostraca (broken and discarded pottery sherds) as well.[118]

The use of these materials varied according to specific task, economic status, and educational level. Waxed wooden tablets were especially suited to trial and error—after making a first attempt at inscribing letters with the pointed end of a stylus, students could use the opposite, flattened end of the utensil to smooth out the wax and erase their mistakes.[119] One late Roman notebook made up of five waxed wooden tablets bound together contains a teacher's model (one involving noun syllabification) and an assortment of exercises by students of different elementary educational levels: some practiced writing individual letters by tracing their form multiple times, others copied out the alphabet in full, still others made a first attempt at names and words.[120]

Letters written on wooden tablets with unwaxed surfaces were more difficult to erase, and thus it makes sense that they were often used for teachers' models. On one second- or third-century CE example (a wooden tablet from Tebtunis, Egypt), a teacher wrote out a hexameter model for his student to copy, "Begin, good hand, beautiful letters and a straight line." He then followed with the exhortation, "Imitate it!" Below the teacher's model are found five consecutive attempts at copying this text, clearly by a student who is still unlettered and unable to check his own work. With each successive time he dutifully wrote out the text (and the exhortation as well!), the student's handwriting deteriorated and became more and more error filled.[121]

Papyri and ostraca made for less expensive and more readily available alternatives. Fifty percent of all surviving school exercises have been found on papyrus: many of these pieces are relatively mediocre quality, not suitable for more formal scribal or literary endeavors.[122] Especially popular for students just beginning to learn how to write individual letters, papyri were also used with great regularity for slightly more advanced exercises involving the copying of the entire alphabet (in forward and/or reverse order) and for "syllabaries" (various repeated combinations of consonants and vowels).[123]

Ostraca were the least expensive and most accessible medium for primary-level exercises. The textured surfaces of ceramic fragments were harder to write on, and the space available for copying words and letters was often more restricted. Nonetheless, their nearly ubiquitous presence in trash heaps behind buildings, in alleyways, and at the outskirts of towns made them a cheap and viable option for little children and their teachers.[124] Among the surviving sherds, we find many cases where students made egregious mistakes in trying to copy their teachers' models, or taking shortcuts to complete assignments.[125]

The trials and errors of young students were on display in more public settings as well. Alphabetic school exercises have been found scratched as graffiti on walls from Egypt to Italy. Just south of modern-day Minya in Middle Egypt, a syllabary written in red letters was discovered on a tomb wall at the cemetery of Beni-Hassan,[126] and several Latin graffiti from first-century Pompeii have been identified as school exercises.[127]

The learning of letters would also have been visible—and audible—to adults outside the school walls. Lessons were reinforced through games and songs. At home, young children were seen with letter blocks made of ivory or wood, or eating cakes specially decorated with alphabetic signs.[128] At other times, the lilting sounds of alphabetic songs were heard, wafting on the breeze in Greek and Roman cities, sung by children, or by their caretakers, for purposes of memorization.[129]

I would suggest that such cultural artifacts and practices—from lessons etched on wood and wax, papyri and pottery, and plastered walls to the sights and sounds of children learning the alphabet through play and musical performance—would have conditioned the reception of the school stories in the *Paidika* among its early readers and hearers. Social memories of school were reinforced through the powers of rote repetition. Among those who had participated in such lessons as children, the reading and writing of letters were skills not only cognitively recalled: they had become "sedimented in the body," physically incorporated into their muscle memory.[130] But even among the larger population—those who had not had such skills drilled into them—there would have been ample opportunity to become habituated visually and aurally to the contours and rhythms of the alphabetic learning taking place in local neighborhoods.[131] These school practices would have marked the young Jesus' experience as conforming in several respects to conventional patterns of Graeco-Roman elementary education.

Yet, in these same stories about Jesus at school—in the very details about his alphabetic calisthenics—readers would have found competing clues that hinted at the Christ child's prodigious virtuosity in the ways of divine wisdom. The young Jesus whom we meet in the *paideutēria* of Zacchaeus and his colleagues is one whose academic performance quickly outstrips that of his peers. Through these stories we track his progress to the top of the class, to higher stages of learning. Not only that—we also see him assuming the role of master and introducing a new, advanced curriculum.

ADVANCED INSTRUCTION

In its fully elaborated narrative form, the *Paidika* shows Jesus rapidly moving past primary school proficiency and acquiring the skills of a student who has graduated to higher studies. This accelerated trajectory of learning begins in chapter 6 when he finally responds to Zacchaeus's promptings by reciting "all the letters from alpha to omega with much proficiency."[132] It continues in chapter 13, when he demands more advanced lessons from his second teacher: "You tell me first what beta is and I shall tell you what alpha is."[133] And it concludes in chapter 14 when, with no need for further instruction, he goes directly to the lectern and, ignoring the book spread open before him, speaks "awe-inspiring words" from memory.[134] The image we are left with is that of a master *rhētōr*—one who has become fluent not only in letters and grammar but also in the art of public speaking. Indeed, there is already a sign that Jesus possesses the power of the spoken word in *Paidika* 6 and 7 when the crowd of onlookers marvels that no teacher has ever uttered "such words" (*toioutoi logoi*),[135] and again when Zacchaeus, stunned by "the lucidity of his word" (*to tranon tou logou*), wonders whether he is "not earthborn" and even perhaps "a god or an angel."[136] Even on this point, the social realities of school life would have served as a crucial point of reference for ancient readers and listeners: the auditory memories of older students struggling to master their declamations through arduous repetition and practice would have set the five-year-old Jesus apart as already particularly precocious in the oratorical arts, as one whose tongue was "even able to tame fire."[137]

What marks off Jesus' power and knowledge more than anything else in these school stories, however, is his mystical manipulation of the letter *alpha* and its form. In chapter 6 of the *Paidika,* after reciting the entire alphabet to his teacher Zacchaeus, Jesus presents an extended discourse on "the order of the first letter/element [*hē tou prōtou stoicheiou taxis*],"[138] exhorting Zacchaeus to pay close attention to how the shape of the letter *alpha* "has slanted lines and a middle stroke, which you see pointing, crossing, intersecting, spreading outward, drawing back, rising up, dancing, darting like arrows, three-marked, double-mouthed, of the same form, of the same thickness, of the same family, corded, yoked, of equal measure, of equal proportion."[139]

Scholars, usually so prone to disagreement, have almost unanimously agreed that the cryptic monologue that follows—with its meditative musings on the lines of the alpha—is "difficult to decipher,"[140] and even at times downright "unintelligible."[141] Despite its complications, however, the text in its current state still gives us important clues about the cultural resonances Jesus' speech would have had for early Graeco-Roman readers.[142] These playful, puzzling words placed in the mouth of the young Jesus would have had at least two interpretive registers among such recipients. The key to this verbal riddle is the Greek word *stoicheia,* which could refer either to "letters" (as the fundamental components of language and speech) or to "elements" (as the fundamental components of the cosmos).[143]

THE ELEMENTS (*STOICHEIA*) OF WRITING: LETTERS AND THE PRACTICE OF PENMANSHIP

On the face of it, Jesus' detailed exposition of "the first letter/element" is firmly grounded in ancient pedagogical practice—specifically, in the instructions on penmanship that young students received about how to write the letters in their proper forms. At several points, Jesus' vocabulary does indeed correspond quite noticeably to the characteristic "lines" (*kanones*) of the letter *alpha.*[144] The opening description of the letter's "slanted lines and a middle stroke, which you see pointing, crossing, intersecting, spreading outward" evokes the image of the uncial (that is, capital) *A.*[145] Other adjectives such as "drawing back, rising up, dancing, darting like arrows," and "corded" may evoke the curves and bow-like shape of the lower-case, cursive *α.*[146]

Indeed, this allusive technique of describing the form of a letter would not have seemed all that strange to a second- or third-century reader. A contemporaneous source from the late second century—Athenaeus's *Banquet of the Learned* (*Deipnosophistae*)—collects examples from three earlier authors who do a similar thing with the letters that spell out the Greek name Theseus (ΘΗΣΕΥΣ).[147] The first is a scene from Euripides (ca. 480–406 BCE) in which an illiterate shepherd tries to describe the letters of the hero's name:

> For I indeed do nothing know of letters,
> But I will tell you all their shapes, and give
> Clear indications by which you may judge.
> There is a circle, round as though it had been
> Worked in a lathe, and in its center space
> It has a visible sign. Then the second
> Has first of all two lines, and these are parted
> By one that cuts them both across the middle.
> The third is a curly figure, wreathed round.
> The fourth contains one line that mounts right up,
> And in a transverse course three others hang
> From its right side. The letter that comes fifth
> Admits of no such easy explanation;
> For there are two diverging lines above,
> Which meet in one united line below.
> The letter that comes last is like the third.[148]

The second account is credited to the tragic poet Agathon (ca. 448–400 BCE):

> The letter that comes first is like a circle,
> Divided by a navel in the middle;
> Then come two upright lines well joined together;
> The third is something like a Scythian bow;
> Next comes a trident placed upon its side;
> And two lines yoked to one lower stem;
> The last again the same as the third.[149]

The third and final citation comes from a work by Theodectes of Phaselus (ca. 380–340 BCE):

> The letter that comes first is a circle,
> With one soft eye; then come two upright lines
> Of equal and exact proportions,
> United by one middle transverse line;
> The third is like a wreathed curl of hair;
> The next a trident lying on its side;
> The fifth two lines of equal length above,
> Which below join together in one base;
> The sixth, as I have said before, a curl.[150]

Athenaeus quotes each of these accounts in succession and then mentions a fourth source known to his second-century readers—Sophocles's *Amphiaraus*—which presented yet another scene of alphabet gymnastics in which an actor performed on stage, "dancing in unison with his explanation of the letters."[151]

When we compare these sources to the *Paidika,* what is striking at first glance is the similar descriptive vocabulary applied to the shapes of letters and the correlative emphasis on numbers (especially integers of twos and threes). Thus, Euripides describes the upsilon (*Y*) as consisting of "two diverging lines above, which meet [*suntrechein*] in one united line below," and Theodectes speaks of the same Greek letter as two lines that "join together" (*sunteinein*) in one base.[152] In the *Paidika,* Jesus similarly describes the lines of the alpha as "intersecting" (*sunagomenoi*).[153] The passage from Agathon describes the eta (*H*) as "two upright lines well joined together [*ezugōmenoi*]" and the upsilon as "two lines yoked [*ezugōmenoi*] to one lower stem." The same root form appears in the *Paidika* when Jesus describes the lines of the alpha as "yoked" together (*zugostatai*). Finally, the adjective *isometroi* ("of equal length or proportions") is used by both Theodectes (twice, in fact, to describe the vertical lines of the letter *H* and the two upper arms of the letter *Y*), and by Jesus in the *Paidika* (with reference to the slanted strokes of the letter *A*).

This common vocabulary describing the shapes of different Greek letters may very well have been derived from school settings where children were taught these forms by way of analogy or comparison to images and objects from everyday life.[154] Aasgaard has likened Jesus' enigmatic speech to the kind of popular jingles used as aids by those just learning to read, and he interprets this scene in *Paidika* 6 as a "parody of reading exercises familiar to anyone having attended the antique school."[155] While I agree there is parody at play here in the *Paidika,* I think the target of the parody is not "reading exercises" in general but rather the repetitive penmanship lessons students received immediately after learning the letter names (a context that perfectly fits the sequencing of the story in the *Paidika*).[156]

The tedious task of learning to write was both an "inscribing" and an "incorporating" practice: that is, penmanship lessons not only produced a written product on the page (or on a tablet or ceramic sherd); they also had an "irreducible bodily component," one that involved both a particular "postural behavior" and a set of finely tuned minor motor skills that, over time, became ingrained as part of the writer's "habitual memory."[157] In this context, the concluding words of Jesus' monologue—"three-marked, double-mouthed, of the same form, of the same thickness, of the same family, . . . of equal measure, of equal proportion"—take on a new significance. The language used here would seem to reinforce the need for manual dexterity—the measured rhythm and control of writing required for producing letter forms with sufficient balance and proportion to meet a schoolmaster's strict standards.[158] Among a literate readership, these remembered (and still practiced) bodily dispositions of writing would have been one important register for the reception of this story.

THE ELEMENTS (*STOICHEIA*) OF THE COSMOS: LETTERS AND PHILOSOPHICAL SPECULATION

But such memories of childhood penmanship lessons would not have been the story's only cultural register. The dual signification of the word *stoicheion* as both "letter" and "element" would have prompted other associations related to the diverse uses of alphabetic signs among adults in the Graeco-Roman world. Letters were used as popular narrative devices in stories,[159] as decorative motifs on small- and large-scale material objects,[160] and as apotropaic devices at ancient gravesites,[161] but they also played an integral role in scientific and philosophical speculation about the world and the nature of divinity.[162]

These philosophical and scientific applications were facilitated by the fact that the Greeks used letters for their system of numbering. All twenty-four alphabetic symbols (along with three additional archaic forms) were juxtaposed in different combinations to cover the gamut of numerical possibilities: alpha equaled one, beta two, and so on. Accordingly, the letters had a wide range of associations as spatial markers of measurement—from labeling architectural blocks of stone in a building project, to quantifying the proportions of the human body, to tracking the incremental daily movement of the sun across the sky.[163]

It was in and through such practices that the alphabet came to be linked, both symbolically and causally, to the time and space of the created cosmos. To manipulate letters in writing and in ritual was to exert (at least potentially) a certain degree of control over the world itself.[164] In antiquity, numbers and letters came to be used for the purpose of divining the will of the gods through a combination of various methods, including isopsephy (numerological prognostication), *notarichon* (alphabetic acrostics), and the casting of lots.[165] The operative assumption—that the alphabet exerted influence over the fabric of existence, that there was a cosmic sympathy between the letters (*stoicheia*) and the elements (*stoicheia*) more broadly conceived—also came to expression in the Graeco-Roman practices of alchemy and astrology.[166] Alchemy combined aspects of chemistry, metallurgy, and metaphysical mysticism: by uniting elements together in various combinations, alchemists sought to establish correspondences between the seven metals, the seven planetary spheres, the seven musical notes, and the seven vowels of the alphabet.[167] In astrology, letters (especially the vowels) were often seen as a key to unlocking the mysteries of the zodiac and the will of the gods encrypted therein.[168] The notion of heaven as a scroll and the stars as its script was a long-standing topos in both ancient Hebrew and Greek literature, from Isaiah to Plotinus.[169] This pair of analogies (heaven-scroll, stars-script) also may have served as background to one of Jesus' sayings in the Gospel of Matthew (5:18), when he observes that not even the smallest letter (iota) would pass from the book of the law until heaven and earth pass away. From there, the association between letters, celestial bodies, and divine agency was a rather small extra step in reasoning.[170]

In antiquity, the Greek vowels held particular significance, due to their perceived resonance with the heavenly spheres, especially the planets, whose movements ruled over the sky. In the early second century, Plutarch wrote on the meaning of a large letter *E* carved in stone at the temple precinct at Delphi. Connecting the "seven vowels in the alphabet" with the seven celestial bodies, he identifies the letter *E* (the second of the vowels) with the sun ("the second planet after the Moon") and with Apollo, the solar deity.[171] Around the same time, Nicomachus of Gerasa notes that practitioners of magic call out with "inarticulate and discordant [lit. "unconsonantal"] sounds" in order to attune themselves to the cosmos and to acquire powers for the purpose of "divine consecration."[172]

It was in the context of such ritual performance that the vowels were called "the seven letters of magicians" and were instrumental in the naming of the gods and lords of the universe in the Greek magical papyri.[173] In assorted spells from Egypt, the seven vowels invoke the name and power of the magician's patron god, and at least in one case the vocalization of their sounds is accompanied by seven different physical actions.[174] For alpha (*A*), the ritual specialist stretches his hands out to the left; for epsilon (*E*), he punches the air with his fist; for eta (*H*), he extends both hands straight ahead; for iota (*I*), he holds his stomach; for omicron (*O*), he touches his toes; for upsilon (*Y*), he looks up into the air and places his hands on his heart; and for omega (*Ω*), he holds his hands on his head.[175]

Similar views of the vowels and their cosmic significance may also be found in Gnostic literature such as the third-century work entitled *Marsanes.* In that text—a fragmentary account of a visionary's ascent to heaven—the vowels are understood to be superior to the semivowels and consonants. They are "the nomenclature of the [gods] and the angels," and are identified with "the three shapes of the soul." The shape of the first, self-begotten soul is that of the seven vowels in order, *AEĒIOUŌ*. The shape of the second soul consists of this same sequence without the initial alpha and the final omega: *EĒIOU.* The shape of the third soul is said to consist of each of the seven vowels repeated three times in order: [*AAA*] *EEE,* [*ĒĒĒ*], *III, OOO, UUU, ŌŌŌ.*[176] The mix of arithmology and alphabetic classification in *Marsanes* has led David Brakke to conclude that, for this Gnostic author, the heavenly ascent described would have been facilitated not only by astrology and the scholastic study of letters but also by ritual practices such as baptism and theurgy.[177]

Finally, one finds a similar set of associations informing early Christian interpretation of biblical texts. In his *Stromata,* Clement of Alexandria comments on the Greek text of Psalm 18:2 in the Septuagint—"The heavens tell each other of the glory of God"—and identifies the vowels as the audible sounds (or sensible types) of that dialogue. On this basis, he then goes on to explain the alpha-omega (*A-Ω*) of Revelation 21:6 as the beginning and end of that heavenly speech, and the ten commandments (enumerated by the vowel *iota, I* = 10) as signifying "the blessed name . . . Jesus [*Iēsous*], who is the Word."[178]

From Pythagorean cosmological speculation to the sciences of alchemy and astrology, and from inscriptions marking sacred precincts to the vocalization of vowels in "magical" spells and biblical interpretation—we find a wide range of practices that would have conditioned early readers' engagement with the story of Jesus in school and his exegesis of the letter *alpha*. In their eyes, what Jesus was doing with the first letter was not simply parsing out the lines of its surface form on the page but also plumbing its depths for eternal wisdom.

Jesus' display of alphabetic wisdom in *Paidika* is also intimately connected with theologies about the power of divine names, commonly attested in pagan, Jewish, and Christian contexts from antiquity. François Bovon has perceptively noted how ancient Christians' theological and symbolic valuation of letters, numbers, and names was "a custom [*habitude*] anchored as much in Greek philosophical reflection as it was in Hebrew scripture."[179] Thus, in one of the so-called magical papyri, the Greek vowels play a distinctive role in prayers not only to Apollo but also to Hermes, Serapis, Orpheus, and the Jewish God, who is identified as *Iaō* (Ιαω).[180] This text and other later spells in Coptic also use *Aeēiouō* (Αεηιυω) alongside *Iaō* as a cipher for the name of the Jewish deity (in effect, as a tertiary adaptation of the Hebrew Tetragrammaton, YHWH).[181] In syncretistic Jewish and Christian sources, the names of angels and other divine intermediaries were also ripe for this kind of alphabetic association: examples include an amulet featuring rows of vowels beside the names of gods and angels,[182] and Christian spells from Egypt designating the four cherubim from Revelation 4:1–8 with names modeled acronymically after the letter *alpha* (*Alpha, Leōn, Phōnē, Anēr*).[183]

What is important to note here is the fact that in the ancient world divine names—and by extension the letters and vowels linked with them—were understood to be specially imbued with the life-giving power of creation. In Genesis and in the Gospel of John, God creates the world by means of a spoken word (*logos*), and by a certain lexical logic this meant that the letters themselves played an instrumental role in bringing the very cosmos into existence.[184] In a second- or third-century Hermetic work called *Poimandrēs,* creation is similarly enacted through "the word [*logos*] of God," which "leap[s] up out of the downward-tending *stoicheia.*"[185] The author here seems to be allegorizing the way words are formed from their constituent elements to present an image of creation. The so-called *Eighth Book of Moses* also portrays the letters (specifically, the vowels) as key agents of *kosmopoieia* ("world creation"), due to their mystical function of invoking the divine name (in this case, Apollo).[186] In the first three centuries CE, we find a number of analogous examples of Jewish and Christian authors who highlight the divine name as instrumental in God's act of creation in Genesis.[187]

Around the time the *Paidika* stories began to circulate, a more sophisticated theology of names and vowels had begun to emerge in certain early Christian communities, with the letter *alpha* as a key hermeneutical component. For one second-century Gnostic Christian author, the alpha in God's name (*Iaō*) represented the hinge of creation.[188] In the third century, Clement of Alexandria understood the extra alpha added to Abraham's name in Genesis 17:5 to signify "knowledge of the one and only God" who brought the world into being.[189] By the late fourth century, John Chrysostom could preach about the alpha as the letter that "holds together" the entire cosmos as its "foundation stone."[190]

The young Jesus' exposition of the letter *alpha* in the *Paidika* should be added to this chorus of voices, as an early witness to Christian mystical speculation on the alphabet's potential for granting insight into the nature of the Creator God. It is not coincidental that the story of Jesus' encounter with Zacchaeus shows an attendant preoccupation with names. In *Paidika* 6.2b, Jesus speaks to Joseph of his own preexistence at the time of his father's birth: "When you were born, I existed and stood by you so that you might be instructed as a father with an instruction given by me, which no other person knows or is able to teach, and (so that) you might bear the salvific name [*to sōtērion onoma*]."[191] Immediately following this, he enters into conversation with "the Jews" and assures them that he knew "what existed before the world was created."[192] Leaving them speechless, Jesus then goes to Zacchaeus's classroom to begin his alphabetic instruction.

In the first half of this chapter, I argued that ancient schools and images of childhood education would have served as important *lieux de mémoire* for early recipients of the *Paidika* accounts about Jesus and his teachers. In the second half, I have suggested other fertile sites of memory for ancient readers trying to make sense of the esoteric "letter lore" in these stories. These sites included philosophy and science, ritual performances of so-called magical spells invoking the names of gods and angels, and the interpretation of biblical passages related to creation.

Yet, in the ancient world, these "memory spaces" (*Erinnerungsräume*) may not have been as sharply differentiated as one might suppose. In fact, there is ample evidence from Greek and Roman sources for tangible links between schools and some of the other social settings I have discussed. For example, alphabetic lessons in the classroom sometimes seem to have been used as a forum for giving young students a foretaste of metaphysical speculation.[193] In the second century CE, Nicomachus of Gerasa compares the grammarians' distinction between vowels and consonants to the philosophical distinction between the soul and the body.[194] More specific evidence comes from the Latin grammarian Terentianus Maurus, who mentions Pythagorean complaints about pedantic schoolmasters who tried to teach about the deeper connections between numbers and letters without the requisite knowledge.[195] A century and a half later, the philosopher Iamblichus is reported to have criticized the Pythagoreans' own use of letter geometries as a basis for deriving philosophical insight: "It is not safe to argue from characters [*charaktēra*]. For . . . the ancient [mode of forming letters] was different from the present mode of forming them."[196] His argument—that such teaching is rendered null and void by changes in handwriting style—takes it for granted that such modes of instruction remained current in the classroom.

The tenor and texture of such "advanced" alphabetical instruction may be reflected in certain grammatical-philosophical commentaries from late antiquity. One example is Proclus's commentary on Euclid's *Elements* (*Stoicheia*), in which the commentator explores the deeper significance of various lines and shapes used to form letters and numbers. Straight lines symbolize "the inflexible, unvarying, incorruptible, unremitting, and all-powerful providence that is present to all things," while through circles the divine Mind "perfect[s] all intelligible essences."[197] Angles are likened to "the coherence that obtains in the realm of divine things . . . the orderliness that leads diverse things to unity."[198] Right angles refer to "the immaculate essences in the divine orders and their particular potencies," while obtuse and acute angles are aligned with divinities in charge of generation and change.[199] The triangle is identified as "the ultimate source of generation and of the production of species among things generated."[200] Hints of this same approach to the geometry of letters may also be found in the writings of the Christian poet Paulinus of Nola (354–431 CE), who meditates on the composition of alpha out of three lines.[201]

If in fact (as the evidence suggests) some philosophically inclined elementary instructors spiced up their lessons about letters with metaphysical footnotes on their forms, then perhaps a new reading of Paul's Letter to the Galatians is in order, a reading that will shed further light on Jesus' knowledge of letters in the *Paidika*. In chapter 4 of his epistle, Paul presents a series of reflections on children and *stoicheia* that seems to critique certain kinds of pedantic classroom practice. He begins by noting how just as children (*nēpioi*) remain subject to their father's guardianship until they reach the age of maturity, so too are human beings "enslaved to the *stoicheia* of the world" while still in their infancy (4:3). Most modern interpreters have argued that Paul used the word *stoicheia* here to refer to humanity's worship of "elemental spirits" (that is, gods associated with the four cosmic elements) before the coming of Christ.[202] Thus, Paul goes on to contrast the Galatians' former and present conditions. Before they knew God in Christ, they were "enslaved to beings that by nature are not gods" (4:8); but now that they have come to know and be known by God, he asks them, "How can you turn back again to the weak and beggarly *stoicheia?*" (4:9). When he concludes by noting that the Galatians continued to observe "special days, and months, and seasons, and years," New Testament scholars have taken this as evidence for calendrical observances related to astrology and the zodiac.[203]

These same scholars, however, have neglected an important aspect of Paul's analogy—namely, the fact that it is grounded in the widely recognized connection between children and *stoicheia* in Graeco-Roman society. The scenario the apostle envisions—of children enslaved to *stoicheia*—would also have prompted among his Galatian readers recollections of learning the letters of the Greek alphabet under the compulsion of their master in the primary school classroom. Thus, in Galatians 3:24–25, Paul represents the law as a *paidagōgos* whose harsh instruction gives way to the teaching of Christ, in whom all are "children of God." When read in this way, Paul's exhortation for them not to return to such "weak and beggarly letters" in Galatians 4:9 is part of an effort to cultivate in his readers an advanced "curriculum" in which *gnōsis*—their knowledge of God and their being known by God—was the age-appropriate lesson plan. In so doing, Paul also lodges a stark critique of alternative uses and observances of the letters/elements, astrological or otherwise.[204]

Read against the background of Paul's Letter to the Galatians, the stories about Jesus' alphabetic lessons in the *Paidika* prove to be both a counterpart and a foil. As I have argued, Jesus' seemingly cryptic and elusive discourse about "the first element" (*to prōton stoicheion*) in *Paidika* 6.4 would have sponsored a set of cultural memories rather similar to those evoked (and then critiqued) by Paul in his reflections on the *stoicheia* in Galatians 4. In the end, however, these two early Christian sources part ways when it comes to their divergent attitudes toward this common set of cultural memories. To emulate the young Jesus depicted in the *Paidika,* ancient readers would have had to eschew the dichotomy Paul sets up between the *stoicheia* and knowledge of God, and instead embrace a vision for divine knowledge that sees these "weak and beggarly letters/elements" as a means toward a salutary end.

Corroborating Evidence—An Actual Community of Second-Century Readers

Up to now, I have employed a kind of audience-oriented criticism to sketch out plausible settings for the reception of the *Paidika* in the Graeco-Roman world. In the absence of specific data about the early interpretation of stories about Jesus' acts of bringing clay birds to life and cursing children, my reconstructions have depended upon a thorough and textured documentation of literary sources, material *realia,* and social practices that together make up a compelling context for understanding how early Christians and others might have made sense of the enigmatic Christ child. In this chapter, I have taken the same tack with regard to the depictions of Jesus interacting with his teachers at school, and I have suggested that these stories would have resonated in particular ways with Greeks and Romans intimately familiar with the contours of alphabetic instruction in the elementary classroom, and with a range of other scientific, philosophical, and religious uses of letters as keys to the mysteries of the cosmos. In other words, to borrow the language of Franz Dornseiff, school exercises and recitations must have functioned as practical sites of "childhood remembrance" (*Kinderinnerung*) for the readers and hearers of such tales.[205] What is remarkable in this present case, however, is the fact that we have corroborating evidence from an actual second-century community of readers who interpreted the *Paidika* along these very lines.

For this evidence, I turn to Irenaeus of Lyons and his treatise *Against Heresies* (ca. 180 CE). In the midst of cataloguing the myriad other groups with whom he had disagreements, Irenaeus pauses to give account of a Christian sect led by a certain man named Marcus.[206] Marcus was a contemporary and disciple of the famous theologian and church reformer Valentinus (ca. 100–ca. 175 CE), who had adapted Gnostic teachings for a more mainstream audience by emphasizing a mystical doctrine of salvation through personal acquaintance or knowledge (*gnōsis*) of God.[207]

Despite Irenaeus's demonizing and distorting accusations against Marcus and his followers, the heresiologist's account gives us enough information to build a reliable impression of an early Christian movement that advocated mystical meditation on the letters as a means of attaining divine insight.[208] Portraying Marcus's prophetic gifts as a form of "magic," Irenaeus describes how the Valentinian leader and his community were accustomed to drawing lots and pronouncing oracles at festival celebrations.[209] As we have already seen, these particular ritual practices were closely linked with forms of letter speculation in antiquity. This connection becomes explicit when Irenaeus turns to Marcus's doctrine about the Father's action of sending forth the divine Word (*Logos*)—a doctrine grounded in a generative theology of letters and names:

> The pronunciation of his name took place as follows: he spoke the first word of it, which was the beginning [of all the rest], and that utterance consisted of four letters. He added the second, and this also consisted of four letters. Next he uttered the third, and this again embraced ten letters. Finally, he pronounced the fourth, which was composed of twelve letters. Thus took place the enunciation of the whole name, consisting of thirty letters, and four distinct utterances. Each of these elements has its own peculiar letters, and character, and pronunciation, and forms, and images, and there is not one of

> them that perceives the shape of that [utterance] of which it is an element. . . . This teacher declares that the restitution of all things will take place, when all these, mixing into one letter, shall utter one and the same sound.[210]

For Marcus, the pronunciation of the Word's name is a creative act: it takes the form of a vocal utterance in which the letters first generate a multiplicity of new sounds, but then are "received up again by the syllable[s] to which [they] belonged,"[211] and resolved into a harmony of one united tonal element.

Marcus illustrated this divine process of generation and reunification with two alphabetic exercises that may very well have been drawn from writing lessons practiced in elementary school settings.[212] The first exercise follows the Pythagorean method of speculation on the letter *delta* (Δ), where the spelling out of each letter in the letter's name produces an endless stream of alphabetic elements: "The word Delta contains five letters, viz., D, E, L, T, A: these letters again, are written by other letters, and others still by others. If, then, the entire composition of the word Delta [when thus analyzed] runs out into infinitude, letters continually generating other letters, and following one another in constant succession, how much faster than that [one] word is the [entire] ocean of letters!"[213] Graphically represented on the page, the successive waves of letters produced in this exercise would take the form of the capital *delta* itself, an ever-expanding triangle with an exponentially widening base.

Marcus's second exercise involved the familiar scholastic practice of pairing letters, starting with the first and last (alpha and omega) and moving through the remainder of the alphabet. In this case, however, these pairs were envisioned as being written on the page in the form of an anthropomorphic "body of truth."

> I wish to show you Aletheia [Truth] herself; for I have brought her down from the dwellings above, that you may see her without a veil, and understand her beauty—that you may also hear her speaking, and admire her wisdom. Behold, then, her head on high, Alpha and Omega; her neck, Beta and Psi; her shoulders with her hands, Gamma and Chi; her breast, Delta and Phi; her diaphragm, Epsilon and Upsilon; her back, Zeta and Tau; her belly, Eta and Sigma; her thighs, Theta and Rho; her knees, Iota and Pi; her legs, Kappa and Omicron; her ankles, Lambda and Xi; her feet, Mu and Nu. Such is the body of Truth, according to this magician, such the figure of the element, such the character of the letter.[214]

In his book *Marcus Magus,* Niclas Förster cites cultural precedents for the pairing of letters and the twelvefold accounting of human body parts in Graeco-Roman astrological practice, where ancient school exercises were adapted and applied both to the classification of the zodiac (the macrocosmos) and to the "iatromedical" study of the body (the microcosmos).[215]

In addition to these exercises, Marcus engages in other mystical manipulations of the alphabet, including numerology and phonetic classification.[216] With respect to phonetics, he adheres to the grammarians' division of the letters into three types—mute (unvoiced), semivowels, and vowels—and associates them with different pairs of heavenly beings, called *aeons.* In this schema, the vowels held a special significance, insofar as they constituted the vocal utterances of the seven heavens: "The first heaven indeed pronounces *alpha;* the next to this *epsilon;* the third *ēta;* the fourth, which is also in the midst of the seven, utters the sound of *iota;* the fifth *omicron;* the sixth *upsilon;* the seventh, which is also the fourth from the middle, utters the elegant *omega.*" But here again, Marcus draws a specific connection to memories of childhood: to his ear, the voweled voices of the seven heavens are echoed back by "infants who have just been born, the cry of whom, as soon as they have issued from the womb, is in accordance with the sound of every one of these elements."[217]

Irenaeus had a different opinion. To him, Marcus's metaphysical musings did not do justice to their divine subject, and their effect was to puncture and pulverize the truth. Thus, he writes that in Marcus's hands the Word of God is "cut up piecemeal into four syllables and thirty elements/letters," and "the greatness of the truly unspeakable power" is pulled to pieces "by means of Alpha and Beta."[218] For Marcus and his followers, however, these methods of mining the *stoicheia* for deeper significance were a means toward attaining genuine divine insight, and as such they fit hand in glove with wider patterns of late ancient scientific and philosophical practice.

Most important for our purposes, these same alphabetical methods directly informed the way Marcus's community understood the stories of Jesus' schooling in the *Paidika.* The evidence again comes from Irenaeus, who claims that this "Marcosian" sect put forward "an unspeakable number of apocryphal and spurious writings, which they themselves have forged," including a variation on one of the *Paidika* teacher tales: "[The Marcosians] bring forward that reckless account—that when the Lord was a boy and learning His letters, the teacher said to Him, as is customary, 'Say Alpha,' and he answered, 'Alpha.' Again, the teacher commanded him to say 'Beta,' but the Lord answered, 'First you tell me what Alpha is, and then I shall tell you what Beta is.' "[219] Irenaeus's allegation of apocryphal composition and forgery was itself probably spurious: it is much more likely that Marcus and his followers were consumers, rather than producers, of such stories. Regardless, it is clear from Irenaeus's testimony that *Paidika* stories were circulating among the members of Marcus's community in either oral or written form, and that they were engaged in interpreting the young Jesus' words in concert with practices of mystical speculation on the form and character of the letters. As a result, we have here evidence of a particular second-century community who read or heard this story of Jesus at school as an allegory of divine knowledge—one that showed how "[Jesus] alone knew the Unknown, which he revealed under its type Alpha."[220]

As it turns out, another Valentinian work, the *Gospel of Truth*,[221] also attests to the fact that more than one *Paidika* teacher story was making the rounds within early Christian communities during the second century CE. Speaking of Christ as an instructor who came to enlighten those who lacked knowledge of the Father, the author of the gospel writes, "He became a pedagogue [Coptic, *jaumaït*], at peace and occupied for a time with places of instruction [*m-ma n-ji sbō*]. He came forward and uttered the word [*sheje*] as [if he were] a teacher [*sah*]. People who thought themselves wise in their hearts [*nsophos nhrēï hm-pouhēt*] came up to him, testing him, but he upbraided them, for they were foolish [*hnpetshoueit*]."[222] The passage suggests the author's familiarity with the *Paidika,* or at least some oral or written component of it.[223] Indeed, the use of the plural form for "places of instruction" (*m-ma n-ji sbō*) would seem to indicate that the author's community knew at least two versions of the school stories.[224] In any case, the image of a young Jesus in the classroom demonstrating a preternatural wisdom that outstrips his teachers would have reinforced the self-perception of the Valentinians as a circle of philosophically inclined Christians organized along the lines of a school or academy.[225]

Ultimately, Irenaeus's witness to the alphabetic proclivities of Marcus and his church and this contemporaneous Valentinian testimony from the *Gospel of Truth* provide a double confirmation of the kind of cultural memory work I have described in this chapter. In the *Gospel of Truth,* we see how Jesus is once again remembered as a student prodigy, a whiz kid who possesses the knowledge and authority of a wise teacher. In the case of the interpretation fostered by Marcus and his community, we observe how Jesus' time as a schoolboy, retold in story, was synchronized with by-now-familiar social practices related to *stoicheia* and their metaphysical manipulation. Thus it was—from primary school lessons on penmanship to more advanced meditations on the meaning of the letters—that ancient readers' recollection and experience of such practices provided a fertile cognitive framework for reimagining the childhood of Jesus and for calibrating their own place within the divinely ordered cosmos.

PART III

Christian-Jewish-Muslim Encounters

6

Jews and Christians

In part 2 of this book, I focused on what the *Paidika* would have communicated to a Graeco-Roman readership about the childhood of Jesus. I now turn to the question of the work's history of interpretation, not only among later Christian readers, but also among Jewish and Muslim communities of reception. The *Paidika* stories were taken up as both shared and contested "sites of memory" for Christians, Jews, and Muslims in a range of cultural encounters. In the process, the stories were often transformed in the context of translation and scribal emendation, scientific and philosophical exchange, and pilgrimage travel related to the cult of the saints. In this chapter I focus on how the *Paidika* tales became tools in the negotiation of Christian and Jewish identity in late antiquity and the Middle Ages. Chapter 7 concludes with an investigation of how Muslims and Arabic-speaking Christians reworked these same traditions. The story units and tale types that served as our plumb line in part 2—the stories about Jesus' miraculous enlivening of the birds, his cursing and other powerful speech acts, and his precocity in school—will continue to guide and frame my analysis throughout the remainder of this book.

Signs of Christian-Jewish Tension in the Paidika

I turn first to the question of the *Paidika*'s intersection with ancient Judaism, both at the time of the stories' early dissemination and after their later collection and transmission in written narrative form(s). Appropriate caution is in order here: a scholarly consensus now holds that in late antiquity the dividing lines between Jewish and Christian communal identities were far less consistent—far more porous and contested—than previous generations of scholars had imagined. The theory of an early "parting of the ways," which held sway in the field for generations, has more recently given way to notions of persistent interaction and various forms of cultural hybridity.[1]

The contents of the *Paidika* give hints that at least some of the stories may have taken shape in the midst of early sibling tensions between ancient Christians and their Jewish neighbors. Indeed, as in the case of early Christian gospels, the *Paidika* can serve as an indirect source for the way certain early followers of Jesus negotiated their rootedness in, but increasing estrangement from, the larger Jewish community and its leadership.

Scholars have long recognized, for example, that the pejorative portrayal of "the Jews" (*hoi Ioudaioi*) in the Gospel of John was part and parcel of an early history in which the Johannine Christians—who were Jews themselves—experienced acute friction and eventually a traumatic rupture with the synagogues where they had initially maintained membership after the death of Jesus.[2] Thus, even as the writer of the fourth gospel shows an intimate familiarity with patterns of Jewish scriptural interpretation and festival celebration, he consistently portrays "the Jews" as enemies of Jesus and his disciples (5:16–18; 6:41; 7:1; 7:13; 8:22–24; 8:48–59; 10:31–33; 11:8; 11:54; 18:38–40; 19:7; 19:38; 20:19), and has Jesus allude to the fact that his followers would eventually be expelled from synagogue worship (9:22; 12:42; 16:2).

By way of comparison, the Gospel of Luke—a work known in some form by the authors of the *Paidika*—only rarely makes mention of "the Jews" as an undifferentiated group within the narrative. Instead, it depicts Jesus in conflict specifically with the Jewish leadership caste, often designated as "the scribes and the Pharisees." This pair of collective actors accuse Jesus of blasphemy (5:21), complain about his willingness to eat and associate with sinners (5:30; 7:30; 15:1–2), become angered by his violations of the Sabbath (6:2; 6:7; 14:1–5), and subject him to cross-examination and ridicule (11:53–57; 16:14). For his part, Jesus gives an unsparing response, especially in Luke 11:39–12:1 where, in a scathing indictment, he tells the Pharisees that they are full of greed and wickedness, labels them fools, and pronounces woe upon them twice (11:39–43) before turning to warn the people against their leaders' hypocrisy. And yet, as in the case of the Gospel of John, the representation of conflict in Luke not only tells us something about the gospel writer's perceptions about the life setting of Jesus; it also evokes (and cloaks) the Lucan community's ongoing tensions with Jewish leadership in the period after Jesus' death.

These tensions are revealed more explicitly in the Acts of the Apostles, Luke's companion volume. Starting in chapter 9 of Acts, "the Jews" again become an almost ubiquitous, antithetical presence: they plot to kill Paul (9:23), they are pleased at James's execution (12:3), they are called blasphemers (13:45; cf. 17:5), they incite persecutions against the believers (13:50), they poison the minds of the Gentiles against the gospel (14:2), they divide cities (14:4), they stone the apostles (14:5 and 14:19), they are filled with jealousy (17:5; also 13:45), they conspire to kill Paul (18:12; 20:19; 23:12; 26:21), and they bring forward public charges and accusations against him before the authorities (21:22; 22:30; 24:9; 25:2; 25:7; 25:24; 26:2–3; 26:7). Interspersed among this litany of negative representations, however, are places where Jews—both individuals and groups—are specifically counted among the faithful (2:5; 2:10; 13:43; 14:1; 16:1; 21:20; 28:24). Indeed, in Acts, the early missionaries Paul, Barnabas, Aquila, and Apollos all pointedly retain and embrace their own Jewish identity (16:20; 18:1; 18:24; 19:34; 21:39; 22:3; 23:6; 26:5). The result of this characterization scheme is a mixed bag,[3] but it has led some scholars to reconstruct the situation of Luke's community in terms not dissimilar to that of the Gospel of John—as another situation in which the nascent church found itself still enmeshed in "inner Jewish struggles."[4]

It is uncertain whether a similar situation pertained in the community or communities that first transmitted the stories about Jesus as a child. In the *Paidika,* the signs of such tensions are more muted. Nonetheless, at several points one finds Jesus clashing with his Jewish counterparts (both children and adults) or engaged in actions that function as implicit critiques of traditional Jewish belief and practice.[5] Such conflict-laden encounters are concentrated especially in the first seven chapters.

Thus, in the story of Jesus and the sparrows (*Paidika* 2–3), we read that "a certain Jew saw the child Jesus doing these things with the other children [that is, making birds out of clay]," went to his father, Joseph, and "accused [*diebalen*] the child Jesus" of violating the Sabbath.[6] After Jesus brings the clay birds to life, the text reports that "the Pharisee" (presumably the "Jew" who had tattled on him two verses earlier) witnessed this action and "announced the news to all his friends."[7] What ensues is another conflict, this time with "the son of Annas the high priest."[8] After questioning Jesus further about violating the Sabbath, Annas's son then destroys Jesus' pools with a willow twig. Jesus' response is a curse that condemns not just the boy himself but also his entire lineage: "May your fruit be rootless and may your shoot be dried up like a young branch charred by a violent wind [*arizos ho karpos sou kai xēros ho blastos sou hōs klados ekkaiomenos en pneumati biaiō*$_i$]."[9]

The language of Jesus' curse of Annas's son in *Paidika* 3.2 would have resonated with an audience familiar with the Septuagint, where Israel is compared to a flowering shoot with roots that bears fruit. In Isaiah 11:1, the prophet declares, "A shoot [*rabdos*] shall come out from the root [*rizē*] of Jesse, and a flower [*anthos*] shall grow out of his root [*rizē*]." Isaiah 27:6 proclaims, "The ones who are coming, the children of Jacob, will blossom [*blastan*], and Israel will bloom [*exanthein*], and the whole world will be filled with its fruit [*karpos*]."[10] Jeremiah calls Israel a "righteous branch" (*anatolē dikaia*) that will spring up for David (23:5), and elsewhere describes the people of Israel "as a tree planted by waters [*hudata*] that sends its roots [*rizai*] out toward moisture" (17:8).[11] The simile paints a topographical portrait not dissimilar to that imagined in the opening vignette of the *Paidika* where Jesus plays by the bank of a stream (*rhuax*) and plays in the waters (*hudata*).[12]

And yet, Jesus' words to the son of Annas conjure up this cluster of fecund images only to turn the reader's mind to corresponding images of prophetic judgment. The language of his curses recalls Isaiah 40:24, where the rulers of the earth are likened to plants whose root (*riza*) is scarcely entrenched in the soil before God "sent a wind [*epneusen*] upon them and they dried up [*exēranthēsan*]."[13] Similar judgments are pronounced against Israel in Ezekiel 17:1–10 and 19:10–14, where vines are planted by water and put forth "branches" (*klēmata*) and "roots" (*rizai*), "fruit" (*karpos*) and "shoot" (*blastos*), only to be dried up (*xērainesthai*) when God sends a burning wind (*anemon*) upon them.[14] Even more compelling linguistic correspondences are found in the Wisdom of Sirach. There the children of the unfaithful are condemned as "an accursed memory" (*eis kataran to mnēmosunon*): they are "branches" (*kladoi*) that "will not take root" (*ou diadōsein . . . eis rizan*) (23:25–26), "unhealthy roots" (*rizai akathartoi*) that are plucked up like reeds "by the banks of a river" (*epi . . . cheilous potamou*) (40:15–16).[15]

In this context, the *Paidika*'s opening scene by the stream, culminating with Jesus' curse of Annas's son, was probably understood by some audiences as a narrative dramatization of these images of divine judgment. The high priest's son embodies an Israel that has fallen out of favor and is destined for the mortal end described in Job: "But a man dies and is gone; . . . a river wastes away and dries up [*xērainesthai*], and a human being lies down and does not rise again [*ou mē anastē*$_i$]" (14:10–12a).[16]

This final imagery from Job may also be lurking in the background of the story about Jesus' curse that takes place two chapters later. After Jesus smites the child who collided into his shoulder, he has a testy exchange with Joseph in *Paidika* 5. There is no explicit reference to "Jews" in the story, but Joseph's words and Jesus' response both contain signs that a context of Jewish controversy with Judaism may have been operative. Joseph appeals to Jesus for clemency and no more acts of cursing, and he uses as justification the fact that "the people suffer and they hate us."[17] The purported context is the grief and anger of the "people" (*laos*) and the "parents" (*goneis*) over their son's death in *Paidika* 4;[18] but in fact the language that Joseph uses coheres closely to patterns of early Christian polemical discourse against Jews. In the synoptic Gospels, one finds the general notion that followers of Jesus are "hated" by the world, just as the prophets were "hated" by the people of Israel.[19] But in the Gospel of John the world's hatred is localized and made concrete in the Jews' hatred of Christ: "But now they have seen and hated both me and my Father. It was to fulfill the word that is written in their law, 'They hated me without a cause' " (John 15:24b–25).

In early Christian apologetic literature contemporaneous with the early circulation of the *Paidika* stories, this theme of Jewish hatred for Christians is developed and notably connected with the theme of Jewish suffering and accursedness. One sees the pattern playing out in Justin Martyr's *Dialogue with Trypho the Jew,* a fictionalized debate that nonetheless gives us crucial information about Christian perceptions and stereotypes of Jews in the second century CE.[20] Throughout the *Dialogue,* Justin repeatedly returns to this theme of alleged Jewish hatred for Christians. He prays for Trypho "and for all other men who hate us."[21] He admits that he is not surprised that Trypho and his confederates "hate us who hold these opinions and who convict you of a continual hardness of heart."[22] Finally, to underscore his point, he cites the words of God spoken to the faithful through Solomon and Isaiah: "They who hate me love death" (Proverbs 8:36); "Say . . . to them that hate you and detest you, that the name of the Lord has been glorified" (cf. Isaiah 66:5).[23] In each case, Justin's contemporary referent for these scriptural passages is the Jews' ongoing rejection of Jesus. The litany of "hate" speech continues, reaching a higher pitch in chapters 133 to 136 of the *Dialogue,* where Justin writes that the Jews not only "despised the word of the Lord" but also "hate and murder us who have believed."[24]

In *Paidika* 5, Joseph emphasizes that the people's hatred is attributable to the fact that they "suffer."[25] In his *Dialogue,* Justin Martyr also notably develops a discourse of deserved Jewish suffering, implicitly connected to the Jews' perceived opposition to Christ and his followers. Thus, in chapter 16, he tells Trypho, who represents the Jewish people, "You alone may suffer that which you now justly suffer. . . . These things have happened to you in fairness and justice, for you have slain the just one, and his prophets before him; and now you reject those who hope in him . . . cursing in your synagogues those who believe in Christ."[26] Here, Justin credits the suffering of the Jews to their hatred of Jesus and his followers, implying that their curses have in fact rebounded upon them. For Justin, the Jews' suffering is especially embodied in the practice of circumcision: it is a physical sign and symbol of their present pain.[27]

One finds a similar discourse of Jewish suffering in Origen's third-century treatise *Against Celsus.* Celsus, a Greek philosopher who lived in the second century and wrote a polemical work against Christians called *The True Word,* used a Jewish spokesperson as a literary device to launch a series of attacks against Christianity. Origen, in his response to Celsus's criticisms, also speaks in pointed terms about the sufferings and disasters the Jewish people and the city of Jerusalem were to experience as a form of divine vengeance due to the wicked deeds they had committed against Jesus.[28] At one point, Origen even recalls an occasion when he attended a debate "with certain Jews" over the proper scriptural understanding of the suffering inflicted upon the Jewish nation versus the suffering of Christ.[29] Throughout, Origen's main point is that Jewish suffering (in the past, in the present, and at the final judgment) is at one and the same time a form of divine punishment and a stark proof of Christ's own divinity and sovereignty.[30]

As shown by Justin Martyr and Origen, the second and third centuries witnessed a campaign by Christian writers to characterize the Jews as a people who had justly suffered on account of their hatred for Jesus and his followers. In the ears of a literate audience familiar with Christian apologetics against Judaism, Joseph's words to Jesus in the *Paidika* may not have been as innocent and sympathetic as contemporary scholars have usually assumed. Instead, they would have carried a sober undertone of polemic for those with ears to hear.

In this context, Jesus' response also would have been taken as a pointed criticism. He tells Joseph, "[While] you may know sensible words, are you not ignorant of where your words come from? . . . These children shall not be raised, and these people shall receive their punishment."[31] The first half of Jesus' statement seems to confirm the underlying judgment present in Joseph's words: he acknowledges that Joseph articulates an insight drawn from familiar (and presumably authoritative) sources. The second half of his statement makes the judgment explicit. The people are assured of their punishment: they will not be raised from the dead at the final hour. Then, as if to punctuate the point, Jesus' words have an instantaneous effect: "And immediately those who were accusing him became blind."[32] For early readers primed by the language of ancient controversy between Jews and Christians, this confluence of themes—blindness, punishment, and disqualification from the resurrection—would have seemed like standard fare.

Here, we might revisit Justin Martyr and Origen one more time to get a fuller sense of how Jesus' words would have evoked the language of Christian-Jewish polemical encounter. In his *Dialogue,* Justin links the paired themes of hatred and blindness, and punishment and accursedness, in reference to the Jews. Addressing Trypho in chapter 134, he writes, "It is better for you to follow God than your imprudent and blind masters."[33] Five chapters later, he speaks of the Jews' participation in the curse of Shem: "the punishment of the sin" would attach itself to their whole lineage.[34] Origen likewise associates blindness especially with the Jews, characterizing Celsus's Jewish spokesperson as the embodiment of that attribute.[35] By accusing Christians of being blind, both Celsus and Celsus's Jew prove themselves to be blind in reality.[36] By using this anonymous Jew as a literary surrogate, Celsus assimilates the Jewish qualities of hatred and blindness: in Origen's eyes, Celsus is like those whom "hostility blinds."[37]

Thus, even in the absence of explicit references to the Jews or their leaders in chapters 4 and 5 of the *Paidika,* one can reasonably infer from the language placed in the mouths of Joseph and Jesus that the *Paidika* tales were forged in the crucible of Christian and Jewish polemical engagement.[38] Assorted clues scattered throughout the other infancy stories support this case. In chapter 6, Jesus pointedly criticizes his teacher Zacchaeus as someone who "do[es] not know the law" despite his legal training. When "the Jews" lament the fact that they had never heard such words spoken by anyone ("neither a teacher of the law nor any Pharisee"), Jesus claims knowledge that trumps that of their "fathers" and their "fathers' fathers."[39] Later in the same chapter, Jesus further calls Zacchaeus a "hypocrite," another common trope in Christian anti-Jewish polemics.[40] In the second half of the *Paidika,* such polemical language becomes less conspicuous.[41] It may be that portions of the work derived from settings where tensions between Jews and Christians were not as much an issue. For the episodes that compose the first half of the *Paidika,* however, there are compelling indications that Christian identity vis-à-vis Judaism was a pressing concern.

What, then, does this say about the communities that first transmitted these stories? Over the past century, a few scholars have tried to identify signs that the *Paidika* may have originated in a "Jewish-Christian" milieu—that is, among groups who recognized Jesus as the Messiah but remained Torah observant.[42] As possible evidence for such a provenance, these scholars highlight the identification of Joseph as Jesus' father (with no particular qualification to account for a virgin birth), the prominent role played by Jesus' brother James, and hints of separation in the text between the Jewish leadership and the general populace.[43] This textual evidence, however, is so meager and our knowledge of actual early Jewish-Christian groups so limited (and so dependent on hostile witnesses) that no definitive conclusions can be drawn on this basis alone.

Undaunted, others have tried to bolster such arguments by pointing out parallels between names and story types in the *Paidika* and in late ancient rabbinic literature. Jacob Neusner has proposed that the teacher Zacchaeus in the *Paidika* may have been loosely based on a real first-century rabbi, Yohanan ben Zakkai.[44] Others have called attention to stories of alphabetic instruction,[45] miracles involving the carrying of water in a cloak,[46] and tales about another first-century rabbi, Hanina ben Dosa, surviving snakebites and stretching beams of wood,[47] all in literature produced by Jewish communities.[48]

Yet, there are significant methodological and chronological problems with these arguments. First of all, in some cases—especially the pair of stories about snakebites—the suggested parallels are tenuous. The rabbinic story about the snake tells how Rabbi Hanina ben Dosa is bitten but remains unaffected, a plot line that differs significantly from the *Paidika* story where Jesus heals his brother James from the serpent's bite. Given such divergence in detail, and given the widespread popularity of snakebite stories in the ancient Graeco-Roman world, there may not be any specific link (literary or otherwise) between the *Paidika* and these rabbinic accounts. To put it simply, the fact that stories with common themes are found in the *Paidika* and in rabbinic sources does not mean that one was necessarily dependent on the other, nor does it mean that the *Paidika* versions of these tales necessarily derived from a Jewish (or Jewish-Christian) provenance.

Second, such attempts to interpret the *Paidika* as dependent on rabbinic tales run into chronological conundrums. One example is the Babylonian Talmud, in which one finds the rabbinic stories about snakebites and stretched beams. Some scholars have shown a persistent tendency to push the date of Talmudic traditions as early as possible on the basis of the names of the rabbis mentioned as the transmitters (or the subjects) of the stories themselves. But given the fact that the contents of this compendium grew by accretion over centuries via processes of oral and literary transmission, and given the strong hand evidenced in their final redaction, it has proven difficult to trace earlier origins for specific textual units. Our only relatively reliable reference point is the redaction of the collection itself, which probably took place between the late sixth and early eighth centuries.[49] To argue, then, that stories in the *Paidika* derive from earlier forms of Talmudic legends is historically untenable, given the evidence in hand.

Another example that raises such chronological difficulties is the *Story of Ahiqar.* The Slavonic, Armenian, Syriac, and Arabic recensions of the text contain variations on a parable about a wolf brought to a schoolhouse and instructed to recite the first letters of the alphabet: the wolf responds instead by listing the names of its most tasty prey (goat kids and lambs).[50] The Ahiqar legend may be traced back to the middle of the first millennium BCE, and while the original tale was not Jewish in origin, there is evidence that Jewish versions cropped up fairly early on in the history of transmission.[51] On this basis, some scholars have cited the story in arguing that the *Paidika* episodes about Jesus' alphabetic lesson were indebted to the *Story of Ahiqar* and by extension to a Jewish (or more specifically, to a Jewish-Christian) provenance.[52]

Unfortunately, such arguments stretch credulity on a couple of fronts: the stories are not similar enough to establish a direct genealogical connection, and there is also the problem that the earliest version of the Ahiqar legend we have (an Aramaic papyrus from Elephantine Island in Egypt) does not contain the story about the wolf at school.[53] Our only attestations of this particular parable come from medieval manuscripts copied by later Christian scribes. Therefore, it is most likely that the parable of the wolf represents an editorial insertion in these "much later and more elaborate recensions."[54] If there is any connection between the schoolroom episodes in the *Paidika* and the *Story of Ahiqar* (and I doubt there is), it is almost certainly not the case that the early *Paidika* drew material from any early Jewish form of the legend.

Another text that has been proposed as possible source material for the *Paidika* is the so-called *Jeremiah Apocryphon,* which contains an episode that bears a striking resemblance to Jesus' miracle of carrying water in his cloak (*Paidika* 10). The protagonist is the scribe Ezra, and the episode is set during his boyhood years:

> Now there were some of the little children of the Hebrews in the school of the Chaldeans receiving instruction, and they totaled seventy children. And there was a child among them whose name was Ezra who was in his mother's arms [and] did not yet know good from evil. When he had reached the age, they sent him to school, and the spirit of the Lord was upon him. The children of the Hebrews and the Chaldeans went to the river at eventide to draw water and sprinkle the school. While they were yet walking one with another on their way to the river, they filled their vessels with water, [and] the vessel that was in Ezra's hand broke. . . . He went down to the water, filled his robe like a vessel with water, raised it upon his shoulder, [and] went

> with the children. And when he reached the school, he put his robe down full of water like a vessel, [and] he sprinkled the school. When he had finished sprinkling it, he took his robe which was dry [and] put it on.[55]

The *Jeremiah Apocryphon* in its present form dates to the early medieval period and contains elements that reflect a Christian context of transmission and redaction.[56] Arthur Marmorstein nonetheless argued for an original Jewish composition: citing a series of thematic correspondences with rabbinic materials, he proposed the third or fourth century CE as an estimated date of origin.[57] Marmorstein's theory has induced later scholars to raise the possibility of Jewish influence over the *Paidika:* some have even proposed that a hypothetical early version of Ezra's miracle story served as source material for the *Paidika.*[58] Unfortunately, the connections cited by Marmorstein and others are often rather generic, and his dating estimate falls into the same anachronistic trap mentioned above with reference to study of the Babylonian Talmud. Such theories have been put forward despite the problems involved in arguing for the influence of a later textual attestation upon an earlier one.

The countervailing notion—namely, that the *Jeremiah Apocryphon,* in its present Christian(ized) form, may in fact belong to the *Paidika*'s later history of reception—remains a cleaner (although by no means obligatory) solution. Proposed by the text's original editors, the idea has been received with unwarranted skepticism in some quarters.[59] Emblematic of this skepticism are two questions posed by Karl Heinz Kuhn in the full expectation that each would elicit a negative answer: "Would a Christian transfer a miracle, the performance of which was attributed to Jesus, to Ezra? And if the [*Jeremiah Apocryphon*] is of Jewish origin, would a Jew read and use the apocryphal gospel?"[60] While Kuhn thinks that the answer to both of these questions is no, I beg to differ. In each case, yes is an eminently viable response.

Two points are worth emphasizing here. First, in late antiquity and the early medieval period, Christians (and for that matter, Muslims as well) did in fact regularly use Jesus' life as a (retroactive and retrospective) model for their literary representation of prophets and other heroes of the faith. In this case, one could easily imagine the payoff—namely, that Ezra, by performing the same miraculous action in his boyhood, would have served as a ready-made christological type, a Hebrew scribe whose action was later fulfilled by the young Jesus. Second, we do in fact also have tangible evidence that at least some late ancient and early medieval Jews actually knew and read certain stories associated with the *Paidika.* The next section of this chapter concentrates on evidence for cultural memory practices related to Jesus' childhood in late ancient Palestine, where a sixth-century account of a pilgrim's travel itinerary gives us a surprising glimpse into different lines of interaction between Christians and Jews related to localized *Paidika* story traditions. The section following shifts the focus to a medieval Jewish work called *Toledoth Yeshu* ("Generations of Jesus"), in which stories from the *Paidika* play a role in the pejorative portrayal of Jesus as a magician.

Pilgrimage and a Paidika *Tradition in Late Ancient Palestine: Christians, Jews, and Localized Memories of Jesus' Childhood at Nazareth*

Sometime around the year 570, a pilgrim journeyed from his home in Piacenza (a town in northern Italy) to the holy places in Palestine.[61] We do not know his name, but his travel diary—called an *Itinerary*—provides us with invaluable information about late ancient pilgrimage and about the local landscapes and peoples he encountered. The Piacenza pilgrim's account describes how, traveling from Constantinople via Syria and Lebanon, he entered northern Palestine, where he began an extensive tour of biblical sites in Galilee.[62]

After making initial stops at Diocaesarea and Cana,[63] he and a traveling companion arrived in Nazareth:

> Thence we came to the city of Nazareth, in which there are many excellent things. In the synagogue there is still the book [*tomus*] from which our Lord was set to learn the ABC's. In the synagogue, too, is the bench upon which our Lord used to sit with the other children. This bench can be moved and lifted up by Christians; but Jews [*Iudaei*] cannot by any means stir it; nor does it permit itself to be carried out of doors. The house of the Blessed Mary is a basilica, and many cures are wrought in it by her garments. In the city the beauty of the Hebrew women [*mulieres Hebraeae*] is so great, that no more beautiful women are found among the Hebrews [*Hebraeae*]; and this they say was granted them by the Blessed Mary, who they say was their mother. And though the Hebrews [*Hebraei*] have no love for Christians [*Christiani*], yet these women are full of charity for them. This province is like paradise [*paradisus*]. In corn and produce it is like Egypt, but it excels in wine and oil, fruits and honey. Millet, too, is unnaturally tall there, higher than the stature of a tall man.[64]

This anonymous pilgrim's brief account of his visit to the town of Nazareth gives us an unexpected glimpse into the dynamics surrounding the social reception of the *Paidika* in sixth-century Palestine. Indeed, we see here how an infancy story tradition—the repeated scene of Jesus at school—was both elaborated upon and localized in the context of pilgrimage practice.

For the Piacenza pilgrim, Christ's childhood in Nazareth is remembered and reimagined in 3-D, specifically through his encounter with local architecture and artifacts that serve as material traces of a treasured past. It was in and through the ritualized act of visiting a "holy site" (*locus sanctus*) that the contours of Jesus' classroom crystallized before this visitor's eyes and became palpable to the touch.[65] Blake Leyerle has perceptively analyzed the *Itinerary* in terms of the pilgrim's preoccupation with the "texture" of his physical environs, which he used as raw "social data" for reconstructing the past.[66] But what makes the Piacenza pilgrim's account especially interesting is the fact that a *synagogue* serves as the privileged site of memory in this case.

Upon entering the synagogue in Nazareth, the pilgrim and his traveling companion see on display the "book" (*tomus*) Jesus reputedly used for his alphabetic exercises. In this context, the Latin word, *tomus,* may actually have referred to a sheet of papyrus, or to several sheets bound in a small volume.[67] As we have seen, along with wooden tablets and ceramic sherds (ostraca), papyri were one of the most commonly attested media used by ancient students for writing in school, from the elementary level to more advanced stages of education.[68] Among literate pilgrims like our friend from Piacenza, the act of gazing upon (and perhaps even touching or holding) the exercise book Jesus himself used would have prompted memories of learning to read as children, experiences now conflated with the stories of Christ's boyhood in the *Paidika.* If the book was written in Hebrew or Aramaic (instead of in Greek or Latin), the book itself—as an *objet de mémoire*—would have had the function of further conflating the Jewish study house with the Hellenistic schoolhouse.[69]

The Piacenza pilgrim's "tactile piety" would have been reinforced by his encounter with "the bench on which [Jesus] sat with the other children" while attending lessons.[70] The almost conspiratorial observation that "Christians can lift the bench and move it about," but that "the Jews are completely unable to move it, and cannot drag it outside," suggests that this artifact was to be touched as well as to be seen. One can imagine that Christians visiting the site engaged in some heavy lifting as a way of physically proving the truth of the gospel in a Jewish worship space. To borrow a phrase from Lactantius, this was a "rite pertaining to the fingers"—not to mention hands and arms—an exclusive act of devotion performed by the strength of one's body in the presence of religious rivals.[71]

The unlikelihood and incongruity of such a scenario has led one scholar, Joan E. Taylor, to conjecture that the pilgrims' hosts—the resident Jewish community in the synagogue—may have even played along by pantomiming their inability to move the bench. In her reconstruction, their motivation may have been a monetary one: namely, for the sake of maintaining a thriving pilgrimage business among their Christian clientele.[72] In the absence of corroborating evidence, Taylor's hypothesis about the social situation surrounding the Piacenza pilgrim's visit must remain an exercise in historical speculation. It certainly runs against the grain of the pilgrim's own perception: he "envision[s] resistance on the part of the Jews."[73] But Taylor's reading at least prompts us to think about the varied forms that such resistance could take.

The complicated and contested nature of late ancient Jewish-Christian interaction is brought out in the very next paragraph of the *Itinerary.* The Piacenza pilgrim, after telling of his visit to a basilica associated with the "house of the Blessed Mary," describes the good looks and kind hospitality of the local Jewish women who welcomed him to town and who claimed to be related to Mary by blood. Such claims may have been another subtle form of resistance: by underscoring biological lineage (something that the pilgrim could not claim) the women were marking their own historical and local prerogative.

The pilgrim remains a visitor and a voyeur: as an outsider he tries to control (and consume) the holy site in visual acts of aesthetic judgment.[74] In his eyes, the stunning beauty of these women mirrors that of Mary herself, and is in turn mirrored by a local landscape that is a verdant paradise where the grain grows tall and the fruit excels that produced in Egypt.[75] Set over against a daily social reality in which (as the pilgrim admits), the Jews "have no love for Christians,"[76] and in which pilgrims' interactions with local populations in Palestine and Samaria could sometimes become quite strained,[77] these effusive descriptions of the Nazarene women fairly jump off the page. What does the Piacenza pilgrim's account tell us about the role that sixth-century Nazarene Jews played in the history of the *Paidika*'s reception?

Some scholars have proposed that the women the pilgrim met in Nazareth were not simply Jews but Jewish Christians, and that this explains both his effusive language and their interest in traditions about Jesus. Simon Claude Mimouni has called attention to a shift in the pilgrim's vocabulary when writing about the Jewish women and their hospitality. While the pilgrim refers to the hapless Jews who cannot move the schoolhouse bench as *Ioudaei* ("Jews" or "Judaeans"), he calls the women who show him kindness *Hebraeae* ("Hebrews"). For Mimouni, this shift requires a special explanation, and as a solution he postulates that the "Hebrews" are in fact "Christians of a Jewish origin—Jewish-Christians," while the "Christians" in the pilgrim's account were "of a pagan background—pagano-Christians."[78] Mimouni was not the first scholar to suggest that Nazareth may have been home to Jewish-Christian groups: in the mid-twentieth century, Bellarmino Bagatti and Emmanuelle Testa had argued for a Jewish-Christian presence at Nazareth from early on, contending that the presence of this community helped explain the rise of *loca sancta* in the region connected with Jesus' life.[79] Unfortunately, the hypotheses of Bagatti, Testa, and Mimouni do not hold up to critical scrutiny. In her book *Christians and the Holy Places,* Taylor effectively dismantles such theories, concluding there is no evidence for Jewish-Christian communities in Nazareth after the second century, nor any evidence showing Christian veneration of sites prior to the fourth century.[80]

Indeed, when it comes to his encounter with the "Hebrew" women, there are more subtle and satisfying ways to account for the Piacenza pilgrim's language patterns. A survey of primary sources suggests that Christians in fact employed the term "Hebrew" as a label or designation with variable meanings. It was sometimes used as a linguistic marker to refer to Jews who spoke Hebrew or Aramaic,[81] or alternatively as a positive evaluative term to identify Jews who were considered to be "good" in the eyes of Christian observers.[82] Most pointedly, however, it was also used as a "biblicizing" term to justify and interpret the persistent presence of Jews at *loca sancta* in Palestine—as a strategic way of mapping (and thereby relegating) Jews onto a Christian past.[83]

Thus, when the Piacenza pilgrim shifts from his scornful dismissal of the "Jews" who are unable to move the bench to his account of the women who treated him with kindness (*caritas*), it makes sense that he would call them *Hebraeae.* By doing so, he was making their hospitality "safe for the contemporary Christian," objectifying them as "a spectacle of entirely scriptural, 'past-tense' import."[84] A line or two later, we glimpse what lies behind this rhetoric of relegation. In trying to make sense of the women's hospitality and charity, the pilgrim notes that "the *Hebraeae* have no love for the Christians."[85] Here we see the rampant linguistic "slippage" that characterized such encounters. In "biblicizing" the "Hebrew" women from Nazareth, the pilgrim will not let his readers forget that he and they remain bound up in larger Jewish-Christian tensions—a context in which charity was often in short supply.[86]

What, then, are the implications of the Piacenza pilgrim's report for our understanding of sixth-century Nazareth as a setting for the reception of the *Paidika* stories related to Jesus' primary education? The *Itinerary* provides striking evidence that both Jews and Christians were familiar with these tales, to the extent that they marked out a specific site—a Jewish synagogue, nonetheless—as the place where Jesus attended school, sat with his classmates, and learned his ABCs. It also shows that the site—along with the stories connected to it—constituted a contested space where the complexity of larger interreligious conflicts played out at a microlevel. The memory of Jesus' childhood was claimed—in subtly competing ways—by local Jewish women and by Christian pilgrims.

Unfortunately, in trying to reconstruct these dynamics, we have only the testimony of a Latin outsider whose visit to the town was all too brief and shaped by an aesthetic mode of perception through which he appropriated holy places for his own purposes.[87] We are therefore left with more questions than answers when it comes to local Jews at Nazareth who would have been intimately familiar with these stories about Jesus' childhood. What we do discover in the Piacenza pilgrim's travel diary is that the local remembrance and retelling of these stories provided a ritualized forum for the negotiation of religious difference between Jews and Christians in late ancient Palestine.

Jesus the Magician in Jewish Polemics: Countermemories of Jesus' Childhood in Toledoth Yeshu

In the case of the Piacenza pilgrim's account, our evidence for Jewish attitudes toward the infancy stories was frustratingly indirect, filtered through the eyes (and biases) of a Christian visitor to Nazareth. Now I turn to a literary source that gives more direct evidence for Jewish knowledge and interpretation of the *Paidika:* a medieval Jewish work called *Sefer Toledot Yeshu,* or the *The Book of the Generations of Jesus.*[88]

Toledoth Yeshu presents an account of Jesus' life and Christian origins from a distinctively polemical Jewish perspective. It is a controversial text—with respect not only to its incendiary contents but also to scholars' differing views on its dating, provenance, and textual history. It survives in multiple recensions, but the exact nature of the genealogical relationships between the different versions remains an open question. The manuscript evidence ranges from fragments of an eleventh-century Aramaic text found in the Cairo Geniza to a score of Hebrew versions copied in early modern and modern Europe (spanning the sixteenth to twentieth centuries), each with its own variations on the central story.[89]

The origins of *Toledot Yeshu*, however, certainly can be traced to a time earlier than these surviving manuscript copies.[90] Around the year 826 CE, Agobard, bishop of Lyons, quotes a long excerpt in his *Letters on Jewish Superstitions;* and about twenty years later his successor, Amulo, also refers to a *Toledot* text in a treatise he wrote entitled *Against the Jews.*[91] Agobard provides a definite date before which the work (or at least a collection of related stories) must have been circulating—in technical terms, a terminus ad quem. The terminus a quo, the date after which the document must have been written, is a bit less certain. The *Toledot* shows knowledge of Nestorius, who was condemned at the Council of Chalcedon in 451 CE, and of the fifth-century Syrian ascetic Simeon Stylites, which would suggest a date of composition sometime after the middle of the fifth century. A reference to the Jewish liturgical poet Eleazar ben Kalir in the final chapter would seem to push the date even later, as he is thought to have lived during the first half of the seventh century (and certainly not before the sixth). And yet, some scholars have suggested that the final two chapters containing these named references were in fact later additions to the text, and have therefore pushed for a date of composition in the early fifth or even the late fourth century.[92]

Another complicating factor is the relationship of *Toledot Yeshu* to the Babylonian Talmud, which was probably collected and edited around the seventh century. There is a general consensus that the contents of the *Toledot* show dependence on certain Talmudic traditions about Jesus, but the nature of that dependence—whether, for instance, it was based on the standardized written form of the Talmud or some other earlier written or oral stratum—is a far from settled matter.[93]

In any case, it is safe to say that certain elements of the *Toledot* narrative took shape sometime between the late fifth and the late eighth or early ninth century, most likely in a milieu where Aramaic was spoken.[94] The manuscript record, however, gives evidence of continued editorial revision through the medieval, early modern, and modern eras, during which time the narrative was expanded and adapted for different communities.[95] In this chapter, I focus on one well-known version of the *Toledot Yeshu,* the Strasbourg manuscript published by Samuel Krauss in his 1902 edition.[96] While the manuscript itself dates to the eighteenth century, it preserves a form of the text that seems to trace its roots to at least the thirteenth or fourteenth century.[97]

For purposes of analysis, the Strasbourg version of *Toledot Yeshu* may be divided into two main sections, with a supplementary section appended at the end.[98] The first section (chapters 1–8), constituting the majority of the work, presents an extended parody of the Gospels.[99] The much shorter second section (chapters 9–10) draws on material from the Acts of the Apostles. Finally, the supplementary section at the end of the work (chapters 11–12) recasts two figures from fifth-century Christian history as Jewish sympathizers.[100]

The beginning of the narrative tells how Miriam (Mary), engaged to be married to a man named Yochanan (John), is unwittingly seduced by Joseph the son of Pandera, who disguised himself as her betrothed. When she becomes pregnant, Yochanan leaves the city and departs for Babylon in shame. Miriam gives birth to a son and names him Yehoshua, or Yeshu (aka Jesus). When the boy reaches an appropriate age she brings him to school so that he might become learned in the law. There, Jesus proves himself both haughty and brilliant. He brazenly walks in front of his teachers with his head uncovered, which his fellow students take as a sign of his illegitimate birth. He also argues with them over the finer points of legal interpretation in the *halakhot* (religious laws) and questions their authority, saying, "Who is the master, and who is the disciple?"[101]

The next set of events in the *Toledot* explains how Jesus acquired his miraculous powers. In those days, we are told, the Jerusalem Temple had a foundation stone on which was engraved the four letters of the divine name in Hebrew (that is, the unutterable Tetragrammaton); and whoever was able to learn that name by heart could do whatever he or she wanted. To guard against such an intrusion, brass statues of dogs (in some versions, lions) were placed at the gate of the Holy of Holies. If anyone tried to enter and memorize those letters, as soon as that person tried to leave the precinct of the Temple the dogs would bark (or the lions would roar), and the person would instantly forget what he or she had seen. Eager to obtain such power, Jesus devised a successful plan to steal the name. Having entered the Temple, he wrote the letters of the name upon a piece of parchment. Then, he made an incision in his thigh and inserted the folded-up parchment under his skin. When he left, the dogs barked and his memory was wiped clean, but he was able to reopen the wound and withdraw the parchment intact. Thus it was, according to the *Toledot,* that he obtained the divine name and the ability to perform extraordinary feats of healing, proclaiming himself as the Messiah.[102]

In response to Jesus' healings and growing group of followers, a delegation of Jewish leaders takes Jesus before Queen Helene, the wife of King Jannaeus, and accuses the would-be Messiah of being a sorcerer (their first public accusation against him).[103] In his own defense, Jesus speaks the divine name and raises a dead man before the queen, who summarily dismisses the case. When Jesus goes to Upper Galilee and gains more followers, however, the Jewish leaders return to the queen to renew their accusation of sorcery (their second public accusation). She responds by sending cavalry to Galilee, but when they try to arrest Jesus again, his followers offer violent resistance. In the presence of these troops, Jesus performs two miracles, the first of which is of particular interest: "Now the men of Galilee were making birds of clay. And (Jesus) spoke the letters of the ineffable Name and they flapped their wings. The same hour they fell down before him."[104] He follows this up by causing a millstone to float upon the waters of the sea and telling the soldiers to return and report these things to their queen.[105]

After Jesus has been accused a second time and Queen Helene once more calls him to court, the Jewish leaders recruit Judas Iscariot to enter the Holy of Holies and smuggle out the divine name in the same way that Jesus did, in order to acquire the same power. This leads to a dramatic confrontation before the queen. In the face of the leaders, Jesus lifts up his hands like the wings of an eagle and begins to fly. Judas does the same, and an aerial battle ensues. Both possess equal power, and thus at first Judas is unable to force Jesus to the ground. But then he has an idea: he decides to defile Jesus (in some manuscripts, he urinates on him; in others, he ejaculates on him), and the result is that both become unclean and lose the power of the divine name. This action is explained as Judas's true betrayal, the act over which Christians weep.[106]

Judas's act of defilement leads into a retelling of Jesus' passion and death. In the *Toledot,* Jesus, now stripped of his power, is beaten with pomegranate staves and then taken to a synagogue in Tiberias, where he is bound to a pillar, given vinegar to drink, crowned with a wreath of thorns, and finally pelted with stones. This public humiliation is interrupted when a group of his followers manage to help him escape, and he takes refuge in the city of Antioch.[107]

Another parodic rendition of the passion narrative follows. When Jesus and his followers return to Jerusalem that same year for the Passover celebration, he enters the city on a colt and goes into the Temple. There, he is betrayed by a disciple named Ga'isa ("Thief")—identified as Judas in other manuscripts—and is seized again by the Jewish leaders, who put him to death, hang him on a carob tree, and then arrange for his burial. After his burial, when Jesus' disciples begin proclaiming that his body is no longer in the grave and that he has ascended into heaven, the leaders investigate and find out that a gardener has removed the body and reburied it somewhere else. In the end, the Jewish leaders exhume his body again and drag it through the streets to demonstrate the falsity of the disciples' claims.[108]

After this, the story shifts to the doings of the disciples after Jesus' death in what amounts to a (much abbreviated) retelling of the Acts of the Apostles from a Jewish perspective. After Jesus' followers flee and disperse to various places (including Mount Ararat, Armenia, and Rome), many end up slain. This adds to the strife between them and the Jewish leaders, which continues for another thirty years until finally the Jewish leaders resolve to separate Jesus' disciples from their midst once and for all. With this goal in mind, they ask a learned man named Elijah—later identified as the apostle Paul—to go to Antioch, to present himself as one of Jesus' disciples, and to form a separatist movement among the Christians (Nazarenes) in that city. This figure manages to obtain the divine name for himself. Accordingly, he begins demonstrating his power to heal the lame and thereby attracts a following. He teaches Christians to profane the Sabbath and instead recognize the first day of the week (Sunday) as holy. In place of the Jewish festivals, he has them celebrate Christian rites, and he instructs them to reject circumcision and to turn the other cheek. These efforts are successful: the Christians separate themselves from Israel, and as a result the purity of Israel is restored.[109]

The Strasbourg version of the *Toledot* then concludes with two final chapters that take well-known personages of Christian late antiquity as their points of departure. The first tells about the rise of a certain Nestorius, a figure whose name would have evoked the famous bishop of Constantinople condemned for christological heresy in the fifth century. The Nestorius in the *Toledot* is conspicuously presented as a "Judaizing" Christian who opposes the teachings of the apostle Paul. In particular, he argues that Christians should be circumcised, just as Jesus was circumcised, and that Jesus came to fulfill the law, not to abolish it.[110] Furthermore, as for those who say that Jesus is God, he accuses them of being idolaters. These teachings lead to a virulent schism among the Christians. In the end, Nestorius goes to Babylonia where he tries to administer the sacraments but is killed by a group of women who oppose him.[111]

The second additional chapter concerns a man named Simeon Kepha, whose story is modeled after the fifth-century Syriac *Life of Saint Simeon the Stylite.* In the *Toledot,* Simeon Kepha is identified as the chief of the Sanhedrin and as a privileged recipient of divine revelation. The Christians envy him for his wisdom and try to compel him to convert on pain of death. He agrees to do so only on the condition that the Christians will refrain from violence against Jews and that they will continue to allow Jews freedom of worship. For the rest of his life Simeon withdraws from society and lives at the top of a tall tower, where he follows an ascetic regimen. His name, Kepha, is explained in terms of his commitment to standing on the "Rock" in fulfillment of Ezekiel's prophecy. Despite his outward conversion, Simeon's ongoing allegiance to the people of Israel is underscored in the narrative: even atop his tower, he remains engaged in composing liturgical poetry for the Jewish communities in Palestine and Babylon, gestures of piety for which he is remembered and honored as Rabbi Simeon.[112]

This plot summary shows that the Strasbourg version of the *Toledot* draws on certain structural elements found in the *Paidika.* In both the *Paidika* and its polemical Jewish counterpart, the miracle with the birds is featured alongside stories emphasizing Jesus' troubled relationships with his teachers in school and the power he acquires through his mastery of letters. Specific verbal details also correspond. For example, the phrase uttered by Jesus to his rabbinic master in chapter 2 of the *Toledot*—"Who is the master, and who is the disciple?"—seems to echo the language in *Paidika* 6.2f, where Jesus tells

Zacchaeus, "I want to instruct you rather than being instructed by you," and *Paidika* 7.2, where Zacchaeus admits, "I thought that I would have him as a student, but I have been found to have him as a teacher."[113] Later versions of the *Toledot* also show dependence upon stories associated with the *Paidika*. Perhaps the clearest example of this may be illustrated by a comparison between MS Vindobona (an expanded recension of the *Toledot* preserved in Vienna) and a Syriac *Life of Mary*.[114] Both texts contain versions of Jesus' bird miracle in which he animates not only birds but also a number of other animals—including oxen and asses—and commands them to stand and walk or fly.[115] Essentially the same story is also found in the *Arabic Gospel of the Infancy*.[116] Thus, the Strasbourg and Vindobona manuscripts both betray signs of Jewish familiarity with early Christian infancy traditions.

It is in this context that we glimpse the role Jewish-Christian polemics and apologetics played in the reception of *Paidika* stories. One of the distinguishing features of Jesus' bird miracle in the Strasbourg *Toledot Yeshu* is its narrative connection to Jewish accusations of magic. In addition to their instrumental role in pushing forward the plot, these accusations had an aetiological function: to explain why the despised Christian Messiah had been able to perform wondrous deeds during his lifetime.

In the Strasbourg version of the *Toledot*, Jesus is accused twice of being a magician. The first time occurs after he has healed a lame man and a leper—"signs" he performs by saying the letters of the divine name over them. After witnessing these acts, the "wise men" among the Jews bring him before Helene the queen and tell her, "This man is a sorcerer, and he deceives the world."[117] The same accusation is lodged a second time a bit later, after Jesus is released from custody. When he continues to perform signs in Upper Galilee, the Jewish leaders approach the queen again, reasserting their charge that "he practices sorcery and thus leads the world astray."[118] Jesus' act of bringing the clay birds to life is the very next miracle he performs, one that serves to confirm the veracity of their accusation. We are told that when the queen's soldiers go to arrest him, they find him "misleading the men of Upper Galilee" by calling himself the son of God and by speaking the letters of the divine name over the birds so that they flap their wings and fly.[119]

In certain other recensions of the *Toledot* these accusations of magic are accentuated even more. A manuscript from Yemen, for example, contains a third allegation about Jesus' identity as a magician (as well as the story of his miracle with the birds).[120] There are also multiple references to Jesus' magical powers in a late recension called the *Tam ū-mūʿād:* for example, in order to perform his miracle with the birds, Jesus is said to have "whispered over them, like snakes and otters hiss" and thus "performed magic."[121] Finally, in a copy preserved in Vienna, one finds other elaborations on this theme. The terms of the first accusation are echoed in Jesus' public defense when he insists to the queen: "I am the Son of God, not a magician."[122] Later, after the second accusation and Jesus' act of bringing the birds to life, the queen herself expresses concern that he was gathering together an anti-Jewish movement "by means of his magic": she then explicitly calls him both a "magician" and a "bastard."[123] Just as in the other recensions, Jesus' possession of the divine name is understood as the source of his magical power. Yet, to this explanation the Vienna manuscript adds another as well: Jesus' wonder-working is also attributed to the fact that "he went to Egypt, stayed there a long time, and learned much magic."[124]

The accusations of magic lodged against Jesus in these versions of the *Toledot* draw on long-standing polemical *topoi* in ancient Judaism—*topoi* that came to expression in literature and social practice. One finds hints of such accusations as early as the second century in the anti-Christian polemics of the Greek philosopher Celsus, who composed a dialogue in which a Jewish interlocutor put forward arguments that Jesus' wonder-working was rooted in his childhood training in magic. According to Origen, Celsus's Jew claimed that Jesus, due to his family's poverty, "hired himself out as a workman in Egypt, and there tried his hand at certain magical powers on which the Egyptians pride themselves," before returning to Israel "full of conceit because of these powers" and giving himself "the title of God."[125] Interestingly enough, in this same context, Celsus's Jew highlights the illegitimacy of Jesus' birth, attributing his parentage to a Roman soldier named Panthera.[126] Hints of similar accusations appear also in Justin Martyr's contemporaneous *Dialogue with Trypho the Jew,* in which Justin reports that Jesus' miracles were viewed by the Jewish people as a form of magic: "For they dared to call him a magician, and a deceiver of the people."[127] While Celsus and Justin Martyr were in the business of creating literary fictions for the purposes of making their own apologetic points, the specific accusations they placed in the mouth of their "imaginary characters" almost certainly reflected actual Jewish polemical rhetoric against the messianic claims made by Christians at the time.[128]

These early sources are not our only witnesses to such polemical rhetoric: it would appear that the ancient Jewish community continued to cultivate similar pejorative portrayals of Jesus under its emerging rabbinic leadership. For evidence, we may turn to the Babylonian Talmud, a collection of stories and legal teachings edited between the late sixth and eighth centuries containing material about Jesus with links to the transmission history of the *Toledot Yeshu.* Given their estimated dates, it is most likely that the *Toledot* draws rather loosely on Talmudic traditions, or that the Babylonian Talmud and the *Toledot* share certain oral or written sources in common, perhaps including Celsus.

Tractate *b. Shabbath* 104b suggests the closest connection to Celsus's earlier polemics and to the elaboration of these themes in the *Toledot.* In a section on proper and improper modes of writing, the Talmudic text presents a statute debating the sinful culpability of anyone who "scratches a mark on his flesh," and then later comments (in the form of a question voiced by Rabbi Eliezer): "Did not Ben Stada bring forth witchcraft from Egypt by means of scratches (in the form of charms) upon his flesh?"[129] The uncensored version of the text continues by supplying other details by way of commentary. First, Ben Stada is identified as "the son of Pandira" (a variant spelling of the name Pandera/Panthera). Second, Pandira is identified as his mother's "paramour"; and finally his mother is identified as "Miriam."[130] For at least some of these rabbinic commentators, this *halakhic* teaching was thought to pertain especially to the figure of Jesus, who is (not so subtly) referred to as one who apprenticed himself in Egypt to train as a magician.[131]

This image of a magician who acquires his power by scratching or making an incision into his flesh is picked up and advanced in the Strasbourg *Toledot Yeshu,* where Jesus steals the divine name by slicing open his thigh and hiding the papyrus with the sacred letters inside. Another detail in *b. Shabbath* 104b suggests an additional, promising connection with the *Toledot.* The Talmudic tractate continues by discussing the legality of "writ[ing] upon writing," and the rabbinic commentators cite as their only example the case of a scribe who mistakenly writes the divine name and then is forced to correct it by tracing over its letters. This confluence of themes in the Talmud became fodder for a creative act of renarration in the *Toledot Yeshu,* where suspicions about Jesus' magical proclivities are likewise connected with his questionable past and the power of the divine name.

A further Talmudic link to the *Toledot* traditions may be found in tractates that mention Jesus' mischief making at school. In *b. Berakoth* 17a–b and *b. Sanhedrin* 103a, Jesus is remembered as a "disciple" who "publicly spoiled his food"—probably a reference to dishonoring one's name through false teachings.[132] In *b. Sanhedrin* 107b and *b. Sotah* 47a, the rabbis comment more specifically on his tense relationship with his teacher, who is identified in both settings as Yehoshua (Joshua) b. Perahya and who is said to have "pushed away" or "repulsed" Jesus "with both hands." Jesus is compared to the legendary figure Gehazi, who (according to some of the sages) "engraved the Divine Name in [the golden calf's] mouth," and who thus received the same treatment at the hands of his teacher, Elisha.[133] Tractate *b. Sanhedrin* 107b also suggests that Jesus spent time in Egypt and that his master Yehoshua excommunicated him on account of idolatry and because he "practiced magic and deceived and led Israel astray."[134]

The fact that this same Yehoshua b. Perahya appeared as Jesus' teacher in certain recensions of the *Toledot Yeshu* shows how these Talmudic texts came to serve as secondary sites of memory for the reception of stories about Jesus' childhood.[135] In some settings, material objects may have also played an accessory role in conditioning Jews to associate Jesus with magical practices. Here, we may note in particular the discovery of so-called Babylonian magic bowls on which the names of Yehoshua b. Perahya and Jesus were inscribed.[136] On one bowl, Yehoshua is presented as "the prime example of a potent magician" who possesses power over female demons.[137] Another bowl contains a curse, written in Jewish Babylonian Aramaic (probably with Sasanian Persian origins), in which the unutterable name YHWH and the name of Jesus are presented as having parallel force. The spell is brought into effect "by the name of I-Am-that-I-Am, the Lord of Hosts (*YHWH Tzevaot*), and by the name of Jesus, who conquered the height and depth by his cross, and by the name of his exalted father, and by the name of the holy spirits forever and in eternity."[138] The production and use of such bowls in ritual contexts would have reinforced perceptions among medieval observers that Jesus was a figure who possessed special "magical" powers and privileges in relation to the divine name.[139]

Toledot Yeshu, then, presents a fascinating example of how the *Paidika* stories were taken up and reinterpreted in practices of Jewish countermemory. In this way, the figure (and scratched body) of the Christ child served as an eminently malleable *lieu de mémoire* for medieval Jewish communities who sought, via acts of renarration, both to mark off their own separate historical identity and to co-opt and reclaim elements of a Christian past.

Redeeming the Redeemer: Anti-Jewish Apologetics and the Scribal Defense of the Christ Child

Jewish portrayals of Jesus as an illegitimate son of Mary and as a dubious practitioner of magic were not hidden from public view, nor did counternarratives such as *Toledot Yeshu* remain completely cloaked in secrecy. From Justin Martyr of Rome and Origen of Alexandria in the second and third centuries, to the ninth-century bishops Agobard and Amulo of Lyons and Hrabanus Maurus of Mainz, to a number of later medieval writers, including Raymund Martin of Catalonia and Porchetus de Salvaticis of Genoa in the thirteenth and fourteenth centuries, we find evidence that Christians from different regions were well familiar with such Jewish polemic.[140] Indeed, the fact that Jews viewed Jesus' miracles as a form of sorcery was well known to early Muslims as well. In one of the verses in the Qur'ān where Jesus' miracle of the birds is cited as a sign of his prophetic status, the voice of God addresses Jesus directly and emphasizes how "I restrained the Children of Israel from [harming] you when you came to them with clear proofs, and those of them who disbelieved exclaimed, 'This is nothing other than mere magic.' "[141]

For their part, Christians also sought to defend Jesus vigorously against such criticism. Their responses typically took literary form—apologetic treatises designed to counter Jewish accounts about Jesus' origins and education as a "youth" (*juvenis*), written to correct the perception that he was "hanged on a stake as an abominable sorcerer" (*veluti magum detestabilem, furca suspensum*).[142]

Treatises such as Agobard's *Against Jewish Superstitions,* however, were not the only forum for Christians in their efforts to vindicate Jesus in the face of Jewish criticisms. One can detect hints of similar apologetics in the work of scribes who sometimes edited Christian texts with an eye toward clearing Jesus' name, while also taking any opportunity to portray Jews in an increasingly negative light. Here, the manuscript history of the *Paidika* is instructive, insofar as it provides us with clues as to how such acts of editorial intervention may have been aimed (at least in part) toward resolving controversies regarding Christ's childhood.[143] I turn now to this heretofore unexplored history of scribal apologetics.

When one studies textual histories, time frame is important. Our earliest manuscripts of the *Paidika* are two Latin and Syriac copies that date to the fifth and sixth centuries, respectively, while the surviving Greek texts range primarily from the eleventh to the fifteenth or sixteenth century. As such, the manuscript record provides evidence for the work of Christian scribes over a period of time relatively contemporaneous with the composition and redaction of the *Toledot Yeshu,* a process that resulted in the dissemination of multiple recensions across the Mediterranean world, from Spain and France in the west to Cairo, Yemen, and Bukhara (contemporary Uzbekistan) in the east.[144] What, then, do scribal additions and omissions tell us about how the written transmission of the *Paidika* might have been inflected by concerns connected with Jewish-Christian polemics and apologetics? In what follows, I highlight details in the manuscript record that indicate such tensions and that hint at how Christian scribes sought to acquit the Christ child of any charges of magic. In this way, the practice of copying and editing texts served as a means whereby the young redeemer himself was effectively redeemed in Christian cultural memory.

Scribal Practice and Anti-Jewish Polemic

Paidika scribes, in and through their emendations of the text, engaged in subtle forms of anti-Jewish polemic. At the beginning of this chapter, I discussed how the earliest Greek form of the *Paidika* (or at least the earliest form available to us) betrays signs of having circulated in an environment where Jewish and Christian social identities remained both under negotiation and in conflict. What we find when we examine the work of later Christian scribes is that they took this earlier textual data and made specific changes and additions geared toward accentuating negative portrayals of Jews and Judaism.

A prime example of this may be observed in changes made to the representation of Annas's son in *Paidika* 3. After Jesus brings the sparrows to life, Annas's son questions him about why he was performing such an act on the Sabbath and then proceeds to destroy the pools Jesus had been making from the stream water. Our earliest Greek text (Gs) simply has Jesus respond with an implicit curse: "May your fruit be rootless and may your shoot be dried up like a young branch charred by a violent wind!"[145] In other Greek versions, however, and in the Latin text of the *Gospel of Pseudo-Matthew*—a medieval work that came to incorporate (and update) chapters from the *Paidika*—Jesus' response is embellished. His words underscore the wickedness of the Jewish boy who had challenged him, an accusation that effectively counters and reverses the representation of Jesus in both the Strasbourg and Cairo Geniza versions of the *Toledot,* where he is consistently referred to as "the wicked one."[146]

Thus, in one later Greek recension (Ga), Jesus conversely addresses Annas's son as "wicked, impious and foolish!" and tells him that he will "dry up like a tree" and that he "shall never produce leaves nor roots nor fruit."[147] In another (Gb), the language of condemnation is intensified. After the child destroys the pools, Jesus turns and calls him "impious and lawless" before cursing him ("you shall dry up like the stick you are holding"). In this case, the narrator makes explicit the fact that Jesus' curse was immediately effective: we are told that the boy "went a little way, fell to the ground, and breathed his last."[148] In yet another Greek recension (Gd) and in a late Latin version, Jesus' speech is even harsher: the son of Annas is now a "Sodomite, impious and foolish," one who has "no roots, head (Lat. leaves), or fruit." The instant Annas's son hears these words he falls down and withers.[149]

Finally, in the Latin *Gospel of Pseudo-Matthew*, the same boy becomes the object of a damning diatribe in which he is demonized as a stock representative of the Jews. In chapter 26 of that gospel, the narrator introduces him as "a son of the devil" (*filius diaboli*). After Annas's son destroys the pools of water, Jesus personally scorns him as a "son of death" (*filius mortis*), a "son of Satan" (*filius satanae*), and a "son of iniquity" (*filius iniquitatis*).[150] As usual, Jesus curses the boy, and he dies. But the *Gospel of Pseudo-Matthew* then inserts a twist in the plot. Mary, distraught at the child's death and his parents' mourning, appeals to her son for clemency. To honor his mother's request, the Christ child raises the boy up, but his method of doing so gives even graver insult: "[Jesus], not wishing to grieve his mother, with his right foot kicked the hinder parts of the dead boy . . . and he who had been dead rose up and went away."[151] Two chapters later, when Jesus and the boy meet again, the pattern of demonization continues as if never interrupted. In a reprise of their first encounter, the boy again breaks the small dams that Jesus had built. Jesus responds by calling him, "O most wicked seed of iniquity! O son of death! O workshop of Satan!"[152]

The son of Annas is not the only target for such encoded scribal judgment against the Jews. In Syriac, Ethiopic, Latin, and later Greek copies of the text, we find other editorial changes that enact forms of anti-Jewish polemic. A case in point is the Syriac version of the story in which Jesus curses the boy who struck his shoulder. After the boy's parents complain and Joseph comes to talk sense to Jesus, the Christ child justifies his actions by pointing out the sinful lineage of that boy's family: "If these were not children of a sinner, they would not be receiving a curse. These shall see their torment."[153]

The operating assumption regarding Jewish inheritance of sin and judgment comes to expression again in the very next chapter when Jesus encounters his first teacher. Speaking to Zacchaeus, he says, "For when I am greatly exalted I shall lay aside that which is mixed in your race [Syr. *gnes*]."[154] While Jesus' words might refer more generally to the sinfulness of humankind, in this context the Jews stand in as the particular target of his approbation. In the Ethiopic version of the same story, Jesus' words are likewise embellished so as to underscore the "fleshly" character of the Jewish teacher's law: thus, he says to Zacchaeus, "I am different from you, and I do not have, like you, a family of flesh. And you are the only one who has been found in the Law."[155] Such rhetoric associating the Jews with "fleshliness" was an old saw dating back to early Christian anti-Jewish polemics.[156]

The Latin *Gospel of Pseudo-Matthew* also provides evidence that Christian scribal emendations were framed with an eye trained on Jewish-Christian tensions surrounding the figure of the Christ child. Immediately after Jesus' curse of the anonymous boy, a crowd of "evildoers" come to Joseph with "accusations" against Jesus, and we are told that "when Joseph saw this, he was in great terror, fearing the violence and uproar of the people of Israel."[157] In the story about Zacchaeus, the teacher tells Joseph and Mary that their regard for their son is in direct conflict with the honor due to "the elders of the whole church [*ecclesia*, "assembly"] of Israel," and shortly thereafter, Jesus responds by telling his teacher, "I am a stranger to your law-courts."[158] One final scribal intervention takes place near the end of Jesus' encounter with his first teacher: marveling at Jesus' alphabetic virtuosity, Zacchaeus is made to exclaim, "I do not know whether he be a wizard [*magus*] or a god; or at least an angel of God speaks in him."[159] In earlier versions of the *Paidika*, Zacchaeus had merely wondered whether Jesus was "either a god or an angel."[160] The addition of a third possibility—that Jesus could possibly be a wizard—sticks out incongruously like a sore thumb, rubbed raw by a long history of polemic friction. Zacchaeus stands in as the literary representative of rabbinic learning. Placed in his mouth, the word "wizard" would have had a special resonance for readers, evoking the kind of controversial language found in the Talmudic texts. It was into this arena of controversy that Christian scribes inserted themselves by painting Jesus' Jewish adversaries in an increasingly negative light and (as I have yet to show) by taking steps to reshape the young Jesus' image in more sanctioned sacramental and theological terms.

Scribal Practice and Theological Apologetics

The flipside of Christian scribes' editorial polemics against Judaism was a collective effort to redeem the Christ child of unsavory associations with magic. In the face of Jewish accusations that Jesus had apprenticed as a magician during his childhood sojourn in Egypt, scribes working in Greek, Latin, Syriac, and other languages began making changes to the text, downplaying the apparent capriciousness of the Christ child's actions and instead highlighting in more standard theological terms his divinity as the incarnate Word, which he was seen to manifest already at a tender age. The figure that emerges through such textual redaction was a young Jesus whose divine power came to expression most clearly and authoritatively through the cross and the sacraments.

I again focus on the three main story types that have served as primary case studies throughout this book. Here, for thematic reasons, I change the order, beginning with the teacher stories, continuing with the miracle of the birds (making comparisons to some of his other wondrous deeds), and concluding with Jesus' curse of the boy who bumped his shoulder.

Just as we saw in the case of how scribal practice reinforced anti-Jewish polemics, the Zacchaeus story also proved fertile ground for theologically motivated editorial apologetics. Greek and Latin scribes went to great lengths to underscore the Christ child's identification with the eternal Creator. In Greek recension A (Ga) and the *Gospel of Pseudo-Matthew,* Jesus' first teacher laments his ignorance by confessing he does not know "the beginning or the end" of Jesus' teaching regarding the first letter, an obvious allusion to Christ's divine identity as alpha and omega.[161] Another Greek recension has Zacchaeus proclaim in wonder that Jesus must be either "a god or an angel *or the creator of everything,*" language that contrasts with Zacchaeus's musings in the *Gospel of Pseudo-Matthew* that Jesus may be a wizard.[162] The late Greek text effectively sanitizes Zacchaeus's statement of any echo of rabbinic accusations found in the Talmud or *Toledot Yeshu.*

In a Syriac *Life of Mary,* the Ethiopic and Georgian versions of the *Paidika,* and the *Armenian Infancy Gospel,* there is evidence that later scribes took steps to read Christ's infancy through the lens of later trinitarian and christological doctrine. The *Life of Mary* incorporates episodes from the *Paidika* into a larger narrative about the lives of Mary and Jesus. It occasionally transposes story elements from one episode to another. This is the case when it retells the tale of Jesus' conversation with the teachers in the Temple. In the *History of the Blessed Virgin Mary,* this story is embellished with characteristic details from the *Paidika* episode about Zacchaeus: the teachers try to teach Jesus the letters *aleph* and *beth,* and Jesus responds by calling them hypocrites due to their lack of true knowledge. He then embarks on his mystical exegesis of the letter forms. The discourse concludes with a final observation about how the letters were "fixed in the form of the Trinity."[163]

A similar pattern of theologization is found in the Slavonic version of the *Paidika.* When Jesus instructs Zacchaeus about the lines of the first letter, he adopts recognizable language from the early Christian Councils of Nicaea (325 CE) and Chalcedon (451 CE) to describe both the letter and, by extension, himself: "Hear now, teacher, and understand how a limit has two lines that you see through the middle. And I passed by the offerings and I magnified saying the tri-hypostatic praise from two natures identical in form and in power, equal in honor. And the same limit has the Arpha [i.e., Alpha]."[164] In the *Armenian Infancy Gospel,* the young Jesus' interpretation of the first two letters, *alaph* and *beth,* is again self-referential, but his vocabulary draws much more specifically on the theology of the incarnation: "The *alaph* signifies the Name, God; and the *beth,* the Word to be born, the Word of God becoming embodied."[165]

Finally, in the Syriac and Ethiopic *Paidika* and in the *Gospel of Pseudo-Matthew,* scribal additions to the Zacchaeus story point ahead to the crucifixion as the salvific fulfillment of Jesus' divine incarnation. Thus, the Syriac editor has Zacchaeus marvel, "It is not right for this one to be this [way] on the Earth; truly this one is worthy of a great cross."[166] The same point pertains in the Ethiopic and in the *Gospel of Pseudo-Matthew:* in the latter, the teacher (in this case, Zacchaeus' preceptor, Levi), after asking whether Jesus ought to live on the earth, affirms, "He ought to be hung on the great cross."[167]

An examination of the story about Jesus and the sparrows shows a pattern of scribal redaction consistent with the christological and soteriological emphasis reflected in the changes made to the Zacchaeus tale. In our earliest Greek recension of the text (Gs), Jesus brings the birds to life by clapping his hands and shouting, "Go, take flight, like living beings."[168] In other versions (Syriac, Georgian, and later Greek and Latin recensions), the words Jesus speaks to the birds are supplemented with an additional phrase: "Go, take flight, *and remember me,* living ones."[169] The textual history is unclear at this point. But if the shorter text (Gs) represents an earlier reading, it is possible that the phrase "and remember me" was a scribal addition meant to reinterpret the story through a sacramental lens: the five-year-old Jesus speaks the Eucharistic words of institution recorded in Luke 22:19 and 1 Corinthians 11:24 ("Do this in remembrance of me"), and the twelve sparrows thus become symbols of the apostles and, by extension, the church writ large.[170]

Jesus' enlivening of the birds was not the only episode to which Christian scribes applied such a sacramental reading. In the early Latin and later Greek versions, one finds similar examples. The first is Jesus' healing of the woodcutter's foot. In Ga and Gd, after healing the man's wound, Jesus says to him, "Rise, split your wood, *and remember me.*"[171] The final phrase does not appear in either Gs or the Syriac. The second is his raising of a sick infant who died. After performing the miracle, Jesus says to the mother, "Take your child *and give it milk and remember me.*"[172] Here the Eucharistic exhortation is combined with an image of nursing often used as a metaphor for the nourishment Christians received through participation in the sacrament. For the scribes and their readers, the insertion of these Eucharistic allusions had the function of redirecting attention away from the young Jesus' miraculous deeds (including the questions that they raised about the possible magical character of these acts) and toward the regularized distribution of Christ's power and grace through sanctioned celebrations of the sacrament.

A Postscript: Scribal Slips and Polemical Parodies

I conclude this chapter with a pair of textual curiosities that shed light on how medieval Christian readers of the infancy stories may have perceived the power Jesus held over his Jewish antagonists. The two examples come from Greek and Syriac sources related to the *Paidika* tradition.

The first relates to the tale about the boy who collides with Jesus' shoulder. Our earliest Greek manuscript (Gs) contains what appears to be a revealing scribal "slip." Where all the other recensions have the Greek term for "shoulder," *ton ōmon*, Gs has a variant form, *ton onomon.*[173] Most likely, what happened was that the scribe simply reduplicated a syllable (and altered a vowel by way of attraction or phonetic confusion). Thus, *ton ōmon* becomes *ton [on]omon.*

This was a common enough occurrence in the textual trade, but what is curious is the final product—a form that ends up being quite close to the Greek word for "name" (*to onoma*). In a manuscript otherwise plagued by errors and linguistic infelicities, one wonders whether medieval readers of this text would have naturally assumed that the resultant form was simply a misspelling or grammatical misrendering of *to onoma*. After all, the *Paidika* itself is a text in which Jesus elsewhere plays around with the concept of names. He tells Zacchaeus that "as for the name with which you are named, you are a stranger" (*to onoma ho*$_i$ *onomazē*$_i$ *allotrios tugchaneis*), and he gives his father, Joseph, the promise (already fulfilled) that he "might bear the salvific name" (*to sōtērion onoma bastasē*$_i$*s*).[174]

Is it possible that readers, already accustomed to nonstandard forms and spellings, would have simply engaged in an act of mental correction when they encountered this error, converting *onomon* to its closest cognate, *onoma* ("name")? If so, they would have been confronted with a scene remarkably reminiscent of Jesus' conflict with Judas in the *Toledot Yeshu*—a scene in which an antagonist seeks to deprive Jesus of the name in his possession (*to onoma autou*) by means of violence. Could it be that this scribal slip may have inadvertently played into some of the cultural assumptions we have already examined regarding Jesus and the power of the divine name? Guy Stroumsa, citing a range of late antique evidence—including Origen, Evagrius, Pseudo-Dionysius, Egyptian magical papyri, and Gnostic literature discovered at Nag Hammadi—has noted how the name of Jesus acquired "the magical virtues of the Divine Name in Judaism," and how Christ himself came to be understood as "the Name of the Father."[175] What I am suggesting is that this widespread notion of Christ as the bearer of the divine name in Christian circles could have served as a ready-made interpretive framework for medieval readings of the scribal error in Gs. Thus, Jesus' subsequent curse of the boy might have been understood as the ultimate comeuppance against his attacker, a confirming sign that the power thought to reside in the name was, indeed and in fact, embodied in the person of Jesus himself.

The second scribal curiosity comes from the medieval Syriac *Life of Mary* mentioned earlier, which preserves several chapters from the *Paidika* (chs. 4, 6–7, 11–16), as well as other stories drawn from the *Protevangelium of James* and the *Assumption of the Virgin*.[176] What is especially interesting is the episode the *Life*'s editor chose to place immediately before the main block of *Paidika* material. The story in question tells of an encounter between a three-year-old Jesus and a boy named Judah who was "afflicted with a devil that vexed him," and who, in his agitation, "would tear the flesh of his own arms and members."[177] When Judah came out to join Jesus and his playmates, the devil instantly departed from him "in the form of a mad dog."[178] In the end, we are informed that the boy would in fact grow up to be Jesus' traitorous disciple Judas Iscariot, the one who "bit our Lord": significantly, the place where Judas was said to have "bitten" (Syr. *n*^{e}*kat*) or "smitten" Jesus was the same place where "the Jews smote our Lord with a spear."[179] A similar episode concerning the three-year-old Judas is also found in the *Arabic Gospel of the Infancy*, where it has the analogous narrative function of introducing the main body of material drawn from the *Paidika*.[180]

How would this story of a childhood Jesus have resonated in later medieval contexts where Jewish counterhistories of Jesus like the *Toledot Yeshu* were circulating? I wonder whether later medieval Syriac- and Arabic-speaking Christians would have understood these images of savage dogs, of Judas tearing his flesh, and of Jews striking Jesus in the *Life of Mary* and the *Arabic Gospel of the Infancy* as parodies of Jewish polemics, as counter-counterhistories. I wonder whether, in the eyes of such readers, Jesus' boyhood exorcism of Judas would have been read as a story that effectively turned the tables on the *Toledot*. After all, in this Christian legend about Jesus' youth, the figure of Judas (along with the Jews who typologically take up his cause) does indeed become the subject of unsparing mockery: his kiss of betrayal is reimagined as the bite of a rabid dog, and he is recast as the would-be antagonist who can only tear at his own flesh in vain.

With these two final examples—a slip of the pen by a sloppy Greek copyist and a Syriac editor's insertion of a story lampooning a young Judas—I close this chapter on a speculative note. In each of these cases, we can see once again how the scribal reception of the *Paidika*, in intended and unintended ways, could potentially become entangled in the endless parries and ripostes of Jewish-Christian apologetics.[181] When read in proximity to one another, the *Toledot Yeshu* and the manuscript history of the *Paidika* attest to the way Jesus' childhood itself sometimes became a sharply contested site of memory, a point of heated polemical encounter for early medieval Jews and Christians.

7

Muslims and Christians

In the often fraught encounters between ancient Christians and Jews, the childhood of Jesus was a contested site of memory. For Jewish polemicists, his formative years marked the beginning of a wayward turn toward magic and misbehavior, while for Christian apologists and scribes it was a period that presaged a miraculous and redemptive adulthood and served as early proof of his identity as the Messiah. When it comes to early medieval cultural encounters between Muslims and Christians, however, the situation proves to be much different.

In the Arabic-speaking world, the *Paidika* stories sponsored a more collaborative and complementary history of reception. Without question, Muslim and Arabic Christian readers still read these infancy tales for their own distinctive theological and social purposes, and they occasionally used such stories to mark off religious difference. Nonetheless, their respective interpretations of Jesus' childhood were shaped by—and in turn helped shape—a shared sensibility, a common cultural heritage that was rooted in four specific areas of practice: (1) scriptural interpretation and commentary, (2) storytelling about prophetic miracles, (3) the production of scientific knowledge, and (4) ascetic discipline. Through these particular practices the Christ child became part of a shared cultural memory among Christians and Muslims in the Islamic Near East.

From Apocryphon to Scripture: The Miracle of the Birds in the Qur'ān and Qurānic Commentary

In early Christianity, the *Paidika* ultimately never found a place in emerging New Testament collections. In the fourth century, church leaders' opinions on the value of the infancy stories were mixed. While Epiphanius of Salamis could favorably cite the childhood miracles as proof that Jesus possessed the spirit as Messiah before the descent of the dove at his baptism,[1] John Chrysostom dismissed the *Paidika* as a collection of fabricated tales and literary inventions.[2] Later Christian writers in the sixth, seventh, and eighth centuries largely echoed Chrysostom's judgment. The *Decretum Gelasianum* and Maximus the Confessor both reassert the narrative's apocryphal character, highlighting its manifest divergences from Matthew, Mark, Luke, and John.[3] Anastasius of Sinai and the author of an anonymous list condemning Manichaean writings viewed the *Paidika* as unequivocally "false" and "demonic."[4]

And yet, even as Christian leaders were busy ghettoizing the *Paidika* as a dubious, extracanonical work, the rise of Islam in the seventh century witnessed a significant shift in the reception of at least one of the childhood miracles of Jesus. Cited twice in the revelatory text of the Qur'ān, the story of the Messiah's miracle of bringing the clay birds to life attained *scriptural* authority for Muslim readers. The first citation appears in Sura 3:49, where Jesus, identified as the "messenger [*rasūl*] to the children of Israel," gives personal witness to his childhood deed: "Lo! I have come to you with a sign from your Lord. Lo! I create for you from clay something like the form of birds and I blow into it and it becomes birds by God's leave. And I heal the blind from birth and the leper and I bring the dead to life by God's leave. And I declare to you what you eat and what you store up in your houses. Surely in that there is a sign for you if you are believers."[5] The second Qur'ānic reference, Sura 5:110, has the divine voice testify to Jesus' wonder-working during his infancy. God addresses Jesus directly: "O Jesus Son of Mary remember my favor to you and your mother, how I strengthened you with the Holy Spirit so that you spoke to mankind when you were in the cradle and when you were of mature age. [Remember] when I taught you the Scripture, Wisdom, the Torah and the Gospel and when you created from clay something resembling the form of birds by My leave and when you blew into it and it became birds by My leave and you healed the blind from birth and the leper by My leave and brought forth the dead by My leave."[6] In each case, Jesus' miracle involving the birds is set alongside his acts of healing the sick and raising the dead as signs of God's favor given to believers. The details largely correspond to the *Paidika* account, with one exception: instead of clapping his hands and then speaking to the birds as a means of animating them, here he brings them to life with his breath.[7]

The divergence in detail suggests that during the early Islamic period the story may have been circulating in the Arabian Peninsula through practices of oral storytelling in which such adaptations were standard procedure. The eminent Islamic historian John Wansbrough has marked the repetition of tales in the Qur'ān as a sign of orality—as "the product of an organic development from originally independent traditions during a long period of transmission."[8] Alternatively, the Qur'ān may have also relied on a written text in a variant form (or a combination of oral and written sources), perhaps deriving from a Syro-Aramaic milieu.[9] In any case, the Qur'ān "seems to expect prior knowledge of the story on the part of the hearers,"[10] and Jesus' gesture of breathing life into an inanimate clay form undoubtedly reflects the way the *Paidika* story was being reread intertextually in relation to the well-known story of Adam's creation in Genesis 2:7, where God "formed man from the dust of the ground and breathed into his nostrils the breath of life; and the man became a living being." As we shall see, this textual memory of Genesis would raise a theological problem for later Muslim commentators—one related to the question of divine agency—that they felt compelled to address and resolve.

Over the past fifty years, a number of scholars engaged in critical study of the Qur'ān and its early transmission, redaction, and standardization have noted evidence for significant cultural interaction between the early followers of Muḥammad and local communities of Jews and Christians. Fred Donner has characterized earliest Islam as something of an ecumenical "believers' movement" that sought to bring other groups with similar monotheistic views together for a common purpose.[11] More recently, in *The Bible in Arabic,* Sidney Griffith has written about the "intertwining" of late ancient Christian and early Islamic scriptural and interpretive traditions (in both oral and written forms).[12] In the context of such interreligious exchange, it should not be surprising to see in the Qur'ān evidence for early Muslims' acquaintance with *Paidika* traditions, along with a range of biblical texts, including the creation account in Genesis and miracle stories from the New Testament.

With its incorporation into the Qur'ān, the story of Jesus and the birds quickly became the subject of detailed commentary by Muslim interpreters, who focused especially on three aspects of the text: (1) the figure of the birds themselves, (2) Jesus' action of "creating" them from clay and bringing them to life, and (3) the emphasis on the fact that Jesus did this "by God's leave."[13]

Our oldest surviving example of this genre of Qur'ānic commentary is an early tenth-century compendium by Abū Ja'far Muḥammad ibn Jarīr al-Ṭabarī (d. 922) from Tabaristan, Persia.[14] In his commentary on Sura 3:49, Ṭabarī focuses primarily on the figure of the birds, and more specifically on the question of how many birds Jesus created. In the Qur'ān, the word in question is *ṭayr,* a noun form that can be read either as singular or as a collective reference to a plural group. Ṭabarī (along with most other early interpreters) understood the term to refer to multiple "birds," but in his commentary he reports on a reader in the Ḥijāz (western Arabia) who took the form as *ṭā'ir* ("bird, flying thing"), an unequivocal singular derived from the same root.[15] In the Arabic of the Qur'ān, long vowels (such as the *alif* in the word *ṭā'ir*) sometimes are not written out, occasionally resulting in divergent interpretations of specific word forms.[16] This variant reading of the term as singular may also have been motivated by a reader's attempt to reconcile the form of *ṭayr* with the noun that precedes it and with which it stands in relationship, *hay'a* ("form, configuration")—thus, "the form of a bird" rather than "the form of birds."[17]

Ṭabarī goes on to cite two earlier authoritative commentators who support this singular reading, albeit with different explanations of the text.[18] The first account, attributed to Ibn Isḥāq (d. 768), situates the story at an "elementary school" (another sign of engagement with *Paidika* traditions) and retells the story with Jesus asking his schoolmates if they would like him to make "a bird (*ṭā'ir*) . . . from this clay." After he makes "the form of a bird" (*hay'at al-ṭā'ir*) and causes it to fly off with the command, "Be a bird [*ṭā'ir,* lit. "flying thing"] by God's leave," the boys report this event to their teachers and Jesus' family is forced to leave town with Mary and her child riding on a donkey.[19]

The second account, attributed to Ibn Jurayj (d. 767 or 768) is even more idiosyncratic. Jesus first asks what kind of "flying thing" (*ṭā'ir*) was hardest to create. When he is told that the hardest was a "bat" (*khuffāsh*) because it consisted of nothing but flesh, Jesus then goes ahead and creates one (the Arabic simply says, "he did it").[20] Here, Ṭabarī offers us a rare glimpse of the way that this particular story from the *Paidika,* remembered and retold in the Qur'ān, ended up being contested (and thereby further transformed) by early Islamic interpreters. In the end, Ṭabarī himself considers the plural reading preferable, and not only because of the grammar involved. For him, the act of creating multiple birds simply made for a much more impressive miracle, worthy of Jesus' prophetic status.[21]

Later commentators on Suras 3:49 and 5:110 from the twelfth through the fourteenth centuries continued to discuss not only the number and kind of flying creatures brought to life through Jesus' miracle but also their direction of flight and ultimate fate. The Persian commentator Rāzī (d. 1209) relates the tradition that Jesus created a bat that "flew between heaven and earth" after Jesus had brought it to life. Rāzī proceeds to report the disputed opinion of Wahb ibn Munabbih (d. 729) that "while it was flying people kept their eyes on it but when it had disappeared from view it dropped down dead."[22] A few decades later, Ibn 'Arabī (1165–1240) presented his own allegorical interpretation of the story: according to him, the birds took off "in the direction of Jerusalem" as a symbol for "a simple and perfect soul" that withdraws from the world and flies toward its holy destination "with wings of love."[23] In Ibn 'Arabī, one observes how a Qur'ānic story connected with the infancy of Jesus could be redeployed in service to Ṣūfī asceticism, a topic to which I return later in this chapter.

Aside from the bird(s)—or bat, depending on your pleasure—two other textual details especially attracted the attention of later Qur'ānic commentators: the verb "create" (*khalaqa*) and the phrase "by God's leave" (*bi-idhnillāh*), which were each used to describe or qualify Jesus' actions in the story. The two details were related in the minds of Muslim interpreters. First, since the act of creation was typically understood as an exclusively divine prerogative, its attribution to Jesus raised potential theological problems for those who would reject Christian claims concerning Jesus' divinity. Second, as a corollary to the first concern, the phrase "by God's leave" came to be understood as an attempt within the Qur'ān to safeguard divine agency and guard against Christian interpretations of Jesus as God incarnate.

Ṭabarī makes no explicit mention of either of these issues, but later Muslim commentators address them head-on. The first to do so was Zamakhsharī, an early twelfth-century Mu'tazilite theologian who was born in Khwārezmia but who lived most of his life in Bukhāra, Samarkand, and Baghdad. Zamakhsharī glosses the verb *khalaqa* ("to create") with another verb, *qaddara*, which means "to determine" or "to make in proportion." Thus, in his eyes, Jesus' action in the Qur'ān should not be confused with a creation ex nihilo but instead should be understood as an act of "fashioning."[24] A contemporary of Zamakhsharī, the Shī'ī scholar Ṭabrisī, offers a similar explanation for the verb, "to create," and then adds a comment on the phrase "by my [i.e., God's] leave" in Sura 5:110: "[The Qur'ān] calls it a 'creation' [*khalq*] because he [Jesus] was making it in proportion [*kāna yuqaddiruhu*], and its statement 'by my leave' [*bi-idhnī*] means, 'You do this by my leave [*idhnī*] and by my decree [*amrī*].' "[25] Later Ṭabrisī goes on to underscore the role of divine agency in this transaction to an even greater extent when he emphasizes that "it became a bird 'by God's leave'—that is, through his decree and will, and not through the action of the Messiah."[26]

Thirteenth- and fourteenth-century Qur'ānic commentators continued along the same lines while expanding the scope of their observations. In his *Great*

Commentary (*al-Tafsīr al-kabīr*), Rāzī provides other acceptable synonyms for the verb *khalaqa* as it was applied to Jesus: it had the meaning not only of *taqdīr* ("to determine") but also of *taswiya* ("to arrange, make regular") and *taṣwīr* ("to fashion, represent).[27]

On the one hand, such interpretations served as an implicit argument against the theology of Arab Christians who, according to Muḥammad's biographer, already were arguing in the ninth century "that (Jesus) is God because he used to raise the dead, heal the sick, declare the unseen, and make clay birds and then breathe into them that they flew away."[28] On the other hand, the fact that the verb *khalaqa* could describe such everyday human actions also seems to have given some Muslim interpreters (including Rāzī) considerable pause about the appropriateness of its use to describe God's activity as Creator. Rāzī reports on a certain Abū 'Abd Allāh al-Baṣrī (d. 970), who advocated that, on this account, the term *al-Khāliq* ("the Creator") should no longer be used as one of the exclusive names for God.[29] His view, however, did not represent a widespread consensus: later commentators such as Ibn Kathīr worked to retain this theological use of the term, arguing quite reasonably that the term could in fact be used in more than one sense.[30]

In his commentary on the phrase "by God's leave," Rāzī observed a subtle difference between the two Qur'ānic accounts of the bird miracle.[31] In 3:49 the phrase is applied only to Jesus' creation of birds out of clay forms, and Rāzī explains that this was done through God's agency—specifically "through God's causing it to exist and his creation of it" (*bi takwīn illāhi wa takhlīqihi*).[32] In 5:110, however, the Qur'ān applies the phrase "by my [i.e., God's] leave" both to Jesus' act of forming the clay birds and to his subsequent act of bringing them to life.[33] For Rāzī, the difference in detail does not change the underlying message: each act is ultimately grounded in the creative power of God. Thus, for example, the breath Jesus breathed into the clay had no special quality in and of itself; rather it was God who was able to create life through that breath "by his power" (*bi-qudratihi*).[34] These insights were echoed in the commentaries of Bayḍāwī and Ibn Kathīr, active in Persia and Syria during the thirteenth century and the fourteenth, respectively.[35]

In this context, the miracle story of Jesus and the birds, transformed and transmitted via Qur'ānic revelation, came to be read as a statement on God's agency in and through the life of Jesus as prophet and Messiah. The breath Jesus breathes into the clay birds reminds Rāzī of the breath—the "pure spirit" (*rūḥ maḥḍ*)—Gabriel breathed into Mary at Jesus' own virginal conception.[36] In the hands of interpreters like Ibn Kathīr, the phrase "by God's leave" came to be applied to Jesus' entire earthly mission insofar as it signaled the fact that he was a prophet sent by God.[37] In this way, the practice of Qur'ānic commentary became a site of memory for recalling this tale from Jesus' childhood as a "sign" (*āya*) of his privileged status as God's messenger (*rasūl*).[38]

Retellings: The Multiplication of Miracle Stories in the Arabic Gospel of the Infancy

During the early Islamic period, point-by-point commentary on Qur'ānic language and theology was not the only mode for the reception of *Paidika* traditions. Jesus' childhood deeds also became the subject for renarration. One sees hints of this in Ṭabarī's reporting of the following *ḥadīth* tradition, which he attributes to Muḥammad's early biographer Ibn Isḥāq:

> Jesus, the blessings of God be upon him, was sitting one day with the boys from the elementary school. He took clay and then said, "Shall I make a bird for you from this clay?" They said, "Can you do that?" He replied, "Yes, by the leave of my Lord." Then he prepared it and when he had made it in the form of a bird he blew into it. Then he said, "Become a bird by the leave of my Lord." So it flew out between the palms of his hands. The boys went off and mentioned that business of his to their teacher and divulged it to the people. Jesus grew and the Children of Israel had in mind to do away with him. So when his mother feared for him she bore him on a little donkey of hers and went off as a fugitive with him.[39]

Most noteworthy about Ṭabarī's account is the narrative setting given for the story: Jesus' miracle of blowing into the form of a bird and bringing it to life takes place in an elementary school, in the presence of his classmates and their teacher. While Jesus' act of breathing into the clay derives from Suras 3:49 and 5:110 in the Qur'ān, it is clear that this *ḥadīth* does not simply adhere to the details of the Qur'ānic account. Instead, there is evidence that the commentator (whether Ṭabarī himself or one of the earlier chain of transmitters) has conflated two stories from the early Christian *Paidika* tradition. Here, the bird and teacher tales come together, combined in an act of creative retelling. This suggests at least some kind of loose dependence on the *Paidika* or one of its variants. Early Muslim knowledge of such stories about Jesus' childhood would have been mediated not only through recitations of the Qur'ān but also through contact with Christian texts and their oral performance, whether in Syriac or in Arabic.[40] Indeed, such cultural and textual contact is attested by one Muslim writer, the thirteenth-century Egyptian jurist Qarāfī, who identifies the "gospel of the childhood" (*injīl al-ṣubūwa*) as the "fifth gospel" (*al-injīl al-khāmis*) of the Christians. In citing the text, Qarāfī observes that "in it are remembered [*dhukira*] the things that originated from

Christ in his state of infancy [*ṭufūla*], . . . and in it there are things added and things omitted."[41]

Syriac and Arabic manuscripts amply attest to the variability of the *Paidika* traditions recalled by Qarāfī. In Syriac, the *Paidika* was transmitted in a variety of forms, most often in narrative compilations that incorporated material also from the *Protevangelium of James* and the *Assumption of the Virgin.*[42] The two oldest surviving Syriac copies date to the fifth and sixth centuries and provide some of our earliest and best readings of the text, although both copies suffer from lacunae.[43] Later, the *Paidika* collection of stories came to be transmitted with—and sometimes included as a constituent component of—medieval versions of the *Life of Mary,* a work that integrated episodes on the Holy Family's flight to Egypt with assorted additional stories about Jesus' childhood miracles.[44]

A single manuscript copy of the *Paidika* translated into Arabic is preserved in the Biblioteca Ambrosiana in Milan.[45] Characterized by its adherence to a short text form matching that of the Syriac, the text abbreviates some chapters (chs. 6–7) and completely omits others, most notably the story of Jesus sowing wheat with his father (ch. 11), the third school episode (ch. 14), and the tale of Jesus with the teachers in the Temple (ch. 17).[46] At the same time, however, it also adds two new miracle accounts into the mix. One narrates a tale in which Jesus plays a game of hide-and-seek with other children and ends up turning them into pigs, monkeys, and wolves.[47] The other tells the story of Jesus' apprenticeship to a dyer of cloth (Jesus throws all the material into the same vat, but the pieces wondrously come out in different colors).[48]

This Arabic translation of the *Paidika* had a cultural impact that went beyond Christian circles. Indeed, these new stories about the Christ child's miraculous proclivities quickly entered Muslim cultural memory as well: they were picked up and incorporated into narratives about the deeds of the Islamic prophets, among whom Jesus was especially honored.[49] One of the earliest examples of this narrative genre was Tha'labī's *Tales of the Prophets* (*Qiṣaṣ al-anbiyā'*). In that eleventh-century work, Tha'labī cites both the hide-and-seek and dye-shop stories from the Arabic *Paidika,* thereby supplying us with definitive evidence that the work was already in circulation at that time.

First, Tha'labī tells the tale about Jesus seeking his friends, who were hiding in their homes because they feared him as a "magician." When he inquired after them, their parents insisted that they were not there and that only "swine" were inside. According to Tha'labī, the words that Jesus uttered in response—"So shall they be"—had an immediate result: "When the door was opened upon them, lo, they were swine indeed."[50] Shortly thereafter,

Tha'labī also relates the story of how Jesus produced fabrics of many colors from a single dye, a miracle that for him testifies to the "all-powerful" and "all-knowing" God.[51]

In addition to the Arabic translation of the *Paidika,* stories about the young Jesus were incorporated into longer, composite narratives similar in format to the above-mentioned Syriac *Life of Mary.* Such was the case with the *Arabic Gospel of the Infancy* (*AGI*), which combined elements from the *Protevangelium of James* (*AGI* 1–10), legends associated with the Holy Family's flight to Egypt (*AGI* 11–35), and stories from the *Paidika* mixed with assorted other childhood tales (*AGI* 36–53).[52] As in the case of the *Paidika* translated into Arabic, the more expansive *AGI* also was known to Muslim readers. One such reader was Kisā'ī, the famous eleventh- or twelfth-century compiler of prophetic traditions. After recounting Jesus' school lesson with one of his teachers, Kisā'ī cites the tale of Jesus and the dyer, a story found in the *AGI.* As in the case of Tha'labī, so too in Kisā'ī: Jesus' miraculous action comes with a theological catch. The Christ child's instruction to the dyer takes the form of the Islamic *shahāda* (the profession of faith), recast in distinctively Christian terms: "Say there is no god but God and that I, Jesus, am His messenger, and you will take out each garment in whatever color you want."[53]

The dissemination of the *AGI* would have been enabled of course by the copying of manuscripts, and indeed three copies of the work are preserved in European libraries. Only one of these is complete: an undated Arabic text at the Bodleian in Oxford.[54] The second and third copies are both fragmentary. One of them dates to the year 1299 and is preserved at the Biblioteca Laurenziana in Florence.[55] Unfortunately, it lacks several important stories, including Jesus' miracle of carrying water in his cloak, his enlivening of the twelve clay birds, his curse of the boy who strikes his shoulder, his two alphabetic lessons in the classroom, and his dialogue with the teachers in the Temple.[56] Because of this, the fragmentary Florence manuscript is of limited value for tracing the reception of the three *Paidika* story units or types I have chosen to highlight in this book. The third version of the *AGI* is in Garshuni (Arabic written in Syriac script) and is preserved in the Vatican Library.[57] It breaks off even earlier than the Florence text,[58] but it is followed immediately in the same manuscript by a Syriac version of the *Paidika,* which includes many (although not all) of the remaining infancy episodes found in the Oxford text. This curious juxtaposition of the *AGI* and the Syriac *Paidika* in a single manuscript may actually provide insight into the way the former took shape, probably via a combination of mix-and-matchable sources, and probably in a bilingual provenance in which both Syriac and Arabic were spoken.[59]

External evidence indicates that certain traditions associated with the *AGI* were circulating in Syria in the ninth century. Around the year 850 CE, Isho'dad of Merv, the bishop of Hadatha, cites a Zoroastrian or Magian prophecy about the virgin birth in his *Commentary on Matthew*: the same prophecy is mentioned in the opening lines of the *AGI* manuscript in Florence, although the relationship (if any) between the two texts is unclear.[60] As I show later in this chapter, however, internal evidence related to the closing chapters of the Oxford text probably suggests a date of written composition sometime between the ninth and the eleventh century, most likely in a Syrian or Mesopotamian provenance.[61] For my analysis and translation of the *AGI* I shall primarily use the complete Oxford version (which I have examined in person), while supplying cross-references to the Florence and Vatican versions in footnotes when appropriate.

The *Paidika* material in the Oxford *AGI* is concentrated toward the end of the work, in chapters 36–53 (translated in Appendix B). The contents of this section are organized as follows:

Ch. 36	Jesus brings clay animals and birds to life
Ch. 37	Jesus creates cloths of many colors in a dyer's shop
Ch. 38	Jesus stretches the wood for doors, pails, beds, and chests (cf. *Paidika* 12)
Ch. 39	Jesus stretches wood for a king's throne
Ch. 40	Jesus turns boys into goats while playing hide-and-seek
Ch. 41	Jesus and his friends playact a king and his court
Ch. 42	Jesus heals a serpent's bite and kills the serpent
Ch. 43	Jesus heals his brother James from a snakebite (cf. *Paidika* 15)
Ch. 44	Jesus raises a boy who had fallen off a roof (cf. *Paidika* 9)
Ch. 45	Jesus carries water from a well in his handkerchief (cf. *Paidika* 10)
Ch. 46	Jesus brings twelve clay sparrows to life by pools of water (cf. *Paidika* 2–3)
Ch. 47	Jesus curses a boy who strikes his shoulder (cf. *Paidika* 4)
Ch. 48	Jesus attends the school with his first teacher, Zacchaeus (cf. *Paidika* 6)
Ch. 49	Jesus attends school with a second (anonymous) teacher (cf. *Paidika* 13)
Ch. 50–53	Jesus talks with the teachers in the Temple (cf. *Paidika* 17)

Two observations on the organization of this material. First, the order of the stories has been rearranged in comparison with earlier versions of the *Paidika*. The tales of Jesus' miracles involving carpentry, healings, raising the dead, and carrying water have been displaced from their original contexts and moved forward in the sequence, while the core stories that have especially occupied our attention in this book—the miracle of the birds, the curse of the boy who strikes Jesus' shoulder, and two of the teacher episodes plus Jesus' visit to the Temple—are clustered together at the very end of the narrative. Second, as in the Syriac *Life of Mary* and in the Arabic *Paidika* discussed above, the *AGI* includes several stories not found in earlier *Paidika* collections: the aforementioned scene in which Jesus produces fabrics of many colors from a single dye,[62] an adapted version of the hide-and-seek tale in which he turns his friends into baby goats,[63] and another story in which he and his playmates engage in role-play, taking on the parts of a king and his royal court.[64]

In the *AGI,* one finds as well the duplication of certain stories, most notably Jesus' repeated miracles involving birds, carpentry, and serpents. The pattern of replication and revision is also found in the Syriac *Life of Mary.* While this may be an indication of orality, it is also possible that the *Paidika* material was incorporated during an earlier stage of written transmission.[65] In the Oxford text, the doubled miracles involving carpentry and the healing of snakebites are presented together in pairs. Thus, chapter 38 presents an adapted version of Jesus' act of bed stretching from *Paidika* 12 (here, he does this trick with wooden doors, pails, and chests as well),[66] and then chapter 39 follows with a story about how Jesus helped Joseph stretch the wood of a king's throne to its proper dimensions.[67] Likewise, chapters 42 and 43 are matched in theme. In chapter 42, Jesus heals a boy—identified later as Simon the Canaanite (aka "the Zealot")—from the bite of a serpent. He does so not by breathing on the wound but by commanding the serpent to suck out the venom, and after this Jesus summarily curses the reptile and it perishes.[68] Chapter 43 then follows with the original story from *Paidika* 15 about Jesus' healing of his brother James from the poison of a viper (which also meets its demise in the end).[69]

Jesus' bird miracle is also duplicated, although the two versions of the tale are not paired in direct sequence. Instead, they form something of a narrative *inclusio,* bracketing (and thereby highlighting) the chapters in which these doubled miracles are clustered. Chapter 36 effectively introduces the section of text containing material drawn from the *Paidika.* It presents the story of Jesus playing in the clay with his friends at the age of seven. In this case, however, it is not just Jesus making the figures of sparrows: all of the children mold "forms like donkeys, cattle, birds, and other animals." When the other boys ask him about his identity as "the son of the Creator," Jesus commands the animals to walk: "And right then [lit. "in that hour"] they began to prance around, and then when he had given them permission, they returned [to their places]. He had made [them] in the form of birds and sparrows. When he ordered them to fly, they flew; and when he ordered them to stand still, they stood still on his hand. He fed them and they ate, and he gave them water and they drank."[70] Ten chapters later, in *AGI* 46, the miracle is recapitulated in a retelling of *Paidika* 2–3, the story of Jesus' enlivening of the twelve sparrows by the stream.[71] For readers attentive to such literary signs, the duplication of this well-known story type—and its use as an *inclusio* to frame the other doubled miracle accounts—would have hinted at the infinite multiplication of Jesus' wondrous deeds as a child. Even the expansive account in the *AGI* is simply the tip of the iceberg, a small selection from a larger body of "miracles, mysteries, and secrets" hidden from public view and too numerous to count.[72]

Jesus and the Teachers in the Temple in the Arabic Gospel of the Infancy

We have already seen in this chapter how one story from the *Paidika*—Jesus' miracle of giving life to the birds—took on a scriptural status in early Islam through its inclusion (twice) in the text of the Qur'ān. In the centuries that followed, the significance and authority of the miracle were repeatedly pressed home by Qur'ānic commentators—from Ṭabarī in the tenth century to Ibn Kathīr in the fourteenth—who drew out its specific theological implications for Islamic teaching. We have also observed the way stories about the Christ child were creatively renarrated in Arabic-speaking settings, a phenomenon attested in the *Arabic Gospel of the Infancy,* as well as in Muslim *Tales of the Prophets*. In each context, literary adaptation and duplication were constructive memory practices through which the repertoire of the Christ child was enhanced and expanded.

As we saw in the story about Jesus and the birds, such memory practices involved an interesting combination of reuse and reinvention. Similar processes are at work in the final episode of the *AGI,* the tale of Jesus' encounter with the teachers in the Jerusalem Temple. This scriptural story about Jesus at the age of twelve is worth more detailed study, as it will demonstrate vividly how the production of the image of the Christ child was reshaped in an Arabic-speaking cultural milieu.[73]

Originally part of the first-century Gospel of Luke (2:41–52), the story about Jesus and the teachers in the Temple was adopted early on, in parts almost verbatim, as the closing chapter of the Greek *Paidika*. It largely retained the same form and function in Syriac translation.[74] The basic plot in each version runs as follows. Unbeknownst to his parents, Jesus stays behind in the Temple at the end of the Passover festival. When Mary and Joseph discover on their way home that Jesus is missing, they return to Jerusalem to find him still engaged in conversation with the teachers in the Temple. Impressed with the boy's facility in explaining the finer points of the law and prophets, the teachers tell Mary she is blessed for having such a son.

In the Arabic version, however, the story is significantly expanded, with the addition of new details about the specific content of Jesus' knowledge. As I shall show, these details were carefully calibrated for a readership acquainted with (and perhaps even well versed in) medieval Arabic science and philosophy. Such scholarly disciplines and practices served as crucial cultural touchstones—and mechanisms of social memory—for the transmission of traditions about Jesus' childhood.

In the *AGI,* the story of Jesus and the teachers in the Temple at first seems to adhere to the same general plot as in the original Lukan version and its early apocryphal retellings. In chapter 50, Jesus stays behind to converse with "the scribes, elders, and scholars of the sons of Israel," and he dumbfounds them with his probing questions and insightful elucidation of "the books, the law, the commandments, the wise sayings, and the mysteries that were in the books of the prophets."[75] Already, however, extra details in the dialogue crop up—details not present in Luke or in the Greek, Latin, and Syriac versions of the *Paidika*—especially the content of Jesus' scriptural exegesis.

It is in chapters 51 and 52 where one finds the major blocks of new, interpolated narrative material. Two teachers are singled out from the crowd gathered around Jesus: "one skilled in astronomy"[76] and another "learned in natural medicine."[77] Each of these scholars opens a dialogue with Jesus by asking the precocious twelve-year-old whether he had studied the requisite curriculum in the scientific discipline. The astronomer asks him whether he had done readings in "astronomical science" (*'ilm al-hay'a*).[78] The physician asks him whether he had studied "medical science" (*'ilm al-ṭibb*).[79] And in each case, Jesus responds to this line of questioning by demonstrating his mastery of technical terminology in the field.

Here, the nature of Jesus' language is noteworthy. His terminology corresponds to the scientific discourse that became current during the renowned Arabic translation movement, which flourished during the eighth, ninth, and tenth centuries CE under the patronage of 'Abbāsid rulers, beginning with the second caliph al-Manṣūr (754–775 CE) and continuing with his successors.[80] Centered in Baghdad but with a much wider geographical impact, the translation movement enabled the preservation and transmission of Greek (and Sasanian) philosophical and scientific knowledge into Arabic linguistic parlance.

Participating side by side in this movement were Muslim and Christian scholars who not only were highly trained in textual study but also became skilled practitioners in applied sciences such as astronomy and medicine. These translators did the yeoman's work of searching out and collecting the writings of Greek authors such as Aristotle in philosophy, Euclid in geometry, Ptolemy in astronomy, and Galen in medicine, and in developing a technical vocabulary in Syriac and Arabic adequate to the task of producing translations that made Greek cultural knowledge accessible to non-Greek-speaking communities living under Islamic rule. Once translated into Arabic, the body of scientific knowledge did not remain static. In fact, many of the translators pursued original research that resulted in revolutionary advances beyond Greek theory and practice.[81] In addition, they began producing handbook summaries for students, and in this way Greek and Arabic scientific knowledge became integrated into school curricula.

In the *AGI,* one finds characteristic vocabulary of such Arabic translators and scientists placed in the mouth of the young Jesus as he speaks with the teachers in the Temple. When the first question to Jesus is posed by "one skilled in astronomy [lit. "the science of the spheres"]" (*ḥakīm māhir fī ʿilm al-aflāk*), Jesus responds by explaining "the number of the spheres [*ʿadad al-aflāk*], and of the celestial bodies [*al-ajrām*]; their natures (*ṭabāʾiʿ*), operations (*afʿāl*), and opposition (*muqābala*); their division into thirds (*tathlīth*), fourths (*tarbīʿ*), and sixths (*tasdīs*); their direct and retrograde course (*istiqāmatuhā wa rujūʿuhā*); their (division into) seconds (*daqāiʿq*) and smaller increments (*shaʿāʾir*); and other things that the intellect cannot grasp."[82] This is the language of the Arabic astronomical handbooks.

Such astronomical handbooks could take different forms. One type was called a *zīj*. Derived from Indian and Greek precedents,[83] a *zīj* most often consisted of tables or charts with accompanying instructions for their use in calculating the positions of stars, planets, and the moon, and thus also for timekeeping within the Islamic world. The *zīj* type of handbook is usually classified under the rubric "mathematical astronomy."[84]

Another type, the *kitab al-hayʾa*—a "book on [astronomical] configuration"—was more theoretical in orientation. It concerned itself with (in the words of a thirteenth-century Egyptian encyclopedist) "the situations of the lower and upper simple bodies, their forms, their positions, their magnitudes, the distances between them, the motions of the orbs and the planets and their amounts . . . [and] their quantities, positions, and inherent motions."[85] The eighth, ninth, and tenth centuries witnessed the emergence and systemization of a corresponding discipline called *ʿilm al-hayʾa,* "the science of [astronomical] configuration." One of the earliest Arabic astronomers was Yaʿqūb ibn Ṭāriq, active during the reign of the ʿAbbasid caliph al-Manṣūr (754–775 CE). Yaʿqūb produced astronomical handbooks of both the *zīj* and the *hayʾa* type, the latter published under the title *The Structure of the Celestial*

Spheres (*Tarkīb al-aflāk*).[86] Other prominent Muslim authors who published astronomical treatises during this period include: Ibn Kathīr al-Farghānī, who wrote *A Comprehensive Collection on the Science of the Celestial Sphere* (*Jawāmiʿ ʿilm al-falak*), also known as his *Book on Astronomical Configuration* (*Kitāb al-hayʾa*); Sahl ibn Bishr, who wrote a treatise on astronomy and mathematics (*Kitāb al-hayʾa wa-ʿilm al-ḥisāb*); ʿUṭārid ibn Muḥammad, author of a *Book on the Structure of the Celestial Spheres* (*Kitāb tarkīb al-aflāk*); Abū Maʿshar (d. 886), author of a *Book on the Configuration of the Celestial Sphere* (*Kitāb hayʾat al-falak*); and Abū Bakr al-Rāzī (d. 925), who composed a *Book on the Configuration of the Cosmos* (*Kitāb hayʾat al-ʿālam*).[87] To this list may be added the famous polymath al-Kindī and the three sons of the astronomer Mūsa ibn-Shākir, known collectively as the Banū Mūsā (d. 873), whose writings included treatises on astronomy, astrology, mathematics, geometry, and mechanics.[88]

One of the most productive astronomical scientists and authors of the time was in fact a Melkite Christian named Qusṭā ibn Lūqā (820–912). A native speaker of Greek from the town of Baalbek (now in modern Lebanon), Qusṭā mastered Syriac and Arabic at a young age and moved to Baghdad, where he became a leading figure in the translation movement and pursued his own scientific pursuits. In the 860s, he was commissioned by the caliph Aḥmad ibn al-Muʿtaṣim to translate Theodosius's *Spherics* (*Kitāb al-ukar*) and Autolycus's *Rising and Setting (of the Fixed Stars)* (*Kitāb al-ṭulūʿ wa al-ghurūb*).[89] In addition, he also produced at least three original astronomical treatises, including an *Introduction* (*Madkhal*), a treatise *On the Configuration of the Spheres* (*Hayʾat al-aflāk*), and a *Book on the Use of the Celestial Globe* (*Kitāb al-ʿamal bi-l-kura al-nujūmiyya*).[90] The second of these original works represents perhaps our earliest extant handbook of theoretical astronomy in the *hayʾa* tradition.[91]

The *Arabic Gospel of the Infancy*'s account of Jesus' teaching in the Temple must be analyzed in relation to the *hayʾa* genre of astronomical literature. When Jesus is asked whether he was well read in "astronomical science" (*ʿilm al-hayʾa*), and when he answers by explicating "the number of the spheres (*ʿadad al-aflāk*), and of the celestial bodies (*al-ajrām*); their natures (*ṭabāʾiʿ*), operations (*afʿāl*), and opposition (*muqābala*)," educated Arabic readers would have recognized this scientific discourse as belonging to such handbooks.

To get a sense of the way the terminology in chapter 51 of the *AGI* evokes the scientific discourse of *ʿilm al-hayʾa,* let us draw some comparisons to certain details found in two astronomical synopses. The first is the aforementioned *Book on the Use of the Celestial Globe* (*Kitāb al-ʿamal bi-l-kura al-nujūmiyya*) by Qusṭā ibn Lūqā. The second is a chapter in *The Keys of the*

Sciences (*Mafātīḥ al-ʿulūm*), written in the late tenth-century (ca. 975–991 CE) by the Muslim scientist Abū ʿAbd Allāh Muḥammad ibn Aḥmad al-Khwārizmī.[92] Khwārizmī's work represents an example of how astronomical knowledge became incorporated into larger compendia of the sciences that summarized and classified the state of individual fields of knowledge. *The Keys of the Sciences* is divided into two parts—the first on Islamic sciences such as jurisprudence (*al-fiqh*), theological discourse (*al-kalām*), and grammar (*al-naḥw*); and the second on foreign sciences such as philosophy (*al-falsafa*), logic (*al-manṭiq*), medicine (*al-ṭibb*), mathematics (*al-ʿadad*), and astronomy (*ʿilm al-nujūm*). In each chapter, the author presents and discusses a vocabulary of scientific terms employed in the field under consideration.

From our survey of *hay'a* texts above, we can already see how Jesus' discourse on "the spheres" (*al-aflāk*) evoked the language commonly featured in the titles of several scientific handbooks during this period. Indeed, in some sources, Qusṭā ibn Lūqā's *Book on the Use of the Celestial Globe* is actually referred to as the *Book of the Use of the Spherical Globe* (*Kitāb al-ʿamal bi-l-kura al-falakiyya*),[93] and this alternative designation fairly reflects its main thematic emphasis. Qusṭā regularly uses the term *falak* or its plural form *aflāk* to describe the lines drawn upon the globe—the "circles" that mark the ecliptic, the equator, the meridian, and the horizon.[94] In discussing the circle (*falak*) of the ecliptic, for example, he divides it into "360 equal parts," and then into further divisions, which he associates with the "hours" (*sāʿāt*) and "minutes" (*daqā'iq*) by which the increments of the globe's rotation (and the sun's revolution) are measured.[95] This conventional geometrical and astrological language is echoed by Jesus in *AGI* 51 when he speaks of the "minutes" (*daqā'iq*) and the other divisions of the *aflāk* (spheres, circles, or orbits).[96] It also finds articulation in Khwārazmī's encyclopedic *Keys of the Sciences,* where he centers his attention on "the circle [or sphere] of the ecliptic" (*falak al-burūj*), which he identifies as "the circle [*al-aflāk*] that the sun traces in its path from the east to the west in one year."[97] Dividing each circle into "twelve sections" to correspond to the signs of the zodiac (also labeled as *al-burūj* in Arabic), he subdivides each section further into thirty degrees (*darajāt*), each degree into sixty minutes (*daqā'iq*), and so on into progressively smaller divisions measured by thirds, fourths, fifths, tenths, elevenths, and on to infinity.[98]

Other linguistic nuances of Jesus' speech in the Temple also resonate with the astronomical writings of Qusṭā ibn Lūqā and Khwārizmī. Here, three more examples will suffice. First, the young Jesus speaks of the "opposition" (*al-muqābala*) of celestial bodies. This is also a concern of Qusṭā ibn Lūqā, although he uses slightly different vocabulary to describe it. In chapter 4 of his *Book on the Use of the Celestial Globe,* he writes that "the earth, by virtue of being spherical [*kuriyya*] and in the middle of the heaven, has its every point lying opposite [*sāmata*] a point of heaven; and every one of its circles [*falak*] which are in heaven has a location of [the earth] lying opposite it. And with respect to the earth, the place that is opposite the line of the equator [*ma'addil al-nahār;* lit. "equalizer of the day"] in heaven is called the line of the equator [*al-istiwā'*]."[99] The Arabic verb *sāmata* functions as a commonly used synonym for the verb *qābala* in astronomical literature: both typically are used to indicate when one celestial body "is positioned opposite to" (or "faces") another celestial body. Like the author of the *AGI,* Khwārizmī favors the verb *qābala:* on the same subject, he speaks about "the line of the earth's equator" (*khaṭ al-istiwā'*) as "the line that stands opposite to [*yuqābil*] the equator [*mu'addil al-nahār*]" of the heavenly realms.[100] Later, when discussing the conditions for a lunar eclipse, Khwārizmī employs the same verbal form when he notes how the eclipse is caused by the earth's passing between the moon and that which "stands opposite to it" (*yuqābaluhu*)—namely, the sun and its rays.[101] The author also applies the adjectival form of this verb (*muqābil*) to describe the opposition between a planet's perigee (*al-ḥaḍīḍ*) and apogee (*al-awj*)—that is, the nearest and farthest points of its elliptical orbit around another celestial body.[102] Later in his treatise, he even gives the word *al-muqābala* its own vocabulary entry, defining it in terms of a position resulting from a movement of 180 degrees in a circular orbit (*niṣf al-falak*).[103]

Second, with respect to the movement of celestial bodies, the Jesus of the *AGI* highlights their direct and retrograde courses (*istiqāmatuha wa rujū'uha*). Similarly, Qusṭa ibn Lūqā speaks of the rising and setting of stars as ascendants and descendants, and how to determine the place where the constellations rise in "a direct orbit" (*falak mustaqīm*).[104] Khwārizmi writes even more specifically about the direct course (*al-istaqāma*) and the return course (*al-rujū'*) of the planets: while he describes their direct course upward "through the successive tiers of the constellations," their return course denotes their path "longitudinally in a direction counter to the tiers of the constellations."[105]

Third and finally, Jesus refers to the analytical division of the planets' orbits into three, four, and six equal parts—*tathlīth* ("a division into three"), *tarbī'* ("a division into four"), and *tasdīs* ("a division into six").[106] The same vocabulary also appears in Khwārizmi's *Keys to the Sciences,* where each term indicates an orbital distance traveled around the sun calculated in fractions—namely, a third, a fourth, or a sixth of the total circumference.[107]

Thus, for medieval Arabic readers, the technical language used by Jesus in the *Arabic Gospel of the Infancy* would have marked him as a child who had precociously mastered "astronomical science" (*'ilm al-hay'a*), as someone with extraordinary command over the knowledge disseminated in *hay'a* handbooks. As Dimitri Gutas and George Saliba have both argued, this astronomical knowledge quickly found its way into Arabic school curricula at the elementary, intermediate, and advanced levels.[108] The academic setting of the story about Jesus and the scholars in the Temple (a story that actually takes the place of the third teacher episode in the *AGI*) would have made eminent sense to readers familiar with practices of scientific instruction during the period of the Graeco-Arabic translation movement and in its immediate wake. Even as this Arabized Jesus displays an intellectual prowess that belies his years, his wisdom concerning the cosmos and its creator is framed in readily recognizable cultural terms.

In the *AGI,* the wisdom of the Christ child is not restricted to his expansive knowledge of the universe (as macrocosmos); it also extends to inner workings of the human body (as microcosmos). After his exchange with the astronomer, Jesus engages in a question-and-answer discussion with a practitioner of "natural medicine" (*ṭibb al-ṭabā'i'*). After this physician queries him about whether he had studied "medical science" (*'ilm al-ṭibb*), Jesus proceeds to explain "about physics [*al-ṭabī'a*], metaphysics [*mā ba'd al-ṭabī'a*], hyperphysics [*mā fawq al-ṭabī'a*], and hypophysics [*mā taḥt al-ṭabī'a*]; about the powers [*quwwāt*] of the body; the humours [*akhlāṭ*] and their functions [*af'āl*]; the limbs [*a'ḍā'*] and bones [*a'ẓām*]; the veins [*'urūq*], arteries [*ṣawārib*], and nerves [*a'ṣāb*]; the [respective] function[s] of heat [*ḥarāra*], dryness [*yubūsa*], cold [*burūda*], and moisture [*ruṭūba*], and what is produced by them; what activities the soul [*al-nafs*] does in the body [*al-jasad*], [including] its perceptions [*ḥawwās*] and powers [*quwwāt*], the faculty of speech, and the operations of anger and desire; the conjunction and separation [of the body and soul]; and other things that the created intellect cannot grasp."[109]

As in the case of his astronomical discourse, the terminology Jesus employs in conversation with the physician presents us with something of a primer in the vocabulary of medieval scientific handbooks written in Arabic during the period of the translation movement. Indeed, the eighth, ninth, and tenth centuries witnessed a veritable renaissance of scholarship in the field of Arabic medicine, again sponsored by the 'Abbasid caliphate. The center of this renaissance in medical research was the city of Baghdad, where the translation of Greek medical literature (especially Galen) received official patronage under the caliph al-Manṣūr and his successors.[110]

At the forefront of this translation effort was the Bukhtīshū' family of physicians. Hailing originally from the town of Jundīshāpūr (modern-day Iran), the members of this Nestorian Christian clan served as official physicians and medical advisers in the court of the caliphs for twelve generations, from the eighth to the eleventh century.[111] They, along with other prominent Nestorian Christian families of medical experts from Jundīshāpūr (such as the Māsawayh and the Ṭayfūrī), played an instrumental role in commissioning Arabic translations from Greek, Syriac, and Persian originals, as well as conducting original research and writing textbooks summarizing their findings.[112]

For my purposes in this chapter—in order to contextualize the medical discourse in the *Arabic Gospel of the Infancy*—I draw comparisons with selected works by the leading scientific translator and author during the early ʿAbbāsid period: the renowned physician, philosopher, and Nestorian Christian theologian, Ḥunayn ibn Isḥāq alʿIbādī (ca. 808–873/7).[113] A frequent and favored recipient of commissions from the Bukhtīshūʿ leadership, Ḥunayn produced an enormous corpus of translations during his professional career in Baghdad, along with a select number of original medical treatises.[114] His level of productivity, critical sensibilities, and skills as a teacher inspired a cottage industry in Graeco-Syriac and Graeco-Arabic scientific and philosophical translation. The students he trained, led by his son Isḥāq ibn Ḥunayn and his nephew Ḥubaysh ibn al-Ḥasan al-Aʿsam, worked alongside him during his lifetime and continued the high standards of his work after his death in the 870s.[115] With Ḥunayn and his well-trained associates—a group that came to be called the "School of Ḥunayn"—the translation movement reached its pinnacle.[116]

While Ḥunayn also translated Greek biblical, philosophical, astronomical, and even meteorological works, he became best known for his exacting translations of the Greek medical corpus, especially Galen.[117] Indeed, in the year 856, at the peak of his scholarly powers, Ḥunayn penned a treatise for the military commander ʿAlī ibn Yaḥyā in which he gave account of all known translations of Galen's writings at that time.[118] In this bibliographical report, he lists 129 works in total and identifies approximately one hundred of them as texts that he and his collaborators had translated into Syriac and/or Arabic.[119] At least nine of these treatises pertained to the subject of anatomy, including *On Anatomical Procedures* (*Kitāb fī ʿamal al-tashrīḥ*), *On the Anatomy of Veins and Arteries* (*Kitāb fī tashrīḥ al-ʿurūq wa al-awrād*), and *On the Anatomy of Nerves* (*Kitāb fī tashrīḥ al-ʿaṣab*).[120]

Through such translations, Galen's theories—on the four bodily humors; on the influence of heat, cold, dryness, and moisture on good and ill health; on the circulatory and nervous systems; and even on the relationship between the physical constitution of the body and the soul[121]—quickly gained currency among Arabic-speaking communities in the Islamic world.[122] It is from this medical (and philosophical) lexicon that the precocious young Jesus draws his vocabulary in the *Arabic Gospel of the Infancy.* Indeed, one sees the same terms highlighted in the titles and chapter headings of the above-mentioned Galenic writings translated by Ḥunayn and his school.

Take, for example, the case of Galen's treatise *On Anatomical Procedures* (*Kitāb fī 'amal al-tashrīḥ*), translated into Arabic around the year 850 as a result of Ḥunayn's text critical work with earlier Greek and Syriac manuscripts and his collaboration with his nephew Ḥubaysh.[123] The treatise features sections on human skeletal structures and the relationship of muscles and ligaments to bones (*'aẓām*) (books 1–2); on the nerves (*ḍawārib*), veins (*al-'urūq*), and arteries (*al-awrād*) in the hands and feet (book 3), and in the heart, lungs, and brain (books 7 and 9); and on the bones and nerves in the neck (book 11). The final three books of the treatise examine in more detail the body's system of veins and arteries (book 13) and the cranial and cervical nerves (books 14–15). As we have already seen, these final topics also were the subject of two separate treatises by Galen dedicated specifically to the study of the blood vessels and the nervous system, made available to an Arabic readership as a result of Ḥunayn's translations.[124]

In addition to his medical contributions in the area of translation, Ḥunayn and his students produced original compositions on human anatomy in which this same Galenic vocabulary was operative. One such book, written at the very end of his life, is his *Questions on Medicine for Students* (*al-Masā'il fī al-ṭibb li-l-muta'allimīn*). Surviving in both Syriac and Arabic, this expansive treatise was begun by Ḥunayn and completed by his nephew Ḥubaysh after his uncle's death.[125] In perhaps our earliest manuscript, a bilingual copy in the Vatican with the Syriac and Arabic in parallel columns, the place where Ḥunayn left off and Ḥubaysh began is explicitly noted: "(Here) end the inquiries of our late master Ḥunayn. (And here) begin the additions which Ḥubaysh the Crippled added."[126]

A careful examination of the Arabic version of Ḥunayn's *Questions* sheds light on Jesus' scientific terminology in the *Arabic Gospel of the Infancy.*[127] Again, let me cite four examples for comparison. First, there is Jesus' language concerning "nature" and the "natural." At the beginning of his dialogue with the doctor he highlights the importance of physics (lit. "nature," *al-ṭabī'a*), metaphysics (lit. "what is after/beyond nature," *mā ba'd al-ṭabī'a*), hyperphysics (lit. "what is above nature," *mā fawq al-ṭabī'a*), and hypophysics (lit. "what is below nature," *mā taḥt al-ṭabī'a*).[128] A similar concern comes to expression on the first page of Ḥunayn's treatise, where he introduces his "theory of natural things" and its relation to the "science of [discerning/curing] illnesses."[129] Indeed, throughout their treatise, Ḥunayn and Ḥubaysh occupy themselves with causes that are "natural" (*ṭabīʿiyya*), "unnatural" (*laysat bi-ṭabīʿiyya*), and "outside the natural" (*khārij ʿan al-ṭabīʿī*).[130] Examples of "things that are natural" (*al-umūr al-ṭabīʿiyya*) are life stages, colors, complexions of the body, and the distinction between males and females. "Things that are not natural" (*al-umūr illātī laysat bi-ṭabīʿiyya*) include air, states of motion and stillness, food and drink, sleep and wakefulness, and sex. Finally, "things outside nature" (*al-umūr al-khārija ʿan al-amr al-ṭabīʿī*) pertain especially to diseases—"the factors which cause them" (*al-asbāb al-fāʿila*) and the abnormal conditions to which they give rise.[131] These three categories have a systematic function for the two authors' organization of medicine (*al-ṭibb*) as a discipline.

Second, in the *AGI,* Jesus also talks about the "powers [*al-qūwāt*] of the body," and about "the humors (*al-akhlāṭ*) and their functions (*al-afʿāl*)."[132] In the opening chapter of his *Questions on Medicine for Students,* Ḥunayn likewise highlights the "humors" (*al-akhlāṭ*) and the "power" (*al-qūwa*) and "functions" (*al-afʿāl*) of the body as three of the seven principal "natural things" (*al-umūr al-ṭabīʿiyya*) pertaining to human anatomy. With respect to each, he asks questions designed to link these aspects closely together. For example, what is the "power" (*qūwa*) of each "humor" (*khalṭ*) and what the "function" (*fiʿl*) of each "power" (*qūwa*)?[133] Later, Ḥunayn and Ḥubaysh both evaluate a person's health and administer remedies for illness principally by assessing his or her "power" (*qūwa*) and the effectiveness of the body's "functions" (*afʿāl*).[134] The "humors" become a subject for extended treatment in several specialized areas: the authors evaluate their role in digestion,[135] their effect on skin color,[136] and their relation to fevers,[137] bodily decay,[138] swelling (including tumors),[139] and discoloration of the urine.[140]

Third, Jesus speaks with clinical knowledge about the "parts" of the body (*al-aʿḍāʾ*), especially the "bones" (*al-aʿẓām*), "veins" (*al-ʿurūq*), "arteries" (*al-ḍawārib*), and "nerves" (*al-aʿṣāb*).[141] For Ḥunayn, the "parts" or "members" (*aʿḍā*) of the body serve as a fourth anatomical feature categorized as one of the seven principal "natural things" (*umūr al-ṭabīʿiyya*).[142] The nerves, veins, and arteries serve the needs of major body parts, such as the brain and heart, while the bones are recognized as a body part that possesses "an innate power" (*qūwa gharīziyya*).[143] All these organs are recognized as having exclusively uniform components, and thus a breach in their integrity results in illness.[144] Veins and arteries (body parts with internal spaces, or cavities) are contrasted with nerves (parts with spaces external to them), and each type of organ, when afflicted, receives treatment in accordance with its natural power (*qūwa*), function (*fiʿl*), and temperature.[145]

This leads us to our fourth and final point of comparison. In the *Arabic Gospel of the Infancy*, Jesus teaches his listeners in the Temple about "heat" (*al-ḥarāra*), "cold" (*al-burūda*), "dryness" (*al-yubūsa*), and "moisture" (*al-ruṭūba*), and the effects these conditions have on the body.[146] At the beginning of his *Questions*, Ḥunayn discusses these four "conditions" (*amzija*) at great length, including their various combinations in relation to the four elements (fire, air, water, and earth) and the four humors (blood, phlegm, yellow bile, and black bile).[147] Health (or sickness) is dependent on the correspondence (or lack thereof) between a person's "hot" (*ḥār*) or "cold" (*bārid*) constitution and the hot and cold seasons of the year.[148] Sickness is caused by unnatural temperatures of the body part; remedies are designed to bring temperature back in line with what is "natural." Throughout the treatise (on almost every other page), Ḥunayn and Ḥubaysh prescribe medicinal cures that either heat or cool, moisten or dry out the body, depending on the person's condition, particular affliction, and internal balance of humors.[149]

In short, this treatise by Ḥunayn and Ḥubaysh supplies the kind of medical curriculum the young Jesus is portrayed as having mastered in the *AGI*. Here, it is important to note that the handbook *Questions on Medicine for Students* was specifically designed for classroom use. Indeed, schools would have been the main cultural crucibles for the transmission and dissemination of Greek scientific knowledge into Arabic. Ḥunayn himself writes about the important role of classroom instruction among his contemporaries and compares their practices to that of the ancient Alexandrians: "[The members of the medical school in Alexandria] would gather every day to read and study one leading text among those [books by Galen], just as our contemporary Christian colleagues gather every day in places of teaching known as *skholē* [...] for [the study of] a leading text by the ancients. As for the rest of the books, they used to read them individually—each one on his own, after having first practiced with those books which I mentioned—just as our colleagues today read the commentaries of the books by the ancients."[150] According to the eleventh-century Muslim author Abū al-Ḥasan ʿAlī Ibn Riḍwān al-Miṣrī (d. 1061), the medieval Arabic curriculum for medical studies was modeled after Alexandria in Galen's time, and preparatory subjects included logic, physics, mathematics, astrology/astronomy, and pharmacology, as well as a basic introduction to language and grammar.[151] This course of study also necessarily incorporated ethics ("the practical branch of philosophy"), since Galen himself had written a treatise entitled *That the Excellent Physician Is a Philosopher.*[152]

In the context of the translation movement and medieval Arabic science, then, it should not be surprising that Jesus' discourse with the teachers moves from astronomy to medicine and then on to more philosophical or psychological matters—including "the effect of the soul on the body" (*fiʿl al-nafs fī al-jasad*) and the "perceptions" (*hawāss*) and "powers" (*qūwāt*) of the soul, such as anger and desire. The transmission of Greek knowledge was yoked to educational practice that assumed such connections. One sees this interdisciplinarity modeled in the literature produced for this curriculum. Here, three examples will suffice.

First, in a commentary on Hippocrates translated by Ḥunayn, the sevenfold structure of the cosmos (including sun, stars, moon, and planetary spheres) is presented as a model for the seven aspects of the human person, body and soul. The same commentary also analyzes causes and cures for diseases, diagnosed in terms of the four elements (fire, air, water, and earth), the four conditions (heat, cold, dryness, and moisture), and the four humors.[153]

Second, in a book by the tenth-century Muslim physician and man of letters ʿArīb ibn Saʿīd of Cordoba (d. ca. 980), the author writes about the physical formation of a human fetus in the womb and the first ten years of a child's life. Notably, he examines the early stages of human development (from the first appearance of nerves, blood, and bone in the fetus to the development of "the power of discrimination" in the ten-year-old child) and connects each stage to the monthly sway of different planets and their distinctive natures (cold and dry, hot and wet, and so on).[154]

A third and final example comes from the corpus of writings by Qusṭā ibn Lūqā. In his treatise *On the Distinction between the Spirit and the Soul* (*Risāla fī al-farq bayn al-rūḥ wa al-nafs*), he discusses the effect (*fiʿl*) the soul has on the movements (*ḥaraka*), sensations (*ḥassās*), and desires (*shahwa*) of the body and then relates this subject to the science of medical treatment and the analysis of human anatomy, including the transmission of nutrients via the blood vessels (*al-ʿurūq*) and the sensory function of the nerves (*al-ʿaṣab*).[155]

In each of these cases, the translator or author takes it for granted that his readers would have had the requisite training in astronomy and/or philosophy to understand the medical instructions contained in his pedagogical work. But if Ibn Riḍwān is to be believed, sometimes this may have been too much to expect, not only of many students but also of their teachers. Commenting on the state of medical training in the eleventh century, he laments the fact that too many so-called physicians relied on quackery and deceit in their actual practice, and that too many medical authors produced works plagued with mistakes and empty sophistry. In light of Galen's high standard that all physicians "seek perfection" and attain the status of philosophers through their multidisciplinary acquisition of knowledge, Ibn Riḍwān wryly notes that "it is evidently difficult for one person to combine all [the qualities] which I mentioned, and consequently, the 'philosopher-physician' is rarely found in any city or at any time."[156] In this context, we begin to see how the Christ child encountered in the Temple among the teachers is "remembered" in the *AGI* as a successful, self-made product of this educational environment, as one who exceptionally combines the astronomer's wide angle of vision with the physician's attention to microscopic detail.

In fact, this way of reading the *AGI* is confirmed by the Qur'ānic commentator Ibn Kathīr, who lived and worked in Damascus during the fourteenth century. In his *Tafsīr,* the Muslim author addresses the question of how to interpret the wondrous deeds of the prophets: "Many of the [scholars] say that God sent each one of the prophets with what suited the people of his period. . . . As for Jesus (on whom be peace), he was sent in the period of physicians and natural scientists. So he brought them signs which nobody could have had access to except were he supported by Him who prescribed the way."[157] Ibn Kathīr then continues by citing examples of Jesus' "power to give life to an inanimate object" (that is, his act of bringing the clay birds to life), as well as his healing of the blind and of lepers and his raising of people from the dead, as examples of works that exceeded even the most advanced training of an Arab physician.[158] Thus it was that by the age of twelve Jesus had attained and surpassed the lofty status of the "excellent physician and complete philosopher" envisioned in turn by Galen, Ḥunayn ibn Isḥāq, and Ibn Riḍwān.[159]

Sufism, the Science of the Letters, and the Ascetic Jesus

The fields of astronomy and medicine were not the only contexts in which this scientific and philosophical renaissance came to expression; nor were they the only lenses through which Arabic readers tried to understand and find application for the *Paidika* stories about Jesus and his teachers. Another (perhaps more surprising) setting for the reception of such stories was medieval Sufism and the Islamic "science of the letters" (*'ilm al-ḥurūf*).[160] It is in this context that we begin to observe the stories of Jesus' childhood reinterpreted in ascetic terms.

As in Greek antiquity, the alphabet became a source of mystical preoccupation for medieval Arabic speakers seeking more profound insights into the divine will. In the Islamic world, there were numerous and diverse practices in which letters played an instrumental role,[161] including divination,[162] geomancy,[163] arithmomancy and numerological portents,[164] alchemy,[165] astrology,[166] the use of talismans and amulets,[167] and even Qur'ānic interpretation.[168] Out of the confluence of these practices—and especially in conjunction with arithmomancy, alchemy, and astrology—emerged a specific discipline and genre of literature that came to be called "the science of the letters."

As its name suggests, this discipline was formulated in many respects after the fashion of a science, albeit one that skirted the edges of the primary institutionalized fields of learning.[169] For theorists and practitioners, *'ilm al-ḥurūf* was "scientific" in both its organization and its application. In the literature produced by experts in this field, the twenty-eight letters are often divided into four groups of seven, with each group associated with one of the basic cosmological elements—fire, air, water, or earth. These letter groups were thought to bring about tangible effects in the world in accordance with their inherent elemental characteristics. One area of practical application was medical care: the heat of the "fire" letters could be used to counteract the ill effects of cold humors, while the coolness of the "water" letters was seen as a remedy for fevers. The system also had links with astrology and astronomy: each letter group was associated with a different planetary or lunar influence, and the efficacy of the system was assumed to derive from the power of the celestial "spheres" (*al-aflāk*).[170]

Late medieval Muslim commentators such as Ibn Kamāl Pasha (d. 1534) make a point of tracing the roots of such letter practices to eminent ancient Greek philosophers and scientists such as Plato, Aristotle, Pythagoras, and Archimedes.[171] As eminent a figure as Ibn Khaldūn (d. 1406) includes *'ilm al-ḥurūf* in the catalogue of sciences he presents in chapter 6 of his *Prolegomena* (*Muqaddima*).[172] There, he seems to associate it with the "intellectual sciences," a category that comprises the seven primary disciplines of logic, arithmetic, geometry, astronomy, physics (including medicine), metaphysics, and music, but also could include "the related sciences of astrology, sorcery, and talismans" to which the science of the letters had close kinship.[173] At the same time, it was also recognized that the different forms of so-called letter magic (*al-sīmiyā'*) also involved an extensive system of exercises (*al-riyyāḍa*, "training, discipline"), with rationales that diverged to a certain extent from "scientific natural principles" (*uṣūl ṭabī'iyya 'ilmiyya*).[174]

In its hybrid character as both intellectual science and devotional discipline, the study of *'ilm al-ḥurūf* found an especially receptive audience among Ṣūfī Muslims, who saw alphabetic speculation as a pathway toward deeper knowledge of the divine.[175] Indeed, most of the surviving literary works of this genre come from authors steeped in the ascetic ethos of Sufism (*al-ṣūfiyya*), which emerged as a religious movement within Islam during the eighth and ninth centuries CE. Early communities developed in the East, especially in Baṣra and

Baghdad, at around the same time that the Graeco-Arabic translation movement was coming into full bloom. The most prominent Ṣūfī scholars of the period—Ḥārith ibn Asad al-Muḥāsibī (Baṣra and Baghdad, d. 857), Sahl ibn ʿAbd Allāh al-Tustarī (Baṣra, d. 896), Abū Saʿīd al-Kharrāz (Baghdad, d. 892 or 899), and al-Junayd ibn Muḥammad (Baghdad, d. 910)—were all contemporaries of Ḥunayn ibn Isḥāq or Qusṭā ibn Lūqā.[176]

Mystics in the Ṣūfī movement sought to cultivate an internal experience of intimacy with God's love through a rigorous program of ascetic training and self-examination—a set of disciplines they called "the science of introspection" (*ʿilm al-bāṭin*). They regarded their methods of acquiring knowledge as "superior to the perceptible sciences," but they also still considered "the latter to be indispensable for leading a God-fearing life."[177] The science of the letters proved to be especially suited to Ṣūfī sensibilities, providing as it did a forum for close textual study, analysis of elemental correspondences (such as the alignment of letters with the humors and the celestial spheres), and meditation on the nature of God and God's revelatory word.

In the tenth and eleventh centuries, Sūfī authors began making systematic attempts to collect earlier writings and produce comprehensive textbooks and summaries as part of a concerted effort to present their way of life as an "orthodox" expression of Islam, and with this we also see the production of handbooks offering instruction in *ʿilm al-ḥurūf*. One of the early examples is a treatise entitled *Explaining the Meaning of the Letters* (*Sharḥ maʿānī al-ḥurūf*) by Abū ʿAbd al-Raḥmān al-Sulamī (937/42–1021 CE).[178] Apart from study trips to Baghdad and the Ḥijāz (western Arabia), Sulamī spent the bulk of his adult life in his native city of Nishapur (Khurasan, Iran), where he was initiated and accredited as a Ṣūfī teacher, founded a Ṣūfī lodge, and composed more than a hundred literary works, the vast majority of which were hagiographies (which is to say, lives of saints), Qur'ānic commentaries, and treatises on "Sufi sayings, manners and customs."[179] His treatise, *Explaining the Meaning of the Letters,* was conceived as an appendix to his major commentary on the Qur'ān (entitled *Ḥaqā'iq al-tafsīr*), and in it he cites earlier authorities, most notably the Ṣūfī poet and martyr Manṣūr al-Ḥallāj (d. 922 CE).[180]

The opening chapters of the treatise are dedicated to establishing foundations. Sulamī begins by grounding the practice of alphabetic interpretation in the authority of the Prophet (chs. 1–4). He does so by citing two sayings whose origins he traces back to Muḥammad through his contemporaries. The first comes via ʿAlī ibn Abī Ṭālib: "Each verse of the Qur'ān has a 'back' [*ẓahr,* i.e., a literal and outer meaning] and a 'belly' [*baṭn,* i.e., a hidden and inner meaning], and each letter [*ḥarf*] has a horizon [*ḥadd,* i.e., a boundary, a definition] and a point of ascent [*maṭla'*, *muṭṭala'*, i.e., an allegory, a symbolism]."[181] The second comes via Abū Bakr: "Learn the alphabet [*Abū Jād*] and its interpretation! Woe unto the scholar who ignores its interpretation! . . . In it are all the wondrous things that there are."[182]

With this exhortation in mind, Sulamī presents an initial interpretation of each Arabic letter in traditional, symbolic terms (chs. 5–7), followed by a long series of quotations from earlier Ṣūfī mystics who commented on the hidden or inner meanings of the letters (chs. 8–21). Thus, for example, in the case of the first letter of the Arabic alphabet, Sulamī first writes, "The *Alif* is God and the gifts of God [*ālā' allāh*]. The *Alif* is a letter drawn from God's names [*asmā' allāh'*]."[183] A few chapters later, he quotes several sayings by Ḥallāj (al-Ḥusayn) in which *alif* is associated with a number of additional themes, including primordial knowledge of the divine will, kingship, the intimacy of God as Confidant, and divine oneness.[184]

The remainder of the treatise (chs. 22–76) consists of a more detailed commentary on each letter, beginning with *alif* and ending with *yā'*. As one might expect, the letter *alif* again receives the most attention—six chapters of commentary, twice that of any other letter.[185] Sulamī's principal method is to take the initial meanings he introduced earlier and explore their mystical dimensions in more depth with the help of the Qur'ān and a range of authoritative Ṣūfī interpreters, whom he calls the "learned divines" (*al-'ulamā' al-rabbāniyyūn*).[186]

In the midst of these interpretations of the letters, Sulamī twice cites stories about Jesus and the alphabet (chs. 6 and 27). He attributes each of the stories to a chain (*isnād*) of earlier Ṣūfī and Muslim witnesses, following the conventional Islamic method of confirming the veracity of reported traditions. The first is traced back to the Prophet Muḥammad himself; the second is attributed to the Prophet's paternal cousin, Ibn 'Abbās.[187] Despite this system of attestation and the changes that took place in the retelling, however, it is almost certain that these stories derive from a reading of the *Arabic Gospel of the Infancy*. Thus, Sulamī's treatise on letters serves as a unique witness to an Islamic cultural memory of Jesus' childhood.

The first story about Jesus cited by Sulamī appears near the beginning of his treatise, in chapter 6. After providing his chain of witnesses (with Muḥammad identified as its ultimate source), he gives the following account:

> The mother of Jesus entrusted him to one of the scribes that he might teach him. The teacher told him, "Write!" Jesus asked, "What shall I write?" He replied, "In the name of God." Jesus asked him, "What does 'in the name' [*bism*] mean?" The teacher answered, "I do not know." So Jesus replied to him, "The

> *Bā'* is God's beauty, the *Sīn* God's exaltedness and the *Mīm* God's kingdom. God [*Allāh*] is the god of the gods. He is the Benefactor [*al-Raḥmān*], merciful in the world to come and in this world, and the Compassionate [*al-Raḥīm*], compassionate in the world to come."[188]

Here, the relationship between Sulamī's story and the *AGI* is rather loose, although a certain structural correspondence with the first teacher episode is evident. As with Zacchaeus in the *AGI* (and in contrast to the earlier Greek and Syriac versions of the *Paidika*), Mary plays an instrumental role in introducing the child to the schoolmaster.[189]

Other details diverge. In Sulamī's treatise, the scribe commands Jesus to write, while in the *Paidika* traditions Jesus is told to recite the letters orally. But it is *what* Jesus is commanded to write that especially marks the way that these Christian stories were being creatively reworked in an Islamic context. The phrase Jesus interprets—"In the name of God, the Benefactor, the Compassionate" (*bismillāh al-raḥmān al-raḥīm*)—is from the opening words of the Qur'ān and serves as a nearly ubiquitous opening formula of blessing in later Islamic texts. By parsing out the three-letter phrase, "in the name of" (*bism*=*bā', sīn, mīm*), Jesus demonstrates how each letter stood for a divine attribute: *bā'* is for God's "beauty" (*bahā'*), *sīn* is for God's "exaltedness" (*sinā'*), and *mīm* is for God's kingdom (*mamlaka*). The young Jesus is thereby introduced as the scientist of letters par excellence, as a mystic whose insight into God's nature extends beyond "this world" to "the world to come."

The second story about Jesus cited by Sulamī accords more closely with the teacher stories in the *AGI*. In chapter 27, after again tracing his chain of witnesses (this time traced back to Ibn 'Abbās), Sulamī relates the following story: "Jesus was sent to the scribes. One of them said to him, 'Say, *Alif*!' which he did. Then he said to him, 'Say, *Bā'*!' Jesus replied, 'Can you not tell me what the *Alif* stands for?' The scribe answered, 'I do not know what it means.' Jesus replied, 'The *Alif* is God [*Allāh*], Mighty and Exalted is He.' "[190] One of the distinctive features of the *AGI* (in contrast to the Greek and Syriac versions of the *Paidika*) is the fact that Jesus' first two teachers order him to pronounce both *alif* and *bā* in succession, and the same is the case here in Sulamī's account.[191] But the end of the story—Jesus' final response—is noticeably different. Sulamī (or perhaps an earlier Ṣūfī interpreter) has adapted it for a new audience and for a new purpose to underscore for like-minded readers the mystery of the letter *alif* and Jesus' role as a guide to its deeper, divine meaning.

In this way, the *Paidika* stories about Jesus' encounters with teachers were integrated into the science of the letters, and the Christ child transformed into an ascetic exemplar.[192] In the eyes of Sulamī and his contemporaries,

Jesus the prophet becomes an advanced Ṣūfī master, a "friend of God" and "elite mystic" whose heart has been enlightened, who has been given "the capacity to understand difficult and obscure passages."[193] He sets the standard for "aspirants and penitents," having achieved a transcendent "station of knowledge" (*maqām al-ma'rifa*) in conversation and communion with the divine.[194] One of the features of this station is the ability to discern the secret meanings of the letters. Another, according to Sulamī, is the ability to communicate with "all creatures, whether they are human beings, jinn, beasts of prey, birds or animals"—that is, to become something of a Doctor Dolittle in dervish dress.[195]

Sulamī's description of the mystic's ability to communicate with animals hints at yet another way he was interpreting stories of Jesus' childhood in an ascetic vein. As I have noted, in the *Arabic Gospel of the Infancy* one finds two versions of the famous miracle story from the *Paidika,* in which the young Jesus brings clay sparrows to life. In one of these Arabic versions, he brings to life not only clay birds but also clay oxen, asses, and other animals. After he does so, he gives the creatures verbal commands, and they obey. He tells the beasts of burden to walk, and they walk; he tells the birds to fly, to stand still, and to eat and drink, and they do just what he asks.[196] Could it be that this story served as inspiration for Sulamī in his portrait of what transcendent knowledge looked like? For a perceptive Ṣūfī exegete, the communicative power that the seven-year-old Jesus holds over animals in this story would only have served as further proof of his advanced station in the divine "science."

Thus it was—from the *Arabic Gospel of the Infancy* to Sulamī's treatise *Explaining the Meaning of the Letters*—stories of Jesus' interaction with teachers (and animals as well) were reread and recontextualized in and through acts of translation, the scientific production of knowledge, and the ascetic disciplines of Ṣūfī study and contemplation. In the end, it was through these practiced sites of memory that medieval Arabic-speaking Christians and Muslims reshaped the Christ child in their own (partially shared) cultural image.

In closing, I should note that Sulamī's science of the letters is not our only attested example of a Muslim author reappropriating *Paidika* stories and the figure of a young Jesus for ascetic ends.[197] Another fascinating case study of such reading practices comes from late medieval and early modern South Asia and the Indian city of Lucknow, where apocryphal tales of Jesus' childhood served as a narrative template for the production of Ṣūfī hagiographical summaries. There, a fifteenth-century Indian Ṣūfī saint named Shah Mīna was commemorated in two separate accounts that both drew on the stories of Jesus learning the alphabet in school.[198] The first was written by a certain

'Abd al-Ḥaqq in 1618,[199] and the second by Irtadā 'Alī Khān in the nineteenth century.[200]

The *topos* of modeling the life of a saint or a hallowed figure after Jesus was not new to Islam. Indeed, there is evidence that as early as the eleventh century hagiographers were drawing on stories of Jesus' childhood in an effort to portray their subjects as preternaturally precocious and to give their lives a prophetic imprimatur. A contemporary of Sulamī, the eminent Shī'ite theologian from Baghdad, Abū 'Abd Allāh Muḥammad ibn Muḥammad, known more commonly as al-Shaykh al-Mufīd (948–1022 CE), wrote a treatise called *The Book of Guidance* (*Kitāb al-irshād*) designed to defend the legitimacy of the twelve imams recognized by Shī'ites as the spiritual successors (*khulafā'*) to Muḥammad, a line of succession beginning with Muḥammad's cousin 'Alī. In his *Book of Guidance,* al-Shaykh al-Mufīd narrates in glowing terms the details of 'Ali's biography, including his miraculous deeds. One of these miracles was the early manifestation of esoteric wisdom as a boy: according to his hagiographer, 'Alī attained "the perfection of his intellect" between the ages of seven and ten, and in this way he followed the "signs" and example of Jesus who was known to have spoken from the cradle as an infant and to have transcended ordinary human understanding.[201]

The early modern accounts of Shah Mīna's life adhere to a similar literary model. But while al-Shaykh al-Mufīd, as a Shī'ite, was concerned principally with the validation of 'Alī's authority as the first of the twelve imams, Shah Mīna's South Asian hagiographers are far more interested in showing how the wisdom of the Indian Ṣūfī saint was the natural fruit of his rigorous commitment to meditation and ascetic renunciation. Another contrast lies in the area of attribution: in marked contrast to al-Shaykh al-Mufīd's explicit citation of Jesus as an exemplar for 'Alī, both 'Abd al-Ḥaqq and Irtadā 'Alī Khān draw on *Paidika* stories without acknowledging their source or mentioning Jesus by name.

Thus, 'Abd al-Ḥaqq, having noted Shah Mīna's early childhood training under his master, Shaykh Qiwām al-Dīn, reports about "the first day that they sent him to school" and essentially proceeds to retell one of the *Paidika* teacher stories with the Ṣūfī saint cast as the main protagonist: "Upon the mention of 'A, B . . . ,' he spoke of spiritual wisdom and divine realities, so that those present were astonished."[202] Irtadā 'Alī Khān's later, more expansive hagiographical account recapitulates the scene, again with Shah Mīna mimetically reenacting the role of the young Jesus: "When at five years he went to school, the teacher said, 'Say "A."' And he said, 'A.' Then the teacher said, 'Say "B."' And he said, 'Why should I be squint-eyed?' In that word he made clear so much truth and gnosis that the teacher and those others present lost their senses."[203] As a result of these words, Mina, the "born saint," was given special honor in the classroom, where he spent his time occupied in meditation.[204]

This story of the saint's rather cryptic response to his teacher's alphabetic instruction is immediately preceded and followed by other recognizable intertextual plays on Christian *Paidika* narratives. Before this school scene, there is a miracle account about birds that obey the young Ṣūfī master's commands: "It is reported by his grandfather that when Shaykh Mina was two or three years old, he said, 'Give me those sparrows that are flying around me.' So the grandfather said, 'Sparrows, Shaykh Mina summons you!' They came and alighted facing the revered master, and they were unable to fly away until he gave them permission to leave."[205] As in the case of Sulamī's description of Ṣūfī sages who have acquired an ability to commune with the animal kingdom, so too in this nineteenth-century life of an Indian saint: in mute imitation of the paradigmatic childhood prophet Jesus, Mina's actions mark him as having attained a select status—he is a "friend of God."

Then, right after his first lesson in the letters, we are told about his continued training, beginning at the age of ten, under Shaykh Qiwām al-Dīn and other masters. At one point, in the presence of a particularly revered teacher, Mina explains a book of Islamic law "in such detail and with such clear points" that the teacher proclaimed that "he had never heard the like before," a scenario closely resembling the third teacher episode in the Greek and Syriac *Paidika*.[206] A short time later, Mina is approached by a group of "distinguished scholars" who "inquire about the stages of the rational and traditional sciences from him," a scene remarkably similar to the expanded story of Jesus in the Temple from the *Arabic Gospel of the Infancy*.[207]

These stories drawn from *Paidika* common stock have a consistent function in Irtadā 'Alī Khān's hagiography—to illustrate for readers the childhood signs of Mina's sainthood, a sainthood marked not only by esoteric wisdom but also by gestures of ascetic renunciation, including fasting, the performance of ablutions, sleep deprivation, and spending nights "sitting up on a high wall" in Stylite fashion. The increasingly rigorous program of spiritual and bodily disciplines reaches its culmination in forty-day-long fasts, another example of how Mina's life, as a hagiographical product, was stitched together in large part from the strands of earlier Christian traditions (infancy or otherwise).

In the end, these case studies of the science of the letters and lives of saints provide striking evidence for the way Ṣūfī social memories of Jesus' childhood were transmitted and creatively transformed via sets of practices shared by Christians and Muslims alike in the Arabic-speaking world and in India. From Baghdad to Lucknow, the production of scientific disciplines and hagiographical narratives served as fertile contexts for new Islamic readings of the early Christian *Paidika,* readings that fostered and facilitated distinctively ascetic memories of the young Jesus.

Epilogue
Reimagining a Young Jesus

In this book, we have traversed a historical landscape populated by "sites of memory" related to the *Paidika* of Jesus. Putting ourselves in the place of early Graeco-Roman readers and hearers of these tales, we made stops in homes and ritual spaces where ceramic toys and figurines littered the floors and lined the shelves, where the chirpings and songs of domesticated birds and of children playing (or praying) reached our ears. Continuing on, we paid visits to athletic stadiums and philosophical academies where competitions of body and soul took place, and to elementary school classrooms where alphabetic instruction opened the door to more esoteric forms of divine learning.

Later our path brought us to an early medieval terrain, where the *Paidika* stories themselves became contested yet also shared sites of memory for Christians, Jews, and Muslims. Accompanying a Latin-speaking traveler, we visited a synagogue in Nazareth, Jesus' former schoolhouse. At this pilgrimage site, Jewish residents and Christians visitors came into uneasy cultural contact. From there, we entered the narrative world of the *Toledot Yeshu* and saw how *Paidika* stories were appropriated for decidedly polemical and parodic purposes—namely, for the production of an alternative Jewish "Life of Jesus." Various Christian scribes, in turn, made changes to their copies of the *Paidika*, both to enhance the young Jesus' divine credentials and to downgrade his

Jewish opponents. Finally, moving across an expansive Arabic and Islamic topography we discovered the diverse and sundry ways in which the figure of the Christ child was recast in the context of prevailing theologies about prophecy and divine sovereignty, scientific advances, ascetic contemplation, and the making of new saints.

Throughout, I have emphasized how readers and hearers would have engaged with the *Paidika* on the microlevel: not primarily with larger macro-narrative contexts, but with the subtle and specific details of story units that evoked concrete connections to contemporary social *realia*. Philip Rousseau and Tomas Hägg have recently noted how biographies in late antiquity were conceived not only in terms of chronological movement, development, and change, not simply as a life story moving ahead "stage by stage," but also in terms of the construction of character portraits, emblematic vignettes capturing moments of action and speech almost like a sequence of snapshot stills.[1] The reception history of the *Paidika* may helpfully be seen in this light.

In fact, the Christ child *was* seen and not just read or heard about. The stories I have traced through Greek-, Latin-, Syriac-, and Arabic-speaking settings were also retold in art, where they were encapsulated and epitomized in visual form, freeze-framed in the eye of the viewer. In the Florentine manuscript of the *Arabic Gospel of the Infancy* (1299 CE), for example, medieval reader-viewers encountered the Christ child in just such a series of portraits.[2]

Dating to the end of the thirteenth century, and probably produced in or around Baghdad, the fragmentary Arabic manuscript preserves a series of exquisitely detailed line drawings that serve as a running visual commentary on the text. On one folio, an adolescent-looking Jesus sits on a stool with a bird perched on his finger, while a donkey, two goats, and two other birds walk toward him (fig. 1).[3] On another, he gestures toward four spritely young goats that look at him expectantly: they are his former playmates, transformed into kids, and now waiting to be changed back into their original human form.[4] The depiction of domesticated animals in the two scenes would have evoked stereotypical images of town and village life in the countryside around Baghdad.[5] On the pages of a medieval codex from the heart of the Islamic world at the fin de siècle of the thirteenth century, Jesus' childhood is captured in still life, made present to Arab Christians (and Muslims) as a visual memento of the sacred past.[6]

Around the same time, visualizations of the young Jesus were also taking place in the Latin West. In a medieval manuscript now preserved in the Biblioteca Ambrosiana in Milan, a succession of *Paidika* scenes accompanies the script.[7] The young Jesus' actions ring familiar, but the clothes and architectural

Figure 1. Jesus animates birds and animals. Florence, Biblioteca Medicea Laurenziana, Or. 387, 26v. On concession of the Ministry for Goods and Cultural Activities. Any further reproduction is prohibited by any means.

Figure 2. Jesus animates a bird. St. Martin's Church, Zillis, Switzerland, Panel 91. Photograph by Stephen J. Davis.

settings conform more closely to medieval European conventions. On the front of one leaf, Jesus—dressed in a long, ragged peasant robe—brings clay birds to life: six of them fly away as a group of children look on.[8] On the reverse, a child falls off the upper story of a building with a wooden balcony: Jesus stands to the right with his hand raised, ready to resurrect the dead boy.[9] Three additional folia show Jesus at school: he arrives holding his writing tablet ready to meet his instructors, who are reimagined as European schoolmarms.[10]

Images of the Christ child were not confined to books and literate audiences: they also sometimes were displayed in churches and other architectural settings. One medieval artist, for example, etched a series of *Paidika* scenes on red clay tiles probably first displayed on the wall of a church (or perhaps a wealthy home) somewhere in the vicinity of Tring, England. Ten tiles survive, of which two show Jesus cursing children: in one, the victim is Annas's son; in the other, the child who attacked Jesus' shoulder. Other tiles feature familiar scenes of Jesus attending school and doing chores around the house.[11]

Another artist painted an image of Jesus bringing clay birds to life on the ceiling of a church in the town of Zillis, high in the Swiss Alps (fig. 2). Set within a larger program of biblical scenes, the image would have prompted parishioners to situate their acts of viewing in relation to the sacred past, but also to local topography and ritual practice (a context for cultural memory I explore more fully in Appendix C).

In such visual representations—that is to say, in and through the ritualized practices of reading, viewing, and worshipping that framed the reception of such images—the Christ child was reshaped and refigured for new eyes.[12] Speaking about the subjectivity of seeing, the art historian James A. Francis has asserted, "It is the viewer's relationship to the object, his or her recognition and reception of it and devotion to it, *that changes the nature of the image itself.*"[13] In these pages, I have suggested that the same held true for ancient and medieval readers and hearers of the *Paidika*. Graeco-Roman audiences found in the stories cues to revisit material and practical sites of memory connected with everyday life, and they used such sites to think about the nature of Jesus' childhood. Later Christians, Jews, and Muslims also appropriated the *Paidika* stories themselves as *lieux de mémoire* for tracking the shifting contours of their own religious and social landscapes. In the midst of this, the enigmatic figure of the young Jesus was constantly reimagined—incrementally remade to conform to the eye and image of the beholder. Ultimately, then, I have written a book not so much about the Christ child himself as about *how,* and *by whom,* he was remembered. It was through such dynamic processes of observation and interpretation that the infancy of Jesus became so malleable—and so memorable—to different generations of readers, hearers, and viewers.[14]

Appendix A
The Greek Paidika

The *Great* Childhood Deeds of *Our Master and Savior* Jesus Christ[1]

1. *I, Thomas the Israelite, considered it necessary to make known to all of the brothers from the Gentiles how many (deeds) our Lord Jesus Christ did after he had been born in our region of Nazareth at the village of Bethlehem. The first of those deeds is the following:*[2]

2.1. The child Jesus was five years old and was playing at the crossing of a stream *after it had rained.* Disturbing the waters, *which were unclean,* he collected (them) into pools and began making them pure and virtuous. *He commanded the waters by the administration of his word [*logos*] alone and not by any deed.* 2.2. Then, taking up the soft clay from the mixture, he fashioned from it twelve sparrows. Now it was the Sabbath when he was doing this, and many children were with him. 2.3. After a certain Jew saw the child Jesus doing these things with the other children, [the Jew] went to his father, Joseph, and accused the child Jesus, saying that he had made clay on the Sabbath, something which was not permitted, and had fashioned twelve sparrows. 2.4. Joseph came and reprimanded him, saying, "Why are you doing these things on the Sabbath?" When Jesus clapped his hands together *with a shout,* the birds flew away in front of everybody, and he said, "Go and fly like living things."[3] Flying, the sparrows went away chirping. 2.5. When the Pharisee saw [this], he was amazed and announced the news to all of his friends.

3.1. The son of Annas the high priest *said to him, "Why are you acting this way on the Sabbath?"* Taking a willing twig, he upset the pools and caused the water that Jesus had collected together to drain out; and he dried up the places where the water had collected. 3.2. When Jesus saw what had happened, he said to him, "May your fruit be rootless and may your shoot be dried up like a young branch charred by a violent wind!" 3.3. And immediately that child dried up.

4.1. Going from that place with his father, Joseph, [a boy],[4] while running, tore into his shoulder.[5] Jesus said to him, "As for you, cursed be your guide [*hēgemōn*]," and immediately the boy died. Right away the people cried out when they saw that he had died and said, "Where was this child born that his word [*rhēma*] becomes a deed?" 4.2. When the parents of the child who had died saw what had occurred, they blamed his father, Joseph, saying, "Since you have this child, how can you possibly live with us in this village? If you want to stay here, teach him to bless and not to curse, *for we have been deprived of our child."*

5.1. Joseph said to Jesus, "Why do you say such things? These people suffer and they hate us." The child said to Joseph, "[While] you may know sensible words [*rhēmata*], are you not ignorant of where your words [*rhēmata*] come from?[6] [. . .][7] These children shall not be raised, and those people shall receive their punishment."[8] And immediately those who were accusing him became blind. 5.2. Then Joseph laid hold of his ear and pulled it forcefully. 5.3. Jesus said to him, "Let it be sufficient for you to seek after me and find me, *and not, on top of this, to strike me,* having laid hold of a natural ignorance. *You have not seen me clearly, as to how I am yours. Look, you know not to give me grief, for I was yours and with regard to you I have been taken into hand.*

6.1. Now a teacher whose name was Zacchaeus, standing [nearby] and hearing Jesus say these things to his father Joseph, was exceedingly amazed. 6.2. He said to Joseph, "Come and give him [to me], brother, so that he may be instructed in letters and so that he may know all knowledge, learn to love his peers, honor old age, and respect his elders, [and] so that he may acquire a desire to have children and likewise instruct them in turn. 6.2a. Joseph said to the teacher, "Who is able to hold sway over this child and instruct him? Do not think that he has the character of a small man,[9] brother. *But the teacher said, "Give him to me, brother, and do not let him concern you."* 6.2b. Staring at them, the child Jesus said to that teacher *the following speech [*logos*], "Since you are a teacher, you were educated in a clever manner,* but as for the name with which you are named, you are a stranger. For I am from outside you, but with a view to my fleshly nobility of birth I am within you. But you, despite being legally trained, do not know the law." He said to Joseph, "When you were born,[10] I existed and stood by you so that you might be instructed as a father with an instruction given by me, which no other person knows or is able to teach, and [so that] you might bear the salvific name."[11] 6.2c. The Jews cried out loudly and said to him, "O what a new and unexpected marvel! The child has perhaps only attained the age of five, and O what words [*rhēmata*] he utters! We have never known anyone to have spoken such words [*logoi*]—neither a teacher of the law nor any Pharisee—like this child has." 6.2d. The child responded to them and said, "Why are you amazed? Or rather, why do you not believe in the things that I said to you? Truly, I know exactly when you, and your fathers, and your fathers' fathers were born, and what existed before the world was created." 6.2e. Having heard this, all of the people were silenced, no longer being able to speak to him. And he, coming to them, began skipping about and saying, "I was playing with you since I know you wonder at small things and are meager in your mental capacities." 6.2f. Now when they seemed to be consoled by the child's exhortation, the teacher said to his father, "Come and lead him to the school [*paideutērion*] and I shall teach him letters." *Joseph took him by the hand and led him to the school.* The teacher, after flattering him, led him into the classroom [*didaskaleion*]. And Zacchaeus wrote for him the alphabet and began to recite the letters in order for him, and he was saying the same letter repeatedly. But the child did not respond to him. The teacher became angry and struck him on the head. Then the child *became irritated and* said to him, "I want to instruct you rather than being instructed by you, since I know the letters you are teaching more accurately and much better than you.[12] These things are to me 'like a noisy gong or clanging cymbal,'[13] which does not offer articulate sound, or informed opinion, or the power of understanding." 6.3. *When he had ceased from his anger,* the child said by himself all the letters from alpha to omega with much proficiency. Staring clearly at the teacher, he said, "Not knowing the alpha, which is in accordance with nature, how do you teach another person the beta? Hypocrite! If you know, first teach me the alpha and then I shall trust you to speak the beta." Then he began to put questions to the teacher regarding the first element. *And he [the teacher] did not have the power to talk with him.* 6.4. With many people listening, he began to say to the teacher, "Listen, teacher, and understand the order[ing] of the first element. Turn your attention to what follows: how it has slanted lines and a middle stroke, which you see pointing, crossing, intersecting, spreading outward, drawing back, rising up, dancing, darting like arrows,[14] three-marked, double-mouthed, of the same form, of the same thickness, of the same family, corded, yoked, of equal measure, of equal proportion. [Such are] the lines possessed by the alpha."[15]

7.1. After he had heard such an exposition, and after Jesus had pronounced such lines of the first letter, the teacher was at a loss regarding such a teaching and such a speech in defense. And the teacher said, "*Woe is me! Woe is me! I, the miserable one, am at a loss.* I caused myself shame when I took this child under my wing. 7.2. Take [him] from me, brother, *for I cannot bear the sternness of his glance nor the clarity of his word [*logos*].* This child is simply not earthborn.[16] He is even able to tame fire. Perhaps this child existed before the creation of the world. What sort of womb bore him? What sort of mother's womb reared him? I do not know. Woe is me, brother! He dumbfounds me. I cannot follow [him] in my mind. I have tricked myself—I, the thrice-wretched one. I thought that I would have him as a student, but I have been found to have him as a teacher. 7.3. *Consider well my shame, friends, because I am an old man and I have been mastered by a child.* I am *to be cast out to die, or* to flee from this village, on account of this child? For I can no longer be seen in the sight of everyone, especially those who have seen that I was mastered by an exceedingly small child. What am I to say or what am

I to tell anyone regarding the lines of the first element, which he presented to me? Truly, I do not know, friends, for I understand neither the beginning nor the end. 7.4. *Therefore, brother Joseph, take him away with good health [*sōtēria*, "salvation"] to your house.*[17] For this child is some great thing—either a god or an angel, or . . . I do not know what I should say."

8.1. The child Jesus laughed and said, "Now let the barren bear fruit and let the blind see; *and you who are foolish in heart, gain understanding, for I come from above so that I may rescue those who are below and call them to the places on high, just as the one who sent me to you commanded me [to do]."* 8.2. Immediately, all who had fallen under his curse were saved, and no one dared to provoke him to anger from then on.

9.1. *Again, after many days,* Jesus was playing with other children as well on a certain upper story of a house. One of the children fell and died. Seeing [what had happened], the other children departed for their own houses and left Jesus alone. 9.2. When the parents of the child who had died arrived, they began accusing Jesus, saying, "You threw our child down." But Jesus said, "I did not throw him down." 9.3. While they were mad with anger and screaming [at him], Jesus came down from the roof, stood by the corpse, *cried out in a loud voice,* and said, "Zeno, Zeno (for this was his name), *arise and* say whether I cast you down." And arising, he said, "No, Lord." Seeing [this], they were amazed. *And again, Jesus said to him, "Sleep now."* And the parents of the child glorified God and bowed down to the child Jesus.

10.1. [=Ga 11] The child Jesus was around seven years old, and he was sent by his mother, Mary, to fetch water. But at the watering place, there was a great crowd, and the pitcher was knocked and it broke. 10.2. Jesus spread out the cloak that he had thrown on and he filled [it] with water and brought [it] to his mother. When Mary saw what Jesus had done *as a sign, she kissed him, saying, "Lord, my God, bless our child." For they were afraid lest someone curse* [baskainein] *him.*[18]

11.1. [=Ga 12] In the season of sowing, when Joseph had begun planting seeds, the child Jesus also planted one measure of wheat. 11.2. His father harvested one hundred great measures and gave them to the poor and to the orphans, *and Joseph took [the harvest] from the seed planted by Jesus.*

12.1. [=Ga 13] [Jesus] came to be around eight years old. When his father, being a carpenter, was working on ploughs and yokes, he received a bed from a certain wealthy man so that he might make it very great and fit for a special purpose. Seeing as one beam, called [the bed rail],[19] was shorter and did not have the [proper] measurement, *Joseph was upset and did not know what to do. Arriving,* the child said to his father, "Place the two pieces of wood down and make them even from your side." 12.2. *Joseph did just as Jesus said to him, and* the child stood on the other side, grabbed hold of the short piece, stretched it, and made it even with the other piece of wood. He said to his father, "*Do not be upset, but* do whatever you want." *Then Joseph hugged him, saying, "Blessed am I because God gave me such a child."*

13.1. [=Ga 14] When Joseph saw his intelligence and mindfulness, he wanted him not to be at a loss when it came to letters. He handed him over to another teacher, and the teacher, after writing for him the alphabet, said, "Say alpha."[20] 13.2. The child said, "You tell me first what beta is and I shall tell you what alpha is."[21] The teacher became angry and struck him. *Jesus cursed him, and* the teacher fell down and died. 13.3. The child went home to his parents, and Joseph, calling his mother, ordered her not to let him out of the house, lest [all] those who were angering him should die.

14.1. [=Ga 15] After some days, once more another teacher said to his father, Joseph, "Come, brother, and give him to me for the purpose of [bringing him to] school, so that with flattery I may teach him letters." *Joseph said to him, "If you have courage, brother, take him with good health [*sōtēria, *"salvation"]." Taking the child, the teacher led him by the hand with fear and much struggle [*agōn*]. But the child went [with him] happily.* 14.2. Entering the classroom, he found a book lying on the lectern. Taking it, he did not read aloud the words written there [*ta gegrammena*], *on account of the fact that they were not from God's law.* Instead, he opened his mouth and quoted awe-inspiring words [*rhēmata*] so that the instructor sitting opposite him listened to him very happily. [The instructor] began exhorting him to say more, and the crowd standing by was frightened by his divinely approved words [*rhēmata*]. 14.3. Joseph ran quickly to the classroom, thinking to himself that the instructor was no longer without experience and that he might suffer. The instructor said to Joseph, "Just so you know, brother: I took your child on as a student, [but] he is full of much grace and wisdom. *Therefore, brother, take him away to your house with good health [*sōtēria, *"salvation"]."* 14.4. *[Jesus] said to the instructor, "Since you have spoken correctly and witnessed correctly, on account of you, even the one who was struck down will also be saved." And straightaway, that instructor was also saved,* and he took the child and led him away to his house.

15.1. [=Ga 16] James went out into the woods to tie up dry sticks *so that loaves of bread might be made.* Jesus also went out with him, and while they were gathering together the sticks, a *venomous* viper bit James on his hand. 15.2. *While he was laid out dying,* the child Jesus ran to James[22] and blew on the bite, and straightaway the bite was healed. The beast was killed, and James was saved.

16.1.[23] *[=Ga 10] Again, when a certain young man was splitting wood in even pieces, he split the base of his foot, and having lost a lot of blood, he died. 16.2. When there was an uproar, Jesus ran and, forcing his way, he came through the crowd and grabbed hold of the foot that had been stricken, and immediately it was healed. He said to the young man, "Go, split your pieces of wood." 16.3. When the crowd saw [this], they were amazed and said, "For he saved many souls from death. And he will be able to save all the days of his life."*

17.1. [=Ga 19][24] When Jesus was twelve years old, his parents went to Jerusalem according to their custom for the festival of the Passover. While they were turning back [to go home], Jesus remained in Jerusalem, and his parents did not know. 17.2. Thinking that he was in the caravan, they traveled a day's journey and [then] began looking for him among their relatives and among those known to them. When they did not find him, they returned to Jerusalem, seeking for him. After three days they found him sitting in the Temple in the midst of the teachers, listening to them and asking them questions. Those who heard him were astonished at how he posed questions[25] to the elders and solved the main points of the law, as well as the songs and parables of the prophets. 17.3. His mother said to him, "Child, what have you done to us? Behold, we have been seeking after you, pained and upset." But Jesus said to them, "For what reason were you seeking after me? Do you not know that it is necessary for me to be in the places that belong to my Father?" 17.4. The scribes and the Pharisees said to Mary, "Are you the mother of this child?" *She said, "I am."* And they said to her, "Blessed are you because the Lord God has blessed the fruit of your womb. For we have never seen or heard of such wisdom of praise and glory of virtue." Arising from there, Jesus followed his mother and was obedient to his parents. She observed everything he said, pondering them in her heart, and Jesus advanced in wisdom and in age and in grace before God and people. To him be the glory . . .

Appendix B
The Arabic Gospel of the Infancy, *Chapters 36–53*[1]

36.[2] When the Lord Jesus had completed seven years since his birth, that day he was with children of the same age (that is, those who were his peers). They were playing in the clay and were making forms like donkeys, cattle, birds, and other animals.[3] Each one of them was proud of what he had fashioned and was pleased with his work. Then the Lord Jesus said to the young boys, "The sculptured images that I fashioned I shall command to walk." The boys said to him, "And are you the son of the Creator?" So the Lord Jesus commanded them to move, and right then [lit. "in that hour"] they began to prance around,[4] and then when he had given them permission, they returned [to their places]. He had made [them] in the form of birds and sparrows. When he ordered them to fly, they flew; and when he ordered them to stand still, they stood still on his hand. He fed them and they ate, and he gave them water and they drank. Those boys went and told their fathers about this. Their fathers said to them, "O you, our children, do not associate with him anymore, for he is a magician. Beware of him, steer clear of him, and, from now on, no longer play with him.

37.[5] On a certain day, the Lord Jesus was running around and playing with the boys, and he passed by the shop of a dyer named Salem. In the shop of this dyer there were many pieces of cloth belonging to the people of the city [that] he wanted to dye. When the Lord Jesus came to the shop of the dyer, he took all of the pieces of cloth and threw them into an earthen jar [full] of indigo. When Salem the dyer came and saw that the pieces of cloth were ruined, he started to shout in a loud voice and argued with the Lord Jesus.[6] He said, "What have you done to me, son of Mary? You have disgraced me before all of the people of the city, for each one of them wanted his item a certain color, and you have come and ruined it all." The Lord Jesus said, "Each piece of cloth you want to change, I shall change its color for you." And immediately, the Lord Jesus began to take out the pieces of cloth from that earthen jar, each of them just like the color that the dyer wanted, until he had taken all of them out. When the Jews saw this miracle and sign, they praised God.

38.[7] Joseph was taking the Lord with him and was going around in each city, for the people used to come to him on account of his trade, so that he would make for them doors, milk pails, beds,[8] and chests. The Lord Jesus was with him wherever he went. Whenever Joseph needed something in his trade for lengthening, shortening, widening, or narrowing—whether it was by a cubit or a span—the Lord Jesus would stretch out his hand to it and it would become just as Joseph wanted. He did not need to make anything with his hand, because Joseph was not skillful in the trade of carpentry.[9]

39.[10] On a certain day, the king of Jerusalem invited him and said to him, "Joseph, I want you to make for me a throne [*sarīr*][11] the size of the place where I sit." He responded to him listening and obedient, and immediately he began making the throne. He remained in the house of the king for two years until he finished the work of that throne. After he had it brought to its place, he found it lacking in size on every side by two spans. When the king saw that, he became angry at Joseph. But Joseph, on account of his fear of the king, spent the night hungry and did not taste anything at all. The Lord Jesus said to him, "Why are you afraid?" And Joseph said, "Because I have ruined all of what I made over the period of two years." The Lord said to him, "Do not be afraid, and do not be anxious, but hold onto the side of the throne and I will hold onto the other side in order to fix it." So Joseph did as the Lord Jesus said to him, and each one pulled from his side, and the throne was fixed. It became the size of that place. When those who were present saw the miracle, they were amazed and praised God. And the wood of that throne was from the wood that was manifested in the time of Solomon, son of David, and it is wood of [different] kinds and shapes.

40.[12] On a certain day, the Lord Jesus went out to the alley and saw the boys gathered together playing. He followed in their footsteps, but those boys, when they saw him, hid from his presence. He came to the door of a house and saw women there, and the Lord Jesus said to them, "Where did the boys go?" Those women said to him, "There is no one here." And he said to them, "Those who are in the furnace, who are they?" The women said to him, "Those are young goat kids." The Lord Jesus cried out and said, "O you goat kids, come out here to your shepherd." So those boys came out like a young goat and began to prance around him. When those women witnessed this they became quite crazed and they were seized with trembling and rushed to bow down to the Lord Jesus beseeching him humbly, saying, "Our Lord Jesus, son of Mary, you are truly the good shepherd for Israel. Have pity on your mothers who are standing before you, the ones who did not doubt you. Indeed, our Lord, you have come for the purpose of healing and not for the purpose of annihilation." The Lord Jesus replied, "The sons of

Israel among the people are like the black-skinned people [*al-sūdān*]."[13] And the women said to him, "Our Lord, you know everything and nothing is hidden from you. Now we ask you and request from your goodness that you return the boys your servants to their original condition. And the Lord Jesus said, "Come on, you boys! Let's go play!" And at that instant, the goats were transformed and became boys in the presence of those women.

41.[14] When it was in the month of Adar,[15] the Lord Jesus gathered together the boys in the manner of a king, and they spread out their clothes on the ground and he sat on them. They wove for him a crown made of flowers and placed it on his head. And they stood in his presence, on his right and on his left, like the guards that stand in the presence of the king. Everyone who crossed the path, the boys would drag forward angrily,[16] saying to him, "Come and bow down to the king, and return to your path."

42.[17] While they were acting this way, some people approached carrying a boy.[18] For this boy had gone off with the [other] boys to the mountain to fetch firewood and had found a partridge nest.[19] He had stretched out his hand to take the eggs from that nest, and a venomous serpent [*ḥayya*][20] had bitten him from the center of the nest, so that he had cried out for help. When his companions came, [he was] stretched out on the ground like a dead person. His family came to carry him and take him to the city.[21] When they arrived at the place where the Lord Jesus was acting like the king and the boys were around him like his attendants, the boys rushed up to the one who had been bitten and said to his family, "Come and greet the king." They did not want to come on account of their sadness, so the boys dragged them forcefully against their will.[22] When they came to where the Lord Jesus was, he said to them, "Why are you carrying this boy?" They said, "A serpent has bitten him." The Lord Jesus said to the boys, "Come let us go kill it." The parents of the boy said, "Let us go, for our son is close to death." The boys replied, saying, "Are you not listening to what the king said, that we will go and kill the serpent? And you contradict him?" So they herded [them] off walking, and when they came to the nest the Lord Jesus said to the boys, "This is the serpent's place?" They said to him, "Yes." Then the Lord Jesus called out and [the serpent] came out without delay and submitted to him. He said to it, "Go and suck out the poison that you injected into that boy." That serpent retreated to where the boy was and sucked out all of its poison. Then the Lord Jesus cursed it, and it burst open at that moment.[23] And he passed his hand over the boy, and he regained his health and began to cry. The Lord Jesus said to him, "Do not cry, for after a short while you will be my disciple." And this was Simon the Canaanite mentioned in the Gospel.

43.[24] Another day, Joseph sent his son James to fetch firewood, and the Lord Jesus went along as his companion. When they arrived at the place where the wood was, he [James] began to gather up the wood, when a venomous viper [*afʿa*] bit him on the hand and caused him to call out and begin crying. When the Lord Jesus saw him in this state, he came up to him and breathed on the spot where the viper had bitten him, and he was healed instantly.

44.[25] On another day, the Lord Jesus was with the boys playing on the roof [of a house], and a certain boy fell down and died instantly. The boys ran away,[26] and the Lord Jesus was left alone on the roof. When the family of that boy came, they said to the Lord Jesus, "You are the one who threw our son off the roof." He said to them, "I did not throw him off." But they began to cry out, saying, "Our son has died and this is the one who killed him." The Lord Jesus said to them, "Do not slander me. If you do not trust me, come and we will ask the boy and he will reveal the truth." Now the Lord Jesus came down and stood over the head of the corpse and cried out in a loud voice, "Zeno, Zeno,[27] who threw you down off the roof?" The dead boy replied, saying, "My Lord, you did not throw me down, it was so-and-so who threw me."[28] So the Lord said to those who were present, "Listen to what he says."[29] And everyone who was present praised God on account of this miracle.[30]

45.[31] On a certain day, the Lady Mary said to the Lord Jesus, "My son, bring me water from the well." When he went to fetch the water and had filled his pitcher, it got bumped, and it broke when it was full. But the Lord laid out his handkerchief and collected the water and brought it in his handkerchief back to his mother. When the Lady Mary saw him, she was amazed at this, and she preserved everything that she saw and remembered it in her heart.

46. Another day, the Lord Jesus was at a rivulet of water, and there were some boys with him who were also making small pools. The Lord Jesus made from the clay twelve sparrows, and he lined them up on the sides of the pool, three on each side. It was the Sabbath that day, and the son of Hanan the Jew came and saw them engaged in this way. He said to them with anger and annoyance, "On the Sabbath day, do you form clay?" And he rushed over and destroyed their pools. But the Lord Jesus clapped his hands over the sparrows that he had made, and they flew [away] chirping. Then the son of Hanan came and destroyed the Lord Jesus' pool as well and dried up its water. So the Lord Jesus said to him, "Just as this water dried up, your life will dry up." At that moment, that boy withered.

47. Again, the Lord Jesus was going with Joseph, and it happened to him by chance that a boy was running and that boy shoved the Lord Jesus so that he fell. [Jesus] said to [the boy], "Just as you tossed me down, you will fall and not get up again." Immediately, the boy fell down and died.

48. There was in Jerusalem a teacher of children named Zacchaeus, and he said to Joseph, "O Joseph, why don't you bring Jesus so that he may learn?" Joseph said to him, "Certainly," and he went and told the Lady Mary, and they took [the boy] and brought him to the teacher. When the teacher saw him, he wrote for him the alphabet and said to him, "Say *Alif*." He [Jesus] said "*Alif*." Then the teacher said to him, "Say *Bayt*," and the Lord Jesus said to him, "Tell me the explanation of the letter *Alif*, and then I shall say *Bayt*." The teacher was about to strike him, so he told him that the *Alif* is such-and-such and the *Bayt* is such-and-such, that among the signs there are straight ones, crooked ones, round ones, and pointed [i.e., dotted] ones, as well as unpointed [i.e., undotted]

ones, and why one letter precedes another. And he began to explain and interpret things that the teacher had not heard about or read about in a book. Then the Lord Jesus said to the teacher, "Listen, so that I may recite (them) to you," and he began to say, "*Alif, Bayt, Gamal, Dalad* . . ." all the way up to *Tau,* reciting fluently. The teacher was amazed and said, "I think that this boy was born before Noah." He turned to Joseph and said to him, "You have brought me a boy so that I might teach him and he is the teacher of teachers." And he said to the Lady Mary, "Your son is not in need of learning."

49. Then they took him to the place of another teacher who was more clever than that [first] teacher. When he saw him, he said to him, "Say *Alif,*" and he said, "*Alif.*" He said to him, "Say *Bayt,*" and the Lord Jesus responded to him, saying, "Tell me what the meaning of *Alif* is, and after that I shall say *Bayt.*" So the teacher raised up his hand to strike him, and immediately his hand withered and he died. Joseph said to Lady Mary, "From now on, we should not allow him to go out of the house, for everyone who comes up against him dies."

50. When he was twelve years old, they brought him up to Jerusalem to the festival. When the festival was over, they returned [home], but the Lord Jesus remained behind in the Temple among the scribes, elders, and scholars of the sons of Israel, posing questions to them and giving them answers on the [subject of] the sciences. He said to them, "Whose son is the Messiah?" They said to him, "He is the son of David." He said to them, "Then how does he call him 'my Lord' in the Spirit, when he said, 'The Lord said to my Lord, sit on my right hand, so that I may place your enemies under your footsteps.' " The chief scribe replied, "Have you read the [holy] books?" The Lord Jesus said to him, "The books, and also what is in the books," and he explained the books, the law, the commandments, the wise sayings, and the mysteries that were in the books of the prophets—something that no created intellect is able to grasp. That scribe said to him, "Until now, I have not grasped nor have I heard this teaching. I wonder what will come of this boy?"

51. A learned man was also there, one skilled in astronomy [*'ilm al-aflāk*], and he said to the Lord Jesus, "Have you done readings in astronomical science [*'ilm al-hay'a*]?" The Lord Jesus responded and told him the number of the spheres,[32] and of the celestial bodies; their natures, operations, and opposition; their division into thirds, fourths, and sixths; their direct and retrograde course; their [division into] seconds and smaller increments; and other things that the intellect cannot grasp.

52. A man learned in natural medicine [*ṭibb al-ṭabā'i'*] was also present among them, and he said to the Lord Jesus, "Have you done readings, my friend, in medical science [*'ilm al-ṭibb*]?" The Lord Jesus responded and spoke at length about physics, metaphysics, hyperphysics, and hypophysics; about the powers of the body; the humors and their functions; the limbs and bones; the veins, arteries, and nerves; the [respective] function[s] of heat, dryness, cold, and moisture, and what is produced by them; what activities the soul does in the body, [including] its perceptions and powers, the faculty of speech, and the operations of anger and desire; the conjunction and separation [of the

body and soul]; and other things that the created intellect cannot grasp. That learned man arose and bowed down before the Lord Jesus and said, "My Lord, from now on, I am your disciple and servant."

53. While they were in the midst of speaking about these and other similar things, the Lady Mary came, after she and Joseph had been searching around for him for three days. She saw him sitting among the scholars asking them questions and giving answers to them, and Lady Mary said to him, "Why have you treated us this way, my son? For your father and I have been inquiring after you to the point of exhaustion." He said, "Why are you two inquiring after me? Don't you know that I am supposed to be in my Father's house?" But they did not understand the words that he spoke to them. The scholars said, "O Mary, is this your son?" When she said, "Yes," they said to her, "Blessed are you, Mary, on account of your giving birth [to him]." The Lord Jesus went home to Nazareth, and he obeyed them in every matter. His mother kept everything he said in her heart, and the Lord Jesus grew in stature and wisdom and grace before God and humankind.

Appendix C
Jesus and the Birds in St. Martin's Church, Zillis, Switzerland

On the ceiling of St. Martin's Church in Zillis, Switzerland, a twelfth-century painted panel displays a familiar scene from early Christian stories about Jesus' childhood (see fig. 2).[1] Jesus is shown as a young boy playing on the bank of a flowing river. Seated between two companions holding clay birds in their hands, the Christ child has just performed a miracle, bringing one of these inanimate figures to life. In the painting, he releases the bird into the air, as the other children look on in mute surprise. On the pigmented surface of the wood, the bird hovers transfixed just above Jesus' outstretched hands.

With a leap of the mind's eye, a visitor to the church, craning her neck to espy this image, might just imagine that the bird is actually about to take flight—out of the frame and out of the confines of the church itself. If that bird were indeed to escape and fly outside, it would soon find itself gliding over another river, the Hinterrhein, which flows north through the Schams Valley (Val Schons) and past Zillis before it plunges into the treacherous Via Mala Gorge on its way to the main branch of the Rhine. In this setting—in the shadow of the Alps, along a historic route of travel and trade through a series of high mountain passes—Christian parishioners since the Middle Ages have filed into St. Martin's and gazed up at this image of Jesus as a young boy.

How would medieval worshippers have made sense of this scene of Jesus and the birds? How would they have understood its placement and presentation within the church at Zillis? How would the details of the painting have prompted viewers to read the significance of this infancy story in relation to local geography, iconography, and religious practice? To seek out answers to these questions, it is important to broaden the scope a bit and place this painting in the context of the architectural and iconographic history of the church, as well as the transmission history of *Paidika* traditions in the Latin-speaking world of medieval Europe.

The current St. Martin's Church in Zillis rests upon the foundations of a late ancient ecclesiastical structure dating to the late fifth century.[2] The first church on the site was built using portions of walls from an earlier Roman-era construction and featured a semicircular apse and a baptistery.[3] After a stage of renovations to the original apse during the reign of Charlemagne (ca. 800 CE), the entire first church was finally dismantled and replaced with a new, single-naved construction early in the twelfth century.[4] It was at this stage that the Romanesque paintings on the ceiling of St. Martin's were commissioned and installed.[5]

The ceiling is made up of 153 panels in total, arranged in seventeen rows of nine panels each, set within a grid of longitudinal and cross-battens (fig. 3, with key).[6] The arrangement of the panels was designed to present to the viewer a terrestrial map of the cosmos, with the events of the Gospels plotted as its key coordinates. In this context, the ceiling has been described as a *topographia christiana* and compared to the four-cornered maps of the world produced by Cosmas Indicopleustes (Alexandria, mid-sixth century) and Beatus of Liébana (northern Spain, late eighth century).[7] The panels along the four borders of the ceiling contain forty-eight watery scenes (1–48) populated by sea monsters, depicted as hybridized creatures with fish tails. These panels mark the perilous edges—the outer boundary and extent—of the known world. On the field inside those borders, ninety-eight panels depicting the life and miracles of Jesus (49–146) and seven more panels on the *Life of St. Martin of Tours* (147–53) occupy and constitute the terra firma. This staged sequence of biblical and hagiographical scenes is arrayed in horizontal rows running from north to south, starting at the eastern end of the ceiling and progressing toward the west. The scenes are presented in separate, bordered panels like successive leaves of an illuminated manuscript. Beginning with the Annunciation and the events leading up to Christ's birth, the majority of the panels follow the lines of the gospel narrative(s) up to the Passion and Jesus' crowning with thorns, before the focus shifts abruptly in the final row, which contains episodes from St. Martin's vita.[8] The central vertical column running from east to west and the central horizontal row running from north to south are each bordered with thicker, ornamented bands, and their intersection forms the shape of a cross—the mark of Christ crucially superimposed upon the *mappa mundi.*

As the only panel not primarily inspired by the canonical Gospels or by the *Life of St. Martin,* the image of Jesus bringing the clay birds to life attracts the observant viewer's attention (Panel 91).[9] Why does this apocryphal scene appear here, and how would medieval visitors to the church have understood its significance in relation to the acts of worship performed in that space?

During the medieval period, collections of infancy stories were transmitted in Latin throughout continental Europe and the British Isles. At a relatively early date, probably sometime in the fourth or fifth century, the Greek *Paidika* was translated into Latin.[10] In the Old Latin version, which survives in a fragmentary fifth-century palimpsest, the story of Jesus' miracle with the birds is featured as the opening episode (as in all other early versions). Later, this Old Latin text was incorporated into a more expansive work called the *Gospel of Pseudo-Matthew,* which by the eleventh century combined four different kinds of material in a unified narrative structure celebrating the role of Mary: (1) an introductory prologue; (2) material translated and adapted from the early Christian *Protevangelium of James* focusing on events leading up to and including Jesus' birth; (3) independent story traditions about the flight of the Holy Family to Egypt; and (4) a collection of stories about Jesus' childhood drawn from the *Paidika* in Latin.[11]

While there is evidence that the *Gospel of Pseudo-Matthew* was originally disseminated in the area of what is now northeast France and southern Germany, by the twelfth century expanded versions of the text—with the *Paidika* material now incorporated—had come to be copied in Austria and Italy as well.[12] Given the fact that Zillis is located along an Alpine pass that constitutes the principal north-south route of travel linking Bregenz in western Austria with Milan in northern Italy, it is therefore not surprising to find evidence for familiarity with this text on the twelfth-century ceiling of St. Martin's. One finds proof of local acquaintance with the *Gospel of Pseudo-Matthew* elsewhere on the ceiling as well. In particular, the painted panels related to the Holy Family's flight to Egypt contain subtle details drawn from the same apocryphal source.[13] On one of the panels (82), Mary sits on the back of a horse or donkey with the Christ child in her lap.[14] The animal walks toward the right, while Mary and child face the viewer in a full-frontal posture. A date palm is depicted just inside the right-hand border of the frame on the right: the branches of the tree bend down to the left toward Mary, and she extends her hand to pluck a cluster of dates hanging from its branches. The adjacent squares fill out the scene. To the left (81), Joseph walks behind holding a whip with three cords in his right hand and carrying a long staff laden with a sack and a water flask over his shoulder. To the right (83), a winged angel strides ahead, looking back over his shoulder at Mary but pointing the way forward with an outstretched right index finger.[15]

At first glance, these three scenes might be taken simply as an elaboration of the basic story as it is found in chapter 2 of the canonical Gospel of Matthew (2:13–18). Indeed, the panel preceding this triad (80) shows Joseph receiving the message communicated by the angel in Matthew 2:13, "Get up [and] take the child and his mother and escape to Egypt." In the church at Zillis, however, a singular detail—the inclining palm tree—marks the sequence at least in part as a visual reading of the later Pseudo-Matthean *Gospel.*[16] In that version of the story, Mary finds herself growing fatigued from the heat of the sun on the third day of their journey through the desert, and seeing a palm tree, she asks Joseph if she can rest in its shade. When they reach the tree and she asks Joseph for some of its fruit to eat, he is first dismayed by its formidable height, but the child

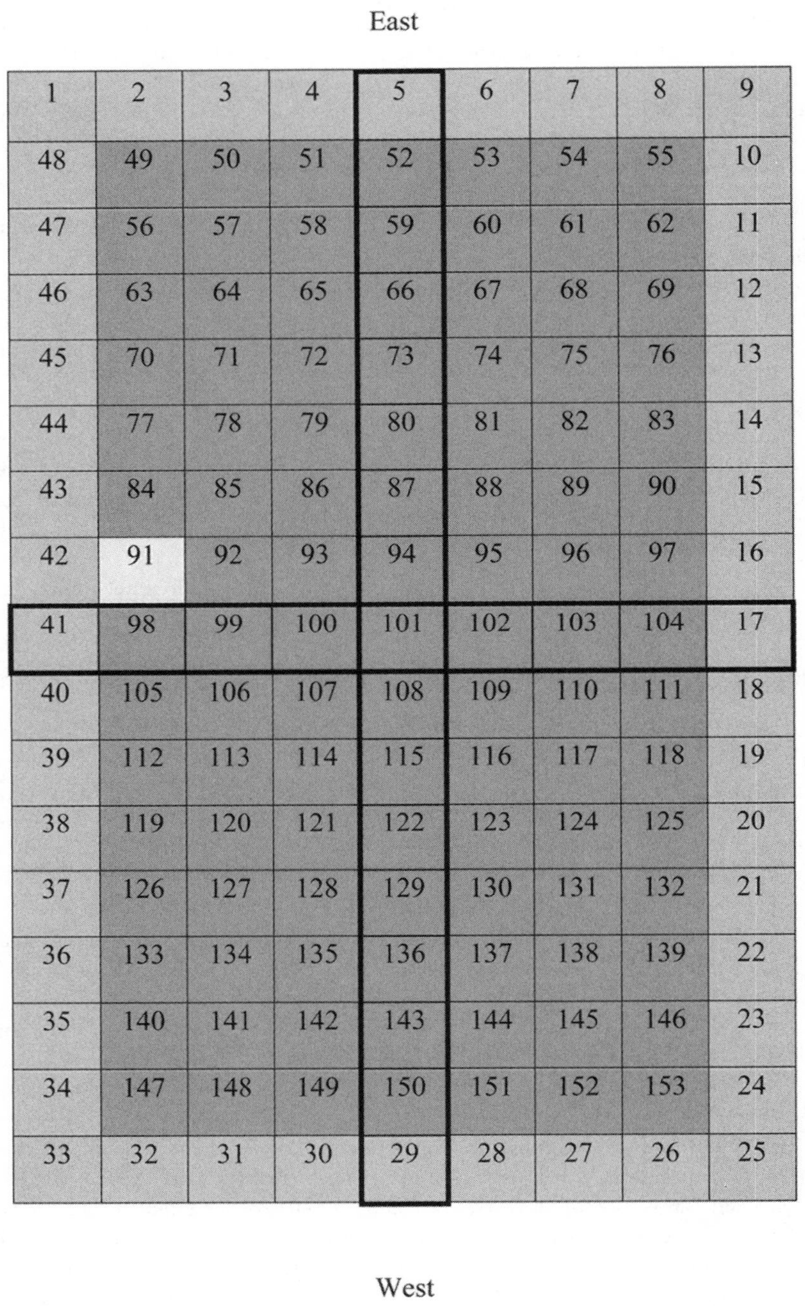

East

1	2	3	4	5	6	7	8	9
48	49	50	51	52	53	54	55	10
47	56	57	58	59	60	61	62	11
46	63	64	65	66	67	68	69	12
45	70	71	72	73	74	75	76	13
44	77	78	79	80	81	82	83	14
43	84	85	86	87	88	89	90	15
42	91	92	93	94	95	96	97	16
41	98	99	100	101	102	103	104	17
40	105	106	107	108	109	110	111	18
39	112	113	114	115	116	117	118	19
38	119	120	121	122	123	124	125	20
37	126	127	128	129	130	131	132	21
36	133	134	135	136	137	138	139	22
35	140	141	142	143	144	145	146	23
34	147	148	149	150	151	152	153	24
33	32	31	30	29	28	27	26	25

West

Figure 3. Plan of the painted ceiling. St. Martin's Church, Zillis, Switzerland. Plan design by Stephen J. Davis.

KEY TO FIGURE 3:

Selected Numbered Panels on the Ceiling of St. Martin's Church

1–48	Watery scenes populated by sea monsters
10–12	Boat scenes
49–146	Scenes from the life of Christ
79	Jesus' dedication as an infant in the Temple
81–83	The Holy Family's flight to Egypt
84	The Holy Family in repose
91	**Jesus animates the birds**
92–93	Jesus speaks with the teachers in the Temple
94–97	John the Baptist
98	The baptism of Jesus
99–102	Jesus' temptation in the desert
101	Scene of Jesus' third temptation
103–4	The wedding at Cana
110–111	Jesus heals the paralytic at the pool at Bethsaida
116	The Samaritan woman at the well
135	The washing of Peter's feet
136–37	The Last Supper
147–53	Scenes from the life of St. Martin

Jesus intervenes and commands the palm to bend its branches down so that his mother can be refreshed. Afterward—the very next day—Jesus blesses the palm, and an angel takes one of its branches to heaven to be planted there "in the paradise of my Father."[17]

The painting of Mary reaching out to take fruit from the palm (82) conflates elements of this account. In the *Gospel of Pseudo-Matthew,* she has the opportunity to dismount and sit down at the base of the tree before Jesus commands it to incline its branches toward her. On the church ceiling in Zillis, the events from the story are compressed and conflated: Mary remains seated on her mount as she plucks the dates from the branches. In this context, the painted panel located at the beginning of the next row—an image of the Holy Family seated in repose (84)—should also be understood as closely connected, insofar as it provides an element of narrative resolution to the earlier three-panel sequence.[18] This fourth panel provides something of a visual pause, perhaps affording the viewer a quiet moment of Marian devotion, before he or she moves on to contemplate the graphically violent sequence of panels on the Massacre of the Innocents that fill the rest of the horizontal row.[19]

The image of Jesus and the birds (91) is located in the very next row, immediately below the image of the Holy Family at rest. There the seated figures of Christ and his two young companions subtly mirror the postures of Jesus, Mary, and Joseph above. The inclusion of this apocryphal scene further confirms that the choices of the artists (and of those who commissioned the art) were informed by readings of the Pseudo-Matthean *Gospel* in its expanded form. Chapters 26 and 27 of that work tell the story of how a four-year-old Jesus, after his family's return from Egypt, "was playing with some children at the bed of the Jordan" on a Sabbath day. Redirecting the river water into pools, he makes twelve sparrows out of the clay. Then, when an onlooker accuses him of violating the Sabbath, Jesus claps his hands and commands the birds to fly. After the birds take wing, he calls after them again, "Go and fly through the earth, and through all the world, and live."[20]

Juxtaposed on its upper edge to the scene of the Holy Family at rest (84), the story of the Christ child's miracle with the birds is bordered on its lower edge by a panel depicting the baptism of Jesus (98).[21] The visual link between these two contiguous panels would have been reinforced by formal and spatial considerations. First, the two scenes mirror one another in their formal layout. As in the adjacent scene with the birds (and in the scene of the Holy Family at rest above it), the baptism presents Jesus in the center of the image flanked by two other figures—in this case, John the Baptist on the left, and an angel on the right.[22] Second, the panels presenting Jesus' miracle with the birds and his baptism are connected by their spatial proximity.

This immediate proximity has the effect of drawing the childhood miracle and the baptism scene together as part of a larger iconographic narrative with Jesus' baptism at its center. On the one hand, the baptism caps a narrative sequence introduced in the previous row, where the panel with Jesus and the birds is followed by two scenes depicting Jesus' encounter with the teachers in the Temple (92–93), and then two more pairs of scenes showing John the Baptist preaching in the desert (with Elijah in 94–95, and with the Lamb of God in 96–97).[23] On the other hand, the baptism effectively begins a new chapter in this visual narrative: it serves as a prelude to Jesus' temptations in the desert where he is finally ministered to by an angel (99–102) and to his miracle of turning water to wine at the wedding at Cana (103–4).[24] All of these scenes occupy the same row, with Jesus' baptism and his miracle of turning water to wine bracketing the temptation panels in the middle. As currently reconstructed, this sequence occupies the central row of the entire ceiling program: set off with a doubled border, these panels compose the horizontal span of the cross that transects the *mappa mundi*.[25]

The formal and spatial factors I have outlined above would also have fostered key thematic and theological connections between Jesus' baptism and his act of bringing the birds to life. The two scenes each in its own way underscore the life-giving character of Jesus as incarnate Word, encountered by the faithful in story and sacrament. And in each, water becomes the medium for this life-giving divine action. I have already noted how the St. Martin's artists used water to provide a framework, a visual structure, for their christological cartography. Around the external border of the ceiling panels, watery scenes encircle the biblical terra firma. While most of these border panels are populated by formidable sea creatures, one also finds three with scenes of human beings in boats (10–12).[26] Scene 12 is fragmentary and difficult to interpret. Of the other two, one shows a man boarding a boat (11), probably a depiction of Jonah's story, understood to prefigure the resurrection in early Christian interpretation (Matthew 12:39–41). The other shows two disciples fishing (10), perhaps meant to evoke the church's missionary calling as "fishers of men" (Matthew 4:19; Mark 1:17), as well as Peter and John's miraculous catch of fish after Jesus' resurrection (John 21:1–14). Indeed, the number of ceiling panels in the church (153 in total) is thought to have been designed as a specific allusion to the number of fish caught in that Johannine story. According to John 21:11, the disciples' net was "full of large fish, a hundred fifty-three of them." Some scholars have surmised that there were originally four panels featuring boat scenes on the ceiling of St. Martin's Church and that these panels may originally have been located at the ends of the column and row that intersect to form the shape of a cross.[27] On the horizontal plane, this would have aligned two of them with the scenes of Jesus' baptism and the miracle of turning water to wine at Cana, which bookend that row within the inner zone of panels.

Interspersed throughout the inner zone—the terra firma of Christ's life—one also finds other scenes in which water plays a central role, including panels featuring the stories of Jesus' healing of the paralytic by the pool at Bethsaida (110–11), his encounter with the Samaritan woman at the well (116), and his washing of St. Peter's feet (135).[28] In addition, a river—the Jordan of biblical story, represented here by a horizontal blue band—serves as the backdrop on a number of panels throughout the visual program, cutting across the landscape and unifying the iconographic narrative.[29] The representation of such a river cutting across this visual *mappa mundi* corresponds to the conventions of medieval cartographers, who often show rivers and their tributaries crisscrossing the world continent and intersecting with the surrounding oceans at various points.[30] In the case of St. Martin's Church in Zillis, these common waters effectively map Jesus' miracle with the birds and his baptism onto the same landscape.

The landscape is populated not only by biblical stories but also by local landmarks and coordinates. Indeed, a close examination of the panel located at the center of the entire painted program (101)—the scene of Jesus' third temptation by the devil from Matthew 4:8–10—shows how this biblical landscape was modeled after the local terrain in and around Zillis. In that painting, as in the two other temptation scenes (99–100), Jesus stands on the right side of the panel. The devil, represented as a black figure with wings, horns, and claws, stands on the left. In this third temptation scene, however, the devil gestures with his left claw toward a pair of mountains in the background. With his right, he points toward a black disk in the foreground. Bordered and inscribed with white lines, the disk contains miniature symbols of buildings and towers, "all the kingdoms of the world" from Matthew 4:8 schematically represented for the viewer.[31]

For a local worshipper gazing up at the ceiling in St. Martin's in the twelfth century, however, the mountain in the background would have attracted special notice, for its contours closely mirror that of the massif Piz Vizan, which overlooks the town of Zillis on the southwest side of the Schams Valley, and which was the first sight a worshipper would have had after leaving the church from its main (western) door.[32] In an article on the early medieval Christianization of the Alps, Randon Jerris has noted how sacred landscapes in this region were often produced via "the appropriation of such diverse topographic features as mountains, rivers, valleys, terraces, and prominent rock outcrops."[33] In St. Martin's Church, on the ceiling panel featuring Jesus' third temptation, the artists mapped the biblical story onto just such a local topography. And, in the process, they plotted the church at Zillis itself at "the very center of the world," at the nexus of the cross that spans the *mappa mundi*.[34] In this way, the rest of the cosmos—from the central terrain populated by gospel stories out to the watery limits of the earth—is envisioned from the privileged vantage point of St. Martin's Church.[35] The river running intermittently through the painted program may be understood to have had a local referent as well: in the eyes of the beholder, the Hinterrhein that carved out the Schams Valley may have been metonymically conflated with the river Jordan and all other rivers of the world. That same river flowed past Jesus as he brought the birds to life and flowed around him as he was baptized by John.

Here one begins to see more clearly how the paintings at St. Martin's Church sponsored local viewing practices that mapped the world of the Gospels onto the physical and sacred topography of Zillis. How would the scene of Jesus' miracle with the birds have been interpreted in such a context? In what other ways would this story about Jesus' childhood have evoked particular cultural associations for parishioners in the twelfth century? For fully textured answers to these questions, I need to revisit what is known about the socio-economic and religious history of Zillis as a settlement and to review the church's iconography in light of that history.

The history of the town and church at Zillis is especially marked by two distinctive kinds of practices—first, travel connected with both trade and pilgrimage; and second, the administration of baptism. Both of these sets of practices find significant correspondence in the ceiling paintings at St. Martin's Church.

From the time of its original establishment during the late Roman period, the town of Zillis gained a reputation as a supply outpost for travelers, tradesmen, and pilgrims making their way through the high Alpine passes on their way northward through the Via Mala Gorge to the main branch of the Rhine, or southward through the Splügen Pass toward Chiavenna and Lake Como. Beginning in the eighth century, the bishop of Chur (only 33.5 kilometers to the north of Zillis) took steps to consolidate his authority over the region, and there was a corresponding increase in security for those navigating the mountain passes. Monasteries established by the bishop began to serve as hospices, offering hospitality and protection to travelers. In this way, the bishop's economic patronage sponsored a rapid growth in the Alpine cult of the saints and an influx of pilgrims to newly established monastic shrines in the region.[36]

Prompted to read the iconography in light of such practices, medieval viewers of the paintings in the Zillis church would have seen traces of the town's history in the iconography. Since the late ancient period, images of the three Magi and the Holy Family had long been associated with pilgrimage and other forms of travel.[37] Accordingly, these scenes, with their interspersed representations of the Magi (71–72) and the Holy Family at rest (84), would have evoked for visitors the town's well-earned reputation as a way station for those making long journeys at high altitude through otherwise inhospitable terrain. In this context, the scene of Jesus' third trial by the devil—explicitly set within a Zillisian landscape and placed at the very crux of the iconographic program—would have simultaneously been read as a warning regarding the notorious hazards and temptations of such travel and as an assurance that St. Martin's Church bore Christ's seal as a safe haven for those resting on their journeys.

Already in late antiquity the church established at Zillis also came to serve as a center for the administration of Christian baptism, as shown by the fifth-century remains of a baptistery discovered in excavations beneath the current architectural structure. Established as one of the oldest *ecclesiae plebeiae* (that is, nonmonastic churches) in central Europe, the boundaries of its parish originally extended over not only the Schams Valley but also the outer Rheinwald as far as Splügen, eighteen kilometers to the south.[38] In the seventh and eighth centuries, the large parish at Zillis was divided into smaller units in order to accommodate the liturgical needs of the communities in outlying areas.[39] During the later medieval period, however, St. Martin's continued to serve as the "mother church" for the entire Schams Valley, and it was there that all children from the valley were taken to be christened.[40] The twelfth-century baptismal font, which still stands in the church choir, provides tangible evidence for the maintenance of such baptismal practice at the time the ceiling paintings were commissioned and in the decades and centuries after.[41]

Apart from the baptism scene itself, various other details in the paintings would have triggered cultural memories of this liturgical history among medieval viewers. Interspersed among the paintings one finds depictions of ritual actions and implements associated with childhood dedication and acts of washing or purification. In the painting of Jesus' infant dedication at the Temple (79), Mary hands the Christ child over to the priest Zechariah. Between them, on a cloth-draped table, sits a cup whose form closely emulates that of the chalice-shaped baptismal font in the choir of St. Martin's. Elsewhere, on the panel where Jesus washes Peter's feet (135), the disciple places his right foot in a basin that follows the same pattern, with a slightly wider design. The sacramental context of this image is reinforced in two adjacent panels of the Last Supper (136–37), where the disciples sit at table with several similarly shaped cups and bowls laid out before them.[42]

In the end, the image of Jesus bringing the birds to life would have contributed significantly to the local perceptions of St. Martin's Church as a privileged site of baptismal practice. In the Latin *Gospel of Pseudo-Matthew,* Jesus' miracle is brought about through his use of both water and word to grant new life to the birds in his keeping. Having first redirected water into pools "by the word of his power," and after taking clay from those pools and shaping that clay in the form of sparrows, he enlivens them by "the voice of his command" to "go, and fly through all the earth."[43] In this form, the Christ child's command echoes his words in Matthew 28:19, where he commands his followers, "Go therefore and make disciples of all nations, baptizing them in the name of the Father and of the Son and of the Holy Spirit."

Hearing such scriptural echoes in the midst of baptismal celebrations in the Zillis church, medieval worshippers gazing at the bird leaving Jesus' hand might have found their eyes drifting down to the adjacent panel showing their Savior's own baptism, and down further still—three rows below in the same column—to another panel capturing Jesus in the act of reaching out to bless young children, an iconographic fulfillment of his gospel exhortation to "let the little children come to me."[44] These visual stimuli would have allowed local parishioners and church visitors to draw tangible connections between the images themselves and the ritual actions taking place in that space. The Jesus presented here is one who paved the way in all respects for the infants brought to St. Martin's for christening: he not only welcomed children into his embrace, he also experienced life as a little child, was dedicated at an altar, and was baptized in a river—a flowing current that could be reimagined just by looking out the church door to the valley below, or by raising one's eyes to the painted panels on the church ceiling. Viewed in this context, the image of Jesus granting life to a bird provides evidence of medieval Christian cultural memory at work. In concert with the other crucially marked scenes from Jesus' life, this miracle helped remind local worshippers of their own social and sacramental history—a history painted into *Paidika* lore high in the Alps.

Abbreviations

AGI	*Arabic Gospel of the Infancy*
ANF	*Ante-Nicene Fathers,* ed. A. Roberts and J. Donaldson
ANRW	*Aufstieg und Niedergang der römischen Welt,* ed. H. Temporini et al.
BIFAO	*Bulletin de l'Institut français d'archéologie orientale*
CANT	I. M. Geerard, *Clavis apocryphorum Novi Testamenti*
CCSA	Corpus Christianorum Series Apocryphorum
CCSL	Corpus Christianorum Series Latina
CGL	*Corpus Glossariorum Latinorum,* ed. G. Goetz
CIL	*Corpus Inscriptionum Latinarum,* ed. T. Mommsen et al.
CSCO	Corpus Scriptorum Christianorum Orientalium
CSEL	Corpus Scriptorum Ecclesiasticorum Latinorum
DT	*Defixionum Tabellae,* ed. A. Audollent
DTA	*Appendix Continens Defixionum Tabellae,* ed. R. Wünsch
EI[2]	*Encyclopaedia of Islam,* second edition, ed. P. J. Bearman et al.
Ep.	*Epistles*
FC	Fathers of the Church
GAS	F. Sezgin, *Geschichte des arabischen Schrifttums*
GCAL	G. Graf, *Geschichte der christlichen arabischen Literatur*
GCS	Die Griechischen Christlichen Schriftsteller
IG	*Inscriptiones Graecae,* ed. W. Dittenberger et al.
LCL	Loeb Classical Library
LXX	Septuagint

NPNF	*Nicene and Post-Nicene Fathers,* ed. P. Schaff and H. Wace
Or.	*Orations*
Paidika	The "Childhood Deeds" of Jesus
PDM	*Papyri Demoticae Magicae*
PG	*Patrologia Graeca,* ed. J. P. Migne
PGM	*Papyri Graecae Magicae,* ed. K. Preisendanz
P.Oxy.	*The Oxyrhynchus Papyri,* ed. B. P. Grenfell et al.
PTS	Patristische Texte und Studien
SB	*Sammelbuch griechischer Urkunden aus Ägypten,* ed. F. Preisigke et al.
SEG	*Supplementum epigraphicum graecum,* ed. J. J. E. Hondius et al.
SGD	D. R. Jordan, "A Survey of Greek Defixiones"
T. Berol.	*Aus den Papyrus der Königlichen Museen,* ed. A. Erman and F. Krebs
TLG	*Thesaurus Linguae Graecae*
TU	Texte und Untersuchungen
UPZ	*Urkunden der Ptolemäerzeit,* ed. U. Wilcken
WUNT	Wissenschaftliche Untersuchungen zum Neuen Testament
ZPE	*Zeitschrift für Papyrologie und Epigraphik*

Notes

Chapter 1. Cultural Memories of a Young Jesus

1. This "core content" that I describe here corresponds to the so-called short recension documented by Burke (*De infantia,* 188–97) and Aasgaard (*Childhood of Jesus,* 14), although each uses a different chapter numbering system to refer to the content of that recension. For a more systematic account of the textual problems related to the short, middle, and long forms of the text, see chapter 2. For a translation of the Greek text (Gs), see Appendix A. Unless otherwise referenced in the notes, all translations of ancient and modern texts are my own.

2. The "intermediate" text of the *Paidika* adds a second miracle account (ch. 16), in which Jesus heals the injured foot of a woodsman (Burke, *De infantia,* 333–35). It is not attested in the earliest short recension, however, and therefore probably represents a later addition.

3. Lambeck, *Commentariorum,* VII.270–73; Burke, *De infantia,* 45–126.

4. Lambeck, *Commentariorum,* VII.270–73. Other scholars followed: see esp. Simon, *Nouvelles observations,* vol. 1, 5–9 (the title and chapters 1 and 6 of the Paris MS); Cotelier, *SS. Patrum,* 2nd ed., vol. 1, 345–46 (the entire Paris text=chapters 1–6 and the opening section of an additional story about Jesus and a dyer); and Fabricius, *Codex apocryphus,* vol. 1, 127–58 (introduction), 159–67 (Paris text, with comparisons to the Vienna version).

5. Esp. the landmark edition by Tischendorf, *Evangelia apocrypha* (1853; 2nd ed. 1876).

6. Beausobre, *Histoire critique,* 366; Ellicott, "Apocryphal Gospels," 193; see also Cowper, *Apocryphal Gospels,* lxxii, who concludes that the *Paidika* is "utterly worthless" (p. 129).

7. Norton, *Evidences,* 375; Stowe, *Origin,* 206 ("ridiculous" and "immoral"); Nicolas, *Études,* 295–99; Variot, *Évangiles apocryphes,* 214–15.

8. Beausobre, *Histoire,* 366 ("violent & vindicatif"); Pons, *Recherches,* 24 ("bizarres et parfois méchants"); Harnack, *Geschichte,* vol. 2.1, 593.

9. The first early modern scholar to argue for a Gnostic provenance was Simon, *Nouvelles observations,* 5–9. In his wake, a whole train of scholars proposed various theories of Gnostic origins or influence: Beausobre, *Histoire,* 366–68; Nicolas, *Études,* 333–35; Meyer, "Erzählung des Thomas," 63–67; Meyer, "Kindheitserzählung des Thomas," 132–42; Bauer, *Leben Jesu,* 87–100. A competing group of scholars during this period argued for Manichaean influence on the *Paidika:* Lardner, *Credibility,* III.435; Giorgi, *Alphabetum Thibetanum,* 383–92; and Variot, *Évangiles,* 44. Mingarelli ("De Apocrypho," 73–155) combined these two theories, arguing for Gnostic origins and a later Manichaean expansion.

10. See Cecchelli, *Mater Christi* (1954); Cullman, "Infancy Gospels" (1963), 363–417; Otero, *Das kirchenslavische Evangelium* (1967), 172–84; Vielhauer, *Geschichte* (1975), 672–77; Schindler, *Apokryphen,* 2nd ed. (1988), 439–41; Rebell, *Neutestamentliche Apokryphen* (1992), 132–36; Baars and Helderman, "Neue Materialien" (1993), 191–226, and (1994), 1–32; Schneider, *Evangelia infantiae* (1995), 34–47; Ceming and Werlitz, *Die verbotenen Evangelien,* rev. ed. (1999), 93–95; and Lapham, *Introduction* (2003), 129–31. Among the scholars who have argued against Gnostic influence are Gero, "Infancy Gospel of Thomas," 46–80; Wilson, "Apokryphen, II," 334–36; Hock, *Infancy Gospels,* 83–103; and Burke, *De infantia,* 124–26, and passim.

11. Hervieux, *New Testament Apocrypha,* 112.

12. Cullman, "Infancy Gospels," 442.

13. Elliott, *Apocryphal New Testament,* 68; see also now Upson-Saia, "Holy Child or Holy Terror?" 2.

14. Hervieux, *New Testament Apocrypha,* 106 and 112; see also Pfeiffer, *Introduction,* 123; Foster, "Apocrypha," 113. On this history of polemic, see Burke, *De infantia,* viii–ix, 51–52, 57–60, 90.

15. Frilingos, "'It Moves Me to Wonder,'" 840–42.

16. Aasgaard, *Childhood,* 2.

17. On this point, see Burke, "'Social Viewing,'" 30, where he associates such derogatory and "anachronistic" comments with "the snobbery in scholars of the Roman classics." Hunter ("Ancient Readers," 262) discusses a similar dismissive tradition among scholars of the Greek novel, who often have assumed that "serious people in antiquity did not take those novels seriously (and certainly did not devote much time to reading them)." Illustrative of this attitude is B. E. Perry (*Ancient Romances,* 5, 56), who characterizes the novel's audience as "children and the poor-in-spirit" and "young or naïve people of little education."

18. Aasgaard (*Childhood,* 1), for example, emphasizes certain "stranger features" of the text.

19. In this context, it is striking that even those early Christians who cite the *Paidika* critically (see chapter 2) do not seem to have raised specific objections to the ethical behavior of the young Jesus depicted in such tales. Kaiser ("Die sogenannte 'Kindererzählung des Thomas,'" 463–68) rightly observes how some later manuscript copyists and translators made changes to the text that were meant to justify or soften the impact of Jesus' actions (indeed, probably a sign of some discomfort on their part), but she also acknowledges that such responses were by no means uniform and that "the individual text witnesses did not change anything essential" (p. 467). Elsewhere, Dzon ("Boys Will Be Boys," 179–225) argues persuasively that medieval readers of infancy gospels in fact would have understood the *Paidika*'s Jesus to embody human childhood in a full sense, both in his behavior and in his physiognomy. Taken all together, the evidence suggests that ancient readers (diverse as they were) were not as disturbed by Jesus' actions in the *Paidika* as modern readers have tended to be (Kaiser, "Die sogenannte 'Kindererzählung des Thomas,'" 468). My perspective differs from that of Upson-Saia ("Holy Child or Holy Terror?" 3), who posits that the image of an angry young Jesus in the *Paidika* most certainly would have been "alarming and offensive" to early Christian audiences. She makes this claim on the basis of literary evidence in which anger is critiqued as an unbecoming emotion. To explain how such stories came to be incorporated in the *Paidika,* Upson-Saia conjectures that they must have originated among opponents of Christianity, and that only later were they adapted by a Christian editor for the purpose of domesticating and defusing such critiques. I find Upson-Saia's argument problematic in two ways. First, she assumes that late ancient Greek society (Christians included) shared a rather undifferentiated perspective on anger, a "wide(-ranging) consensus" (ibid., 11, 14) built almost exclusively on the testimony of a philosophical and patristic elite. Second, to explain how such "embarrassing" scenes found their way into the work of a Christian author, she depends on a text-critical argument from silence: without citing explicit evidence, she presumes that the stories simply must have originated from extra-Christian polemical sources. As a result, she leaves little room for alternative discursive uses and functions of anger, such as I explore in chapter 4.

20. See especially the scholarship of Beryl Rawson, Sarah Pomeroy, Ville Vuolanto, Ada Cohen, Christian Laes, and Cornelia Horn, among others.

21. Bradley, "Wet-nursing at Rome," 201–29; French, "Birth Control," 1355–62; Bradley, "The Nurse and the Child at Rome," 137–56; Dasen and Ducate-Paarmann, "La naissance," 377–405; Hänninen, "From Womb to Family," 49–59; Dasen, "Blessing or Portent?" 61–73; Dasen, "Roman Birth Rites," 199–214; Dasen, "Childbirth and Infancy," 291–314.

22. Garnsey, "Child Rearing in Ancient Italy," 48–65; Pilch, "'Beat his ribs,'" 101–13; Harlow and Laurence, *Growing Up;* Laes, "Childbeating in Antiquity," 75–89; Bakke, "Upbringing of Children," 145–63; Huskinson, "Growing Up in Ravenna," 55–80; Dolansky, "Togam virilem sumere," 47–70.

23. Kurylowicz, "Adoption," 61–75; Boswell, *Kindness of Strangers*; Kunst, "Adoption," 87–104; McGinn, "Widows, Orphans," 617–32; Corbier, "Child Exposure," 52–73; Miller, *Orphans of Byzantium;* Tate, "Christianity," 123–41; Hübner and Ratzan,

eds., *Growing Up Fatherless;* Bernstein, "Adoptees," 331–53; Kotsifou, "Papyrological Perspectives on Orphans," 339–73.

24. On the education of children in the ancient world, two classic studies are Marrou, *Histoire de l'éducation* (1948); and Jaeger, *Early Christianity and Greek Paideia* (1961). But see also (in chronological order): Beck, *Bibliography of Greek Education;* Wiedemann, *Adults and Children,* 143–75; Kleijwegt, *Ancient Youth,* 75–134; Riché, "Réflexions," 17–38; Hopkins, "Everyday Life," 25–30; Robb, *Literacy and Paideia;* Cribiore, *Writing, Teachers, and Students;* Bloomer, "Schooling in Persona," 57–78; Vössing, *Schule und Bildung;* Legras, *Éducation;* Rawson, "Education," 81–98; Cribiore, *Gymnastics of the Mind;* Too, ed., *Education;* Gibson, "Learning," 103–29; Kalogeras, "Role of Parents and Kin," 133–43; Watts, *City and School;* Lalanne, *Une éducation grecque;* Marinescu, Cox, and Wachter, "Paideia's Children," 101–14; Katz, "Educating Paula," 115–27; and Joyal, McDougall, and Yardley, eds., *Greek and Roman Education.*

25. Watts, "Infant Burials," 372–83; Huskinson, "Decoration," 114–15; Huskinson, *Roman Children's Sarcophagi;* Huskinson, "Iconography," 233–38; Dimas, *Untersuchungen;* Strubbe, "Epigrams," 45–95; Scott, *Archaeology of Infancy;* Hummel, *Das Kind;* King, "Commemoration of Infants," 117–54; McWilliam, "Children among the Dead," 74–98; Pearce, "Infants, Cemeteries," 125–42; Norman, "Death and Burial of Roman Children" (parts I and II); Oakley, "Death and the Child," 163–94; Rawson, "Death, Burial, and Commemoration," 277–97; Huskinson, "Disappearing Children?" 91–103; Huskinson, "Constructing Childhood," 323–38; Sorabella, "Eros and the Lizard," 353–70; Holman, "Sick Children," 143–70; Horn, "Approaches to the Study of Sick Children," 171–98; Talbot, "Death and Commemoration," 283–307.

26. On evidence for children with disabilities, see, e.g., Grasl, "Behinderte in der Antike," 118–26; Amundsen, "Medicine," 3–22; Garland, *Eye of the Beholder;* Edwards, "Cultural Context of Deformity," 79–92; Gourevitch, "Au temps," 459–73; Allély, "Les enfants malformés et considérés comme prodigia," 127–56; Allély, "Les enfants malformés et handicapés," 73–101; Gourevitch, "L'enfant handicapé à Rome," 459–77; Dasen, "'All children are dwarfs,'" 49–62; Kelly, "Deformed Child," 199–226; Mustakallio and Laes, eds., *Dark Side of Childhood.*

On problems and attitudes related to the sexual and physical abuse of children, see, e.g., Bakke, *When Children Became People,* 140–49; Kleijwegt, "Exposed," 113–26; Blondiaux et al., "Rickets and Child Abuse," 209–15; Laes, "When Classicists Need to Speak Up," 30–59; Horn and Martens, *"Let the Little Children Come to Me,"* 217–21, 225–32; Martens, "'Do Not Sexually Abuse Children,'" 227–54.

27. Ariès, *L'enfant et la vie familiale* (1960), trans. Baldick, under the title *Centuries of Childhood* (1962).

28. For critiques of Ariès's thesis, see Kleijwegt, *Ancient Youth;* and Eyben, *Restless Youth.*

29. On children in early Christian discourse, see Clark, "The Fathers and the Children," 1–27; Gould, "Childhood," 39–52; Eyben, "Early Christian View of Youth," 239–55; Strange, *Children in the Early Church;* Leyerle, "Appealing to Children," 243–70; Guroian, "Ecclesial Family," 61–77; Steenberg, "Children in Paradise," 1–22; Hennessy, *Images of Children in Byzantium;* and Horn and Phenix, eds., *Children in Late Ancient Christianity.*

On children's roles in early Christian ecclesiastical and monastic practice, see MacCoull, "Child Donations," 409–15; Eyben, "Young Priests," 102–20; Papaconstantinou, "Notes sur les actes de donation d'enfants," 83–105; Papaconstantinou, "Theia oikonomia," 511–26; Peters, "Offering Sons to God," 285–95; Jacobs and Krawiec, "Fathers Know Best?" 257–63; Krawiec, "'From the Womb of the Church,'" 283–307; Richter, "What's in a Story?" 237–64; Vuolanto, "Children and Asceticism," 119–32; Papaconstantinou, "Child or Monk?" 169–81; Hillner, "Monks and Children," 773–91; Greenfield, "Children in Byzantine Monasteries," 253–81; Schroeder, "Queer Eye," 333–47; Horn and Martens, *"Let the Little Children Come to Me,"* 301–45; Vuolanto, "Choosing Asceticism," 255–92; Horn, "Raising Martyrs and Ascetics," 293–316; Schroeder, "Children and Early Egyptian Monasticism," 317–38; Doerfler, "The Infant, the Monk and the Martyr," 243–58; Schroeder, "Monastic Family Values," 21–8; Schroeder, "Child Sacrifice," 269–302.

30. Hock, *Infancy Gospels,* 98–9.

31. Chartrand-Burke, "Infancy Gospel" (2001); Burke, *De infantia* (2010).

32. Chartrand-Burke, "Infancy Gospel," 316–65 (ch. 7: "A Child's Life in Roman Antiquity"), and 366–405 (ch. 8: "Children as Adults Saw Them"). These chapters are streamlined considerably and combined into a single chapter in the published version: see Burke, *De infantia,* 223–89. Chapter 5 includes sections on "Children in Roman Antiquity" (pp. 225–47), "Idealized Childhood" (pp. 247–68), and "The Infancy Gospel of Thomas and the Idealized Child" (pp. 268–89). See also Burke's articles "'Social Viewing' of Children" (2010), 29–43, and "Depictions of Children in the Apocryphal Infancy Gospels," 388–400.

33. Chartrand-Burke, "Infancy Gospel," 45, 382–83; Burke, *De infantia,* 69, 252.

34. Ps.-Apollodorus, *Library* (*Bibliotheca*) 2.4.8–9: Frazer, LCL, I.174–77; see also the story about Apollo slaying Python while in his mother's arms in Ps.-Apollodorus, *Library* 1.4.1 (Frazer, LCL, I.26–27).

35. On Si-Osiri, see Griffith, *Stories,* 44, 50; see also Griffith (*Stories,* 24) and Meyer ("Kindheitserzählung," 135) on the Egyptian story about the high priest Neneferkaptah animating clay models. On Moses, see Philo of Alexandria, *Life of Moses* 1.5.21 (Colson and Whitaker, LCL, VI.287); and Perrot, "Les récits d'enfance," 497–504.

36. Burke, *De infantia,* 223–24; Chartrand-Burke, "Infancy Gospel," 316.

37. Burke, *De infantia,* 246; Chartrand-Burke, "Infancy Gospel," 364.

38. Burke, *De infantia,* 58, 88, 113, 120, 125, 221, 224–25, 250–61 (on "Idealized Children in Ancient Biography"), 268–84 ("The Infancy Gospel of Thomas and Ancient Biography"), and 287–88; Chartrand-Burke, "Infancy Gospel," 380–94. For other treatments of the *Paidika* in relation to ancient biographies of child heroes whose actions foreshadow their adult careers, see Variot, *Évangiles apocryphes,* 222; Michaelis, *Die apocryphen Schriften,* 96–111; Gero, "Infancy Gospel," 77; and Hock, *Infancy Gospels,* 96–97; Klauck, *Apocryphal Gospels,* 73–78; Frilingos, "No Child Left Behind," 49; Kaiser, "Jesus als Kind," 266–67. For broader discussions of this literary motif, see Talbert, "Prophecies of Future Greatness," 129–41; Carp, "Puer senex," 736–39; and Cox, *Biography in Late Antiquity,* esp. 22–23, 34.

39. Burke, *De infantia,* 224, 261–68 (on "Idealized Children in Funerary Art"); Chartrand-Burke, "Infancy Gospel," 371–80.

40. Burke, *De infantia,* 224.

41. Ibid., 264 and 285; Chartrand-Burke, "Infancy Gospel," 376, 399; see also Huskinson, *Roman Children's Sarcophagi,* 81, 93.

42. Lévi-Strauss, *Totemism,* 89; see also Brown, *Body and Society,* 153; Burke, "Depictions of Children," 395; and my discussion of Chris Frilingos's scholarship later in this chapter.

43. Horn and Martens, *"Let the Little Children Come to Me,"* 75.

44. Ibid., 76, 130, 180, cf. 196, where stories about Jesus at play are said to give access to "the mundane," presenting "a rather common picture of children at play in a Jewish or Greco-Roman context."

45. Ibid., 131.

46. Ibid., 130.

47. Aasgaard, *Childhood,* 53–54; see also his articles "From Boy to Man," 3–20, and "Uncovering Children's Culture," 1–27.

48. Aasgaard, *Childhood,* 53–54.

49. Ibid., 53–72. In emphasizing rural life as a primary point of reference, Aasgaard follows the work of Bagatti, "Nota sul Vangelo," 486–87.

50. Aasgaard, *Childhood,* 73–85.

51. Ibid., 82–85. It should be noted that Aasgaard is somewhat equivocal regarding Jesus' "rebelliousness": on the one hand, he concludes that most cases of disobedience and tension are "solved within the story" and therefore "not fundamental" to it (p. 82); on the other hand, he acknowledges that "not all social and cultural tension in [the *Paidika*] is resolved" and that "some traces of protest and offense remain" (p. 83).

52. Ibid., 166–95 (quote at 171).

53. Ibid., 167–68.

54. For an early and influential example of this critique, see Brown, *Cult of the Saints* (1981). Ramsey MacMullen tried to reclaim the "popular" as an operative category in his book *The Second Church* (2009), but his work is an exception that proves the rule.

55. Aasgaard, *Childhood,* 192–213.

56. Ibid., 193. Aasgaard advocates a similar approach elsewhere in his scholarship: in particular, see his articles, "Children in Antiquity and Early Christianity," 24–26, 36–37; and "Uncovering Children's Culture," 1–27. It should be noted that François Bovon had earlier proposed that the *Paidika* may have been inspired by the "curiosity of children" (*curiosité des enfants*) about early gaps in the story record about Jesus' childhood years: see Bovon, "Évangiles canoniques et évangiles apocryphes" (1980), 25.

57. Burke, *De infantia,* 124.

58. Kaiser, "Jesus als Kind," 264–66.

59. Ibid., 268–69. Like Burke, Kaiser identified Aasgaard's main problem as a lack of supporting primary evidence.

60. Ibid., 266–67. Kaiser draws on Cullmann and Rebell's respective observations regarding the "übermütigen Götterknaben" ("high-spirited sons of the gods") and the "Trickster-Jesus": see Cullmann, "Kindheitsevangelien," 352; and Rebell, *Neutestamentliche apokryphen,* 135.

61. Kaiser, "Jesus als Kind," 269. For a similar conjecture related to the medieval reception of the *Paidika,* see Dzon, "Boys Will Be Boys," 217 ("Perhaps medieval adults acquired more patience when hearing about how even the Christ Child created difficulties for those around him").

62. Kaiser, "Jesus als Kind," 269.

63. Aasgaard, *Childhood,* 92. In her more recent article "Die sogenannte 'Kindheitserzählung des Thomas'" (2011), Kaiser continues to emphasize the theme, "Jesus as Child" (see esp. pp. 468–79), but she also recognizes in the work "the combination of two concepts or narrative strategies: . . . [1] the representation of the child as an adult in miniature, . . . and [2] the representation of the child as child" (p. 472).

64. Ibid., 99–102 (quotes from pp. 101–2); on Jesus' gender socialization in the *Paidika,* see pp. 103–12 (=ch. 7, "Jesus from Boy to Man").

65. Frilingos, "No Child Left Behind," 27–54. This article was written just prior to the publication of Aasgaard's book (as well as prior to Kaiser's essay), but in it Frilingos shows an acquaintance with Aasgaard's research from the latter's conference papers and published articles.

66. Ibid., 32.

67. Ibid., 40, 42, 46–49, 53. Frilingos (p. 53, note 102) calls attention to the work of Winkler (*Constraints of Desire,* 101–26) on the negotiation of tradition, education, and violence in Longus's ancient novel, *Daphnis and Chloe.* In highlighting the *Paidika*'s "conflicted view of learning and corporal punishment," Frilingos (pp. 36–38) also points out similar cultural negotiations at work in Lucian of Samosata's *The Dream* (ch. 3: Macleod, *Lucian,* 22–25), where Lucian recounts making sculpted models in school and being punished by his uncle/tutor, who hits him with a stick when he accidently breaks a writing slab.

68. Frilingos, "No Child Left Behind," 34, note 28. In that same note, Frilingos cites Leyerle's article "Appealing to Children," in which she analyses John Chrysostom's portrayal of children (especially those found in his scriptural commentaries) in terms of adult "problems of cultural reproduction" (p. 270).

69. Burke, *De Infantia,* 224.

70. Aasgaard, *Childhood,* 193.

71. Frilingos ("No Child Left Behind," 38–39) employs the postcolonial category of hybridity in analyzing the figure of Jesus in the *Paidika,* drawing on Homi Bhabha's "in-between" spaces of contradictions and ambivalence to describe how Jesus' performance of *paideia* both participated in and posed a challenge to Greek cultural and political norms: see esp. Bhabha, *Location of Culture;* and Pratt, *Imperial Eyes,* 1–11. I apply postcolonial language to a similar but slightly different purpose here: to describe a contestation of power and authority related to the representation of the young Jesus as simultaneously embodying the culturally recognizable characteristics of child, of adult, and of hero-god. To borrow the language of Stephon Slemon ("Unsettling the Empire," 108), the figure of the Christ child becomes "a place of ambivalence: between systems, between discursive worlds, implicit and complicit" in all of them. Bhabha (*Location of Culture,* 85) describes something analogous in his concept of "the elliptical *in-between,* where the shadow of the other falls upon the self."

72. Bhabha, *Location of Culture,* 136 (cf. 127, 240); see also Benita Parry, "Problems in Current Theories of Colonial Discourse," in *Post-colonial Studies Reader,* 36–44, at 41–42.

73. For the palimpsest metaphor, I am indebted to Spivak, "Can the Subaltern Speak?" 24–28.

74. Here, I disagree with Burke (*De Infantia,* 280; cf. "The Infancy Gospel of Thomas," 314), who believes that "any assessment of the christology behind the text must be made without thought to the fact that Jesus is here presented as a child." In my description of christology in the *Paidika,* I am self-consciously avoiding the exclusively binary terminologies (i.e., humanity on the one hand; divinity on the other) that characterized the later doctrinal debates of the fourth and fifth centuries. Instead, I want to read the stories' multifaceted representation of the young Jesus in relation to the gradated ontological and ethical hierarchies that permeated Graeco-Roman worldviews in the early centuries of the Common Era. On the role that such social and cosmological hierarchies played in shaping ancient Christian thought during this period, see Martin, *Inventing Superstition.* For a similar recognition of how christological dynamics were at work in later Western medieval reception of the *Paidika,* albeit in more binary, Chalcedonian terms, see Dzon, "Boys Will Be Boys," 184, and passim.

75. For an earlier example of how sociological scholarship on cultural memory has been applied to the early Christian cult of the martyrs, see Castelli, *Martyrdom and Memory.*

76. On Halbwachs's scholarship and his impact on the history of memory studies as a discipline, see Erll, *Kollektives Gedächtnis,* 14–18; and "Cultural Memory Studies," 1–15. Erll (*Kollektives Gedächtnis,* 19–22) also documents the importance of Halbwachs's contemporary Aby Warburg (1866–1929), whose work on "the afterlife of antiquity" (*das Nachleben der Antike*) and whose famous exhibit Mnemosyne (1924–1929) contributed to the formation of "collective memory" as a subject of sociological study and archival practice: see also Warburg, *Erneuerung der heidnischen Antike* and *Bilderatlas Mnemosyne;* Kany, *Mnemosyne als Programm;* Diers, "Mnemosyne," 79–94; and Ginzburg, "Kunst und soziales Gedächtnis," 63–127.

77. Halbwachs, *Les Cadres sociaux de la mémoire* (Eng. trans. in *On Collective Memory,* 37–189). Later, he published case studies of collective memory in relation to communities of musicians and the Christian topography of the Holy Land: see "La Mémoire collective chez les musiciens," 136–65 (Eng. trans. in *The Collective Memory,* 158–86); and *La Topographie légendaire* (Eng. trans. of the conclusion in *On Collective Memory,* 193–235). Halbwachs's final major study was published posthumously: *La Mémoire collective* (Eng. trans. in *The Collective Memory,* 22–157).

78. This was not a completely new insight, as Sigmund Freud had already made similar observations in his development of the concept of "screen memories": see Freud, "Über Deckerinnerungen," 215–30; trans. J. Strachey, "Screen Memories," 299–322.

79. Halbwachs, *Cadres sociaux,* ch. 3 (*On Collective Memory,* 49).

80. Halbwachs, *Mémoire collective,* ch. 2 (*The Collective Memory,* 69).

81. See, e.g., Halbwachs, *Mémoire collective,* ch. 2 (*The Collective Memory,* 72), where he reflects on his shifting memories of his father: "The image I have of my father continuously evolved over time, not only because my remembrances of him while he

lived accumulated but also because I myself changed and my perspective altered as I occupied different positions in my family and, more important, in other milieus."

82. Halbwachs, *Cadres sociaux,* preface (*On Collective Memory,* 38).

83. Halbwachs, *Mémoire collective,* ch. 1 (*The Collective Memory,* 31).

84. Halbwachs, *Mémoire collective,* ch. 1 (*The Collective Memory,* 46; see also pp. 35–41 on "childhood remembrances," and pp. 41–44 on "adult remembrances"). For Halbwachs's treatment of the family as a collective domain for memory construction in his earlier work, see *Cadres sociaux,* ch. 5 (*On Collective Memory,* 54–83).

85. Thus, Halbwachs wrote in *La Mémoire collective* (ch. 2; *The Collective Memory,* 71): "But how many of the remembrances that we believe genuine, with an identity beyond doubt, are almost entirely forged from false recognitions, in accordance with others' testimony and stories! A framework cannot produce of itself a precise and picturesque remembrance. But, in this case, the framework has been buoyed up with personal reflection and family remembrances: the remembrance is an image entangled among other images, a generic image taken back into the past."

86. Halbwachs, *Topographie légendaire.* In his book *Cadres sociaux* (ch. 4; *On Collective Memory,* 52–53), he had originally introduced the concept of "the localization of memory," but had not yet explored its implications for material spaces.

87. Halbwachs, *Topographie légendaire,* conclusion (*The Collective Memory,* 202, 204).

88. Halbwachs, *La Mémoire collective,* ch. 4 (*The Collective Memory,* 133).

89. Halbwachs, *La Mémoire collective,* ch. 4 (*The Collective Memory,* 140).

90. See, e.g., Bloch, "Mémoire collective," 73–83; Gedi and Elam, "Collective Memory," 30–50; Confino, "Collective Memory," 1386–1403; and Klein, "On the Emergence of Memory," 127–50. See especially Confino, "Memory and the History of Mentalities," 77–84, on "the unbearable lightness of interpretation" (p. 83) when it comes to the deployment of memory as a category of historical analysis.

91. Erll, "Cultural Memory Studies," 2–3; Harold Marcuse, "Collective Memory: Definitions," at http://www.history.ucsb.edu/faculty/marcuse/classes/201/CollectiveMemoryDefinitions.htm.

92. Erll, "Cultural Memory Studies," 4–5, quote at 5; see also Olick, "Collective Memory," 336. The systematization of memory studies as a multidisciplinary field has played an important role in this refinement of approaches: see especially the work of Der Gießener Sonderforschungsbereich 434, which from 1997 to 2008 sponsored a series of publications on various "Erinnerungskulturen" ("Cultures of Remembrance"), ranging from Roman antiquity to the modern Palestinian-Israeli conflict: for an overview with bibliography, see Erll, *Kollektives Gedächtnis,* 34–39; and http://www.uni-giessen.de/erinnerungskulturen/home/index.html.

93. Nora, *Les lieux de mémoire* (Eng. trans. *Realms of Memory*). For concise summaries of Nora's project, see Nora, "Between Memory and History," 7–24; and Erll, *Kollektives Gedächtnis,* 23–27.

94. Connerton, *How Societies Remember.* For another example of how "social memory" has been used an analytical term, see Fentress and Wickham, *Social Memory.*

95. Connerton, *How Societies Remember,* 72ff.

96. Ibid., 74.

97. See esp. J. Assmann, "Kollektives Gedächtnis," 9–19; *Das kulturelle Gedächtnis* (Eng. trans. *Cultural Memory*), esp. 48–66; "Collective Memory and Cultural Identity," 125–33; and *Religion und kulturelles Gedächtnis* (Eng. trans. *Religion and Cultural Memory*), esp. 1–30. Assmann actually proposed two different terms—"communicative memory" and "cultural memory"—to account for (1) short-term, experiential memory mediated through oral communication, and (2) longer-term memory processes mediated through formalized ritual and/or writing. This sharp dichotomy, however, fails to do full justice to the messy details involved in historical processes of transmission, as illustrated by the persistence of certain oral traditions that sometimes exceed the three- or four-generation threshold Assmann sets up as a limit for "communicative" memory. As we shall see in the case of the *Paidika,* oral processes of transmission probably ran concurrently with the transmission of written texts across multiple centuries. For this reason, I adopt the term "cultural memory" in its very broadest sense, to accommodate both a generational and cross-generational timeframe. For me, it serves as a synonym for "social memory," and demarcates the diversity of oral, written, and ritual practices through which the past was shaped for present-day consumption in late antiquity and the early medieval period.

98. A. Assmann, *Erinnerungsräume,* 147–339, quote at 149; see also A. Assmann and J. Assmann, "Das Gestern im Heute," 114–40.

99. A. Assmann, *Erinnerungsräume,* 179–218, esp. 213ff.; see also A. Assmann, "Texte, Spuren, Abfall," 96–111; and Erll, *Kollektives Gedächtnis,* 137–40 (on the social processes of storage, circulation, and recall). Elsewhere in her scholarship, Aleida Assmann also shows how such insights about histories of reuse might extend to "written folklore," which she characterizes as a kind of "compilation literature" (*Kompilationsliteratur*) and a "literature of reuse" (*Wiedergebrauchsliteratur*): A. Assmann, "Schriftliche Folklore," 175–93, esp. 177 and 181.

100. A. Assmann, *Erinnerungsräume,* 218–40, quote at 228. Assmann (pp. 226–27) also notes the way that images functioned for Aby Warburg as "the paradigmatic memory-media" (*die paradigmatischen Gedächtnismedien*) insofar as they are nearer to the "impression power of memories" (*die Einprägungskraft des Gedächtnisses*).

101. A. Assmann, *Erinnerungsräume,* 298–338, quote at 312.

102. On physical settings for remembrance in the ancient world, analyzed through a Halbwachsian lens, see also Alcock, *Archaeologies,* esp. 19–32.

103. Erll, *Kollektives Gedächtnis,* 138; see also p. 136, where she notes that "the producers and recipients of a memory-medium perform an active work of construction [*aktive Konstruktionsarbeit*]" marked by acts of selection, encoding/decoding, and meaning-making connected with what is remembered. According to Erll (p. 142, quoting Halbwachs), the "memory-forming power" (*gedächtnisbildende Macht*) of such media often goes unacknowledged: it is "like the air we breathe" (*wie die Luft, die wir einatmen*), prompting us to make imaginative connections between past events and present experience without our even realizing we are doing it.

104. On the "linguistic turn" and the problems it poses for historians, see especially Elizabeth Clark's pathbreaking article, "The Lady Vanishes," 1–31.

105. Erll, *Kollektives Gedächtnis,* 143–93, at 159.

106. Ibid., 158.

107. On "intermediality," see Erll, *Kollektives Gedächtnis,* 171. For a discussion of how texts and images stamp (and are stamped by) personal and collective remembrance, see Erll, *Kollektives Gedächtnis,* 161–64; cf. Halbwachs, *The Collective Memory,* 23–24; and Welzer, *Das kommunikative Gedächtnis,* 39.

108. On the constructive character of remembrances and their role in the production and maintenance of individual and social identity, see Schmidt, "Memory and Remembrance," 191–201. Kammen (*Mystic Chords of Memory,* 3) makes the observation that "societies in fact reconstruct their pasts rather than faithfully record them, and . . . they do so with the needs of contemporary culture clearly in mind—manipulating the past in order to mold the present."

Chapter 2. Texts and Readers

1. Fish, *Is There a Text in This Class?*

2. See also the work of Najman ("Traditionary Processes"), who critiques the prevailing assumptions among biblical scholars who "operate with an overly simplistic, unilinear conception" of their subject matter, thinking in terms of "organized unities of familiar kinds—texts, books, collections." Instead, Najman wants to ask: "What makes texts into unities?" In reassessing the ways such "textual unities" are constructed, Najman focuses especially on Nietzsche's notion of the authorial "personality" or "figure" and Foucault's "author function," both of which recognize these categories as constructed in and through the process of reading: see Nietzsche, "Homer and Classical Philology," 145–70; and Foucault, "What Is an Author?" 205–22. Najman ("Configuring the Text," 3–22) also explores how such notions of "textual unity" are connected with constructions of authorial and genre unity. On processes of editorial revision and textual fluidity in early Christianity, see also Czachesz, "Rewriting and Textual Fluidity in Antiquity," 426–41.

3. Aasgaard (*Childhood,* 113–36) has a whole chapter entitled "Intertextuality—Reflections of the Bible," where he argues that the influence of biblical texts (from specific references to more general allusions and themes) is "considerably stronger than has been previously observed" (p. 113).

4. Gero ("Infancy Gospel," 47) sees in these stories "the patent retrojection of synoptic miracles into the period of the Childhood."

5. On seeking and finding, cf. Matthew 7:7–11 and Luke 11:9–13. On his birth and origins, cf. Luke 11:27. In addition to such gospel references and allusions, Aasgaard (*Childhood,* 118–20) also notes Zacchaeus's allusion to the Pauline phrase "noisy gong and clanging cymbal" (*Paidika* 6.2ff.; Burke, *De infantia,* 316–17; cf. 1 Corinthians 13:1).

6. Matthew 21:18–19; Mark 11:12–14.

7. Burke (*De infantia,* esp. 203–4) has proposed that the editor of the earliest Greek recension of the text may have been exclusively acquainted with the author of Luke-Acts: In addition to the *Paidika*'s clear reliance on Luke 2 in chapter 17, he also notes the similarities between Jesus' healing of the man bitten by a snake in chapter 15 and the story of the snake-bitten Paul on the island of Malta in Acts (28:3–6), the companion volume to Luke. Geert van Oyen ("Rereading the Rewriting," 482–505) has

argued, however, for a broader (and more variegated) relationship between the *Paidika* and the New Testament writings.

8. Burke, *De infantia,* 203; Aasgaard, *Childhood,* 115–18; also Schmahl, "Lk 2,41–52 und die Kindheitserzählung," 249–58; Jonge, "Sonship, Wisdom, Infancy," 347–48. Outside this final pericope, however, the evidence for exclusive dependence on Luke is elusive. On this subject, Kaiser ("Jesus als Kind," 263–64) observes that any such privileged connection with the Gospel of Luke seems to have been lost on later recipients of the *Paidika.*

9. See, e.g., Cullmann, "Kindheitsevangelien," 330; Vielhauer, *Geschichte,* 674; Chartrand-Burke, "Completing the Gospel," 109–16; Kaiser, "Jesus als Kind," 260–63.

10. Burke writes that even "the author of the Luke-Acts would have recognized a kinship between his work and the 'heretical' infancy gospel" (Chartrand-Burke, "Completing the Gospel," 112–13; also Aarde, "Kindheidsevangelie van Tomas as 'n heroïese mite"; Aarde, "Kindheidsevangelie van Tomas—historiese allegorie," 461–89; and Kaiser, "Jesus als Kind," 263).

11. Pertinent ancient analogies to such "gap filling" are rabbinic and philosophical techniques of midrash (Andrew Jacobs, *per litt.,* December 31, 2012). The image of later readers and authors seeking to "fill gaps" in earlier narratives also conforms to Wolfgang Iser's phenomenology of reading processes, according to which readers naturally seek to fill "spots of indeterminacy," "blanks," and "gaps" in the texts they encounter: see Iser, *Act of Reading;* also Fowler, *Let the Reader Understand,* 34, 46, 134–38, 144, 153–54, 174, 181, 213–18; and Aichele et al., *Postmodern Bible,* 32. When it comes to the *Paidika,* however, this impulse to fill gaps should be understood as only part of the picture (see also Kaiser, "Jesus als Kind," 260–61).

12. Aasgaard (*Childhood,* 114) acknowledges that using the canonical categories such as "Old Testament" and "New Testament" in relation to the second century is "anachronistic," but he nonetheless still tries to apply them, "in a loose sense, to writings that were fairly widespread and generally well regarded at the time, and most of which were later included in the canon of the churches." The vagueness of his language on this point underscores his problematic operating assumption that the text's readers would have been familiar with the full range of biblical allusions that he identifies, and it prevents him from asking more specific questions about readership and audience: e.g., who would have been equipped to interpret the stories in these terms, and how readers or hearers not so equipped would have made sense of the stories.

13. Harris (*Ancient Literacy*) sets 15 percent as a high-water mark, but even that is probably unduly generous. While Harris acknowledges probable variations between the demographics of cities and provinces, his methods and figures have nonetheless been critiqued in some quarters as too focused on quantitative considerations and not sufficiently attuned to questions of context (e.g., the nature of the texts being read, the relation of reading to writing, and complications caused by different cultural contexts and the phenomenon of multilingualism): see, e.g., Beard et al., eds., *Literacy;* Curchin, "Literacy," 461–76; and more recently, Johnson and Parker, eds., *Ancient Literacies.* For general discussions of literacy in ancient Christian and early medieval contexts, see Gamble, *Books and Readers,* esp. 2–10, and 247–48, notes 8 and 10; and McKitterick, ed., *The Uses of Literacy,* esp. 1–10 ("Introduction").

14. Gamble, *Books and Readers,* chs. 3–5.

15. I would simply caution against the undue expectations scholars sometimes bring to the table regarding high levels of biblical literacy and/or theological fluency among the *Paidika*'s early audience. To presume that readers or hearers had ready access to and command of such a wide range of biblical texts conflicts with what we know about the way texts circulated among early Christian communities in the first three centuries, and it also imports a restrictive set of assumptions about where these stories would have been encountered. Such patterns of reading/reception would pertain only to early Christian *literati* who had unusual access to textual sources in their personal libraries (a rare scenario, and one that seems suspiciously similar to the social setting of modern historians), or to church communities with large numbers of biblical codices in their collections and with thoroughly regularized lectionary readings that allowed for maximal access to biblical books (an anachronistic scenario that retrojects later conditions and practices to the second- or third-century ecclesiastic milieu). Even if there were a handful of early Christian cognoscenti and communities equipped to read these childhood stories with such intertextual dexterity, these scenarios do not represent all the settings for how stories/texts were encountered during the period in which the *Paidika* began to circulate, nor do they exhaust the range of reading and listening modes that would have contributed to these stories' transmission and interpretation (for more on this, see my discussion later in this chapter).

James A. Francis ("Visual and Verbal Representation," 285–305) has voiced a similar caution with respect to both textual and visual evidence: "[A] fundamental assumption has been that early Christian images represent theological statements and systems and that they exist to communicate those concepts to the viewer. They are traditionally interpreted by literal reference to Scripture, as if they could be no more than mere 'illustrations' of a text. Certainly our current understanding of the fluidity of pre-Constantinian Christianity should make us cautious in using as a guide to interpretation a canon or theology that was developed later. More fundamentally, we should question the assumption that theologies must predominate in anything considered Christian" (pp. 297–98). In this context, it is relevant to note that the *Paidika* itself shows a relative paucity of "theologically-loaded titles such as Lord, Messiah, Christ, or Saviour" (Burke, *De infantia,* 200).

16. Gero, "Infancy Gospel," 59; Hock, *Infancy Gospels,* 84–85; Burke, *De infantia,* 46–56; Voicu, "Ways to Survival," 404–5. The first published manuscript, a fragmentary text from Vienna (*Philos. gr. 162 [olim 144],* dated pre-1455 CE) did not identify the work as a gospel but presented its contents as originating from "Thomas the Israelite": see Lambeck, *Commentariorum,* VII.270–73; Hunger, *Katalog,* vol. 1, 265; Burke, *De infantia,* 46–47, 129–31. This attribution led to the text's identification as the "Gospel of Thomas" by Mingarelli ("De Apocrypho Thomae Evangelio," 73–155) and Thilo, *Codex apocryphus,* vol. 1, lxxiii–xci, 277–315.

17. In his *Refutation of All Heresies,* Hippolytus of Rome mentions "the *Gospel* entitled *According to Thomas,* which states expressly, 'The one who seeks me will find me in children from seven years of age and onwards. For there, hiding in the fourteenth aeon, I am revealed' " (Hippolytus, *Refutation of All Heresies* 5.7.20 (cf. *Gospel of Thomas* 4): ed. Wendland, GCS 26 (1916; repr. 1977), 83; trans. Attridge, in *Nag*

Hammadi Codex II, 2–7, vol. 1, 103; for a fuller discussion, see Burke, *De infantia,* 38–41).

18. Early copies in Latin, Syriac, and Georgian versions all lack it, an indication that this mark of authorship was a secondary addition: Burke, *De infantia,* 205–7; also Hock, *Infancy Gospels,* 84–85; Gero, "Infancy Gospel," 59.

19. Examples are ubiquitous: see, for instance, Davies (*Infancy Gospels,* xxix–xxx), who acknowledges that "we need to be careful to distinguish between the radically different sorts of books that are all being labeled with the same word [i.e., gospel]," but still goes on to assert that the so-called *Infancy Gospel of Thomas* is "more akin to the biblical gospels than any of the other 'gospels' of which we know." Gero ("Infancy Gospel," 59), Hock (*Infancy Gospels,* 84–85), Kaiser ("Jesus als Kind," 253–57), and Burke (*De infantia,* 39) are all well aware that the title "gospel" is not original, but they continue to use it to conform to contemporary conventions (although Kaiser places the title in scare quotes throughout). One prominent exception to this pattern is found in the work of Sever Voicu, whom I shall discuss further below: see esp. Voicu, "Notes," 119–32; "Histoire," 191–204; "Verso," 7–85; and "La traditione latine," 13–21.

20. Amsler, "Les *Paidika Iesou,*" 434–45; see also Voicu, "Notes," 121–22; Voicu, "Verso," 55–59; Otero, *Das kirchenslavische Evangelium,* 37–38; Gero, "Infancy Gospel," 59; and Hock, *Infancy Gospels,* 84–85. In the title, the adjectival form, *paidika,* is not accompanied by a noun, so another translation is quite possible, e.g., "The Childhood Miracles of Jesus" or "The Childhood Stories of Jesus."

21. The earliest extant Greek copy, an eleventh-century manuscript from Jerusalem, bears a more elaborate heading in which this core title is evident: "The Mighty Childhood Deeds of Our Master and Savior Jesus Christ" (*Ta Paidika megaleia tou despotou hēmōn kai sōtēros Iēsou Christou*): Burke, *De infantia,* 303; Aasgaard, *Childhood,* 219. The designation *Paidika* is also attested in later medieval Greek recensions. See, e.g., recension Ga: "An Account on the Childhood Deeds [*paidika*] and Mighty Deeds [*megaleia*] of our Lord [*kurios*] and Saviour Jesus Christ" (Burke, *De infantia,* 340–41); and recension Gb: "A Writing of the Holy Apostle Thomas on the Childhood Conduct of the Lord [*peri tēs paidikēs anastrophēs tou kuriou*]" (Burke, *De infantia,* 454–55). For a discussion, see also Voicu, "Verso," 58.

22. Voicu, "Verso," 62; see also pp. 58–59, where he discusses the Syriac and Georgian evidence. The title (along with the opening chapter) is absent in the earliest Latin version but attested in later manuscripts.

23. Epiphanius of Salamis, *Panarion* 51.20.2–3 (Holl, GCS 31.2 [1980], 277–78; trans. Williams, 45, but modified slightly by Burke, *De infantia,* 7). Both Voicu ("Verso," 41) and Burke (*De infantia,* 7) express doubts about whether Epiphanius was referring to a written text.

24. John Chrysostom, *Homily 17 on John* (*PG* 59.110); Burke, *De infantia,* 6.

25. *Decretum Gelasianum* (Dobschütz, *Decretum,* 51; also Burke, *De infantia,* 7–8). Interestingly, a later list of Manichaean books interpolated into a heresiological treatise by Timothy of Constantinople identifies "the so-called Childhood Deeds [*Paidika*] of the Lord" as a Manichaean composition written against the doctrine of the incarnation (*PG* 86.21CE; Burke, *De infantia,* 10–11). This interpolation took place sometime after the eighth century CE.

26. Maximus the Confessor, *Life of the Virgin* 62 ("l'enfance du Christ"): Esbroeck, CSCO 478, 77.27–78.28 (Georgian text); CSCO 479, 52.19–53.8 (French translation); also Burke, *De infantia,* 8–9.

27. Anastasius Sinaita, *Hodegos* 13 (*PG* 89.229C; also Burke, *De infantia,* 9–10): "the so-called childhood miracles [*paidika thaumata*] of Christ."

28. George Syncellus, *Chronographia, anno 5505:* Mosshammer, 384–85; trans. Adler and Tuffin, 385–86, slightly modified by Burke, *De infantia,* 11–13. As part of his larger commentary on the *anno mundi* 5505 ("five years from the Incarnation of God"), Syncellus distinguishes the "variety of gospels [that] have been composed, of which only four have been adjudged by the blessed apostles to be received by the Church," from "the childhood deeds [*paidika*] of our Saviour . . . [which] include reports about the miracles performed by the creator of the ages up until his twelfth year of age according to the flesh."

29. Euthymius Zigabenus (*Commentary on the Four Gospels,* on John 2:11: *PG* 129.1153B) makes reference to "the so-called childhood miracles [*paidika thaumata*] of Christ."

30. Dover, *Greek Homosexuality,* esp. 16–17. On Plato's use of the term, see also Gonzalez, "How to Read a Platonic Prologue," 25–35; and Morgan, "Inspiration," 56–7. On Xenophon's vocabulary of *paidika,* see Dover, *Greek Homosexuality,* 54, 63–64, 87; and Percy, "Reconsiderations," 13–63, at 38.

31. Dio Chrysostom (ca. 40–ca. 120 CE), *Oration* 3.93 (Cohoon, LCL, I.146).

32. Plutarch (ca. 46–120 CE), *Pelopidas* 28.10 (Lindskog and Ziegler, vol. 2.2, 94).

33. Aelius Aristides (117–181 CE), *To Kapitōn* (*Pros Kapitōna*) 326 (Dindorf, II.430); and *To Demosthenes on Exemptions from Public Duties* (*Pros Dēmosthenē peri ateleias*) 15 (Dindorf, II.623).

34. Lucian (ca. 125–after 180 CE), *Icaromenippus* 2 (Harmon, LCL, II.268–322).

35. Dio Cassius (ca. 150–235 CE), *Roman History* 49.39.2; 57.19.5; 59.11.1; 64.4.2; 69.11.2; 72.14.3; 78.32.3; 79.15.1 (Boissevain, II.319, 581, 629; III.103, 231, 296, 440, 467).

36. Herodian (ca. 170–240 CE), *Roman History* 3.10.6 (Stavenhagen, 96).

37. Flavius Philostratus (ca. 170–247 CE), *Life of Apollonius* 6.11, 7.42, 8.7 (Kayser, I.219, 295, 303); and *Lives of the Sophists* 2.23 (Kayser, II.107); see also Flavius Philostratus, *Heroïkos* 16.2 (Kayser, II.148; trans. Aitken and MacLean, *Philostratus,* 235).

38. Diogenes Laertius (fl. 3rd cent. CE), *Lives of Eminent Philosophers* 2.19, 2.64, 5.3, 8.86, 9.25 (Long, I.65, 84, 198; II.434, 450).

39. Philo of Alexandria (20 BCE–50 CE), *On the Contemplative Life* 61 (Cohn and Reiter, VI.62).

40. Josephus (37–100 CE), *Jewish Antiquities* 17.44 (Niese, IV.77); and *Jewish War* 1.489 (Niese, VI.112).

41. Clement of Alexandria (ca. 150–ca. 215 CE), *Paedagogus* 3.8.44.1 (Mondésert et al., SC 158, 96).

42. Hippolytus (170–235 CE), *Refutation of All Heresies* 5.26.23 (Marcovich, 205).

43. Origen of Alexandria (ca. 185–254 CE), *Against Celsus* 8.9 (Borret, SC 150, 194; trans. Chadwick, 459).

44. Eusebius of Caesarea (ca. 263–339 CE), *Life of Constantine* 1.7.2 (Winkelmann, 18).

45. John Chrysostom (ca. 347–407 CE), *Homilies on 2 Corinthians* 26.4 (*PG* 61.586); *Homilies on the Epistle to Titus* 5.4 (*PG* 62.693).

46. Plutarch, *On the Fortunes of Alexander* 9.1 (Perrin, LCL, VII.408–9).

47. Plutarch, *Pompeius* 8.6–7 (Perrin, LCL, V.135; also Ziegler, *Plutarchi vitae parallelae*, vol. 3.2, 284).

48. On the infancy tales about Jesus as a species of ancient biography, see also Cox, *Biography*, 85.

49. Burke, *De infantia*, 250–61, 268–84; see also Chartrand-Burke, "*Infancy Gospel of Thomas*," in *Non-Canonical Gospels*, 134–7. For a discussion of "Imperial Children in Biography and Panegyric," see also Weidemann, *Adults and Children*, 49–83 (ch. 2).

50. Burke, *De infantia*, 283, note 1 (where he refers to these childhood tales as "a class apart"). Burke mentions Onesicritus's lost work, *How Alexander Was Brought Up*, as a possible *comparandum* (see also Pelling, "Childhood and Personality," 218).

51. Burke, *De infantia*, 283.

52. Ibid., 284, citing Doty, "Concept of Genre," 446 (Burke misidentifies the page number as p. 46).

53. Price, "Implied Reader Response," 909–38; see also Goldhill, "Genre," 185–200. Recognizing the variety of extratextual factors that contribute to genre formation, Goldhill writes, "Genre cannot be fully accounted for in purely formal literary terms: audience, context of performance, circulation of texts, and self-aware critical discussion all play a role" (pp. 186–87).

54. Najman, "Idea of Biblical Genre," 307–22. Drawing on Bakhtin's notion of genre diversity in speech (from "rigid and trite" to "more flexible, plastic, and creative"; Bakhtin, *Speech Genres*, 78), Najman emphasizes how new genres are produced through "the transformation of one or several old genres: by inversion, by displacement, by combination" (p. 308). This diversity is a function of the fact that genres are generated through readers' continual attempts to classify texts. Najman follows Walter Benjamin's *Origin of German Tragic Drama* in proposing the metaphor of genre as "a constellation of features or elements" that "depend for their legibility on our interests as readers" (p. 316).

55. For the concept of "reading cultures," I am indebted to William A. Johnson: see especially his publications "Toward a Sociology of Reading," 593–627, and *Readers and Reading Culture*, esp. 1–16. Johnson evaluates activities of reading not just in cognitive terms but also as "the negotiated construction of meaning" within particular social and cultural contexts (Johnson, "Toward a Sociology of Reading," 603; *Readers and Reading Culture*, 12). In this context, he draws comparisons to other analogous anthropological and ethnographic categories for analyzing such cultures of literacy, including Shirley Heath's "literacy events" and Brian Street's "literary practices" (Johnson, "Toward a Sociology of Reading," 601; *Readers and Reading Culture*, 9–10). Heath ("What No Bedtime Story Means," 50) writes about "occasions in which written language is integral to the nature of participants' interactions and their interpretive processes and strategies". Street ("Literacy Practices," 61) makes note of "both behavior

and conceptualizations related to the use of reading and/or writing" (cf. Street, ed., *Cross-Cultural Approaches,* 12–13). I also utilize here R. D. Grillo's broader concept of "communicative practices," which encompasses not only readerly modes of activity but also oral-aural ones: with this term, Grillo targets "the social activities through which language or communication is produced" and "the way in which these activities are embedded in institutions, settings or domains" (Grillo, *Dominant Languages,* 15; cited by Johnson, "Toward a Sociology of Reading," 601–2; and *Readers and Reading Culture,* 10).

56. Johnson, "Toward a Sociology of Reading," 601.

57. On the recitation of ancient narrative prose literature, see, e.g., Wesseling, "Audience," 71–73.

58. On the modification of houses and apartments to serve as worship spaces, see White, *Building God's House.* On the late Roman household as "both a private *and* public space," see Sessa, *Formation of Papal Authority,* 24.

59. See, e.g., the "Isidora to Asklepiades Dossier," Letters 16–20 (28–27 BCE): Bagnall and Cribiore, *Women's Letters,* pars. 417–19.

60. See, e.g., *P.Oxy.* VI.930, on a certain student from Oxyrhynchos named Ptolemaios who was reading book 6 of the *Iliad* when his tutor left him, perhaps to pursue other employment. On this text and the use of Homer (esp. the *Iliad*) in ancient education, as illuminated by papyrological finds, see Cribiore, *Gymnastics of the Mind,* 48, 194–97.

61. See, e.g., Lucian's criticism of a wealthy provincial from Syria who entertained his guests with readings after dinner but did not understand the contents due to insufficient study: Lucian, *The Ignorant Book Collector* (*Adv. Indoct.,* ca. 170 CE): Harmon, LCL, III.173–212. For a case where the reading of a text led to intellectual debate, see Plutarch, *Against Colotes* 2 (*Moralia* 1107F): Babbitt; LCL, XIV.190–3). These and other examples are discussed in Johnson, "Toward a Sociology of Reading," 613–18; and D. J. Allan, "Ἀναγιγνώσκω," 248–49.

62. It should be noted that scholarly study was not always a solitary pursuit. Pliny the Younger (*Ep.* 3.5.11–12: Radice, LCL, I.176–77) reports that his uncle, Pliny the Elder, used to have a lector read a book to him during dinner while dictating notes to another servant and while hosting guests who would occasionally interrupt to correct mispronounced words, much to Pliny's annoyance (discussed by Johnson, "Toward a Sociology of Reading," 616–17).

63. Pachomian, *Praecepta* 139–40: Boon, *Pachomiana latina,* 49–50; also Bacht, *Vermachtnis* II.112–13 and 220–23; Wipszycka, "Review of Books," 171–72 (cited by Cribiore, *Gymnastics of the Mind,* 177).

64. Jauss, *Toward an Aesthetic of Reception,* 39 (my emphasis). Both Jauss and Johnson ("Toward a Sociology of Reading," 612–15) are interested in the "aesthetics" of reading and reception.

65. For a helpful deconstruction of these kinds of dichotomies, see Parker, "Books and Reading Latin Poetry," 192. The subject of spoken vs. silent reading has been something of an obsession among students of ancient literature (including historians of early Christianity), ever since Norden (*Die antike Kunstprosa,* vol. 1, 6), Balogh ("'Voces paginarum,'" 84–109, 202–40), and Hendrickson ("Ancient Reading," 182–96) called

attention to the passage in Augustine's *Confessions* (6.3.3) where the Latin author recalls observing with some curiosity Ambrose's practice of reading in silence. Balogh's thesis that such silent reading was rare in the Graeco-Roman world and that it was inhibited by *scriptio continua* (the practice of writing Greek literary texts without spaces between words) has enjoyed a robust afterlife in the field even though it has been effectively debunked by a number of subsequent scholars. For selected examples of this continued dependence on an overdetermined dichotomy between silent and spoken reading, see Saenger, "Silent Reading," 367–414; Saenger, *Spaces Between Words;* Achtemeier, "*Omne verbum sonat,*" 3–27; Gamble, *Books and Readers,* 203–4; Cavallo and Hild, "Buch," II.815; Thomas, "Writing, Reading," 30; Kivy, *Performance of Reading,* esp. 10–18; and Johnson, *Readers and Reading Culture,* 4–9. For studies citing convincing evidence against Balogh and his adherents, see Wohleb, "Beitrag," 111–12; Clark, "Ancient Reading," 698–700; McCartney, "Notes," 184–87; Turner, *Greek Manuscripts;* Di Capua, "Osservazioni," 59–99; Stanford, *Sound of Greek*; Knox, "Silent Reading," 421–35; Allan, "'Αναγιγνώσκω," 1–14; Starr, "*Lectores,*" 337–43; Schenkeveld "Letter," 13; Schenkeveld, "Prose Usages," 129–41; Burnyeat, "Letter," 15; Burnyeat, "Postscript," 74–76; Slusser, "Reading Silently," 499; Horsfall, "Review," 81–85; Gilliard, "More on Silent Reading," 689–96; Gilliard, "Letter," 19; Johnson, "Function," 65–68; Johnson, "Toward a Sociology of Reading," esp. 594–600; Gavrilov, "Reading Techniques," 56–73; Carruthers, *Book of Memory,* 212–15; and Parker, "Books and Reading," esp. 90ff.

66. Gamble, *Books and Readers,* 205–31, quote at 205.

67. Gamble, *Books and Readers,* 231–37, quotes at 234. Even when he briefly addresses so-called apocryphal literature in a discussion of miniature codices, he merely takes this as evidence for an "edifying" kind of popular use (pp. 239–41).

68. Gamble, *Books and Readers,* 237–41, quotes at 239–41.

69. The current consensus holds that early Christian attempts to define hard-and-fast boundaries for the New Testament canon really began in earnest only during the fourth century: see Sundberg, "Towards a Revised History," 452–61; Metzger, *Canon,* 209–47; Gamble, "New Testament Canon," 267–94; MacDonald, *Formation,* 137–227. In a recent article, David Brakke has advanced these discussions about scripture and canon by turning his gaze toward the realm of practice—specifically, what was done with texts and who was doing it: see Brakke, "Scriptural Practices," 263–80.

70. For a critique of the use of the category of religion when applied to the study of the Greek and Roman worlds, see Nongbri, *Before Religion.*

71. Froma Zeitlin ("Religion," 106) has lamented the "lack of attention to Jewish and Christian works of prose fiction that were written in Greek," but notes that "recent trends in criticism have argued for a more multicultural view of the ancient Mediterranean in its diversity of religious beliefs and practices and have suggested a greater fluidity in the assessment of mutual interests and influences."

72. One notable example from late antiquity is Apuleius's borrowing and supplementation of earlier stories about a man physically transformed into an ass: Apuleius, *The Golden Ass* (*Metamorphoses*): Aldington and Gaselee, LCL; Zimmerman, *Apulei Metamorphoseon;* cf. Ps.-Lucian, *Lucius,* or *The Ass:* Harmon and Macleod, LCL, VIII.52–145. Augustine of Hippo models his *Confessions* after Apuleius and acknowledges his awareness of such tales in his *City of God* (18.18: Dombart and Kalb, II.278;

trans. FC 24, 106–7). On the reading of ancient romances as a catalyst for the production of new or expanded narrative prose works, see Hunter, "Ancient Readers," 263–64; and Price, "Implied Reader Response," 909–38. On how the authors of early Christian acts novellae drew on and adapted motifs from Greek romances, as well as from earlier acts literature, see Pervo, *Profit with Delight;* Burrus, *Chastity as Autonomy;* Perkins, *Suffering Self;* Cooper, *Virgin and the Bride;* Price, "Implied Reader Response," 909–38; Hock, Chance, and Perkins, eds., *Ancient Fiction;* Pervo, "Ancient Novel," 685–711; Thomas, *Acts of Peter;* Burrus, "Mimicking Virgins," 49–88; and Whitmarsh, "Introduction," 13 (cf. 55, 83).

73. There is evidence for Christian editorial redaction of the novels *Joseph and Asenath* (ed. Reinmuth; trans. Humphrey) and *Apollonius, King of Tyre:* (ed. Kortekaas, *Historia Apollonii Regis Tyri;* trans. Sandy, in *Collected Ancient Greek Novels,* 736–72; see also Kortekaas, *Story of Apollonius;* and Kortekaas, *Commentary*). The historian Socrates Scholasticus identifies the author of the novel *Aethiopica* (Heliodorus) with a Christian bishop of that name in Trikka (in Thessaly, Greece), and in so doing seems to indicate not only his familiarity with this kind of literature but also an attempt to "sanitize" the texts for Christian consumption: Socrates Scholasticus, *History of the Church* 5.22.51 (Hansen, GCS, n.s. 1, 302; trans. *NPNF*, ser. 2, vol. 2, 132); quote from Zeitlin, "Religion," 94; see also Whitmarsh, "Introduction," 13.

74. Three examples are the Latin *Gospel of Ps.-Matthew* (Gijsel and Beyers, *Libri de nativitate,* CCSA 9–10); the *Armenian Infancy Gospel* (trans. Terian); and the *Arabic Gospel of the Infancy* (Thilo, *Codex apocryphus,* vol. 1, 65–131; trans. *ANF* 8.405–15; see also chapter 7 in this book).

75. Hunter, "Ancient Readers," 269; also Shiner, *Proclaiming,* esp. 171–90 (ch. 9, "Including the Audience").

76. *Apollonius, King of Tyre* is preserved in Latin but has roots in a Greek original that probably dates to the third century CE: see the discussion in Hunter, "Ancient Readers," 269–70.

77. *Paidika* 2.5; 4.1; 6.1; 6.2c; 6.2e; 6.4; 7.1; 9.3; 14.2; 16.3; 17.2 (Burke, *De infantia,* 305, 307, 309, 313–15, 319–21, 325, 331, 335–37). Gero ("Infancy Gospel," 59) includes miracle stories with the "astonishment of bystanders noted" as a distinct subcategory in his formal classification of the *Paidika* narrative material. Similar observations have been made about the role of the disciples and crowds in the early Christian gospels (esp. Mark) and acts literature and their relation to either implied or actual readers: see, e.g., Tannehill, "Disciples in Mark," 386–405; Malbon, "Disciples/Crowds/Whoever," 104–30; and Williams, *Other Followers of Jesus.* The reconstruction of reader roles in such studies is frequently rather one- or two-dimensional, with only the diametrical postures of imitation or resistance imagined as possibilities for "ideal" or "implied" readers. Moore and Sherwood have lodged a sharp and effective critique against the way most biblical scholars have adopted reader-response methodologies only to produce an army of "lockstep goose-stepping . . . readerly cyborgs . . . programmed by historical authors to read in rigidly predetermined ways": see "Biblical Studies 'after' Theory . . . Part One," 26–27; and also their two follow-up articles, "Biblical Studies 'after' Theory . . . Part Two," 87–113; and "Biblical Studies 'after' Theory . . . Part Three," 191–225. Their collaboration has resulted in a cowritten monograph: *The Invention of the Biblical*

Scholar (2011). In my attempt to track the *Paidika* and its history of interpretation, I am conscious of the need to avoid the pitfalls Moore and Sherwood highlight by identifying (1) the specific sociocultural locations in which readers are situated, and (2) the way such locations would have framed a spectrum of readerly postures and perceptions.

78. I borrow language from Hunter, "Ancient Readers," 267–68, who argues that such details reveal how narratives sometimes "lay claim to the methods and purposes of oral story-telling and—to greater and lesser degrees—advertise and exploit this constructed in-betweenness for various literary purposes." For a similar reader-oriented analysis, see Morgan, "Reader and Audiences," 85–103.

79. Achilles Tatius, *Leucippe and Clitophon* 8.4–7, 8.15–18; cf. 3.14: ed. Gaselee, LCL, 396–411, 440–53 (cf. 438–41); trans. Winkler, in *Collected Ancient Greek Novels,* 170–284, at 269–84, esp. 270–74, 281–84 (cf. 215–16).

80. See Bowie, "Ancient Readers," 101–2, for a discussion of two mosaics found in a house at Daphne near Syrian Antioch dated to the Severan period (193–235 CE) with scenes dramatizing the protagonists from the novel *Metiochus and Parthenope.* These scenes are drawn from the literary account, from the characters' personification on the local stage, or from some combination of the two (e.g., reading performances in the home involving *prosōpopoiia*). Whatever the case, the mosaics provide convincing evidence for how Graeco-Roman households served as contexts for the dissemination and interpretation of such stories, sometimes in interaction with extradomestic settings and practices.

81. Aasgaard (*Childhood,* 169–71) is laudably aware of the various contexts in which storytelling took place in late antiquity: from individuals reading written texts in their own private studies to communal settings in which stories are recited aloud, including places of worship, households, workspaces, private parties (*symposia*), and public venues such as marketplaces, fairs, and taverns. While he envisages and explores the implications of each of these possibilities, he also specifically privileges the household as "the most probable setting" (p. 171) for the transmission of the *Paidika.*

82. Alikin, *Earliest History,* 62–65 (quotes at pp. 65 and 63). Alikin does offer a small caveat, noting that Christians tried "to make their activities at the symposium serviceable to the building up of their Christian identity and morals" (p. 65), but in doing so she seems to disregard how ethical formation within community also played a role in broader symposium practices among non-Christians or mixed constituencies: on this point, see Aune's comparison of Plutarch and Paul in his article "Septem sapientium convivium," 51–105, esp. 87. On the relation between early Christian gatherings and Hellenistic practices, see also Rouwhorst, "Roots," 295–308.

83. Alikin, *Earliest History,* 183 (cf. 288). On the use of the banquet table as a setting for philosophical discourse and teaching, see also Smith, *From Symposium to Eucharist,* 256–58 ("Social Bonding: Table Talk as a Mode of Teaching"). On "anecdotes" as "the glue and ideological underpinning of literate exchange" in "the oral environments of the symposium," as well as in other settings for performance and dialogue, see Goldhill, "Anecdote," 111.

84. *Apostolic Tradition* 26 (quotes at 26.2 and 26.10): Dix, *Treatise,* 45–52 (quotes at pp. 45 and 47). On the dating of the text, see Bradshaw, *Search,* 78–80.

85. *Apostolic Tradition* 35.3–36.1: Dix, *Treatise,* 62.

86. Methodius, *Symposium* 5.3 (Musurillo, SC 95, 148; trans. *ANF* 6.326, slightly modified).

87. Methodius, *Symposium* 10.6 (Musurillo, SC 95, 300–302; trans. *ANF* 6.350).

88. Hägg, "Orality," 66; repr. in Mortensen and Eide, *Parthenope,* 134.

89. Hägg, "Orality," 66; repr. in Mortensen and Eide, *Parthenope,* 135.

90. Hägg (*Novel,* 93) writes: "The ability to read, and read easily and for pleasure, in a milieu where true literacy was not common, no doubt carried with it the obligation to read aloud to members of the household, to a circle of friends, perhaps even to a wider audience." In putting forward this hypothesis, Hägg is interested in accounting for the supposed "wider circulation of the novel" (a circulation not evidenced by documentary sources), but I think his key insight relates to the social agency possessed by the literate elite.

91. Hunter, "Ancient Readers," 262.

92. Ibid., 264–67, quote at 267; cf. Swain, *Hellenism and Empire,* 118ff. Hunter acknowledges that the variety of narrative forms produced may reflect "the expectation of a diverse and complex audience response," and by extension perhaps even "a diverse and complex audience" (p. 270), but he does not flesh out the methodological assumptions behind a move from a diversity in literary form to a diversity in audience constituency. Bowie ("Ancient Readers," 92ff.) similarly argues that both the "intended" and the "actual" readership of Greek and Roman novels generally fit the profile of a highly educated readership on the basis of intertextual considerations, citation evidence, and the conformity of papyri to high literary writing types and book formats. In his earlier article, "Readership of Greek Novels," 435–59, Bowie had acknowledged that "[t]here are indeed, overall, a number of points which could support the notion that the readership of the novel may have spilled over from the class of *pepaideumenoi* who read other literary works to a slightly wider circle," but he was not convinced that such a nonelite readership would have been "typical" (p. 441). For other scholars who interpret the production and reception of ancient narrative literature as primarily the provenance of the elite, see Stephens, "Who Read the Ancient Novels?" 405–18 (esp. 415); Dowden, "Roman Audience," 419–34; Cooper, *Virgin and the Bride,* esp. 23 and 67; and Johnson, *Readers and Reading Culture.*

93. On literacy and orality as a "continuum . . . mediated by memory" and as an "exchange that uses the currency of memory," see Small, *Wax Tablets,* xiii–xiv.

94. In the case of the novel, Scobie (*Apuleius and Folklore,* 1–73) has argued that "professional itinerant story-tellers, *fabulatores* or profane *aretalogoi*" may have been instrumental in the "early stages" of the genre's development (cited by Hägg, "Orality," 49; repr. in Mortensen and Eide, *Parthenope,* 111). Elsewhere, Hägg (*Narrative Technique,* 332) had argued that the novels themselves were originally designed for oral delivery. In the case of the *Paidika,* see especially Gero ("Infancy Gospel," 56), who analyzes the stories as "the fixation in writing of a cycle of oral tradition." His assumption that the *Paidika* "had a long period of oral transmission behind it" leads him to conclude that "the first versions . . . were not written down before the fifth century" (ibid.). This late dating has not achieved consensus among historians. I address implications for dating in more detail later in this chapter.

95. According to Havelock (*Muse Learns to Write,* 41), one can discern elements of "oralized language" even in literate societies: drawing on Luria's ethnography of literate and nonliterate cognition, Havelock (pp. 40–41) speaks of an oral "consciousness," closely tied to "the model of operation of the memory," which in the context of reading performances is shaped by "the coordination of rhythmic patterns with the physical motions of the body" (see also Luria, *Cognitive Development;* and Havelock, *Greek Concept,* 39–40). On the performance of stories via "a totality of words, gestures, and look," see Aasgaard, *Childhood,* 25. On the rise of performance criticism in New Testament studies, see Rhoads, "Performance Criticism . . . Part I," 118–33, and "Performance Criticism . . . Part II," 164–84. Finally, for a fascinating exploration of reading as performance (even in its solitary and/or silent manifestations), see Kivy, *Performance of Reading.*

96. For a helpful discussion of the "conceptional" and "medial" aspects of oral and written discourse, see Bakker, "How Oral Is Oral Composition?" 29–47. Bakker (p. 32) describes both orality and writing as "gradient" insofar as their respective properties may be plotted at various locations on a "continuum," and then applies these insights to the study of Homer. Hägg ("Orality," 49; repr. in Mortensen and Eide, *Parthenope,* 111) notes the "long coexistence and reciprocity of orality and literacy in the archaic and classical periods" but then contrasts that to the more "bookish" Hellenistic culture. While this contrast may be helpful for tracing a cultural shift of emphasis toward textuality in the later period, it has the unfortunate consequence of seeming to relegate "orality" to the classical past and obscuring the ways in which texts themselves continued to be mediated in oral-aural settings. Hägg and Rousseau ("Introduction," in *Greek Biography,* 1–2) also appropriately recognize the blurring of the distinction between the categories of oral and written in their discussion of the more "rhetorical" form of the panegyric versus the more "bookish product" of the biography when they speak of "the transgression of the boundaries between them, their interaction and coalescence." Similar observations have been made with respect to the *Paidika.* Ron Cameron (*Other Gospels,* 123) envisions a process in which episodes "circulated from the oral to the written tradition and back again with relative fluidity." J. K. Elliot (*Apocryphal New Testament,* 63; cf. *Apocryphal Jesus,* 3) proposes that the various collections of *Paidika* tales "encapsulat[ed] in writing at various points in history . . . a developing cycle of oral tradition." These perspectives are favorably cited by Aasgaard (*Childhood,* 30), who likewise emphasizes that "the differences between oral and written should not be overestimated" (p. 25).

97. Hägg, "Orality," 59–64; repr. in Mortensen and Eide, *Parthenope,* 127–31.

98. Two important previous investigations of evidence for orality in the *Paidika* have been published by Gero and Aasgaard, both of whom recognize oral and written processes of transmission as compatible and intersecting. Gero ("Infancy Gospel," 46–80) is concerned with "the phases of oral transmission prior to and simultaneous with the various written versions" (p. 47), and acknowledges that "the recording of the [*Paidika*] stories did not remove them from the sphere of oral circulation and transmission; though of course the literary versions do depend on each other, they also seem to draw on the *vox viva* of the still-circulating oral material" (pp. 56–57). Aasgaard (*Childhood,* 14–34, esp. 23–25) proposes an "oral/written approach" to the study of the *Paidika,* one which recognizes that "the Greek variants may even reflect separate written mani-

festations of oral transmission." An early example of this folkloric approach to the *Paidika* was a long untitled article by Tollius in *Monatliche Unterredungen*, 537–610: Tollius compared the *Paidika* to "similar childhood tales from German folklore" (Burke, *De infantia*, 47). In the nineteenth and early twentieth centuries, several scholars also drew attention to nontextual evidence related to the transmission of the infancy tales: see Hofmann, *Leben Jesu;* Meyer, "Erzählung des Thomas," 63–67; Meyer, "Kindheitserzählung," 132–42; and Donehoo, *Apocryphal and Legendary Life of Christ* (for a discussion of their scholarship, see Burke, *De infantia*, 63–67).

99. On the way oral performance techniques intersected with matters of punctuation and paragraphing, see also Bryan, *Preface to Mark*, 78 and 80.

100. On the relation between cognitive memory, the oral-aural reading of early Christian narratives in group settings, and the adaptations of texts within the context of performance, see Czachesz, "Rewriting," 426–41; on the role of "serial recall," see Rubin, *Memory*, 175–76.

101. The most prominent example of such a linking device is the retroactive amnesty granted in *Paidika* 8.2 (Burke, *De infantia*, 334–35) to those whom Jesus had previously cursed, an amnesty that seems a non sequitur in that it only lasts until chapter 13 when Jesus curses the second teacher. It should be noted in this context that even the connections between the repeated teacher stories are rather minimal, limited to the insertion of a singular adjective: "*another* master" (13.1) or "*another* teacher" (14.1). In *Paidika* 14.3, Burke's insertion of the linking adverb "too" in the phrase "suspecting that this teacher too was no longer inexperienced" is gratuitous and not reflected in the Greek text (Burke, *De infantia*, 330).

102. Aasgaard, *Childhood*, 27. James Francis ("Visual and Verbal Representation," 301) writes that "[t]exts appropriated through hearing do not possess the fixity of those assimilated and conceptualized according to modern practices of reading." On the fluidity of transmitted content as a feature of oral settings, see also Koskenniemi and Lindqvist, "Rewritten Bible," 11–39, esp. 29; and Czachez, "Rewriting," 426–41.

103. Olrik, *Principles*, 41–61 (=ch. 3, "The Structure of the Narrative: The Epic Laws"), esp. p. 52 ("§ 74. The Law of Three"); see also Olrik, "Epic Laws," 129–41. Gero ("Infancy Gospel," 62–64) highlights the "triplicate" version of the teacher tale as "a common folkloric device" (cf. Burke, *De infantia*, 100). For the application of Olrik's study of oral folklore to early Christian acts novellae, see MacDonald, *Legend and the Apostle*, 26–34; and Davis, *Cult of Saint Thecla*, 14.

104. *Paidika* 6.2f (Burke, *De infantia*, 315–17).

105. *Paidika* 6.4 (Burke, *De infantia*, 319–21; Aasgaard, *Childhood*, 28). See also the twofold repetition of the prefix *homo*- in the same passage: "of equal measure, of equal proportions" (*isometrous, isomerous:* Burke, *De infantia*, 318–19).

106. See especially the Syriac ("Go, fly, and be mindful of me, you who are alive") and the Latin ("Go, fly over the earth and throughout the whole world, and live"): cited by Gero, "Infancy Gospel," 64–65. This same tripartite command is also evident in Greek recensions A, B, and D (Burke, *De infantia*, 344–45 [Ga], 402–3 [Gd], 456–7 [Gb]). The Gs recension (*Paidika* 2.4: Burke, *De infantia*, 304–5) has the command in bipartite form.

107. Gero ("Infancy Gospel," 66) cites the Slavic ("Arise, split the wood, and remember me"), the Latin ("Arise and chop [alt. find] wood, and remember me"), and Greek

recension A ("Rise, split your wood, and remember me": Burke, *De infantia,* 370–71 [Ga 10.2]). Once again, the Gs recension has a bipartite command: "Go, split your wood" (*Paidika* 16.2; Burke, *De infantia,* 334–35).

108. Gero ("Infancy Gospel, 66–67) also notes the triplicate format of Jesus' words in later stories about Jesus' raising of a dead infant and a dead workman, attested in Greek recension A (Ga 17.1 and 18.1: Burke, *De infantia,* 382–85) and in the Slavic version.

109. See, e.g., the *inclusio* framing Jesus' description of the first letter: "[I]t has slanted lines and a middle stroke. . . . [Such are] the lines possessed by the alpha" (*Paidika* 6.4; Burke, *De infantia,* 319). This detail is noted by Aasgaard, *Childhood,* 28.

110. Note the recollection and anticipation of past and future acts of healing in *Paidika* 16.3, where the crowd exclaims, "For he saved many souls from death. And he will be able to save all the days of his life" (Burke, *De infantia,* 335). The retroactive amnesty granted to Jesus' previous cursing victims in *Paidika* 8.2 (Burke, *De infantia,* 323) would also fall under this category.

111. The first person is used only in the opening chapter, in a section of text that represents a later addition: "I, Thomas the Israelite" (*Paidika* 1; Burke, *De infantia,* 302–3).

112. This is not to mention the implicit dialogue between Jesus and the teachers in the Temple: "After three days they found him sitting in the Temple in the midst of the teachers, listening to them and asking them questions" (*Paidika* 17.2: Burke, *De infantia,* 335).

113. See Shiner (*Proclaiming,* 4), who notes that the same Greek word, *hupokrinō,* was employed (in the middle voice) for the activities of "acting on a stage, the delivery of an oration, and expressive reading."

114. Mournet, *Oral Tradition,* 132. In analyzing oral elements in the *Testaments of the Twelve Patriarchs,* a second-century work that also features biographical forms of narration, Mournet (ibid.) distinguishes "performance oriented words such as 'speak,' 'say,' and 'tell' " from "visually oriented words related to the silent reading and visual interaction with a text."

115. *Paidika* 6.2e and 17.2 (Burke, *De infantia,* 315, 335–37).

116. Aasgaard, *Childhood,* 29.

117. Paxson, *Poetics,* esp. 12–13; also Haworth, *Deified Virtues,* 42–54.

118. On *prosōpopoiia* in the *Satyricon,* see Patimo, "Una seduta deliberante," 47–60; see also the book review by Grillo, in the *Bryn Mawr Classical Review* 2011.03.72 (http://bmcr.brynmawr.edu/2011/2011–03–72.html). On *prosōpopoiia* in Chariton and Plutarch, see Myers, "Prosopopoetics and Conflict," 585–86. Myers also points out relatively contemporaneous instances of "speech in character" in Philo (*The Life of Moses* 1.54–57; 1.173–75; 1.201–3; cf. 1.158; *On Abraham* 1.4–5; *On Dreams* 1.176; 2.134); and in the novel *Joseph and Aseneth* (11.3–14.16–18; trans. in Charlesworth, *Old Testament Pseudepigrapha,* II.217–25). Much work has also been done on the use of *prosōpopoiia* (or *ēthopoiia*) in the first-century letters of Paul: see Stowers, *A Reading of Romans;* Stowers, "Romans 7:7–25," 180–202; and Sampley, *Paul,* 210–12. Paula Fredriksen ("Historical Integrity," 69–70) notes that Paul's use of "speech in character" in Romans 7 was recognized as such by Augustine in his *Notes on Romans* (44.1–46.6).

119. Myers, "Prosopopoetics and Conflict," 580–96, quote at 584.

120. Ibid., 591. In this context, Myers also cites evidence for the way ancient rhetoricians included "age as a category that should guide how one crafts a speech for a character" (pp. 591–92, note 34): see, for example, Aristotle, *Rhetoric* 2.12–14 (Freese, LCL, 246–57); Quintilian, *Institutes* 3.8.50–54 (Russell, LCL, II.138–43); and Aelius Theon, *Progymnasmata* 65 (Patillon, 8–9).

121. Myers, "Prosopopoetics and Conflict," 587. For other studies of orality in the Fourth Gospel, see Dewey, "Gospel of John," 239–52; Thatcher, "John's Memory Theatre," 73–91; Boomershine, "Medium and Message," 92–120; Wire, "Jesus Retold," 121–32; and Labahn, "Scripture *Talks,*" 133–54. The importance of oral performance has been noted in the study of other early Christian gospels as well: see, e.g., Longenecker, "A Humorous Jesus?" 179–204.

122. For a bibliography of scholarship in support of this dating of composition, see Burke, *De infantia,* 202–3, note 3.

123. Vindobensis 563, fol. 132r–v, 135r–v, 141r–v, 142r–v, 171r–v, 176r–v: ed. Tischendorf, *De evangeliorum apocryphorum,* 214–15; and *Evangelia apocrypha,* 2nd ed., xliv–xlvi. The folia with the erased text of the *Paidika* were overwritten and incorporated into another codex during the eighth century CE: for a detailed discussion of these fragments and their dating, see Philippart, "Fragments palimpsestes latins," 391–411; Lowe, *Codices latini antiquiores,* 14; and Burke, *De infantia,* 145–46.

124. British Museum Add. 14484, fol. 12v–16r (=SyrW): ed. Wright, *Contributions,* 6–11 (English translation), 11–16 (Syriac text). The British Museum copy lacks sections from Jesus' classroom encounter with Zacchaeus (6.2d; 6.3–7.3; 8.2) and the third teacher scene (14.3–4) (Burke, *De infantia,* 162–63).

125. Göttingen, Universitätsbibliothek, syr. 10, fol. 1v–4v (SyrG): first noted by Duensing, "Mitteilungen 58," 637; partially used as a basis for Meyer's translation in "Kindheitserzählung," 93–102; fully collated in relation to the British Museum manuscript by Baars and Heldermann, "Neue Materialien," *Oriens Christianus* 77 (1993), 191–226; 78 (1994), 1–32. In the Göttingen copy, the following material is omitted: parts of Jesus' encounter with the boy who bumps into his shoulder (4.2; 5.2–3) and of the first teacher scene with Zacchaeus (6.1; 6.2c; 6.3–4; most of 7), all of the second and third teacher scenes (14–15), and parts of Jesus' meeting with the teachers in the Temple (17) (Burke, *De infantia,* 163–64).

126. Aasgaard, *Childhood,* 14–15; Burke, *De infantia,* 174, 188–95. Also important for the reconstruction of the short recension has been analysis of the Ethiopic and Georgian versions of the infancy story collection, along with the early medieval Latin *Gospel of Ps.-Matthew*, which contains a section drawn from a *Paidika*-source: see Burke, *De infantia,* 146–49 (Latin Ps.-Matthew), 168–69 (Georgian version), 170–71 (Ethiopic version). Lucas van Rompay's work on the Ethiopic text has been instrumental for defining the parameters of this short recension: see his article "De ethiopische versie," 119–32. The Ethiopic *Paidika* material corresponds to chapter 8 in the *Miracles of Jesus* (*Ta'amra 'Iyasus*): ed. Grébaut, "Les miracles de Jésus," 555–652, at 625–42 ("Huitième miracle, Miracles de l'enfance"). For the Georgian version, see Kekelidze, *Monumenta Hagiographica Georgica,* vol. 1, 115–17; and Melikset-Bek, "Fragment grusinskoi versii," 315–20; Latin trans. Garitte, "Le fragment géorgien," 513–20. The *pars altera* of

the Latin *Gospel of Ps.-Matthew* (LM; Tischendorf, *Evangelium apocrypha,* 2nd ed., 93–112) corresponds to the translation in the fifth-century Latin palimpsest in Vienna, albeit in an expanded and interpolated form: both are witnesses of what Burke calls the "First Latin Version," which originally circulated independently from the *Gospel of Ps.-Matthew* (Canal, "Antiguas versions Latinas," 431–73; Gijsel, *Die unmittelbare Textüberlieferung;* and Gijsel, *Pseudo-Matthaei Euangelium*). A number of later European language versions preserve elements of this First Latin Version, either based on a direct dependence (Irish) or by way of the *pars altera* of *Ps.-Matthew* (German, Danish, Provençal, Old English): for a bibliography of editions and commentary, see Burke, *De infantia,* 148 (notes 3–7) and 149 (notes 1–5).

127. Peeters (*Évangiles apocryphes,* vol. 2, i–lix) was influential in pushing for an early theory of Syriac origins. This theory has been rejected by Gero ("Infancy Gospel," esp. 56ff.), Burke (*De infantia,* 174–88), and others.

128. There are four recensions of Greek *Paidika* (labeled A, B, D, and S). Recensions A and B, and the Latin text of recension D, were originally edited by Tischendorf, *Evangelia apocrypha.* The Greek text of recension D was first published by Delatte, "Évangile de l'enfance," 264–71. Each of these editions has now been superseded by Burke, who also produced an edition of recension S, the earliest of the extant Greek copies: see Burke, *De infantia,* 301–27 (Gs), 339–89 (Ga), 391–451 (Gd), and 453–63 (Gb). For a summary of the *Paidika*'s transmission, which is "anything but easy to describe," see Voicu, "Ways to Survival," 411–13.

129. Burke, *De infantia,* 214–19.

130. Jerusalem, Bibliothēkē tou Patriarcheiou: Codex Sabaiticus 259 (1089/1090 CE): ed. and trans. Burke, *De infantia,* 302–37 (cf. 127–28); see also Aasgaard, *Childhood,* 219–32 (text), 233–42 (translation). My translation of this text is presented in Appendix A.

131. Aasgaard (*Childhood of Jesus,* 15) argues that it is based on "an old archetype (probably ca. fifth century)."

132. Justin Martyr, *Dialogue with Trypho* 88.8 (Marcovich, 224; trans. Burke, *De infantia,* 26; discussed on pp. 26–28).

133. Justin Martyr, *Dialogue with Trypho* 88.8 (Marcovich, 224; trans. Burke, *De infantia,* 26).

134. *Paidika* 12.1 (Burke, *De infantia,* 324–27, quote at 326–27). In the late nineteenth century, Zahn (*Geschichte,* II.771–72) argued that Justin was directly dependent on the *Paidika* account. This viewpoint was subsequently rejected by a number of late nineteenth- and early twentieth-century scholars (Burke, *De infantia,* 27, note 2).

135. *Acts of Thomas* 3 and 17 (Bonnet, *Acta apostolorum apocrypha,* vol. 2.2, 102–4 and 124–25; trans. James, *Apocryphal New Testament,* at 448 and 454). In chapter 2 of that same work, Thomas's carpentry trade is mentioned in the context of Jesus' identity as "the son of Joseph the carpenter" (Bonnet, vol. 2.2, 101–2; trans. James, 448).

136. An early papyrus containing the Gospel of Mark (p^{45}, third cent. CE) appears to have the alternative reading, "the son of the carpenter" (Nestle-Aland, *Novum Testamentum Graece,* 26th edition, 105). While this variant could suggest an early reading that the Gospel of Matthew later picked up, the editors of the Nestle-Aland critical edition see it as a secondary variant in the Markan manuscript tradition (possibly influenced by

the phrasing of Matthew): see Hooker, *Gospel According to Saint Mark,* 152–53; and Collins, *Mark,* 287–88, 291. Both Hooker and Collins note the pejorative connotations sometimes attached to the social status of carpenters in antiquity: see, e.g., Origen, *Against Celsus* 6.34 and 6.36 (Borret, SC 147, 262 and 266–68; trans. Chadwick, 350 and 352), where he defends Jesus against Celsus's charge that the Christian Messiah was only a lowly craftsman: see also Metzger, *Textual Commentary,* 2nd ed., 75–76.

137. This conclusion is strengthened by the fact that no other ancient Christian authors make reference to the story about Jesus' carpentry miracle from the *Paidika.*

138. *Epistle of the Apostles* 4 (Schmidt, *Gespräche Jesu,* 29; trans. Müller, 253); see also Burke, *De infantia,* 29. Schmidt, Müller, and Hornschuh (*Studien*) all support a second-century dating although they differ over the issue of probable provenance (Egypt or Asia Minor). While the *Epistle* is preserved in a fourth- or fifth-century Coptic manuscript, there is a lacuna at the beginning of that text: the first six chapters (including this passage) are only preserved in a much later but fortunately complete Ethiopic version.

139. *Paidika* 13 (Burke, *De infantia,* 329).

140. *Epistle of the Apostles* 4; cf. 1–3 (Schmidt, *Gespräche Jesu,* 29; trans. Müller, 253).

141. Gero ("Infancy Gospel," 56, note 1), Voicu ("Verso," 44 and 47), Bagatti ("Nota," 483), and Burke (*De infantia,* 29) have all questioned whether the author of the *Epistle* had access to this *Paidika* pericope in written form.

142. The pointed citation of this passage, including the author's emphatic assertion regarding the "reality" of the events described, may hint that the story itself was being used for a different purpose by the groups with whom he was in disagreement.

143. *Gospel of Truth* 19.17–32 (Attridge, *Nag Hammadi Codex I,* vol. 1, 86–87 [my translation]; see also Layton, *Gnostic Scriptures,* 254). There is an ongoing debate over whether the author of the anonymous *Gospel of Truth* should be identified as Valentinus himself, or one of his followers: see Brakke, *Gnostics,* 99–105.

144. On Valentinus's presentation of his own teaching authority in terms of an "intellectual pedigree" or "academic lineage," see Brakke, *Gnostics,* 103–4. On the way such philosophical or school-based constructions of authority came into conflict with ecclesiastical and episcopal structures, see also Davis, *Early Coptic Papacy,* 17–28.

145. See esp. *Paidika* 6–8 and 14 (Burke, *De infantia,* 309–23, 331–33).

146. Layton (*Gnostic Scriptures,* 254) notes that the Coptic word *jaumaït,* translated by Attridge as "guide" (*Nag Hammadi Codex I,* vol. 1, 87), was a close equivalent to the Greek term *paidagogos,* which usually referred to "a trained slave who accompanied schoolchildren to the classroom and supervised their conduct."

147. Valentinus, *Fragment A,* in Hippolytus of Rome, *Refutation of All Heresies* 6.42.2 (Völker, *Quellen,* 59 [=Frag. 7]; trans. Layton, *Gnostic Scriptures,* 230–31).

148. Immediately after mentioning the Logos's appearance in "places of instruction," the author of the *Gospel of Truth* goes on to describe how "little children" (*nkouï shēm*) also came to him, "those to whom the knowledge [*psaune*] of the Father belongs" (*Gospel of Truth* 19.28–30: Attridge, *Nag Hammadi Codex I,* vol. 1, 86–7). I am not raising again the old saw of "Gnostic origins" here (a theory thoroughly debunked by Burke, *De infantia,* passim) but rather am speaking to one of many ancient interpretive applications of the *Paidika* stories.

149. Layton (*Gnostic Scriptures,* 267–69) associates Marcus (Mark) with an "eastern" Valentinian school, primarily centered in Alexandria.

150. Irenaeus, *Against Heresies* 1.20.1 (=1.13.1 in *TLG*); Rousseau and Doutreleau, SC 264, 288–89 (my translation); *ANF* 1.344–5; see also Burke, *De infantia,* 3–5.

151. Ibid.

152. Irenaeus, *Against Heresies* 1.14.5 (=1.8.6 in *TLG*): ed. Rousseau and Doutreleau, SC 264, 220–21; *ANF* 1.337.

153. Irenaeus, *Against Heresies* 1.20.1 (=1.13.1 in *TLG*): ed. Rousseau and Doutreleau, SC 264, 288–89.

154. Irenaeus, *Against Heresies* 1.20.1 (=1.13.1 in *TLG*): ed. Rousseau and Doutreleau, SC 264, 289.

155. Ibid.

156. Irenaeus, *Against Heresies* 1.20.1 (=1.13.1 in *TLG*): Rousseau and Doutreleau, SC 264, 288.

157. Gero, "Infancy Gospel," 62–64, quote at 63; also Burke, *De infantia,* 5.

158. Syriac *Paidika* 14.1–2 (ed. Wright, *Contributions,* 15 [Syriac text], 10 [English translation]): "The scribe said to him: 'Say Alaph,' and Jesus said (it). And the scribe next wanted him to say Beth; and Jesus said to him: 'Tell me first what Alaph is, and then I will tell thee concerning Beth.' " See also Tony Burke's edition of Vatican Syr. 159 (1622/1623 CE): Burke, "The *Infancy Gospel of Thomas* from an Unpublished Syriac Manuscript," 225–99 (text and translation, pp. 265–99).

The earliest Greek recension diverges in certain crucial ways. The teacher's first admonition in Irenaeus ("Say alpha": *Against Heresies* 1.20.1 [=1.13.1 in *TLG*]; Rousseau and Doutreleau, SC 264, 289) matches *Paidika* 13.1 ("Say alpha": Burke, *De infantia,* 328–29), but Jesus' compliant response is notably absent. Nor do we find in the Greek the teacher's second admonition to pronounce the letter beta. Finally, the Greek order of the letters is flipped in Jesus' final statement: "You tell me first what beta is and I shall tell you what alpha is" (*Paidika* 13.2; Burke, *De infantia,* 329).

159. On this point, see, e.g., Cameron, *Other Gospels,* 122. Burke (*De infantia,* 5) notes, however, that "Irenaeus only discusses the Marcosians' interpretation of Jesus' statement in Luke 2,49, not the entire story," which may suggest that this juxtaposition is not founded on a common textual source. Gero ("Infancy Gospel," 63–64) thinks Irenaeus was referring to the written text. Otero (*Das kirchenslavische Evangelium,* 176–77) proposes that the Marcosians' tale may have been based not on the *Paidika* itself but rather on the *Epistula Apostolorum.*

160. There is no secure data on the *Paidika* from the third century CE. The Syriac version of the *Acts of Thomas* (ch. 79) refers to the fact that Jesus "went to school" and "taught his teacher," but these details are absent from the Greek text, which suggests that they are probably later editorial editions that cannot be traced to the original third-century text. For the Syriac, see Wright, *Apocryphal Acts,* vol. 1, 248 (Syriac text); vol. 2, 215 (English translation). The Greek text has been edited in Lipsius and Bonnet, *Acta apostolorum apocrypha,* vol. 2.2, 194. For a translation and commentary, see Klijn, *Acts of Thomas,* 2nd rev. ed., 157ff.; for a comparison of the Syriac and Greek versions of this passage, see Burke, *De infantia,* 30–31.

161. Epiphanius of Salamis, *Panarion* 51.20.2–3 (Holl, GCS 31.2, 2nd ed., 277–78; also Burke, *De infantia,* 7).

162. Epiphanius of Salamis, *Panarion* 51.20.2–3 (Holl, GCS 31.2, 2nd ed., 277–78).

163. John Chrysostom, *Homily 17 on John* (*PG* 59.110); also Burke, *De infantia,* 6.

164. John Chrysostom, *Homily 17 on John* (*PG* 59.110). As Amsler ("Les *Paidika Iesou,*" 442–45) points out, Chrysostom extends his argument against the veracity of such childhood miracle accounts in two later sermons, where he defends the claim in the Gospel of John (2:11) that Jesus performed the first of his miracles in Cana of Galilee: see John Chrysostom, *Homilies 21.1–2 and 23.1 on John* (*PG* 59.129–30 and 139).

165. For some reason, Voicu ("Verso," 41–42; cf. "Histoire de l'enfance," 191) is of two minds about the significance of Epiphanius's and Chrysostom's testimony: he raises questions about whether the former depended on a written source, while arguing that the latter must have had a text of the *Paidika* at his disposal.

166. As further evidence for the standardization of the full *Paidika* narrative, see the sixth-century *Decretum Gelasianum,* which has possible connections with earlier Roman traditions and includes the "Book of the Infancy of the Savior" (*Liber de infantia salvatoris*) in a list of apocryphal works: ed. Dobschütz, *Decretum,* 51; trans. Schneemelcher, *New Testament Apocrypha,* vol. 1, 38; also Burke, *De infantia,* 7–8.

167. *Questions of Bartholomew* 2.11 (ca. fourth century): ed. Vassiliev, *Anecdota graeco-byzantina,* vol. 1, 12; trans. Burke, *De infantia,* 31. For a critical French translation of the text, see Kaestli, "Questions de Barthélemy," 255–305; also Kaestli and Cherix, *L'évangile de Barthélemy,* 29–134. In addition to the Greek, there are surviving Slavonic and Latin recensions: see Moricca, "Un nuovo testo"; and Bonwetsch, "Die apokryphen Fragen," 1–42. Wilmart and Tisserant ("Fragments grecs et latins") have identified this text with the eponymous gospel mentioned by Jerome in the prologue of his *Commentary on Matthew* and later condemned in the *Decretum Gelasianum*

168. *History of Joseph the Carpenter* 17: trans. Robinson, *Coptic Apocryphal Gospels,* 137–38 (Bohairic), 154–55 (Sahidic). For the complete Bohairic edition, see Lagarde, *Aegyptiaca,* 1–37 (trans. Robinson, 130–47). Four different sets of Sahidic fragments survive: three are reproduced and/or translated by Robinson (pp. 147–59); the fourth was edited by Lefort ("À propos de l'histoire," 201–23). The Arabic version was edited by Battista and Bagatti (*Edizione critica*). For discussions of the text's history of publication, see Perez, "Joseph the Carpenter," 1371–74; and Elliott, *Apocryphal New Testament,* 111–17. Translations of the Sahidic, Bohairic, and Arabic versions of the relevant passage are arranged in parallel and discussed by Burke, *De infantia,* 32–33. The dating of this work remains uncertain: Morenz (*Geschichte*) gives the fourth century as his estimate, while Boud'hors ("Histoire," 28) opts for a later, seventh-century dating.

169. This detail also appears in a late recension of the *Acts of Andrew and Matthias* (Cod. Mosquensis RGB gr. 129, fol. 122v–56v; fifteenth century CE) which incorporates elements of the *Paidika* stories and may be partially dependent on the *Questions of Bartholomew*: Vinogradov, "Die zweite Rezension," 31–33. Burke (*De infantia,* 17–25) reproduces the Greek text with emendations based on communication with J.-D. Kaestli, and supplies an English translation along with an analytical discussion.

170. On the basis of the evidence that I have discussed above, Gero ("Infancy Gospel," 56, note 1) concludes that the stories in the *Paidika* were not written down in extended narrative form before the fifth century. He envisions a complex process of transmission in several stages, beginning in the second century when individual teacher tales were written down but remained in oral circulation, continuing with a "tunnel period" of oral transmission from the second to the sixth centuries that witnessed the expansion of narrative material; and concluding with the standardization of written versions in the sixth century, with some continued expansion until the tenth. Burke (*De infantia,* 94) and Aasgaard (*Childhood,* 7, note 37) find Gero's late dating of the written composition to be too "cautious." I am in agreement with Gero's characterization of a complex mix of smaller oral and written traditions during the first three or four centuries of transmission, but I think the testimony of Epiphanius and Chrysostom, while not absolutely definitive, strongly suggests the existence of an identifiable written collection of stories already in the fourth century.

171. Amsler ("Les *Paidika Iesou,*" 457) draws a similar conclusion, noting the way that early witnesses such as Irenaeus and the *Epistle of the Apostles* attest merely "un apophthegme probablement isolé." In this context, he likewise casts doubt on a second-century date for the *Paidika* and instead argues for a fourth-century date for the circulation of a more fleshed-out narrative version.

172. In some ways, my approach is analogous to form-critical methodologies, especially insofar as I focus on literary forms and the social settings for their oral and written transmission. In this, I follow Gero ("Infancy Gospel," 46–80, esp. 57ff.), who analyzes independent story units and classifies them according to three types: (1) simple short miracle stories with no saying attached and no synoptic parallels; (2) healings and other miracles in the form of apophthegms; and (3) curses or imprecations (seen as "healings in reverse"). Despite his general concern with the larger scope of the plot, Burke (*De infantia,* 201) also acknowledges that the *Paidika* "reads more like a compilation of stories than a freely-composed narrative" and that "[i]ts stories may have once circulated independently, just as episodes attested in later branches of the infancy gospel trajectory once did." For an accessible introduction to form criticism as a discipline, see McKnight, *What Is Form Criticism?* Classic monographs include Dibelius, *Formgeschichte* (trans. Woolf, *From Tradition to Gospel*); and Bultmann, *Geschichte der synoptischen Tradition* (trans. Marsh, *History of the Synoptic Tradition*). For a more recent adaptation of form critical methods, helpfully framed in relation to "how ancient readers reread texts," see Melugin, "Recent Form Criticism Revisited," 46–64, quote at 60.

In contradistinction to form critics' traditional preoccupation with the recovery of textual origins, however, I am more interested in the role that such forms and settings played in processes of reception and interpretation (both oral and written) moving forward in time in successive attempts "to restructure and give meaning to the past" (Hamrit, "Nachträglichkeit"). As such, my inquiry bears a certain resemblance to Sigmund Freud's conception of *Nachträglichkeit* ("afterwardsness") as interpreted by Jacques Lacan ("Fonction et champ," 81–166), or to Benjamin's understanding of *Nachleben* ("afterlife") as read by Gerhard Richter (*Afterness,* esp. 1–6).

Chapter 3. Bird-Watching

This chapter is a considerably revised version of my article "Bird Watching in the *Infancy Gospel of Thomas*: From Child's Play to Rituals of Divine Discernment."

1. *Paidika* 2.1 (Burke, *De infantia,* 303).

2. *Paidika* 2.2 (Burke, *De infantia,* 303).

3. *Paidika* 2.3 (Burke, *De infantia,* 303–5).

4. *Paidika* 2.4 (Burke, *De infantia,* 305). In the other Greek versions (Ga, Gb, Gd), Jesus calls them "living ones" and exhorts them to "[r]emember me" (ch. 2.4): Burke, *De infantia,* 344–45 (Ga), 402–3 (Gd), and 456–57 (Gb,=ch. 3.2).

5. *Paidika* 2.4 (Burke, *De infantia,* 305).

6. For bibliography and discussion related to the transmission of these traditions, see Schneemelcher, *New Testament Apocrypha,* vol. 1, 439–43, 456–59; and Burke's website: http://www.tonyburke.ca/infancy-gospel-of-thomas/.

7. *Questions of Bartholomew* 2.11 (Vassiliev, *Anecdota graeco-byzantina,* vol. 1, 12); see also Burke, *De infantia,* 31; and Elliott, *Apocryphal New Testament,* 652–72.

8. Qur'ān 3:49 and 5:110 (Pickthall, *Meaning,* 69–70, 158, translation modified); see my discussion in chapter 7.

9. Cartlidge and Elliott, *Art and the Christian Apocrypha,* 98–99, 107–8, and fig. 4.21. For further bibliography and discussion, see Appendix C.

10. Here, I borrow language from Walter Benjamin (*Arcades Project,* 460), who writes, "Historical 'understanding' is to be grasped, fundamentally, as an afterlife [*Nachleben*] of that which is understood" (cited by Richter, *Afterness,* 3).

11. Nora, "Between Memory and History," 19.

12. Olick and Levy ("Collective Memory," 921–36) speak of "collective memory" as "an active process of sense-making through time."

13. Thompson, *Glossary,* 268–70.

14. Hock (*Infancy Gospels,* 105) also rejects the synoptic stories as primary intertexts. However, his own solution—that sparrows are naturally associated with water and rainy weather—is no more satisfying, especially since there is no mention of rain in the earliest Greek recension (Gs). One finds the detail that Jesus was playing after a rainstorm only in later Greek and Slavonic versions of the *Paidika.* For the later Greek versions, see Burke, *De infantia,* 341 (Ga), 401 (Gd), and 455 (Gb). For the Slavonic text, see Rosén, *Slavonic Translation,* 48 (translated by T. Allen Smith at http://www.tonyburke.ca/infancy-gospel-of-thomas/the-infancy-gospel-of-thomas-slavonic/).

It should be noted that some late medieval Latin scribes observed the verbal connection between the *Paidika* and Jesus' synoptic teachings about *strouthia,* and sought to underscore it by making a subtle alteration to the wording of the *Paidika*—namely, by adding the promise, "nobody shall kill you" (*a nemine mortem invenietis*) at the end of Jesus' words to the sparrows (Late Latin *Paidika* 4:2; ed. Tischendorf, *Evangelia Apocrypha,* 2nd ed., 168; trans. *ANF* 8.400). This late Latin insertion perhaps was meant to echo Jesus' promise in Matthew 10:29 that "not one of them will fall to the ground" on account of God's providence. It may also have served as an implicit apologetic against a tradition in Islamic commentary on the Qur'ān, which claimed that the birds in fact died after they had flown out of sight (al-Tha'labī, *'Arā'is:* trans. Brinner, *Lives of the*

Prophets, 653–74; Renard, *Friends of God,* 93 and 296, note 8; see also my discussion in chapter 7).

15. Aasgaard, *Childhood,* 128; see also Bauckham, "Imaginative Literature," 797; and Baars and Helderman, "Neue Materialien," *Oriens Christianus* 77 (1993), 205–11.

16. *Paidika* 2.1 (Burke, *De infantia,* 303); cf. Genesis 1:6–10 (LXX; ed. Rahlfs, vol. 1, 1).

17. *Paidika* 2.2 (Burke, *De infantia,* 303); cf. Genesis 2:7 (LXX; ed. Rahlfs, vol. 1, 3).

18. Aasgaard, *Childhood,* 128.

19. Another possible biblical intertext for the appearance of sparrows in this story is Proverbs 26:2 (LXX; Rahlfs, vol. 2, 230): "Just like birds [*ornea*] and sparrows [*strouthoi*] fly, idle words [*mataia*] do not fall upon anyone." The Greek substantive plural adjective *mataia*—"idle" or "vain" (words)—in the Septuagint translation stands in for the Hebrew *qillah hinam* ("groundless curses"). Therefore, the Greek word used here may have originally carried a range of associations, from false accusations to undeserved execrations. In this context, it is noteworthy that the story of Jesus' miracle with the birds parallels the structure of this verse from Proverbs. His release of the vivified sparrows into the air is immediately followed first by a public accusation (lodged by the high priest Annas's son) that this miracle had violated the Sabbath, and second by Jesus' cursing of the high priest's son for destroying the pools that he had formed. It is uncertain, however, whether any ancient readers made a link between these words in Proverbs and the accusation in the story. If they did, Jesus' release of the birds would have been understood as an act designed to show that this accusation was an empty one. If readers further connected Proverbs' allusion to cursing practices with Jesus' subsequent act of causing his accuser to wither, they would have had to understand the fulfillment of Proverbs in ironic terms. In the *Paidika,* Jesus' own curses are proven to be far from idle: they fall upon the other child (and later his teachers) with very real and deadly effect.

20. Klein, *Child Life,* 9–10 and pls. VIII–IX.

21. For discussions of ancient toy animal figurines made from clay and other materials such as wood, bone, metal, and stone, see Lazos, *Paizontas,* esp. 415–18; Ricotti, *Giochi e giocattoli;* Fittà, *Giochi e giocattoli,* esp. 48–89; Fittà, *Da Roma per gioco,* 8–25; and Fluck, "Puppen—Tiere—Bälle," 1–21. On the relationship between such toys and children's care for live animals, see Bradley, "Sentimental Education," 523–57, esp. 538–39.

The transmission history of the *Paidika* also bears witness to the relevance of such toy usage as an interpretive context for later readers, editors, and translators of the text. In the *Arabic Gospel of the Infancy* (*AGI*), the story about Jesus' actions of molding birds out of clay and making them come alive is repeated twice (in two quite different versions). While the second telling of the tale (*AGI* 46) draws most directly on the story as it appears in the Greek text, the first telling (*AGI* 36) adds crucial new details. Most notably, Jesus does not limit his craftsmanship to sparrows; instead, he creates a whole menagerie of creatures out of clay, including "images of asses, oxen, birds, and other animals": see Thilo, *Codex apocryphus,* 110, 122. For a fuller discussion of the *Arabic Gospel of the Infancy,* see chapter 7; for a translation, see Appendix B.

22. On the funerary evidence for animal and bird figurines, see especially Oakley, "Death and the Child," 163–94, esp. 174–79.

23. Newark, N.J., The Newark Museum, Eugene Schaefer Collection, 1950, 50.212, 50.292, 50.367.A–C, 50.638–40, 50.647, 50.649–50, 50.720–21 (Oakley, "Death and the Child," 176, 302–3, cat. 118). Other examples of horse figurines preserved in collections housed in Syracuse, Corinth, Rome, and New York are documented by Klein, *Child Life,* 9 and pl. VIII (A–D).

24. Examples include two terracotta figurines of roosters in the Ashmolean Museum, Oxford (Fittà, *Giochi e giocattoli,* 72, figs. 121–22); four terracotta figurines of birds (two roosters, a duck, a pigeon) in the Germanisches Zentralmuseum, Mainz, Germany (Ricotti, *Giochi e giocattoli,* 26, fig. 14); and two children's rattles in the form of a rooster and a hen in the Kurpfälzisches Museum, Heidelberg (Filtzinger, Planck, and Cämmerer, *Die Römer in Baden-Württemberg,* 289, fig. 116). Three smaller limestone figurines of birds (two roosters and one pigeon) are preserved at the Wallraf Richartz Museum, Cologne: Museo di Antichità, *Da Roma per gioco,* 21 (also on cover).

25. British Museum, London: Fittà, *Giochi e giocattoli,* 72, cat. 124.

26. A set of Roman terracotta figurines in Colchester, England, may have been designed expressly for children's play: Alcock, *Life in Roman Britain,* 100–101. In Palestine, a clay bird on wheels found in a Roman tomb attests to the popularity of such toys during the first and second centuries CE: Zias, "Roman Tomb," 63–65; cited by Pitarakis, "Material Culture," 228.

27. Grandjouan, *Athenian Agora,* 25; Pitarakis, "Material Culture," 220–22, figs. 18 (dog) and 19 (rooster); see also the bird rattles from the fourth century CE documented in the American School of Classical Studies publication *Birds of the Athenian Agora,* esp. 7 and 9, figs. 12 (=inv. T 1423) and 17 (=inv. T 1854).

28. For an Egyptian example of a clay rattle in the form of a bird, see Török, *Coptic Antiquities* I, 54, K 6 Taf. LXXV. For an example of "a wooden bird-shaped pull toy fitted with a pair of wheels" discovered at Gerzah (ancient Philadelphia) in the Fayum, see Gabra, *Le Caire,* 98; Gabra, *L'art copte en Égypte,* 218, nos. 270a–b and 271; and Gabra and Eaton-Krauss, *Treasures,* 143, no. 89a–c.

29. Fluck, "Puppen—Tiere—Bälle," 19, and cat. no. 13. Fluck comments on the special association birds seem to have had for children: "Vögel scheinen für Kinder von besonderer Bedeutung gewesen zu sein. Sie sind wie kein anderes Tier auf vielen Kindergrabstelen im gesamten römischen Reich präsent" (p. 19).

30. Pitarakis, "Material Culture," 218.

31. Huizenga, *Homo Ludens,* 9–10.

32. Ibid., 10.

33. *Arabic Gospel of the Infancy* 36 (Thilo, *Codex apocryphus,* 110); see my translation in Appendix B.

34. Klein, *Child Life,* 10–12.

35. Cohen, "Introduction," 19, note 65; see also Lazos, *Paizontas,* 439–59.

36. Lazenby, "Greek and Roman Household Pets," esp. 249–52 and 299–301.

37. For a discussion of most of these sources in relation to broader patterns of pet keeping in antiquity, see Bradley, "Sentimental Education," 523–57. On the popularity of birds as pets in Greek cultural contexts, see also Pollard, *Birds,* esp. 15–16.

38. Plautus (254–184 BCE), *The Captives* 1002–3 (Nixon, LCL, I.562); see also Varro (116–27 BCE; *On Agriculture* 3.5–11; Hooper and Ash, LCL, 446–89) on the cultivation of aviaries at wealthy estates.

39. Ovid (43 BCE–17/18 CE), *Metamorphoses* 13.831–3 (F. J. Miller, LCL, II.286–87); Columella (4–70 CE), *On Agriculture* 8.8.9–10 (Forster and Heffner, LCL, II.366–67); see also Jennison, *Animals for Show and Pleasure,* 101, 122–23, 131–35. Later, in the fourth century CE, the Greek writer Libanius (314–394 CE) also recalls caring for pigeons (*peristerai*) as a small boy: see Libanius, *Autobiography* 5 (= *Oration* 1.5; Norman, LCL, I.56–57); also Marinescu, Cox, and Wachter, "Paideia's Children," 107, note 8.

40. Pliny the Elder (23–79 CE), *Natural History* 10.120 (Rackham, LCL, III, 368–69).

41. Pliny the Younger (61–ca. 112 CE), *Ep.* 4.2.3–4 (Radice, LCL, I.244–45). In Petronius's first-century novel the *Satyricon* 46 (Heseltine, LCL, 78–79), a father kills his son's pet birds for a very different reason: the ragman Echion is driven to distraction by his son's obsession with his birds and secretly kills three of the boy's favorite goldfinches to quell his frustration.

42. Catullus (ca. 84–ca. 54 BCE), *Poems* (*Carm.*) 2–3 (Cornish and Goold, LCL, 2–5).

43. For a markedly erotic reading of the poem, see Thomson, *Catullus,* 203. Gaiser (*Catullus,* 37) reserves judgment on the question of whether a double entendre is operative in Catullus's sparrow poems.

44. Marcus Cornelius Fronto (ca. 100–170), *To Friends* (*Ad amicos*) 1.12 (Haines, LCL, I.172).

45. Augustine, *Confessions* 1.19.30 (Watts, LCL, 56–59, my translation).

46. Lamberton and Rotroff, *Birds of the Athenian Agora,* 10–11, and fig. 19 (= inv. P 16912). Other bowls from the fifth and fourth centuries feature a boy tempting a bird with a piece of cake (Oakley, "Death and the Child," 280, cat. no. 91), a girl chasing a bird with a toy roller (Oakley, "Death and the Child," 280, cat. no. 92), and another boy offering a bird a grasshopper as a snack (Fittà, *Giochi e giocattoli,* 67, fig. 107). See also the Attic red-figured *lekythos* (ca. 420–390 BCE) by Aison showing a girl with a pet bird, discussed by Pollard, *Birds,* fig. 24.

47. See the two identical molds from the second century BCE, preserved in Munich, Staatliche Antikensammlungen und Glypothek, 5444 and 5424: Reeder, "Some Hellenistic Terracottas," 82, figs. 68 and 69.

48. Baltimore, The Walters Art Gallery, 48.1714; and Paris, Louvre, D 466: Reeder, "Some Hellenistic Terracottas," 81, fig. 66; and 82–83, fig. 70.

49. Pompeii, Regio I, Insula 9.3, Room 10, center of north wall, SAP inv. no. 41661: Wallace-Hadrill, *Houses and Society,* 192 (for an architectural plan of the building, see 191, fig. A.2; for a photo of this painting in situ, see http://www.pompeiiinpictures.com /pompeiiinpictures/R1/1%2009%2003%20p4.htm).

50. Pompeii, Regio I, Insula 9.3, Room 6, north portico of the garden area: for photos of the sculpture taken in 1952 at the time of excavation, see http://www.pompeiiin pictures.com/pompeiiinpictures/R1/1%2009%2003%20p2.htm.

51. For examples from Jerusalem and Madeba, see Bliss, *Excavations at Jerusalem, 1894–1897,* 253–55; Saller and Bagatti, *Town of Nebo,* 237–38, pl. 40.3; Lux, "Eine altchristliche Kirche," 170, 172, 177, and pls. 31b, 35c. For a discussion of the evidence for these practices not only in early Byzantine Palestine but also in ancient Egyptian,

Nabataean, Greek, Roman, and Hebrew cultures, see Hübner, *Spiele und Spielzeug,* 28–37, esp. 28 and 31. On late medieval and early modern representations of people (esp. children) using bird tethers, see Brednich, "Vogel am Faden," 573–97 (with fourteen figures).

52. This evidence also crossed over lines of religious communities: on Jewish children's epitaphs with depictions of birds found in second- to fourth-century CE Roman catacombs, see Williams, "Image and Text," 328–50, esp. 344 and 346–50.

53. Cohen, "Introduction," in *Constructions of Childhood,* 20.

54. Huskinson, *Roman Children's Sarcophagi,* 88.

55. Plutarch, *Consolation to his Wife* 10 (*Moralia* 611E; De Lacy and Einarson, LCL, VII.600–601);

56. Two examples come from the Catacomb of Praetextatus (mid- to late third century CE): on one, Psyche appears with a large bird, flanked on the right by Cupid and a hare; on the other, she receives a peacock while a second bird alights beneath her chair (Huskinson, *Roman Children's Sarcophagi,* 52–54, cat. nos. 7.4 and 7.5). On another sarcophagus from Taormina, Psyche stands beside the seated figure of the deceased child and holds a bird in her hand (Museo del Teatro inv. no. 57 [undated]: Huskinson, *Roman Children's Sarcophagi,* 52–54, cat. no. 7.8).

57. For representative examples of type 1, see Oakley, "Death and the Child," 169, cat. 68; Fittà, *Giochi e giocattoli,* 65–66, 68, figs. 103–4, 112; Fittà, *Da Roma per gioco,* 20; Bradley, "Sentimental Education," 528–29, pls. XIII–XV, figs. 5, 7, and 8; and Kleiner, "Women and Family Life," 545–54 and pls. XIV–XV, esp. 553, and pl. XV, fig. 4.

58. For representative examples of type 2, see Oakley, "Death and the Child," 3, 180–81, 183–84, cat. no. 124, and figs. 1, 23, and 25; Clairmont, *Classical Attic Tombstones,* 1993, vol. 1, 188–89, no. 0.869a; Grossman, "Forever Young," 309–22, esp. 315; Kleiner, *Roman Group Portraiture,* 174 and fig. 66; Alcock, *Life in Roman Britain,* 100 (on two Roman tombstones at York that show young girls cradling birds in their hands); Ricotti, *Giochi e giocattoli,* cover image; Romiopoulou, *Ellēnorōmaïka Glypta,* 74, cat. no. 74; Fittà, *Giochi e giocattoli,* 69, fig. 113; Huskinson, *Roman Children's Sarcophagi,* 58, cat. no. 8.26; Froschauer and Harrauer, *Spiel am Nil,* 19, fig. 19; and also *Ägypten—Schätze aus dem Wüstensand,* 75, cat. no. 6.

59. For representative examples of type 3, see Oakley, "Death and the Child," 182, fig. 22; Clairmont, *Classical Attic Tombstones,* 1993, vol. 1, 412, 415, cat. no. 1.690 and 1.694; Grossman, "Forever Young," 318 and fig. 16.8.

60. For representative examples of type 4, see Dinahet, "L'image de l'enfance," 93–94, fig. 4; Reeder, "Some Hellenistic Terracottas," 85, fig. 76 (cf. fig. 77); Oakley, "Death and the Child," 189–90, cat. no. 126; Huskinson, *Roman Children's Sarcophagi,* 24, 58, 66, cat. 1.47, 8.22, 9.43; Bradley, "Sentimental Education," 537 and pls. XV and XIX, figs. 8 and 13; Fittà, *Giochi e giocattoli nell'antichità,* 66, fig. 106; and Museo di Antichità Collezioni Archeologiche, *Da Roma per gioco,* 19.

61. For example, on one Greek funerary stele dated ca. 340 BCE, a young girl is depicted standing and holding a doll and a bird, while a small Maltese dog springs up at her feet (Oakley, "Death and the Child," introduction frontispiece, and 181, cat. 124). On another Attic gravestone, a girl named Plangon also holds a doll and a bird in her hands: she is accompanied by a pet duck, and on a wall near her hang knucklebones

and other playthings (Munich, Staatliche Antikensammlungen und Glyptothek GL 199: Clairmont, *Classical Attic Tombstones,* 1993, vol. 1, 188–89, no. 0.869a; Grossman, "Forever Young," 315). Also from Greece: a second-century CE funerary stele of a girl named Olympia holding a bird in the Archaeological Museum in Athens (Romiopoulou, *Ellēnorōmaïka Glypta,* 74, cat. no. 74). From second- and fourth-century Rome: a statue of a girl holding a bird (Rome, Galleria Collonna: Fittà, *Giochi e giocattoli,* 69, fig. 113), and a sarcophagus relief of a young boy holding a bird, with another at his feet (ca. 320 CE; Vatican Museums, Galleria Lapidaria, no. 9256: Huskinson, *Roman Children's Sarcophagi,* 58, cat. 8.26). From Oxyrhynchus in Egypt: a late ancient stele of a boy who kneels while holding a bird (Recklinghausen, Ikonenmuseum, Inv. 511: Froschauer and Harrauer, *Spiel am Nil,* 19, fig. 19; see also *Ägypten—Schätze aus dem Wüstensand,* 75, cat. no. 6).

62. Connerton, *How Societies Remember,* 72; cf. 59.

63. Malibu: The J. Paul Getty Museum (ca. 100 BCE): Oakley, "Death and the Child," 189–90, cat. 126; Bradley, "Sentimental Education," 537 and pl. XIX, fig. 13.

64. Bradley, "Sentimental Education," 529 and pl. XV, fig. 8.

65. The sculpted face of a gravestone from Delos shows a boy named Zosas playing with a rooster: with his right hand he holds what looks like a bunch of grapes over the bird's head (Dinahet, "L'image de l'enfance," 93–94, fig. 4). A grave stele from Smyrna dated to the second or first century BCE shows a child kneeling and holding a loaf of bread or some other edible item away from a hungry and aggressively inquisitive rooster (Pfuhl and Möbius, *Die ostgriechischen Grabreliefs,* 211, no. 804, pl. 117; Bieber, *Sculpture,* 137, fig. 539; Reeder, "Some Hellenistic Terracottas," 85, fig. 76). For similar late Roman examples depicting children trying to keep grapes away from their winged pets, see Huskinson, *Roman Children's Sarcophagi,* 24, 58, and 66; cat. 1.47 (Ostia, Azienda 10); cat. 8.22 (Paris, Louvre inv. no. Ma 952, 280 CE); cat. 9.43 (Rome, Museo Nazionale Romano, inv. no. 75184).

66. Rome, Catacomb of Domitilla (third cent. CE): Fittà, *Giochi e giocattoli,* 66, fig. 106; also *Da Roma per gioco,* 19.

67. Bradley, "Sentimental Education," 536, and pl. XVIII, fig. 12.

68. On the social importance of memorial practices that took place at cemeteries in the early Christian era, see MacMullen, *Second Church.*

69. Nilsson, *Minoan-Mycenaean Religion,* 333–35.

70. Merker, *Sanctuary,* 193.

71. Daems, "Terracotta Figurines," 230, 235–36, figs. 1–2; Burkholder, *Arabian Collection,* 205, and fig. 44b (third cent. BCE–first cent. CE); Karvonen-Kannas, *Seleucid and Parthian Terracotta Figurines,* 110–11, and pl. 85, figs. 700–704, 707, 709, and 713 (second cent. BCE–second cent. CE); Ingen, *Figurines from Seleucia,* 333–36, cat. nos. 1547–73; pls. LXXX–LXXXI, figs. 594–97 (second cent. BCE–second cent. CE); Downey, *Terracotta Figurines,* 189, 205–8, cat. nos. 158–59, figs. 148–49 (second–third cent. CE).

72. Merker, *Sanctuary,* 43, 126, 265, 268–69, 278 (V9 and V10).

73. Herodotus, *Persian Wars* 1.159 (Godley, LCL, I.200–201); cited by Pollard, *Birds,* 146.

74. Aelian, *Varia Historia* 5.17 (Wilson, *Historical Miscellany,* LCL 486, 224–25); cited by Pollard, *Birds,* 146.

75. The fifth-century *Life and Miracles of Saint Thecla* describes how pilgrims to Hagia Thekla in Seleukia would feed grain to local pigeons and bring birds to the saint's shrine as sacrificial offerings, and how, in the atrium of the shrine, children would be seen playing with various species of birds (Dagron, *Vie et miracles,* 133–34). One of the miracle accounts in that collection (*Miracle* 24: Dagron, *Vie et miracles,* 350–53) even relates how a young toddler was healed of an eye ailment after a crane lanced his eye with its beak.

76. Pinch, *Magic in Ancient Egypt,* 96. For a transcription and translation of this papyrus, see Quirke, *Egyptian Literature,* 77–89.

77. Griffith, *Stories,* 24; Meyer, "Kindheitserzählung," 132–42, at 135; Burke, *De infantia,* 69.

78. For examples, see *PGM* IV.296–466 (Preisendanz, I.82–88; Betz, 44–47); Kambitsis, "Une nouvelle tablette," 213–23, and plates; and Martinez, *P.Michigan XVI.* For further discussion of the use of such clay figurines, see Faraone, "Binding and Burying," 165–220; Ritner, *Mechanics,* 113–36, 159–62; Pinch, *Magic in Ancient Egypt,* 90–103; and Davis, "Forget Me Not," 248–59.

79. *PGM* I.4–5, 26–7 (Preisendanz, I. 2–4; Betz, 3).

80. *PGM* I.24–25, 29, 39–40 (Preisendanz, I.4; Betz, 3–4).

81. *PGM* I.59–64 (Preisendanz, I.6; Betz, 4); cf. *PGM* IV.3125–71 (Preisendanz, I.174–76; Betz, 98–99), instructions for the making of a phylactery in which "a wild white-faced [falcon]" is sacrificed to a statue with the heads of a falcon, a baboon, and an ibis.

82. *PGM* I.64–97 (Preisendanz, I.6; Betz, 4–8).

83. *PGM* XLVIII.1–21, esp. 1–8 (Preisendanz, II.181; Betz, 282).

84. *PGM* XII.376–96 (Preisendanz, II.82–83; Betz, 166–67).

85. *PGM* IV.475–829, esp. lines 795–99 (Preisendanz, I.88–100, esp. 100; Betz, 48–54, esp. 53).

86. *PGM* XIII.81–9 (Preisendanz, II.91; Betz, 174); see also *PGM* XIII.455 (Preisendanz, I.109; Betz, 184). A similar set of instructions for bird vocalizations and clapping is found in *PGM* XIII.594–602 (Preisendanz, II.115; Betz, 187). I thank Elizabeth Davidson for calling my attention to the ritual function of clapping in these spells.

87. *PGM* XIII.148–61 (Preisendanz, II.94; Betz, 176).

88. *PGM* XIII.230–34 (Preisendanz, II.98–99; Betz, 179).

89. *PGM* XIII.234–343, esp. 247–48, 260–61, 277–82 (Preisendanz, II, 99–105, esp. 100–101; Betz, 179–81, esp. 179–80).

90. *Paidika* 2.4, 9.3, 15.2 (Burke, *De infantia,* 305, 325, 333).

91. *PGM* III.187–262, at 198–201 (Preisendanz, I.40–44, at 40; Betz, 23–26, at 23).

92. *PGM* III.202–3 (Preisendanz, I.40; Betz, 24).

93. *Paidika* 2 and 15 (Burke, *De infantia,* 303–5 and 333).

94. See, e.g., *PGM* VII.540–78 (Preisendanz, II.24–6; Betz, 133–34). Sarah Iles Johnston ("Charming Children," 97–117) cites this spell and lists numerous other examples in analyzing the social role of children as divinatory agents. For two earlier studies of child mediums in the ancient world, see Hopfner, "Kindermedien," 65–74; and Dodds, *Ancient Concept,* 185–205. Finally, Dornseiff (*Alphabet,* 20) also notes the account of children who served as blindfolded soothsayers under the emperor

Didius Julianus (193 CE), an account recorded in the late Roman *Augustan History* (7.10).

95. Plutarch, *On the Oracles at Delphi* 12, 17, 22 (=400A, 402D, 405D) (Babbitt, *Moralia,* LCL, V.288–9, 304–5, 320–1).

96. Johnston, *Ancient Greek Divination,* 109–43, esp. 128–32.

97. Brent, *Imperial Cult,* 21; "Auspicium," 154. Cicero (*On the Laws* 2.31; Keyes, LCL, 408–9) identifies the right of augurs as "the highest and most important authority in the state," the authority to adjourn legal councils and committees and to rescind their decisions.

98. Tertullian, *On the Pallium* 6 (PL 2.1050A; *ANF* 4.12). Tertullian lists "the bird-gazer" alongside "the first teacher of the forms of letters, the first explainer of their sounds, the first trainer in the rudiments of arithmetic, the grammarian, the rhetorician, the sophist, the medical man, the poet, the musical timebeater, (and) the astrologer" as public figures in Carthaginian society who are deemed worthy to be vested with the philosopher's mantle (*pallium*). Accordingly, he argues that the *pallium* is suitable clothing for the Christian as well, since he or she is a member of a "divine sect and discipline" (ibid.; see also Dunn, *Tertullian,* 41).

99. Pease, "Auspicium," 154.

100. Holland, *Janus,* 1–20; Taylor, "Tiber River Bridges," 4.

101. Virgil, *Aeneid* 9 (Fairclough and Goold, LCL, II.114–17).

102. See, e.g., Servius (late fourth century CE), *Commentary on the Aeneid* (*Serv. Aen.*) 9.24 (Thilo and Hagen, *Servii Grammatici,* 311).

103. Cicero, *On Divination* 2.76–77 (Falconer, 456–59); cf. Cicero, *On the Nature of the Gods* 2.3.9–10 (Rackham, LCL, I.130–33).

104. See the discussion of Livy in Brent, *Imperial Cult,* 28; also Liebeschuetz, *Continuity and Change,* 56–65.

105. Suetonius, *Augustus* 7 (Rolfe, LCL, I.130–31); Brent, *Imperial Cult,* 112–13.

106. Cicero, *On Divination* 1.107–8 (Falconer, 338–41); see also Marcus Cornelius Fronto, *To Emperor Lucius Verus* (*Ad Verum Imperator*) 2.1.11 (Haines, LCL, 141: "Between Romulus and Remus, as they took the auguries on separate hills, birds decided the question of sovereignty").

107. Pollard, *Birds,* 122.

108. Beginning in the period of the Republic, the emperor's own reputation as a divine ruler was further grounded in stories about the posthumous apotheosis and divinization of Romulus, who became identified with the early Roman deity Quirinus in local cultic parlance and practice: Fishwick, *Imperial Cult,* vol. 1.1, 51–55. On Caesar's promotion of himself as a "new Romulus," see Burkert, "Caesar und Romulus-Quirinus," 356–76; Weinstock, *Divus Julius,* 175–99; and Fishwick, *Imperial Cult,* vol. 1.1, 56–59, 67–68.

109. Peppard, *Son of God,* 115–24.

110. *Protevangelium of James* 9.6 (Hock, *Infancy Gospels,* 48–49; = ch. 9.1, in Tischendorf, *Evangelia apocrypha,* 18; Schneemelcher, *New Testament Apocrypha,* I.429–30).

111. Peppard, *Son of God,* 123.

112. In some ways, this narrative Christianization of "pagan" ritual gestures in the *Paidika* may be likened to the rhetorical strategies of second- and third-century early

Christian apologists who sought to represent Christianity as the fulfillment of Greek philosophical practice. A similar sociological dynamic also prevailed in later saints' cults, where literary *vitae* and collections of miracles presented the power of Christian holy men and women in competition (or "co-opetition") with rival cultic figures, including Greek gods and other saints. For examples, see Davis, *Cult of St. Thecla,* 73–80 and 133–36; on the concept of "co-opetition" in modern sociology, see Brandenburger and Nalebuff, *Co-opetition.*

113. On the sedimentation of social memory in bodies, places, and practices, see Connerton, *How Societies Remember.*

114. Various scholars have compared the *Paidika* to ancient biographies of heroes and holy men whose childhood years "are seen as anticipations of their future greatness" (Aasgaard, *Childhood,* 49; also Hock, *Infancy Gospels,* 96–97; and Burke, *De infantia,* 281–84).

Chapter 4. Cursing

1. I would like to offer a belated apology to both friends for my ill-advised acts of youthful aggression.

2. *Paidika* 3.1 (Burke, *De infantia,* 305).

3. *Paidika* 3.2 (Burke, *De infantia,* 307).

4. *Paidika* 4 (Burke, *De infantia,* 307).

5. *Paidika* 13.2 (Burke, *De infantia,* 329). This despite the fact that Jesus earlier had seemingly renounced his cursing ways at the end of his encounter with his first teacher, Zacchaeus, in chapter 8, where Jesus declares, "Now let the barren bear fruit and let the blind see," and right away, "all those who had fallen under his curse [*hupo tēs kataras*] were saved" (*Paidika* 8.1–2; Burke, *De infantia,* 323). Jesus' similar declaration of amnesty in *Paidika* 14.2, where he says, "[E]ven the one who was struck down will also be saved" (Burke, *De infantia,* 333), is probably a secondary addition to the text.

6. Numerous painted Greek ceramic bowls and figurines show children playing knucklebones, an everyday game in which participants tossed five *astragali* (hocks or ankle bones) of a sheep: see the examples preserved at the J. Paul Getty Museum in Malibu, CA (inv. 79.AF.171; 81.AC.5; 96.AE.28: http://www.getty.edu/art/exhibitions/coming_of_age/0z25636701.html), at the National Archaeological Museum in Athens (inv. 12112 and 14868), at the Staatliche Museen in Berlin (Poplin, "Les jeux," 46–47; and Horn and Martens, *"Let the Little Children Come to Me,"* 190). For additional examples of terracottas and vases showing young girls playing with knucklebones or holding bags that contained them, preserved in Boston (Museum of Fine Arts, Terracottas 01.7841 and 03.897), London (British Museum, Terracotta D161), and New York (Metropolitan Museum of Art, Vase 06.1021.119), see Klein, *Child Life,* 18 and pl. XIX A–D.

7. A Roman sarcophagus belonging to a young boy named Aemilius Daphnus shows groups of boys playing with nuts on the ground: British Museum, Sc. 2321 (Rawson, *Marriage, Divorce, and Children,* fig. 4a). Another sarcophagus (Paris, Louvre) from the same period depicts four boys rolling nuts down an inclined board: Veyne, "Roman Empire," 16.

8. On the practice of skimming sherds over water, see Minucius Felix, *Octavius* 3.5–6 (Rendall, LCL, 318–19). Examples of ball and team sports include two Greek

painted vases with scenes of boys throwing balls to or at each other (Klein, *Child Life,* 18–20 and pl. XX B and E), a Greek marble relief in the National Archaeological Museum in Athens showing boys holding sticks facing off in teams (Plati, *Playing,* 27; also Klein, *Child Life,* 20 and pl. XXI B); a second-century CE Roman tomb painting of older boys throwing and catching a ball (Veyne, "Roman Empire," 15), and a child's sarcophagus relief in the Louvre showing girls throwing a ball against a wall (Veyne, "Roman Empire," 16). For a discussion of such material evidence for children's play, see Horn and Martens, *"Let the Little Children Come to Me,"* 190–91; also Golden, *Children and Childhood,* 53–56.

9. Wiedemann, *Adults and Children,* pl. 20; cited by Horn and Martens, *"Let the Little Children Come to Me,"* 191–92.

10. Golden, *Children and Childhood,* 53–55; Wiedemann, *Adults and Children,* 147.

11. On "Greco-Roman ball games and team sports," including evidence for young people's participation in these activities, see Crowther, *Sport in Ancient Times,* 154–59.

12. Wiedemann, *Adults and Children,* 147–53. For references to ball sports in the writings of Latin authors, see Martial, *Epigrams* 14.45–48 (Bailey, LCL, III.244–47); and Pliny the Younger, *Ep.* 2.17.12 (Radice, LCL, I.136–37).

13. Harris, *Sport in Greece and Rome,* 95.

14. On the timing of the boys' competitions at Olympia relative to those of the men, see Miller, *Ancient Greek Athletics,* 125. For a discussion about images of children engaged in athletic exercises found on vases and other material artifacts, see Klein, *Child Life,* 23.

15. Within the Olympian precinct, the deified personification of *Agōn* was honored with a statue, a muscular figure shown holding a weight or dumbbell in each hand: see Pausanias, *Description of Greece* 5.26.3 (Jones, LCL, II.540–41). For evidence related to agonistic local festivals in Greece and Italy, see Arnold, "Agonistic Features"; "Local Festivals of Euboea," 385–92; "Local Festivals at Delos," 452–58; "Festivals of Rhodes," 432–36; and "Agonistic Festivals in Italy and Sicily," 17–22.

16. On age classifications for boys at Greek athletic games, see especially Klee, *Zur Geschichte,* 46–48; Crowther, "Age-Category," 304–8; Golden, *Children and Childhood,* 69–70; Golden, *Sport and Society,* 104–9; Miller, *Ancient Greek Athletics,* 248; Kyle, *Sport and Spectacle,* 117; and Crowther, "Observations," 343–64. At the Asclepieia held at Epidaurus, there seem to have been three age divisions, two for boys and one for older youth—*paides Puthikoi* (approx. age 12–14), *paides Isthmikoi* (age 14–17), and *ageneioi* (age 17–20). However, one should expect that, in practice, there would have been considerable variation from venue to venue.

17. The third-century CE Baths of Caracalla in Rome include a series of floor mosaics depicting scenes of boxers in the midst of pugilistic competition; some wear crowns of victory on their heads and one carries a palm wreath in his left hand (see Friedländer, *Sittengeschichte Roms,* 785; Baus, *Kranz,* 40).

18. Pindar, *Nemean Odes* 5 (Race, LCL, II.46–47); also Robbins, "Nereids," 25–33.

19. Pausanias, *Description of Greece* 6.2.10–11 (Jones, LCL, IV.178–79); Golden, *Sport in the Ancient World,* 48.

20. On the difficulty of determining the age of the boys and youth participating in Greek festival games, see Golden, *Children and Childhood,* 67–69.

21. Pausanias, *Description of Greece* 6.14.1 (Jones, LCL, IV. 242–44).

22. In certain locales, it is conceivable that the minimum age may have been younger than twelve.

23. Citing a range of epigraphic evidence, Henri Marrou (*History,* 117) argues that, at certain places in the Greek world, "physical education accompanied literary education from the time the child was seven or eight." However, elsewhere (p. 389, notes 1 and 3) he admits that the surviving evidence (especially during the Graeco-Roman period) is equivocal on this point. On the relationship between athletic training in gymnasia and competition in the games, see Nijf, "Athletics and *Paideia,*" 203–28.

24. Jason König (*Athletics and Literature,* 48) notes that children would most often receive their training in the smaller *palaistrai,* but that there are numerous documented exceptions. On evidence for the inclusion (or exclusion) of children at gymnasia in different settings, see also Delorme, *Gymnasion,* 262–66; and Gauthier, "Notes," 4–7.

25. Thus, Aristotle counsels that "children must be turned over to the *gymnastai* and the *paidotribai,* for the one works with the condition of the body, the other with its actions" (Aristotle, *Politics* VIII.3.2 [= 1338b]: Rackham, LCL, 644–45; the translation cited here is that of Miller, *Arete,* 152). On the training of boys at *gymnasia* and *palaistrai* under the supervision of *gymnastai, paidotribai,* and *sophronistai* (who were charged with monitoring good behavior), see also Guhl and Koner, *Life,* 212–15.

26. Brunet, "Olympic Hopefuls," 227–29; quote from Kyle, *Sport and Spectacle,* 246.

27. Lucian of Samosata, *Anacharsis* (*Concerning Gymnasia*) 24 (Steindl, *Luciani Scytharum colloquia,* 67–68; Macleod, *Luciani opera,* II.250; trans. Sweet, *Sport and Recreation,* 253).

28. Clement of Alexandria, *Paedagogus* 3.10.51.1 (Mondésert et al., SC 158, 110; *ANF* 4.311).

29. Flavius Philostratus, *On Gymnastics* (*De gymnastica*) 46 (Kayser, *Flavii Philostrati opera,* II.287; trans. Sweet, *Sport and Recreation,* 224).

30. Ps.-Plutarch, *The Education of Children* (*De liberis educandis*) 11 (*Moralia* 8) (Babbitt, LCL, I.36–39; Berry, "The *De Liberis Educandis* of Pseudo-Plutarch," 387–99).

31. König, *Athletics and Literature,* 61. Elaborating on this point, König writes, "*Paides* and ephebes and *gymnasion* officials also often played central roles within agonistic ritual, and their integration into the fabric of festival timetables was often carefully regulated, through instructions set out in detail at the time of foundation in inscribed decrees" (p. 67).

32. On the relationship between athletic and literary contests in gymnasia and at Greek festival games, see Nijf, "Athletics and *Paideia,*" 215ff.

33. Miller, *Ancient Greek Athletics,* 83–86.

34. Arnold, "Agonistic Festivals," 246–48. At the Sebasta or Augustalia festival in Naples, a musical and dramatic component was added shortly after Augustus's death in the early first century CE, and the awarding of prizes for the writing and recitation of poetry achieved special renown and continued to be observed well into the third century CE. At the Capitolia festival in Rome, established in 98 CE and held every five years thereafter, the poetry contest gained an even greater prominence: there, at the close of competition, the emperor himself would bestow a wreath of olive and oak leaves on the victor.

35. *IG* 4, 2012.

36. Schmitz, "Agon," in *Dictionary*, I.74; also Trapido, "Language," 18–26.

37. For a discussion of *agōn* as a feature of "play and law" in various cultural contexts, see Huizenga, *Homo Ludens,* 76–88. On the element of competition (*agōn*) in the classical Greek *polis,* see Arnason and Murphy, eds., *Agon, Logos, Polis:* see especially the editors' "Introduction," 8–14, and Arnason's article, "Autonomy and Axiality," 198, where he discusses "the agonistic character of political life—exemplified by disputes in law-courts and assemblies—and the strong emphasis on mutual criticism and debate between rival schools of thought."

38. Meyer, *Legitimacy and Law,* 19. David J. Cohen (*Law, Violence, and Community,* 22) likewise emphasizes that Athenian litigation was "shaped by the larger political and social enterprise of defining, contesting, and evaluating hierarchies and allegiances in an agonistic society."

39. Aristotle, *Rhetoric* 1.11.1–29 (1370b–71b) (Freese, LCL, 14–29); also Cohen, *Law, Violence, and Community,* 66–67, 119.

40. Alexander, *Case for the Prosecution;* see also the review by Dyck in *Bryn Mawr Classical Review* 2003.09.37. Later, during the early Christian period, public disputations not in the courts were even modeled after agonistic judicial exchanges. Thus, in the third century CE, Origen of Alexandria (ca. 185–254) writes about his interrogation of a certain Heracleides on his view of Christ and describes it as an *anakrisis,* a legal term that usually refers to "the preliminary cross-examination of the disputants and their evidence by a magistrate before the matter goes to a court for trial" (Origen of Alexandria, *Dialogue with Heracleides* 1.16–17: Scherer, *Entretien d'Origène avec Héraclide,* SC 67, 54; see also Scherer, *Entretien d'Origène avec Héraclide et les évêques ses collègues,* 120); Lim, "Religious Disputation," 209–10 (quote here from 210, note 21). On the function of the *anakrisis* in Athenian law, see MacDowell, *Law,* 239–42.

41. On Greek sophists engaged in legal and forensic activity, see Philostratus, *Lives of the Sophists* 1.19; 1.21; 2.1 (=Olearius pp. 511, 516–17, 555) (Kayser, *Flavii Philostrati opera,* I.24–25, 29–31, 63–64; Wright, LCL, 62–65, 74–79, 156–59); also Russell, *Greek Declamation,* 12–13. For a discussion of Roman rhetoricians and teachers who were also active in courtroom settings, see Winterbottom, "Schoolroom and Courtroom," 59–70.

42. Winterbottom, "Schoolroom and Courtroom," 59.

43. Russell, *Greek Declamation,* 12, 40, 48.

44. Quintilian, *Institutes* 10.5.19–20 (Russell, LCL, IV.364–67). Elsewhere in the same treatise, sharply criticizing teachers "who think that declamation in general is in every way distinct from forensic cases," Quintilian considers it absurd to get passionate about a speech, "unless we are seeking to prepare ourselves by a sort of mock battle for genuine perils and a real engagement!" (*Institutes* 2.10.8, see also 2.10.4 and 2.10.12: Russell, LCL, I.326–29). In discussing Quintilian's critique of other schoolteachers, Jeffrey Walker (*Rhetoric and Poetics,* 97) emphasizes that Quintilian's operative "rhetoric of agonistic competition" extended to his assertions of superiority over other teaching rivals.

45. See Bourdieu (*Outline of a Theory of Practice,* 72) for a discussion of *habitus.*

46. *Paidika* 2.3–4 (Burke, *De infantia,* 303–5).

47. *Paidika* 3.1–3 (Burke, *De infantia,* 305–7).

48. *Paidika* 4.1 (Burke, *De infantia,* 307).

49. *Paidika* 4.2–5.3 (Burke, *De infantia,* 307–9).

50. *Paidika* 6–8 (Burke, *De infantia,* 309–23).

51. *Paidika* 13–14 (Burke, *De infantia,* 329–33).

52. *Paidika* 14.1 (Burke, *De infantia,* 331).

53. *Paidika* 14.3–4 (Burke, *De infantia,* 331–33). It should be noted that certain elements of this cursing motif (esp. in 13.2, 14.1, and 14.4) are unique to Greek recension S (Gs: see Appendix A), and thus they may reflect a strategy of scribal redaction and interpretation designed to highlight the agonistic function of cursing in the second and third teacher tales.

54. *Paidika* 6.2b–c (Burke, *De infantia,* 311–13).

55. *Paidika* 6.2f (Burke, *De infantia,* 315–17).

56. *Paidika* 6.4–7.1 (Burke, *De infantia,* 319–21).

57. *Paidika* 7.2–3 (Burke, *De infantia,* 321).

58. *Paidika* 4.1 (Burke, *De infantia,* 307).

59. Hock, *Infancy Gospels,* 109; Aasgaard, *Childhood,* 234.

60. Burke, *De infantia,* 196. Here, I have some doubts about Burke's text-critical assessment of Jesus' curse in *Paidika* 4.1. Noting that Jesus' curse in Greek recension S (Gs) diverges in wording from the early Syriac and Latin versions, Burke regards it as an "aberrant" (and thus interpolated) reading. While I concur with both Burke (ibid.) and Voicu ("Notes," 131; "Verso," 24) that in other places Gs most certainly shows evidence of some later interpolations (e.g., the material corresponding to Ga 1 and 10), I contend that according to the principle of *lectio difficilior* (the prioritization of the more difficult reading) the language found in recension S of *Paidika* 4.1—especially the use of the verb *erragē* and the noun *hēgemōn*—reflects an earlier provenance and that the Latin and Syriac versions (and the other Greek recensions) probably reflect later redactional activity designed to smooth out the rough edges of the text.

61. Aasgaard, *Childhood,* 234. In his 2001 dissertation Burke also translated the verb *erragē* as "bumped" (Chartrand-Burke, "Infancy Gospel of Thomas," 226), but in his 2010 critical edition he revises his translation and opts for the phrase "tore into" (Burke, *De infantia,* 306).

62. Peeters, *Évangiles apocryphes,* I.167.

63. Marcus Aurelius, *Meditations* 6.20.1 (Farquharson, *Meditations,* 106; here I modify Long's translation). Farquharson reads *tē*$_i$ *kefalē*$_i$ as an instrumental dative: thus, he understands the other person's blow as having been administered "with his head" (p. 107) in this scenario.

64. On the following, see Poliakoff, *Combat Sports,* 38–46.

65. Scholiast on Homer, *Iliad* 23.711 (Poliakoff, *Combat Sports,* 34 and 38).

66. For examples of early Egyptian wall paintings and reliefs (ca. 2000–1150 BCE) from Beni Hasan (ca. 2000 BCE), El Amarna (ca. 1350 BCE), Thebes (late fourteenth cent. CE), and Medinet Habu (ca. 1182–1151 BCE) showing wrestling moves that incorporated shoulder and neck holds, see Poliakoff, *Combat Sports,* 5 (fig. 1), 26–27 (figs. 7–11), 31 (fig. 15), 46 (fig. 41), 49 (fig. 48), 51 (figs. 50–51). For a selection of Greek ceramic vases (sixth–fourth cent. BCE) showing similar wrestling maneuvers, see

Poliakoff, *Combat Sports,* 14 (fig. 4), 24 (fig. 6), 29 (fig. 12), 36–37 (figs. 22–23), 38 (figs. 25–26), 39–41 (figs. 29–31), 44 (fig. 37), and 48 (fig. 45).

67. Beck, *Album,* pl. 27, no. 149 (Museo Nazionale RC 2066).

68. Ibid., pls. 36–37, figs. 193 (Paris, Louvre CA 1684), 194 (Oxford, Ashmolean Museum 1911.257), 195 (Hamburg, Museum für Kunst und Gewerbe 1900.518), 197a (Turin, Museo di Antichita 4123), and 197c (London, British Museum E 94).

69. *P.Oxy.* 3.466; Poliakoff, *Combat Sports,* 51–53 and fig. 52.

70. On imitation of athletic and gladiatorial contests in children's play, see Wiedemann, *Adults and Children,* 147–53. Newby (*Greek Athletics,* 41–42) has pointed to the depiction of children in athletic scenes on Roman sarcophagi from the second and third centuries CE as evidence for "the imitation of such contests within childhood pursuits and education" (on this subject, see also Huskinson, *Roman Children's Sarcophagi,* 16–19). For further examples of the portrayal of athletes (both adults and children) in Roman sculptured reliefs, see Aravantinou, "Un frammento," 67–84; and Castagnoli, "Il capitello," 1–30.

71. Newby, *Greek Athletics,* 54 (commenting on a second-century CE mosaic in the baths near the Porta Marina in Ostia). For images and discussions of specific bath mosaics depicting wrestlers and other athletes in Italy, Gaul, and North Africa, see Newby, 45–87, esp. fig. 3.1 (bath complex at Pompeii, ca. 41–54 CE, Claudian period), fig. 3.2 (palaestra of the baths of Neptune, Ostia, ca. 139 CE), fig. 3.3 (baths of Porta Marina, Ostia, ca. 117–138 CE), fig. 3.4 (Terme Marittime at Ostia, ca. 193–211 CE), and fig. 3.5 (inn at Ostia, ca. 193–211 CE). In an early third-century CE painting of two wrestlers in the latrines of a bath complex in Vienna, Gaul, one is shown reaching out with his left hand to grab the shoulder or neck of his opponent (Musée Gallo-Romain de Saint-Romain-en-Gal; Newby, pl. 2a).

72. Flavius Philostratus (ca. 170–247 CE), *On Gymnastics* (*De gymnastica*) 27 (Kayser, *Flavii Philostrati opera,* II.274–75). In the case of young girls, Philostratus notes that this process of being "broken in" extends to the additional *agōn* of producing offspring.

73. Vallois, "APAI," 250–71; Speyer, "Fluch," 1160–1288.

74. On the various materials used for the recording of curses, see Gager, *Curse Tablets,* 3–4; and Ogden, "Binding Spells," 10–12. For examples of curses on public monuments and graves, see Parrot, *Malédictions et violations;* Robert, "Malédictions funéraires grecques," 241–89; Strubbe, "Cursed be he that moves my bones," 33–59; Strubbe, "Curses against Violation of the Grave," 70–128; Strubbe, *Arai epitymbioi.* For selected examples on papyri, see *PGM* V.304–69 (Preisendanz, 190–92; Betz, 106–7), XL.1–18 (Preisendanz, 177–78; Betz, 280), and LVIII.1–14 (Preisendanz, 186; Betz, 285); Meyer and Smith, *Ancient Christian Magic,* 187–96, 207–8, 210–12, 215–18, 224 (nos. 88–92, 101, 103–4, 106–8, 111); and Björck, *Der Fluch,* esp. 131–38 (=*PGM* CIX). For examples on ostraca (broken sherds of pottery), see Preisendanz, *Papyri Magicae Graecae,* II, Ostraca 1 and 5; and Gager, *Curse Tablets,* 21, note 5.

75. Major collections and bibliographies of *defixiones* include: Wünsch, *Appendix* (=*DTA*); Audollent, *Defixionum Tabellae* (=*DT*); Preisendanz, "Die griechischen und lateinischen Zaubertafeln," *Archiv fur Papyrusforschung* 9 (1930), 119–54, and 11 (1933),

153–64; Wortmann, "Neue magische Texte," 56–111; Jordan, "Survey," 151–97 (=SGD); and Kropp, *Defixiones*.

76. Gager, *Curse Tablets,* 4–5; Dickie, *Magic,* 48.

77. On the deposition of curses in underground graves and sanctuaries, or in bodies of water such as lakes, seas, rivers, and streams, see Gager, *Curse Tablets,* 18–21.

78. Jordan, "Survey," 152, 157 (on the Athenian grave), and 187 (on the Nubian grave). Curse tablets have also been found in children's sarcophagi from Rome, from around the year 400 CE: Wünsch, *Sethianische Verfluchungstafeln,* 3; and Jordan, "Survey," 152.

79. Christopher Faraone (*Ancient Greek Love Magic,* 30, 43–55) evaluates *erōs* magic as "a specialized extension of cursing rituals" due to the fact that its effects were understood in terms analogous to the effects of certain diseases; yet, one important difference between common Greek curses and erotic spells lay in the fact that "the former torture their victims with fever or pain until they die, while the latter do so only until they yield" (Faraone, *Ancient Greek Love Magic,* 55, citing Kuhnert, "Feuerzauber," 37–54). On cultural memory and the construction of gender in ancient love spells, see also Davis, "Forget Me Not," 248–59.

80. Kagarow, *Griechische Fluchtafeln,* 55–58; Gager, *Curse Tablets,* 21.

81. Schwertheim, *Inschriften,* vol. 1, no. 500, lines 13–14 (=*SEG* 28.943); Strubbe, "Cursed be he that moves my bones," 41 (cf. 53–54, note 84).

82. Faraone, "Agonistic Context," 8 and 26, note 38.

83. Gager, *Curse Tablets,* 180–3 (no. 84) (=*SEG* 30.326; SGD 21); see also Elderkin, "Two Curse Inscriptions," 382–95; Jordan, "Hekatika," 62–65; Versnel, "Religious Mentality," 22–23; Versnel, "Beyond Cursing," 66.

84. Comparetti, "Varietà epigraphiche siceliote," 197–200 (=*SEG* 4.61; SGD 115); trans. Versnel, "Beyond Cursing," 64–65; see also Gager, *Curse Tablets,* 192–93 (no. 93).

85. *DT* 155; trans. Ogden, "Binding Spells," 6–7.

86. Lucian of Samosata, *Alexander the False Prophet* 5 (Macleod, *Luciani opera,* II.333).

87. Dickie, *Magic and Magicians,* 221–22.

88. Apuleius, *Apology* 42 (Hunink, I.65–66).

89. Apuleius, *Apology* 44 (Hunink, I.66–67); also Hopfner, "Die Kindermedien," 66. Hopfner (pp. 72–73) notes that in antiquity the prepubescent years were seen as a prime "physiologisch-pathologisches Moment" that facilitated a "nervöse, hysterische" state of mind best suited for the reception of visions—a melancholic disposition compared to epileptic illness.

90. Hippolytus, *Refutation of All Heresies* (*Haer.*) 28.41–42 (cited by Dickie, *Magic,* 242).

91. For a catalogue of Graeco-Egyptian examples, see Hopfner, "Die Kindermedien," 67–70.

92. *PDM* xiv.1–92 (third cent. CE) (Griffith and Thompson, *Demotic Magical Papyrus,* recto, cols. I/1–III/35; Betz, *Greek Magical Papyri,* 195–200). In the case of one fourth-century papyrus—a "procedure of Solomon" (*PGM* IV.850–929: Preisendanz,

102–4; Betz, 55–56)—the vision of the boy medium is brought about with no external props: the magician simply summons the gods to "inspire" and "enter into" the boy, with the result that they will "reveal" themselves to him and accomplish his request.

93. Johnston, "Charming Children," 97–117.

94. *Paidika* 6.3 (Burke, *De infantia,* 319).

95. *Paidika* 7.2 (Burke, *De infantia,* 321).

96. *DTA* 55: Eidinow, *Oracles,* 359–60.

97. *DTA* 84: "I bind Androkleidēs and his evil tongue, and his evil heart, and his evil spirit, and his workshop, and I bind his children [*hoi paides*]" (Eidinow, *Oracles,* 369–70); *DTA* 102: "I am sending a letter to the gods below and Persephonē, conveying Tibitis, the daughter of Choirinē, who has done me wrong, and her daughter, her husband, and three children [*ta paidia*], two girls and a boy [*arren*]" (Eidinow, *Oracles,* 378–79); *DTA* 47: "I register Hermeia, deeds, business, spirit, hands, children [*(. . . tek)na*], work of workshop and if anyone is working for Hermeia . . . I register Biotē, hands, feet, spirit, tongue, workshop, children [*tekna*] and everything that belongs to her" (Eidinow, *Oracles,* 391); and NGCT 23: "I bind Theoxenos the buttock-less to Pluto and Persephone and Kleita and . . . and Eupolis and Dēmētria the mother still of his child [*(p)ais*] and Hierokleides himself and selected children [*tekna*]" (Eidinow, *Oracles,* 443–44).

98. *DT* 92: Eidinow, *Oracles,* 404.

99. On the practice of cursing as a preemptive means of managing sources of risk and neutralizing perceived threats, see Eidinow, *Oracles,* esp. 225–37.

100. Faraone, "Agonistic Context," 10–11. The other two kinds of agonistic curses in his four-type classification scheme relate to commercial and amatory relationships.

101. Ibid.

102. SGD 91 (Sicily, ca. fifth century BCE): Miller, "Studies," 65–108; Gager, *Curse Tablets,* 76–77, no. 17; Faraone, "Agonistic Context," 12. For another example of a spell targeting choral directors, see *DTA* 34 (Greece, Attika, fourth or third century BCE): Gager, *Curse Tablets,* 49, no. 1.

103. *DT* 15 (Apheca [also Fiq], Syria, third century CE): Audollent, *Defixionum Tabellae,* 21–26; Gager, *Curse Tablets,* 51–53, no. 4; see also Ganszyniec, "Magica," 164; Robert, *Études épigraphiques,* 99–102; Maricq, "Notes philologiques," 360–68. An earlier set of third-century BCE Attic curses, all written in the same hand, target an "actor" (*hypokritēs: DTA* 45; Gager, *Curse Tablets,* 50, no. 2), as well as *didaskaloi* and *hupodidaskaloi,* terms that probably designate theatrical instructors or choral teachers (*DTA* 33–34; Faraone, "Agonistic Context," 12, and 27–28, note 49; see also my discussion below). See also the theatrical rivalry attested in *DT* 110 (Raraunum, Gaul, late third century CE): Gager, *Curse Tablets,* 74–75, no. 16; Egger, "Fluchtafeln," 348–69; and Versnel, "'May he not be able to sacrifice . . . ,'" 247–48, and 269.

104. SGD 24–28, esp. 24–26 (Greece, Athens, third century CE): Jordan, "*Defixiones,*" 205–55 (nos. 1–5), esp. 214–18 (nos. 1–3); Faraone, "Agonistic Context," 12.

105. SGD 24 (Jordan, "*Defixiones,*" 214–15, no. 1; Gager, *Curse Tablets,* 44, 50–51, no. 3).

106. SGD 28 (Jordan, "*Defixiones,*" 219–20, no. 5).

107. SGD 29 (Jordan, "*Defixiones,*" 221–23, no. 6; Faraone, "Agonistic Context," 12–13).

108. For the curses from Corinth and Isthmia, see Jordan, "*Defixiones,*" 214; Faraone, "Agonistic Context," 13 and 28, note 54. For the curse from Oxyrhynchus, see SGD 157 (fourth century CE; Wortmann, "Neue magische Texte," 108–9; *Bonner Jahrbücher des Rheinischen Landesmuseums in Bonn* 168 [1968], no. 12; Gager, *Curse Tablets,* 44, 59–60, no. 8). The lead tablet from Oxyrhynchus (Gager, *Curse Tablets,* 60) calls upon the daimons to bind "the 365 limbs and sinews of those athlete runners under [name missing], to whom Taeias gave birth, and under Ephous, to whom Taeias gave birth, so that they might have neither power nor strength."

109. For curses related to gladiatorial races and competitions, see esp. Gager, *Curse Tablets,* 44–46, 53–74 (nos. 5–7, 9–15); Faraone, "Agonistic Context," 12–13; and Futrell, *Roman Games,* 203–4. Almost all of these arena curses seek to prevent the horse from running (*trechein*): for example, one lead tablet from Carthage asks the *daimōn* of one untimely dead to "[b]ind their running, their power, their soul, their onrush, their speed. Take away their victory, entangle their feet, hinder them, hobble them, so that tomorrow morning in the hippodrome they are not able to run or walk about, or win, or go out of the starting gates, or advance either on the racecourse or track, but may they fall with their drivers" (*DT* 237; *CIL* 8.12508; Delattre, "Inscriptions imprécatoires," 297–300; Gager, *Curse Tablets,* 60–62, no. 9). Another spell from Carthage includes a list of the charioteer's body parts to be bound, including his shoulders, arms, elbows, wrists, and eyes (*DT* 242; Faraone, "Agonistic Context," 13). Finally, in a later Syrian curse from the fifth or sixth century CE, the sight of the *daimones* and spirits of those who have died violently is meant to prevent the rival charioteers from competing, from squeezing over into another lane, and from colliding with the favored team: the final words of the imprecation call for those same charioteers to be broken, dragged, and destroyed by the divine agents who were overseeing the race (*SEG* 34.1437; SGD 192; Rengen, "Deux défixions," 213–34; Gager, *Curse Tablets,* 56–58, no. 6).

110. *Paidika* 10.2 (Burke, *De infantia,* 327). It should be noted that the verb used here, *baskainein* ("to bewitch"), is also used by Paul in Galatians 3:1 ("You foolish Galatians! Who has bewitched you?") in the context of his repeatedly referring to the Jewish law as a "curse" (*katara;* see Galatians 3:10–14). This commentary about Mary's fear for Jesus' safety only appears in Greek recension S (Gs): it is absent from Ga, Gb, Gd, and other language versions. For this reason, Burke (*De infantia,* 326, note 2) has suggested that this sentence "may have been added by a sensitive redactor anxious to emphasize Jesus' more exemplary behavior." I find this explanation somewhat dissatisfying, since the notion of Jesus' susceptibility to an anonymous curse would have actually been more problematic in later periods when christological orthodoxies had become formalized. Another possibility is worth considering: that this commentary represents a *lectio difficilior* (the "more difficult reading"). In such a case, it would be an early component of the story subsequently censored and thus not otherwise preserved in the manuscript record. If Burke is correct and this comment was in fact a secondary addition, then it would in any case have been framed by the redactor's familiarity with the Mediterranean agonistic cursing practices that I have described in this chapter (or alternatively, with the Greek and Jewish polemical traditions I discuss in chapter 6).

111. *Paidika* 3.4 (Burke, *De infantia,* 307).

112. It should be noted that this wording of the curse appears in only one recension of the Greek text (Gs); all other versions substitute the phrase "You shall no longer go your way!" (Burke, *De infantia,* 306, note 5). As I seek to show, however, the specific language used in Jesus' curse of the boy is best explained by an earlier dating.

113. Liddell and Scott, *Greek-English Lexicon,* 763; Bauer, *Greek-English Lexicon,* 343.

114. *IG* 3, 1086 (Dittenberger, *Inscriptiones Atticae,* 255). The editor estimates a date of ca. 80 CE, but the argument on which this dating depends remains uncertain (*incertum*).

115. *IG* 7, 3196 (Dittenberger, *Inscriptiones Graecae Megaridis, Oropiae, Boeotiae,* 594–95); see also relevant examples from Delphi (*SEG* 1.187; ca. 260 BCE); and Argos (Vollgraff, "Novae inscriptiones," 253, line 35; see also the editor's commentary on p. 255: "*hêgemones* sunt praecentores chororum puerorum").

116. Julius Pollux, *Onomasticon* 4.106 (Dindorf, *Iulii Pollucis Onomasticon,* 210). Synonyms include *choropoiia* and *choropoios* (the formation or arrangement of a chorus), *chorostasia* (the establishment of a choral group), *choreusai* (to form or perform a chorus), *ho topos hou hē paraskeuē tou chorou* (the place where the chorus prepares or practices), *korufaios chorou* (the chief singer or head of a chorus), *chorēgia* and *chorēgion* (the office of choral director), *chorēgos* (one who directs or funds a choral troupe), and *didaskalos, hupodidaskalos,* and *chorodidaskalos* (various titles for the choral teachers). The final few terms listed here—*chorēgos, didaskalos, hupodidakalos,* and *chorodidaskalos*—seem to have functioned as direct synonyms for *hēgemōn chorou,* and thus it is especially significant that among the corpora of Greek curse tablets we have examples that specifically invoke these same titles in targeting choral leaders as the intended victims of agonistic spells. For an early binding curse against *choregoi,* see SGD 91 (Sicily, ca. fifth century BCE; Miller, "Studies," 65–108; Gager, *Curse Tablets,* 76–77, no. 17). For a pair of lead disks containing curses against *didaskaloi* and *hupodidaskaloi,* see *DTA* 33–34 (third century BCE; Wünsch, "Appendix," in *IG* 3.3, 5). Faraone ("Agonistic Context," 12) discusses each of these *defixiones* as evidence for the "unmistakable" agonistic ethos that prevailed during the classical and Hellenistic periods, and cites a second-century CE Latin *defixio* against a mime actor named Sosio as an indication that similar practices associated with theatrical and musical competition continued into the late Roman period. For a further discussion of such terminology in the context of "choregic" competition, see Eidinow, *Oracles,* 56–64.

117. Eidinow, *Oracles,* 232; see also pp. 235–36, where she discusses the cycle of perceived "risk and causes of misfortune" that played into reciprocal patterns of cursing in antiquity. Commenting on a curse writer who warns, "If anyone has cursed me . . . I curse in turn all my enemies," she notes that "attempting to neutralize the source of risk, he resorted to a curse and became a sourse of risk and misfortune for someone else" (p. 236). The curse she comments on here is NGCT 24 (Oxford, Ashomolean Museum, inv. G.514.3; early fourth century BCE; Jordan, "Three Curse Tablets," 115–17; Eidinow, *Oracles,* 444).

118. Meijer, *Stoic Theology,* 5–7; Long, *Stoic Studies,* 233, 245, 270; Campbell, "Self-Mastery," 327–40. On the ancient Stoic debate between Chrysippus and Cleanthes over "how the spirit [*pneuma*] emanates from the *hegemonikon* when it reveals itself in the

act of walking," see Arnim, *Stoicorum veterum fragmenta,* II.836 (quote here from Meijer, *Stoic Theology,* 5, note 26; cf. Dragona-Monachou, *Stoic Arguments,* 53).

119. Epictetus (55–135 CE), *Discourses* 1.15; 3.3, 5, 9–10, 22; 4.4–5 (Oldfather, LCL, I.106; II.28, 40, 66, 74–76, 136, 328–32): for Epictetus, the goal of lived philosophy was to keep one's "governing principle" (*hēgemonikon*) in conformity with nature. Marcus Aurelius (121–180 CE), *Meditations* 2.2; 5.3, 11, 26; 6.8; 7.16, 22, 28, 33, 55, 75; 8.43, 48, 61; 9.7, 15, 22; 10.24; 11.20; 12.1, 14, 33 (Farquharson, *Meditations,* 20–22, 74–76, 84, 90, 98, 124–26, 128, 130, 138, 146, 160, 162–64, 168, 174, 178, 179, 204, 228–30, 234–36, 240–42, 250). Marcus Aurelius emphasizes the need to keep control of the *hēgemonikon* and advocates a program of contemplative withdrawal to prevent it from getting distracted or severed from universal nature: in this way he urges his reader to "honor your governing self [*to hēgemonikon sou*] alone and the divine element within you [*to en soi theion*]" (12.1).

120. On the mind as the "dominant part" (*to hēgemonikon*) of the soul and as identifiable with the divine "breath" or "spirit" (*pneuma*), see, e.g., Philo (20 BCE–50 CE), *Allegorical Interpretation of Genesis* (*Legum allegoriarum*) 1.39–40 (Colson and Whitaker, LCL, I.170–72); *On the Unchangeableness of God* (*Quod deus sit immutabilis*) 45 (Colson and Whitaker, LCL, III.32); *Who Is the Heir of Divine Things?* (*Quis rerum divinarum heres*) 55 (Colson and Whitaker, LCL, IV.310); *On the Special Laws* (*De specialibus legibus*) 4.69 (Colson and Whitaker, LCL, VIII.48); and *Questions and Answers on Genesis* 4.117 (Marcus, LCL, Supplement 1, 401). On 4 Maccabees (first or second century CE), see my discussion later in this chapter.

121. Plutarch (46–120 CE), *On Moral Virtue* (*De virtute morali*) 3 (*Moralia* 441C–442A) (Pohlenz, *Plutarchi moralia,* III.129–31; Hembold, LCL, VI.22–27). Plutarch notes the agreement among philosophers "in supposing virtue to be a certain disposition of the governing portion [*to hēgemonikon*] of the soul."

122. For example, see Clement of Alexandria (ca. 150–215 CE), *Stromata* 2.11.51.6 (Früchtel, Stählin, and Treu, GCS 52.15 [1960], II.141; Mondésert, SC 38, 65; *ANF* 2.359), where Clement writes, "Reason, the governing principle [*to hēgemonikon*], remaining unmoved and guiding the soul, is called its pilot. For access to the Immutable is obtained by a truly immutable means." For other similar uses of the term, see *Stromata* 4.6.39–40; 4.8.63; 5.14.92, 104, 133; 6.6.47; 6.16–18; 7.7.35–36; 8.4.14 (Früchtel, Stählin, and Treu, GCS 52.15 [1960], II.265–66, 277, 388, 395, 417, 455, 499–518; III.27–28, 88).

123. Philo of Alexandria, *On the Creation of the World* (*De opificio mundi*) 30 (Colson and Whitaker, LCL, I.24–25); and *On the Special Laws* (*De specialibus legibus*) 2.61–62 (Colson and Whitaker, LCL, VII.346–47).

124. Philo of Alexandria, *On the Creation of the World* (*De opificio mundi*) 69 (Colson and Whitaker, LCL, I.54); cf. 75 and 100 (Colson and Whitaker, LCL, I.58 and I.80); also see *On Flight and Finding* (*De fuga et inventione*) 69 (Colson and Whitaker, LCL, V.46). The same correspondence of human and divine mind is also highlighted in Philo's treatise *On Special Laws* (1.18; Colson and Whitaker, LCL, VII.108), where he writes that it would be "quite ridiculous to deny that if the mind in us, so exceedingly small and invisible, is yet the ruler of the organs of sense, the mind of the universe, so transcendently great and perfect, must be the King of kings."

125. 4 Maccabees 1:30 and 7:16 (Rahlfs, I.1158 and I.1167). See also 4 Maccabees 13:4 (ed. Rahlfs, I.1175), where the author lauds the "supremacy of mind" (*hē hēgemonia tēs dianoias*) exhibited by the seven martyred brothers, which allowed them to "prevail over" (*perigignesthai*) and "master" (*epikratein*) their emotions even in the face of torture.

126. Plutarch, *On the Defects of the Oracles* (*De defectu oraculorum*) 29 (*Moralia* 425F–26A) (Babbitt, LCL, V.434).

127. Plutarch, *Platonic Questions* 2.2 (*Moralia* 1001B–C) (Hubert, *Plutarchi moralia,* vol. 6.1, 117; see also Cherniss, LCL, vol. 13.1, 32–35).

128. Marcus Aurelius, *Meditations* 9.22 (Farquharson, 180; my translation).

129. On the task of properly ordering and directing one's *hēgemonikon,* see Marcus Aurelius, *Meditations* 8.43 and 9.7 (Farquharson, 160–61 and 174–75).

130. For examples of where Marcus Aurelius uses mnemonic language in reference to the divine *hēgemonikon,* see *Meditations* 7.75 and 8.48 (Farquharson, 146–47 and 162–63).

131. Philo of Alexandria, *Every Good Man Is Free* (*Quod omnis probus liber sit*) 20 (Colson and Whitaker, LCL, IX.20–21).

132. Epictetus, *Discourses* 2.17.23 (Oldfather, LCL, I.342–45).

133. Epictetus, *Discourses* 3.26.29–39 (Oldfather, LCL, II.236–41).

134. Philo of Alexandria, *On the Creation of the World* (*De opificio mundi*) 78 (Colson and Whitaker, LCL, I.60–63, quote at 63).

135. Philo of Alexandria, *On Husbandry* (*De agricultura*) 54–59 (Colson and Whitaker, LCL, III.136–39).

136. Philo of Alexandria, *Allegorical Interpretation* (*Legum allegoriarum*) 3.224 (Colson and Whitaker, LCL, I.452–53).

137. Riginos, *Platonica,* 41–49; Lefkowitz, *Lives,* 67; Burke, *De infantia,* 256.

138. Philo of Alexandria, *Every Good Man Is Free* (*Quod omnis probus liber sit*) 144–46 (LCL, IX. 92–95).

139. Epictetus, *Discourses* 3.21.1–3 (Oldfather, LCL, II.122–25).

140. Epictetus, *Discourses* 3.21.12 (Oldfather, LCL, II.126–27).

141. Pfitzner, *Paul and the Agon Motif;* Brändl, *Der Agon bei Paulus.*

142. Romans 15:30 and Philippians 2:27–30; see also 1 Thessalonians 2:3, where Paul boasts of his courage "to declare to you the gospel of God in spite of great opposition [*en pollō*$_i$ *agōni*]," and Philippians 4:3, where he names two women (Euodia and Syntyche) who have "participated in the contest together" (*sunathlein*) with him.

143. Philippians 3:12–16; see also 1 Corinthians 9:24–25; Galatians 2:2; and Philippians 2:16.

144. 1 Corinthians 9:24–27.

145. 1 Timothy 1:18 and 6:11.

146. 2 Timothy 2:5.

147. Colossians 1:29–31 and 2:18.

148. Colossians 4:12.

149. Ephesians 6:12.

150. Clement of Alexandria, *Stromata* 2.20.110.1–3 (Früchtel, Stählin, and Treu, GCS 52.15 [1960], II.173; Mondésert, SC 38, 118; *ANF* 2.371, modified); see also

Stromata 5.14.93 (Früchtel, Stählin, and Treu, GCS 52.15 [1960], III.387–88; Boulluec, SC 278, 178 [= 5.14.92.5–93.3]), where Clement reads book 10 of Plato's *Laws* in light of the testimony of Ephesians 6:12. About a century later, Methodius of Olympus (d. ca. 311 CE) draws a similar analogy in speaking about the soul's contest with lustful impulses in terms of a "wrestling match" (*palē*) against an array of "opponents [*antagōnistai*] who are strong and many in number" (*Symposium,* Epilogue, lines 107–17 [=sect. 300]: Musurillo, SC 95, 330; also Bonwetsch, GCS 27 [1917], 140 [Epilogue=ch. 11]).

151. Origen of Alexandria, *On Prayer* (*De oratione*) 29.2 (=257) (Koetschau, GCS 3 [1899], 382).

152. Origen of Alexandria, *On Prayer* (*De oratione*) 30.2 (=257) (Koetschau, GCS 3 [1899], 394).

153. John Chrysostom, *Address on Vainglory and the Right Way for Parents to Bring Up Their Children* 68 (Schulte, *S. Joannis Chrysostomi De inani Gloria,* 23; trans. Laistner, in *Christianity and Pagan Culture,* 113–14).

154. Philo of Alexandria, *On the Creation of the World* (*De opificio mundi*) 165 (Colson and Whitaker, LCL, I.130–31); *Allegorical Interpretation of Genesis* (*Legum allegoriarum*) 3.110 (Colson and Whitaker, LCL, I.374–75); and Epictetus, *Discourses* 2.22.25 (Oldfather, LCL, I.400–401).

155. *Paidika* 5 (Burke, *De infantia,* 307–9). Jesus' statement, "They will not raise them up [*kakeina ouk anastēsontai*]," has usually been interpreted as a reference to the parents' inability to raise their children who have died (Burke, *De infantia,* 308, note 1; and Aasgaard, *Childhood,* 234–35). However, the neuter plural form of *ta paidia* ("children") does not appear as an antecedent anywhere in chapter 4 or 5: the only references are to the (singular) child who died as a result of Jesus' curse. To find a mention of "children" in the plural, one needs to go all the way back to chapter 2, the story of Jesus and the birds (a pericope that may have circulated independently from this curse story in the early stages of the text's history). Therefore, I think it is preferable to opt for a more obvious neuter plural antecedent, found just a line or two earlier in Jesus' references to "wise words" (*phronima rhēmata*). In my reading of the text, Jesus' reference to the parents inability to "raise up for themselves" (*anistasthai*) words of wisdom, should be understood as a double entendre: not only are they struck dumb (in both senses) in Jesus' presence, they also are unable to resurrect their son due to the fact that his *hegemon* or "rational faculty" is cursed.

156. Philo of Alexandria, *On the Sacrifices of Cain and Abel* (*De sacrificiis Abelis et Caini*) 22 (Colson and Whitaker, LCL, II.108–9). Elsewhere, the Alexandrian author applies a similar allegorical reading strategy to scriptural stories and other examples taken from everyday life to illustrate the damaging and disruptive effects of "blind guides" who distract a mind from its true governing function. Two examples will suffice. In his treatise *On the Unchangeableness of God* (111–13; Colson and Whitaker, LCL, III.64–67), Philo allegorizes Genesis 39:1 by personifying pleasure as Potiphar's wife and the mind as Joseph, who is thrown into the "prison of the passions." There he encounters the "governor" (*hēgemōn*) of the prison (Potiphar), who represents "the concentration and composite of various and sundry vices, combined together in one form." In his essay *On Husbandry* (31–33; Colson and Whitaker, LCL, III.122–25), he likens an untrained mind to an inexperienced herdsman who contends with his

cattle. When this "guide" (*hēgemōn*) is shown to be inexperienced, he runs after the cattle, trying to catch them and bring them under control. However, the herd ("our senses") refuse to come to heel under the guidance of such a lazy and careless shepherd ("the mind"), and they accordingly "shake off restraint, and get unruly, going at random where they have no business to go."

157. Epictetus, *Discourse* 29.7 (Oldfather, LCL, II.510–11).

158. Matthew 4:1–11; Mark 1:12–13; Luke 4:1–3.

159. Deuteronomy 27:1–14.

160. This juxtaposition of the verbs "bless" and "curse" may have also evoked the language of Deuteronomy 30:19 LXX—"I have set before you life and death, the blessing [*eulogia*] and the curse [*katara*]."

161. In Galatians 3:13, Paul follows this with a similar curse formula, "Cursed [*epikataratos*] is everyone who hangs on a tree," which is a reformulation of Deuteronomy 21:23 ("anyone hung on a tree is under God's curse").

162. 4 Maccabees 2.

163. 4 Maccabees 2:19–22.

164. Upson-Saia ("Holy Child or Holy Terror?") focuses on the problematic associations of Jesus' anger in some of the *Paidika* stories; here, I shift the attention to the way Jesus' curse may have in fact prompted ancient audiences to read anger onto the boy's initial physical aggression.

165. Gager, *Curse Tablets,* 184–85, no. 86; also Lattimore, *Themes,* 116–17; Robert, "Malédictions funéraires," 246–49, 279, and 288 (note 9).

166. Gager, *Curse Tablets,* 185–87, no. 87; also Wilhelm, "Zwei Fluchinschriften," Beiblatt, cols. 9–18; Deissmann, *Licht vom Osten,* 315–26 (Eng. trans. *Light from the Ancient East,* 423–35); Bergmann, "Rachgebete," 503–7; and Roussel and Launey, *Inscriptions de Délos,* no. 2532.

167. Gager, *Curse Tablets,* 191, no. 91; see also Ramsey, *Bearing,* 358–61. Other curses citing Deuteronomy survive in other languages as well. A Babylonian Jewish Aramaic curse bowl of unknown date from Mesopotamia records several curses from Deuteronomy 28 and 29 (28:22, 28, 35; 29:19), as well as texts of judgment from Exodus (22:23), Leviticus (26:29), the Psalms (69:24), and Micah (7:16–17) in calling for the death of its victim: see Gager, *Curse Tablets,* 205–7, no. 109; also Naveh and Shaked, *Amulets and Magic Bowls,* 174–79, no. 9. A late ancient Coptic papyrus (sixth century CE or earlier) records a Christian curse against a woman named Alo in which "the curses of the Law and Deuteronomy" are invoked: Michigan 3565 (Worrell, "Coptic Magical and Medical Texts," 13–16; trans. in Meyer and Smith, *Ancient Christian Magic,* 211–12, no. 104).

168. Greek *Paidika* 3.2 (Burke, *De infantia,* 307).

169. Greek *Paidika* 3.3 (Burke, *De infantia,* 307). Manuscript S has the otherwise unattested form of *ekkomenos,* for which Burke substitutes *ekkaiomenos* ("scorched"), correcting his earlier more problematic reading of *ekkomizomenos* ("carried out") (Burke, *De infantia,* 307; cf. Chartrand-Burke, "Infancy Gospel," 152 and 226). Aasgaard's reconstruction of *ekkeomenos* ("let off") is not feasible (see Aasgaard, *Childhood,* 220).

170. Gero, "Infancy Gospel," 60; Hock, *Infancy Gospels,* 93.

171. Matthew 21:19; cf. 24:32, where Jesus reflects on how the "branch" (*klados*) of a fig tree becomes "tender" (*apalos*) when it puts forth its leaves.

172. Mark 11:12–14, 20–24.

173. Greek *Paidika* 4 (Burke, *De infantia,* 307).

174. Greek *Paidika* 2.1 (Burke, *De infantia,* 303).

175. Greek *Paidika* 7.2 (Burke, *De infantia,* 321). See also *Paidika* 2.1 (Burke, *De infantia,* 303), where a later redactor has added the comment that Jesus' action of purifying the water in the pools was accomplished "by the administration of his word alone and not by any deed" (*katastasei logou monon kai ouk ergō$_i$*).

176. Austin, *How to Do Things with Words.* On the pragmatic function(s) of speech in culturally specific linguistic and ritual settings, see also Tambiah, "Magical Power of Words," 175–208; and Janowitz, *Icons of Power,* esp. xx–xxii.

177. Connerton, *How Societies Remember,* 58–59.

178. Mitchell (*Meaning,* 7–8, 174) has observed that the "automatic" character of biblical blessings and curses derives from the fact that God (or a privileged representative of God) is the speaker of the words (see also Janowitz, *Icons of Power,* 20).

179. Greek *Paidika* 4.1 (Burke, *De infantia,* 307).

180. The inscription (*I.Portes* 10) uses this phrase to refer to a contest in rhetoric held at a gymnasium or festival venue: for a discussion of such *logikoi agones,* see Nijf, "Athletics and *Paideia,*" 215 and note 44; also Ziebarth, *Aus dem griechischen Schulwesen,* 136–47.

Chapter 5. Learning Letters

1. *Paidika* 6–8 (Burke, *De infantia,* 309–23).

2. *Paidika* 13 (Burke, *De infantia,* 329).

3. *Paidika* 14 (Burke, *De infantia,* 331–33).

4. This hypothesis is supported by the prominence and repetition of teacher episodes throughout the narrative structure. Burke (*De infantia,* 199) concludes that "it is quite likely that [the *Paidika*] was built around this key episode."

5. *Paidika* 17 (Burke, *De infantia* 335–37). Chapter 17 in recension Gs corresponds to chapter 19 in Ga and Gd (Burke, *De infantia,* 385–89, 447–51), but the pericope is absent in Gb. The story of Jesus and the teachers in the Temple also appears in the final chapter of the Syriac *Paidika:* see Wright, *Contributions,* 11 (English trans.) and 16 (Syriac text); Baars and Heldermann, "Neue Materialien" (1994), 27–30; Burke, "The *Infancy Gospel of Thomas* from an Unpublished Syriac Manuscript," 294–99 (ch. 19); for a discussion of the different recensions, see Burke, *De infantia,* 162–66. On the relationship between *Paidika* 17 and Luke 2:41–52, see Aasgaard, *Childhood,* 115–18; Kaiser, "Jesus als Kind," 260–64; and Burke, *De infantia,* 182–88.

6. Dornseiff, *Alphabet,* 18 ("Die Beschäftigung mit den Buchstaben war also etwas, das ein Wesentliches der Kindheit bezeichnet, und daß Kindheitserinnerungen auf assoziativem Weg zu Faktoren im religiösen Leben der Erwachsenen werden können, ist bekannt").

7. The standard edition of the *Hermeneumata* has long been that of Goetz, *Corpus Glossariorum Latinorum* (=*CGL*), volume 3. This work has now been supplemented by Dionisotti, "From Ausonius' Schooldays?" 83–125, who edits an additional version found in a Vienna manuscript. For a discussion of these handbooks, see also Hopkins, "Everyday Life," 25–30; and Cribiore, *Gymnastics,* 15ff.

8. Dionisotti, "From Ausonius' Schooldays?" 86–87, 123. Dionisotti documents eight different redactions and presents a compelling case for a Gallic provenance.

9. Ibid., 86; see also p. 93, where the author describes the colloquia as "exercises in the vocabulary and idiom of everyday life."

10. Dionisotti (ibid., 93) compares the selection and distribution of scenes in five of the eight different extant versions and labels the scene types under the following headings: Getting up, School, Business/Social, Lunch, Preparing Dinner, Baths, Dinner, Bedtime. The centrality of the "School" scenario can be demonstrated by its frequency of occurrence: it appears in four out of the five parallel texts, and is thus the second-most commonly attested episode after the opening vignette, "Getting up" (which appears in all five).

11. Cribiore, *Gymnastics,* 16. The idealization of moral goals is witnessed, for example, in the *Hermeneumata Stephani* where the child's cleanliness and physical hygiene is emphasized as "what a free boy ought to learn," and where "paying attention to others" is described as "how we make progress" (Goetz, *CGL,* III.380.35–38 and 381.2–34; trans. Hopkins, "Everyday Life," 25 and 26).

12. *Hermeneumata Stephani* (Goetz, *CGL,* III.380.40–59; trans. Hopkins, "Everyday Life," 26); see also Chartrand-Burke, "The Infancy Gospel of Thomas," 342. It is unclear in the text whether the tutor is to be identified with the child's slave (also mentioned in the text), or whether the slave and the tutor are to be regarded as two different people. In another handbook (*Hermeneumata Celtes* 19–22: Dionisotti, "From Ausonius' Schooldays?" 99), it is the boy's slave who accompanies him to school and who supplies him with "tablets and a case for pencils, a ruler, an abacus, and counting tokens." On the familial role of the tutor in helping the student to prepare for school, see also *Colloquia Monacensia* 2 (Goetz, *CGL,* III.646; trans. Hopkins, "Everyday Life," 26): "I go out of my bedroom with my tutor [Gk. *paedagogos;* Lat. *paedagogus*] and my nurse [Gk. *hē trophos;* Lat. *nutrix*] to greet my father and my mother. I greet them both and kiss them both."

13. *Hermeneumata Stephani* (Goetz, *CGL,* III.377.9–17).

14. *Hermeneumata Celtes* 21–22 (Dionisotti, "From Ausonius' Schooldays?" 99).

15. *Hermeneumata Einsidlensia* (Goetz, *CGL,* III.225.25–35; trans. Cribiore, *Gymnastics,* 15 ["I take out the stylus and sit down at my place: I erase and copy according to the model. Afterwards, I show my writing to the teacher, who makes every kind of correction"]).

16. *Hermeneumata Einsidlensia* (Goetz, *CGL,* III.225.35–43 and 226.7–23; trans. Cribiore, *Gymnastics,* 15); also *Hermeneumata Stephani* (Goetz, *CGL,* III.381.2–34; trans. Hopkins, "Everyday Life," 26); and *Hermeneumata Celtes* 20–21 (Dionisotti, "From Ausonius' Schooldays?" 98–99): "He [the schoolmaster] gives me a model [Gk. *analogion;* Lat. *manuale*] and orders me to read five pages from it. I read accurately and with noble style. Then he gives it to another" (my translation).

17. *Hermeneumata Einsidlensia* (Goetz, *CGL,* III.225.56–226.6; trans. Cribiore, *Gymnastics,* 15).

18. *Hermeneumata Celtes* 40–42 (Dionisotti, "From Ausonius' Schooldays?" 101; my translation).

19. *Hermeneumata Celtes* 39 (Dionisotti, "From Ausonius' Schooldays?" 100–101; Hopkins, "Everyday Life," 26).

20. Cicero, *Letters to Friends* (*Ad Familiares*) 261.1 (=VII.25.1), to M. Fabius Gallus (August 45 CE) (ed. Bailey, LCL, II.440; trans. Wiedemann, *Adults and Children,* 87). In the second century, Dio Chrysostom (*Or.* 15: Cohoon, LCL, II.160–61) also observes that "so far as obeying and being thrashed are concerned, you can go on and assert that the boys who take lessons of schoolmasters are likewise their servants and that the gymnastic trainers are slavemasters of their pupils."

21. Cicero, *Letter to Quintus* (*Ad Quintum Fratrem*) 25.4 (=III.5.4) (Bailey, LCL 462, 182 [my translation]; see also Wiedemann, *Adults and Children,* 87).

22. Marcus Aurelius, *Meditations* 1.7 (Farquharson, *Meditations,* 4–7); see also Wiedemann, *Adults and Children,* 96.

23. Marcus Aurelius, *Meditations* 1.17 (Farquharson, *Meditations,* 18–19).

24. Augustine, *Ep.* 104.7 (409 CE) (PL 33.391; *NPNF*, ser. 1, vol. 1, 429); Wiedemann, *Adults and Children,* 106.

25. Augustine, *Confessions* 1.14–15 (Skutella and Verheijen, CCSL 27, 12–13; *NPNF*, ser. 1, vol. 1, 49). As Wiedemann (*Adults and Children,* 202) observes, "Beating plays a major part in Augustine's memories of his schooldays."

26. Augustine, *Confessions* 1.15 (Skutella and Verheijen, CCSL 27, 13; *NPNF*, ser. 1, vol. 1, 49); see also Origen of Alexandria's comments about "the pains inflicted on those who are being educated by fathers and teachers and schoolmasters" (*Against Celsus* 6.56: Borret, SC 150, 318; trans. Chadwick, 372). Commenting on the use of corporal punishment in Graeco-Roman educational settings, Marrou (*History,* 159) observes that "the terrible schoolmaster, stick in hand" was "the characteristic figure that stayed in the memory of the men who had been educated at these little schools." For a recent reassessment of ancient evidence related to disciplinary violence against children, see Laes, "Childbeating in Roman Antiquity," 75–89.

27. Harris, *Ancient Literacy,* 135.

28. Kleijwegt, *Ancient Youth,* 76–83; contra Marrou, *History,* 305. Kleijwegt (p. 79) argues strongly against Marrou's assertion that the establishment of public schools in "every important city" was a priority among ancient authorities, noting the lack of evidence to support this claim.

29. Harris, *Ancient Literacy,* 233; Booth, "Schooling of Slaves," 11–19.

30. In the study of pilgrimage practice and the shrine centers, "catchment area" refers to "the geographical and demographic extent of [a particular shrine's] appeal" (Frankfurter, "Introduction," in *Pilgrimage and Holy Space,* 7). I adopt this phrase here to refer to the demographic compass of images and assumptions related to education in the ancient world.

31. Beck, *Album,* 9–10 (quotes from p. 9). On Chiron's reputation as Achilles's instructor, see Marrou, *History,* 26–27, 473–74. Attic-style amphorae, cups, and vases from Greece feature scenes of Apollo being brought to Chiron for instruction (Beck, *Album,* 11–12, nos. 2–26 and 30; and pls. 1–4, figs. 1–19). In a circa first-century CE painting from Herculaneum, Chiron teaches Achilles how to play the lyre (Beck, *Album,* 12, nos. 27–28, and pl. 4, figs. 20–21; Elia, *Pitture murali,* 25, no. 25 [9019], fig. 5), and

in a late Roman bronze relief he shows him how to hunt and throw a javelin (Simon, "Karren," in Helbig and Speier, *Führer,* II.357–60, no. 1546).

32. Ps.-Apollodorus, *Library* (*Bibliotheca*) 3.10.3 and 3.13.3–8 (Frazer, LCL, II.14–17 and 64–77); see also Johansen, "Achill bei Cheiron," 181–205; and Beck, *Album,* 9–10.

33. Ps.-Justin Martyr, *On the Sole Government of God* (*De monarchia*) 6 (Otto, *Corpus,* III.154–56; *ANF* 1.293); Lactantius, *Divine Institutes* 1.10.2 (Heck and Wlosok, I.37; *ANF* 7.19); Lactantius, *Epitome of the Divine Institutes* 8.1 (Heck and Wlosok, 9; *ANF* 7.226); and Gregory of Nazianzus, *Or.* 43.12 (*Funerary Oration on St. Basil the Great*) (*PG* 35.509).

34. Beck, *Album,* 10.

35. Ibid., 13, no. 46; pl. 6, fig. 30.

36. Ibid., 13, no. 37; pl. 4, fig. 25; another fifth-century BCE *skyphos* showing Linus teaching Iphicles is preserved in Schwerin, Germany (ibid., 13, no. 47; pl. 6, fig. 31).

37. Ibid., 13, nos. 38–41; pls. 5–6, figs. 26–29. The first of these—an Attic cup from Vulci, Italy—shows the rest of the boys in the classroom scattering as Heracles attacks Linus. Heracles's conflict with Linus remained well known to storytellers and collectors of tales like Ps-Apollodorus (*Library* 1.3.2: Frazer, LCL, I.16–17), and another second-century author, Pausanias (*Description of Greece* 2.19.8; Jones, LCL, I.346–47), reports on a grave of "Linus the poet" outside the city of Argos in Greece.

38. Tacitus, *Annals* 11.14 (Moore, LCL, III.270–71).

39. Tatian, *Oration Addressed to the Greeks* 41.1 (Whittaker, 72–75); and Origen of Alexandria, *Against Celsus* 1.16 (Borret, SC 132, 118; trans. Chadwick, 18).

40. Klein (*Child Life,* 28–31, and pls. XXVIII–XXXII) and Beck (*Album,* 14–20, nos. 31–75, and pls. 10–16, figs. 53–84) catalogue relevant examples of Attic red- and black-figure ware and other ceramic finds, and provide helpful photographic documentation of different scene types.

41. New York, Metropolitan Museum, 17.230.10 (Klein, *Child Life,* 29, pl. XXIX; Beck, *Album,* 15 and 19, no. 58, and pl. 11, figs. 58–60).

42. For a description and image, see García, *Pupils,* 66–67 (fig. 36); also Helbig, *Wandgemälde,* no. 1463.

43. Webster, *Ancient History,* 569; Wiedemann, *Adults and Children,* 343, pl. 4; Chartrand-Burke, "Infancy Gospel," 342–43, fig. 7.3.

44. Trier, Rheinisches Landesmuseum, INV 9921: Johnston, *Private Life,* par. 112, fig. 52; Bonner, *Education,* 56, fig. 9; Avrin, *Scribes,* 171, pl. 147; Small, *Wax Tablets,* 149; Cüppers, *Römer,* 492–94.

45. Small (*Wax Tablets,* 149) surmises that this third student is arriving late for class; if so, ancient viewers may have been meant to understand the scene's tranquility to be short-lived! Or perhaps the third student is a depiction of the deceased, and the afterlife is being reimagined as a classroom where divine wisdom is imparted? If so, the student's arrival is a blessed homecoming of sorts: a child who has died returns to a pathway of learning that had been prematurely interrupted in life.

46. For a discussion of the evidence for the educational use of such varied architectural settings in both Hellenistic and Roman contexts, see Cribiore, *Gymnastics,* 25–34; García, *Pupils,* 57–64; and Bloomer, *School of Rome,* 13–14. On the more formal "lecture rooms" discovered during the archaeological excavations at Kom el-Dikka in Alexandria

(dating from the fourth to the seventh century CE), see McKenzie, *Architecture*, 150, 171, 207–8 (fig. 358), 212–15 (figs. 366–70), and 220.

47. *Paidika* 6.2f and 14.1 (Burke, *De infantia*, 315 and 331). In the second episode (*Paidika* 13.1–3; Burke, *De infantia*, 329), it is clear that Jesus also received instruction somewhere other than his home (since he "went home to his parents" after he cursed the teacher), but the text does not give any further information about this location.

48. Clement of Alexandria, *Who Is the Rich Man That Shall Be Saved?* 3e (Butterworth, LCL, 340; *ANF* 2.601). Clement's language resembles that of the first-century BCE historian Diodorus Siculus, who speaks of Athenians as a people "who offer their country as a school for the common use of humankind" (*Library of History* 13.27: Oldfather, LCL, V.194–95 [translation modified]).

49. *Paidika* 2f (Burke, *De infantia*, 315–17).

50. Cribiore, *Gymnastics*, 18–19; Cribiore, *Writing*, 17. On the *didaskaleion* of Tothes in Memphis, see *UPZ*, I.78.9–14. On the *grammatodidaskaleion* of Malankomas in the Fayum, see *SB*, III.7268. On the *didaskaleion* of the *grammatodidaskalos* Dionysios in Oxyrhynchus, see *P.Oxy.* LXIV, col. IV.18–20 (315/316 CE). Another papyrus from Oxyrhynchus (*P.Oxy.* LVII.3952; dated 610 CE) suggests that there were at least two *didaskaleia* in that city during the early seventh century CE and that these institutions may have been public rather than private in character.

51. Evans, *War*, 170.

52. Mommsen, *CIL*, IV.360, 3732, 3735, 3736; IV.362, 2730, 3739; also García, *Pupils*, 70. The irregular form *poveri* is used in place of the standard Latin plural form, *pueri*.

53. García, *Pupils*, 70.

54. *CIL*, IV.5207–11, 9089–94; García, *Pupils*, 78.

55. García, *Pupils*, 77.

56. Ibid., 82.

57. *Hermeneumata Stephani* (Goetz, 380.40–59; Hopkins, "Everyday Life," 26).

58. *Paidika* 9.1–3 (Burke, *De infantia*, 323–25).

59. *Paidika* 9.1 (Burke, *De infantia*, 323). Burke translates *ti dōma huperoͅon* as "a certain roof of an upstairs room," supplying the word "roof" even though it does not appear in the Greek. He does so presumably because later in the story we are told that Jesus "comes from the *stegē*" after the child's parents arrive on the scene. The word *stegē* commonly means the "roof" of a building, but it can also refer to a "chamber" or "room," or alternatively to a "house" or "dwelling," either of which would make sense in this context. Here, I take it as a synonym for *dōma*, referring to the room from which the child fell.

60. *Paidika* 9.2–3 (Burke, *De infantia*, 325).

61. Aasgaard (*Childhood*, 42) observes that the Zeno episode "is more loosely tied to the preceding [chapters]," citing the phrase "many days later" as evidence for the pericope's temporal detachment. It should be noted that the time transition indicated by "many days later" is minor compared to the transitions in *Paidika* 10.1 and 12.1, which indicate the passing of whole years in Jesus' life, from age five to age seven in *Paidika* 10.1 (Burke, *De infantia*, 325), and then again to age eight in *Paidika* 12.1 (Burke, *De infantia*, 327).

62. *Paidika* 9.1 (Burke, *De infantia,* 323).

63. The adverb *palin* appears at the beginning of *Paidika* 16.1 (Burke, *De infantia,* 333); see also *Paidika* 14.1 (Burke, *De infantia,* 331), where *palin* follows the phrase "after some days" (*kai meth' hēmeras*) in marking the transition between the second and third teacher tales (*Paidika* 13 and 14).

64. *Paidika* 9.1 (Burke, *De infantia,* 323).

65. *Paidika* 2.1 and 6.2e (Burke, *De infantia,* 303 and 315).

66. Horn and Martens, *"Let the Little Children Come to Me,"* 201.

67. Jerome (ca. 347–420 CE), *Apology against Rufinus* 1.30 (Lardet, SC 303, 82; *NPNF*, ser. 2, vol. 3, 498).

68. On this approximate age range, see Kleijwegt, *Ancient Youth,* 89. While the majority of scholars understand seven to have been the typical starting age for children's education outside the home, Wiedemann (*Adults and Children,* 164) contends that during the Roman period "schoolmasters began by teaching five- or six-year-olds the Greek alphabet" as preparation for "learning the Latin alphabet later."

69. Cribiore, *Gymnastics,* 19–20.

70. Harris (*Ancient Literacy,* 234) argues that the definition of this three-tiered system became especially marked in the second century CE, citing as evidence Apuleius's *Florida* 20.3 (Helm, *Apulei Opera,* II.2, 40–41). For other examples of scholars who talk about these three tiers of ancient education, see Marrou, *History,* 142–216 (on primary, secondary, and higher education in Hellenistic Greek society), and 265–91 (on primary, secondary, and higher education in Roman society); Kleijwegt, *Ancient Youth,* 88–123; Cribiore, *Writing,* 13–17; and García, *Pupils,* 27. It should be noted that ancient authors sometimes employed this tripartite classification schema as a normative attempt to understand the psychology of children and youth at different stages of development. Of course, both in theory and in practice, there was much more variation than this schema would seem to admit. Some ancient writers parsed the educational process down to smaller (and more numerous) increments or age-divisions: see Wiedemann, *Adults and Children,* 165, who cites a passage from Rufinus's translation of Origen's *Commentary on Numbers* (27.13) as one example. In practice, there was often a great deal of overlap of activities and interaction between students of different ages within individual classroom settings, as indicated by the *Hermeneumata* colloquia (Cribiore, *Gymnastics,* 38).

71. An alternative title for such an elementary-level instructor was *grammatistēs.*

72. Cribiore, *Writing,* 13–17. The first two levels correspond to Marrou's category of "primary education" (*History,* 142–59, 265–73), while the third level corresponds to his categories of "secondary education" (pp. 160–85, 274–83) and "higher education" (pp. 194–216, 284–91).

73. Marrou, *History,* 143–44; Cribiore, *Writing,* 16.

74. Cribiore, *Writing,* 14, 16–17.

75. *Kathēgētēs* seems to be used as the primary term: it is used ten times to refer to Zacchaeus (*Paidika* 6.1–7.1), two times to refer to the second teacher (13.2), and six times to refer to the third teacher (14.1–4). However, *didaskalos* is also applied to each teacher: three times to Zacchaeus (*Paidika* 6.2f–6.4), twice to the second teacher (13.2), and once to the third teacher (14.1). In his translation, Burke (*De infantia,* 302–36)

renders *kathēgētēs* as "teacher" and *didaskalos* as "master." For a discussion of these titles, see also Paul Foster, "Educating Jesus," 24.

76. García (*Pupils,* 49–55) cites several graffiti and other epigraphic evidence for "the precarious economic conditions" of teachers living at the poverty line or scraping to make it by in ancient Rome (quote at p. 54).

77. *Paidika* 6.2b (Burke, *De infantia,* 311–13).

78. Cribiore (*Gymnastics,* 48, 58, 105–9) and Harris (*Ancient Literacy,* 135 and 246) both emphasize that ancient Greek and Roman fathers shouldered a range of educational responsibilities, from providing certain forms of pedagogy in the home, to recruiting qualified teachers, to funding the economic cost of their children's schooling. On the continued involvement of families in their children's education during the Byzantine period, see Kalogeras, "Role of Parents," 133–43.

79. *Paidika* 6.2f and 14.1 (Burke, *De infantia,* 315 and 331).

80. On ancient attitudes toward flattery (and its opposite, frank speech), see Ribbeck, *Kolax,* 1–114; and Fitzgerald, ed., *Friendship.* The first three articles in the latter volume are especially pertinent to this question: Konstan, "Friendship," 7–19; Glad, "Frank Speech," 21–59; and Engberg-Pedersen, "Plutarch," 61–81. For discussions of flattery in ancient primary sources, see, e.g., Aristotle, *Nicomachean Ethics* 4.3.29 (=1125a), 4.6.9 (=1127a), and 8.8.1 (=1159a) (Rackham, LCL, 224, 238, and 480–81); Julius Pollux, *Onomasticon* 6.122–3 (Bethe, II.34).

81. Konstan, "Friendship," 12–13 (quote at 13); also Glad, "Frank Speech," 21–59. Other authors wrote orations contrasting flattery with the "frank speech" (*parrhēsia*) characteristic of true friendship: see, e.g., Horace (65–8 BCE), *Ep.* I.17.19 and I.18.1–4 (Fairclough, LCL, 362 and 368); Dio Chrysostom (ca. 40–ca. 120 CE), *Or.* 3.2 (Cohoon, LCL, I.104–5); Maximus of Tyre (second century CE), *Oration* 14 (Trapp, 118–25); and Themistius (317–ca. 390 CE), *Oration* 22 (Maisano, 735–75). These works are discussed in Glad, "Frank Speech," 25; and Konstan, "Frankness," 16–17.

82. Plutarch, *How to Tell a Flatterer from a Friend* 2 and 16 (Babbitt, *Moralia,* LCL, I.266–69 and 314–15).

83. Lucian, *On Salaried Posts in Great Houses,* or *The Dependent Scholar* (*De Mercede conductis*) 38 (Harmon, LCL, 130, 411).

84. *Paidika* 6.2f (Burke, *De infantia,* 317).

85. *Paidika* 13.2 (Burke, *De infantia,* 329).

86. Wiedemann, *Adults and Children,* 28, citing Juvenal, *Satires* 1.15 (Ramsay, LCL, 2–3).

87. Horace, *Ep.* II.1.70–71 (on his teacher L. Orbilius Pupillus) (Fairclough, LCL, 402–3). Another former student (the poet Domitius Marsus) was moved to commemorate the same teacher's disciplinary whip and rod in a poem: see Suetonius, *Lives of the Grammarians* 9 (Rolfe, LCL, II.408–11); Evans, *War,* 169.

88. Lucian, *The Dream* 2–3 and 16 (Macleod, *Lucian,* 22–25); for other references, see Booth, "Punishment," 65–73.

89. *T. Berol.* inv. 13234 (Erman and Krebs, *Aus den Papyrus,* 233; Cribiore, *Writing,* 205, cat. no. 134; trans. Cribiore, *Gymnastics,* 69).

90. I want to thank Andrew Jacobs for his helpful comments on corporal punishment as a kind of moral formation. On "the conflicted view of learning and corporal

punishment" as part and parcel of Greek *paideia* in Lucian and the *Paidika,* see Frilingos, "No Child Left Behind," 35–40 (quote at 38); also Frilingos, "'It Moves Me to Wonder,'" 825–52. On the cultural values of *paideia* in both the Greek East and Latin West, see Borg, "Glamorous Intellectuals," 157–76; and Ewald, *Philosoph.*

91. Wiedemann, *Adults and Children,* 27.

92. Diogenes Laertius (fl. third century CE), *Lives of Eminent Philosophers* 10.2–4 (Long, II.494–95; Hicks, LCL, II.528–33); cited by Harris, *Ancient Literacy,* 135, see also 237–38. Cribiore (*Gymnastics,* 59) notes that "[a]ccusing someone of being a schoolteacher, or having a schoolteacher as a father, was a common insult." A. D. Booth ("Some Suspect Schoolmasters," 1–20) catalogues evidence for the general disregard shown the profession.

93. Reporting on the policies of the second-century emperor Antoninus Pius (86–161 CE), the *Digesta Iustiniani* (50.4.11.4) notes that "those who taught basic education to boys could not benefit from immunity [from liturgies]" (*eos, qui primis litteris pueros inducunt, non habere vacationem:* Krueger and Mommsen, available online at http://webu2.upmf-grenoble.fr/Haiti/Cours/Ak/Corpus/d-50.htm#4; trans. Kleijwegt, *Ancient Youth,* 80, note 21). See also the discussion in Laes, "School-teachers," 109–27.

94. Cribiore, *Gymnastics,* 73, echoing the observations of the fourth-century CE Greek writer Libanius, *Or.* 25.46 and 43.17 (Foerster, *Libanii opera,* I.559 and III.346).

95. *Paidika* 6.2f and 13.2 (Burke, *De infantia,* 317 and 329).

96. Plautus, *Bacchides* 440–1 (Nixon, LCL, 353–54); Cribiore, *Gymnastics,* 156.

97. Plautus, *Bacchides* 447–8 (Nixon, LCL, 354).

98. Juvenal, *Satire* 7.213–14 (Ramsay, LCL, 154–55); Cribiore, *Gymnastics,* 156, note 98.

99. Libanius, *Oration* 58 (Foerster, *Libanii opera,* IV.175–200; Cribiore, *Gymnastics,* 49); Prudentius, *On the Crown* (*Peristephanon Liber*) 9.47–50 (Thomson, LCL, II.224–25; Cribiore, *Gymnastics,* 156–57). In one of his sermons, Basil of Caesarea also makes a reference to "irrational children, who break the writing tablets when the teacher finds fault with them" (*Homily* 8.67c: *PG* 31. 317B; trans. Holman, *The Hungry Are Dying,* 189; discussed by Cribiore, *Gymnastics,* 157).

100. Plautus, *Bacchides* 444 (Nixon, LCL, 354), with a nod to Seinfeld.

101. *Paidika* 7.1 and 7.3 (Burke, *De infantia,* 321).

102. *Paidika* 7.2 (Burke, *De infantia,* 321).

103. Horace, *Ep.* I.18 (Fairclough, LCL, 368–69); Philodemus, *On Frank Speech* (*De libertate dicendi*), fr. 83 (Konstan, 86–7; see also Glad, "Frank Speech," 40). Frilingos ("No Child Left Behind," 49) mentions other examples of students surpassing their teachers found in ancient literature.

104. For this heading, I borrow the title of a practical guide to phonics and spelling written for parents, students, and teachers: Margaret Bishop's reference book, *The ABC's and All Their Tricks.*

105. For a bibliography on ancient literacy (including a section entitled "Alphabet") covering the period since Harris's landmark study, *Ancient Literacy* (1989), see Werner, "Literacy Studies," 333–84.

106. *Paidika* 6.2–3 (Burke, *De infantia,* 311–19).

107. *Paidika* 13.1–2 (Burke, *De infantia,* 329).

108. *Paidika* 14.1–2 (Burke, *De infantia,* 331).

109. *Hermeneumata Einsidlensia* (Goetz, *CGL,* III.225.56–226.6; trans. Cribiore, *Gymnastics,* 15).

110. See Julius Pollux (*Onomasticon* 2.8–10: Bethe, I.82–83) and Censorinus (*Birthday Book* 14.3–4: Sallmann, 25–26; trans. Parker, 28), who both draw on Hippocrates's division of childhood into seven-year age groupings: *paidion* (up to age 7), *pais* (ages 7–14), and *meirakion* (ages 14–21). Aristotle (*Politics* VII.15 and VIII.3–4 [1336a–37a; VIII.1338a–39b]: Rackham, LCL, 624–33, 642–53) makes reference to an age classification system similar to that of Hippocrates, counseling that children should remain at home until the age of seven. Citing this evidence, Marrou (*History,* 147) unequivocally states, "Up to the age of seven the child stayed at home and was looked after by the womenfolk. . . . The school period began when the child reached the age of seven and in theory lasted until he was fourteen." Burke (*De infantia,* 236) follows Marrou on this point almost without qualification: "At the age of seven most children, both Roman and Jewish, began primary school."

111. Juvenal, *Satire* 14.10–14 (Ramsay, LCL, 264–65).

112. Cribiore, *Gymnastics,* 2. As an example, Censorinus (*Birthday Book* 14.2: Sallman, 25; trans. Parker, 27–28) also reports on Varro's theory that human life was divided into "five equal stages, each one fifteen years long, except the last," with the first two stages being childhood (ages 1–15) and adolescence (ages 16–30).

113. Quintilian, *Institutes* 1.1.15–18 (ed. and trans. Russell, LCL, I.70–73); Harris, *Ancient Literacy,* 240.

114. Wiedemann, *Adults and Children,* 164.

115. Herodas, *Mime* 3.22–23 (Knox, LCL, 104; trans. Buck at http://www.elfinspell.com/Mimes.html#refchap3); also Hock, *Infancy Gospels,* 117; Foster, "Educating Jesus," 24; García, *Pupils,* 42; Cribiore, *Gymnastics,* 175.

116. Quintilian, *Institutes* 10.1.15 and 10.2.2 (Russell, LCL, IV.258–59 and IV.322–23); Cribiore, *Gymnastics,* 132.

117. These two methods are noted by Quintilian (*Institutes* 1.1.27: Russell, LCL, I.76–79). The quote here is from García (*Pupils,* 38), who identifies the first method as having a Greek origin and the second as having derived from Latin tradition.

118. Cribiore, *Writing,* 57–69, 173–284 (nos. 1–412). The organization of Cribiore's catalogue follows an ascending schema of eleven educational levels, identified according to the curricular content of the exercises: letters of the alphabet (nos. 1–40); alphabets (nos. 41–77); syllabaries (nos. 78–97); lists of words (nos. 98–128); writing exercises (nos. 129–74); short passages (nos. 175–232); long passages (nos. 233–324); *scholia minora* (nos. 325–43); compositions, paraphrases, and summaries (nos. 344–57); grammar (nos. 358–78); and notebooks (nos. 379–412).

119. Small, *Wax Tablets,* 145–46.

120. Cribiore, *Writing,* 279, no. 400; Cribiore, *Gymnastics,* 43–44.

121. Cribiore, "Schooltablet," 263–70; Cribiore, *Writing,* 205–6, no. 136; Cribiore, *Gymnastics,* 133. Cribiore (*Writing,* 68) accounts for ten such notebooks and nineteen individual tablets dating to the Roman period, and twelve notebooks and forty-one individual tablets dating to the Byzantine period. One tablet contains a teacher's model affirming the virtues of alphabetic instruction: "Letters are the greatest beginning

of understanding"; below, the halting and truncated handwriting of a student shows how difficult that beginning could be (T. Louvre inv. AF 1195; Cribiore, *Writing,* 211, no. 160; *Gymnastics,* 39–40, fig. 8). For another example of a wise maxim copied as a school exercise, see Bonner, *Education,* 175, fig. 20; and García, *Pupils,* 41, fig. 21.

122. Cribiore, *Writing,* 57–60.

123. Ibid., 191–96 (nos. 78–97); see also Dornseiff, *Alphabet,* 67 and 70. One example of a syllabary is found in a book of Greek school exercises (*un livre d'écolier*) on papyrus from the third century BCE (Guéraud and Jouguet, *Un livre d'écolier;* Cribiore, *Writing,* 269, no. 379). Students often reused papyri, as in the case of a writing exercise written on the back of a personal letter (*P.Med. Copto* inv. 76.24 [seventh or eight century CE]; Pernigotti, "I papyri copti," 96–97, no. 13; Cribiore, *Writing,* 190, no. 75).

124. According to Cribiore (*Writing,* 69–70), among surviving exercises, one-third of those for the learning of individual letters and over half of those for alphabetic memorization have been found on ostraca.

125. On one Roman-era example from Upper Egypt, a student named Kametis tried to write the first four letters of the Greek alphabet in forward and reverse order, but on the return pass he mixed up the order of the beta and the gamma (O.MU 2309; Cribiore, *Writing,* 185, no. 51; Cribiore, *Gymnastics,* 168, fig. 24). For another example of student error, this time probably caused by phonetic confusion, see O.Col. 348, Acc. 64.2.179 (Cribiore, "Fun," 165–68, with figure). For an example of a student shortcut, see O.ROM inv. 906.8.522 (second century CE; Cribiore, *Writing,* 184, no. 44; Cribiore, *Gymnastics,* 165–66), where a slightly more advanced student was asked to write the entire alphabet twice in forward and reverse sequence. The trick was to do it by pairing opposite letters, beginning with alpha and omega, continuing with beta and psi, and so on; but judging from the ink, this particular student simply wrote the entire alphabet in succession once from left to right and then turned around and wrote them in the same order, only this time from right to left. The early Christian writer Jerome makes reference to this kind of alphabetic school exercise and underscores its mnemonic objective (Jerome, *Commentary on Jeremiah* 5.27.2–3; Reiter, CCSL 74 [1960], 245–46 [on Jeremiah 25:26]; also García, *Pupils,* 37). For similar school exercises involving the use of the alphabet for the purposes of versification, see Cribiore, *Writing,* nos. 48, 56, 61, 66, and 287.

126. Champollion, *Monuments,* II.459–60, no. 10; Cribiore, *Gymnastics,* 23–24.

127. *CIL* IV, 164, and nos. 2514–48, 5452–5506, 6904–10, and 9263–9312. According to García (García, *Pupils,* 37), the characters were "usually traced on the lower part of the wall," and thus "show that the writers were children, or adults who bent down to trace them" at children's eye level.

128. On the use of blocks and dice for alphabetic instruction, see Quintilian, *Institutes* 1.1.26 (Russell, LCL, 76–77); Jerome, *Ep.* 107.4 (Hilberg, CSEL 55, 294; *NPNF,* ser. 2, vol. 6, 191); and Manser, "Der hl. Ambrosius," 401. Clement of Alexandria (*Stromata* 5.8.48.8; Früchtel, Stählin, and Treu, GCS 52.15, 3rd ed., 359; Boulluec, SC 278, 104 [= 5.8.49.1]; *ANF* 2.456) also alludes to children's play with letters (*stoicheia*). On the use of cakes for a similar pedagogical purpose (and as an incentive for mastering such lessons), see Horace, *Satires* 1.1.25–26 (Fairclough, LCL, 6–7); and Jerome, *Ep.* 128.1 (Hilberg, CSEL 56, 156–57). These sources are cited and discussed by Dornseiff (*Alphabet,* 17–18) and Cribiore (*Gymnastics,* 164).

129. On the use of a song (*canticum*) for the learning of the alphabet, see Jerome, *Ep.* 107.4 (Hilberg, CSEL 55, 294). Cribiore (*Gymnastics,* 165) discusses this passage but cites the number of the epistle incorrectly. Cribiore also notes a play entitled *Alphabet Show* or *Grammatical Science* (*Grammatikē theōria*) written by the fifth-century BCE Athenian poet Callias, which included a scene where a chorus of twenty-four women, each associated with a Greek letter, sings a dramatized "lesson" on the alphabet and their syllabic combinations: see Athenaeus, *Banquet of the Learned* (*Deipnosophistae*) 10.453d–f (Olson, LCL, V.170–75; Kaibel, II.485–86 [= 10.79]; trans. Yonge, III.715–16); also Svenbro, *Phrasikleia,* 183–86; and Jacob, *Web.* Later, in the second century CE, the sophist Herodes Atticus (ca. 101–77 CE) is said to have employed twenty-four slaves, each with a name beginning with a separate letter of the alphabet, to help in the (musical?) instruction of his "dyslexic" (*dysgrammatos*) son: see Philostratus, *Lives of the Sophists* 2.1 (= 558; Kayser, *Flavii Philostrati opera,* I.66; Wright, LCL, 164–65).

130. Connerton, *How Societies Remember,* 72; also Carruthers, *Book of Memory,* 60–69, esp. her observations about the "somatic nature of memory images" (p. 63), formed through patterns of repetition akin to the training of a dancer's muscles (pp. 68–69).

131. See Carruthers, *Book of Memory,* 64, on "associational connections . . . formed by habit."

132. *Paidika* 6.3 (Burke, *De infantia,* 319).

133. *Paidika* 13.2 (Burke, *De infantia,* 329).

134. *Paidika* 14.2 (Burke, *De infantia,* 331).

135. *Paidika* 6.2c (Burke, *De infantia,* 315).

136. *Paidika* 7.2 and 7.4 (Burke, *De infantia,* 321 and 323).

137. *Paidika* 7.2 (Burke, *De infantia,* 321).

138. *Paidika* 6.4 (Burke, *De infantia,* 319).

139. *Paidika* 6.4 (Burke, *De infantia,* 319); cf. Aasgaard, *Childhood,* 224–25 and 236–37.

140. Burke, *De infantia,* 319, note 8; see also Aasgaard (*Childhood,* 237, notes 9 and 10), who twice describes words in the passage as "difficult to make sense of"; and Hock (*Infancy Gospels,* 119), who similarly evaluates this passage as "most difficult."

141. James, *Apocryphal New Testament,* 62; and Aasgaard, *Childhood,* 145. Along these lines, David Frankfurter ("The Magic of Writing," 211) connects Jesus' letter mystification with a Greek cultural "fascination with the hieroglyph" (see also Frilingos, "No Child Left Behind," 48, note 87).

142. One of the complications is a text critical one: a number of scholars have viewed the Greek text as corrupt at this point. For examples of attempts at reconstructing a "cleaner" reading of this passage, see Hoffmann, *Das Leben Jesu,* 222–23; Tischendorf, *Evangelia Apocrypha,* 2nd ed., 145–46; Meyer, "Kindheitserzählung," 138; and Delatte, "Évangile," 267–68. Such editorial emendations have largely proven dissatisfying: see Hock, *Infancy Gospels,* 119; and Burke, *De infantia,* 319, note 8.

143. Barry (*Greek Qabalah,* 47) writes: "The Greeks used the same word, *stoicheia* (from *steichō*, 'to march in a row'), to denote not only atomic elements as the order of essential constituents of matter, but also alphabetic letters, since they occurred in a sequence and were the essential constituents of speech."

144. *Paidika* 6.4 (Burke, *De infantia,* 319). I follow Aasgaard (*Childhood,* 145) in interpreting Jesus' words in relation to "pedagogical strategies and experiences," and agree with him that Jesus' vocabulary refers to "the form of the letter alpha, either written as the uncial A . . . or as cursive α."

145. On "block capitals" as an integral part of the first lessons at school in Latin-speaking settings, see Petronius, *Satyricon* 58.7 (Heseltine, LCL, 124–25); and Harris, *Ancient Literacy,* 252; contra Daniel, "Liberal Education," 158–59.

146. It is also possible that these descriptions have the stylus strokes of a capital alpha in mind (Andrew Jacobs, *per litt.,* December 31, 2012). Aasgaard (*Childhood,* 145) reads some of the terms in this passage as referring not to the letter alpha but to "numbers and words" and to "diacritical signs." On these points, his analysis is not as well supported. Given Jesus' explicit final statement in *Paidika* 6.4 (Burke, *De infantia,* 319), I think that the terminology in question has the letter alpha as its primary referent throughout.

147. Athenaeus, *Banquet* 10.454b–f (Olson, LCL, V.174–79; Kaibel, II.487–88 [= 10.80]; trans. Yonge, II.717–18).

148. Athenaeus, *Banquet* 10.454b–c (Olson, LCL, V.174–77; Kaibel, II.487 [= 10.80]; trans. Yonge, II.717 [modified]). The citation is from Euripides, *Fragment* 382 (Snell and Kannicht, *Tragicorum Graecorum Fragmenta,* V.1, 429–30; Collard and Cropp, LCL, VII.420–21).

149. Athenaeus, *Banquet* 10.454d (Olson, LCL, V.176–77; Kaibel, II.487–88 [= 10.80]; trans. Yonge, II.717 [modified]). The citation is from Agathon, *Telephos,* fr. 4 (Nauck, *Tragicorum Graecorum Fragmenta,* 2nd ed., 764); discussed by Cribiore, *Gymnastics,* 160; and Aasgaard, *Childhood,* 144–45.

150. Athenaeus, *Banquet* 10.454e–f (Olson, LCL, V.176–79; Kaibel, II.488 [= 10.80]; trans. Yonge, II.718 [modified]). The citation is from Theodectes, fr. 6 (Nauck, *Tragicorum Graecorum Fragmenta,* 2nd ed., 803–4).

151. Athenaeus, *Banquet* 10.454f (Olson, LCL, V.178–79; Kaibel, II.488 [= 10.80]; trans. Yonge, II.718).

152. Athenaeus, *Banquet* 10.454c and 10.454e (Olson, LCL, V.176–77 and V.178–79; Kaibel, II.487 and 488 [= 10.80]; trans. Yonge, II.717 and 718).

153. *Paidika* 6.4 (Burke, *De infantia,* 319).

154. The fact that this letter tradition was preserved in a work of Euripides may strengthen this argument for the cultivation of such vocabularies in scholastic milieus. As Cribiore notes (*Gymnastics,* 179), Euripides was part of "the cultural package of students at the primary level . . . gained by copying a short text as an exercise in penmanship, [and] enriched when he attempted to read the same text with syllables and words separated." As evidence, she cites a first-century wax tablet with Euripides's *Trojan Women* divided into syllables as an aid to students (*T. Berol.* inv. AM 17651; Cribiore, *Writing,* 216, no. 182), and a third-century BCE papyrus with school exercises containing short passages from two of Euripides's other works (*Phoenissae* and *Ino*) (Cribiore, *Writing,* 269, no. 379).

155. Aasgaard, *Childhood,* 144–46 (quote at 146).

156. On the widespread custom of drilling the forms of the letters after thorough memorization of their names, see Dionysius of Halicarnassus, *On Literary Composi-*

tion 25.211 (Roberts, 268–69); Quintilian, *Institutes* 1.1.24 (Russell, LCL, I.76–77); and Harris, *Ancient Literacy,* 240. In some cases, penmanship may have been "taught side by side with the syllabic method" (Cribiore, *Gymnastics,* 176–77; see pp. 176–81 for evidence on wax tablets and papyri).

157. On writing as a physical, mnemonic discipline: see Connerton, *How Societies Remember,* 72–77; see also J. Assmann (*Religion and Cultural Memory,* 89), who calls writing a "memory technique." I want to resist the opposition Assmann sets up between writing and the body when he suggests writing "takes the place of the body as a practice of memory" (*Religion and Cultural Memory,* 91). On writing as a set of socially learned bodily dispositions and skills, see the work of Marcel Mauss and Pierre Bourdieu on *habitus:* Mauss, "Les techniques du corps"; Bourdieu, *Outline;* and Bourdieu and Wacquant, *Invitation.*

158. Quintilian (*Institutes* 1.1.27; Russell, LCL, I.76–79) mentions how schoolmasters would sometimes physically guide the hands of their pupils in tracing the lines of the letters they were learning (see also García, *Pupils,* 38).

159. Brian McNeil ("Jesus and the Alphabet," 126–28) discusses a proverb involving school and letters in the *Story of Aḥiḳar,* arguing that it may have been a source for the tales of Jesus and the teachers in the *Paidika.*

160. Dornseiff (*Alphabet,* 158–68) catalogues numerous examples of ancient objects adorned with letters, including ceramic vases (I.1–24), pieces of stone (II.1–30 and IV.7), architectural bricks (III.1–10), terracotta figurines (IV.1 and 6), lead and wooden tablets (IV.2–3), bronze objects (IV.4–5 and 8), and wall surfaces (V.1–9). The provenance of these objects ranges widely, from amphitheaters (II.5; III.3) and baths (II.8; III.1–2), to funerary settings (I.14, 20; II.11, 14, 28, 30) and worship spaces (II.6–7, 9, 16, 17; III.4). One of these objects may have been associated with a local school: a terracotta lamp from Pompeii molded in the form of a bald-headed man with a scroll in his hand (perhaps a "Schulmeister") is adorned with the first six letters of the Greek alphabet (αβγδεζ) (Naples Museum, inv. 109, 411; Dornseiff, *Alphabet,* 167 [IV.6]).

161. On evidence for the use of letters to ward off baleful influence in funerary practice, including by Christians, see Dornseiff, *Alphabet,* 75–77; Dieterich, "ABC-Denkmäler," 202–28; and Rossi, "Vaso," 125–46.

162. Along these lines, Paulissen ("Jésus à l'école," 169) has analyzed the three school scenes as illustrating "different facets" of Jesus' divinity in narrative progression (see also Burke, "Depictions of Children," 395). According to Paulissen's analysis, the first story emphasizes his place (*taxis*) in the divine (i.e., trinitarian) hierarchy, the second highlights his power (*dunamis*) to perform miracles, and the third features his divine inspiration as an interpreter. In my analysis, I focus less on the theological aspects of Jesus' representation in these stories and more on the way that his learning of letters would have been contextualized by discrete sets of educational and ritual practices in the late ancient world.

163. Dornseiff, *Alphabet,* 15–16, 62. In keeping with such solar observation, letters were also used as chronological markers: on the wall of a temple dedicated to the god Serapis (Stratonikeia, western Asia Minor), a late second-century grammarian left behind a poem comprising twelve verses and 365 characters (the number of months and days in the year), with letters associated with each verse and numbered according

to the days of the month (Kaibel, *Epigrammata Graeca,* 495–96 [epigram no. 1096; 189 CE]).

164. Such a connection between writing and the world was consonant with the thought of Pythagorean philosophers, who derived numerical and alphabetical significance from the structure of the universe (*ta panta,* "the Entirety"). Thus, Aristotle describes how the Pythagoreans "came to believe . . . that the elements of numbers [*ta tōn arithmōn stoicheia*] are the elements of everything [*tōn ontōn stoicheia pantōn*]" (*Metaphysics* I.5.1–2 [985b–86a]; Treddenick, LCL, 32–33 [translation modified]; Barry, *Greek Qabalah,* 28–29). In his late second- or early third-century commentary on Aristotle's *Metaphysics,* Alexander of Aphrodisias comments, "The universe corresponds to the twenty-four letters [*stoicheia*], because the constellations add up to twelve, the planets to eight, and the elements [*stoicheia*] to four" (Alexander of Aphrodisias, *Commentary on Aristotle's Metaphysics* 814 [=N 6; Arist. P. 1093a]: ed. Hayduck, 835; see also Dornseiff, *Alphabet,* 88, note 2).

165. Barry, *Greek Qabalah,* 60. Artemidorus uses numbers and letters for prognoses of death: see his *Interpretation of Dreams* (*Oneirocritica*) 2.70 (Pack, 196–203); also Bouché-Leclercq, *Histoire,* I.320; and Dornseiff, *Alphabet,* 99–100. Ancient alphabetic acrostics are attested in Jewish texts (e.g., Jeremiah 1–4; Ps.-Nahum 1; Wisdom of Solomon 31:10–31; Sirach 51:13–29; and Psalms 9, 10, 25, 34, 37, 111, 112, 119, 145) and in Greek literature (e.g., the *Alexander Romance,* the *Sybilline Oracles,* and Origen's *Commentary on Psalms*): see Dornseiff, *Alphabet,* 27, 137, 146–51. Finally, there are several examples from antiquity where letters were used on dice, *astragaloi,* and roulette wheels in oracular contexts: e.g., Pausanias, *Description of Greece* 7.25.10 (Jones, LCL, III.326–27); Ammianus Marcellinus, *History* 29.1.28–32 (Rolfe, LCL, III.202–7); Dornseiff, *Alphabet,* 151–55; and Heinwetter, *Würfel- und Buchstabenorakel.* On acrostics, palindromes, and figure writing, see also Habinek, "Situating Literacy," 114–40.

166. See, e.g., Zosimus of Panopolis' treatise *On the Letter Omega* (late third or early fourth century CE), in which he highlights the letter's alchemical and astrological properties: in chapter 1, for example, the author associates omega with the planet Saturn (Kronos) and with sulfur (*to theion,* a play on words with the adjective *theios,* "divine"; trans. Jackson, 16–17 and 41, note 8; Berthelot and Ruelle, *Collection,* vol. 2.3, 228; Barry, *Greek Qabalah,* 47). For a critical edition of Zosimus's writings, see Mertens, *Les alchimistes grecs. Tome IV.1.* For concise, helpful introductions to ancient alchemy and astrology, with translations of selected relevant texts, see Luck, *Arcana Mundi,* 307–58 (ch. 5, "Astrology"), and 359–78 (ch. 6, "Alchemy").

167. Berthelot, *Introduction,* 74; Barry, *Greek Qabalah,* 44–47; Dornseiff, *Alphabet,* 125. Many surviving alchemical handbooks are marked up with geometric shapes and cryptic alphabetic (or numerical) symbols: see, e.g., Berthelot and Ruelle, *Collection,* I.156, fig. 29; and "Textes grecs," 79–80. On the early history of alchemy, see Lindsay, *Origins of Alchemy;* also Halleux, "Alchemy."

168. Barry, *Greek Qabalah,* 58, 116; Dornseiff, *Alphabet,* 84–85. In his *Arts of Grammar* (ch. 6: Uhlig, 9–16; Lallot, *La grammaire,* 44–47), Dionysius of Thrace (ca. 170–ca. 90 BCE) apportions each of the zodiacal signs to one of three different categories of letters: "voiced" (*phōnēenta* = vowels), "semivoiced" (*ēmiphōna* = continuant consonants, or semivowels), and "voiceless" (*aphōna* = plosive consonants) (see also Kemp, "*Tekhne*

Grammatike," 343–63). There has been some debate over the authenticity of Dionysius's authorship of this work, but see Robins ("Dionysius Thrax," 67, note 1), for a generally positive appraisal (apart from "a few spurious later additions"). In excerpts from Vettius Valens (second century CE; Bassus, Cumont, Martin, and Oliver, *Catalogus*, IV.146–49), one finds a similar commentary on such astrological correspondences, with pairs of letters (alpha-nu, beta-xi, gamma-omicron, etc.) matched to the twelve zodiacal signs. In his *Anthology* (ed. Pingree), the same author presents mathematical interpretations of the constellations where the letters are read as numbers. For another example of commentary on the letters and their phonetic classification, see Philo of Alexandria, *Questions and Answers on Genesis* 4.117 (Marcus, LCL, Supplement 1, 399–401), where the author likens the vowels to the mind, the semivowels to the senses, and the consonants to the body.

169. Isaiah 34:4; Plotinus, *Enneads* 3.1.6 (Armstrong, LCL, III.26–29); see also Julian of Halicarnassus (Usener, "Aus Julian," in *Kleine Schriften*, IV.321–39; cited by Dornseiff, *Alphabet*, 89–91).

170. See, e.g., *PGM* XIII.1–734 (Preisendanz, 86–120; Betz, 172–89); also Philo of Alexandria (ca. 30 BCE–45 CE), *On the Creation of the World* 126 (Colson and Whitaker, LCL, I.98–99); discussed by Dornseiff (*Alphabet*, 43–44) and Barry (*Greek Qabalah*, 65).

171. Plutarch, *On the E at Delphi* 4 (=386A–B) (Babbitt, *Moralia*, LCL, V.206–7); Barry, *Greek Qabalah*, 39–40. The base of a statue dedicated to Apollo in Syrian Antioch carries an inscription with all seven vowels (Perdrizet, "Une inscription d'Antioche," 62; also Deubner, in *Archiv für Religionswissenschaft* 9 [1906], 146; Weinreich, "Heros," 66ff.; and Dornseiff, *Alphabet*, 45–46). Elsewhere in antiquity, vowel sequences marked oracular verses associated with the same god: Eusebius, *Preparation of the Gospel* 11.6 (Mras, GCS 43.2, 13–20); Macrobius, *Saturnalia* 1.19 (Kaster, SCBO, 109–12; see also Kaster's three-volume edition in LCL).

172. Nicomachus of Gerasa, *Manual of Harmony* (*Enchiridion*) 6 (Jan, *Musici Scriptores Graeci*, 277 [cf. the editor's comments on p. 228]; trans. Gersh, *From Iamblichus to Ereugena*, 295); see also Dieterich, *Mithrasliturgie*, 34; Dornseiff, *Alphabet*, 52; and Barry, *Greek Qabalah*, 38–39.

173. *PGM* LXIII.1–7 (second or third cent. CE; Preisendanz, II.196; Betz, 294–95).

174. *PGM* XIII.760–820 (Preisendanz, II.122–24; Betz, 190–91); discussed by Barry, *Greek Qabalah*, 48; and Dornseiff, *Alphabet*, 42.

175. *PGM* XIII.824–42 (Preisendanz, II.124–25; Betz, 191). The practice of hymning the vowels is independently attested by a first-century BCE Alexandrian source: Demetrius, *On Style* 71 (Roberts, LCL, 347). On the performative context indicated by such sources, see Barry, *Greek Qabalah*, 37–38; and Dornseiff, *Alphabet*, 42–43, 47. In contrast to the orality of vowels, Dornseiff (p. 61) argues that the consonants had more of a written provenance, due to the fact that they were harder to pronounce.

176. *Marsanes* NHC X.1.26–30 (Pierson, *Nag Hammadi Codices IX and X*, 292–305; Robinson et al., *Nag Hammadi Library*, 466–68). This conforms to the phonetic hierarchy established by Dionysius of Thrace (*Art of Grammar* 6: Uhlig, 9–16; Lallot, 44–47). In *Marsanes* (NHC X.1.30), the consonants submit to "the hidden gods" and to the vowels "by means of beat and pitch and silence and impulse."

177. Brakke, *Gnostics,* 82.

178. Clement of Alexandria, *Stromata* 6.16.141.6–145.7 (Früchtel, Stählin, and Treu, GCS 52.15, 503–6; Descourtieux, SC 446, 342–50; *PG* 9.812; *ANF* 2.514). The Gnostic *Books of Jeu* (third century CE) likewise interpret the alpha and omega of Revelation in light of the ritualized practice of using vowel sounds to call upon the name of God. In the first *Book* (ch. 40; Schmidt, *Books of Jeu,* 90), the heavenly hosts call upon the name of God with a sequence of letters that starts with "ααα ωωω" and includes the other Greek vowels, each repeated three times. In the second *Book* (ch. 50; Schmidt, *The Books of Jeu,* 124), these same hosts invoke the Father with sequences of vowels repeated seven times (ωωωωωωω [εεε] εεεε υυυυυυυ) and proclaim that "the entirety has come from the *alpha* and will return to [the *omega*]." The second- or third-century Gnostic text, *Pistis Sophia* (IV.136: ed. Schmidt, 353), also has Jesus call upon the Father with a series of vowels (α ε η ι υ ω) and with the name ιαω (probably a Greek equivalent to the Hebrew Tetragrammaton). For a discussion of these sources, see Dornseiff, *Alphabet,* 40–41, 48, 82 (cf. 122).

179. Bovon, "Names and Numbers," 267.

180. *PGM* XIII.1–734 (Preisendanz, II.86–120; Betz, 172–89); also Dieterich, *Abraxas,* 173, 177–78, 182, 185, 197–98, 201, 204; and Dornseiff, *Alphabet,* 37, 45–47, 60. On the name Iaō, see Scholem, *Origins of the Kabbalah,* 32–33, note 55.

181. See, e.g., *PGM* XIII.39 (Preisendanz, II.89; Betz, 173); Meyer and Smith, *Coptic Texts,* 87, 92, 99, 101, 114, 231, 234; Barry, *Greek Qabalah,* 48–49. At Sinai and elsewhere, stone inscriptions have been discovered with sequences of the seven vowels repeated in forward or reverse order (from alpha to omega and from omega to alpha), and these may derive from analogous practices of divine petition (Dornseiff, *Alphabet,* 50–51, 58).

182. *PGM* X.36–50 (Preisendanz, II.53; Betz, 150); Deissmann, *Licht vom Osten,* 341; Dornseiff, *Alphabet,* 59.

183. Meyer and Smith, *Coptic Texts,* 98, 102, 118, 391; see also Barry, *Greek Qabalah,* 148–52; Dornseiff, *Alphabet,* 65; Erman and Krebs, *Aus dem Papyrus,* 262. The names of the four incorporeal creatures thus form an acrostic or *notarikon* on the first Greek letter. In the same corpus of spells, the twenty-four elders from Revelation are reimagined as heavenly figures and are assigned names beginning with the twenty-four letters of the Greek alphabet (Meyer and Smith, *Coptic Texts,* 118, 333).

184. Genesis 1:1–2:4; John 1:1–18. In Greek philosophical literature, this logic traces back to Plato, who imagines that God created the world by "forming a shape like the letter *chi* (X)," bending the ends inward and fastening them to form "two circles, one inner and one outer" (Plato, *Timaeus* 35a–36d: Bury, LCL, VII.64–73; trans. Lee, 72–73; cited by Barry, *Greek Qabalah,* 159–60).

185. *Poimandrēs* 10 (Nock and Festugière, *Corpus Hermeticum,* I.10; Layton, *Gnostic Scriptures,* 454); also Dornseiff, *Alphabet,* 119.

186. *PGM* XIII.1–734 (Preisendanz, II.86–120; Betz, 172–89); also Dieterich, *Abraxas,* 185.

187. The *Book of Jubilees* (first century CE) speaks about the power of an oath made "by the praiseworthy, illustrious, and great, splendid, marvelous, powerful, and great name which made the heavens and the earth and everything together" (*Jubilees* 36:7:

VanderKam, I.198 [Ethiopic text]; II.238 [English trans.]; also Charles, *Book of Jubilees,* 176–77). Likewise, in the contemporaneous *Prayer of Manasseh,* it was by means of God's "terrible and glorious name" that the divine word "closed the abyss and sealed it" at the moment of creation (*Prayer of Manasseh* 1:3: Horst and Newman, 166). For a fuller discussion of the divine name in Jewish sources, see Janowitz, *Icons of Power,* 26–28. The first-century Christian author of *1 Clement* echoes this theme, identifying the divine name as "the primal source of all creation" (*1 Clement* 59.3; Holmes, *Apostolic Fathers,* 3rd ed., 122–25). Guy Stroumsa ("Nameless God," 230–43) notes how Christian "theologies of the name" were grounded in long-standing Jewish attitudes and practices.

188. *Pistis Sophia* IV.136 (Schmidt, 353; trans. Horner, 180); also Barry, *Greek Qabalah,* 49. A later scribe also appended a section at the end of the first book of *Pistis Sophia,* in which he presents a mystical reading of God's name in which the letter *alpha* predominates: "This is the name of the Deathless One *AAA* ŌŌŌ. And this is the name of the sound by which the Perfect Man was moved *III.* But these are the interpretations of the names of these Mysteries. The first is *AAA.* Its interpretation is *PhPhPh.* The second is *MMM* or ŌŌŌ. Its interpretation is *AAA.* The third is *PsPsPs.* Its interpretation is *OOO.* The fourth is *PhPhPh.* Its interpretation is *AAA.* He who is upon the throne is *AAA.* This is the interpretation of the second *AAAA AAAA AAAA.* This is the interpretation of the whole name" (Schmidt, 126; trans. Horner, 62). For discussions of this text, see Barry, *Greek Qabalah,* 49 and 107; Dornseiff, *Alphabet,* 40–41. See also *PGM* IV.475–829 (the so-called *Mithras Liturgy*), which identifies the seven-voweled divine name of AEĒIOUŌ as the "first origin of my origin" (Preisendanz, I.88–100; Betz, 48–54; cited by Janowitz, *Icons of Power,* 81–2).

189. Clement of Alexandria, *Stromata* 5.1.8.6 (Früchtel, Stählin, and Treu, GCS 52.15, 331; Boulluec, SC 278, 36–38 [= 5.1.8.5–7]; trans. *ANF* 2.446). In the Greek LXX, Abraham's name change involves the addition of a single alpha (from Abram to Abraam).

190. John Chrysostom, *Homily 9 on the Epistle to the Hebrews* (*PG* 63.77). Dornseiff (*Alphabet,* 21 and 29) cites this source and also discusses a later Greek *Alphabetarion on the Passion of Christ* in which the letter *alpha* is read in similar terms as the "beginning (*archē*) of the world."

191. *Paidika* 6.2b (Burke, *De infantia,* 313, my emphasis). Immediately prior to this, Jesus had criticized Zacchaeus's inadequacy as a teacher by telling him, "As for the name with which you are named, you are a stranger."

192. *Paidika* 6.2d (Burke, *De infantia,* 315).

193. Diels (*Elementum,* 44) believed that astrological applications of the word *stoicheion* derived directly from such grammatical instruction, while Dornseiff (*Alphabet,* 15–16) argued that such astrological and grammatical applications developed concurrently in ancient Greek culture. For continuations of this debate over the origins of the term, see Voll-Graff, "Elementum," 89–115; Koller, "Stoicheion," 161–74; and Burkert, ΣΤΟΙΧΕΙΟΝ, 167–97. For a more recent treatment of the linguistic and cosmological aspects of *stoicheia,* see Falcon, *Aristotle,* 48–51.

194. Nicomachus of Gerasa, *Excerpts* 6 (Jan, *Musici scriptores Graeci,* 276–78; trans. Levin, 194–95); Dornseiff, *Alphabet,* 33.

195. Terentianus Maurus, *On Letters* 247–78 (Cignolo, I.21–23); Dornseiff, *Alphabet,* 114–15.

196. Proclus, *Commentary on Plato's Timaeus,* book 3 (*Tim.* 36d) 226B–C (Diehl, II.278; trans. Taylor, II.141); Barry, *Greek Qabalah,* 166–67.

197. Proclus, *Commentary on the First Book of Euclid's Elements* 108, cf. 147–58 (trans. Morrow, 88, cf. 117–25).

198. Proclus, *Commentary on the First Book of Euclid's Elements* 128–29 (Morrow, 104).

199. Proclus, *A Commentary on the First Book of Euclid's Elements* 132–34 (Morrow, 106–7).

200. Proclus, *A Commentary on the First Book of Euclid's Elements* 166 (Morrow, 131). In reference to these passages, Barry (*Greek Qabalah,* 169) writes, "The symbolism referred to would have automatically attached to those Greek letters with simple geometric forms, such as *gamma* or *tau* (the right angle), *delta* (the triangle), *iota* (the perpendicular line), *lambda* (the acute angle) and *omicron* (the circle)." Dornseiff (*Alphabet,* 22) notes Porphyry's similar treatment of the letter *delta,* as reported by Eusebius of Caesarea, *Preparation of the Gospel* 3.7.4 (Mras, GCS 43.1, I.124).

201. Paulinus of Nola, *Carmen* 19.645–47: *Alpha crucem circumstat et phi, tribus utraque virgis / littera diversam trina ratione figuram / perficiens quia perfectum est mens una, triplex vis* (Hartel, GSEL 30, 140); see also Theodosius of Alexandria's sixth-century treatise *On Grammar* (ed. Goettling, 4; Dorseiff, *Alphabet,* 21), which includes a similar commentary on the letter *alpha*'s "three lines."

202. See, e.g., Wink, "Elements," 225–48; Betz, *Galatians,* 204–5, 215–17; Schweizer, "Slaves," 455–68; Martyn, "Christ, the Elements of the Cosmos, and the Law," 16–39; Martyn, *Galatians,* 393–406, 411–12; Boer, "Meaning," 204–24; and Engberg-Pedersen, *Cosmology and Self,* 90–92.

203. See, e.g., Boer, "Meaning," 216–17, 222–24.

204. See also Clement of Alexandria (*Stromata* 5.8.48.8–49.1; Früchtel, Stählin, and Treu, GCS 52.15, 359–60; Boulluec, SC 278, 104; *ANF* 2.456), who links children's instruction in the twenty-four letters (*stoicheia*) with the knowledge of the cosmological elements (*stoicheia*), referring to "the arrangement of the letters/elements [*stoicheia*] and the world [*kosmos*]."

205. Dornseiff, *Alphabet,* 57.

206. Irenaeus, *Against Heresies* 1.20 (=1.13–22 *TLG*) (Rousseau and Doutreleau, SC 264, 288–95; *ANF* 1.334–47); Dornseiff, *Alphabet,* 35, 126–33. For a comprehensive discussion of Irenaeus and other sources on the life and teachings of Marcus, see Förster, *Marcus Magus,* esp. 54–388. On the question of provenance, Layton (*Gnostic Scriptures,* 268) associates Marcus with Alexandria, while Markschies (*Valentinus Gnosticus?* 262, note 20) argues for an Asian or Gallic provenance. Förster (*Marcus Magus,* 395) concludes that the evidence for geography is equivocal, insofar as it presents a "mixture of western and eastern motifs" (*Mischung aus westlichen und östlichen Motiven*) and yields "no clear affiliation . . . in one or the other direction" (*keine eindeutige Zugehörigkeit . . . zu der einen oder der anderen Richtung*).

207. Layton, *Gnostic Scriptures,* 217–22.

208. For a later account of Marcus's speculations on the alphabet, probably dependent on Irenaeus, see Ps.-Tertullian, *Against All Heresies* 5 (Kroymann, CSEL 47, 222; CCSL 2, 1407–8; *ANF* 3.653 [modified]): "After these there were not wanting a Marcus

and a Colorbasus, composing a novel heresy out of the Greek alphabet. For they affirm that without those letters truth cannot be found; nay more, that in those letters is comprised the whole plenitude and perfection of truth (*plenitudinem et perfectionem veritatis; plērōma kai teleiōsis alētheias*); for this was why Christ said, 'I am the Alpha and the Omega.' . . . These men run through their Ω, Ψ, X Φ, Υ, T—through the whole alphabet, indeed, up to A and B—and compute ogdoads and decads. So we may grant it useless and idle to recount all their trifles" (cf. Dornseiff, *Alphabet*, 71 and 81).

209. Irenaeus, *Against Heresies* 1.13.4 (Rousseau and Doutreleau, SC 264, 197–200; *ANF* 1.335). For a detailed commentary on this passage, see Förster, *Marcus Magus*, 126–31.

210. Irenaeus, *Against Heresies* 1.14.1 (Rousseau and Doutreleau, SC 264, 208–10; *ANF* 1.336); Förster, *Marcus Magus*, 163–206, esp. 192–205.

211. Irenaeus, *Against Heresies* 1.14.2 (Rousseau and Doutreleau, SC 264, 212; *ANF* 1.336); Förster, *Marcus Magus*, 213–15.

212. Barry (*Greek Qabalah*, 115 and 117) explicitly compares Marcus' alphabetical methods to those of a grammarian, and Dornseiff (*Alphabet*, 34–35) likewise makes note of his employment of grammatical categories.

213. Irenaeus, *Against Heresies* 1.14.2 (Rousseau and Doutreleau, SC 264, 213–14; *ANF* 1.336–37); Förster, *Marcus Magus*, 218–20. The Pythagoreans interpreted the triangular letter *delta* (Δ) as the "the ultimate source of generation and of the production of species among things generated" (*archē geneseōs kai tēs tōn genētōn eidopoiias*): Proclus, *Commentary on the First Book of Euclid's Elements* 166: trans. Morrow, 131; cf. the citation of Porphyry on this subject by Eusebius of Caesarea, *Preparation of the Gospel* 3.7.4 (Mras, GCS 43.1, 124). The sixth-century anonymous treatise *On the Mystery of the Greek Letters* likewise identifies the letter *delta* as a "type" (*tupos*) of "creation" (*ktisis*) and connects it with the text of Genesis 1:1 ("In the beginning God created heaven and earth"), associating its base line with "the earth" (Copt. *pkah*) and its upper strokes with "the heaven of the heavens" (*tpe n-mpēue*): see *On the Mystery of the Greek Letters* 12 and 13 (Bandt, *Traktat*, 122 and 126). For a discussion, see Dornseiff, *Alphabet*, 22.

214. Irenaeus, *Against Heresies* 1.14.3 (Rousseau and Doutreleau, SC 264, 215–17; *ANF* 1.337). On this "body of truth," see Barry, *Greek Qabalah*, 108–11; and Förster, *Marcus Magus*, 220–28.

215. Förster, *Marcus Magus*, 222–26, with numerous textual and documentary examples cited in notes 137–42.

216. Irenaeus, *Against Heresies* 1.14.5–6; 1.15.1–2 (Rousseau and Doutreleau, SC 264, 220–26, 232–41; *ANF* 1.337–39). The six-letter Greek name for Jesus (*Iēsous*), for example, is understood to be "arithmetically symbolical." For commentary, see Förster, *Marcus Magus*, 233–64 and 312–43. On the wider use of numerology/arithmology in early Christian theology, including Valentinian contexts, see Kalvesmaki, "Formation"; and "Theology."

217. Irenaeus, *Against Heresies* 1.14.7–8 (Rousseau and Doutreleau, SC 264, 228–29; *ANF* 1.338); see also Barry, *Greek Qabalah*, 41; Dornseiff, *Alphabet*, 82–83; Förster, *Marcus Magus*, 277–79, 281–84.

218. Irenaeus, *Against Heresies* 1.15.5 and 1.16.3 (Rousseau and Doutreleau, SC 264, 249, and 261–62; my translation); Förster, *Marcus Magus*, 356–60.

219. Irenaeus, *Against Heresies* 1.20.1 (Rousseau and Doutreleau, SC 264, 288–89; *ANF* 1.344–45).This version of the story seems to conflate elements found in *Paidika* 6 and 13. There are, however, key differences in comparison with both accounts. First, in the "Marcosian" version, Jesus actually responds to the teacher by repeating the letter *alpha.* Second, the teacher asks him to recite the letter *beta.* Third, Jesus' final statement ("First tell me what Alpha is, and then I will tell you what Beta is") does not match either *Paidika* 6.3 ("First teach me the alpha and then I shall trust you to speak of the beta") or 13.2 ("You tell me first what beta is and I shall tell you what alpha is").

220. Irenaeus, *Against Heresies* 1.20.1 (Rousseau and Doutreleau, SC 264, 289; *ANF* 1.345).

221. Attridge and MacRae, in *Nag Hammadi Codex I,* I.55–117 (text and translation), and II.39–135 (notes); trans. Attridge and MacRae, in Robinson et al., *Nag Hammadi Library,* 40–51. For a critical edition, see Malinine et al., *Evangelium Veritatis;* trans. Layton, *Gnostic Scriptures,* 253–64 (with supplemental alterations).

222. *Gospel of Truth* I, 3.19 (Attridge and MacRae, *Nag Hammadi Codex I,* I.86–87; trans. Attridge and MacRae, in Robinson et al., *Nag Hammadi Library,* 41); see also Tite, *Valentinian Ethics,* 258–59.

223. Attridge and MacRae (*Nag Hammadi Codex I,* II.55) make the observation that this passage is "possibly an allusion to Luke 2:46–49 or to a non-canonical infancy gospel." The Gnostic *Tripartite Tractate* also may allude to these stories about Jesus' teaching in childhood: "About the [one] who appeared in flesh, they believed without any doubt that he is the Son of the unknown God. . . . Before he had taken them up, and while he was still a child, they testified that he had already begun to preach" (*Tripartite Tractate* I,5.133.27–28; Attridge and Pagels, in *Nag Hammadi Codex I,* I.330–31; trans. Attridge and Mueller, in Robinson et al., *Nag Hammadi Library,* 101). On the appearance of the *Logos* in the form of an infant or newborn child in early Christian literature (including Gnostic texts), see Markschies, *Valentinus Gnosticus?* 207–12.

224. It is noteworthy that a reference to Jesus' education is also found in the Syriac version of the *Acts of Thomas* (ch. 79: Wright, *Apocryphal Acts,* I.248 [Syriac text]; II.215 (English trans.]), which celebrates the fact that Jesus "was reared that the perfect rearing might be seen in him; and went to school that through him perfect wisdom might be known; he taught his teacher, because he was the true teacher and the master of the wise." This passage implies knowledge of at least one of the teacher episodes from the *Paidika,* in either oral or written form. The Syriac recension, however, contains later emendations, so it is unclear whether this detail was original. The Greek version does not contain any reference to Jesus' schooling: instead, it notes only that Jesus "was raised up through infancy so that the full maturity may be manifest through his adulthood" (Greek *Acts of Thomas* 79; Lipsius and Bonnet, *Acta apostolorum apocrypha,* vol. 2.2, 194). For a discussion of both versions, see Burke, *De infantia,* 30–31.

225. On the Valentinians' self-identification in terms of a philosophical school, see McGuire, "Valentinus and the *Gnostike Hairesis*"; Lüdemann, "History," 129; Markschies, "Valentinian Gnosticism," 401–38; Dunderberg, *Beyond Gnosticism,* 3–4; and Tite, *Valentinian Ethics,* 213–16, 258–59.

Chapter 6. Jews and Christians

1. See, e.g., Becker and Reed, eds., *Ways That Never Parted;* and Boyarin, *Border Lines.*

2. For this reconstruction of the Johannine community's history, see especially Brown, *Gospel according to John,* esp. I.lxvii–lxxix; and Martyn, *History and Theology.* The literature on this subject is voluminous, but for assessments of the state of the question over the past two decades, see Smith, *Theology,* 48–56; Rissi, "'Juden,'" *ANRW* 2.26.3, 2099–41; Reinhartz, "Johannine Community," 111–38; Bieringer, Pollefyt, and Vandecasteele-Vanneuville, eds., *Anti-Judaism;* Diefenbach, *Konflikt Jesu;* and Reinhartz, "Gospel of John," 99–116. Assumptions about a Jewish background to the Gospel of John have also motivated attempts among source critics to reconstruct an earlier "Jewish Christian" form of the gospel: see, e.g., Siegert, *Erstenwurf;* and Siegert, *Synopse.*

3. This apparent ambivalence has led Gaston ("Anti-Judaism," 153) to call Luke-Acts "one of the most pro-Jewish and one of the most anti-Jewish writings in the New Testament." Since the nineteenth century, the majority of scholars have seen the anti-Jewish elements in the text as predominating: see, e.g., Overbeck, *Kürze Erklärung;* Baur, "Über Zweck," 59–178; Conzelmann, *Theology of St. Luke;* Haenchen, *Acts of the Apostles;* and Sanders, *Jews in Luke-Acts.* Other scholars have argued that the anti-Jewish character of Luke-Acts has been overstated in this history of scholarship, pointing out places where the Pharisees and the Jewish community are portrayed more positively: see especially the work of Jervell: "Das gespaltene Israel," 68–96; "Acts of the Apostles," 17–32; *Unknown Paul;* "Church of Jews," 11–20; and "God's Faithfulness," 29–36. A similar perspective is put forward in Brawley, *Luke-Acts and the Jews.*

These polar approaches have led Joseph B. Tyson to seek a middle way. Drawing on Wolgang Iser's concept of the "implied reader," Tyson argues that the ambiguous presentation of the Jews in Luke-Acts was connected with the fact that this two-volume work was designed for an audience with relatively limited acquaintance with, but a deep affinity for, Jewish religious life—a social posture that he associates with Gentile "Godfearers": see Tyson, "Jews and Judaism," 19–38; *Images of Judaism;* and *Luke, Judaism, and the Scholars.*

4. Brawley, *Luke-Acts and the Jews,* 4, commenting on the work of Tiede (*Prophecy and History*), Juel (*Luke-Acts,* 7, 31, 68, 100, 101–12, 115–20), and Salmon, "Hypothesis."

5. On Jewish-Christian tensions reflected in the *Paidika,* see Wilde, *Treatment of the Jews,* 220; Schonfield, *Readings,* 13–14, 18–19; and Wilson, *Related Strangers,* 84–85 (discussed by Burke, *De infantia,* 83–84, 103).

6. *Paidika* 2.3 (Burke, *De infantia,* 303–5).

7. *Paidika* 2.4–5 (Burke, *De infantia,* 305).

8. *Paidika* 3.1 (Burke, *De infantia* 305). Annas may have originally been identified as "the scribe" (*grammateus*) rather than the "High Priest" (*archiereus*) in the early text tradition, as reflected in selected Greek (Ga, Gb, Gd), Syriac (SyrW), Ethiopic, and Irish versions of the *Paidika* and in the *Protevangelium of James.* As such, the reading of "High Priest" would have been "a change made likely to bring Annas' title into accord

with the adult Jesus accounts" (Burke, *De infantia,* 305, note 8; cf. 344, note 3; and 404, note 1).

9. *Paidika* 3.2 (Burke, *De infantia,* 307). Amsler ("Les *Paidika Iesou,*" 452–58) likewise reads the story about the pools of water in chapters 2 and 3 as an anti-Jewish polemic, but (in support of a later date for the *Paidika*) he argues that the story may have had its roots in the tensions between the Christian and Jewish communities in fourth-century Antioch.

10. Isaiah 11:1 and 27:6 (LXX; Rahlfs, II.581 and II.599).

11. Jeremiah 17:8 and 23:5 (LXX; Rahlfs, II.692 and II.683).

12. *Paidika* 2.1 (Burke, *De infantia,* 303).

13. Isaiah 40:24 (LXX; Rahlfs, II.620).

14. Ezekiel 17:1–10 and 19:10–14 (LXX; Rahlfs, II.796–97 and II.801); see also Hosea 9:16 (LXX; Rahlfs, II.498), where Ephraim has been "dried up at his roots and no longer produces fruit" (*tas rizas autou exēranthē, karpon ouketi mē enegkē$_i$*).

15. Wisdom of Sirach 23:25–26 and 40:15–16 (LXX; Rahlfs, II.417 and II.447); cf. Wisdom of Solomon 4:3–5 (LXX; Rahlfs, II.349), where the children of the ungodly are "young boughs" or "shoots" (*kladoi*) uprooted by the violent strength of the wind (*hupo bias anemone edrizōthēsetai*) and without "fruit" (*karpos*).

16. Job 14:10–12a (LXX; Rahlfs, II.294). For similar images, see also Job 15:29–34 and 18:16–19.

17. *Paidika* 5 (Burke, *De infantia,* 307).

18. *Paidika* 4.1–2 (Burke, *De infantia,* 307).

19. Matthew 24:9; Mark 13:3; Luke 1:69–71 and 6:22–23.

20. On the fictional character of the dialogue, see, e.g., Sanders, *Schismatics;* and Johnson, *Among the Gentiles,* 366, note 7; *pace* Horner (*Listening to Trypho,* 107 and back jacket).

21. Justin Martyr, *Dialogue with Trypho* 35.8 (Marcovich, 129; *ANF* 1.212).

22. Justin Martyr, *Dialogue with Trypho* 39.1 (Marcovich, 134; *ANF* 1.214).

23. Justin Martyr, *Dialogue with Trypho* 61.5 and 85.8 (Marcovich, 176 and 218; *ANF* 1.228 and 242).

24. Justin Martyr, *Dialogue with Trypho* 133.38 and 133.40 (Marcovich, 301; *ANF* 1.266); cf. 134.34–35 and 136.3 (Marcovich, 303 and 306; *ANF* 1.267 and 268).

25. *Paidika* 5.1 (Burke, *De infantia,* 307).

26. Justin Martyr, *Dialogue with Trypho* 16.2–4 (Marcovich, 96–97; *ANF* 1.202, modified).

27. Justin Martyr, *Dialogue with Trypho* 19.2 (Marcovich, 100; *ANF* 1.203). For a more detailed discussion of Justin's view of Jewish circumcision, see Jacobs, *Christ Circumcised,* ch. 2.

28. Origen of Alexandria, *Against Celsus* 2.25 (Borret, SC 132, 354; Chadwick, 90).

29. Origen of Alexandria, *Against Celsus* 1.55 (Borret, SC 132, 224–28; Chadwick, 50).

30. Origen of Alexandria, *Against Celsus* 2.8 and 4.22 ("One fact, then, which proves that Jesus was something divine and sacred, is this, that Jews should have suffered on His account now for a lengthened time calamities of such severity") (Borret, SC 132, 298–300; SC 136, 234–38; Chadwick, 71–73 and 198–99).

31. *Paidika* 5.1 (Burke, *De infantia,* 309).

32. *Paidika* 5.1 (Burke, *De infantia* 307).

33. Justin Martyr, *Dialogue with Trypho* 134.1 (Marcovich, 301; *ANF* 1.266).

34. Justin Martyr, *Dialogue with Trypho* 139.1 (Marcovich, 309; *ANF* 1.269).

35. Origen, *Against Celsus,* 1.32 and 2.57 (Borret, SC 132, 162–64 and 420; Chadwick, 31–32 and 111).

36. Origen, *Against Celsus* 2.79 (Borret, SC 132, 474; Chadwick, 127). It is significant that Origen goes on to note that "they, *whether Jews or Greeks,* who lead astray those that follow them, accuse us of seducing men" (my emphasis).

37. Origen, *Against Celsus* 4.74 (Borret, SC 136, 368; Chadwick, 243).

38. At least one later scribe acknowledged this comment in an editorial addition he made to his manuscript of the *Paidika:* a variant reading in a fourteenth century manuscript from Mount Athos in Greece (*Cod. Vatopedi 37* = MS V, recension A) accentuates the reaction of a crowd of "Jews" who look on and are "very afraid and disturbed" by Jesus' judgment (Burke, *De infantia,* 348, note 5).

39. *Paidika* 6.2b–d (Burke, *De infantia,* 313–15).

40. *Paidika* 6.3 (Burke, *De infantia,* 319). The roots of this particular polemical trope may be traced to Luke 12:1 and 13:14–17 (cf. Matthew 22:18 and 23:13–36).

41. See, e.g., *Paidika* 17.4 (Burke, *De infantia,* 337), where the scribes and Pharisees bless Mary for being Jesus' mother.

42. Throughout this chapter, I use the adjectival phrase "Jewish-Christian" in two different ways. When I use it to modify nouns such as "encounter," "tensions," "controversy," and "conflict," I am referring to the often polemical interchanges between churches and synagogues through which increasingly separate "Jewish" and "Christian" theological and social identities were formed in late antiquity. When I use it (or the noun phrase "Jewish Christians") to refer to groups or social milieus, I am referring to (historically elusive) communities of Jesus followers—whether ethnic Jews or so-called Judaizing Gentiles—who adhered to the requirements of the Mosaic Law.

43. Nicolas, *Études,* esp. 290–94, 333–35; Wilde, *Treatment of the Jews,* 220; also Schonfield, *Readings,* 13–14, 18–19. For more recent arguments in favor of a Jewish-Christian provenance, see Voicu, "Verso," 7–95; Aarde, "Infancy Gospel," 826–50; Aarde, "Ebionite Tendencies," 353–82. There is a vast literature on evidence related to the history of "Jewish Christianity" in late antiquity: see, e.g., Schoeps, *Theologie und Geschichte;* Klijn and Reinink, *Patristic Evidence;* Pritz, *Nazarene Jewish Christianity;* Taylor, "Phenomenon," 313–34; Mimouni, "Pour une definition," 171–82; Klijn, *Jewish-Christian Gospel Tradition;* Mimouni, *Judéo-christianisme ancien;* Mimouni and Jones, eds., *Judéo-christianisme;* Boyarin, *Border Lines;* Marcus, "Jewish Christianity," 87–102; Becker and Reed, eds., *Ways That Never Parted;* Marcus, "Jewish Christianity," 87–102; Paget, "Definition," 22–52; Jackson-McCabe, ed., *Jewish Christianity Reconsidered;* Finley, "Ebionites"; and Boyarin, "Rethinking Jewish Christianity."

44. Neusner, "Zacchaeus/Zakkai," 57–59.

45. *Story of Ahiqar* (trans. Conybeare, Harris, and Smith Lewis, *Story of Aḥiḳar,* 23 [Slavonic], 54 [Armenian], 84 [Syriac], and 117 [Arabic]). The episode in question involves the brief tale of a wolf that is brought to school and told to recite the alphabet but refuses to follow the teacher's instruction. In their introduction (pp. lxxxiii–lxxxiv),

Conybeare and Harris claim that this story provides "a very strong confirmation of this theory of a lost Hebrew original," but see my skeptical comments below. On the relation of this legend (and its possible Jewish connections) to the *Paidika,* see McNeil, "Jesus and the Alphabet," 126–28; and Burke, *De infantia,* 102–3.

46. A story about a young Ezra carrying water in his cloak is preserved in the *Jeremiah Apocryphon* (Kuhn, "Coptic Jeremiah Apocryphon," 95–135, 291–350; for the Ezra story, see pp. 309–10). The Garshuni version of the text was published by Mingana and Harris, "New Jeremiah Apocryphon," *Woodbrooke Studies,* I.148–91 (English translation), 192–233 (facsimile) (the story about Ezra is on pp. 177–78); see also Leroy and Dib, "Un apocryphe carchouni"; and Kuhn, "Apokryphon of Jeremiah," 170–71.

47. Evans (*Noncanonical Writings,* 234) cites stories in the Tosefta and the Babylonian Talmud about Hanina ben Dosa (*t. Berakhot* 3,20; *b. Berakhot* 33a; *b. Ta'anit* 25a); see also Burke, *De infantia,* 102–3.

48. In summarizing the history of scholarship, Burke (*De infantia,* 57–58, 68, 83–84, 89, 102–3, 111, 116, 125–26, 199–200, 208–10, 284) helpfully identifies and discusses publications on the question of Jewish-Christian origins for the *Paidika.* Burke himself seems favorably disposed to this theory, but in most of these cases he treats the question only in passing and refrains from a full critical engagement with some of the problematic historical issues I address.

49. Sternberger, *Einleitung,* 191–223, esp. 203. A similar dilemma applies to the *Tosefta,* the other source for the story of Rabbi Hanina ben Dosa's snakebite: based in part on the *Mishna* (ca. 200 CE), it was necessarily compiled later, probably sometime around the end of the third century or the beginning of the fourth; some estimates, however, have even pushed the date as late as the fifth century (Stemberger, *Einleitung,* 153–66).

50. *Story of Ahiqar* (trans. Conybeare, Harris, and Smith Lewis, *Story of Aḥiḳar,* 23 [Slavonic], 54 [Armenian], 84 [Syriac], and 117 [Arabic]).

51. Lindenberger, "Introduction," to his translation in Charlesworth, *Old Testament Pseudepigrapha,* II.479.

52. McNeil, "Jesus and the Alphabet," 126–28; Burke, *De infantia,* 102–3.

53. Berlin, Königliche Museen (now part of Altes Museum), P.13446 (trans. Lindenberger, in Charlesworth, *Old Testament Pseudepigrapha,* II.494–507).

54. Lindenberger, "Introduction," in Charlesworth, *Old Testament Pseudepigrapha,* 480.

55. *Jeremiah Apocryphon:* Kuhn, "Coptic Jeremiah Apocryphon," 309–10 (Coptic version); cf. Mingana and Harris, "New Jeremiah Apocryphon," in *Woodbrooke Studies,* I.177–78 (Garshuni version: "And the children of the Hebrews and the children of the Chaldeans used to go every day and carry water on their shoulders for their teachers. When they went one day to carry water, the jar of Ezra fell down and broke. . . . [Ezra] took off his mantle and went into the sea, and filled it with water as if it were a jar; then he placed it on his shoulder and walked with his fellow-students, and not a single drop fell from it. When he reached the scribes, he began to sprinkle the place with water from his mantle; then he put it on immediately, and it was as dry as before.")

56. Kuhn, "Apokryphon of Jeremiah," 170–71.

57. Marmorstein, "Quellen," 327–37. On scholarship relating this work to the category of Jewish pseudepigrapha, see Charlesworth, *Pseudepigrapha,* 88–91; and Herder, *Paralipomena Jeremiae,* 87–88.

58. Discussed by Burke, *De infantia,* 83–84, 89.

59. Mingana and Harris ("New Jeremiah Apocryphon," in *Woodbrooke Studies,* I.125–38) originally argued that the *Paidika* was a source for the Ezra story as it appears in medieval manuscripts of the *Jeremiah Apocryphon.* Burke (*De infantia,* 84) is among those who view their historical arguments with suspicion, but he does not give any reasons for this evaluation.

60. Kuhn, "Coptic Jeremiah Apocryphon," 101–2.

61. The Latin text was originally edited by Geyer in CSEL 39, 157–218. Later, he published an emended version along with a second recension in CCSL 175, 127–53 (original, longer recension), 155–74 (second, shorter recension). For a more recent critical edition, see Milani, *Itinerarium Antonini Placentini.* For English translations, see Stewart, *Of the Holy Places;* and Wilkinson, *Jerusalem Pilgrims,* rev. ed., 129–51. The name Antoninus was ascribed to this pilgrim as a result of confusion with the martyr Antoninus of Placentinus, who is mentioned in the first chapter of the *Itinerary.* The date of ca. 570 CE is based on the assumption that the work was written after the end of Justinian's reign in 565 (in the opening chapter of the *Itinerary,* the pilgrim speaks of "the time of Justinian's reign" as if it is in the past), but before war was renewed with Persia in 572 (the pilgrim is able to go to Mesopotamia without hindrance in chapter 46). On the basis of the pilgrim's reference to an earthquake in Beirut that had taken place "recently" (*Itinerary* 1), Solzbacher (*Mönche, Pilger und Sarazenen,* 144) argues for an earlier, alternative date: he suggests a time frame around the occurrence of two known earthquakes in 551 and 555. For a summary of these dating considerations, see Caner et al., *History and Hagiography,* 252, note 1. For earlier critical studies of the Piacenza pilgrim, see Geyer, *Kritische und sprachliche Erläuterungen;* Grisar, "Zur Palästinareise," 760–70; Grisar, "Nochmals das Palästinaitinerar," 776–78; and Vermeer, *Observations.*

62. Piacenza pilgrim, *Itinerary* 1–3 (Geyer, CSEL 39, 159–61; CCSL 175, 129–30; Stewart, *Of the Holy Places,* 1–4; cf. Wilkinson, *Jerusalem Pilgrims,* 129–31).

63. Piacenza pilgrim, *Itinerary* 4 (Geyer, CSEL 39, 161; CCSL 175, 130; Stewart, *Of the Holy Places,* 4; cf. Wilkinson, *Jerusalem Pilgrims,* 131).

64. Piacenza pilgrim, *Itinerary* 5 (Geyer, CSEL 39, 161–62; CCSL 175, 130–31; trans. Stewart, *Of the Holy Places,* 4–5, modified; cf. Wilkinson, *Jerusalem Pilgrims,* 131–32). For discussions of evidence related to the history of pilgrimage to Nazareth in late antiquity, see Maraval, *Lieux saints et pèlerinages,* 293; Taylor, *Christians and the Holy Places,* 226–29; and Bitton-Ashkelony, *Encountering the Sacred,* 28.

65. On the optical and tactile dimensions of early Christian pilgrimage practice in Palestine and elsewhere, see Frank, *Memory of the Eyes,* 118–33, with a discussion of the Piacenza pilgrim on pp. 119–20. On the localization of the holy as a mode of physical "presence" (*praesentia*) among Latin-speaking pilgrims, see Brown, *Cult of the Saints,* 88–90.

66. Leyerle, "Landscape as Cartography," 132–33, where she discusses the Piacenza pilgrim in relation to Philip Pearce's concept of "texture" (Pearce, "Route Maps," 145),

and Maurice Halbwachs's understanding of the role of "social data" in the constitution of "religious memory" (Halbwachs, *On Collective Memory,* 119). Leyerle also discusses the Piacenza pilgrim in her article "Pilgrims to the Land," 353–57.

67. Glare, *Oxford Latin Dictionary,* 1948; Souter, *Glossary,* 422; cf. Liddell and Scott, *Greek-English Lexicon,* 1804 (Gk. *tomos*).

68. See my discussion in chapter 5.

69. Debary and Turgeon ("Introduction," 5) define "objects of memory" (*objets de mémoire*) as artifacts that serve "to recall the past" (*remémorer le passé*), but that in doing so become something other than what they were initially. I am indebted to Andrew Jacobs (*per litt.,* December 31, 2012) for his insight on how the language of the script presented in the book would have crucially inflected the Piacenza pilgrim's experience of the synagogue as a place tied to conceptions of both past and present.

70. I borrow the phrase "tactile piety" from Wilken, *Land Called Holy,* 116.

71. Lactantius (*Divine Institutes* 5.19.29; PL 6.617A–B) speaks disapproving of pagan acts of worship as "rites pertaining to the fingers only" (*ritus ad solos dactulos pertinens*); see also MacMullen, *Paganism,* 63; and Wilken, *Land Called Holy,* 301, note 56.

72. Taylor, *Christians,* 228–29 and 328.

73. Jacobs, *Remains of the Jews,* 128.

74. On the "aestheticization of the Jew" in the Piacenza pilgrim's account, see Jacobs, *Remains of the Jew,* 124–31. Jacobs notes how the pilgrim's "reduction of material realities to aesthetic judgment inscribes at once distance and appropriation" (p. 124) and uses language of "consumption" to describe his "sensory and aesthetic experience of Palestinian Jews" (p. 130).

75. Piacenza pilgrim, *Itinerary* 5 (Geyer, CSEL 39, 161–62; CCSL 175, 131; trans. Stewart, *Of the Holy Places,* 161–62; cf. Wilkinson, *Jerusalem Pilgrims,* 131–32).

76. Ibid.

77. In chapter 8 of his *Itinerary,* the pilgrim describes how, while he was passing through village streets in Samaria, "the Jews followed us with straw, burning our footsteps," and how "these people have such a hatred for Christ that they will scarcely give an answer to Christians" (*Itinerary* 8: Geyer, CSEL 39, 164–65; CCSL 175, 133; trans. Stewart, *Of the Holy Places,* 7–8; cf. Wilkinson, *Jerusalem Pilgrims,* 133–35).

78. Mimouni, *Judéo-christianisme ancien,* 64; Mimouni, "Pour une definition," 171–82. As evidence, he cites examples of early Christian authors occasionally using the term "Hebrews" as a way of referring to "Jewish-Christians": see, e.g., the *Letter of Clement to James* 1.1 (trans. in Schneemelcher, *New Testament Apocrypha,* 496), where Jesus' brother James is called the bishop of "the holy church of the Hebrews" (cf. Ps.-Clementine *Homily* 11.35: Siouville, *Les Homélies Clémentines,* 260). See also *Gospel of Philip* 55.27–28 (Layton, *Nag Hammadi Codex II, 2–7,* I.150; trans. in Robinson, *Nag Hammadi Library,* 143); for commentary, see Siker, "Gnostic Views," 286; and Harvey, *True Israel,* 141.

79. Bagatti, "Ritrovamenti," 5–44; Bagatti, "Gli altari," 64–94; Bagatti, "I battisteri," 213–27; Bagatti, "Probabile figura," 61–6; Bagatti, *Excavations in Nazareth,* vol. 1; Testa, "Le grotte mistiche," 5–45; Testa, *Il simbolismo,* esp. 78–94.

80. Taylor, *Christians,* esp. 1–17, 221–67.

81. Examples include Acts 6 and Origen of Alexandria's *Against Celsus* 3.5–8 (Borret, SC 136, 20–28; Chadwick, 131–33); discussed by Harvey, *True Israel*, 129–43, esp. 129–30 and 139. Commenting on the contrasting use of "Hebrews" and "Hellenists" in Acts 6, Bruce (*Paul*, 42) writes, "The distinction was probably linguistic and cultural: the Hebrews, in that case, attended synagogues where the service was conducted in Hebrew and used Aramaic as their normal mode of speech."

82. Melito of Sardis, *On the Pascha* 94.714 (Perler, SC 123, 116); *Apology of Aristides* 2.3–4 (Pouderon and Pierre, SC 470, 188–91); Origen of Alexandria, *Against Celsus* 3.5–8 (Borret, SC 136, 20–28; Chadwick, 131–33). Commenting on Origen's terminology, Lange (*Origen and the Jews*, 31) writes, "*Ioudaios*, in many mouths, was a sneering expression, even perhaps a term of abuse; *Hebraios*, on the other hand, was a liberal's word, leaning over backwards to give no offence." Harvey (*The True Israel*, 132 and 141) notes that the term "Hebrew" was also used to designate Jews who were "conservative," "traditional," and "non-innovative" in orientation, but see Cohen (*Beginnings*, 71, note 5), who sharply critiques Harvey's monograph as "insufficiently rigorous" and observes that a more comprehensive terminological study is a desideratum.

83. See Jacobs, *Remains of the Jews*, 26–36, for a discussion of Eusebius of Caesarea's "textual 'mapping' of contemporary Jews into a Christian past" (p. 36). Jacobs sees Eusebius's "terminological fuzziness" in using the term "Hebrew" as a "conceptual tour de force by which (he) demonstrates the mastery and totality of his Christian historical vision" (p. 31).

84. Jacobs, *Remains of the Jews*, 36.

85. Piacenza pilgrim, *Itinerary* 5 (Geyer, CSEL 39, 162; CCSL 175, 131; trans. Stewart, *Of the Holy Places*, 5; cf. Wilkinson, *Jerusalem Pilgrims*, 132).

86. On Jewish-Christian tensions that surfaced in the context of pilgrimage practice, see also Leyerle, "Pilgrims," 356; and Dietz, *Wandering Monks*, esp. 33 and 37.

87. On the Piacenza pilgrim's "strategies of aestheticization and appropriation," see again Jacobs, *Remains of the Jews*, 124 (cf. 127–31, 136).

88. The title, *Toledot Yeshu*, is often translated as *History of Jesus* or *Life of Jesus:* see, e.g., Silberstein, *Mapping Jewish Identities;* and Schäfer, *Mirror of His Beauty*. For a brief introduction to the work, see Dan, "Toledot Yeshu," 28–29. The word *toledot* (sometimes transliterated as *toledoth, toldot,* or *toldoth*) is a plural noun in Hebrew, meaning "genealogies" or "generations," and in this context, it is used as the title for the book of Genesis. Here, I opt for the latter translation, *Generations of Jesus*, because it better conveys the fact that the work is concerned not only with Jesus' birth and life story but also with the early history of the church during the period after his death (see also Tolan, *Saracens*, 17ff.).

89. Peter Schäfer is currently heading a project aimed at producing a synoptic edition of *Toledot Yeshu:* for a preliminary report, see Schäfer, Meerson, and Deutsch, *Toledot Yeshu*, esp. Schäfer's "Introduction," 1–11. Until Schäfer's edition is published, the most comprehensive work on the *Toledot* remains Krauss, *Das Leben Jesu;* but see also Di Segni, *Vangelo*.

The first analysis of the manuscript evidence by Erich Bischoff was published by Krauss in *Das Leben Jesu*, 27–37. According to their analysis, the surviving manuscripts were divided into five different families or types. These types were labeled according to their signature publications or text collections (Wagenseil, De Rossi, Huldreich), their language (Modern Slavic) or their place of origin (Cairo). Schonfield (*According to the Hebrews,* 31–32) critiqued their methodology as "arbitrary" and argued the five groups could be distilled down to two essential text types: *Toledot Yeshu* proper and *Toledot Minor* (a shorter narrative focusing primarily on Jesus' passion and resurrection). More recently, Di Segni ("La tradizione testuale," 83–100; and *Vangelo,* 29–42, 203–19) has proposed a different classification system of three text types, based on the name of the authority said to preside over Jesus' trial: (1) a Pilate group, consisting primarily of Aramaic texts from the Cairo Geniza, which he regards as the earliest recension with a possible Syrian provenance (Higger, "Ma'aseh Yeshu," 143–52; trans. Basser, "Acts of Jesus," 273–82; see also Schonfield, *According to the Hebrews,* 205–7; Samuel Krauss, "Mount of Olives," 170, note 6 [in Hebrew]; and Gero, "Nestorius Legend," 108–20); (2) a Helena group, consisting of various Hebrew and Judaeo-Arabic texts (see also Legásse, "La légende juive des Apôtres et les rapports judéo-chrétiens dans le haut Moyen Age," 99–132; Legásse, "La légende juive des Apôtres et les rapports judéo-chrétiens dans le Moyen Age occidental," 121–139); and (3) a Herod group, represented by a single manuscript published by J. J. Huldreich (see also Leiman, "Scroll of Fasts," 187–92). For a clear discussion of Di Segni's text types, see Newman, "Death of Jesus," 59–60. For an analysis of extant Judaeo-Arabic versions of *Toledot Yeshu* and a discussion of its textual history in that language, see also Goldstein, "Judeo-Arabic Versions," 9–42.

90. Krauss, *Das Leben Jesu,* 19. In the introduction to his edition of a late version of the *Toledot,* Schlichting (*Die verschollene Toledot-Jeschu-Fassung,* 2) notes that the dates proposed for the *Toledot* traditions have ranged widely, from untenably early (e.g., Voltaire's claim for a first-century composition) to quite late (e.g., Klausner's tenth-century estimate): see Voltaire, *Nouveaux mélanges,* 309; and Klausner, *Jesus von Nazareth,* 65. On Voltaire's engagement with ancient traditions about Jesus' childhood, considered in the context of eighteenth-century scholarship, see Barbu, "Voltaire and the *Toledoth Yeshu,*" 617–27; and Rosset, "'False' and 'True,'" 628–40.

91. Krauss, *Das Leben Jesu,* 5–6; Goldstein, *Jesus,* 147. Horbury ("Critical Examination," 438ff.) and Barbu ("Voltaire and the *Toledoth Yeshu,*" 620) note that Amulo uses a text type different from that in the version cited by Agobard.

92. Most recently, see Ben Ezra ("An Ancient List," 481–96), who argues for the possibility of a late fourth- or early fifth-century dating for *Toledot Yeshu* on the basis of internal references to Christian liturgical festivals. In Fiebig's review of Krauss's *Das Leben Jesu* (pp. 506–8), he argued for a possible earlier date despite the fact that the *Toledot* refers to the name of Nestorius. Similarly, Krauss and Horbury (*Jewish-Christian Controversy,* 12, note 31) observe that some versions of the *Toledot* refer to the practice of tonsuring clergy (a development first found in the sixth century), but they dismiss this detail as a later addition.

93. On the *Toledot*'s dependence on the Babylonian Talmud (Bavli), see Krauss, *Das Leben Jesu,* 9, 181–94, who states unequivocally, "The *Toledot* is based essentially on the *Talmud*; without the *Talmud* there is also no *Toledot*" (Das Toldoth gründet sich wesentlich auf dem Talmud, ohne Talmud gäbe es auch kein Toldoth"; p. 9). Some scholars have tried to argue, to the contrary, that the *Toledot Yeshu* influenced the formation of the Bavli, an argument that assumes a very early composition for the *Toledot*:

see, e.g., Maier, *Jesus von Nazareth,* 129; Gero, "Apocryphal Gospels," 3991–93; Gero, "Nestorius Legend," 120; and Gero, "Jewish Polemic," 165, note 5. Over against such views and in support of the consensus that the *Toledot Yeshu* in fact "elaborated on the Talmudic kernel with great creativity," see also Rubenstein, *Stories,* 272, note 94.

94. On this operative date range see Krauss, *Das Leben Jesu,* 242 and 246; Krauss and Horbury, *Jewish-Christian Controversy,* 12; and Newman, "Death of Jesus," 61–62. While Krauss acknowledged this four-century time span between the terminus a quo and the terminus ad quem, he generally favored a date early in that period, circa fifth or sixth century. In some of his work, Horbury tries to narrow this date range slightly, placing the composition of the *Toledot* between the fourth and the seventh centuries: see esp. Horbury, "Depiction," 281–86; cf. Gero, "Critical Examination." Other scholars have come to similar conclusions. Schonfield (*According to the Hebrews,* 225–27) assigns the finalized version of the *Toledot* to the eighth century, although he argues for the existence of a so-called *Ur-Toledot* at least as early as the late fourth century. Goldstein (*Jesus,* 163) prefers a sixth- or seventh-century dating, right around the time that the Babylonian Talmud was being redacted. On the probable Syrian/Aramaic provenance of the *Toledot,* see Krauss, *Das Leben Jesu,* 246–47, who notes that the Strasbourg manuscript he edited was primarily a Hebrew text, but with a number of Aramaic sentences. Sokoloff ("Date and Provenance," 25) has analyzed the Aramaic dialect in the Geniza fragments containing parts of the *Toledot* narrative, concluding that the linguistic evidence "strongly points to the provenance of the Aramaic *Toledot Yeshu* as being Jewish Babylonia, and its time of composition towards the middle of the first millennium CE." For an argument that the work originated in Palestine but was reworked in Babylonia, see Alexander, "Jesus and His Mother," 599–604.

95. On the text as "a process of extended evolution" rather than a "single composition," see Di Segni, *Vangelo,* 218; and Newman, "Death of Jesus," 59. This process of copying and redaction has continued into the twentieth century with variant versions such as the *Tam ū-mū'ād,* a late version of the *Toledot* preserved only in modern copies and edited by Schlichting (*Die verschollene Toledot-Jeschu-Fassung*). While Schlichting argued that it probably had textual roots in the medieval period, he also observed that the *Tam ū-mū'ād,* "mostly in handwritten circulation, experienced an organic growth well into the nineteenth century" (pp. 38–44, quote at 42).

96. MS Strasbourg (an exemplar of the Wagenseil text type): Krauss, *Das Leben Jesu,* 38–50 (Hebrew text), 50–64 (German translation); for an English translation (with some summarized sections), see Schofield, *According to the Hebrews,* 35–61. For a Hebrew edition incorporating all six texts published by Krauss, see Eisenstein, *Otsar vikuhim,* 227–35. See also Alexander, "Jesus and His Mother," 605–16, who provides English translations of three recensions (Wagenseil, De Rossi, and Huldreich) in synoptic parallel: Wagenseil text = Wagenseilus, *Tela Ignea Satanae;* De Rossi text = Horbury, "Critical Examination," 152–205 (MS Schwager XI.59; Jewish Theological Seminary of America in New York); and Huldreich text = Huldricius, *Historia Jeshuae Nazareni.*

97. Horbury, "Strasbourg Text," 49–59.

98. I follow Krauss's chapter numbering system (used in the text of his German translation but absent in his edition of the Hebrew); in my notes, however, I also cross-reference the different chapter organization employed by Schonfield in his English translation.

99. Bammel ("Christian Origins," 328) writes that "the stories are quite clearly meant to be a travesty of the corresponding Christian stories, to disqualify them by making them ridiculous." Alexander ("Jesus and His Mother," 577–79) also characterizes the *Toledot* tales as parodic.

100. On these sections of text, see Horbury, "Depiction," 280–86.

101. *Toledot Yeshu* 1–2 (MS Strasbourg): Krauss, *Das Leben Jesu,* 38–40 (Hebrew text), 50–52 (German translation); = ch. 1 in Schonfield, *According to the Hebrews,* 35–39; quote at 1.28, p. 37.

102. *Toledot Yeshu* 3–4 (MS Strasbourg): Krauss, *Das Leben Jesu,* 40–41 (Hebrew), 53–54 (German); = ch. 2 in Schonfield, *According to the Hebrews,* 39–41.

103. The events of the *Toledot* narrative are set around the year 90 BCE: Helene is otherwise known in historical sources as Salome Alexandra (Goldstein, *Jesus,* 149).

104. The bird story appears in three of the *Toledot* manuscripts edited by Krauss, *Das Leben Jesu,* 42 and 54 (MS Strasbourg, ch. 5), 72 and 98 (MS Vindabona, ch. 8), and 119 and 124 (MS Adler, ch. 5), as well as in a parallel text from Shem-Ṭob Ibn Shaprut's *Touchstone* (Krauss, *Das Leben Jesu,* 147 and 148) and in the late *Toledot* recension called the *Tam ū-mū'ād* (ch. 15.34–35, = sect. 137: Schlichting, *Die verschollene Toledot-Jeschu-Fassung,* 110 and 111).

105. *Toledot Yeshu* 4–5, quote at 5 (MS Strasbourg): Krauss, *Das Leben Jesu,* 41–42, at 42 (Hebrew), 54–55, at 54 (German); = ch. 3.1–20 in Schonfield, *According to the Hebrews,* 41–43, quote at 3.16, p. 43 (modified).

106. *Toledot Yeshu* 5 (MS Strasbourg): Krauss, *Das Leben Jesu,* 42–43 (Hebrew), 55 (German); = ch. 3.21–31 in Schonfield, *According to the Hebrews,* 43–45.

107. *Toledot Yeshu* 5–6 (MS Strasbourg): Krauss, *Das Leben Jesu,* 43–44 (Hebrew), 55–56 (German); = ch. 3.32–43 in Schonfield, *According to the Hebrews,* 45–47.

108. *Toledot Yeshu* 6–8 (MS Strasbourg): Krauss, *Das Leben Jesu,* 44–46 (Hebrew), 56–59 (German); = ch. 4–5 in Schonfield, *According to the Hebrews,* 48–53. When Jesus is confronted by the Jewish leaders, they repeatedly ask him his name, and he responds four different times with four different names (Mathai, Naki, Buni, and Netser). This exchange provides the opportunity for textual word plays through which his accusers give the meaning of those names a negative twist. After Jesus' death, the leaders try to hang him on several trees, which all break because he was said to have uttered the divine name over them in anticipation of these events: only the carob tree was able to bear his weight, since he had not uttered the divine name over it.

109. *Toledot Yeshu* 9–10 (MS Strasbourg): Krauss, *Das Leben Jesu,* 46–48 (Hebrew), 59–62 (German); = ch. 6 in Schonfield, *According to the Hebrews,* 53–58. In a copy of the *Toledot* in Leipzig (Cod. hebr. B.H. 27, fols. 206a–11b), the Elijah character is identified as Simeon Kepha, and thus becomes an amalgam of Peter and Paul. For a discussion of the calendrical correspondence between the Jewish and Christian festivals counterposed in the text, see Ben Ezra, "Ancient List," 481–96.

110. On earlier traditions about Jesus' circumcision, see Jacobs, *Christ Circumcised.*

111. *Toledot Yeshu* 11 (MS Strasbourg): Krauss, *Das Leben Jesu,* 48–49 (Hebrew), 62 (German); = ch. 7 in Schonfield, *According to the Hebrews,* 58–59.

112. *Toledot Yeshu* 12 (MS Strasbourg): Krauss, *Das Leben Jesu,* 49–50 (Hebrew), 62–64 (German); = ch. 8 in Schonfield, *According to the Hebrews,* 59–61.

113. *Toledot Yeshu* 2 (MS Strasbourg): Krauss, *Das Leben Jesu,* 39 (Hebrew), 52 (German); = ch. 1.28 in Schofield, *According to the Hebrews,* 37; cf. *Paidika* 6.2f and 7.2 (Burke, *De infantia,* 317 and 321). With respect to the role that letters play in the *Toledot,* Krauss (*Das Leben Jesu,* 16), emphasizes the way that the narrative presents "ein Spiel mit den evangelischen Namen, . . . mit Alphabeten und Gematria's."

114. Budge, *History of the Blessed Virgin Mary,* I.67–77; II.71–82; Geerard, *Clavis apocryphorum,* no. 94.

115. Budge, *History of the Blessed Virgin Mary,* I.70; II.76; MS Vindobona, ch. 8 (Krauss, *Das Leben Jesu,* 72 [Hebrew], 97 [German]). In his edition of the *Tam ū-mūʿād,* Schlichting (*Die verschollene Toledot-Jeschu-Fassung,* 2) discusses the inclusion of Jesus' miracle of the birds in terms of the mutual influence of Christian, Jewish, and Islamic traditions.

116. *AGI* 36 (Thilo, *Codex apocryphus,* 110); see my translation in Appendix B. I discuss this work in more detail in chapter 7.

117. *Toledot Yeshu* 4 (MS Strasbourg): Krauss, *Das Leben Jesu,* 41 (Hebrew), 54 (German); = ch. 3.2 in Schonfield, *According to the Hebrews,* 41.

118. *Toledot Yeshu* 5 (MS Strasbourg): Krauss, *Das Leben Jesu,* 42 (Hebrew), 54 (German); = ch. 3.12 in Schonfield, *According to the Hebrews,* 42.

119. *Toledot Yeshu* 5 (MS Strasbourg): Krauss, *Das Leben Jesu,* 42 (Hebrew), and 54 (German); = ch. 3.13–16 in Schonfield, *According to the Hebrews,* 42–43.

120. MS Adler (A), ch. 4, 5, 6: Krauss, *Das Leben Jesu,* 119 (Hebrew), 124–25 (German); see also Alexander ("Jesus and His Mother," 592–93), who observes that "given the lateness of this *Toledot* manuscript (possibly 19th century), and its provenance (Yemen) it might well be that it is [the Qur'ānic] appropriation of the apocryphal Christian tale to which the *Toledot* is reacting." On the possibility of a "three-way dynamic . . . between the Jesus traditions in Christianity, Judaism and Islam" (ibid.), see Alexander, "*Toledot Yeshu,*" 137–58.

121. *Tam ū-mūʿād* 15.34–35 (= sect. 137): Schlichting, *Die verschollene Toledot-Jeschu-Fassung,* 110–11. On the association of whispering and magical practice, see Luck, *Arcana Mundi,* 55, 74, 106–7, 250, 279, 292, 342–44.

122. MS Adler (A), ch. 7: Krauss, *Das Leben Jesu,* 71 (Hebrew), 96 (German).

123. MS Adler (A), ch. 9: Krauss, *Das Leben Jesu,* 76 (Hebrew), 102 (German).

124. MS Vindobona, ch. 11: Krauss, *Das Leben Jesu,* 78 (Hebrew), 104 (German).

125. Origen, *Contra Celsum* 1.28 (Borret, SC 132, 150–53; Chadwick, 28–31); also Schäfer, *Jesus,* 19.

126. Origen, *Contra Celsum* 1.32 (Borret, SC 132, 162–65; Chadwick, 31–32); also Schäfer, *Jesus,* 19. In the fourth century CE, Eusebius of Caesarea (*Eclogae propheticae* III.10: Gaisford, 11) also passes on reports about Jewish claims that Jesus "was fathered from a panther [*ek panthēros*]."

127. Justin Martyr, *Dialogue with Trypho* 69.7 (Marcovich, 191; *ANF* 1.233).

128. Krauss (*Das Leben Jesu,* 2) observes that Celsus, in his attacks on Christianity, was reproducing "Jewish opinions" ("jüdische Ansichten"). It is noteworthy that the accusations of magic in Celsus's treatise are concentrated especially in the first two chapters, where they are placed in the mouth of the anonymous Jewish interlocutor. On Celsus's Jew as a rhetorical figure, see Andresen, *Logos und Nomos,* 22 (note 32), 214–15; and Gallagher, *Divine Man,* 49–53. On the relation of

Celsus's polemic to actual Jewish perspectives in late antiquity, see Bammel, "Der Jude des Celsus," I.265–83; Miura-Stange, *Celsus und Origenes,* 126, note 1; Lange, *Origen and the Jews,* 64–70; Setzer, *Jewish Responses,* 147–50; Wilson, *Related Strangers,* 278–73; Cook, *Interpretation,* 27–28; and Paget, *Jews,* 275–77. For arguments that Celsus relied, at least in part, on written Jewish sources, see Lods, "Étude sur les sources juives," 1–33; Pichler, *Streit,* 50–52; and Stanton, *Jesus and Gospel,* 149–53. For a discussion of the representation of Jewish perspectives in both Justin Martyr and Celsus/Origen, see Maier, *Jesus,* 250–54.

129. *b. Shabb.* 104b (Epstein, *Babylonian Talmud,* vol. 2.1, 502–4).

130. *b. Shabb.* 104b (Epstein, *Babylonian Talmud,* vol. 2.1, 504). The rabbis quoted in the uncensored commentary wrestle over the identity of Stada: while Rabbi Hisda identifies this name with the true husband of Miriam, another rabbinic voice argues that it refers to the mother herself, who "has been unfaithful to [lit. "turned away from"—*satath da*] her husband."

131. For an early discussion of this reference to Jesus as an original feature of *b. Shabb.* 104b, see Herford, *Christianity in Talmud,* 37–41. Meier (*Jesus,* 198, 204, 209–10) argues against the identification of Jesus with Ben Stada/Ben Pandera, and instead sees it as a later development influenced by knowledge of *Toledot Yeshu.* More recently, however, Schäfer (*Jesus,* 15) has argued strenuously that the text "indeed refers to the Jesus of the New Testament story" and that "it presents . . . a highly ambitious and devastating counternarrative."

132. *b. Ber.* 17a–b (Epstein, *Babylonian Talmud,* vol. 1.1, 103); *b. Sanh.* 103a (Epstein, *Babylonian Talmud,* vol. 4.3, 701); see also Herford, *Christianity,* 57–61; and Schäfer, *Jesus,* 26 and 30.

133. *b. Sanh.* 107b (Epstein, *Babylonian Talmud,* vol. 4.3, 734–35; see p. 735, note 4, for the uncensored text); *b. Sot.* 47a (Epstein, *Babylonian Talmud,* vol. 3.3, 246). The majority of scholars have viewed these references to Jesus as original to the Talmud: see, for example, Herford, *Christianity,* 52–54; Eisler, *IĒSOUS,* I.491; Bammel, "Christian Origins," 317–55; and Schäfer, *Jesus,* 34 and 155, notes 1–7. For arguments to the contrary, see Maier, *Jesus,* 116–17, 124–28, 228.

134. Schäfer, *Jesus,* 34.

135. See, for example, the summary account in Shem-Ṭob Ibn Shaprut's *Touchstone:* ed. Krauss, *Das Leben Jesu,* 146–47 (Hebrew) and 147–49 (German). On the role of Yehoshua b. Perahya in the *Toledot* traditions, see Krauss, *Das Leben Jesu,* 185; Ginzberg, *Ginze Schechter,* I.329; Horbury, "Trial of Jesus," 104ff.; Maier, *Jesus,* 295, note 291; Falk, "Qeta' hadash,'" 3109; Boyarin, "Qeriah metuqqenet," 250, and Schäfer, *Jesus,* 38.

136. Schäfer, *Jesus,* 38; Reiner: "From Joshua to Jesus," 258–60.

137. Montgomery, *Aramaic Incantation Texts,* nos. 8 (1, 6, 8), 9 (1.2f.), 17 (1.8, 10), 32 (1.4), and 33 (1.3), pp. 154ff., 161, 190, 225 (commentary on pp. 226–28), and 230; also Naveh and Shaked, *Amulets and Magic Bowls,* 158–63 (bowl 5); Shaked, "Poetics of Spells," 173–95; Levene, *Corpus of Magic Bowls,* 31–9 (bowls M50 and M59); quote in Schäfer, *Jesus,* 38.

138. Levene, "'. . . and by the name of Jesus . . . ,'" 287 (text) and 290 (translation). Montgomery (*Aramaic Incantation Texts,* 23, bowl 34, 1.2) has published another Bab-

ylonian magical bowl with an inscription invoking "Jesus the healer" (*Yeshua' asya*); see also Schäfer, *Jesus,* 38.

139. On Jesus' ancient reputation as a magician, see Smith, *Jesus the Magician;* and Bammel, "Jesus der Zauberer," II.3–14.

140. For a fuller list and discussion of known Christian witnesses to such Jewish "anti-Gospel" traditions, see Krauss, *Das Leben Jesu,* 5–8; also Schonfield, *According to the Hebrews,* 29–30. In the case of *Toledot Yeshu,* historians have argued that such Jewish stories were "read by erudite medieval Christian scholars and polemicists" (Barbu, "Voltaire and the *Toledoth Yeshu,*" 620; see also Horbury, "Critical Examination," 4–9).

141. Qur'ān 5:110 (Pickthall, *Meaning,* 158–59, modified). Given that fragments of the *Toledot* have been discovered in Cairo, Yemen, and Bukhara (contemporary Uzbekistan), it is not unreasonable to suppose that it (or sources on which it was based) became known to both Christians and Muslims living in these areas.

142. Agobard of Lyons, *Epistola de Judaicis Superstitionibus.* For the Latin text, see PL 104.87; Enge, "De Agobardi," 15; and Krauss, *Das Leben Jesu,* 5. For an English translation, see Mead, *Did Jesus Live 100 BC?* 290–91; and Schonfield, *According to the Hebrews,* 209–10.

143. My analysis of the intentional scribal emendation of the *Paidika* for specific apologetic purposes may be compared in certain respects to Bart Ehrman's analysis of New Testament manuscripts in *The Orthodox Corruption of Scripture.* But while Ehrman focused on the way that intra-Christian theological debates influenced the editing of New Testament writings, I am interested in the relationship between Jewish-Christian controversy and the manuscript history of the *Paidika.*

144. Schonfield, *According to the Hebrews,* 29–30.

145. *Paidika* 3.1–2 (Burke, *De infantia,* 305–7).

146. *Toledot Yeshu* 5–6 (Strasbourg MS): Krauss, *Das Leben Jesu,* 56–57, 60; Schonfield, *According to the Hebrews,* 48, 54. For the Cairo Geniza text, see Higger, "Ma'aseh Yeshu," 143–52; trans. Basser, "The Acts of Jesus," 273–80, esp. 277–80.

147. Ga 3.2 (Burke, *De infantia,* 344–47).

148. Gb 2.2–3 (Burke, *De infantia,* 454–55). In this account, Jesus' encounter with Annas's son occurs right before the bird miracle.

149. Gd 3.2–3 (Burke, *De infantia,* 404–5); Late Latin *Paidika* 4.3 (= *Vatic. lat.* 4578, fourteenth cent. CE: Tischendorf, *Evangelia apocrypha,* 2nd ed., 168). For a critical edition of the Slavonic *Paidika,* see Rosén, *Slavonic Translation;* trans. Smith, at http://www.tonyburke.ca/infancy-gospel-of-thomas/the-infancy-gospel-of-thomas-slavonic/; see ch. 3.2, where the son of Annas is identified as an "impure, senseless Sodomite."

150. *Gospel of Pseudo-Matthew* 26 (Tischendorf, *Evangelia apocrypha,* 2nd ed., 94–95; *ANF* 8.378).

151. *Gospel of Pseudo-Matthew* 26 (Tischendorf, *Evangelia apocrypha,* 2nd ed., 95; *ANF* 8.378): this episode should be given the title "Jesus kicks ass." On the text and its transmission, see Jan Gijsel, *Die unmittelbare Textüberlieferung;* Gijsel, *Libri de Nativitate Mariae,* CCSA 9, 37–515. On the so-called Egyptian prelude to *Pseudo-Matthew,* see Norelli, "Gesù ride," 653–84.

152. *Gospel of Pseudo-Matthew* 28 (Tischendorf, *Evangelia apocrypha,* 2nd ed., 96; *ANF* 8.378).

153. Syriac *Paidika* 5.1: Wright, *Contributions*, 12 (Syriac); 7 (English). I cite here the translation of Vat. Syr. 159 by Burke, "The *Infancy Gospel of Thomas* from an Unpublished Syriac Manuscript," 272–73. My thanks to him for making his edition and translation available to me prior to publication.

154. Syriac *Paidika* 6.2b: Wright, *Contributions*, 13 (Syriac); 8 (English); ed. and trans. Burke, "The *Infancy Gospel of Thomas* from an Unpublished Syriac Manuscript," 276–77. Throughout this scene (see esp. 6.2e and 7.2), the Syriac text emphasizes Zacchaeus's feebleness of mind and lack of mental control, another topos probably drawn from the common stock of early Christian anti-Jewish polemics.

155. Ethiopic *Paidika* 7 (Grébaut, "Les miracles de Jésus," 630; trans. Poirier, at http://www.tonyburke.ca/infancy-gospel-of-thomas/the-infancy-gospel-of-thomas-ethiopic/).

156. See, e.g., Jacobs, *Remains of the Jews;* Jacobs, *Christ Circumcised;* Drake, "Sexing the Jew"; Fredriksen, *Augustine and the Jews;* and Davis, "Biblical Interpretation," 53.

157. *Gospel of Pseudo-Matthew* 29 (Tischendorf, *Evangelia apocrypha,* 2nd ed., 96–97; *ANF* 8.378–79).

158. *Gospel of Pseudo-Matthew* 30 (Tischendorf, *Evangelia apocrypha,* 2nd ed., 97–100, at 98; *ANF* 8.379). Additional episodes in the Prologue to Gd and the Late Latin text also carry hints of Christian allegations against Jews as spiritually dead and quarrelsome. In one instance, Jesus sees "the children of the Hebrews playing" and takes a salted fish and throws it into the water, saying, "Shake off the salt and swim in the water" (Gd Prologue 4: Burke, *De infantia,* 394–95; cf. Late Latin *Paidika* 1.4: ed. Tischendorf, *Evangelia apocrypha,* 2nd ed., 165; for a discussion of the "Egyptian prologue," see Norelli, "Gesù ride"). This story may constitute both a criticism of Judaism as a "dead" faith and a proselytizing witness that Jews need Christian baptism to come to life. A second example presents a variant on the story of the sparrows. When walking through the streets of a city, Jesus laughs when he sees twelve sparrows swoop down from a wall "fighting amongst themselves" before falling unexpectedly into the lap of "the teacher" (Gd Prologue 5: Burke, *De infantia,* 396–97; cf. Late Latin *Paidika* 2.1: Tischendorf, *Evangelia apocrypha,* 2nd ed., 165).

159. *Gospel of Pseudo-Matthew* 31 (Tischendorf, *Evangelia apocrypha,* 2nd ed., 102; *ANF* 8.380).

160. *Paidika* 7.4 (Gs) (Burke, *De infantia,* 322–23); Syriac *Paidika* 7.4 (Wright, *Contributions,* 14 [Syriac]; 9 [English]; also Burke, "The *Infancy Gospel of Thomas* from an Unpublished Syriac Manuscript," 284–85).

161. Ga 7.3 (Burke, *De infantia,* 364–65); *Gospel of Pseudo-Matthew* 31 (Tischendorf, *Evangelia apocrypha,* 2nd ed., 102; *ANF* 8.380). In the latter text, it is actually Zacchaeus's preceptor Levi who utters these words.

162. Gd 7.4 (Burke, *De infantia,* 420–21). The Christ child's divine identity is also highlighted elsewhere in Ga and Gd in the story of Jesus' healing of the woodcutter's foot, where the crowd reacts by worshipping him and proclaiming, "Truly, perhaps God dwells in him" (Ga/Gd 10.3: Burke, *De infantia,* 370–71, 426–27). Burke (*De infantia,* 370, note 3) notes that the manuscripts vary at this point. In one case (MS V), the word "perhaps" has been omitted: God unequivocally dwells in Jesus. In another (MS α), the crowd instead proclaims, "Truly the spirit of God dwells in this child." One sees a simi-

lar emphasis on the Christ child's divinity in the *History of Joseph the Carpenter,* an Egyptian work from perhaps the fourth or fifth century CE. In that text, Joseph, on his deathbed, recalls Jesus' healing of the boy bitten by a serpent (Jesus' brother James in *Paidika* 15; Burke, *De infantia,* 332–33), and then prays to Christ, addressing him as "O Lord and my God," and "my Lord, my God and Saviour, most surely the Son of God" (*History of Joseph the Carpenter* 17: Robinson, *Coptic Apocryphal Gospels,* 137–38 [Bohairic], 154–55 [Sahidic]; Elliott, *The Apocryphal New Testament,* 116 [Arabic]; see also Burke, *De infantia,* 32–33).

163. *History of the Blessed Virgin Mary:* Budge, I.68 (Syriac text), and II.74 (English).

164. Slavonic *Paidika* 6.4 (Rosén, *Slavonic Translation,* 60; trans. Smith).

165. *Armenian Infancy Gospel* 20.3 (Terian, *Armenian Gospel,* 93–94). On the Armenian traditions, see also Calzolari, "Les récits," 560–87.

166. Syriac *Paidika* 7.2 (Burke, "The *Infancy Gospel of Thomas* from an Unpublished Syriac Manuscript," 282–83).

167. Ethiopic *Paidika* 6 (=*Miracles of Jesus* 8.6: Grébaut, "Les miracles de Jésus," 629–30); *Gospel of Pseudo-Matthew* 31 (Tischendorf, *Evangelia apocrypha,* 2nd ed., 101; trans. *ANF* 8.380).

168. Greek *Paidika* 2.4 (Gs) (Burke, *De infantia,* 304–5).

169. Ga 2.4 = Gd 2.4 = Gb 3.2 (Burke, *De infantia,* 344–45, 402–3, 456–57); Syriac *Paidika* 2.4 ("Go, fly, and be mindful of me, little ones": Wright, *Contributions,* 11 [Syriac]; 6 [English]; ed. and trans. Burke, "The *Infancy Gospel of Thomas* from an Unpublished Syriac Manuscript," 268–69); Georgian *Paidika* 2.4 (Garitte, "Le fragment géorgien," 517); Late Latin *Paidika* 8 and 15 (Tischendorf, *Evangelia apocrypha,* 2nd ed., 174 and 179).

170. One sees this apostolic interpretation already operative in the early Christian *Gospel of Bartholomew* (ch. 2.11: Vassiliev, *Anecdota graeco-byzantina,* vol. 1, 12), where Mary declares to the disciples, "In your likeness God formed the sparrows and sent them to the four corners of the world." The date and provenance of the work remain uncertain, although fourth-century Egypt has been tentatively proposed as a possibility: see also Kaestli, "Questions de Barthélemy," in Bovon and Geoltrain, *Écrits apocryphes chrétiens,* I.255–305; Kaestli and Cherix, *L'évangile de Barthélemy,* 29–134; and Burke, *De infantia,* 31.

171. Ga 10.2 and Gd 10.2 (Burke, *De infantia,* 370–71, 426–27).

172. Ga 17.1 and Gd 17.1 (Burke, *De infantia,* 382–83, 444–45). On milk and nursing as Eucharistic metaphors, see Davis, *Coptic Christology in Practice,* 191–97.

173. *Paidika* 4.1 (Burke, *De infantia,* 307); see also Aasgaard, *Childhood,* 221, note 12. Both Burke and Aasgaard record this form with a rough breathing over the initial omicron, but in my transcription I omit this on the assumption that at the time this manuscript was written (eleventh century CE) the pronunciation of such rough breathings had already fallen out of use, along the lines of what has now become the convention in Modern Greek.

174. *Paidika* 6.2b (Burke, *De infantia,* 313).

175. Stroumsa, "A Nameless God," 238–39, quotes at 239.

176. Budge, *History of the Blessed Virgin Mary,* I.67–77; II.71–82; Burke, *De infantia,* 164–65.

177. Budge, *History of the Blessed Virgin Mary,* I.65–66; II.70–71.

178. Ibid., I.66; II.71.

179. Ibid., I.66; II.71 (see also notes 2 and 4). In the *Arabic Gospel of the Infancy* (Thilo, *Codex apocryphus,* 108), Judas "wanted to bite the Lord Jesus but was not able to do so; nevertheless, he did strike [*ḍaraba*] Jesus on his right side and Jesus wept [*bakiya*]." Here, the story is retold in a way that alludes to both the enigmatic story of the boy who struck Jesus on his shoulder (*Paidika* 4: Burke, *De infantia,* 307; cf. *AGI* 47: Thilo, *Codex apocryphus,* 122) and the story of Jesus weeping in the Gospel of John (11:35).

180. *AGI* 35 (Thilo, *Codex apocryphus,* 108; *ANF* 8.412); for my translation, see Appendix B.

181. It is unknown whether this scribal error originated with the production of this eleventh-century manuscript, or whether the manuscript inherited a mistake made earlier in the *Paidika*'s history of textual transmission. Could such a scribal misreading have been partially inspired by knowledge of stories about the possession of the divine name, like that found in the *Toledot?* Or alternatively, if traced to an earlier point in the text's history, could such a misreading have served as inspiration for an elaborated Jewish legend explaining the source of Jesus' "magical" power? Unfortunately, we lack definitive answers to such questions: any direct source connection between this manuscript of the *Paidika* and the *Toledot* tradition must remain speculative in the absence of further evidence. What I am arguing for is an environment in which apologetic reading strategies were ready to hand for Christians (and Jews) speculating about Jesus' childhood.

Chapter 7. Muslims and Christians

1. Epiphanius of Salamis, *Panarion* 51.20.2–3 (Holl, GCS 31.2, 277–78; Williams, II.45); Burke, *De infantia,* 7. For another positive assessment of the *Paidika*'s value, especially in relation to the testimony of the Gospel of Luke, see Georgius Syncellus, *Chronographia, anno 5505* (eighth–ninth cent.) (Mosshammer, *Georgii Syncelli Ecloga Chronographica,* 384–85; Adler and Tuffin, *Chronography,* 385–86); Burke, *De infantia,* 11–13.

2. John Chrysostom, *Homilies on John* 17 (*PG* 59.110; *NPNF*, ser. 2, vol. 14, 60); Burke, *De infantia,* 6; see also Voicu, "Histoire de l'enfance," 191; and Voicu, "Verso," 41–42.

3. *Decretum Gelasianum* (Dobschütz, 51; Schneemelcher, *New Testament Apocrypha,* I.38); Maximus the Confessor, *Life of the Virgin* 62 (Esbroeck, CSCO 478, 77.27–78.28 [text]; and CSCO 479, 52.19–53.8 [translation]).

4. Anastasius of Sinai, *Hodegos* 13: *PG* 89.229C; Burke, *De infantia,* 9–10. List of Manichaean books: *PG* 86.21C; Burke, *De infantia,* 11. See also Euthymius Zigabenus's twelfth-century commentary on John (*Commentarius: PG* 29.1153B; Burke, *De infantia,* 14), in which the author writes about "the childhood miracles of Christ" and calls them a "forgery."

5. Qur'ān 3:49: trans. Robinson, *Christ in Islam,* 142.

6. Qur'ān 5:110: trans. Robinson, *Christ in Islam,* 142.

7. For a discussion of the relationship between the Qur'ān and the *Paidika,* see Robinson, *Christ in Islam,* 143–44.

8. Wansbrough, *Quranic Studies,* 47; see also Mourad, "On the Qur'ānic Stories," 13–24. According to the folk narrative "laws" of Olrik and Lord, doubled and tripled stories or scenes are a common feature of oral tradition: Olrik, "Epic Laws," 131–41; and Lord, *Singer of Tales.*

9. On possible Syriac influence over the language and content of the Qur'ān, see Luxenberg, *Syro-Aramaic Reading.*

10. Robinson, *Christ in Islam,* 144. Robinson argues that the repetition of the phrase "by God's leave" in Sura 5:110 may be related to the accusation against Jesus that he was performing the act on the Sabbath as in the *Paidika,* but see also my discussion below regarding the negotiation of divine agency.

11. Donner, *Muhammad and the Believers;* see also Shoemaker, *Death of a Prophet.* Technically, Donner (pp. 145–93) argues that "Islam," as a unifying label for adherents to Muḥammad's message, did not formally emerge until later, under the leadership of 'Abd al-Malik in the late seventh or early eighth century; prior to that, participants in the movement typically called themselves "believers" (*mu'minūn*) rather than "submitters" (*muslimūn*). For other, earlier reconstructions of Islam as a product of a Jewish and Christian environment, see Lüling, *Über den Ur-Qur'ān* (on an alleged Jewish-Christian *Vorlage*); and Cook and Crone, *Hagarism* (on possible Jewish roots); see also Robinson, *Christ in Islam,* 33–34.

12. Griffith, *Bible in Arabic,* esp. ch. 7.

13. I rely principally on a pair of studies by Neal Robinson: "Creating Birds," 1–13, and *Christ in Islam,* 142–55 (text), and 210–12 (notes). His article examines five different Muslim commentators (Ṭabarī, Zamakhsharī, Rāzī, Bayḍāwī, and Ibn Kathīr), ranging from the tenth to the fourteenth century; in his book he revisits two of them (Zamakhsharī and Rāzī) in some detail. In this chapter, I supplement the list with an examination of two other commentators from the twelfth and thirteenth centuries—Ṭabrisī and Ibn 'Arabī—whose interpretations of the bird miracle are included in Abū Wandī, *'Īsā wa Maryam,* 273 (Ṭabrisī) and 276 (Ibn 'Arabī). Where relevant, I also cite this edition for the five authors treated by Robinson.

14. Ṭabarī (d. 922), *Jāmi' al-bayān,* III.190 (on Sura 3:49), and VII.83 (on Sura 5:510); see also Abū Wandī, *'Īsā wa Maryam,* 74 (on 3:49) and 258 (on 5:110). On Ṭabarī's biography and writings, see Bosworth, "al-Ṭabarī," *EI*[2], X.11–15.

15. Ṭabarī, *Jāmi' al-bayān,* III.190; Abū Wandī, *'Īsā wa Maryam,* 74.

16. See, e.g., the opening verse (Sura 1:1) where the divine attribute, *al-raḥmān* (the Beneficent), is written without an elongated *alif* (*al-raḥman*), a pattern repeated throughout the Qur'ān. In the case of *ṭā'ir,* the reader in the Ḥijāz may have assumed that the *alif* was not written and that the *yā'* that follows it—perhaps unpointed in his text—was a *hamza.*

17. Pickthall (*Meaning,* 69–70, 158) supports this singular reading in his translation of both 3:49 and 5:110.

18. Robinson ("Creating Birds," 4–5) notes that Rāzī and Bayḍāwī each also identify earlier interpreters who supported the singular reading of *ṭā'ir* (Nāfi' and Ya'qūb, respectively): see Rāzī, *Tafsīr,* II.451ff. and III.468ff. (Abū Wandī, *'Īsā wa Maryam,* 94–96 [on 3:49], and 267 [on 5:110]); Bayḍāwī, *Anwār al-tanzīl,* 74 and 166.

19. By the early medieval period, the image of Mary and Jesus on a donkey had become the iconic representation of the Holy Family's flight to Egypt: see Lyster, Hulsman, and Davis, *Be Thou There.*

20. Ṭabarī, *Jāmiʿ al-bayān,* III.190; Abū Wandī, *ʿĪsā wa Maryam,* 74.

21. Robinson, "Creating Birds," 4.

22. Rāzī, *Tafsīr,* II.451ff. (trans. Robinson, "Creating Birds," 5); Abū Wandī, *ʿĪsā wa Maryam,* 95.

23. Ibn ʿArabī, *Tafsīr,* I.349–50; Abū Wandī, *ʿĪsā wa Maryam,* 276 (on 5:110).

24. Zamakhsharī (d. 1144), *al-Kashshāf,* I.431 (on 3:49). Robinson ("Creating Birds," 7–9; *Christ in Islam,* 145) notes that in his commentary on Sura 2:21, where God is notably the agent of the action, Zamakhsharī (*al-Kashshāf,* I.209) similarly interprets the verb *khalaqa* in terms of bringing something into being "by proportioning it and making it regular" (*ʿalā taqdīrin wa istiwāʾin*), as in the case of fashioning a sandal. On Zamakhsharī's life and literary production, see Versteegh, "al-Zamakhsharī," 431–34.

25. Ṭabrisī, *Majmaʿ al-bayān:* Abū Wandī, *ʿĪsā wa Maryam,* 273 (on 5:110). On Ṭabrisī's role in the Shīʿī community as a scholar, jurist, and martyr, see Kohlberg, "al-Ṭabrisī (Ṭabarsī)," 40–41.

26. Ṭabrisī, *Majmaʿ al-bayān:* Abū Wandī, *ʿĪsā wa Maryam,* 273 (on 5:110).

27. Rāzī, *Tafsīr,* II.451ff.; Abū Wandī, *ʿĪsā wa Maryam,* 94–96 (on 3:49). Rāzī's commentary on the use of the verb *khalaqa* in Sura 2:21 may be found at *Tafsīr,* I.209. For his discussion of the verb *khalaqa,* Rāzī relied heavily on the work of the tenth-century philologist Ibn al-Anbārī (d. 940) (Robinson, "Creating Birds," 7–9).

28. Ibn Hishām (d. 833), *Sīrat al-nabī:* trans. Guillaume, *Life of Muhammad,* 271; Robinson, *Christ in Islam,* 144. This biography of Muḥammad is attributed (and probably traces its oral roots) to the eighth-century figure Ibn Isḥāq (d. 761 or 767), but the surviving written version was edited by Ibn Hishām in the ninth century.

29. Ibn Hishām, *Sīrat al-nabī:* trans. Guillaume, *Life of Muhammad,* 271; Robinson, *Christ in Islam,* 144.

30. Ibn Kathīr (d. 1372): *Tafsīr,* I.99. Rāzī (*Tafsīr,* I.209) also quotes from Qāḍī ʿAbd al-Jabbār (d. 1025) in support of this view.

31. Robinson, "Creating Birds," 11.

32. Rāzī, *Tafsīr,* II.451ff.; Abū Wandī, *ʿĪsā wa Maryam,* 95 (on 3:49).

33. Rāzī, *Tafsīr,* III.468ff.

34. Rāzī, *Tafsīr,* II.451ff.; Abū Wandī, *ʿĪsā wa Maryam,* 95 (on 3:49); see also Robinson, "Creating Birds," 11.

35. Bayḍāwī (d. 1286), *Anwār al-tanzīl,* 74; Ibn Kathīr (d. 1372), *Tafsīr,* II.41 (on 3:49); II.678ff. (on 5:110).

36. Rāzī, *Tafsīr,* II.451ff.; Abū Wandī, *ʿĪsā wa Maryam,* 95 (on 3:49). This connection between breath or wind (*rīḥ*), spirit (*rūḥ*), and the role of Gabriel in Jesus' conception is also found in the writings of Muslim apologists such as Shibāb al-Dīn al-Qarāfī (1228–1285), who wrote a *Response* to Paul of Antioch's Christian *Letter to a Muslim Friend in Sidon:* see Qarāfī, *al-Ajwiba,* 79–88; see also Samuel Noble's forthcoming Yale University dissertation, "Muslim-Christian Polemic in 7th/13th Century Egypt."

37. Ibn Kathīr (d. 1372), *Tafsīr,* II.41; Robinson, "Creating Birds," 11.

38. Qur'ān 3:49; see also Ibn Hishām (d. 833), *Sīrat al-nabī:* trans. Guillaume, *Life of Muhammad,* 274, where Jesus' bird miracle is understood by Muḥammad's biographer as "a sign to men and a confirmation of his prophethood" (see also pp. 253 and 276 for similar readings of the story). In Arabic commentary on the Qur'ān, the word *āya* could mean both a textual "verse" (as in the Bible or the Qur'ān) and a "sign" or "miracle" (as a manifestation of the prophets' witness to humanity concerning God): each sense carried with it an association with divine revelation.

39. Ṭabarī, *Jāmi' al-bayān,* III.190ff.; Abū Wandī, *'Īsā wa Maryam,* 74; trans. Robinson, "Creating Birds," 4–5.

40. As cited above, another tradition attributed to Ibn Isḥāq (d. 761 or 767) but preserved in Ibn Hishām's ninth-century *Life of Muḥammad* (trans. Guillaume, 271) shows how early Muslims were familiar with the way that Christians at Najrān in southwest Arabia purportedly cited Jesus' bird miracle in support of their claims about Christ's divinity. On Christian-Muslim engagement in Syriac-speaking contexts, see Griffith, "Disputes with Muslims," 251–73; also Griffith, "Disputing with Islam," 29–54.

41. Qarāfī, *al-Ajwiba:* Awaḍ, 104–5, quotes at 104.

42. For a discussion of the textual evidence, see Burke, *De infantia,* 162–66.

43. Göttingen, Universitätsbibliothek, Syr. 10 (fifth or sixth cent.: Baars and Heldermann, "Neue Materialien"). London, British Library, Add. 14484 (sixth cent.: Wright, *Contributions,* 11–16 [Syriac], 6–11 [English]).

44. See, e.g., Vatican Syr. 159, fol. 237v–39v (1622/23 CE; Burke, "*Infancy Gospel of Thomas* from an Unpublished Syriac Manuscript," 265–99); the version of the *Life of Mary* edited by Budge, *History of the Blessed Virgin Mary* (= *CANT* 94); and another version of the *Life of Mary* (= *CANT* 95), which interpolates stories of the Holy Family's flight to Egypt alongside material from the *Paidika* (heretofore, only the Holy Family material has been published: see Mingana, "Vision of Theophilus," 1–92). A number of unpublished manuscripts related to the *Life of Mary* remain to be studied: for assessments and discussion, see Mimouni, "Les Vies de la Vierge," 211–48, esp. 239–42; and Burke, *De infantia,* 164–65.

45. Milan, Biblioteca Ambrosiana, G 11 sup. (undated): ed. Noja, "À propos du texte arabe," 335–41; French trans. Noja, "L'Évangile arabe apocryphe," 681–90; see also Moraldi, *Nascita e infanzia,* 50; and Moraldi, *Vangelo arabo apocrifo,* 28.

46. Burke, *De infantia,* 167 (these omitted chapters correspond to Ga 12, 15, and 19).

47. Arabic *Paidika* 6: Noja, "À propos du texte arabe," 338; Noja, "L'Évangile arabe apocryphe," 687.

48. Arabic *Paidika* 11: Noja, "À propos du texte arabe," 340; Noja, "L'Évangile arabe apocryphe," 688–89.

49. On the role of Jesus and other biblical prophets in the Qur'ān and early Islam, see Tottoli, *Biblical Prophets.*

50. Tha'labī, *'Arā'is* (Brinner, 650).

51. Tha'labī, *'Arā'is* (Brinner, 652); see also Renard, *Friends of God,* 33–34.

52. Burke, *De infantia,* 166. In Arabic, this collection of infancy stories was (perhaps for the first time) designated as a "gospel," conforming to Qur'ānic and Muslim linguistic usage of the term *injīl.* This point is noted by Gero, "Infancy Gospel," 59.

53. Kisā'ī, *Tales of the Prophets* (Thackston, 332–33); also Tha'labī, *'Arā'is* (Brinner, 647–48); Newby, *Making,* 208–9; and Renard, *Friends of God,* 33–34. On the Islamic profession of faith, see Gimaret, "Shahāda," 201; and Lindsay, *Daily Life,* 140–41.

54. Oxford, Bodleian Library, Oxon. Bodl. Or. 350 (undated): ed. Sike, *Evangelium infantiae.* In this book, I generally cite J. C. Thilo's 1832 edition, which corrected certain errors in Sike: see Thilo, *Codex apocryphus,* xxvi–xliv (introduction), 65–131 (Arabic text and Latin translation); trans. *ANF* 8.405–15.

55. Florence, Biblioteca Laurenziana, Or. 387, 1299 CE: ed. Provera, *Vangelo arabo* (with Italian translation); Genequand, "Vie de Jésus en arabe," 191–204.

56. The Florence text follows closely the order of the Syriac *Life of Mary* (Budge, *History of the Blessed Virgin Mary*), which also does not include these stories from the *Paidika.*

57. Vatican, Syr. 159. Peeters (*Évangiles apocryphes,* vol. 2, 1–68) incorporated this Garshuni text into his French translation of the Oxford manuscript of the *AGI.*

58. Provera (*Vangelo arabo,* 23) seems to take this cut-off point as the extent of "the original part [*la parte originale*] of the *Arabic Gospel of the Infancy.*" However, the fact that the Vatican manuscript leaves off in mid-sentence obviates against this argument. Instead, the truncation of the text is more likely due to the loss of folia at the end of a manuscript sometime in the history of transmission.

59. See Peeters's introduction to the "rédaction syro-arabe" of the work in *Évangiles apocryphes,* vol. 2, i–xxix.

60. Isho'dad of Merv, *Commentary on Matthew* 2 (Gibson, *Commentaries,* I.19–20 [English]; II.lb–lg [Syriac]); cf. *AGI* 1 (Florence, Biblioteca Laurenziana, Or. 387, 2r–v; Provera, *Vangelo arabo,* 66–67). For analysis of the connection between Isho'dad and the Florence *AGI,* see Peeters, *Évangile apocryphes,* II.xi–xii; Provera, *Vangelo arabo,* 20; Elliott, *Apocryphal New Testament,* 100; Horn, "Apocryphal Gospels in Arabic," 599; and Burke, *De infantia,* 166, note 6.

61. I have found theories about Egyptian interpolations in the Oxford MS—advocated or assumed by Provera (*Vangelo arabo,* 23–24) and Burke (*De infantia,* 167)—to be insufficiently supported. The stories about the Holy Family's sojourn in Egypt remain remarkably generic and nonlocalized in comparison with local Egyptian traditions: cf. Lyster, Hulsman, and Davis, *Be Thou There,* esp. ch. 3 (Davis, "Ancient Sources," 133–62); Davis, "Hermeneutic of the Land," 329–36; and Davis, *Coptic Christology in Practice,* 125–48. The only specific geographical reference is to the tree at Maṭarīya (near Cairo), and this could easily be explained through the dissemination of miracle stories and literary "itineraries" associated with pilgrimage travel. There is also ample evidence for cultural contact between Syrians and Egyptians in the early medieval period, exemplified not only by the composition of Syriac works on the Holy Family in Egypt (e.g., *Vision of Theophilus:* ed. Mingana), but also by institutions such as the Monastery of the Syrians in Wādī al-Naṭrūn and practices such as the exchange of patriarchal letters (Innemee and Van Rompay, "La présence des Syriens," 167–202; Heijer, "Relations," 923–38).

62. *AGI* 37: Thilo, *Codex apocryphus,* 110–12; Peeters, *Évangiles apocryphes,* II.45–46; Provera, *Vangelo arabo,* 110 (=ch. 35); cf. the *Armenian Infancy Gospel* 21.1–14 (trans. Terian, 99–104).

63. *AGI* 40: Thilo, *Codex apocryphus,* 114–16; Peeters, *Évangiles apocryphes,* II.48–50; Provera, *Vangelo arabo,* 114–16 (=ch. 39); see also Budge, *History of the Blessed Virgin Mary,* I.70–72; II.76–78. As noted above, the Arabic *Paidika* contains a variation on this tale in which Jesus' playmates are transformed into pigs, monkeys, and wolves: see Arabic *Paidika* 6 (Noja, "À propos du texte arabe," 338; trans. Noja, "L'Évangile arabe apocryphe," 687).

64. *AGI* 41: Thilo, *Codex apocryphus,* 116; Peeters, *Évangiles apocryphes,* II.50; Provera, *Vangelo arabo,* 116–18 (=ch. 40); see also Budge, *History of the Blessed Virgin Mary,* I.72; II.78.

65. Tony Burke, *per litt.,* January 15, 2013.

66. *AGI* 38: Thilo, *Codex apocryphus,* 112; Peeters, *Évangiles apocryphes,* II.46–47; Provera, *Vangelo arabo,* 112 (=ch. 37).

67. *AGI* 39: Thilo, *Codex apocryphus,* 112–14; Peeters, *Évangiles apocryphes,* II.47–48; Provera, *Vangelo arabo,* 112–14 (=ch. 38).

68. *AGI* 42: Thilo, *Codex apocryphus,* 116–18; Peeters, *Évangiles apocryphes,* II.50–53; Provera, *Vangelo arabo,* 118–20 (=ch. 41); see also Budge, *History of the Blessed Virgin Mary,* I.72–73; II.78–79.

69. *AGI* 43: Thilo, *Codex apocryphus,* 118–20; Peeters, *Évangiles apocryphes,* II.54; see also Budge, *History of the Blessed Virgin Mary,* I.72–73; II.78–79. Note that while these two snake stories are also found in the Syriac *Life of Mary,* they are not paired together in that text and appear in the opposite order, with the story about Jesus' brother James coming much earlier in the narrative.

70. *AGI* 36: Thilo, *Codex apocryphus,* 110; Peeters, *Évangiles apocryphes,* II.44–45; Provera, *Vangela arabo,* 110 (=ch. 34); see also Budge, *The History of the Blessed Virgin Mary,* I.70; II.76.

71. *AGI* 46: Thilo, *Codex apocryphus,* 122; Peeters, *Évangiles apocryphes,* II.56–57.

72. *AGI* 54: Thilo, *Codex apocryphus,* 128; Peeters, *Évangiles apocryphes,* II.64–65.

73. *AGI* 50–53: Thilo, *Codex apocryphus,* 124–28; Peeters, *Évangiles apocryphes,* II.62–64.

74. *Paidika* 17 (Burke, *De infantia,* 335–37); cf. Syriac *Paidika* 19 (ed. Wright, *Contributions,* Syr. 16 [text], 11 [translation]).

75. *AGI* 50: Thilo, *Codex apocryphus,* 124–26; Peeters, *Évangiles apocryphes,* II.62.

76. *AGI* 51: Thilo, *Codex apocryphus,* 126; Peeters, *Évangiles apocryphes,* II.63.

77. *AGI* 52: Thilo, *Codex apocryphus,* 126–28; Peeters, *Évangiles apocryphes,* II.63.

78. *AGI* 51: Thilo, *Codex apocryphus,* 126; Peeters, *Évangiles apocryphes,* II.63.

79. *AGI* 52: Thilo, *Codex apocryphus,* 126–8; Peeters, *Évangiles apocryphes,* II.63.

80. The definitive work on the history of the translation movement was written by Gutas, *Greek Thought;* see also O'Leary, *How Greek Science Passed,* esp. 155–75; and Goodman, "Translation," 477–97. Several later commentators—including al-Akhbārī, Ṣā'id al-Andalusī, Ibn Abī Uṣaybi'a, and Ibn al-Nadīm—all comment on the instrumental role of al-Manṣur: see Gutas, *Greek Thought,* 30–31.

81. On the rise of new observational techniques in astronomy during the ninth and tenth centuries, see Saliba, *History,* 15–16. On the production of revolutionary works in medicine, astronomy, mathematics, physics, and philosophy in the tenth and eleventh centuries, see Gutas, *Greek Thought,* 152–53.

82. *AGI* 51: Thilo, *Codex apocryphus,* 126; Peeters, *Évangiles apocryphes,* II.63.

83. Prominent examples of earlier precedents include a no-longer-extant Sanskrit text translated into Arabic under the caliph al-Manṣūr (known in Arabic as *Zīj al-Sindhind al-kabīr*), and Ptolemy's *Handy Tables* (translated into Arabic under the title *al-Qānūn fī ʿilm al-nujūm*): see the discussion in Ragep, "Astronomy."

84. See, e.g., King, "Astronomy," 276ff.

85. Ibn al-Akfānī, *Irshād* (Witkam, *De Egyptische arts,* 408).

86. Sezgin, *GAS,* VI.125; Saliba, *History,* 16.

87. These examples are catalogued and discussed by Saliba (*History,* 16–17), and Gutas (*Greek Thought,* 119–20, 133–34).

88. On al-Kindī, see Endress, "Die wissenschaftliche Literatur," 428; Vaglieri and Celentano, "Trois epîtres," 523–62; and Saliba, *History,* 55. On the Banū Mūsā, see Hill, "Mūsā, banū," 640–41; Pingree, "Banū Mūsā," III.7.716–17; Rāshid, *Les mathématiques;* Casulleras, "Banū Mūsā," 92–94; Darrbagh, "Banū Mūsā"; and Masood, *Science and Islam.*

89. Gutas, *Greek Thought,* 125–26; Sezgin, *GAS,* V.154; and VII.73 (no. 1); Gabrieli, "Nota," 353–54; and Wilcox, "Transmission."

90. The latter two works by Qusṭā ibn Lūqā are still extant. A copy of his *Kitāb hay'at al-aflāk* survives in Oxford's Bodleian collection (Bodleian MS Arabic 879); for a discussion, summary, and partial translation of Qusṭā's *Kitāb fī al-ʿamal bi-l-kura al-nujūmiyya,* see Worrell, "Qusṭā ibn Lūqā," 285–93. Qusṭā's introductory treatise is no longer extant: the medieval Arabic bibliographers Ibn al-Nadīm, Ibn al-Qifṭī, and Ibn Abī Uṣaybiʿa refer to two different introductory titles, and it is unclear whether these were two separate compositions or variations of the same work. Finally, Qusṭā ibn Lūqā has been credited with the authorship of another extant work, entitled *On the Use of the Spherical Astrolabe* (*Kitāb fī al-ʿamal bi-l-asṭurlāb al-kurī*) (Leiden MS Or. 51.2; *Handlist,* 12), but the authenticity of the authorial attribution remains in doubt. For a bibliographical discussion (and various enumerations) of Qusṭā's astronomical works, see Kheirandish, "Qusṭā ibn Lūqā," 948–49. For discussions of his larger theological and scientific œuvre, see Graf, *GCAL,* II.30–2; and Isbir, *Risāla,* esp. 5–17.

91. Saliba, *History,* 17, although he notes that this work is alternatively attributed to the Banū Mūsā in one source.

92. Khwārizmi, *Mafātīḥ al-ulūm* (*Keys of the Sciences*): ed. Vloten. Little is known about this author, who should not be confused with the famous mathematician Abū Jaʿfar Muḥammad ibn Mūsā al-Khwārizmī. For a discussion of the *Keys of the Sciences* and other works belonging to this classificatory genre, see Hill, "Mathematics," 250.

93. Worrell, "Qusṭā ibn Lūqā," 285, note 5.

94. Qusṭā ibn Lūqā, *Book on the Use of the Celestial Globe* 1 (trans. Worrell, "Qusṭā ibn Lūqā," 287).

95. Qusṭā ibn Lūqā, *Book on the Use of the Celestial Globe* 1 and 3 (trans. Worrell, "Qusṭā ibn Lūqā," 287–88). Worrell seems to misread/mistranslate the phrase *fī al-daqā'iq.* Instead of meaning "to be exact" (as Worrell would have it), I believe this phrase actually refers to the minutes of a circle, with each minute representing one-sixtieth of the total circumference, or a half degree (*daraja*) of a circle (Lane, *Arabic Lexicon,* III.896). Thus, an amended translation of the passage in question would read something

like the following: "And the sun revolves once in a day and a night and a division-part of 360 is a division-part of that rotation *into the minutes* which the sun has travelled in the circle of the ecliptic on that day" (Worrell, 288, modified, with the italics marking my substitution).

96. *AGI* 51: Thilo, *Codex apocryphus,* 126; Peeters, *Évangiles apocryphes,* II.63. In addition to "minutes" (*daqā'iq*), Jesus also refers to *sha'āyir,* which in other contexts can connote a sixth of a unit of measurement (Lane, *Arabic Lexicon,* IV.1561).

97. Khwārizmi, *Mafātīḥ al-ulūm* (Vloten, 215).

98. Ibid. For another use of the term "minutes" (*daqā'iq*) as an astronomical unit of measurement, see Khwārizmi, *Mafātīḥ al-ulūm* (Vloten, 224), where he presents a method of verifying "genuine planets" by determining "if there is between the sun and the planet sixteen minutes (*daqīqa*) and no less"; but if there is more than sixteen degrees between the planet and the sun, then he notes that there is "conflagration" (*al-iḥtirāq*). For examples of Khwārizmi's use of "degrees" (*darajāt*) as units of measurement, see the text at Vloten, 226–27 and 233.

99. Qusṭā ibn Lūqā, *Book on the Use of the Celestial Globe* 4 (trans. Worrell, "Qusṭā ibn Lūqā," 288, modified slightly).

100. Khwārizmi, *Mafātīḥ al-ulūm* (Vloten, 215).

101. Ibid. (Vloten, 223).

102. Ibid. (Vloten, 221); see also pp. 226–27, where Khwārizmi uses this same adjective in speaking about how a sign of the zodiac stands opposite (*muqābil*) to its astrological house.

103. Ibid. (Vloten, 232).

104. See the summary of Qusṭā ibn Lūqā, *Book on the Use of the Celestial Globe* (*Kitāb al-'amal bi-l-kura al-nujūmiyya*), chs. 25–32, in Worrell, "Qusṭā ibn Lūqā," 291–92.

105. Khwārizmi, *Mafātīḥ al-ulūm* (Vloten, 221–22). In the chapter of his *Prolegomena* (*Muqaddima*) dedicated to astronomical science (*'ilm al-hay'a*), Ibn Khaldūn (d. 1406) also refers specifically to the "retrograde and direct motions of the stars" (*al-rujū' wa al-istiqāmat li-l-kawākib*) as fundamental data for determining their epicycles (Ibn Khaldūn, *Prolegomena* 6.21; trans. Rosenthal, III.137). An Arabic edition of this text, edited by Khalīl Shihāda and Suhayl Zakkār, is available online at http://www.muslimphilosophy.com, along with Rosenthal's translation.

106. *AGI* 51: Thilo, *Codex apocryphus,* 126; Peeters, *Évangiles apocryphes,* II.63.

107. Khwārizmi, *Mafātīḥ al-ulūm* (Vloten, 232).

108. On the integration of Ptolemaic astronomy and astrology into school curricula, see Gutas, *Greek Thought,* 15. One example, discussed by Saliba (*History,* 33–39), is Naṣīr al-Dīn al-Ṭūsī's twelfth-century treatise *A Memento on the Science of Astronomy* (*Tadhkira fi 'ilm al-hay'a*), which was written without complex mathematical proofs so as to make it "suitable for school instruction" at an introductory level. The medieval author, Ibn al- Akfānī (*Irshād al-Qāṣid:* ed. Sprenger, 85; cited by Saliba, *History,* 34), notes that different astronomical handbooks were used at different levels of the curriculum: "As for these texts which are devoid of geometric proofs and which are devoted to the description of these matters without proofs the introductory one (*mukhtaṣara*) among them is the *Tadhkira* of Khwāja Naṣīr al-Dīn al-Ṭūsī, the intermediate is the *Hay'a* of (Mu'ayyad al-Dīn) al-'Urḍī, and the elaborate (*mabṣūta*) is the *Nihāyat al-Idrāk* of

al-Quṭb al-Shīrāzī." The production of numerous commentaries on such texts also serves as evidence for their use in the classroom (Saliba, *History,* 34, 37, and 45–46, note 51).

109. *AGI* 52: Thilo, *Codex apocryphus,* 126–28; Peeters, *Évangiles apocryphes,* II.63.

110. The two definitive works on Arabic and Islamic medicine are Ullmann, *Islamic Medicine;* and Pormann and Savage-Smith, *Medieval Islamic Medicine;* but see also Isaacs, "Arabic Medical Literature," 342–63.

111. Graf, *GCAL,* II.109–12; Savage-Smith, "Ṭibb," 452b; also Goodman, "Translation," 480.

112. On the prominent cultural role of these multilingual families of physicians, see Gutas, *Greek Thought,* 31, 34, 118, 133, 135; see also Whipple's earlier article, "Role of the Nestorians," 313–23.

113. With respect to Ḥunayn's translation work, Isaacs (*Arabic Medical Literature,* 344–45) calls him "the Erasmus of the Arabic Renaissance."

114. For a bibliography, see Graf, *GCAL,* II.122–29.

115. On this "school" and the translation work of Isḥāq and Ḥubaysh, see Bergsträsser, *Ḥunain ibn Isḥāḳ und seine Schule;* and Graf, *GCAL,* II.129–32. Another prominent figure in this school of Ḥunayn's disciples was 'Īsā ibn Yaḥyā, who translated, among other works, Galen's treatise *On the Difference Between Similar Body Parts* (Gk. *Peri tēs tōn homoiomerōn sōmatōn diaphoras;* Ar. *Kitāb Jālīnūs fī ikhtilāf al-a'ḍā' al-mutashābiha al-ajzā'*): ed. Strohmaier, *Galen: Über die Verschiedenheit.*

116. Gutas, *Greek Thought,* 124; see also Mijallī, *Ḥunayn ibn Isḥāq.*

117. For a list of translations produced by Ḥunayn's "school," see Salama-Carr, *Traduction,* 69–75; and also Sa'di, "Biobibliographical Study," 409–46. Sa'di organizes his bibliography in four sections: (1) nonmedical translations, including philosophical works by Plato, Aristotle, Galen, and others (pp. 423–25); (2) medical translations, including Hippocrates and Galen (pp. 425–34); (3) original nonmedical works (pp. 434–37); (4) original medical works (pp. 437–42). Ḥunayn is credited with having translated the Greek Old Testament (the Septuagint) into Arabic, but unfortunately it is no longer extant: Strohmaier, "Ḥunayn b. Isḥāḳ," III.578 (col. 2); and Griffith, *Church in the Shadow of the Mosque,* 119–20. On Ḥunayn's translations of Aristotle's philosophical and other works, see Peeters, *Aristoteles Arabus.* On his translations of astronomical and meteorological treatises, see Sa'di, "Biobibliographical Study," 424; and Daiber, *Kompendium;* see also Ḥunayn's translation of a Pseudo-Galenic treatise edited by Bergsträsser (*Pseudogaleni in Hippocratis*), a work in which knowledge of the macrocosmos (e.g., astronomy and meteorology) is closely linked with knowledge of the microcosmos (e.g., human anatomy). One also observes the confluence of such interests in Ḥunayn's studies of human vision, where he follows Galen in seeing a connection between the structure of the eye and the surrounding air or *pneuma:* Eastwood, *Elements of Vision.*

118. Bergsträsser, *Ḥunain ibn Isḥāq: Über die syrischen und arabischen Galen-Übersetzungen;* Bergsträsser, *Neue Materialien;* see also Meyerhof, "Les versions syriaques et arabes," 33–51; Meyerhof, "New Light," 685–724; and Walzer, "D̲j̲ālīnūs," III.402 (col. 2).

119. Strohmaier, "Ḥunayn b. Isḥāḳ," III.578 (col. 2).

120. Gutas, *Greek Thought,* 119, 134, 144.

121. On this topic, see Biesterfeldt, *Galens Traktat.*

122. Galen's medical ideas and language were also conveyed through the translation of other ancient Greek authors, whose writings had been subsequently redacted through a Galenic lens: for an example relevant to Ḥunayn's corpus, see Filius, ed., *Problemata Physica.*

123. Two complete Arabic translations of this work survive: Oxford, Bodleian MS. Marsh 158 (=Summary Catalogue 9153); and London, British Museum, Additional MS. 23406 (1482 CE). Of the fifteen books in the treatise, only the first eight books and the first five chapters of the ninth book are extant in Greek; for the remainder, scholars must rely on the Arabic translation made by Ḥunayn and Ḥubaysh. For an edition of the surviving Greek text, see Kühn, *Claudii Galeni opera omnia,* II.215–731; a corresponding English translation was published by Singer, *Galen on Anatomical Procedures.* A critical edition of the first nine books of Ḥunayn's Arabic version has been produced by Garofalo (*Anatomicarum administrationum libri*). An Arabic edition of books 9–15, along with a German translation, was published by Simon (*Sieben Bücher*); for a corresponding English translation, see Duckworth, Lyons, and Towers, *Galen on Anatomical Procedures.*

124. For the Greek text of Galen's two treatises *On the Anatomy of Veins and Arteries* (*Kitāb fī tashrīḥ al-ʿurūq wa al-awrād*) and *On the Anatomy of Nerves* (*Kitāb fī tashrīḥ al-ʿaṣab*), see Kühn, *Claudii Galeni opera omnia,* II.779–830 and II.831–56. On their translation into Syriac and Arabic, see Iskandar, "An Attempted Reconstruction," 235–58; see also Gutas, *Greek Thought,* 119.

125. For a critical edition of the Arabic based on eight MSS, see Ḥunayn ibn Isḥāq, *al-Masāʾil fī al-ṭibb li-l-mutaʿallimīn* (ed. Abū Riyyān et al.; trans. Ghalioungui, *Questions on Medicine*). There are three extant Syriac manuscripts of this work preserved in Louvain, Birmingham, and Vatican City. The first two are twentieth-century copies. Louvain CSCO Syr. 21 dates to 1904 (Halleux, "Les manuscripts syriaques," 35–48; cf. Chabot, "Version syriaque," 80–143). Mingana Syr. 589 in Birmingham dates to 1932 but is based on an earlier copy, also made in 1904 (Mingana, *Catalogue,* cols. 1125–28). The third manuscript, Vatican Syr. 192, is considerably older: its recent editors Wilson and Dinkha (*Hunain*) argue for an eleventh-century date, although it just as easily could be from the twelfth century; see also Degen, "Oldest Known Manuscript," 63–71.

126. Ḥunayn and Ḥubaysh, *Questions:* Wilson and Dinkha, *Hunain,* 92 (fol. 129v). In Vat. Syr. 192, the beginning of the manuscript is missing. This missing portion is not accounted for in the work's pagination, and the numbering of the folia for the rest of the work is out of proper order: thus, Ḥunayn is credited with writing folia 107r–29v (the beginning of the surviving text), while Ḥubaysh is credited with the rest, which is composed of folia 129v–51v, followed by folia 1r–106v. The Syriac manuscript in the Mingana collection also contains a notice as to where Ḥunayn's work ended: in that text, he is credited with folia 22a–35a, while Ḥubaysh is credited with folia 35a–112a (Wilson and Dinkha, *Hunain,* xvi).

127. In what follows, I cite both the Cairo critical edition edited by Abū Riyyān et al. (*Masāʾil*) and the facsimile of Vat. Syr. 192 reproduced by Wilson and Dinkha, which includes an unedited Arabic version. Although Vat. Syr. 192 lacks the opening and closing sections of the text and although Wilson and Dinkha mistakenly omit folio 80r and reproduce folio 80v twice (pp. 499 and 501), their edition has the advantage of giving

readers access to both the parallel Syriac text and an English translation based on the Syriac. All translations of the Arabic are my own, although readers may also refer to Ghalioungui's translation.

128. *AGI* 52: Thilo, *Codex apocryphus,* 126; Peeters, *Évangiles apocryphes,* II.63.

129. Ḥunayn and Ḥubaysh, *Questions:* Abū Riyyān et al., 1; section missing in Wilson and Dinkha.

130. Ibid.: Abū Riyyān et al., 36–40, 58–59, 207, 214–15; Wilson and Dinkha, 12–15, 38–39, 340–41, 358–59. Pharmaceutical remedies are thus designed to return "the nature of the human body to its own nature" (*ṭabī'at badan al-insān ilā ṭabī'atihi*) (Abū Riyyān et al., 250; Wilson and Dinkha, 428–29).

131. Ibid.: Abū Riyyān et al., 225–26; Wilson and Dinkha, 378–79.

132. *AGI* 52: Thilo, *Codex apocryphus,* 126; Peeters, *Évangiles apocryphes,* II.63.

133. Ḥunayn and Ḥubaysh, *Questions:* Abū Riyyān et al., 2–3 (cf. 13); section missing in Wilson and Dinkha.

134. Ibid.: Abū Riyyān et al., 33–34, 47–50, 59–60, 92–93, 95–96, 97–99, 114–15, 120–21, 122–23, 229–31; Wilson and Dinkha, 6–7, 22–23, 40–41, 56–59, 100–101, 104–5, 108–11, 138–39, 150–51, 154–55, 384–87.

135. Ibid.: Abū Riyyān et al., 131–32, 235–36; Wilson and Dinkha, 174–75, 420–21.

136. Ibid.: Abū Riyyān et al., 231–34; Wilson and Dinkha, 388–95.

137. Ibid.: Abū Riyyān et al., 260–61, 261–62, 272–86; Wilson and Dinkha, 448–49, 452–53, 482–527.

138. Ibid.: Abū Riyyān et al., 266–67; Wilson and Dinkha, 466–67.

139. Ibid.: Abū Riyyān et al., 288–91; Wilson and Dinkha, 534–41.

140. Ibid.: Abū Riyyān et al., 294–334; Wilson and Dinkha, 548–609 (text breaks before the end in this edition).

141. *AGI* 52: Thilo, *Codex apocryphus,* 126; Peeters, *Évangiles apocryphes,* II.63.

142. Ḥunayn and Ḥubaysh, *Questions:* Abū Riyyān et al., 2; section missing in Wilson and Dinkha.

143. Ibid.: Abū Riyyān et al., 9–11; section missing in Wilson and Dinkha; see also Ebied and Young, "Manuscript," 264–69, especially where they cite a brief section on the tongue as an organ "composed of soft flesh, veins (*awrida*), small arteries (*shariyyānāt*), and numerous nerves (*a'ṣāb*)" (p. 267).

144. Ḥunayn and Ḥubaysh, *Questions:* Abū Riyyān et al., 30–31 (cf. 250–52); Wilson and Dinkha, 2–3 (cf. 432–33).

145. Ibid.: Abū Riyyān et al., 101–3, 114–20; Wilson and Dinkha, 116–19, 138–49.

146. *AGI* 52: Thilo, *Codex apocryphus,* 126–28; Peeters, *Évangiles apocryphes,* II.63.

147. Ḥunayn and Ḥubaysh, *Questions:* Abū Riyyān et al., 2–9; section missing in Wilson and Dinkha.

148. Ibid.: Abū Rīyān et al., 25–26; Wilson and Dinkha, 10–11.

149. Ibid.: Abū Riyyān et al., 80–81, 88–92, 93–94, 96–97, 98–99, 99–101, 114–15, 139–44, 179, 191–93, 202–3, 203–4; Wilson and Dinkha, 78–79, 92–99, 102–3, 106–7, 110–11, 112–15, 138–39, 188–95, 272–73, 296–99, 324–25, and 326–29.

150. Bergsträsser, *Ḥunain ibn Isḥāq über die syrischen und arabischen Galen-Übersetzungen,* 18.19–19.1; textual corrections in Bergsträsser, *Neue Materialien,* 17; trans. Gutas, *Greek Thought,* 15.

151. Ibn Riḍwān, *Useful Book* (*al-Nāfiʿ*): MS. 4026, fol. 12b.11–16b.12 and MS. Arberry 17.8–20.10; trans. Iskandar, "Attempted Reconstruction," 253–56 (see also his discussion of the preparatory curriculum on pp. 247–48).

152. Ibid.

153. Ed. Bergsträsser, *Pseudogaleni in Hippocratis;* see also Sālim, *Kitāb Jālīnūs.*

154. ʿArīb ibn Saʿīd of Cordoba (d. ca. 980), *Kitāb khalq al-janīn* (Ullmann, *Islamic Medicine,* 112–14).

155. Qusṭā ibn Lūqā, *Risāla fī al-farq* (ed. Isbir, 65–68).

156. Ibn Riḍwān, *Useful Book* (*al-Nāfiʿ*): trans. Iskandar, "An Attempted Reconstruction," 255.

157. Ibn Kathīr, *Tafsīr,* II.41; trans. Robinson, "Creating Birds," 11.

158. Ibn Kathīr, *Tafsīr,* II.41; trans. Robinson, "Creating Birds," 11–12. Here, Ibn Kathīr is alluding to (and partially quoting from) the Qur'ān 5:110.

159. Ibid. It should also be noted that in this same context Ibn Riḍwān singles out Ḥunayn, along with Muḥammad al-Rāzī, as one of "the most celebrated physicians who were thought by people to have completed (their studies) in the art of medicine" (Iskandar, "Attempted Reconstruction," 256).

160. Important studies of this subject include Fahd, *La divination arabe;* Ullmann, *Die Natur- und Geheimwissenschaften;* Ḥamdān, *ʿIlm al-ḥurūf;* Gril, "Science of Letters," II.105–219; Lory, *La science des lettres;* Böwering, "Sulamī's Treatise," 339–97; and Melvin-Koushki, "Quest."

161. See Böwering, "Sulamī's Treatise," 341–43, where the author discusses the practices I list here, as well as more practical uses of the Arabic letters in commercial settings, such as systems of financial accounting; see also Souissi, "Ḥisāb al-ghubār," 468–69; Sabra, "ʿIlm al-ḥisāb," 1138–41; and Souissi, "ʿIlm al-handasa," 411–14.

162. Fahd, *La divination arabe;* Fahd and Regourd, "Zā'ird̲ja," 404–5.

163. Geomancy is a subspecies of divination in which markings or patterns in rocks or sand on the ground are interpreted as having a special (sometimes alphabetic) significance: see Fahd, *La divination arabe,* 196–204; Fahd, "Khaṭṭ," 1128–30; Hughes, "Daʿwah," 72–78.

164. In addition to their numerological use in astrology, letters were interpreted as numerals in the production of chronograms—writings, often inscriptions, that presented significant past or future dates in encoded form: on their use in Arabic cultural contexts, see Colin, "Ḥisāb al-d̲jummal," 468; also Heinrichs and Knysh, "Ramz," 426–30.

165. Fahd, "Khawāṣṣ al-Ḳurʾān," 1133–34.

166. Pingree, "Ḳirān," 130–31; Pingree, "ʿIlm al-hay'a," 1135–38; see also Kunitzsch, "Nud̲jūm," 97–105; and Fahd, "Nud̲jūm," 105–8.

167. Fahd, "Ḥurūf," 595–96; Fleisch, "Ḥurūf al-hid̲jā'," 596–600; Welch, "Al-Ḳur'ān," 412–14.

168. On the interpretation of the "mysterious letters" that mark the beginning of twenty-nine Qur'ānic suras, traditionally called the "openers of the suras" (*fawātiḥ al-suwar*), see Hirschfeld, *New Researches,* 101–3; Nöldeke, Schwally, Bergsträsser, and Pretzl, *Geschichte,* II.68–78; Bauer, "Über die Anordnung der Suren," 1–20; Goosens, "Ursprung," 191–226; Jeffery, "Mystic Letters," 247–60; Seale, "Mysterious Letters,"

276–79; Jones, "Mystical Letters," 5–11; Cachia, "Bayḍāwī on the *Fawātiḥ?*" 218–31; Bellamy, "Mysterious Letters," 267–85; and Massey, "Mysterious Letters," 471–76. On traditions that Muḥammad was an expert in letter speculation, see Nyberg, "Några," 30–40; cited by Tor Andrae, *In the Garden of Myrtles,* 19–20.

169. See esp. Melvin-Koushki's helpful discussion of the role that lettrism played in the classification of the sciences: "Quest," 209–16.

170. See, e.g., Ibn Khaldūn, *Prolegomena* (*Muqaddima*) 6.28 (=III.137–91): trans. Rosenthal, III.171–227, esp. pp. 171–76; Fahd, "Ḥurūf," 595–96.

171. *Sharḥ al-mī'īn* (Istanbul, Topkapı Sarayı, MS. Ahmet III 1609/3, fol. 46): cited by Fahd, "Ḥurūf," 595–96.

172. Ibn Khaldūn, *Prolegomena* (*Muqaddima*) 6.28: trans. Rosenthal, III.171.

173. Ibn Khaldūn, *Prolegomena* (*Muqaddima*) 6.18: trans. Rosenthal, III.111–18. Ibn Khaldūn asserts that *'ilm al-ḥurūf* "is clearly a kind of sorcery," and therefore, following his logic, it would be rightly categorized as a subdivision of the "intellectual sciences."

174. Ibn Khaldūn, *Prolegomena* (*Muqaddima*) 6.28: trans. Rosenthal, III.176. On *al-sīmiyā'* and its classification as an "occult science," see Melvin-Koushki, "Quest," 210.

175. Melvin-Koushki, "Quest," 183–204.

176. Zarcone et al., "Taṣawwuf (a.)," 313–32. Standard studies of Sufism and Ṣūfī literature include monographs by Gramlich (*Wunder; Sendschreiben; Schlaglichter; Islamische Mystik; Nahrung der Herzen; Weltverzicht*), Meier (*Essays*), and Ritter (*Ocean of the Soul*); see also Andrae (*In the Garden of Myrtles*), Baldick (*Mystical Islam*), and Smith (*Studies*). On the above-mentioned early figures associated with Baṣra and Baghdad, see Arnaldez, "al-Muḥāsibī," 466–67; Böwering, "Sahl al-Tustarī," 840–41; Madelung, "al-Kharrāz," 1083–84; and Arberry, "al-Djunayd," 600.

177. Zarcone et al., "Taṣawwuf (a.)," 313–32; see also Baldick, *Mystical Islam,* 40, on the way that the early Ṣūfī author al-Tustarī discusses the religious life as one of the four main branches of science, alongside medicine, astrology, and alchemy.

178. The standard Arabic edition was published by Böwering and Orfali, *Sufi Treatises;* for an English translation, see Böwering, "Sulamī's Treatise," 339–97, translation at 370–93. On later medieval developments in the science of the letters (*'ilm al-ḥurūf*) after Sulamī, including the two leading literary lights of the early thirteenth century, Abū l-'Abbās Aḥmad b. 'Alī al-Būnī (d. 1225) and Ibn al-'Arabī (d. 1240), and the late-fourteenth-century Ḥurūfiyya movement, see Lory, *La science des lettres,* 54–58, 91–136.

179. Böwering and Orfali, *Sufi Treatises,* 9–11 (quote at 11).

180. Ibid., 20–22. Partly on account of his reliance on earlier authors, Baldick (*Mystical Islam,* 58) gives a rather negative assessment of Sulamī's originality, a judgment that fails to take account of some of the interesting ways Sulamī engages with alphabetic hermeneutics and traditions about Jesus' childhood.

181. Sulamī, *Explaining the Meaning of the Letters* 3: ed. Böwering and Orfali, *Sufi Treatises,* 1 (Arabic page numbering); trans. Böwering, "Sulamī's Treatise," 370–71.

182. Sulamī, *Explaining the Meaning of the Letters* 4: ed. Böwering and Orfali, *Sufi Treatises,* 1–2 (Arabic page numbering); trans. Böwering, "Sulamī's Treatise," 371.

183. Sulamī, *Explaining the Meaning of the Letters* 5, cf. 7 ("The *Alif* signifies God's gifts"): ed. Böwering and Orfali, *Sufi Treatises,* 2 (Arabic page numbering); trans. Böwering, "Sulamī's Treatise," 371, cf. 372.

184. Sulamī, *Explaining the Meaning of the Letters* 11, 12, 15, 18: ed. Böwering and Orfali, *Sufi Treatises,* 3–4 (Arabic page numbering); trans. Böwering, "Sulamī's Treatise," 373–74.

185. Sulamī, *Explaining the Meaning of the Letters* 22–27: ed. Böwering and Orfali, *Sufi Treatises,* 5–6 (Arabic page numbering); trans. Böwering, "Sulamī's Treatise," 375–77.

186. Sulamī, *Explaining the Meaning of the Letters* 21: ed. Böwering and Orfali, *Sufi Treatises,* 5 (Arabic page numbering); trans. Böwering, "Sulamī's Treatise," 375.

187. One finds close parallels to Sulamī's material on Jesus in Tha'labī, *'Arā'is* (trans. Brinner, 647–48).

188. Sulamī, *Explaining the Meaning of the Letters* 6: ed. Böwering and Orfali, *Sufi Treatises,* 2 (Arabic page numbering); trans. Böwering, "Sulamī's Treatise," 372 (modified slightly).

189. *AGI* 48: Thilo, *Codex apocryphus,* 122–24; cf. *Paidika* 6.1–2f (Burke, *De infantia,* 309–19); and the Syriac *Paidika* 6 (Wright, *Contributions,* 12ff. [Syriac], 7ff. [English]; Burke, "The *Infancy Gospel of Thomas* from an Unpublished Syriac Manuscript," 272–81).

190. Sulamī, *Explaining the Meaning of the Letters* 27: ed. Böwering and Orfali, *Sufi Treatises,* 6 (Arabic page numbering); trans. Böwering, "Sulamī's Treatise," 377.

191. *AGI* 48–49: ed. Thilo, *Codex apocryphus,* 122–24. In contrast, the Greek *Paidika* has the first teacher (Zacchaeus) simply write out the entire alphabet (*ho alphabētos*), while the second teacher only tries to teach him the letter *alpha* before Jesus responds, "You tell me first what beta is and I shall tell you what alpha is" (*Paidika* 6.2f and 13.1–2: Burke, *De infantia,* 317 and 329). The Syriac (6.2f) differs slightly. In the first teacher episode, we are told that the schoolmaster Zacchaeus "began to tell him (the letters) from Alaph" and went through "the whole alphabet" (ed. and trans. Wright, *Contributions,* 14 [Syriac], 8–9 [English]). In the second teacher episode (14), the Syriac resembles more closely the *AGI* and Sulamī's account(s) insofar as Jesus' teacher tries to get him to say both aleph and beth (ed. and trans. Wright, *Contributions,* 15 [Syriac], 10 [English]).

192. In his study of the Ṣūfī ethic of world renunciation, Gramlich (*Weltverzicht,* 87–89 and 368) describes Jesus as an "Idealgestalt des Asketentums" and as "das Vorbild der Asketen"; see also his monograph, *Die Wunder der Freunde Gottes* (1987), where he presents a phenomenology of miracles attributed to prophets, saints, and other "friends of God." Gramlich's twofold typology of "Machtwunder" ("miracles of power") and "Huldwunder" ("miracles of grace") includes a number of subcategories that match Jesus' biographical portrait—miracles related to pregnancy and birth; special powers related to knowledge and perception; extraordinary control over the natural world (both inanimate objects and animate creatures), and the ability to heal the sick and raise the dead. For specific examples pertaining to Jesus: see Gramlich, *Wunder,* 29, 39, 65, 76, 80, 83, 109, 114, 148, 166, 194, 343, 351, 353, 359, 382.

193. Sulamī, *Explaining the Meaning of the Letters* 1: ed. Böwering and Orfali, *Sufi Treatises,* 1 (Arabic page numbering); trans. Böwering, "Sulamī's Treatise," 370. Jesus' status as messenger (*rasūl*) and prophet (*nabi'*) in Islam gave him special authorization for this role: later, in chapter 20 (ed. Böwering and Orfali, *Sufi Treatises,* 5; trans. Böwering, "Sulamī's Treatise," 375), Sulamī underscores the fact that "the realities of the letters, well-protected in God's presence, can only be discovered by God's messengers and the

elite of His prophets," and quotes a passage from the Qur'ān (72:26–27) in support of this point. On the status of the "friends of God" in Sufism, see Baldick, *Mystical Islam,* 37–40 (on Ṭustari and his view that "God's friends" are elected prior to birth), and 82–85 (on Ibn 'Arabī, who considered Jesus the seal or consummation of a general cycle of "friends" prior to the life of Muḥammad).

194. Sulamī, *Explaining the Meaning of the Letters* 19: ed. Böwering and Orfali, *Sufi Treatises,* 5 (Arabic page numbering); trans. Böwering, "Sulamī's Treatise," 374–75.

195. Sulamī, *Explaining the Meaning of the Letters* 19: ed. Böwering and Orfali, *Sufi Treatises,* 5 (Arabic page numbering); trans. Böwering, "Sulamī's Treatise," 375.

196. *AGI* 36: Thilo, *Codex apocryphus,* 110; Peeters, *Évangiles apocryphes,* II.44–45.

197. For other examples, see Renard, *Friends of God,* 29–35.

198. Ernst and Lawrence, *Sufi Martyrs,* 51–57; Renard, *Friends of God,* 29.

199. 'Abd al-Ḥaqq's brief summary of Shah Mīna's life (from his *Akhbār al-akhyār*) is translated by Ernst and Lawrence, *Sufi Martyrs,* 52–53.

200. Irtadā 'Alī Khān's somewhat longer account of Shah Mīna's life is also translated by Ernst and Lawrence, *Sufi Martyrs,* 53–56.

201. Al-Shaykh al-Mufīd, *Book of Guidance* 1.7: ed. Ḥusayn al-A'āmī, 161; trans. Howard, 229–31; see also Renard, *Friends of God,* 35.

202. Ernst and Lawrence, *Sufi Martyrs,* 52.

203. Ibid., 53.

204. Ibid. Actually, according to Irtadā 'Alī Khān's account, Mina was designated a saint even prior to birth. While he was still in his mother's womb, people heard words of meditation and Qur'ānic recitation coming from her belly.

205. Ibid.

206. Ibid.; cf. *Paidika* 14 (Burke, *De infantia,* 331–33; Wright, *Contributions,* 15 [Syriac], and 10 [English]; also Burke, "The *Infancy Gospel of Thomas* from an Unpublished Syriac Manuscript," 292–93 [-ch. 15]).

207. Ernst and Lawrence, *Sufi Martyrs,* 53; cf. *AGI* 50–53 (Thilo, *Codex apocryphus,* 124–28; Peeters, *Évangiles apocryphes,* II.62–64). The fact the encounter takes place around the saint's twelfth year provides an additional compelling point of correspondence.

Epilogue: Reimagining a Young Jesus

1. Hägg and Rousseau, "Introduction," 3; see also Hägg, *Art of Biography,* 172–80.

2. Provera, *Vangelo arabo;* Voicu, *Vangelo arabo.* For other studies of this manuscript and its images, see Redin, "Miniatures," 55–71; Baumstark, "Ein apokryphes Herrenleben," 249–71; Cartlidge and Elliott, *Art and the Christian Apocrypha,* 74; Ceccanti, "Aspetti iconografici," 248; Dzon, "Jesus and the Birds," 216–18.

3. MS Laurenziano orientale 387, fol. 26v: Provero, *Vangelo arabo,* between pp. 32 and 33 (corresponding text at p. 110; =ch. 34).

4. MS Laurenziano orientale 387, fol. 29r: Provero, *Vangelo arabo,* between pp. 32 and 33 (corresponding text at p. 114; =ch. 39).

5. The depiction of livestock in scenes depicting everyday life is also characteristic of al-Wasīṭī's illuminated copy of *Maqāmāt al-Ḥarīrī* preserved at the Bibliothèque nationale in Paris (MS arabe 5847, dated 1237 CE): see esp. folio 138, which features a

village scene with realistic background details including "a cow, two pairs of goats, a chicken and a rooster," details not mentioned in the accompanying text itself (Grabar, "The 1237 Manuscript," 13; also Grabar, *Illustrations,* 95). Redin ("Miniatures," esp. 61, 64, 71) has compared the style and content of the Florentine *Arabic Gospel of the Infancy* with nearly contemporaneous extant copies of the *Maqāmāt.* On style, Arnold (*Painting in Islam,* 59) has also noted "several characteristics common" to both the *AGI* in Florence and the *Maqāmāt* of Ḥarīrī, including "robes covered with the same large patterns, made up of convoluted, conventionalized flowers and stems" and angels with "long pointed wings, which are very narrow at the end where they are joined on to the shoulder-blade." With regard to content, the *Maqāmāt* presents a series of tales about a "roguish and peripatetic hero" named Abu Zayd, who is shown in the accompanying illustrations observing groups of young pupils in school settings and meeting with crowds of learned men, confounding them with indecipherable riddles (quote by Grabar, "The 1237 Manuscript," 7). A number of illustrated versions of the *Maqāmāt* (including the Paris MS arabe 5847) were produced in and around Baghdād during the thirteenth century, and the iconographic similarities mentioned by Redin and Arnold are an important reason why scholars have proposed a Mesopotamian provenance for the Florence manuscript of the *Arabic Gospel of the Infancy.*

6. On the realistic features of Arabic book art during the thirteenth century as an appeal to the sensibilities of reader-viewers, see Grabar, "The 1237 Manuscript," 14, who writes that in the *Maqāmāt* al-Wasīṭī "wanted his viewers to see and recognize a specific world and to be amused by it, but did not feel compelled to depict every detail of every feature." In her book *Arab Social Life,* Guthrie highlights the way that the images accompanying the *Maqāmāt* texts evoked "aspects of urban life" (pp. 107–34) and "aspects of rural life" (pp. 135–49): for her, the illustrations reflected "everyday events in the Near East" (p. 18) and were thus designed to appeal to "the taste of an Arab audience" (p. 199).

7. For a facsimile of this manuscript, see Della Croce, *Canonical Histories.*

8. Milan, Bibliotheca Ambrosiana, L58 sup, fol. 13r.

9. Milan, Bibliotheca Ambrosiana, L58 sup, fol. 13v.

10. Milan, Bibliotheca Ambrosiana, L58 sup, fol. 16r–v and 17r; Cartlidge and Elliott, *Art and the Christian Apocrypha,* 115. There are also scenes of Jesus healing a woodsman's foot, retrieving water for his mother in his cloak, sowing seeds and doing carpentry work with his father, and healing his brother James from a snakebite (Milan, Bibliotheca Ambrosiana, L58 sup, fol. 14r–v, 15r–v, and 17v). For an analysis of the Ambrosian manuscript in comparison with other medieval illuminations of *Paidika* stories, see Sheingorn, "Reshapings."

11. Eight are in the British Museum in London: M&ME (Medieval & Modern Europe) 1922, 4–12, nos. 1–8 (http://www.britishmuseum.org/explore/highlights/highlight_objects/pe_mla/t/the_tring_tiles.aspx). The other two are in the Victoria and Albert Museum in London, C.470–1927 (http://collections.vam.ac.uk/item/O70759/tile-tring-tiles/). Cursing scenes: London, British Museum, Tring Tiles 1–2. School scenes: London, British Museum, Tring Tiles 2a (conflated with the scene of the boy jumping on Jesus' shoulder) and 4a–b. Household chores: London, Victoria and Albert Museum, Tring Tile 1b (fetching water from the well); and London, British Museum, Tring Tile

5b–6a (stretching the plank of wood). The finely preserved state of the tiles has led scholars to surmise that they were originally installed in a monumental or private setting. The small-scale scenes decorating the tile faces were produced by means of the painstaking *sgraffito* method: the medieval artist covered the tiles with white slip, carefully etched the details of the figures through the slip, scraped away background areas, and finally fired the tiles to produce an almost three-dimensional effect (Casey, "Fourteenth-Century Tring Tiles," 6–7).

12. On revisualizations of the Christ child in illuminated Latin manuscripts, see Sheingorn, "Reshapings," 254–92. For a case study of how an image of Jesus' miracle with the sparrows was reinterpreted in a Western medieval church, see Appendix C.

13. Francis, "Visual and Verbal Representation," 285 and 296 (my emphasis).

14. In my descriptive language here, I draw on the sociological work of Niklas Luhmann and on the visual theory of James A. Francis. On the subject of observation (*Beobachtung*), Luhmann (*Aufsätze und Reden,* 321; Luhmann, *Wissenschaft,* 95) writes that "everything that exists does so only because it is observed" (*alles was ist, ist nur, weil es beobachtet wird*), and in this context urges a shift of attention "from the observation of *what* to the observation of *how*" ("von der Beobachtung des *Was* zur Beobachtung des *Wie*") (his emphasis). Francis ("Visual and Verbal Representation," 285) emphasizes "the dynamic nature of seeing and being seen, the variety of ways of seeing and the ability of images to convey multiple meanings"; see also Jaś Elsner (*Art and the Roman Viewer,* 51) on "the many possibilities for additional creative and subversive interpretations which images inevitably evoke in different viewers and in different times"; and Roland Barthes (*Camera Lucida,* 12) on "the variety of modes in which (an image) can be seen" (discussed in Francis, "Visual and Verbal Representation," 288).

Appendix A: The Greek Paidika

1. This translation is based on the critical Greek edition published by Burke, *De infantia,* 303–37 (=Gs). Throughout, I indicate secondary material (content not attested in the short form of the text) in *italics.* In the notes below, I provide (on a selective basis) some alternative readings attested in the Syriac text published by Wright, *Contributions,* 6–11 (trans.), 11–16 (text) (=SyrW). I make less frequent reference to other language versions here: see Burke for a more detailed account of such variants, including those attested in Latin (L), Ethiopic (Eth), and Georgian (Geo).

2. This first chapter (or variants thereof) appears in the Greek manuscript tradition but not in the earliest versions of the Latin and Syriac, and on this account, it represents a later addition to the *Paidika.*

3. SyrW, Geo, Ga, Gb, and Gd add: "and remember me" (Burke, *De infantia,* 304, note 4).

4. This reconstruction follows the Syriac. The Greek (Gs) simply has *ekeinos* ("that one"), and Burke (*De infantia,* 306, note 2) conjectures that a preceding phrase indicating Jesus' antagonist was a boy was left out of that version of the text.

5. In place of the Greek noun for "shoulder" (*ōmon*) Gs has the variant spelling *onomon* at this point: see my discussion of this scribal error in chapter 6.

6. SyrW: "If the words of my Father were not wise, he would not know [how] to instruct children."

7. Two words are uncertain here (*epipenta diēgēsan*).

8. SyrW: "And again he said, 'If these were children of the bedchamber, they would not receive curses. These shall not see torment.' "

9. SyrW: "that he is equal to a small cross."

10. Gs actually has the middle form, *egennēsō,* but the other versions (SyrW, Ga, etc.) have constructions with a passive meaning.

11. There are significant variations in Syriac, Latin, Georgian, Ethiopic, and later Greek versions. SyrW: "And that cross of which you have spoken, he shall bear it, whose it is. For when I am greatly exalted, I shall lay aside that which is mixed of your race." For the other variants, see Burke, *De infantia,* 313, note 7.

12. SyrW: "A smith's anvil, being beaten, can learn, and it has no feeling."

13. 1 Corinthians 13:1.

14. Burke leaves this word (*belephetountas*) untranslated.

15. Jesus' exegesis of the letter *alpha* differs in certain details in the Syriac and Latin versions.

16. The Syriac, Latin, and Ethiopic versions add a comment emphasizing that Jesus (or his disciples) is worthy (or destined for) "a great cross" (Burke, *De infantia,* 320, note 6).

17. This language of *sōtēria* is unique to Gs: the Greek word had a range of meanings, from "good health" (or "safety") to "salvation" (cf. 14.1 and 14.4).

18. SyrW: "But his mother Mary was astonished at all that she was seeing."

19. One word is missing in the text. Recension A (Ga 13.1; Burke, *De infantia,* 373) includes the word *enēlaton* ("bed rail") at this point, and I supply it here between brackets.

20. SyrW adds: "And Jesus said [it]. And the scribe next wanted him to say *Beth.*"

21. In SyrW, the order of the letters here is reversed: "Tell me first what *Aleph* is, and then I will tell you about *Beth.*"

22. The subject and object are mixed up in Gs, but corrected here.

23. Chapter 16 appears only in Gs and the other Greek recensions of the text (and not in the earliest Latin and Syriac versions). Therefore, like chapter 1, it represents a secondary addition to the *Paidika.*

24. Cf. Luke 2:41–52.

25. Or, "spoke from memory."

Appendix B: The Arabic Gospel of the Infancy, *Chapters 36–53*

1. This translation is based on the Arabic edition of MS Oxon. Bodl. Or. 350, an undated text edited originally by Sike (*Evangelium infantiae*) and then corrected by Thilo, *Codex apocryphus,* 65–130, at 110–28 (= *Arabic Gospel of the Infancy,* chs. 36–53). The chapters included here consist of the material corresponding to the contents and biographical time frame covered by the *Paidika* tales. In the notes, I provide selected variant readings from the incomplete text of the *Arabic Gospel of the Infancy* (*AGI*) preserved in Florence (Biblioteca Laurenziana, Or. 387, 1299 CE), and edited by Provera,

Vangelo arabo, 108–22 (where chapters 33–41 correspond to the material in *AGI* 35–42). For the Oxford MS, I use the abbreviation O; and for the Florence MS, I use the abbreviation F.

2. O 36=F 34 (Provera, *Vangelo arabo,* 110).

3. F: "riding animals [*dawābb*], donkeys, cattle, and birds."

4. F: "race about" (*yatarakkaḍuna*)

5. O 37=F 35 (Provera, *Vangelo arabo,* 110).

6. F adds "for he wanted to make each one of them an individual color."

7. O 38=F 37 (Provera, *Vangelo arabo,* 112).

8. F provides the correct form, *asirra.*

9. F: "Jesus would stretch out his hand to it and it would become what he wanted. Joseph did not need to make anything with his hand and Joseph was skilled in his trade."

10. O 39=F 38 (Provera, *Vangelo arabo,* 112–14).

11. The word *sarīr* can also mean "bed."

12. O 40=F 39 (Provera, *Vangelo arabo,* 114–16).

13. F adds "who grab hold of the far side of the cloud to die."

14. O 41=F 40 (Provera, *Vangelo arabo,* 116–18).

15. F: *Iyyār.*

16. F: "would bring him into his presence."

17. O 42=F 41 (Provera, *Vangelo arabo,* 118–20). The version of the story preserved in F differs in several details.

18. In F, the boy is fifteen years old and named Simon.

19. In F, the boy hears a sound in a tree or bush that he thinks is the call of a bird and reaches his hand in to take it.

20. F: *afʿan* ("viper").

21. In F, the family intends to take him to Jerusalem to see a doctor.

22. F describes how the family greeted Jesus crying because their son was in great pain on account of the inflammation in his hand.

23. The entire scene in which the serpent sucks out the poison and then is killed is not present in F.

24. This episode does not appear in F.

25. O 44=F 42 (Provera, *Vangelo arabo,* 120–22). The version of the story in F exhibits several embellishments.

26. In F, they first conspire to frame Jesus for the crime of killing the boy, which leads to a dialogue between Jesus and a government administrator called in to identify and punish the wrongdoer.

27. In F, the boy's name is Tūzā.

28. In F, the boy fingers five perpetrators by name (Addī, Rahbī, Wardī, Mardī, and Mūsā) and identifies them as the ones who had conspired to frame Jesus for the crime.

29. In F, Jesus raises the boy, gets him on his feet, and returns him safe and sound to his family.

30. In F, the people voice their praise and identify Jesus as being twelve years old when he performed this miracle.

31. O 45–53 do not appear in F, which generally follows the order of stories in the Syriac *Life of Mary* (Budge, *History of the Blessed Virgin Mary,* I.77ff.; II.82ff.). After

the Zeno story (F 42), the next episode is interrupted by a lacuna after only a line or two (F 43), and the text resumes with an account of Jesus' raising of the widow's son from Nain (F 44: Provera, *Vangelo arabo,* 122; cf. Luke 7:11–17).

32. Or, "orbits."

Appendix C: Jesus and the Birds in St. Martin's Church, Zillis, Switzerland

1. St. Martin's Church in Zillis, Panel 91. The numbering system for the St. Martin ceiling panels was established by Erwin Poeschel (see note 6).

2. There was a Roman settlement at Zillis's location from at least the fifth century CE. Sources first identify this town by the name Ciranes in the first half of the ninth century: Simonett, "Zillis."

3. Simonett, "Ist Zillis die Römerstation Lapidaria?" 21–31, and pls. 1–8; and Jerris, "Cult Lines and Hellish Mountains," 85–108, esp. 86 and 103 (note 18). Jerris notes that the Roman settlement at Zillis functioned as "an important supply depot along critical transalpine routes utilizing the San Bernardino and Splügen Passes" (p. 103, note 18).

4. Murbach, *Painted Romanesque,* 10–12; Rudloff, *Zillis,* 14–15; Nay, *St. Martin's Church,* 7–9.

5. On recent attempts to date the paintings using dendrochronological methods, see Ruoff and Seifert, "Neustes zur Datierung," 170–71; and Garcia, "Les diverses dimensions," 234.

6. The numbering of individual panels in the accompanying chart is based on the system of classification established by Poeschel, *Die romanischen Deckengemälde,* 80–93. Poeschel labels the vertical columns with lowercase letters (a–i) and the vertical columns with capital Roman numerals (I–XVII). In more recent scholarship, the vertical columns have been classified by Roman numeral (I–IX) and the horizontal rows by capital letter (A–P): see, e.g., the foldout chart and photo spread in Rudloff, *Zillis,* 166–69. For a chart with labels and color formatting designed to highlight panel groupings by theme, see Nay, *St. Martin's Church,* inside back cover.

7. Myss, *Kirchendecke,* esp. 17–26. For other treatments of the iconographic program at Zillis in light of medieval worldviews and modes of biblical interpretation, see Rahn, "Die biblischen Deckengemälde," 103–21; Poeschel, *Die romanischen Deckengemälde;* Murbach, *Painted Romanesque Ceiling,* 14–34; Rudloff, *Zillis,* 22–161; Eggenberger, "Zum Bildprogramm," 162–66.

8. The Crucifixion and Resurrection, conspicuously absent on the ceiling, may have originally been rendered in the apse and/or on the walls of the church. If so, these paintings were lost during the sixteenth century when the choir of the church was replaced (1509) and when Reform-minded church leaders replastered the interior of the nave apart from the ceiling. The fact that the ceiling paintings survived, a miracle in its own right, may be attributed in part to the formidable seven-meter height of the panels: their inaccessibility may have initially served as a deterrent to the iconoclastic reach of local Reformers. However, in 1574 the roof frame was replaced, and in 1820 repair work was done to the ceiling, and at one of these times the sequence of the ceiling panels became disordered. This situation was remedied during restoration work from 1938 to 1940, performed

by restorer Henri Boissonnas and overseen by Josef Kemp and Erwin Poeschel. Since 1992, there have been renewed efforts to preserve the paintings using climatization methods and antifungal treatments: Böhm et al., "Climate Control," 9.

According to Poeschel (*Die romanischen Deckengemälde,* 7–11, 18–19), the restoration of the paintings that took place from 1938 to 1940 involved an attempt to reestablish the original order of the painted panels on the basis of iconographic principles—the outer zone according to a system of "kosmographischen Darstellungen" (p. 11), and the inner zone according to "christologischen Grundgedanken" (p. 19). It is not possible to confirm with 100 percent certainty that the current reconstructed order reflects the original, medieval design, and this is especially the case with the interchangeable watery scenes occupying the outer zone. However, the narrative character of the biblical and hagiographical scenes occupying the inner zone provided a much more reliable basis and template for reconstructing the original order. My analysis here presumes that the restored configuration does in fact give historians basic access to the way that the paintings would have been "read" in the twelfth century CE. In notes below, I acknowledge and discuss an alternative reconstruction of the original program by Nay (*St. Martin's Church in Zillis,* 14–15).

9. St. Martin's Church, Zillis, Panel 91 (Poeschel, *Die romanischen Deckengemälde,* 88).

10. Burke, *De infantia,* 144–60, 222.

11. For text and commentary on the *Gospel of Pseudo-Matthew,* see Tischendorf, *Evangelia apocrypha,* 2nd ed., 51–112; and Gijsel, *Pseudo-Matthaei Evangelium Textus et Commentarius,* CCSA 9. The original form of *Pseudo-Matthew,* which dates to around the seventh or eighth century CE, did not contain the material from the Old Latin text of the *Paidika.* The earliest evidence for the inclusion of this material in *Pseudo-Matthew* comes from an eleventh-century manuscript in the Bibliothèque nationale in Paris: BN Lat. 1772 (Burke, *De infantia,* 146). Tischendorf included the *Paidika* material in his early edition of *Pseudo-Matthew,* despite its absence from many of the manuscripts. In light of this, however, he labeled that section as the *pars altera* (pp. 93–112). The connection between the Old Latin version and this *pars altera* was demonstrated by Voicu in his article "Verso," 29–34. For a fuller analysis of the transmission and development of these textual traditions, see Gijsel, *Die unmittelbare Textüberlieferung.* On the proliferation of other Latin texts on Jesus' childhood, see also Schneemelcher, *New Testament Apocrypha,* I.456–9; and James, *Latin Infancy Gospels.*

12. Gijsel, *Die unmittelbare Textüberlieferung,* 17–27.

13. Cartlidge and Elliott, *Art and the Christian Apocrypha,* 98–99, and figs. 4.16 and 4.18; Garcia, "Les diverses dimensions," 228–34.

14. St. Martin's Church, Zillis, Panel 82 (Poeschel, *Die romanischen Deckengemälde,* 87).

15. St. Martin's Church, Zillis, Panels 81 and 83 (Poeschel, *Die romanischen Deckengemälde,* 87).

16. On the palm tree in the *Gospel of Pseudo-Matthew* (and in the Qur'ān), see Mourad, "From Hellenism to Christianity and Islam," 206–16.

17. *Gospel of Pseudo-Matthew* 20–21: Tischendorf, *Evangelia apocrypha,* 2nd ed., 82–84; and Gijsel, *Libri de Nativitate Mariae,* vol. 1, CCSA 9, 459–69.

18. St. Martin's Church, Zillis, Panel 84 (Poeschel, *Die romanischen Deckengemälde,* 87).

19. The panel depicting the Holy Family in repose has been catalogued as Panel 91. The sequence of scenes connected with the Massacre of the Innocents appears on Panels 85–90.

20. *Gospel of Pseudo-Matthew* 26–27 (=*pars altera*): ed. Tischendorf, *Evangelia apocrypha,* 2nd ed., 93–96.

21. St. Martin's Church, Zillis, Panel 98 (Poeschel, *Die romanischen Deckengemälde,* 88).

22. In this respect, a further link may be made with the miracle scene placed below the baptism of Jesus in the same column: probably a representation of Jesus' encounter with the centurion at Capernaum from Matthew 8:5–13, the panel shows Jesus, accompanied by a disciple on the left, facing the centurion, who stands just inside the right border with part of another face (representating his cohort) peeking into the frame behind him.

23. St. Martin's Church, Zillis, Panels 92–97 (Poeschel, *Die romanischen Deckengemälde,* 88).

24. St. Martin's Church, Zillis, Panels 99–104 (Poeschel, *Die romanischen Deckengemälde,* 88).

25. Nay (*St. Martin's Church,* 14–15) has proposed an alternative reconstruction of the medieval iconographic program that accentuates the crucial placement of this baptism scene to an even greater extent: specifically, he argues that the panel with Christ's baptism originally stood at the center of the entire ceiling and that its relocation away from that central location after the Reformation came as a response to local controversies with newly established Baptist congregations in the Grison region (Nay, *per litt.,* March 23, 2010).

26. St. Martin's Church, Zillis, Panels 10–12 (Poeschel, *Die romanischen Deckengemälde,* 82–83). Panel 12 is fragmentary and therefore difficult to interpret with any specificity.

27. In the ceiling's current restored state, not all of the outer border panels are original. During the 1938–1940 restoration work, some were produced as copies to replace panels that were damaged or lost at an earlier stage in the church's history. These copies were modeled on motifs found in the surviving panels; however, the decision not to add a fourth boat scene to the program may have been an oversight on the restorers' part.

28. St. Martin's Church, Zillis, Panels 110–11, 116, 135 (Poeschel, *Die romanischen Deckengemälde,* 89–91). Panels 110 and 116—the healing at the pool of Bethsaida and the encounter with the Samaritan woman—are located in the two consecutive rows below the wedding at Cana. The scenes lie on a diagonal running leftward and down toward the central vertical column of the cross.

29. The horizontal blue band to which I refer appears on more than half of the 105 inner-zone panels, often tying together panel groups unified by theme. It should be noted that this band conspicuously lacks the wavy horizontal lines used to identify deep bodies of water in some of the panels, including the seas in the outer zone, the Sea of Galilee in the scene where Jesus casts the demons into the swine (108), and the pool of Siloam where Jesus heals the paralytic at Capernaum (110); and indeed, it may have functioned

on one level as a generic background motif or a mode of representing a distant horizon. In a number of contexts, however, it seems likely that it would have had a more specific topographical function, and that viewers would have been prompted to understand the blue band as representing a river—perhaps a flowing stream in contrast to deeper waters without a constant current. In the scene of Christ's baptism, these two modes of representing water seem to be combined: the deeper water in which Jesus stands overlaps with the horizontal blue band in the background, which may be seen here as the channel of the Jordan.

30. See, e.g., the famous eighth-century map of Beatus of Liébana, which depicts continents as a central landmass divided up by numerous rivers (including the Jordan): Rudloff, *Zillis,* 32–33; Myss, *Kirchendecke,* 22–26.

31. Garcia ("Les diverses dimensions," 207, note 18) compares the architecture represented on this disk to the cityscapes of Jerusalem found in the background of other panels (nos. 52–53, 85–86, 92, 100, 112, 132, 134).

32. Simonett, "Eine Schamser Landschaft," 116–19; Garcia, "Les diverses dimensions," 206–9.

33. Jerris, "Cult Lines and Hellish Mountains," 98.

34. Garcia, "Les diverses dimensions," 209.

35. In some respects, the perspective established in the ceiling program is similar to that of the famous cover image of the *New Yorker* magazine that presents the reader with a prototypically Manhattan-centric map of the world (*View of the World from 9th Avenue,* March 29, 1976). With respect to the Zillis paintings, Garcia ("Les diverses dimensions," 206) writes of how the viewer's perspective is drawn toward "the center of this space, the fixed place from where one contemplates the imagined (and imaginary) world."

36. Jerris, "Cult Lines and Hellish Mountains," 91–92.

37. On the Magi as archetypes for Christian pilgrims, see, e.g., Vikan, "Pilgrims in Magi's Clothing," 97–107; Webb, *Medieval European Pilgrimage,* 160; and Davis, *Coptic Christology in Practice,* 153–80. On the Holy Family's journey as a model for pilgrimage, see Davis, "Ancient Sources," 133–62; Davis, *Coptic Christology in Practice,* 125–48; and Blick and Tekippe, *Art and Architecture,* 205.

38. Poeschel, "Baugeschichte," 21. According to Müller ("Vom Baptisterium," 26), the strategic location of early baptisteries at Zillis and at other principal sites in the region implies the patronage of the bishop at Chur.

39. Jerris, "Cult Lines and Hellish Mountains," 90.

40. Nay, *St. Martin's Church,* 11.

41. The importance of baptismal practice to the history of the church at Zillis has led one scholar to propose an alternative reconstruction of the original painted program. As mentioned above, Nay (*St. Martin's Church,* 14–15) has argued that the scene of Christ's baptism in fact originally occupied the central place among the panels on the ceiling of St. Martin's. According to this reconstruction, the baptism would have been flanked in the central row (i.e., along the horizontal span of the cross) by scenes related to John the Baptist on the left and the three temptation scenes on the right. The shift that this reconstruction would entail means that Jesus' miracle with the birds, along with the panel showing the Holy Family at rest above it, would have been aligned with

Christ's baptism in the central column of panels (i.e., along the vertical beam of the cross).

42. Garcia, "Les diverses dimensions," 207, note 18. Outlines of chalices are also found etched onto the dark disk to which the devil gestures in the third temptation scene (101) at the very center of the ceiling program. The artists' use of the same figure with sacramental overtones on other panels may have been designed to communicate a transformation from worldly sign to sacramental symbol.

43. *Gospel of Ps.-Matthew* 26–27: Tischendorf, *Evangelia apocrypha,* 2nd ed., 88–90.

44. Matthew 19:13–14; Mark 10:13–14; Luke 18:16.

Bibliography

Editions, Collections, Objects, and Translations

Abū Wandī, Riyaḍ, et al., eds. *'Īsā wa Maryam fī al-Qur'ān wa al-tafāsīr.* Amman: Dār al-Shurūq, 1996.

Achilles Tatius. *Leucippe and Clitophon.* Ed. and trans. S. Gaselee. LCL. London: W. Heinemann; New York: G. P. Putnam's Sons, 1917. Trans. J. J. Winkler, in *Collected Ancient Greek Novels,* ed. B. P. Reardon, 170–284.

Acts of Andrew and Matthias (late Greek recension). Cod. Mosquensis RGB gr. 129, fols. 122v–56v (fifteenth century CE). Ed. A. Vinogradov, "Die zweite Rezension der Actorum Andreae et Matthiae apud Anthropophagos [BHG 110B]," *Christianskij Vostok* 3 (2001), 11–105 (section derived from the *Paidika* at 31–3). This section has been edited and translated with emendations by Burke, *De infantia,* 17–25.

Acts of Thomas (Greek). Ed. M. Bonnet. *Acta apostolorum apocrypha.* Volume 2.2, 99–288. Leipzig: Mendelssohn, 1903; repr. Hildesheim: Olms, 1972. Trans. M. R. James, *The Apocryphal New Testament,* 447–511. Oxford: Clarendon, 1924.

Aelian. *Varia Historia* (*Historical Miscellany*). Ed. N. G. Wilson. LCL 486. Cambridge, Mass.: Harvard University Press, 1997.

Aelius Aristides. *Works.* Ed. W. Dindorf, *Aristides.* 3 volumes. Leipzig: Reimer, 1829; repr. Hildesheim: Olms, 1964.

Aelius Theon. *Progymnasmata.* Ed. and trans. M. Patillon, with G. Bolognesi, 1–9. Paris: Belles Lettres, 1997.

Agobard of Lyons. *Epistola de Judaicis Superstitionibus.* PL 104.77–100. Ed. R. Enge, "De Agobardi episcopi Lugdunensis cum Judaicis contention." Ph.D. dissertation, Leipzig, 1888.

Alexander of Aphrodisias. *Commentary on Aristotle's Metaphysics.* Ed. M. Hayduck. Berlin: G. Reimer, 1891.

Ammianus Marcellinus. *History.* Ed. J. C. Rolfe. LCL. 3 volumes. Cambridge, Mass.: Harvard University Press; London: William Heinemann, 1935–1939.

Anastasius of Sinai. *Hodegos* (*Viae Dux*). *PG* 89.39–310.

Ante-Nicene Fathers. Ed. A. Roberts and J. Donaldson. 10 volumes. New York: Christian Literature, 1885–1897. [=*ANF*]

Antoninus Pius. *Digesta Iustiniani.* Ed. P. Krueger and T. Mommsen. 2 volumes. Berlin: Weidmann, 1870.

Apollonius, King of Tyre. Ed. G. A. A. Kortekaas, *Historia Apollonii Regis Tyri: Prolegomena, Text Edition of the Two Principal Latin Recensions, Bibliography, Indices and Appendices.* Groningen: Bouma's Boekhuis, 1984. Trans. G. N. Sandy, in *Collected Ancient Greek Novels,* ed. B. P. Reardon, 736–72. Berkeley: University of California Press, 1989; rev. ed., 2008.

Apology of Aristides. Ed. and trans. B. Pouderon and M-J. Pierre, with B. Outtier and M. Guiorgadzé. SC 470. Paris: Cerf, 2003.

Apostolic Tradition. Ed. and trans. G. Dix, *The Treatise on the Apostolic Tradition of St. Hippolytus of Rome.* London: SPCK, 1937. Repr. with corrections by Henry Chadwick: London: Alban, 1992.

Apuleius. *Apologies.* Ed. V. Hunink. 2 volumes. Amsterdam: J. C. Gieben, 1997.

———. *The Golden Ass* (*Metamorphoses*). Ed. M. Zimmerman, *Apulei Metamorphoseon Libri XI.* Oxford: Oxford University Press, 2012. Ed. and trans. W. Aldington and S. Gaselee. LCL. London: W. Heinemann; New York: G. P. Putnam's Sons, 1928.

———. *Opera.* Ed. R. Helm. 3 volumes. Leipzig: B. G. Teubner, 1919–1921.

Arabic Gospel of the Infancy. Oxford, Bodleian Library, Oxon. Bodl. Or. 350 (undated). Original ed. H. Sike, *Evangelium infantiae, vel Liber apocryphus de infantia Servatoris, ex manuscript edidit, ac Latina versione et notis illustravit Henricus Sike.* Trajecti ad Rhenum; Utrecht: F. Halma and G. van de Water, 1697. Corrected ed. J. C. Thilo, *Codex apocryphus Novi Testamenti.* Volume 1, xxvi–xliv (introduction), 65–131 (Arabic text and Latin translation). Leipzig: F. C. G. Vogel, 1832. English trans. *ANF* 8.405–15. Florence, Biblioteca Laurenziana, Or. 387 [32] (1299 CE). Critical ed. Mario E. Provera, *Il Vangelo arabo dell'infanzia secondo il Ms. Laurenziano orientale (n. 387).* Jerusalem: Franciscan, 1973. French trans.: G. Genequand, "Vie de Jésus en arabe." In *Écrits apocryphes chrétiens,* ed. Bovon and Geoltrain, volume 1, 191–204. Italian trans. S. J. Voicu, *Vangelo arabo.*

'Arīb ibn Sa'īd of Cordob. *Kitāb khalq al-janīn wa-tadbīr al-ḥabālā wa-l-mawlūdin.* Ed. Ullmann, *Islamic Medicine,* 112–14.

Aristotle. *Metaphysics.* Ed. and trans. H. Treddenick. LCL. Cambridge, Mass.: Harvard University Press; London: William Heinemann, 1935–1936.

———. *Nicomachean Ethics.* Ed. H. Rackham. LCL. Rev. ed. Cambridge, Mass.: Harvard University Press; London: William Heinemann, 1934.

———. *Politics*. Ed. and trans. H. Rackham. LCL. Cambridge, Mass.: Harvard University Press, 1932; repr. 1972.

———. *Rhetoric*. Ed. and trans. J. H. Freese. LCL. London: W. Heinemann; New York: G. P. Putnam's Sons, 1926.

Armenian Infancy Gospel. Trans. A. Terian. Oxford and New York: Oxford University Press, 2008.

Arnim, H. F. A. van, ed. *Stoicorum veterum fragmenta*. 4 volumes. Leipzig: B. G. Teubner, 1903–1924.

Artemidorus. *Interpretation of Dreams* (*Oneirocritica*). Ed. R. Pack. Leipzig: B. G. *Teubner*, 1963.

Athenaeus. *Banquet of the Learned* (*Deipnosophistae*). Ed. and trans. S. Douglas Olson. LCL. 8 volumes. Cambridge, Mass.: Harvard University Press, 2006–2012. Ed. G. Kaibel. 2 volumes. Biblotheca scriptorium Graecorum et Romanorum Teubneriana. Stuttgart: Teubner, 1965–1968. Trans. C. D. Yonge. 3 volumes. London: Henry G. Bohn, 1854.

Attridge, Harold, ed. *Nag Hammadi Codex I (The Jung Codex)*. 2 volumes. Nag Hammadi Studies 22–23. Leiden: Brill, 1985.

Audollent, Auguste, ed. *Defixionum Tabellae*. Paris: Albert Fontemoing, 1904. [=*DT*]

Augustine. *The City of God*. Ed. B. Dombart and A. Kalb. 2 volumes. Stuttgart: Teubner, 1981. Trans. G. G. Walsh et al. 3 volumes. FC 8, 14, 24. Washington, D.C.: Catholic University of America Press, 1950–1954.

———. *Confessions*. Ed. M. Skutella and L. Verheijen. CCSL 27. Turnhout: Brepols, 1981. Ed. and trans. W. Watts. LCL. Cambridge, Mass.: Harvard University Press; London: William Heinemann, 1977. English trans. *NPNF*, ser. 1, vol. 1.

Babylonian Talmud. Ed. and trans. I. Epstein. 35 volumes. London: Soncino, 1935–1952; repr. 1961. Online edition: *Soncino Babylonian Talmud*. Teaneck, N.J.: Talmudic Books, 2010/2011.

Basil of Caesarea. *Homily* 8, *In Time of Famine and Drought* (*Homilia dicta tempore famis et siccitatis*). *PG* 31.304–28. Trans. Susan R. Holman, *The Hungry Are Dying: Beggars and Bishops in Roman Cappadocia*, 183–92. Oxford: Oxford University Press, 2001.

Bassus, D., H. Cumont, A. Martin, and A. Olivier, eds. *Catalogus Codicum Astrologicorum Graecorum*. Volume 4. Brussels: Henri Lamertin, 1903.

Bayḍāwī, ʿAbdallah ibn ʿUmar al-. *Anwār al-tanzīl wa asrār al-taʾwīl*. Beirut: N.p. 1911.

Book of Jubilees. Ed. and trans. J. C. VanderKam. 2 volumes. Louvain: Peeters, 1989. Trans. R. H. Charles. London: SPCK; New York: Macmillan, 1917.

Books of Jeu and the Untitled Text in the Bruce Codex. Ed. C. Schmidt. Nag Hammadi Studies 13. Leiden: Brill, 1978.

Budge, E. A. Wallis, ed. *The History of the Blessed Virgin Mary and the History of the Likeness of Christ*. 2 volumes. London: Luzac, 1899.

Catullus. *Poems* (*Carm.*). Ed. and trans. F. W. Cornish and G. P. Goold. LCL. Rev. ed. Cambridge, Mass.: Harvard University Press; London: William Heinemann, 1978.

Censorinus. *The Birthday Book* (*De die natali*). Ed. N. Sallmann. Leipzig: B. G. Teubner, 1983. Trans. H. N. Parker. Chicago: University of Chicago Press, 2007.

The Childhood Deeds of Jesus. See under *Paidika*.

Charlesworth, James H., ed. *The Old Testament Pseudepigrapha.* 2 volumes. Garden City, N.Y.: Doubleday, 1985.
Cicero. *Letter to Quintus (Ad Quintum Fratrem).* Ed. and trans. D. R. Shackleton Bailey, LCL 462. Cambridge, Mass.: Harvard University Press, 2002.
———. *Letters to Friends (Ad Familiares).* Ed. and trans. D. R. Shackleton Bailey. LCL 205, 216, 230. 3 volumes. Cambridge, Mass.: Harvard University Press, 2001.
———. *On Divination.* Ed. and trans. W. A. Falconer. LCL. Cambridge, Mass.: Harvard University Press; London: William Heinemann, 1964.
———. *On the Laws.* Ed. and trans. C. W. Keyes. LCL. London: William Heinemann, 1928.
———. *On the Nature of the Gods.* Ed. and trans. H. Rackham. LCL. Cambridge, Mass.: Harvard University Press; London: William Heinemann, 1933, repr. 1979.
Clement of Alexandria. *Paedagogus.* Ed. C. Mondésert et al. SC 70, 108, 158. Paris: Cerf, 1960–1970.
———. *Stromata.* Ed. L. Früchtel, O. Stählin, and U. Treu. GCS. 4 volumes. Third ed. Berlin: Akademie, 1960–1980. Ed. C. Mondésert. SC 30, 38, 278–279, 428, 446, 463. Paris: Cerf, 1951–2001. English trans. *ANF* 2.
———. *Who Is the Rich Man That Shall Be Saved?* Ed. and trans. G. W. Butterworth. LCL, 270–367. Cambridge, Mass.: Harvard University Press, 1968.
Columella. *On Agriculture.* Ed. and trans. E. S. Forster and E. H. Heffner. LCL. 3 volumes. Cambridge, Mass.: Harvard University Press; London: William Heinemann, 1941–1955.
Corpus Vasorum Antiquorum. Paris: H. Champion, 1922–.
Daiber, Hans, ed. *Ein Kompendium der aristotelischen Meteorologie in der Fassung des Ḥunain ibn Isḥāq.* Ed. H. J. Dossaart Lulofs. Aristoteles Semitico-Latinus, Prolegomena et Parerga I. Amsterdam and Oxford: North-Holland, 1975.
Decretum Gelasianum. Ed. E. von Dobschütz, *Das Decretum Gelasianum de libris reciipiendis et non recipiendis in kritischem Text herausgegeben und untersucht.* TU 38.4. Leipzig: J. C. Hinrichs, 1912. Trans. W. Schneemelcher, *New Testament Apocrypha,* volume 1, 38–40.
Delattre, R. P., ed. "Inscriptions imprécatoires trouvées à Carthage," *Bulletin de correspondance hellénique* 12 (1888), 294–302.
Demetrius. *On Style.* Ed. and trans. W. R. Roberts. LCL. London: William Heinmann, 1973.
Dio Cassius. *Roman History.* Ed. U. P. Boissevain. *Cassii Dionis Cocceiani historiarum Romanarum quae supersunt.* 5 volumes. Berlin: Weidmann, 1895–1931. Third ed., 2002 (vol. 4 only).
Dio Chrysostom. *Orations.* Ed. and trans. J. W. Cohoon. LCL. 5 volumes. London: Heinemann; New York: G. P. Putnam's Sons, 1932–1952.
Diodorus Siculus. *Library of History.* Ed. and trans. C. H. Oldfather. LCL. 12 volumes. London: William Heinemann; New York: G. P. Putnam's Sons, 1933–1967.
Diogenes Laertius. *Lives of Eminent Philosophers.* Ed. H. S. Long, *Diogenis Laertii vitae philosophorum.* 2 volumes. Oxford: Clarendon, 1964. Ed. and trans. R. D. Hicks. LCL. 2 volumes. Cambridge, Mass.: Harvard University Press; London: William Heinemann, 1950.

Dionysius of Halicarnassus, *On Literary Composition*. Ed. and trans. W. Rhys Roberts. London: Macmillan, 1910.

Dionysius of Thrace. *Art of Grammar* (*Ars Grammatica*). Ed. E. Uhlig, 5–100. Leipzig: B. G. Teubner, 1883; repr. Hildesheim: G. Olms, 1965. Ed. and trans. J. Lallot, *La grammaire de Denysle Thrace*. Second ed. Paris: CNRS, 1998.

Dittenberger, G., ed. *Atticae aetatis Romanae*. 3 volumes. Berlin: Georg Reimer, 1878–1897. [=*IG* 3]

———. *Inscriptiones Graecae Megaridis, Oropiae, Boeotiae*. Berlin: Georg Reimer, 1892. [=*IG* 7]

Dittenberger, G., et al., eds. *Inscriptiones Graecae*. Berlin: Reimer, 1897–. [=*IG*]

Elliott, J. K., ed. *The Apocryphal New Testament: A Collection of Apocryphal Christian Literature in an English Translation*. Oxford: Clarendon, 1993.

Epictetus. *Discourses*. Ed. and trans. W. A. Oldfather. LCL. 2 volumes. Cambridge, Mass.: Harvard University Press; London: William Heinemann, 1926–1928; repr. 1998.

Epiphanius of Salamis. *Panarion*. Ed. K. Holl. GCS 31.2. Second ed. Berlin: Akademie, 1980. Trans. F. Williams, *The Panarion of Epiphanius of Salamis*. 2 volumes. Nag Hammadi and Manichaean Studies 35–36. Leiden and New York: Brill, 1991.

Epistle of the Apostles. Ed. C. Schmidt, *Gespräche Jesu mit seinen Jüngern nach der Auferstehung: Ein katholisch-apostolisches Sendschreiben des 2. Jahrhunderts*. TU 42. Leipzig: J. C. Hinrichs, 1919. Trans. C. D. G. Müller, "Epistula Apostolorum," in *New Testament Apocrypha*, volume 1, rev. ed., trans. R. M. Wilson, 249–84. Louisville: Westminster/John Knox, 1991.

Erman, A., and F. Krebs, eds. *Aus den Papyrus der Königlichen Museen*. Berlin: W. Spemann, 1899. [=*T. Berol.*]

Euripides. *Euripidis Tragoediae*. Ed. A. Nauck. 3 volumes. Leipzig: B. G. Teubner, 1857–1912.

———. *Fragments*. Ed. C. Collard and M. Cropp. LCL. Volumes 7–8. Cambridge, Mass.: Harvard University Press, 2008.

———. *Trojan Women*. Ed. and trans. D. Kovacs. LCL. Volume 4, 14–143. Cambridge, Mass.: Harvard University Press, 1999.

Eusebius of Caesarea. *Eclogae propheticae*. Ed. T. Gaisford, *Eusebii Pamphili Episcopi Caesariensis Eclogae Propheticae*. Oxford: Typographeo Academico, 1842.

———. *Life of Constantine*. Ed. F. Winkelmann, *Eusebius Werke, Band 1.1: Über das Leben des Kaisers Konstantin*. GCS. Berlin: Akademie, 1975. Second ed., 1989.

———. *Preparation of the Gospel* (*Praeparatio evangelica*). Ed. K. Mras. 2 volumes. GCS 43.1–2. Berlin: Akademie, 1954–1956.

Euthymius Zigabenus. *Commentary on the Four Gospels* (*Commentarius in quattuor Evangelia*). *PG* 29.

Faulkner, William. *Requiem for a Nun*. New York: Random House, 1951.

Flavius Philostratus. *Lives of the Sophists*. Ed. C. L. Kayser, *Flavii Philostrati opera*. 2 volumes. Leipzig: Teubner, 1871; repr. Hildesheim: Olms, 1964. Ed. and trans. W. C. Wright. LCL. London: William Heinemann; New York: G. P. Putnam's Sons, 1922.

———. *Opera*. Ed. C. L. Kayser. 2 volumes. Leipzig: Teubner, 1870; repr. Hildesheim: Olms, 1985.

———. *On Gymnastics* (*De gymnastica*). Ed. C. L. Kayser, *Flavii Philostrati opera*. Volume 2, 261–93. Leipzig: B. G. Teubner, 1871; repr. Hildesheim and New York: G. Olms, 1985.

———. *On Heroes*. Trans. E. B. Aitken and J. K. B. MacLean. Atlanta: Society of Biblical Literature, 2002.

Galen. *Galens Traktat "Dass die Kräfte der Seele den Mischungen des Körpers folgen" in arabischer Übersetzung*. Ed. H. H. Biesterfeldt. Wiesbaden: F. Steiner, 1973.

———. *On Anatomical Procedures*. Ed. C. G. Kuhn. Volume 2, 215–731. Leipzig: K. Knoblauch, 1821–1833. Trans. Charles Singer, *Galen on Anatomical Procedures*. London and New York: Oxford University Press, 1956. Critical edition of books 1–9 of the Arabic, translated by Ḥunayn ibn Isḥāq: Ivan Garofalo, ed., *Anatomicarum administrationum libri qui supersunt novem: Earundem interpretatio arabica Hunaino Isaaci filio ascripta*. 2 volumes. Annali dell' Istituto Universitario Orientale di Napoli. Naples: Istituto Universitario Orientale, 1986–2000. Arabic edition and German translation of books 9–15: Max Simon, ed. *Sieben Bücher Anatomie des Galen*. 2 volumes. Leipzig: J. C. Hinrichs, 1906. Reprinted in the series Islamic Medicine 16–17. Frankfurt am Main: Institute for the History of Arabic-Islamic Science at the Johann Wolfgang Goethe University, 1996. English translation of books 9–15: W. L. H. Duckworth, M. C. Lyons, and B. Towers, eds., *Galen on Anatomical Procedures: The Later Books*. Cambridge: Cambridge University Press, 1962.

———. *On the Anatomy of Nerves* (*Kitāb fī tashrīḥ al-ʿaṣab*). Ed. C. G. Kühn, *Claudii Galeni opera omnia*. Volume 2, 831–56.

———. *On the Anatomy of Veins and Arteries* (*Kitāb fī tashrīḥ al-ʿurūq wa al-awrād*). Ed. C. G. Kühn, *Claudii Galeni opera omnia*. Volume 2, 779–830.

———. *On the Difference Between Similar Body Parts* (Gk. *Peri tēs tōn homoiomerōn sōmatōn diaphoras;* Ar. *Kitāb Jālīnūs fī ikhtilāf al-aʿḍāʾ al-mutashābiha al-ajzāʾ*). Arabic translation by ʿĪsā ibn Yaḥyā. Ed. G. Strohmaier, *Galen: Über die Verschiedenheit der homoiomeren Körperteile*. Berlin: Akademie, 1970.

———. *Opera*. Ed. C. G. Kühn, *Claudii Galeni opera omnia*. 20 volumes. Leipzig: K. Knoblauch, 1821–1833.

George Syncellus. *Chronographia, anno 5505*. Ed. A. A. Mosshammer, *Georgii Syncelli Ecloga Chronographica*. Biblioteca scriptorium Graecorum et Romanorum Teubneriana. Leipzig: B. G. Teubner, 1984. Trans. W. Adler and P. Tuffin, *The Chronography of George Synkellos: A Byzantine Chronicle of Universal History from the Creation*. New York and Oxford: Oxford University Press, 2002.

Goetz, George, ed. *Corpus Glossariorum Latinorum*. Volume 3. Leipzig: B. G. Teubner, 1892. [=*CGL*]

Gospel of Philip. Ed. B. Layton, *Nag Hammadi Codex II, 2–7*. Volume 1, 142–214. Leiden: Brill, 1989. Trans. W. W. Isenberg, in *Nag Hammadi Library*. Fourth ed., ed. J. M. Robinson et al., 139–60. Leiden: Brill, 1996.

Gospel of Ps.-Matthew (Latin). Ed. J. Gijsel and R. Beyers, *Libri de nativitate*. CCSA 9–10. Turnhout: Brepols, 1997.

Gospel of Thomas (Coptic text). Original ed. A. Guillaumont et al., *Evangelium nach Thomas*. Leiden: Brill, 1959. Critical ed. B. Layton, *Nag Hammadi Codex II, 2–7*.

Volume 1. Nag Hammadi Studies 20, 52–92 (even pages). Leiden: Brill, 1989. Trans. Thomas O. Lambdin, 53–93 (odd pages).

Gospel of Thomas (Greek fragments). Ed. and trans. H. W. Attridge, "The Gospel According to Thomas. Appendix: The Greek Fragments." In *Nag Hammadi Codex II, 2–7.* Volume 1, ed. B. Layton. Nag Hammadi Studies 20, 95–120. Leiden: Brill, 1989.

Gospel of Truth. Ed. and trans. H. W. Attridge and G. MacRae, S. J., *Nag Hammadi Codex I (The Jung Codex),* ed. H. Attridge. Volume 1, 55–117 (text and translation). Volume 2, 39–135 (notes). Nag Hammadi Studies 22–23. Leiden: Brill, 1985. Trans. Attridge and MacRae, in *Nag Hammadi Library.* Fourth ed., ed. J. M. Robinson et al., 38–51. Leiden and New York: Brill, 1996. Ed. M. Malinine et al., *Evangelium Veritatis: Codex Jung.* 2 volumes. Zürich: Rascher, 1956–1961. Trans. Bentley Layton, *The Gnostic Scriptures,* 253–64. Garden City, N.Y.: Doubleday, 1987.

Gregory of Nazianzus. *Oration* 43 (*Funerary Oration on St. Basil the Great*). *PG* 35.493–606. English translation: http://people.ucalgary.ca/~vandersp/Courses/texts/cappadoc/gnazor43.html (accessed July 10, 2013).

Grenfell, B. P., et al., eds. *The Oxyrhynchus Papyri.* 77 volumes. London: Egypt Exploration Society, 1898–2011. [=*P.Oxy.*]

Griffith, F. L., and H. Thompson, eds. *The Demotic Magical Papyrus of London and Leiden.* London: Grevel, 1904.

Guéraud, O., and P. Jouguet, eds. *Un livre d'écolier du IIIe avant J.-C.* Cairo: Imprimerie de l'Institut français d'archéologie orientale, 1938.

Hermeneumata Celtes. See Dionisotti, "From Ausonius' Schooldays?"

Hermeneumata Einsidlensia. See Goetz, *Corpus Glossariorum Latinorum,* volume 3.

Hermeneumata Stephani. See Goetz, *Corpus Glossariorum Latinorum,* volume 3.

Herodas. *Mime.* Ed. and trans. A. D. Knox. LCL. London: William Heinemann; New York: G. P. Putnam's Sons, 1929. Trans. M. S. Buck. New York: Private printing, 1921. Available at http://www.elfinspell.com/Mimes.html#refchap3 (accessed July 10, 2013).

Herodian. *Roman History.* Ed. K. Stavenhagen, *Herodiani ab excessu divi Marci libri octo.* 1–223. Leipzig: B. G. Teubner, 1922; repr. Stuttgart: B. G. Teubner, 1967.

Herodotus. *The Persian Wars.* Ed. A. D. Godley. LCL. 4 volumes. London: William Heinemann; New York: G. P. Putnam's Sons, 1921–1924; repr. Cambridge, Mass.: Harvard University Press, 1960–1963.

Hippolytus of Rome. *Refutation of All Heresies.* Ed. P. Wendland. GCS 26. Berlin: Akademie, 1916; repr. 1977. English trans. *ANF* 5.9–153.

———. *Refutation of All Heresies.* Ed. M. Marcovich, *Hippolytus: Refutatio omnium haeresium.* PTS 25, 53–417. Berlin: De Gruyter, 1986.

History of Joseph the Carpenter. Sahidic fragments ed. L.-Th. Lefort, "À propos de *l'Histoire de Joseph le Charpentier,*" *Le Muséon* 66 (1953), 201–23. Bohairic text ed. P. de Lagarde, *Aegyptiaca,* 1–37. Göttingen: Hoyer, 1883. Trans. F. Robinson, *Coptic Apocryphal Gospels: Translations with the Texts of Some of Them.* Texts and Studies 4.2, 130–59. Arabic text ed. A. Battista and B. Bagatti, *Edizione critica del testo arabo della "Historia Iosephi fabri lignarii" e recerche sulla sua origine.* Studii Biblici Franciscani Collectio Minor 20. Jerusalem: Franciscan, 1978.

Horace. *Epistles*. Ed. and trans. H. Rushton Fairclough. LCL. Cambridge, Mass.: Harvard University Press, 1961.

———. *Satires*. Ed. and trans. H. Rushton Fairclough. LCL. Rev. ed. Cambridge, Mass.: Harvard University Press, 1961.

Ḥunayn ibn Isḥāq. *Ein Kompendium der aristotelischen Meteorologie in der Fassung des Ḥunain ibn Isḥāq*. Ed. H. Daiber. Aristoteles Semitico-Latinus, Prolegomena et Parerga I, ed. H. J. Dossaart Lulofs. Amsterdam and Oxford: North-Holland, 1975.

Ḥunayn ibn Isḥāq. *On the Syriac and Arabic Translations of Galen*. Ed. G. Bergsträsser, *Ḥunain ibn Isḥāq: Über die syrischen und arabischen Galen-Übersetzungen*. Abhandlungen für die Kunde des Morgenlandes XVII.2. Leipzig: F. A. Brockhaus, 1925.

Ḥunayn ibn Isḥāq (trans.). *Pseudogaleni in Hippocratis de Septimanis Commentarium ab Hunaino quod fertur Arabice versum*. Ed. G. Bergsträsser. Leipzig and Berlin: B. G. Teubner, 1914; repr. Frankfurt am Main: Institute for the History of Arabic-Islamic Science at the Johann Wolfgang Goethe University, 1996.

Ḥunayn ibn Isḥāq and Ḥubaysh ibn al-Ḥasan, *al-Masā'il fī al-ṭibb li-l-muta'allimīn*. Arabic critical edition: Muḥammad 'Alī Abū Riyyān, Mursī Muḥammad 'Arab, and Jalāl Muḥammad Mūsā. Cairo: Dar al-Jāmi'āt al-Miṣriyya, 1978. English trans. P. Ghalioungui, *Questions on Medicine for Scholars by Hunayn ibn Ishaq*. Cairo: Al-Ahram Center for Scientific Translations, 1980. Edition of bilingual Syriac-Arabic MS Vat. Syr. 192: E. Jan Wilson and S. Dinkha, eds., *Hunain ibn Ishaq's "Questions on Medicine for Students": Transcription and Translation of the Oldest Extant Syriac Version (Vat. Syr. 192)*. Studi e Testi 459. Vatican City: Biblioteca Apostolica Vaticana, 2010.

Ibn al-Akfānī. *Irshād al-qāṣid ilā asnā al-maqāṣid*. Ed. A. Sprenger. Fascicule 1. Volume 6. Number 21. Bibliotheca Indica; Calcutta: Asiatic Society of Bengal, 1849. Ed. J. J. Witkam, *De Egyptische arts Ibn al-Akfānī*. Leiden: Ter Lugt Pers, 1989.

Ibn 'Arabī. *Tafsīr al-Qur'ān al-karīm*. 2 volumes. Beirut: Dār al-yaqẓa al-'arabiyya, 1968.

Ibn Hishām, 'Abd al-Malik. *Sīrat al-nabī*. Trans. A. Guillaume, *The Life of Muhammad: A Translation of Ibn Isḥāq's Sīrat rasūl Allāh*. New York: Oxford University Press, 1955, repr. 1967.

Ibn Kathīr, Abū al-Fidā' Ismā'īl. *Tafsīr al-Qur'ān al-'aẓīm*. 7 volumes. Beirut: Dār al-Andalus lil-Ṭibā'a wa al-Nashr, 1966.

Ibn Khaldūn. *Prolegomena (Muqaddima)*. Trans. Franz Rosenthal. Second ed. 3 volumes. Princeton: Princeton University Press, 1967. An Arabic edition of this text, ed. Khalīl Shihāda and Suhayl Zakkār (Beirut: Dar al-Fikr, 2001), along with Rosenthal's translation, is available online at http://www.muslimphilosophy.com (accessed July 10, 2013).

Ibn Riḍwān. *Useful Book on the Quality of Medical Education (Al-Nāfi' fī kayfiyyat ta'līm ṣinā'at al-ṭibb)*. MS. 4026, fol. 12b.11–16b.12 and MS. Arberry 17.8–20.10. Excerpt translated by Iskandar, "An Attempted Reconstruction," 253–56.

Infancy Gospels of James and Thomas. Trans. R. Hock. The Scholars Bible 2. Santa Rosa, Calif.: Polebridge, 1995.

Infancy Gospel of Thomas. See under *Paidika*.

Irenaeus. *Against Heresies.* Ed. A. Rousseau and L. Doutreleau. 5 volumes. SC 100, 152–53, 210–11, 263–64. English trans. *ANF* 1.

Isho'dad of Merv. *Commentary on Matthew.* Ed. and trans. M. D. Gibson, *The Commentaries of Isho'dad of Merv, Bishop of Ḥadatha (ca. 850 A.D.) in Syriac and English.* 2 volumes. Horae Semiticae 5–6. Cambridge: Cambridge University Press, 1911.

James, M. R. *Apocryphal New Testament.* Oxford: Clarendon, 1924.

———. *Latin Infancy Gospels.* Cambridge: Cambridge University Press, 1927.

Jeremiah Apocryphon. Coptic text ed. and trans. K. H. Kuhn, "A Coptic Jeremiah Apocryphon," *Le Muséon* 83 (1970), 95–135, 291–350. Garshuni version ed. and trans. A. Mingana and R. Harris, "A New Jeremiah Apocryphon," *Bulletin of the John Rylands Library* 11 (1927), 329–42, 352–95; repr. in *Woodbrooke Studies,* vol. 1 (Cambridge: W. Heffer and Sons, 1927), 125–38 (introduction), 148–91 (English translation), and 192–233 (facsimile).

Jerome. *Apology against Rufinus.* Ed. and trans. Pierre Lardet. SC 303. Paris: Cerf, 1983. English trans. *NPNF,* ser. 2, vol. 3.

———. *Commentary on Jeremiah.* Ed. S. Reiter. CCSL 74 (1960).

———. *Epistles.* Ed. I. Hilberg. CSEL 55 (1912). English trans. *NPNF,* ser. 2, vol. 6.

John Chrysostom. *Address on Vainglory and the Right Way for Parents to Bring Up Their Children.* Ed. F. Schulte, *S. Joannis Chrysostomi De inani Gloria et de educandis liberis.* Monasterii Guestfalorum: Ex Officina Societatis Typographiae Guestfalorum, 1914. Trans. M. L. W. Laistner, in *Christianity and Pagan Culture in the Later Roman Empire,* 85–122. Ithaca: Cornell University Press, 1951.

———. *Homilies. PG* 56–63. English trans. *NPNF 14* (selected homilies).

Jordan, David R. "A Survey of Greek Defixiones Not Included in the Special Corpora." *Greek, Roman, and Byzantine Studies* 26.2 (1985), 151–97. [=SGD]

———. "Three Curse Tablets." In *The World of Ancient Magic: Papers from the First International Samson Eitrem Seminar at the Norwegian Institute at Athens, 4–8 May 1997,* ed. D. R. Jordan, H. Montgomery, and E. Thomassen, 115–24. Bergen: Norwegian Institute at Athens, 1999.

Joseph and Asenath. Ed. E. Reinmuth. Tübingen: Mohr Siebeck, 2009. Trans. C. Burchard, in *The Old Testament Pseudepigrapha,* ed. J. H. Charlesworth, volume 2, 177–201 (introduction), 202–47 (translation). Garden City, N.Y.: Doubleday, 1985. Trans. E. M. Humphrey. Sheffield: Sheffield Academic, 2000.

Josephus. *Opera.* Ed. B. Niese. 7 volumes. Berlin: Weidmann, 1885–1895.

Julius Pollux. *Onomasticon.* Ed. W. Dindorf, *Iulii Pollucis Onomasticon.* Leipzig: Kuehn, 1824. Ed. E. Bethe. 3 volumes. Leipzig: B. G. Teubner, 1900–1937.

Justin Martyr. *Dialogue with Trypho.* Ed. M. Marcovich. Berlin and New York: Walter de Gruyter, 1997.

Juvenal. *Satires.* Ed. and trans. G. G. Ramsay. LCL. Rev. ed. Cambridge, Mass.: Harvard University Press, 1940; repr. 1999.

Kaibel, George, ed. *Epigrammata Graeca ex lapidibus conlecta.* Berlin: G. Reimer, 1878.

Kisā'ī. *The Tales of the Prophets* (*Qisas al-anbiyā'*). Trans. W. Thackston. Boston: Twayne, 1978.

Khwārizmi, Abū 'Abd Allāh Muḥammad ibn Aḥmad al-. *Mafātīḥ al-'ulūm* (*The Keys of the Sciences*). Ed. G. Van Vloten. Leiden: Brill, 1895.

Kropp, Amina. *Defixiones: Ein aktuelles Corpus lateinischer Fluchtafeln.* Speyer: Kartoffeldruck Kai Broderson, 2008.

Lactantius. *Divine Institutes.* Ed. E. Heck and A. Wlosok. 4 volumes. Leipzig: K. G. Saur; Berlin: De Gruyter [vols. 2–4], 2005–2011. PL 6.11–1016. English trans. *ANF* 7.

———. *Epitome of the Divine Institutes.* Ed. E. Heck and A. Wlosok. Stuttgart and Leipzig: B. G. Teubner, 1994. English trans. *ANF* 7.

Layton, Bentley. *Gnostic Scriptures.* Garden City, N.Y.: Doubleday, 1987.

Layton, Bentley, ed. *Nag Hammadi Codex II, 2–7.* 2 volumes. Leiden: Brill, 1989.

Levene, Dan. "'. . . and by the name of Jesus . . .': An Unpublished Magic Bowl in Jewish Aramaic," *Jewish Studies Quarterly* 6 (1999), 283–308.

———. *A Corpus of Magic Bowls: Incantation Texts in Jewish Aramaic from Late Antiquity.* London: Kegan Paul, 2003.

Libanius. *Autobiography* (= *Oration* 1). Ed. and trans. A. F. Norman. LCL. Volume 1, 51–337. Cambridge, Mass.: Harvard University Press; London: William Heinemann, 1992.

———. *Opera.* Ed. R. Foerster. 12 volumes. Hildesheim and New York: G. Olms, 1985–1998.

Life and Miracles of Saint Thecla. Ed. Gilbert Dagron, *Vie et miracles de Sainte Thècle.* Brussels: Sociètè des Bollandistes, 1978.

Life of Mary (Syriac). Ed. E. A. Wallis Budge, *The History of the Blessed Virgin Mary and the History of the Likeness of Christ.* Volume 1, 67–77 (Syriac text). Volume 2, 71–82 (English translation). London: Luzac, 1899.

London, British Museum, M&ME 1922, 4–12, nos. 1–8. http://www.britishmuseum.org/explore/highlights/highlight_objects/pe_mla/t/the_tring_tiles.aspx (accessed July 11, 2013).

London, Victoria and Albert Museum, C.470–1927. http://collections.vam.ac.uk/item/O70759/tile-tring-tiles/ (accessed July 11, 2013).

Lucian of Samosata. *Alexander the False Prophet.* Ed. M. D. Macleod, *Luciani opera.* Volume 2, 331–59.

———. *Anacharsis* (*Concerning Gymnasia*). Ed. Erwin Steindl, *Luciani Scytharum colloquia, quae inscribuntur Toxaris, Scytha, Anacharsis cum scholiis,* 54–79. Leipzig: BSB Teubner, 1970. Ed. M. D. Macleod, *Luciani opera.* Volume 2, 237–60. Oxford: Clarendon, 1974.

———. *The Dream.* Ed. and trans. M. D. Macleod, *Lucian: A Selection,* 22–33. Warminster: Aris and Phillips, 1991.

———. *Icaromenippus.* Ed. A. M. Harmon. LCL. Volume 2, 268–322. Cambridge, Mass.: Harvard University Press, 1915; repr. 1960.

———. *The Ignorant Book Collector* (*Adv. Indoct.*). Ed. and trans. A. M. Harmon. LCL. Volume 3, 173–212. Cambridge, Mass.: Harvard University Press; London: William Heinemann, 1960.

———. *Lucian: A Selection.* Ed. and trans. M. D. Macleod. Warminster: Aris and Philips, 1991.

———. *On Salaried Posts in Great Houses,* or *The Dependent Scholar* (*De Mercede conductis*). Ed. and trans. A. M. Harmon. LCL 130, 411–81. Cambridge, Mass.: Harvard University Press; London: William Heinemann, 1921.

Macrobius. *Saturnalia*. Ed. R. A. Kaster. Scriptorum Classicorum Bibliotheca Oxoniensis. Oxford: Clarendon, 2011. Ed and trans. R. A. Kaster. LCL. 3 volumes. Cambridge, Mass.: Harvard University Press, 2011.

Marcus Aurelius. *Meditations*. Ed. and trans. A. S. L. Farquharson, *The Meditations of the Emperor Marcus Aurelius*. Volume 1. Oxford: Clarendon, 1944; repr. 1968. Trans. G. Long, at http://classics.mit.edu/Antoninus/meditations.6.six.html (accessed July 10, 2013).

Marcus Cornelius Fronto. *Correspondence*. Ed. and trans. C. R. Haines. LCL. 2 volumes. Rev. ed. Cambridge, Mass.: Harvard University Press; London: William Heinemann, 1929.

Marsanes (NHC X.1.1–68). Ed. B. A. Pierson. *Nag Hammadi Codices IX and X*, Nag Hammadi Studies 15, 229–347. Leiden: Brill, 1981. Trans. B. A. Pierson, in *The Nag Hammadi Library in English*. Fourth rev. ed., ed. J. M. Robinson et al., 460–71. Leiden: Brill, 1996.

Martial, *Epigrams*. Ed. and trans. D. R. Shackleton Bailey. LCL. 3 volumes. Cambridge, Mass.: Harvard University Press, 1993.

Maximus of Tyre. *Orations*. Ed. M. B. Trapp. Bibliotheca scriptorium Graecorum et Romanorum Teuberiana. Stuttgart: Teubner, 1994.

Maximus the Confessor. *Life of the Virgin*. Ed. and trans. M. van Esbroeck, *Maxime le Confesseur: Vie de la Vierge*. 2 volumes. CSCO 478–79. Louvain: Peeters, 1986.

Melito of Sardis. *On the Pascha*. Ed. and trans. O. Perler. SC 123. Paris: Cerf, 1966.

Methodius of Olympia. *Symposium*. Ed. G. Nathanael Bonwetsch. GCS 27. Leipzig: J. C. Hinrichs, 1917. Ed. H. Musurillo. SC 95. Paris: Cerf, 1963.

Meyer, Marvin W., and Richard Smith, eds. *Ancient Christian Magic: Coptic Texts of Ritual Power*. San Francisco: HarperSanFrancisco, 1994; repr. Princeton: Princeton University Press, 1999.

Minucius Felix, *Octavius*. Ed. and trans. G. H. Rendall. LCL. London: William Heinemann, 1966.

Mommsen, Theodore, et al., eds. *Corpus Inscriptionum Latinarum*. Berlin: G. Reimer, 1893–. [= *CIL*]

Montgomery, James A. *Aramaic Incantation Texts from Nippur*. Philadelphia: University Museum, 1913.

Nauck, A., ed. *Tragicorum Graecorum Fragmenta* (*TrGF*). Second ed. Leipzig: B. G. Teubner, 1889; repr. Hildesheim and New York: G. Olms, 1983.

Naveh, J., and S. Shaked. *Amulets and Magic Bowls*. Jerusalem: Hebrew University, Magnes Press; Leiden: Brill, 1985.

Nicene and Post-Nicene Fathers. Ed. P. Schaff and H. Wace. First and Second series. New York: Christian Literature Co., 1886–1900. [=*NPNF*].

Nicomachus of Gerasa. *Excerpts*. Ed. K. Jan, *Musici scriptores Graeci*. Leipzig: B. G. Teubner, 1895; repr. Hildesheim: Olms, 1962. Trans. F. R. Levin. Grand Rapids, Mich.: Phanes, 1994.

———. *Manual of Harmony* (*Enchiridion*). Ed. C. Jan, *Musici scriptores Graeci*. Leipzig: B. G. Teubner, 1895. Trans. S. Gersh, *From Iamblichus to Ereugena*. Leiden: Brill, 1978.

Novum Testamentum Graece. Ed. Eberhard and Erwin Nestle, and Barbara and Kurt Aland. 26th ed. Stuttgart: Deutsche Bibelgesellschaft, 1979; repr. 1991.

On the Mystery of the Letters. Ed. C. Bandt, *Der Traktat "Vom Mysterium der Buchstaben."* TU 162. Berlin and New York: Walter de Gruyter, 2007.

Origen of Alexandria. *Against Celsus*. Ed. M. Borret, *Origène: Contre Celse*. 5 volumes. SC 132, 136, 147, 150, 227. Paris: Cerf, 1967–1976.

———. *Dialogue with Heracleides*. Ed. J. Scherer, *Entretien d'Origène avec Héraclide*. SC 67. Paris: Cerf, 1960.

———. *On Prayer* (*De oratione*). Ed. P. Koetschau, *Origenes Werke*, volume 2. GCS 3.295–403. Leipzig: J. C. Hinrichs, 1899. Trans. W. A. Curtis, at http://www.ccel.org/ccel/origen/prayer (accessed July 10, 2013).

Ovid. *Metamorphoses*. Ed. and trans. F. J. Miller. LCL. Volume 2. Cambridge, Mass.: Harvard University Press; London: William Heinemann, 1976.

Pachomiana latina. Ed. A. Boon. Louvain: Bureaux de la Revue, 1932.

Paidika (Arabic). Milan, Biblioteca Ambrosiana, G 11 sup. (undated). Ed. S. Noja, "À propos du texte arabe d'un évangile apocryphe de Thomas de la Ambrosiana de Milan," in *Yad-Nama: In Memoria di Alessandro Bausani*, ed. B. Scarcia Amorette and L. Rostagno, volume 1, 335–41. Rome: Bardi Editore, 1991. French trans. S. Noja, "L'Évangile arabe apocryphe de Thomas de la 'Biblioteca Ambrosiana' de Milan (G 11 sup)," in *Biblische und Judaistische Studien: Festschrift für Paolo Sacchi*, ed. A. Vivian. Judentum und Umwelt 29, 681–90. Frankfurt am Main: Peter Lang, 1990.

Paidika (Ethiopic). *Miracles of Jesus* (*Ta'amra 'Iyasus*). Ed. S. Grébaut, "Les miracles de Jésus: Texte éthiopien publié et traduit," *Patrologia Orientalis* 12.4 (1919), 555–652, at 625–42 ("Huitième miracle, Miracles de l'enfance"). Trans. Paul-Hubert Poirier, at http://www.tonyburke.ca/infancy-gospel-of-thomas/the-infancy-gospel-of-thomas-ethiopic/ (accessed July 10, 2013).

Paidika (Georgian). Ed. Kornelius Kekelidze, *Monumenta Hagiographica Georgica*. Volume 1, 115–17. Sak'art': Rk. Gz. sammart'velos tipo-lit., 1918. Ed. Leon Melikset-Bek, "Fragment grusinskoi versii 'Djetsiva Hrista' [A Fragment of the Georgian Version of the 'Infancy of Christ']," *Hristianskii Vostok* 6.3 (1917–1920), 315–20. Latin trans. G. Garitte, "Le fragment géorgien de l'Évangile de Thomas," *Revue d'histoire ecclesiastique* 51.1 (1956), 513–20 (Latin translation, 516–20 [=chs. 2–7]). English trans. T. Burke, at http://www.tonyburke.ca/infancy-gospel-of-thomas/the-infancy-gospel-of-thomas-georgian/ (accessed July 10, 2013).

Paidika (Greek). Critical ed. Tony Burke, *De infantia Iesu evangelium Thomae graece*. CCSA 17. Turnhout: Brepols, 2010.

Paidika (Latin). *Gospel of Pseudo-Matthew* (*pars altera*). An early Latin text is attested in two forms: (1) *Vindobonensis* 563 (LV): Vienna, Österreichische Nationalbibliothek, lat. 563; and (2) the so-called *pars altera* of the *Gospel of Ps.-Matthew* (LM): ed. Tischendorf, *Evangelium apocrypha*. Second ed., 93–112. A later Latin text (LT) has also been edited by Tischendorf, *Evangelium apocrypha*. Second ed., 164–80.

Paidika (Slavonic). Ed. Aurelio de Santos Otero, *Das kirchenslavische Evangelium des Thomas*. PTS 6. Berlin: De Gruyter, 1967. Ed. Thomas Rosén, *The Slavonic Translation of the Apocryphal Infancy Gospel of Thomas*. Acta Universitatis Upsaliensis, Studia Slavica Upsaliensia, 39. Uppsala: Uppsala University; Stockholm: Almqvist and Wiksell

International, 1997. Trans. T. Allan Smith, at http://www.tonyburke.ca/infancy-gospel-of-thomas/the-infancy-gospel-of-thomas-slavonic/ (accessed July 10, 2013).

Paidika (Syriac). British Museum Add. 14484, fol. 12v–16r (=SyrW): ed. and trans. W. Wright, *Contributions to the Apocryphal Literature of the New Testament, collected and edited from Syriac Manuscripts in the British Museum, with an English translation and notes,* 6–11 (English translation), 11–16 (Syriac text). London: Williams and Norgate, 1865. Göttingen, Universitätsbibliothek, syr. 10, fol. 1v–4v (SyrG): ed. W. Baars and J. Heldermann, "Neue Materialien zum Text und zur Interpretation des Kindheitsevangeliums des Pseudo-Thomas," *Oriens Christianus* 77 (1993), 191–226; 78 (1994), 1–32. Vat. Syr. 159: ed. and trans. Tony Burke, "The *Infancy Gospel of Thomas* from an Unpublished Syriac Manuscript: Introduction, Text, Translation, and Notes," *Hugoye: Journal of Syriac Studies* 16.2 (2013), 225–99. French trans. Paul Peeters, *Évangiles apocryphes.* Volume 2, 288–311 (partial). Paris: A. Picard, 1914.

Paulinus of Nola. *Carmina.* Ed. W. Hartel. GSEL 30. Vienna: F. Tempsky, 1894.

Pausanias. *Description of Greece.* Ed. and trans. W. H. S. Jones. LCL. 5 volumes. London: William Heinemann; New York: G. P. Putnam's Sons, 1918–35; repr. Cambridge, Mass.: Harvard University Press, 1992.

Pernigotti, Sergio. "I papyri copti dell'Università Gattolica di Milano: I." *Aegyptus* 65 (1985), 67–105.

Petronius, *Satyricon.* Ed. and trans. M. Heseltine. LCL. Cambridge, Mass.: Harvard University Press, 1956. Rev. ed. London: William Heinemann; New York: Macmillan, 1969; repr. 2005.

Philippart, G. "Fragments palimpsests latins du Vindobonensis 563 (Ve siècle?): Évangile selon S. Matthieu, Évangile de Nicodème, Évangile de l'enfance selon Thomas," *Analecta Bollandiana* 90 (1972), 391–411.

Philo of Alexandria. [*Writings.*] Ed. and trans. F. H. Colson, G. H. Whitaker, and R. Marcus, *Philo.* LCL. 12 volumes. Cambridge, Mass.: Harvard University Press, 1929–1962.

Philodemus. *On Frank Speech* (*De libertate dicendi*). Ed. and trans. D. Konstan et al. Texts and Translations 43. Graeco-Roman Series 13. Atlanta: Scholars, 1998.

Piacenza pilgrim. *Itinerary.* Original ed. P. Geyer, *Itinera Hierosolymitana saeculi III–VII.* CSEL 39, 157–218. Vienna and Prague: F. Tempsky; Leipzig: G. Freytag, 1898. Emended ed. Geyer, *Itineraria et alia geographica.* CCSL 175, 127–53 (the original, longer recension), 155–74 (a second, shorter recension). Turnhout: Brepols, 1965. Critical ed. C. Milani, *Itinerarium Antonini Placentini: Un viaggio in Terra Santa del 560–570 d. C.* Milan: Vita e pensiero, 1977. Trans. A. Stewart, *Of the Holy Places Visited by Antoninus Martyr (Circ. 560–570 A.D.).* London: Palestine Pilgrims' Text Society, 1887. Trans. J. Wilkinson, *Jerusalem Pilgrims before the Crusades. Newly Translated with Supporting Documents and Notes.* Rev. ed., 129–51. Warminster: Aris and Phillips, 2002.

Pindar. *Nemean Odes.* Ed. and trans. W. H. Race. LCL. 2 volumes. Cambridge, Mass.: Harvard University Press; London: William Heinemann, 1937.

Pistis Sophia. Ed. and trans. C. Schmidt. Nag Hammadi Studies 9. Leiden: Brill, 1978. Trans. G. Horner. London: SPCK, 1924.

Plato. *Timaeus*. Ed. and trans. R. G. Bury. LCL. Volume 7. London: William Heinemann; New York: G. P. Putnam's Sons, 1929. Trans. D. Lee. London: Penguin, 1977.

Plautus. *Bacchides*. Ed. and trans. P. Nixon. LCL. Cambridge, Mass.: Harvard University Press; London: William Heinemann, 1916.

———. *The Captives*. Ed. and trans. P. Nixon. LCL. Volume 1, 459–567. London: William Heinemann; New York: G. P. Putnam's Sons, 1916.

Pliny the Elder. *Natural History*. Ed. and trans. H. Rackham. LCL. Volume 3. Cambridge, Mass.: Harvard University Press; London: William Heinemann, 1940.

Pliny the Younger. *Epistles*. Ed. and trans. B. Radice. 2 volumes. LCL. Cambridge, Mass.: Harvard University Press, 1969.

Plotinus. *Enneads*. Ed. and trans. A. H. Armstrong. LCL. 7 volumes. Cambridge, Mass.: Harvard University Press, 1966–1988.

Plutarch. *Lives*. Ed. B. Perrin. LCL. 11 volumes. Cambridge, Mass.: Harvard University Press; London: Heinemann, 1914–1926.

———. *Moralia*. Ed. F. C. Babbitt. Trans. B. Einarson and P. H. de Lacy. LCL. 17 volumes. London: William Heinemann; New York: G. P. Putnam's Sons, 1926–1969; repr. Cambridge, Mass.: Harvard University Press, 1969–2004.

———. *On the Defects of the Oracles* (*De defectu oraculorum*). Ed. and trans. F. C. Babbitt, *Moralia*. LCL. Volume 5, 347–501.

———. *On the E at Delphi* 4. Ed. and trans. F. C. Babbitt, *Moralia*. LCL. Volume 5, 198–253. London: William Heinemann, 1936.

———. *On Moral Virtue* (*De virtute morali*). Ed. M. Pohlenz, *Plutarchi moralia*. Volume 3, 127–56. Leipzig: Teubner, 1929; repr. 1972. Ed. and trans. W. C. Hembold. LCL. Volume 6, 22–27.

———. *Pelopidas*. Ed. C. Lindskog and K. Ziegler. *Plutarchi vitae parallelae*. Volume 2.2, 60–105. Leipzig: Teubner, 1914–1939. Second ed., 1968.

———. *Platonic Questions*. Ed. C. Hubert, *Plutarchi moralia*. Volume 6.1, 113–42. Leipzig: Teubner, 1954; repr. 1959. Ed. and trans. H. Cherniss. LCL. Volume 13.1. Cambridge, Mass.: Harvard University Press, 1976.

Poimandrēs. Ed. A. D. Nock and A. J. Festugière, *Corpus Hermeticum*. Second ed. Volume 1, 7–19. Paris: Belles Lettres, 1960. Trans. B. Layton, *Gnostic Scriptures*, 452–59.

Prayer of Manasseh. Ed. P. W. van der Horst and J. H. Newman. Berlin: de Gruyter, 2008. Syriac versions, ed. A. Gutman and W. van Peursen, *The Two Syriac Versions of the Prayer of Manasseh*. Piscataway, N.J.: Gorgias, 2011.

Preisendanz, Karl. "Die griechischen und lateinischen Zaubertafeln." *Archiv für Papyrusforschung* 9 (1930), 119–54; and 11 (1933), 153–64.

Preisendanz, Karl, ed. *Papyri Graecae Magicae: Die griechischen Zauberpapyri*. 3 volumes. Stuttgart: Teubner, 1928–1931. Second ed., 1973–1974. Trans. H. D. Betz et al., *The Greek Magical Papyri in Translation*. Second ed. Chicago: University of Chicago Press, 1992. [=*PGM*]

Preisigke, F., et al., eds. *Sammelbuch griechischer Urkunden aus Ägypten*. Berlin: de Gruyter, 1913–. [=*SB*]

Proclus. *A Commentary on the First Book of Euclid's Elements*. Ed. G. Friedlein, *Procli Diadochi in Primum Euclidis Elementorum Librum Commentarii*. Leipzig: B. G. Teubner, 1873; repr. Hildesheim: Olms, 1967. Trans. G. R. Morrow. Princeton: Princeton University Press, 1970.

———. *Commentary on Plato's Timaeus.* Ed. E. Diehl. 3 volumes. Leipzig: B. G. Teubner, 1903–1906. Trans. T. Taylor. 2 volumes. London: Black, Young, and Young, 1820.

Protevangelium of James. Ed. and trans. R. F. Hock, *The Infancy Gospels of James and Thomas,* 31–77. Santa Rosa, Calif.: Polebridge, 1995. Ed. Tischendorf, *Evangelia apocrypha.* Second ed., 1–50. Trans. W. Schneemelcher, *New Testament Apocrypha.* Volume 1, 421–39.

Prudentius. *On the Crown* (*Peristephanon liber*). Ed. and trans. H. J. Thomson. LCL. 2 volumes. Cambridge, Mass.: Harvard University Press, 1949–1953; repr. 1993–1995.

Ps.-Apollodorus. *Library* (*Bibliotheca*). Ed. and trans. J. G. Frazer. LCL. 2 volumes. Cambridge, Mass.: Harvard University Press; London: William Heinemann, 1921; repr. 1989.

Ps.-Aristotle. *The Problemata Physica Attributed to Aristotle: The Arabic Version of Ḥunain ibn Isḥāq and the Hebrew Version of Moses ibn Tibbon.* Ed. L. S. Filius. Leiden: Brill, 1999.

Ps.-Clement. *Homilies.* Ed. André Siouville, *Les Homélies Clémentines.* Paris: Rieder, 1933, repr. Lagrasse: Verdier, 1991.

———. *Letter of Clement to James.* Trans. G. Strecker, in *New Testament Apocrypha,* ed. W. Schneemelcher, volume 2, 496–503.

Ps.-Galen. *Pseudogaleni in Hippocratis de Septimanis Commentarium ab Hunaino quod fertur Arabice versum.* Ed. G. Bergsträsser. Leipzig and Berlin: B. G. Teubner, 1914; repr. Frankfurt am Main: Institute for the History of Arabic-Islamic Science at the Johann Wolfgang Goethe University, 1996.

Ps.-Justin Martyr. *On the Sole Government of God* (*De monarchia*). Ed. J. C. T. Otto, *Corpus apologetarum Christianorum saeculi secondi.* Third ed. Volume 3, 126–58. Jena: F. Mauke, 1876–1881. English trans. *ANF* 1.290–93.

Ps.-Lucian. *Lucius,* or *The Ass.* Ed. and trans. A. M. Harmon and M. D. Macleod. LCL. Volume 8, 52–145. London: W. Heinemann; New York: Macmillan, 1967.

Ps.-Plutarch. *The Education of Children* (*De liberis educandis*). Ed. and trans. F. C. Babbitt. LCL. Volume 1, 1–69. Cambridge: Harvard University Press, 1927; repr. 2000.

Ps.-Tertullian, *Against All Heresies.* Ed. E. Kroymann, CSEL 47 (1942), 213–26. English trans. *ANF* 3.649–54.

Qarāfī, Shibāb al-Dīn al-. *al-Ajwiba al-fākhira 'an al-as'ila al-fājira.* Ed. Bikr Zakī Awaḍ. Silsilat muqāranat adyān 1. Cairo: Kulliyyat uṣūl al-dīn, 1986.

Questions of Bartholomew. Ed. A. Vassiliev, *Anecdota graeco-byzantina.* Volume 1, 10–22. Moscow: Universitatis Caesareae, 1893. French trans. J.-D. Kaestli, "Questions de Barthélemy," in *Écrits apocryphes chrétiens,* ed. F. Bovon and P. Geoltrain, volume 1, 255–305.

Quintilian. *Institutes* (*Institutio Oratoria*). Ed. D. A. Russell. LCL. 5 volumes. Cambridge, Mass.: Harvard University Press, 2001.

Qur'ān. Ed. and trans. M. M. Pickthall, *The Meaning of the Glorious Qur'ān.* Beirut: Dar al-Kitab al-Lubnani, 1970.

Qusṭā ibn Lūqā. *Book on the Use of the Celestial Globe* (*Kitāb al-ʿamal bi-l-kura al-nujūmiyya*). Summarized and partially translated in Worrell, "Qusṭā ibn Lūqā," 285–93.

———. *Risāla fī al-farq bayn al-rūḥ wa al-nafs*. Ed. ʿAlī Muḥammad Isbir. Damascus: Dar al-Yanābiʿ, 2006.

Rāzī, Fakhr al-Dīn al-. *al-Tafsīr al-kabīr*. 8 volumes. Beirut: N.p., 1978.

Rengen, W. van. "Deux défixions contre les bleus à Apamée (VIe siècle apr. J.-C.)." In *Apamée de Syrie: Bilan des recherches archéologiques, 1973–1979: Aspects de l'architecture domestique d'Apamée*, ed. J. Balty, 213–34. Brussels: Centre belge de recherches archéologiques à Apamée de Syrie. Paris: Diffusion de Boccard, 1984.

Roussel, P., and M. Launey, eds. *Inscriptions de Délos, nos. 1497–2879: Décrets, dédicaces, listes, catalogues, textes divers, postérieurs à 166 av. J-C.* Paris: H. Champion, 1937.

Sālim, Muḥammad Salīm, ed. *Kitāb Jālīnūs fī al-isṭaqsāt ʿalā raʾy Abqrāṭ*. Cairo: al-Hayʾa al-miṣriyya al-ʿāma li-l-kitāb, 1987.

Schneemelcher, Wilhelm, ed. *New Testament Apocrypha*. 2 volumes. Trans. R. M. Wilson. London: Lutterworth, 1963. Rev. ed. Louisville: Westminster/John Knox, 1991.

Septuagint. Ed. A. Rahlfs, *Septuaginta*. 2 volumes. Stuttgart: Deutsche Bibelgesellschaft, 1979.

Servius. *Commentary on the Aeneid* (*Serv. Aen.*). Ed. G. Thilo and H. Hagen, Servii Grammatici qui feruntur in Vergilii Carmina Commentarii. Leipzig: B. G. Teubner, 1883.

Shaykh al-Mufīd, al- (Abū ʿAbd Allāh Muḥammad ibn Muḥammad). *Book of Guidance* (*Kitāb al-irshād*). Ed. Ḥusayn al-Aʿāmī. Beirut: Muʾassasat al-Aʿlamī lil-Maṭbūʿāt, 1979. Trans. I. K. A. Howard. Elmhurst, N.Y.: Tahrike Tarsile Qurʾan, 1981.

Shem-Ṭob Ibn Shaprut. *Touchstone*. Ed. Krauss, *Das Leben Jesu*, 146–47 (Hebrew text), and 147–49 (German translation).

Snell, B., and R. Kannicht, eds. *Tragicorum Graecorum Fragmenta*. 5 volumes. Göttingen: Vandenhoeck und Ruprecht, 1971–2004.

Socrates Scholasticus. *History of the Church*. Ed. G. C. Hansen. GCS, n.s. 1. Berlin: Akademie, 1995. English trans. *NPNF*, ser. 2, vol. 2.

Story of Ahiqar. Trans. F. C. Conybeare, J. R. Harris, and A. S. Lewis, *The Story of Aḥiḳar*. London: C. J. Clay and Sons, 1898. Second ed.: Cambridge: Cambridge University Press, 1913. Trans. J. M. Lindenberger, in *The Old Testament Pseudepigrapha*, volume 2, ed. J. H. Charlesworth, 479–93. London: Darton, Longman and Todd, 1985.

Suetonius. *Augustus*. Ed. and trans. J. C. Rolfe. LCL. Volume 1, 121–287. London: William Heinemann; New York: Macmillan, 1914.

———. *Lives of the Grammarians*. Ed. and trans. J. C. Rolfe, LCL. 2 volumes. London: William Heinemann; New York: Macmillan, 1914–1930.

Sulamī, Abū ʿAbd al-Raḥmān al-. *Explaining the Meaning of the Letters* (*Sharḥ maʿānī al-ḥurūf*). Ed. Gerhard Böwering and Bilal Orfali, *Sufi Treatises of Abū ʿAbd al-Raḥmān al-Sulamī (d. 412/1021)*. Recherches publiées sous la direction de l'Institut de lettres orientales de Beyrouth. Nouvelle série: Langue arabe et pensée islamique, Tome XXII. Beirut: Dar al-Machreq Éditeurs, 2009. Trans. Gerhard Böwering, "Sulamī's Treatise on the Science of the Letters (*ʿilm al-ḥurūf*)," 370–93.

Supplementum epigraphicum graecum. Ed. J. J. E. Hondius et al. Amsterdam: J. C. Gieben, 1923– .

Ṭabarī, Abū Ja'far Muḥammad ibn Jarīr al-. *Jāmi' al-bayān fī tafsīr al-Qur'ān.* 30 parts in 12 volumes. Beirut: Dār al-ma'rifa lil-ṭibā'a wa nashr, 1978.

Ṭabrisī, al-. *Majma' al-bayān fī tafsīr al-Qur'ān.* Excerpt ed. Abū Wandī et al., *'Īsā wa Maryam,* 273–76.

Tacitus. *Annals.* Ed. and trans. C. H. Moore. LCL. 4 volumes. London: William Heinemann; New York: G. P. Putnam's Sons, 1925–1937.

Tatian. *Oration Addressed to the Greeks.* Ed. and trans. M. Whittaker. Oxford: Clarendon, 1982.

Terentianus Maurus. *On Letters.* Ed. C. Cignolo. Volume 1.11–23. Bibliotheca Weidmanniana 6. Collectanea grammatical latina 2. Hildesheim: Olms, 2002.

Tertullian. *On the Pallium.* PL 2.1029–50. English trans. *ANF* 4.5–12.

Tha'labī, al-. *'Arā'is al-majālis fī qisas al-anbiyā' or Lives of the Prophets as Recounted by . . . al-Tha'labī.* Trans. William Brinner. Leiden: Brill, 2002.

Themistius. *Orations.* Ed. R. Maisano. Classici greci. Turin: Unione tiporafico-editrice torinese, 1995.

Theodosius of Alexandria. *On Grammar.* Ed. K. W. Goettling. Leipzig: Libraria Dykiana, 1822.

Thilo, Johann Carl. *Codex apocryphus Novi Testamenti.* Volume 1. Leipzig: F. C. G. Vogel, 1832.

Tischendorf, Constantine von, ed. *Evangelia apocrypha.* Leipzig: Avenarius and Mendelssohn, 1853. Second ed., 1876.

Toledot Yeshu. MS Strasbourg (Wagenseil text type): ed. Krauss, *Das Leben Jesu,* 38–50 (Hebrew text), 50–64 (German translation). English trans. (with some summarized sections): H. Schofield, *According to the Hebrews,* 35–61; see also http://www.essene.com/History&Essenes/toled.htm (accessed July 10, 2013). MS Adler: ed. Krauss, *Das Leben Jesu,* 118–21 (Hebrew text), 122–28 (German translation). For a Hebrew edition incorporating all six texts published by Krauss, see J. D. Eisenstein, *Otsar viḳuhim* (New York: N.p., 1928), 227–35. The so-called Pilate text type has been edited by Michael Higger, "Ma'aseh Yeshu," *Horeb* 3 (1936), 143–52. English trans. H. W. Basser, "The Acts of Jesus," in *The Frank Talmage Memorial Volume,* ed. B. Walfish, 273–82. Haifa: Haifa University Press, 1993. A later, expanded version of the *Toledot* has been edited by G. Schlichting, *Die verschollene Toledot-Jeschu-Fassung Tam ū-mū'ād. Einleitung, Text, Übersetzung, Kommentar, Motivsynopse, Bibliographie.* WUNT 24. Tübingen: Mohr, 1982.

Tripartite Tractate. Ed. and trans. H. Attridge and E. H. Pagels, in *Nag Hammadi Codex I (The Jung Codex),* ed. H. Attridge. Volume 1, 192–337. Trans. H. W. Attridge and D. Mueller, in *Nag Hammadi Library,* fourth ed., ed. J. M. Robinson et al., 58–103. Leiden: Brill, 1996.

Valentinus. *Fragment A* (preserved in Hippolytus of Rome, *Refutation of All Heresies* 6.42.2). Ed. W. Völker, *Quellen zur Geschichte der christlichen Gnosis.* Sammlung ausgewählter kirchen- und dogmengeschichtlicher Quellenschriften, n. s., no. 5, 59 (=Frag. 7). Tübingen: Mohr Siebeck, 1932. Trans. B. Layton, *Gnostic Scriptures,* 230–31.

Varro, *On Agriculture.* Ed. and trans. W. D. Hooper and H. B. Ash. LCL, rev. ed., 446–89. Cambridge, Mass., and London: Harvard University Press, 1935; repr. 2006.

Vettius Valens. *Anthology.* Ed. D. Pingree. Leipzig: B. G. Teubner, 1986. Draft English trans. M. Riley, http://www.csus.edu/indiv/r/rileymt/Vettius%20Valens%20entire.pdf (accessed July 10, 2013). Partial French trans. J. F. Bara. Leiden: Brill, 1989. Partial English trans. R. Schmidt, ed. R. Hand. Berkeley Springs, W.Va.: Golden Hind, 1994.

Virgil. *Aeneid.* Ed. and trans. H. R. Fairclough and G. P. Goold. LCL, vol. 2. Cambridge, Mass., and London: Harvard University Press, 2000.

Vision of Theophilus. Ed. and trans. A. Mingana, "Vision of Theophilus," *Woodbrooke Studies* 3.1 (1931), 1–8 (introduction), 8–43 (English translation), 44–92 (Syriac text).

Vollgraff, Guilielmus. "Novae inscriptiones Argivae (cont.)." *Mnemosyne* 47 (1919), 252–70.

Wilcken, U., ed. *Urkunden der Ptolemäerzeit (ältere Funde).* 2 volumes. Berlin: de Gruyter, 1927–1934. [=*UPZ*]

Wilhelm, A. "Zwei Fluchinschriften." *Jahrshefte des Österreichischen archäologischen Instituts* 4 (1901), Beiblatt, cols. 9–18.

Worrell, William H. "Coptic Magical and Medical Texts." *Orientalia* 4 (1935), 1–37 and 184–92.

Wortmann, Dierk. "Neue magische Texte." *Bonner Jahrbücher des Rheinischen Landesmuseums in Bonn* 168 (1968), 56–111.

Wünsch, Richard. *Appendix Continens Defixionum Tabellae in Attica Regiona Repertas. IG* 3.3. Berlin: G. Reimer, 1897. [=*DTA*]

Zamakhsharī, Abū al-Qāsim Jādullah Maḥmūd ibn ʿUmar al-. *al-Kashshāf ʿan ḥaqāʾiq al-tanzīl wa ʿuyūn al-aqāwīl fī wujūh al-taʾwīl.* 4 volumes. Beirut: N.p., n.d.

Zosimus of Panopolis. *Mémoires authentiques.* Ed. M. Mertens, *Les alchimistes grecs. Tome IV.1.* Second ed., ed. R. Halleux. Paris: Les Belles Lettres, 2002.

———. *On the Letter Omega.* Ed. and trans. H. M. Jackson. Missoula, Mont.: Scholars, 1978.

Secondary Literature

Aarde, A. G. van. "Ebionite Tendencies in the Jesus Tradition: The Infancy Gospel of Thomas Interpreted from the Perspective of Ethnic Identity." *Neotestamentica* 40.2 (2006), 353–82.

———. "The Infancy Gospel of Thomas: Allegory or Myth—Gnostic or Ebionite." *Verbum et ecclesia [Skrif en kerk]* 26 (2005), 826–50.

———. "Die Kindheidsevangelie van Tomas as 'n heroïese mite van die God-kind Jesus in die konteks van die Ebionitiese vroeë Christendom" ("The Infancy Gospel of Thomas as a heroic myth of the God-child Jesus in the context of Ebionite Early Christianity"). Ph.D. thesis, University of Pretoria, 2005.

———. "Die Kindheidsevangelie van Tomas—historiese allegorie of mite in die vorm van 'n biografiese diskursiewe evangelie?" *HTS Teologiese Studies / Theological Studies* 61.1–2 (2005), 461–89.

Aasgaard, Reidar. *The Childhood of Jesus: Decoding the Apocryphal Infancy Gospel of Thomas*. Eugene, Ore.: Cascade, 2009.

———. "Children in Antiquity and Early Christianity: Research History and Central Issues." *Familia (UPSA, Spain)* 33 (2006), 23–46.

———. "From Boy to Man in Antiquity: Jesus in the Apocryphal Infancy Gospel of Thomas." *THYMOS: Journal of Boyhood Studies* 3 (2009), 3–20.

———. "Uncovering Children's Culture in Late Antiquity: The Testimony of the *Infancy Gospel of Thomas*." In *Children in Early Christianity*, ed. C. B. Horn, 1–27. Tübingen: Mohr Siebeck, 2009.

Achtemeier, Paul. "*Omne verbum sonat:* The New Testament and the Oral Environment of Late Western Antiquity." *Journal of Biblical Literature* 108 (1990), 3–27.

Ägypten—Schätze aus dem Wüstensand: Kunst und Kultur der Christen am Nil: Katalog zur gleichnamigen Ausstellung im Gustav-Lübcke-Museum Hamm. Wiesbaden: L. Reichert, 1996.

Aichele, George, et al. (Bible and Culture Collective). *The Postmodern Bible*. New Haven and London: Yale University Press, 1995.

Alcock, Joan. *Life in Roman Britain*. Stroud: Tempus, 2006.

Alcock, Susan. *Archaeologies of the Greek Past: Landscape, Monuments, and Memories*. Cambridge: Cambridge University Press, 2002.

Alexander, Michael. *The Case for the Prosecution in the Ciceronian Era*. Ann Arbor: University of Michigan Press, 2003.

Alexander, Philip. "Jesus and His Mother in the Jewish Anti-Gospel (the *Toledot Yeshu*)." In *Infancy Gospels: Stories and Identities*, ed. C. Clivaz et al., 588–616.

———. "The *Toledot Yeshu* in the Context of Jewish-Muslim Debate." In *Toledot Yeshu ("The Life Story of Jesus") Revisited*, ed. P. Schäfer, M. Meerson, and Y. Deutsch, 137–58.

Alikin, Valeriy A. *The Earliest History of the Christian Gathering: Origin, Development and Content of the Christian Gathering in the First to Third Centuries*. Supplements to the Vigiliae Christianae. Leiden: Brill, 2010.

Allan, D. J. "Ἀναγιγνώσκω and Some Cognate Words." *Classical Quarterly* 74 (=n.s. 30.1) (1980), 244–51.

Allély, A. "Les enfants malformés et considérés comme prodigia à Rome et en Italie sous la République." *Revue des études anciennes* 105 (2003), 127–56.

———. "Les enfants malformés et handicapes a Rome sous le principat." *Revue des études anciennes* 106.1 (2004), 73–101.

Amsler, Frédéric. "Les *Paidika Iesou*, un nouveau témoin de la rencontre entre judaïsme et christianisme à Antioche au IVe siècle?" In *Infancy Gospels: Stories and Identities*, ed. C. Clivaz et al., 433–58.

Amundsen, D. W. "Medicine and the Birth of Defective Children: Approaches of the Ancient World." In *Euthanasia and the Newborn: Conflicts Regarding Saving Lives*, ed. R. C. McMillan et al., 3–22. Dordrecht: Reidel, 1987.

Andrae, Tor. *In the Garden of Myrtles: Studies in Early Islamic Mysticism*. Trans. B. Sharpe. SUNY Series in Muslim Spirituality in South Asia. Albany: State University of New York Press, 1987.

Andresen, Karl. *Logos und Nomos: Die Polemik des Kelsos wider das Christentum.* Berlin: W. de Gruyter, 1955.

Aravantinou, M. Bonanno. "Un frammento di sarcofago romano con fanciulli atleti nei Musei Capitolani: Contributo allo studio dei sarcofagi con scene di palestra." *Bollettino d'Arte* 15 (1982), 67–84.

Arberry, A. J. "al-Djunayd, Abu 'l-Ḳāsim b. Muḥammad b. al-Djunayd al-Khazzāz al-Ḳawārīrī al-Nihāwandī." *EI*[2] 2 (1963), 600.

Ariès, Philippe. *L'enfant et la vie familiale sous l'Ancien Régime.* Paris: Plon, 1960. English translation: *Centuries of Childhood: A Social History of Family Life,* trans. R. Baldick. New York: Vintage, 1962.

Arnaldez, R. "al-Muḥāsibī, Abū 'Abd Allāh al-Ḥārith." *EI*[2] 7 (1991), 466–67.

Arnason, Johann P. "Autonomy and Axiality: Comparative Perspectives on the Greek Breakthrough." In *Agon, Logos, Polis: The Greek Achievement and its Aftermath,* ed. J. P. Arnason and P. Murphy, 155–206.

Arnason, Johann P., and Peter Murphy, eds. *Agon, Logos, Polis: The Greek Achievement and Its Aftermath.* Stuttgart: Franz Steiner, 2001.

Arnason, Johann P., and Peter Murphy. "Introduction." In *Agon, Logos, Polis: The Greek Achievement and Its Aftermath,* ed. J. P. Arnason and P. Murphy, 8–14.

Arnold, Irene Ringwood. "Agonistic Features of Local Greek Festivals Chiefly from Inscriptional Evidence." Ph.D. dissertation, Columbia University, 1927.

———. "Agonistic Festivals in Italy and Sicily." *American Journal of Archaeology* 64.3 (1960), 245–51.

———. "Festivals of Ephesus." *American Journal of Archaeology* 76.1 (1972), 17–22.

———. "Festivals of Rhodes." *American Journal of Archaeology* 40.4 (1936), 432–36.

———. "Local Festivals at Delos." *American Journal of Archaeology* 37.3 (1933), 452–8.

———. "Local Festivals of Euboea, Chiefly from Inscriptional Evidence." *American Journal of Archaeology* 33.3 (1929), 385–92.

Arnold, Thomas W. *Painting in Islam: A Study of the Place of Pictorial Art in Muslim Culture.* Second ed. Piscataway, N.J.: Gorgias, 2004.

Ashcroft, B., G. Griffiths, and H. Tiffin, eds. *Post-colonial Studies Reader.* London and New York: Routledge, 1995.

Assmann, Aleida. *Erinnerungsräume: Formen und Wandlungen des kulturellen Gedächtnisses.* Munich: C. H. Beck, 1999.

———. *Der lange Schatten der Vergangenheit: Erinnerungskultur und Geschichtspolitik.* Munich: C. H. Beck, 2006.

———. "Schriftliche Folklore: Zur Entstehung und Funktion eines Überlieferungstyps." In *Schrift und Gedächtnis: Beiträge zur Archäologie der literarischen Kommunikation,* ed. A. Assmann, J. Assmann, and C. Hardmeier, 175–93. Munich: Wilhelm Fink, 1983.

———. "Texte, Spuren, Abfall: Die wechselnden Medien des kulturellen Gedächtnisses." In *Literatur- und Kulturwissenschaften: Positionen, Theorien, Modelle,* ed. H. Böhme and K. R. Scherpe, 96–111. Reinbek bei Hamburg: Rowohlt, 1996.

Assmann, Aleida, and Jan Assmann. "Das Gestern im Heute: Medien und soziales Gedächtnis." In *Die Wirklichkeit der Medien: Eine Einführung in die Kommunikation-*

swissenschaft, ed. K. Merten, S. J. Schmidt, and S. Weischenberg, 114–40. Opladen: Westdeutscher, 1994.

Assmann, Jan. "Collective Memory and Cultural Identity" (trans. John Czaplicka). *New German Critique* 65 (1995), 125–33.

———. "Kollektives Gedächtnis und kulturelle Identität." In *Kultur und Gedächtnis,* ed. J. Assmann and T. Hölscher, 9–19. Frankfurt am Main: Suhrkamp, 1988.

———. *Das kulturelle Gedächtnis: Schrift, Erinnerung und politische Identität in frühen Hochkulturen.* Munich: Beck, 1992. English trans.: *Cultural Memory and Early Civilization: Writing, Remembrance, and Political Imagination.* Cambridge: Cambridge University Press, 2011.

———. *Moses the Egyptian: The Memory of Egypt in Western Monotheism.* Cambridge, Mass.: Harvard University Press, 1997.

———. *Religion und kulturelles Gedächtnis: Zehn Studien.* Munich: C. H. Beck, 2000. English trans.: *Religion and Cultural Memory: Ten Studies,* trans. R. Livingstone. Stanford: Stanford University Press, 2006.

Aune, David E. "Septem sapientium convivium (Moralia 146B–164D)." In *Plutarch's Ethical Writings and Early Christian Literature,* ed. H. D. Betz, 51–105. Leiden: Brill, 1978.

Austin, J. L. *How to Do Things with Words.* Cambridge, Mass.: Harvard University Press, 1962.

Avrin, Leila. *Scribes, Script, and Books: The Book Arts from Antiquity to the Renaissance.* London: British Library, 1991.

Baars, Wilhelm, and Jan Helderman. "Neue Materialien zum Text und zur Interpretation des Kindheitsevangelium des Pseudo-Thomas," *Oriens Christianus* 77 (1993), 191–226, and 78 (1994), 1–32.

Bacht, H. *Das Vermachtnis des Ursprungs: Studien zum frühen Monchtum.* 2 volumes. Wurzburg: Echter, 1972–1983.

Backe-Dahmen, A. *Die Welt der Kinder in der Antike.* Zaberns Bildbände zur Archäologie. Mainz am Rhein: Zabern, 2008.

Bagatti, Bellarmino. "I battisteri della Palestina." In *Actes du 5e Congrès International d'Archéologie Chrétienne, Aix-en-Provence, 13–19 septembre 1954,* 213–27. Vatican City and Paris: Pontificio Istituto di archeologia cristiana, 1957.

———. *Excavations in Nazareth.* Volume 1. Trans. E. Hoade. Jerusalem: Franciscan, 1969. Originally published as *Gli scavi di Nazaret.* Publications of the Studium Biblicum Franciscanum 17. Jerusalem: Tip. dei PP. Francescani, 1967.

———. "Gli altari paleo-christiani della Palestina." *Liber Annuus* 7 (1957), 64–94.

———. "Nota sul Vangelo di Tommaso Israelita." *Euntes Docete* 29 (1976), 482–89.

———. "Probabile figura del Precursore in un graffito di Nazaret." *Oriens Antiquus* 3 (1964), 61–66.

———. "Ritrovamenti nella Nazaret evangelica." *Liber Annuus* 5 (1955), 5–44.

Bagnall, Roger S., and Raffaella Cribiore, with E. Ahtaridis, eds. *Women's Letters from Ancient Egypt, 300 BC–AD 800.* Ann Arbor: University of Michigan Press, 2006.

Bakhtin, Mikhail. *Speech Genres and Other Late Essays.* Trans. V. W. McGee. Austin: University of Texas Press, 1986.

Bakke, O. M. "Upbringing of Children in the Early Church: The Responsibility of Parents, Goal and Methods." *Studia Theologica: Nordic Journal of Theology* 60.2 (2006), 145–63.

———. *When Children Became People: The Birth of Childhood in Early Christianity.* Minneapolis: Fortress, 1995.

Bakker, Egbert J. "How Oral Is Oral Composition?" In *Signs of Orality: The Oral Tradition and Its Influence in the Greek and Roman World,* ed. E. A. MacKay. Mnemosyne 188, 29–47. Leiden: Brill, 1999.

Balch, David L., and Carolyn Osiek, eds. *Early Christian Families in Context: An Interdisciplinary Dialogue.* Grand Rapids, Mich., and Cambridge: Eerdmans, 2003.

Baldick, Julian. *Mystical Islam: An Introduction to Sufism.* New York: New York University Press, 1989.

Balogh, Josef. "'Voces paginarum': Beiträge zur Geschichte des lauten Lesens und Schreibens." *Philologus* 82 (1927), 84–109, 202–40.

Bammel, Ernst. "Christian Origins in Jewish Tradition." *New Testament Studies* 13 (1966–67), 317–35. Reprinted in *Judaica: Kleine Schriften.* Volume 1. WUNT 37, 220–38. Tübingen: Mohr, 1986.

———. "Jesus der Zauberer." In *Judaica: Kleine Schriften.* Volume 2. WUNT 91, 3–14. Tübingen: Mohr, 1997.

———. *Judaica: Kleine Schriften.* 2 volumes. WUNT 37 and 91. Tübingen: Mohr, 1986–1997.

———. "Der Jude des Celsus." In *Judaica: Kleine Schriften.* Volume 1. WUNT 37, 265–83. Tübingen: Mohr, 1986.

Bandt, Cordula, ed. *Der Traktat "Vom Mysterium der Buchstaben."* TU 162. Berlin and New York: Walter de Gruyter, 2007.

Barbu, Daniel. "Voltaire and the *Toledoth Yeshu*: A Response to Philip Alexander." In *Infancy Gospels: Stories and Identities*, ed. C. Clivaz et al., 617–27.

Barry, Kieren. *The Greek Qabalah: Alphabetic Mysticism and Numerology in the Ancient World.* York Beach, Me.: Samuel Weiser, 1999.

Barthes, Roland. *Camera Lucida: Reflections on Photography.* Trans. R. Howard. New York: Hill and Wang, 1981.

Basser, H. W. "The Acts of Jesus." In *The Frank Talmage Memorial Volume.* Ed. B. Walfish, 273–82. Haifa: Haifa University Press, 1993.

Bauckham, Richard. "Imaginative Literature." In *The Early Christian World,* ed. P. F. Esler, 791–812. London and New York: Routledge, 2000.

Bauer, H. "Über die Anordnung der Suren und über die geheimnisvollen Buchstaben im Qoran." *Zeitschrift der Deutschen Morgenländischen Gesellschaft* 75 (1921), 1–20.

Bauer, Walter. *Greek-English Lexicon of the New Testament and Other Early Christian Literature.* Second ed. Chicago: University of Chicago Press, 1979.

———. *Das Leben Jesu im Zeitalter der neutestamentlichen Apokryphen.* Tübingen: Mohr, 1909.

Baumstark, Antoine. "Ein apokryphes Herrenleben in mesopotamischen Federzeichnungen vom Jahre 1299." *Oriens Christianus,* n.s. 1 (1911), 249–71.

Baur, Ferdinand C. "Über Zweck und Veranlassung des Römerbriefs und die damit zusammengehängenden Verhältnisse der römischen Gemeinde." *Tübinger Zeitschrift für Theologie* (1836), 59–178.

Baus, Karl. *Der Kranz in Antike und Christentum: Eine religionsgeschichtliche Untersuchung mit besonderer Berücksightigung Tertullians (Teildruck).* Bonn: Hanstein, 1940.

Beard, Mary, et al., eds. *Literacy in the Roman World.* Ann Arbor, Mich.: Journal of Roman Archaeology, 1991.

Bearman, P. J., et al., eds. *Encyclopaedia of Islam.* Second ed. 13 vols. Leiden: Brill, 1954–2009. [=*EI*[2]]

Beausobre, Isaac de. *Histoire critique de Manichée et du manichéisme.* Amsterdam: J. Frédéric Bernard, 1734.

Beazley, J. D. *Attic Red-Figure Vase-Painters.* Second ed. 3 volumes. Oxford: Clarendon, 1963.

Beck, Frederick A. G. *Album of Greek Education: The Greeks at School and at Play.* Sydney: Cheiron, 1975.

———. *Bibliography of Greek Education and Related Topics.* Sydney: Cheiron, 1986.

Becker, Adam H., and Annette Yoshiko Reed, eds. *Ways That Never Parted: Jews and Christians in Late Antiquity and the Early Middle Ages.* Tübingen: Mohr Siebeck, 2003.

Bellamy, J. "The Mysterious Letters of the Qur'an." *Journal of the American Oriental Society* 93 (1973), 267–85.

Ben Ezra, Daniel Stökl. "An Ancient List of Christian Festivals in *Toledot Yeshu:* Polemics as Indication for Interaction." *Harvard Theological Review* 102.4 (2009), 481–96.

Benjamin, Walter. *The Arcades Project.* Trans. H. Eiland and K. McLaughlin. Cambridge, Mass.: Harvard University Press, 1999.

———. *The Origin of German Tragic Drama.* London: NLB, 1977.

Bergmann, J. "Die Rachgebete von Rheneia." *Philologus* 70 (1911), 503–7.

Bergsträsser, Gotthelf. *Ḥunain ibn Isḥāḳ und seine Schule: Sprach- und literargeschichtliche untersuchungen zu den arabischen Hippokrates- und Galen-übersetzungen.* Leiden, Brill, 1913.

———. *Neue Materialien zu Ḥunain ibn Isḥāq's Galen-Bibliographie.* Abhandlungen für die Kunde des Morgenlandes XIX.2. Leipzig: F. A. Brockhaus, 1932.

Bernstein, N. "Adoptees and Exposed Children in Roman Declamation: Commodification, Luxury, and the Threat of Violence." *Classical Philology* 104.3 (2009), 331–53.

Berry, Edmund G. "The *De Liberis Educandis* of Pseudo-Plutarch." *Harvard Studies in Classical Philology* 63 (1958), 387–99.

Berthelot, M. *Introduction à l'étude de la chimie des ancients et du moyen âge.* Paris: Georges Steinheil, 1893.

Berthelot, M., and C. E. Ruelle. *Collection des anciens alchimistes grecs.* 3 volumes. Paris: Georges Steinheil, 1887–1888.

Besques, Simone Mollard. *Catalogue raisonné des figurines et reliefs en terre cuite grecs, étrusques et romaines.* 4 volumes. Musée du Louvre, Département des antiquités grecques et romaines. Paris: Éditions des Musées nationaux, 1963.

Betz, Hans Dieter. *Galatians: A Commentary on Paul's Letter to the Churches in Galatia.* Hermeneia. Philadelphia: Fortress, 1979.

Bhabha, Homi. *Location of Culture.* London: Routledge, 1994; repr. 2004.

Bieber, Margarete. *The Sculpture of the Hellenistic Age.* Rev. ed. New York: Columbia University Press, 1961.

Bieringer, Reimund, Didier Pollefyt, and Frederique Vandecasteele-Vanneuville, eds. *Anti-Judaism and the Fourth Gospel.* Louisville: Westminster/John Knox, 2001.

Biesterfeldt, H. H. *Galens Traktat "Dass die Kräfte der Seele den Mischungen des Körpers folgen" in arabischer Übersetzung.* Wiesbaden: F. Steiner, 1973.

Bishop, Margaret M. *The ABC's and All Their Tricks: The Complete Reference Book of Phonics and Spelling.* Fenton, Mich.: Mott Media, 1986; repr. 2006.

Bitton-Ashkelony, Bruria. *Encountering the Sacred: The Debate on Christian Pilgrimage in Late Antiquity.* Berkeley: University of California Press, 2005.

Björck, G. *Der Fluch des Christen Sabinus: Papyrus Upsaliensis 8.* Uppsala: Almqvist and Wiksell, 1938.

Blick, Sarah, and Rita Tekippe. *Art and Architecture of Late Medieval Pilgrimage in Northern Europe and the British Isles.* Leiden: Brill, 2005.

Bliss, F. J. *Excavations at Jerusalem, 1894–1897.* London: Committee of the Palestine Exploration Fund, 1898.

———. "Report on the Excavations at Tell Sandahannah." *Palestine Exploration Fund: Quarterly Statement* (1900), 319–34.

Bloch, Marc. "Mémoire collective, tradition et coutume: À propos d'un livre recent." *Revue de synthése historique* 40 (1925), 73–83.

Blondiaux, G., J. Blondiaux, F. Secousse, A. Cotton, P.-M. Danze, and R.-M. Flipo. "Rickets and Child Abuse: The Case of a Two Year Old Girl from the 4th Century in Lisieux (Normandy)." *International Journal of Osteoarchaelogy* 12 (2002), 209–15.

Bloomer, W. Martin. *The School of Rome: Latin Studies and the Origins of Liberal Education.* Berkeley: University of California Press, 2011.

———. "Schooling in Persona: Imagination and Subordination in Roman Education." *Classical Antiquity* 16 (1997), 57–78.

Boer, Martinus C. de. "The Meaning of the Phrase *ta stoicheia tou kosmou* in Galatians." *New Testament Studies* 53.2 (2007), 204–24.

Böhm, Christine Bäuer, Konrad Zehnder, Heinz Domeisen, and Andreas Arnold. "Climate Control for the Passive Conservation of the Romanesque Painted Wooden Ceiling in the Church of Zillis (Switzerland)." *Studies in Conservation* 46.4 (2001), 251–68.

Bonner, C. *Studies in Magical Amulets, Chiefly Graeco-Egyptian.* Ann Arbor: University of Michigan Press, 1950.

Bonner, Stanley F. *Education in Ancient Rome: From the Elder Cato to the Younger Pliny.* Berkeley: University of California Press, 1977.

Bonwetsch, G. N. "Die apokryphen Fragen des Bartholomäus." *Nachrichten von der Königlichen Gesellschaft der Wissenschaften zu Göttingen* (Geschäftliche Mitteilungen,Gesellschaft der Wissenschaften Philologisch-Historische Klasse; Göttingen: Dieterich, 1897), 1–42.

Boomershine, Thomas E. "The Medium and Message of John: Audience Address and Audience Identity in the Fourth Gospel." In *The Fourth Gospel in First-Century Media Culture,* ed. A. Le Donne and T. Thatcher, 92–120.

Booth, Alan D. "Punishment, Discipline and Riot in the Schools of Antiquity." *Echos du monde classique* 17 (1973), 107–14.

———. "The Schooling of Slaves in First-Century Rome." *Transactions and Proceedings of the American Philological Association* 109 (1979), 11–19.

———. "Some Suspect Schoolmasters." *Florilegium* 3 (1981), 1–20.

Borg, Barbara. "Glamorous Intellectuals: Portraits of *pepaideumenoi* in the Second and Third Centuries AD." In *Paideia: The World of the Second Sophistic,* ed. B. E. Borg, volume 2, 157–76. Millennium-Studien zu Kultur und Geschichte des ersten Jahrtausends n. Chr. Berlin and New York: Walter de Gruyter, 2004.

Boswell, John. *The Kindness of Strangers: The Abandonment of Children in Western Europe from Late Antiquity to the Renaissance.* New York: Pantheon, 1988.

Bosworth, C. E. "al-Ṭabarī, Abū D̲j̲afar Muḥammad b. D̲j̲arīr b. Yazīd." *EI*[2] 10 (1998), 11–15.

Bouché-Leclercq, A. *Histoire de la divination dans l'antiquité.* 4 volumes. Paris: E. Leroux, 1879–1882.

Boud'hors, Anne. "Histoire de Joseph le charpentier." In *Écrits apocryphes chrétiens,* ed. Bovon and Geoltrain, volume 2, 25–59.

Bourdieu, Pierre. *Outline of a Theory of Practice.* Trans. R. Nice. Cambridge: Cambridge University Press, 1977.

Bourdieu, Pierre, and Loïc J. D. Wacquant. *An Invitation to Reflexive Sociology.* Chicago: University of Chicago Press, 1992.

Bovon, François. "Évangiles canoniques et évangiles apocryphes: La naissance et l'enfance de Jésus." *Bulletin des faculties catholiques de Lyon* 58 (1980), 19–30.

———. "Names and Numbers in Early Christianity." *New Testament Studies* 47 (2001), 267–88.

Böwering, Gerhard. "Sahl al-Tustarī, Abū Muḥammad b. 'Abd Allāh b. Yūnus b. 'Īsā b. 'Abd Allāh b. Rafī'." *EI*[2] 8 (1995), 840–41.

———. "Sulamī's Treatise on the Science of the Letters *('ilm al-ḥurūf)*." In *In the Shadow of Arabic: The Centrality of Language to Arabic Culture: Studies Presented to Ramzi Baalbaki on the Occasion of His Sixtieth Birthday,* ed. B. Orfali, 339–97. Leiden: Brill, 2011.

Bowie, Ewen. "The Ancient Readers of the Greek Novels." In *The Novel in the Ancient World,* ed. G. Schmeling, 87–106.

———. "The Readership of Greek Novels in the Ancient World." In *The Search for the Ancient Novel,* ed. J. Tatum, 435–59.

Bowman, Vibiana, ed. *Scholarly Resources for Children and Childhood Studies: A Research Guide and Annotated Bibliography.* Lanham, Md.: Scarecrow, 2007.

Boyarin, Daniel. *Border Lines: The Partition of Judaeo-Christianity.* Philadelphia: University of Pennsylvania Press, 2004.

———. "Qeriah metuqqenet shel ha-qeta' he-hedash shel 'Toledot Yeshu.'" *Tarbiz* 47 (1978), 249–52.

———. "Rethinking Jewish Christianity: An Argument for Dismantling a Dubious Category (to Which Is Appended a Correction of My *Border Lines*)." *Jewish Quarterly Review* 99 (2009), 7–36.

Bradley, Keith R. "The Nurse and the Child at Rome: Duty, Affect and Socialisation." *Thamyris* 1.2 (1994), 137–56.

———. "The Sentimental Education of the Roman Child: The Role of Pet-Keeping." *Latomus* 57.3 (1998), 523–57.

———. "Wet-nursing at Rome: A Study in Social Relations." In *The Family in Ancient Rome,* ed. B. Rawson, 201–29.

Bradshaw, Paul F. *The Search for the Origins of Christian Worship: Sources and Methods for the Study of Early Liturgy.* Second ed. Oxford and New York: Oxford University Press, 2002.

Brakke, David. *The Gnostics: Myth, Ritual, and Diversity in Early Christianity.* Cambridge, Mass., and London: Harvard University Press, 2010.

———. "Scriptural Practices in Early Christianity: Towards a New History of the New Testament Canon." In *Invention, Rewriting, Usurpation: Discursive Fights over Religious Traditions in Antiquity,* ed. J. Ulrich, A.-C. Jacobsen, and D. Brakke, 263–80. Early Christianity in the Context of Antiquity, volume 11. Frankfurt am Main: Berlin, 2012.

Brandenburger, A., and B. Nalebuff. *Co-opetition.* New York: Doubleday, 1996.

Brändl, Martin. *Der Agon bei Paulus: Herkunft und Profil Paulinischer Agonmetaphorik.* WUNT 2. Reihe. Band 222. Tübingen: Mohr Siebeck, 2006.

Brawley, Robert T. *Luke-Acts and the Jews: Conflict, Apology, and Conciliation.* Society of Biblical Literature Monograph Series 33. Atlanta: Scholars, 1987.

Brednich, Rolf Wilhelm. "Vogel am Faden: Geschichte und Ikonographie eines vergessenes Kinderspiels." In *Festschrift Matthias Zender: Studien zu Volkskultur, Sprache und Landesgeschichte,* ed. E. Ennen and G. Wiegelmann. Volume 1, 573–97, with 14 figures. Bonn: Ludwig Röhrscheid, 1972.

Brent, Allen. *The Imperial Cult and the Development of Church Order: Concepts and Images of Authority in Paganism and Early Christianity before the Age of Cyprian.* Supplements to Vigiliae Christianae. Boston and Leiden: Brill, 1999.

Brown, Peter. *The Body and Society: Men, Women, and Sexual Renunciation in Early Christianity.* New York: Columbia University Press, 1988.

———. *The Cult of the Saints: Its Rise and Function in Latin Christianity.* Chicago: University of Chicago Press, 1981.

Brown, Raymond E. *The Gospel according to John.* 2 volumes. Anchor Bible 29–29A. Garden City, N.Y.: Doubleday, 1966–1970.

Bruce, F. F. *Paul: Apostle of the Heart Set Free.* Grand Rapids, Mich.: Eerdmans, 1977.

Brunet, Stephen. "Olympic Hopefuls from Ephesos." *Journal of Sport History* 30 (2003), 219–35.

Bryan, C. *A Preface to Mark: Notes on the Gospel in Its Literary and Cultural Settings.* Oxford: Oxford University Press, 1997.

Bultmann, Rudolf. *Die Geschichte der synoptischen Tradition.* Göttingen: Vandenhoeck und Ruprecht, 1961. English trans.: *History of the Synoptic Tradition.* Trans. J. Marsh. New York: Harper and Row, 1963.

Bunge, Marcia J., ed. *The Child in the Bible.* Grand Rapids, Mich., and Cambridge: Eerdmans, 2008.

Burke, Tony (Chartrand-Burke). "Completing the Gospel: The Infancy Gospel of Thomas as a Supplement to the Gospel of Luke." In *The Reception and Interpretation of the Bible in Late Antiquity: Proceedings of the Montréal Colloquium in Honour of Charles Kannegiesser, 11–13 October 2006*, ed. L. DiTommaso and L. Turcescu, 101–19. Leiden: Brill, 2008.

———. *De infantia Iesu evangelium Thomae graece.* CCSA 17. Turnhout: Brepols, 2010.

———. "Depictions of Children in the Apocryphal Infancy Gospels." *Studies in Religion / Sciences Religieuses* 41.3 (2012), 388–400.

———. "The *Infancy Gospel of Thomas.*" In *The Non-Canonical Gospels,* ed. P. Foster, 126–38. London and New York: T. and T. Clark, 2008.

———. "The Infancy Gospel of Thomas: The Text, Its Origins, and Its Transmission." Ph.D. dissertation, University of Toronto, 2001.

———. "The *Infancy Gospel of Thomas* from an Unpublished Syriac Manuscript: Introduction, Text, Translation, and Notes." In *Hugoye: Journal of Syriac Studies* 16.2 (2013), 225–99.

———. " 'Social Viewing' of Children in the Childhood Stories of Jesus." In *Children in Late Ancient Christianity,* ed. C. B. Horn and R. R. Phenix, 29–43.

Burkert, Walter. "Caesar und Romulus-Quirinus." *Historia* 11 (1962), 356–76.

———. "ΣΤΟΙΧΕΙΟΝ: Eine Samasiologische Studien." *Philologus* 13 (1959), 167–97.

Burkholder, G. *An Arabian Collection: Artifacts from the Eastern Province.* Las Vegas: GB Publications, 1984.

Burnyeat, M. F. "Letter to the Editor." *Times Literary Supplement* (April 19, 1997), 15.

———. "Postscript on Silent Reading." *Classical Quarterly* 47 (1997), 74–76.

Burridge, R. A. *What Are the Gospels? A Comparison with Graeco-Roman Biography.* Cambridge: Cambridge University Press, 1992. Second ed.: Grand Rapids, Mich.: Eerdmans, 2004.

Burrus, Virginia. *Chastity as Autonomy: Women in the Stories of the Apocryphal Acts.* Studies in Women and Religion 23. Lewiston, Pa.: Edwin Mellon, 1987.

———. "Mimicking Virgins: Colonial Ambivalence and the Ancient Romance." *Arethusa* 38 (2005), 49–88.

Cachia, P. J. E. "Bayḍāwī on the *Fawātiḥ.*" *Journal of Semitic Studies* 13 (1968), 218–31.

Calzolari, Valentina. "Les récits apocryphes de l'enfance dans la tradition arménienne." In *Infancy Gospels: Stories and Identities*, ed. C. Clivaz et al., 560–87.

Cameron, Ron. *The Other Gospels: Non-Canonical Gospel Texts.* Philadelphia: Westminster, 1982.

Campbell, Keith. "Self-Mastery and Stoic Ethics." *Philosophy* 60 (no. 233) (1985), 327–40.

Cancik, Hubert, and Helmuth Schneider, eds. *Der neue Pauly: Enzyklopädie der Antike.* 16 volumes. Stuttgart: J. B. Metzler, 1996–2003.

Canal-Sánchez, José Maria. "Antiguas versions Latinas del Protoevangelio de Santiago." *Ephemerides Mariologicae* 18 (1968), 431–73.

Caner, Daniel, with contributions by Sebastian Brock, Richard M. Price, and Kevin van Bladel. *History and Hagiography from the Late Antique Sinai.* Liverpool: Liverpool University Press, 2010.

Carp, Teresa C. "Puer senex in Roman and Medieval Thought." *Latomus* 39 (1980), 736–9.

Carruthers, Mary. *The Book of Memory: A Study of Memory in Medieval Culture.* Second ed. Cambridge: Cambridge University Press, 2008.

Cartlidge, David R., and J. K. Elliott. *Art and the Christian Apocrypha.* London: Routledge, 2001.

Casey, Mary F. "The Fourteenth-Century Tring Tiles: A Fresh Look at Their Origin and the Hebraic Aspects of the Child Jesus' Actions." *Peregrinations: International Society for the Study of Pilgrimage Art* 2.2 (2007), 1–53, available online at http://peregrinations.kenyon.edu/vol2_2.pdf (accessed July 10, 2013).

Castagnoli, F. "Il capitello della Pigna Vaticana." *Bullettino della Commissione Archeologica Comunale di Roma* 71 (1943–1945), 1–30.

Castelli, Elizabeth A. *Martyrdom and Memory: Early Christian Culture Making.* New York: Columbia University Press, 2004.

Casulleras, Josep. "Banū Mūsā." In *The Biographical Dictionary of Astronomers,* ed. T. Hockey et al., 92–94. New York: Springer, 2007.

Cavallo, G., and F. Hild. "Buch." In *Der neue Pauly: Enzyklopädie der Antike,* ed. H. Cancik and H. Schneider, volume 2, 809–16.

Ceccanti, Melania. "Aspetti iconografici dell'infanzia di Gesù nella miniature Toscana dal XII al XV secolo." *Medioevo e Rinascimento* 19 (n.s. 16) (2005), 229–55.

Cecchelli, Carlo. *Mater Christi: La Vita di Maria nella storia nella legenda nella commemorazione Liturgica.* Volume 3. Rome: Farrari, 1954.

Ceming, Katharina, and Jürgen Werlitz. *Die verbotenen Evangelien: Apokryphe Schriften.* Rev. ed. Augsburg: Pattloch, 1999.

Chabot, J. B. "Version syriaque de traits médicaux dont l'original arabe n'a pas été retrouvé." *Notices et extraits des manuscrits de la Bibliothèque nationale et autres bibliothèques* 43 (1954), 80–143.

Champollion, J. F. *Monuments de l'Égypte et de la Nubie.* Volume 2. Ed. G. Maspero. Paris: Fermin Didot, 1889.

Charlesworth, James H. *The Pseudepigrapha and Modern Research, with a Supplement.* Chico, Calif.: Scholars, 1981.

Chartrand-Burke, Tony. See Burke, Tony.

Clairmont, C. *Classical Attic Tombstones.* 6 volumes. Kilchberg, Switzerland: Akanthus, 1993–1995.

Clark, Elizabeth. "The Lady Vanishes: Dilemmas of a Feminist Historian after the 'Linguistic Turn.'" *Church History* 67.1 (1998), 1–31.

Clark, Gillian. "The Fathers and the Children." In *The Church and Childhood,* ed. D. Wood. Studies in Church History 31, 1–27. Cambridge: Blackwell, 1994.

Clark, W. P. "Ancient Reading." *Classical Journal* 26 (1931), 698–700.

Clermont-Ganneau, C. S. "Royal Ptolemaic Inscriptions and Magic Figures from Tell Sandahannah." *Palestine Exploration Fund: Quarterly Statement* (1901), 54–58.

Clivaz, Claire, Andreas Dettwiler, Luc Devillers, and Enrico Norelli, with Benjamin Bertho, eds. *Infancy Gospels: Stories and Identities*. WUNT 281. Tübingen: Mohr Siebeck, 2011.

Cohen, Ada. "Introduction: Childhood between Past and Present." In *Constructions of Childhood,* ed. A. Cohen and J. B. Rutter, 2–22.

Cohen, Ada, and Jeremy B. Rutter, eds. *Constructions of Childhood in Ancient Greece and Italy.* Princeton: American School of Classical Studies at Athens, 2007.

Cohen, David J. *Law, Violence, and Community in Classical Athens.* Cambridge and New York: Cambridge University Press, 1995.

Cohen, Shaya J. D. *The Beginnings of Jewishness: Boundaries, Varieties, Uncertainties.* Berkeley: University of California Press, 1999.

Colin, G. S. "Ḥisāb al-d̲j̲ummal." *EI*[2] 3 (1971), 468.

Collins, Adela Yarbro. *Mark.* Hermeneia 55. Philadelphia: Fortress, 2007.

Comparetti, D. "Varietà epigraphiche siceliote." *Archivio Storico per la Sicilia Orientale* 16–17 (1919–1920), 197–200.

Confino, Alon. "Collective Memory and Cultural History: Problems of Method." *American Historical Review* 102.5 (1997), 1386–1403.

———. "Memory and the History of Mentalities." In *Companion to Cultural Memory Studies,* ed. A. Erll and A. Nünning, 77–84.

Connerton, Paul. *How Societies Remember.* Cambridge: Cambridge University Press, 1989.

Conze, Alexander. *Attischen Grabreliefs.* 4 volumes. Berlin: W. Spemann, 1893–1922.

Conzelmann, Hans. *The Theology of St. Luke.* New York: Harper, 1960.

Cook, John Granger. *The Interpretation of the New Testament in Greco-Roman Paganism.* Tübingen: Mohr Siebeck, 2000.

Cook, Michael, and Patricia Crone. *Hagarism: The Making of the Islamic World.* Cambridge and New York: Cambridge University Press, 1977.

Cooper, Kate. *The Virgin and the Bride: Idealized Womanhood in Late Antiquity.* Cambridge, Mass.: Harvard University Press, 1996.

Corbier, Mireille. "Child Exposure and Abandonment." In *Childhood, Class and Kin in the Roman World,* ed. S. Dixon, 52–73.

Corsaro, William A. *The Sociology of Childhood.* Second ed. Thousand Oaks, Calif.: Pine Forge, 2004.

Cotelier, Jean Baptiste. *SS. Patrum qui temporibus apostolicis floruerunt.* Second ed. Volume 1. Antwerp: Leclerc, 1698.

Cowper, Benjamin Harris. *The Apocryphal Gospels and Other Documents Relating to the History of Christ.* London; Williams and Norgate, 1867.

Cox, Patricia L. *Biography in Late Antiquity: A Quest for the Holy Man.* Transformation of the Classical Heritage 5. Berkeley and Los Angeles: University of California Press, 1983.

Crawford, Sally, and Gillian Shepherd, eds. *Children, Childhood and Society.* Oxford: Archaeopress, 2007.

Cribiore, Raffaella. "Fun with the Alphabet." *Journal of the History of Childhood and Youth* 1.2 (2008), 165–68, with figure.

———. *Gymnastics of the Mind: Greek Education in Hellenistic and Roman Egypt.* Princeton: Princeton University Press, 2001.

———. "A Schooltablet from the Hearst Museum." *ZPE* 107 (1995), 263–70.

———. *Writing, Teachers, and Students in Graeco-Roman Egypt.* American Studies in Papyrology 36. Atlanta: Scholars, 1996.

Crowther, Nigel B. "The Age-Category of Boys at Olympia." *Phoenix* 42.4 (1988), 304–8.

———. "Observations on Boys, Girls, Youths and Age Categories in Roman Sports and Spectacles." *International Journal of the History of Sport* 26 (2009), 343–64.

———. *Sport in Ancient Times.* Praeger Series on the Ancient World. Westport, Conn., and London: Praeger, 2007.

Cullmann, Oscar. "Infancy Gospels." In *New Testament Apocrypha,* volume 1, ed. E. Hennecke and W. Schneemelcher, trans. R. M. Wilson, 363–417. London: Lutterworth, 1963. Rev. ed., 439–43. Louisville: Westminster/John Knox, 1991.

———. "Kindheitsevangelien." In *Neutestamentliche Apokryphen,* volume 1: *Evangelien und Verwandtes,* sixth ed., ed. W. Schneemelcher, 330–72. Tübingen: Mohr, 1990.

Cultural History of Childhood and Family. 6 volumes. Oxford and New York: Berg, 2010.

Cüppers, Heinz, ed., with contributions by H. Bernhard et al. *Die Römer in Rheinland-Pfalz.* Stuttgart: Theiss, 1990; repr. Hamburg: Nikol, 2005.

Curchin, Leonard A. "Literacy in the Roman Provinces: Qualitative and Quantitative Data from Central Spain." *American Journal of Philology* 116.3 (1995), 461–76.

Czachesz, István. "Rewriting and Textual Fluidity in Antiquity: Exploring the Socio-Cultural and Psychological Context of Earliest Christian Literacy." In *Myths, Martyrs, and Modernity: Studies in the History of Religions in Honour of Jan N. Bremmer,* ed. J. Dijkstra, J. Kroesen, and Y. Kuiper, 426–41. Leiden: Brill, 2010.

Daems, Aurelie. "The Terracotta Figurines from ed-Dur (Umm al-Qaiwain, U.A.E.): The Animal Representations." *Arabian Archaeology and Epigraphy* 15.2 (2004), 229–39.

Dan, Joseph. "Toledot Yeshu." In *Encyclopaedia Judaica,* second ed., ed. M. Berenbaum and F. Skolnik, 28–29. Detroit: Gale Virtual Reference Library, 2006.

Daniel, R. W. "Liberal Education and Semiliteracy in Petronius." *ZPE* 40 (1980), 153–59.

Darrbagh, J. al-. "Banū Mūsā." In *Complete Dictionary of Scientific Biography*, available online at http://www.encyclopedia.com/topic/Banu_Musa.aspx (accessed July 10, 2013).

Dasen, Véronique. "'All children are dwarfs': Medical Discourse and Iconography of Children's Bodies." *Oxford Journal of Archaeology* 27.1 (2008), 49–62.

———. "Blessing or Portent? Multiple Births in Ancient Rome." In *Hoping for Continuity,* ed. K. Mustakallio et al., 61–73.

———. "Childbirth and Infancy in Greek and Roman Antiquity." In *A Companion to Families in Ancient Greece and Rome,* ed. B. Rawson, 291–314.

———. "Roman Birth Rites of Passage Revisited." *Journal of Roman Archaeology* 22 (2009), 199–214.

Dasen, Véronique, and S. Ducate-Paarmann. "La naissance et la petite enfance dans l'Antiquité: Bibliographie selective." In *Naissance et petite enfance dans l'Antiquité: Actes du colloque de Fribourg, 28 novembre–1er décembre 2001,* ed. V. Dasen, 377–405. Fribourg: Academic; Göttingen: Vandenhoeck und Ruprecht, 2004.

Dasen, Véronique, and Thomas Späth, eds. *Children, Memory, and Family Identity in Roman Culture.* Oxford: Oxford University Press, 2010.

Davis, Stephen J. "Ancient Sources for the Coptic Tradition." In W. Lyster, C. Hulsman, and S. J. Davis, *Be Thou There,* ed. G. Gabra, 133–62.

———. "Biblical Interpretation and Alexandrian Episcopal Authority in the Early Christian Fayoum." In *Christianity and Monasticism in the Fayoum Oasis,* ed. Gawdat Gabra, 45–61. Cairo and New York: American University of Cairo Press, 2005.

———. "Bird Watching in the *Infancy Gospel of Thomas:* From Child's Play to Rituals of Divine Discernment." In *Portraits of Jesus: Essays in Christology,* ed. S. E. Myers, 125–53. Tübingen: Mohr Siebeck, 2012.

———. *Coptic Christology in Practice: Incarnation and Divine Participation in Late Antique and Medieval Egypt.* Oxford: Oxford University Press, 2008.

———. *The Cult of Saint Thecla: A Tradition of Women's Piety in Late Antiquity.* Oxford: Oxford University Press, 2001.

———. *The Early Coptic Papacy: The Egyptian Church and Its Leadership in Late Antiquity.* Cairo and New York: American University in Cairo Press, 2004.

———. "Forget Me Not: Memory and the Female Subject in Ancient Binding Spells." In *Women and Gender in Ancient Religions: Interdisciplinary Approaches,* ed. S. P. Ahearne-Kroll, P. A. Holloway, and J. A. Kelhoffer, 248–59. Tübingen: Mohr Siebeck, 2010.

———. "A Hermeneutic of the Land: Biblical Interpretation in the Holy Family Tradition." In *Coptic Studies on the Threshold of a New Millennium: Proceedings of the Seventh International Congress of Coptic Studies,* ed. M. Immerzeel and J. van der Vliet, 329–36. Louvain: Peeters, 2004.

Debary, Octave, and Laurier Turgeon. "Introduction: Entre objets et mémoires." In *Objets et memoires,* ed. O. Debary and L. Turgeon, 1–12. Paris: Éditions de la Maison des sciences de l'hommes; Québec: Les Presses de l'Université Laval, 2007.

Degen, Rainer. "The Oldest Known Manuscript of Hunayn b. Ishaq." In *Symposium Syriacum 1976, célébré du 13 au 17 Septembre 1976 au Centre Culturel "Les Fontaines" de Chantilly: Communications.* Orientalia Christiana Analecta 205, 63–71. Rome: Pontifical Oriental Institute, 1978.

Deissmann, Adolf. *Licht vom Osten: Das Neue Testament und die neuentdeckten Texte der hellenistisch-römischen Welt.* Second and third eds. Tübingen: Mohr, 1909. English trans.: *Light from the Ancient East: The New Testament Illustrated by Recently Discovered Texts of the Graeco-Roman World.* London and New York: Hodder and Stoughton, 1911.

Delatte, A. "Évangile de l'enfance de Jacques: Manuscrit No. 355 de la Bibliothèque Nationale." In *Anecdota Atheniensia, vol. 1, Textes grecs inédits relatifs à l'histoire des religions,* 264–71. Paris: Edouard Champion, 1927.

Della Croce, Angelo, with A. M. Ceriani. *Canonical Histories and Apocryphal Legends Relating to the New Testament.* Milan: J. B. Pogliani, 1873.

Delorme, Jean. *Gymnasion: Étude sur les monuments consacrées à l'éducation en Grèce, des origines à l'Empire romain.* Paris: Boccard, 1960.

Dewey, J. "The Gospel of John in Its Oral-Written Media World." In *Jesus and the Johannine Tradition,* ed. R. T. Fortna and T. Thatcher, 239–52. Louisville: Westminster/John Knox, 2001.

Di Capua, F. "Osservazioni sulla lettura e sulla preghiera ad alta voce press gli antichi." *Rendiconti dell' Accademia di Archeologia, Lettere e Belle Arti di Napoli,* n.s. 28 (1953), 59–99.

Di Segni, Riccardo. "La tradizione testuale delle Toledòth Jéshu: Manoscritti, edizioni a stampa, classificazione." *Rassegna Mensile di Israel* 50 (1984), 83–100.

———. *Il Vangelo del ghetto.* Rome: Newton Compton, 1985.

Dibelius, Martin. *Die Formgeschichte des Evangeliums.* Tübingen: Mohr Siebeck, 1919; second ed., 1933. Trans. B. L. Woolf under the title *From Tradition to Gospel.* New York: Charles Scribner's Sons, 1965.

Dickie, Matthew W. *Magic and Magicians in the Greco-Roman World.* New York and London: Routledge, 2001.

Diefenbach, Manfred. *Konflikt Jesu mit den "Juden": Ein Versuch zur Lösung der johanneischen Antijudaismus-Diskussion mit Hilfe des antiken Handlungsverständnisses.* Münster: Aschendorff, 2002.

Diels, Hermann. *Elementum: Eine Vorarbeit zum griechischen und lateinischen Thesaurus.* Leipzig: B. G. Teubner, 1899.

Diers, Michael. "Mnemosyne oder das Gedächtnis der Bilder: Über Aby Warburg." In *Memoria als Kultur,* ed. O. G. Oexle, 79–94. Göttingen: Vandenhoeck und Ruprecht, 1995.

Dieterich, Albrecht. "ABC-Denkmäler." In *Kleine Schriften,* 202–28. Leipzig and Berlin: B. G. Teubner, 1911.

———. *Abraxas: Studien zur Religionsgeschichte des spätern Altertums.* Leipzig: B. G. Teubner, 1891.

———. *Kleine Schriften.* Leipzig and Berlin: B. G. Teubner, 1911.

———. *Mithrasliturgie.* Leipzig: B. G. Teubner, 1903.

Dietz, Maribel. *Wandering Monks, Virgins, and Pilgrims: Ascetic Travel in the Mediterranean World, A.D. 300–800.* University Park: Pennsylvania State University Press, 2005.

Dimas, Stephanie. *Untersuchungen zur Themenwahl und Bildgestaltung auf römischen Kindersarkophagen.* Münster: Scriptorium, 1998.

Dinahet, Marie-Thérèse le. "L'image de l'enfance à l'époque hellenistique: La valeur de l'exemple delien." In *Les Pierres de l'Offrand: Autour de l'oeuvre de Christoph W. Clairmont,* ed. G. Hoffmann with A. Lezzi-Hafter, 90–106. Zürich: Akanthus, 2001.

Dionisotti, A. C. "From Ausonius' Schooldays? A Schoolbook and Its Relatives." *Journal of Roman Studies* 72 (1982), 83–125.

Dixon, Suzanne, ed. *Childhood, Class, and Kin in the Roman World.* London and New York: Routledge, 2001.

Dodds, E. R. *The Ancient Concept of Progress and Other Essays on Greek Literature and Belief.* Oxford: Clarendon, 1973.

Doerfler, Maria E. "The Infant, the Monk and the Martyr: The Death of Children in Eastern Patristic Thought." *Le Muséon* 124.3–4 (2011), 243–58.

Dolansky, F. "Togam virilem sumere: Coming of Age in the Roman World." In *Roman Dress and the Fabrics of Roman Culture,* ed. J. Edmondson and A. Keith, 47–70. Toronto: University of Toronto Press, 2008.

Donehoo, James DeQuincey. *The Apocryphal and Legendary Life of Christ, being the . . . Apocryphal Gospels and other extra canonical literature which pretends to tell of the life and words of Jesus Christ.* New York and London: Macmillian, 1903.

Donner, Fred. *Muhammad and the Believers: At the Origins of Islam.* Cambridge, Mass.: Harvard University Press, 2010.

Dornseiff, Franz. *Das Alphabet in Mystik und Magie.* Second ed. Leipzig and Berlin: B. G. Teubner, 1925.

Doty, W. G. "The Concept of Genre in Literary Analysis." In *The Society of Biblical Literature: Proceedings 1972: Book of Seminar Papers for 108th Annual Meeting,* volume 2, ed. L. C. McGaughy, 413–48. Atlanta: Scholars, 1972.

Dover, K. J. *Greek Homosexuality.* Cambridge, Mass.: Harvard University Press, 1978; repr. 1989.

Dowden, Ken. "The Roman Audience of *The Golden Ass.*" In *The Search for the Ancient Novel,* ed. J. Tatum, 419–34.

Downey, Susan B. *Terracotta Figurines and Plaques from Dura-Europos.* Ann Arbor: University of Michigan Press, 2003.

Dragona-Monachou, Myrto. *The Stoic Arguments for the Existence and the Providence of the Gods.* Athens: National and Capodistrian University of Athens, Faculty of Arts, 1976.

Drake, Susanna L. "Sexing the Jew: Early Christian Constructions of Jewishness." Ph.D. dissertation, Duke University, 2008.

Duensing, Hugo. "Mitteilungen 58." *Theologische Literaturzeitung* 36 (1911), 637.

Dunderberg, Ismo. *Beyond Gnosticism: Myth, Lifestyle, and Society in the School of Valentinus.* New York: Columbia University Press, 2008.

Dunn, Geoffrey D. *Tertullian.* London: Routledge, 2004.

Dyck, Andrew R. Review of Michael Alexander, *The Case for the Prosecution in the Ciceronian Era.* In *Bryn Mawr Classical Review* 2003.09.37.

Dzon, Mary. "Boys Will Be Boys: The Physiology of Childhood and the Apocryphal Christ Child in the Later Middle Ages." *Viator* 42.1 (2011), 179–225.

———. "Jesus and the Birds in Medieval Abrahamic Traditions." *Traditio* 66 (2011), 189–230.

Dzon, Mary, and Theresa M. Kennedy. *The Christ Child in Medieval Culture: Alpha es et O!* Toronto: University of Toronto Press, 2012.

Eastwood, Bruce Stansfield. *The Elements of Vision: The Micro-Cosmology of Galenic Visual Theory According to Ḥunayn Ibn Isḥāq.* Transactions of the American Philosophical Society, volume 72, part 5. Philadelphia: American Philosophical Society, 1982.

Ebied, R. Y., and M. J. L. Young. "A Manuscript of Ḥunayn's *Masā'il fī 'ilm al-ṭibb* in the Leeds University Collection." In *Ḥunayn ibn Isḥāq: Collection d'articles publiée à l'occasion du onzième centenaire de sa mort,* Arabica XXI.3, 264–69. Leiden: Brill, 1975.

Edwards, M. L. "The Cultural Context of Deformity in the Ancient Greek World: 'Let There Be a Law That No Deformed Child Shall Be Reared.' " *Ancient History Bulletin* 10.3–4 (1996), 79–92.

Eggenberger, Christoph. "Zum Bildprogramm." In Rudloff, *Zillis,* 162–66.

Egger, R. "Die Fluchtafeln von Rome (Deux Sèvres): Ihre Entzifferung und ihre Sprache." *Abhandlungen der österreichischen Akademie der Wissenschaften, Phil.-hist. Klasse* 240 (1962), 348–69.

Ehrman, Bart. *The Orthodox Corruption of Scripture: The Effect of Early Christological Controversies on the Text of the New Testament.* New York: Oxford University Press, 1993.

Eidinow, Esther. *Oracles, Curses, and Risk among the Ancient Greeks.* Oxford: Oxford University Press, 2007.

Eisenstein, J. D. *Otsar viḳuhim.* New York: N.p., 1928.

Eisler, R. *IĒSOUS BASILEUS OU BASILEUSAS: Die messianische Unabhängigkeitsbewegung vom Auftreten Johannes des Täufers bis zum Untergang Jakobs des Gerechten nach der neuerschlossenen Eroberung von Jerusalem des Flavius Josephus und den christlichen Quellen.* 2 volumes. Heidelberg: C. Winter, 1929–1930. English trans.: *The Messiah Jesus and John the Baptist according to Flavius Josephus' Recently Discovered Capture of Jerusalem and the Other Jewish and Christian Sources.* Trans. A. H. Krappe. New York: L. MacVeagh, Dial, 1931.

Elderkin, G. W. "Two Curse Inscriptions." *Hesperia* 6 (1937), 382–95.

Elia, O. *Pitture murali e mosaic nel Museo Nazionale di Napoli.* Rome: La Libreria dello stato, 1932.

Ellicott, Charles John. "Apocryphal Gospels." In *Cambridge Essays,* volume 1, 153–208. London: John W. Parker and Son, 1856.

Elliot, J. K. *The Apocryphal Jesus: Legends of the Early Church.* Oxford: Oxford University Press, 1996.

———. *The Apocryphal New Testament: A Collection of Apocryphal Christian Literature in an English Translation.* Oxford: Clarendon, 1993.

Elsner, Jaś. *Art and the Roman Viewer: The Transformation of Art from the Pagan World to Christianity.* Cambridge: Cambridge University Press, 1995.

Endress, G. "Die wissenschaftliche Literatur." In *Grundriß der arabischen Philologie,* ed. W. Fischer and H. Gätje, volume 2, 400–506, and volume 3, 3–152. Wiesbaden: Reichert, 1982–1992.

Engberg-Pedersen, Troels. *Cosmology and Self in the Apostle Paul: The Material Spirit.* Oxford: Oxford University Press, 2010.

———. "Plutarch to Prince Philopappus on How to Tell a Flatterer from a Friend, In *Friendship, Flattery, and Frankness of Speech,* ed. J. T. Fitzgerald, 61–81.

Epiphanius, *Panarion.* Ed. K. Holl, *Ancoratus und Panarion.* 3 volumes. GCS 25, 31, 37. Leipzig: Akademie, 1915–1933.

Erll, Astrid. "Cultural Memory Studies: An Introduction." In *A Companion to Cultural Memory Studies,* ed. Erll and Nünning, 1–15.

———. *Kollektives Gedächtnis und Erinnerungskulturen: Eine Einführung.* Stuttgart: J. B. Metzler, 2005.

Erll, Astrid, and Ansgar Nünning, eds. *Medien des kollektiven Gedächtnisses: Konstruktivität—Historizität—Kulturspezifität.* Berlin: De Gruyter, 2004.
Erll, Astrid, and Ansgar Nünning, with Sara B. Young, eds. *Cultural Memory Studies: An International and Interdisciplinary Handbook.* Berlin and New York: Walter de Gruyter, 2008.
Erman, Adolf, and Fritz Krebs. *Aus dem Papyrus der königlichen Museen.* Berlin: W. Spemann, 1899.
Ernst, Carl W., and Bruce B. Lawrence. *Sufi Martyrs of Love: The Chishti Order in South Asia and Beyond.* New York: Palgrave Macmillan, 2002.
Evans, Craig. *Noncanonical Writings and New Testament Interpretation.* Peabody, Mass.: Hendrickson, 1992.
Evans, John K. *War, Women and Children in Ancient Rome.* London and New York: Routledge, 1991.
Ewald, B. C. *Der Philosoph als Leitbild: Ikonographische Untersuchungen an römischen Sarkophagreliefs.* Mitteilungen des Deutschen Archäologischen Instituts, Römische Abteilung, Ergänzungsheft 34. Mainz: P. von Zabern, 1999.
Eyben, Emiel. "The Early Christian View of Youth." In *Satura Lanx: Festschrift für Werner A. Krenkel,* ed. C. Klodt, 239–55. Hildesheim and New York: G. Olms, 1996.
———. *Restless Youth in Ancient Rome.* London and New York: Routledge, 1993.
———. "Young Priests in Early Christianity." *Jahrbuch für Antike und Christentum* 22 (Münster: Aschendorff, 1995), 102–20. Volume title: *Panchaia: Festschrift für Klaus Thraede,* ed. M. Wacht.
Fabricius, Johann Albert. *Codex apocryphus Novi Testamenti.* Volume 1. Hamburg: B. Schiller, 1703. Second ed., 1719.
Fahd, Toufic. *La divination arabe: Études religieuses, sociologiques et folkloriques sur le milieu natif de l'Islam.* Leiden: Brill, 1966.
———. "Ḥurūf." *EI*[2] 3 (1971), 595–96.
———. "Khaṭṭ." *EI*[2] 4 (1978), 1128–30.
———. "Khawāṣṣ al-Ḳur'ān." *EI*[2] 3 (1971), 1133–34.
———. "Nudjūm." *EI*[2] 8 (1995), 105–8.
Fahd, Toufic, and A. Regourd. "Zā'irdja." *EI*[2] 11 (2002), 404–5.
Falcon, Andrea. *Aristotle and the Science of Nature: Unity without Uniformity.* Cambridge: Cambridge University Press, 2005.
Falk, Ze'ev. "Qeta' hadash mi-'Toledot Yeshu.'" *Tarbiz* 46 (1978), 3109.
Faraone, Christopher A. "The Agonistic Context of Early Greek Binding Spells." In *Magika Hiera,* ed. C. A. Faraone and D. Obbink, 3–32.
———. *Ancient Greek Love Magic.* Cambridge, Mass., and London: Harvard University Press, 1999.
———. "Binding and Burying the Forces of Evil: The Defensive Use of 'Voodoo Dolls' in Ancient Greece." *Classical Antiquity* 10.2 (1991), 165–220.
Faraone, Christopher A., and D. Obbink, eds. *Magika Hiera.* New York and Oxford: Oxford University Press, 1991.
Fentress, James, and Chris Wickham. *Social Memory.* Oxford: Blackwell, 1992.

Fiebig, P. Review of Krauss, *Das Leben Jesu*. In *Theologische Literaturzeitung* 29 (1904), 506–8.

Fildes, V. A. *Breasts, Bottles and Babies: A History of Infant Feedings*. Edinburgh: Edinburgh University Press, 1986.

———. *Wet Nursing: A History from Antiquity to the Present*. Oxford and New York: Basil Blackwell, 1988.

Filtzinger, Philipp, Dieter Planck, and Bernhard Cämmerer, eds. *Die Römer in Baden-Württemberg*. Stuttgart and Aalen: Konrad Theiss, 1976.

Finley, Gregory C. "The Ebionites and 'Jewish Christianity': Examining Heresy and the Attitudes of Church Fathers." Ph.D. dissertation, Catholic University of America, 2009.

Fischer, W., and H. Gätje, eds. *Grundriß der arabischen Philologie*. 3 volumes. Wiesbaden: Reichert, 1982–1992.

Fish, Stanley. *How to Write a Sentence: And How to Read One*. New York: HarperCollins, 2011.

———. *Is There a Text in This Class? The Authority of Interpretive Communities*. Cambridge, Mass.: Harvard University Press, 1982.

Fishwick, Duncan. *The Imperial Cult in the Latin West: Studies in the Ruler Cult of the Western Provinces of the Roman Empire*. 2 volumes. Leiden: Brill, 1987.

Fittà, Marco. *Giochi e giocattoli nell'antichità*. Milan: Leonardo Arte, 1997.

Fitzgerald, John T., ed. *Friendship, Flattery, and Frankness of Speech: Studies on Friendship in the New Testament World*. Leiden and New York: Brill, 1996.

Fleisch, H. "Ḥurūf al-hiḏjā'." *EI*[2] 3 (1971), 596–600.

Fluck, Cäcilia. "Puppen—Tiere—Bälle: Kinderspielzeug aus dem spätantiken bis frühislamzeitlichen Ägypten." In *Spiel am Nil: Unterhaltung im Alten Ägypten*, ed. H. Froschauer and H. Harrauer, 1–21. Vienna: Phoibos, 2004.

Förster, Niclas. *Marcus Magus*. WUNT 114. Tübingen: Mohr Siebeck, 1999.

Foster, Paul. "Educating Jesus: The Search for a Plausible Context." *Journal for the Study of the Historical Jesus* 4.1 (2006), 7–33.

Foster, Richard J. "The Apocrypha of the Old and New Testaments." In *A New Catholic Commentary on Holy Scripture*, ed. R. C. Fuller, L. Johnston, and C. Kearns, 109–14. London: Nelson, 1969.

Foucault, Michel. "What Is an Author?" In *Aesthetics, Method, and Epistemology*, volume 2, ed. James D. Faubion, trans. J. V. Harari, and modified by R. Hurley, 205–22. New York: New Press, 1998.

Fowler, Robert M. *Let the Reader Understand: Reader-Response Criticism and the Gospel of Mark*. Minneapolis: Fortress, 1991.

Francis, James A. "Visual and Verbal Representation: Image, Text, Person, and Power." In *A Companion to Late Antiquity*, ed. Philip Rousseau, 285–305. London: Wiley-Blackwell, 2009.

Frank, Georgia. *The Memory of the Eyes: Pilgrims to Living Saints in Christian Late Antiquity*. Berkeley: University of California Press, 2000.

Frankfurter, David. "The Magic of Writing and the Writing of Magic: The Power of the Word in Egyptian and Greek Traditions." *Helios* 21 (1994), 189–221.

Frankfurter, David, ed. *Pilgrimage and Holy Space in Late Antique Egypt*. Leiden: Brill, 1998.

Fredriksen, Paula. *Augustine and the Jews: A Christian Defense of Jews and Judaism.* New York: Doubleday, 2008; New Haven: Yale University Press, 2010.

———. "Historical Integrity, Interpretive Freedom: The Philosopher's Paul and the Problem of Anachronism." In *St. Paul among the Philosophers,* ed. J. D. Caputo and L. M. Alcoff, 61–73. Bloomington: Indiana University Press, 2009.

French, V. "Birth Control, Childbirth, and Early Childhood." In *Civilization of the Ancient Mediterranean: Greece and Rome,* volume 1, ed. M. Grant and R. Kitzinger, 1355–62. New York: Charles Scribner's Sons, 1988.

Freud, Sigmund. "Über Deckerinnerungen." *Monatsschrift für Psychiatrie und Neurologie* 6.3 (1899), 215–30. English trans.: "Screen Memories," trans. J. Strachey. In *The Standard Edition of the Complete Psychological Works of Sigmund Freud, Volume III 3 (1893–1899): Early Psycho-Analytic Publications,* 299–322. London: Hogarth Press and the Institute of Psycho-Analysis, 1962.

Frey, Jörg, and Jens Schröter, with Jakob Spaeth, eds. *Jesus in apokryphen Evangelienüberlieferungen: Beiträge zu ausserkanonischen Jesusüberlieferungen aus verschiedenen Sprach- und Kulturtraditionen.* Tübingen: Mohr Siebeck, 2010.

Friedländer, L. *Sittengeschichte Roms.* Vienna: Phaidonausgabe, 1934.

Frilingos, Chris. "'It Moves Me to Wonder': Narrating Violence and Religion under the Roman Empire." *Journal of the American Academy of Religion* 77.4 (2009), 825–52.

———. "No Child Left Behind: Knowledge and Violence in the *Infancy Gospel of Thomas.*" *Journal of Early Christian Studies* 17.1 (2009), 27–54.

Froschauer, Harald, and Hermann Harrauer, eds. *Spiel am Nil: Unterhaltung im Alten Ägypten.* Vienna: Phoibos, 2004.

Futrell, Alison. *The Roman Games: A Sourcebook.* Oxford and Malden, Mass.: Blackwell, 2006.

Gabra, Gawdat. *Le Caire: Le musée copte et les anciennes églises.* Cairo: Egyptian International, 1996.

Gabra, Gawdat, and Marianne Eaton-Krauss. *The Treasures of Coptic Art in the Coptic Museum and the Churches of Old Cairo.* Cairo: American University in Cairo Press, 2006.

Gabrieli, G. "Nota biobibliographica su Qusṭā ibn Lūqā." *Rendiconti della Reale Accademia dei Lincei: Classe di Scienze Morali, Storiche e Filologiche,* ser. V., 21 (1912), 341–82.

Gager, John G. *Curse Tablets and Binding Spells from the Ancient World.* New York and Oxford: Oxford University Press, 1992.

Gaisser, Julia Haig. *Catullus.* Oxford and Malden, Mass.: Wiley-Blackwell, 2007.

Gallagher, Eugene V. *Divine Man or Magician? Celsus and Origen on Jesus.* Society of Biblical Literature, Dissertation Series, number 64. Chico, Calif.: Scholars, 1982.

Gamble, Harry Y. *Books and Readers in the Early Church: A History of Early Christian Texts.* New Haven and London: Yale University Press, 1995.

———. "The New Testament Canon: Recent Research and the Status Quaestionis." In *The Canon Debate,* ed. L. M. McDonald and J. A. Sanders, 267–94. Peabody, Mass.: Hendrickson, 2002.

Ganszyniec, R. "Magica." *Byzantinisch-Neugriechische Jahrbücher* 3 (1922), 164.

———. "Sur deux tablettes de Tell Sandahannah." *Bulletin de correspondance hellénique* 48 (1924), 516–21.
Garcia, Hugues. "Les diverses dimensions d'apocryphité: Le cas du cycle de la Nativité de Jésus dans le plafond peint de l'Église Saint-Martin de Zillis." *Apocrypha* 15 (2004), 201–34.
García y García, Laurentino. *Pupils, Teachers and Schools in Pompeii: Childhood, Youth and Culture in the Roman Era.* Ed. Maria Elisa García Barraco. Rome: Bardi Editore, 2005.
Garland, R. *The Eye of the Beholder: Deformity and Disability in the Graeco-Roman World.* Ithaca: Cornell University Press, 1995.
Garnsey, P. "Child Rearing in Ancient Italy." In *The Family in Italy from Antiquity to the Present,* ed. D. I. Kertzer and R. P. Saller, 48–65. New Haven and London: Yale University Press, 1991.
Gaston, Lloyd. "Anti-Judaism and the Passion Narrative in Luke and Acts." In *Anti-Judaism in Early Christianity,* ed. P. Richardson, D. Granskou, and S. G. Wilson, volume 1, 127–53. Waterloo: Wilfrid Laurier University, 1986.
Gauthier, P. "Notes sur le rôle du gymnase dans les cites hellénistiques." In *Stadtbild und Bürgerbild im Hellenismus,* ed. M. Wörrle and P. Zanker, 1–10. Munich: C. H. Beck, 1995.
Gavrilov, A. K. "Reading Techniques in Classical Antiquity." *Classical Quarterly* 47 (1997), 56–73.
Gedi, Noa, and Yigal Elam. "Collective Memory: What Is It?" *History and Memory* 8.1 (1996), 30–50.
Geerard, I. M. *Clavis apocryphorum Novi Testamenti.* Turnhout: Brepols, 1992. [= *CANT*]
Gero, Stephen. "Apocryphal Gospels: A Survey of Textual and Literary Problems." *ANRW* 2.25.5 (1988), 3969–96.
———. "The Infancy Gospel of Thomas: A Study of the Textual and Literary Problems." *Novum Testamentum* 13 (1971), 46–80.
———. "Jewish Polemic in the Martyrium Pionii and a 'Jesus' Passage from the Talmud." *Journal of Jewish Studies* 29.2 (1978), 164–68.
Gero, Stephen (Gerö). "The Nestorius Legend in the *Toledoth Yeshu.*" *Oriens Christianus* 59 (1975), 108–20.
Geyer, Paul. *Kritische und sprachliche Erläuterungen zu Antonini Placentini Itinerarium.* Augsburg: P. J. Pfeiffer, 1892.
Gibson, C. A. "Learning Greek History in the Ancient Classroom: The Evidence of the Treatises on Progymnasmata." *Classical Philology* 99 (2004), 103–29.
Gießener Sonderforschungsbereichs 434. http://www.uni-giessen.de/erinnerungskulturen/home/index.html (accessed July 10, 2013).
Gijsel, Jan. *Die unmittelbare Textüberlieferung des sogenannten Pseudo-Mattäus.* Brussels: AWLSK, 1981.
Gilliard, Frank D. "Letter to the Editor." *Times Literary Supplement* (8 August 1997), 19.
———. "More on Silent Reading in Antiquity: *Non omne verbum sonabat.*" *Journal of Biblical Literature* 112 (1993), 689–96.
Gimaret, Daniel. "Shahāda." *EI*[2] 9 (1997), 201.

Ginzberg, Louis. *Ginze Schechter: Genizah Studies in Memory of Doctor Solomon Schechter. Volume 1: Midrash and Haggadah.* New York: Jewish Theological Seminary of America, 1928; repr. New York: Hermon, 1969.

Ginzburg, Carlo. "Kunst und soziales Gedächtnis: Die Warburg-Tradition." In *Spurensicherung: Die Wissenschaft auf der Suche nach sich selbst,* 63–127. Berlin: Wagenbach, 1995.

———. *Spurensicherung: Die Wissenschaft auf der Suche nach sich selbst.* Berlin: Wagenbach, 1995

Giorgi, Agostino Antonio. *Alphabetum Thibetanum: Missionum apostolicarum commodo editum.* Rome: Societas missionum ad exteros, 1762. Repr. Cologne: Editiones Una Voce, 1987.

Glad, Clarence E. "Frank Speech, Flattery, and Friendship in Philodemus." In *Friendship, Flattery, and Frankness of Speech,* ed. J. T. Fitzgerald, 21–59.

Glare, P. G. W., ed. *Oxford Latin Dictionary.* Oxford: Clarendon, 1982.

Golden, Mark. *Children and Childhood in Ancient Athens.* Baltimore: Johns Hopkins University Press, 1990.

———. "Continuity, Change and the Study of Ancient Childhood." *Classical Views / Echos du monde classique* 36 (1992), 7–18.

———. *Sport and Society in Ancient Greece.* Cambridge: Cambridge University Press, 1998.

———. *Sport in the Ancient World from A to Z.* London and New York: Routledge, 2004.

Goldhill, Simon. "The Anecdote: Exploring the Boundaries between Oral and Literate Performance in the Second Sophistic." In *Ancient Literacies,* ed. W. A. Johnson and H. N. Parker, 96–113.

———. "Genre." In *The Cambridge Companion to the Greek and Roman Novel,* ed. T. Whitmarsh, 185–200. Cambridge: Cambridge University Press, 2008.

Goldstein, Miriam, "Judeo-Arabic Versions of *Toledot Yeshu.*" *Ginzei Qedem* 6 (2010), 9–42.

Goldstein, Morris. *Jesus in the Jewish Tradition.* New York: Macmillan, 1950.

Gonzalez, Francisco J. "How to Read a Platonic Prologue: *Lysis* 203a–207d." In *Plato as Author: The Rhetoric of Philosophy,* ed. A. N. Michelini, 15–44. Cincinnati Classical Studies. Leiden and Boston: Brill, 2003.

Goodman, L. E. "The Translation of Greek Materials into Arabic." In *Religion, Learning and Science in the 'Abbasid Period,* ed. M. J. L. Young et al., 477–97.

Goosens, E. "Ursprung und Bedeutung der koranischen Siglen." *Der Islam* 13 (1923), 191–226.

Gould, Graham. "Childhood in Eastern Patristic Thought: Some Problems of Theology and Theological Anthropology." In *The Church and Childhood,* ed. D. Wood, Studies in Church History 31, 39–52. Cambridge: Blackwell, 1994.

Gourevitch, D. "Au temps des lois Julia et Papia Poppaea, la naissance d'un enfant handicapé est-elle une affaire publique ou privée?" *Ktema* 23 (1998), 459–73.

———. "L'Enfant handicapé à Rome: Mise au point et perspectives." *Medicina nei Secoli* 18 (2006), 459–77.

Grabar, Oleg. "The 1237 Manuscript of the Maqamat of Hariri." Introduction to *Maqāmāt al-Ḥarīrī*. Illustrated by Y. al-Wasiti. Facsimile edition. Volume 2, 7–17. London: Touch@rt, 2003.

———. *Illustrations of the Maqamat.* Chicago: University of Chicago Press, 1984.

Gradel, Ittai. *Emperor Worship and Roman Religion.* Oxford: Oxford University Press, 2002.

Graf, Georg. *Geschichte der christlichen arabischen Literatur.* 5 volumes. Vatican City: Biblioteca apostolica vaticana, 1944–1952. [=*GCAL*]

Gramlich, Richard. *Islamische Mystik: Sufische Texte aus zehn Jahrhunderten.* Stuttgart: Kohlhammer, 1992.

———. *Nahrung der Herzen: Abū Ṭālib al-Makkīs Qūt al-qulūb.* 4 volumes. Stuttgart: Steiner, 1992–1995.

———. *Schlaglichter über das Sufitum.* Stuttgart: Steiner, 1990.

———. *Sendschreiben al-Qušayrīs über das Sufitum.* Stuttgart: Steiner, 1989.

———. *Weltverzicht: Grundlagen und Weisen islamischer Askese.* Wiesbaden: Harrassowitz, 1997.

———. *Wunder der Freunde Gottes: Theologien und Erscheinungsformen des islamischen Heiligenwunders.* Stuttgart: Steiner, 1987.

Grandjouan, Clairève. *The Athenian Agora: Results of the Excavations Conducted by the American School of Classical Studies at Athens. Volume 6: Terracottas and Plastic Lamps of the Roman Period.* Princeton: American School of Classical Studies at Athens, 1961.

Grasl, H. "Behinderte in der Antike: Bemerkungen zur sozialen Stellung und Integration." *Tyche* 1 (1986), 118–26.

Greenfield, R. "Children in Byzantine Monasteries: Innocent Hearts or Vessels in the Harbor of the Devil?" In *Becoming Byzantine,* ed. A. Papaconstantinou and M.-A. Talbot, 253–81.

Griffith, F. L. *Stories of the High Priests of Memphis.* Oxford: Clarendon, 1900.

Griffith, F. L., and H. Thompson, eds. *The Demotic Magical Papyrus of London and Leiden.* London: Grevel, 1904.

Griffith, Sidney H. *The Bible in Arabic: The Scriptures of the "People of the Book" in the Language of Islam.* Princeton: Princeton University Press, 2013.

———. *The Church in the Shadow of the Mosque: Christians and Muslims in the World of Islam.* Princeton: Princeton University Press, 2008.

———. "Disputes with Muslims in Syriac Christian Texts: From Patriarch John (d. 648) to Bar Hebraeus (d. 1286)." In *Religionsgespräche im Mittelalter,* ed. F. Niewohner, Wolfenbütteler Mittelalter-Studien 4, 251–73. Wiesbaden: Harrassowitz, 1992.

———. "Disputing with Islam in Syriac: The Case of the Monk of Bêt Hālê and a Muslim Emir." *Hugoye* 3.1 (2000), 29–54.

Gril, Denis. "The Science of Letters." In *Ibn al-'Arabi: The Meccan Revelations,* ed. M. Chodkiewicz, trans. C. Chodkiewicz and D. Gril, volume 2, 105–219. New York: Pir, 2002–2004.

Grillo, Luca. Book Review of F. Gasti, ed., *Il Romanzo latino.* In *Bryn Mawr Classical Review* 2011.03.72 (http://bmcr.brynmawr.edu/2011/2011-03-72.html).

Grillo, R. D. *Dominant Languages: Language and Hierarchy in Britain and France.* Cambridge: Cambridge University Press, 1989.

Grisar, Hartmann. "Nochmals das Palästinaitinerar des Anonymus von Piacenza." *Zeitschrift für katholische Theologie* 27 (1903), 776–78.

———. "Zur Palästinareise des sogenannten Antoninus Martyr." *Zeitschrift für katholische Theologie* 26 (1902), 760–70.

Grossman, Janet Burnett. "Forever Young: An Investigation of the Depictions of Children on Classical Attic Funerary Monuments." In *Constructions of Childhood,* ed. A. Cohen and J. B. Rutter, 309–22.

Guhl, Erst Karl, and W. Koner. *The Life of the Greeks and Romans Described from Ancient Monuments.* Trans. F. Hueffer. New York: D. Appleton, 1896.

Guroian, Vigen. "The Ecclesial Family: John Chrysostom on Parenthood and Children." In *The Child in Christian Thought,* ed. M. J. Bunge, 61–77. Grand Rapids, Mich.: Eerdmans, 2001.

Gutas, Dimitri. *Greek Thought, Arabic Culture: The Graeco-Arabic Translation Movement in Baghdad and Early 'Abbāsid Society (2nd–4th/8th–10th centuries).* London and New York: Routledge, 1998.

Guthrie, Shirley. *Arab Social Life in the Middle Ages: An Illustrated Study.* London: Saqi, 1995.

Habinek, Thomas. "Situating Literacy at Rome." In *Ancient Literacies,* ed. W. A. Johnson and H. N. Parker, 114–40.

Hadnot, Ira J. "Lenzer Champions Growing Field of Children's Studies." *Dallas Morning News* (June 21, 1998), J1.

Haenchen, Ernst. *The Acts of the Apostles: A Commentary.* Oxford: Basil Blackwell, 1971.

Hägg, Tomas. *The Art of Biography in Antiquity.* Cambridge: Cambridge University Press, 2012.

———. *Narrative Technique in Ancient Greek Romances: Studies of Chariton, Xenophon Ephesius, and Achilles Tatius.* Stockholm: Svenska Institutet i Athen; Lund: P. Åström, 1971.

———. *The Novel in Antiquity.* Berkeley: University of California Press, 1983.

———. "Orality, Literacy, and the Readership of the Early Greek Novel." In *Contexts of Pre-Novel Narrative: The European Tradition,* ed. R. Eriksen, Approaches to Semiotics 114, 47–81. Berlin: Mouton de Gruyter, 1994. Reprinted in *Parthenope: Studies in Ancient Greek Fiction (1969–2004),* ed. L. B. Mortensen and T. Eide, 109–40. Copenhagen: Museum Tusculanum, 2004.

Hägg, Tomas, and Philip Rousseau. "Introduction: Biography and Panegyric." In *Greek Biography and Panegyric in Late Antiquity,* ed. T. Hägg, P. Rousseau, and C. Høgel, 1–28. Berkeley: University of California Press, 2000.

Hägg, Tomas, Philip Rousseau, and C. Høgel, eds. *Greek Biography and Panegyric in Late Antiquity.* Berkeley: University of California Press, 2000.

Halbwachs, Maurice. *Les Cadres sociaux de la mémoire.* Paris: F. Alcan, 1925. English trans.: *On Collective Memory,* trans. L. A. Coser, 37–189. Chicago: University of Chicago Press, 1992.

———. *La Mémoire collective.* Paris: Presses Universitaires de France, 1950. English trans.: *The Collective Memory,* trans. F. J. Ditter Jr. and V. Y. Ditter, 22–157. New York: Harper and Row, 1980.

———. "La Mémoire collective chez les musiciens." *Revue philosophique* 3–4 (1939), 136–65. English trans.: *The Collective Memory,* trans. F. J. Ditter Jr., and V. Y. Ditter, 158–96. New York: Harper and Row, 1980.

———. *La Topographie légendaire des évangiles en terre sainte: Étude de mémoire collective.* Paris, Presses Universitaires de France, 1941. English trans.: *On Collective Memory,* trans. L. A. Coser, 193–235. Chicago: University of Chicago Press, 1992.

Halleux, A. de. "Les manuscripts syriaques du C.S.C.O." *Le Muséon* 100 (1987), 35–48.

Halleux, Robert. "Alchemy." In *The Oxford Classical Dictionary,* ed. S. Hornblower and A. Spawforth. Oxford: Oxford University Press, 2005. E-reference edition online at http://www.oxford-classicaldictionary3.com/entry?entry=t111.e260 (accessed August 19, 2012).

Ḥamdān, 'Abd al-Ḥamīd Ṣāliḥ. *'Ilm al-ḥurūf wa aqṭābuhu.* Cairo: Maktabat Madbūlī, 1990.

Hamrin, Jacqueline. "Nachträglichkeit." *PSYART: A Hyperlink Journal for the Psychological Study of the Arts.* July 16, 2008. Available at http://www.psyartjournal.com/article/show/hamrit-nachtrglichkeit (accessed January 12, 2013).

Hänninen, Marja-Leena. "From Womb to Family: Ritual and Social Conventions Connected to Roman Birth." In *Hoping for Continuity,* ed. K. Mustakallio et al., 49–59.

Harlow, Mary, and Ray Laurence. *Growing Up and Growing Old in Ancient Rome: A Life Course Approach.* London and New York: Routledge, 2002.

Harlow, Mary, and Ray Laurence, eds. *Cultural History of Childhood. Volume 1: In Antiquity.* Oxford and New York: Berg, 2010.

Harlow, Mary, Ray Laurence, and Ville Vuolanto, "Past, Present and Future in the Study of Roman Childhood." In *Children, Childhood and Society,* ed. S. Crawford and G. Shepherd, 5–14.

Harnack, Adolf. *Geschichte der altchristlichen Literatur bis Eusebius.* Volume 2.1. Leipzig: J. C. Hinrichs, 1897.

Harris, H. A. *Sport in Greece and Rome.* London: Thames and Hudson, 1972.

Harris, William. *Ancient Literacy.* Cambridge, Mass.: Harvard University Press, 1989.

Harvey, Graham A. P. *The True Israel: Uses of the Names Jew, Hebrew and Israel in Ancient Jewish and Early Christian Literature.* Leiden: Brill, 1996.

Havelock, Eric A. *The Greek Concept of Justice from Its Shadow in Homer to Its Substance in Plato.* Cambridge, Mass.: Harvard University Press, 1978.

———. *The Muse Learns to Write: Reflections on Orality and Literacy from Antiquity to the Present.* New Haven and London: Yale University Press, 1986.

Haworth, Kenneth R. *Deified Virtues, Demonic Vices, and Descriptive Allegory in Prudentius' "Psychomachia."* Amsterdam: A. M. Hakkert, 1980.

Heath, Shirley. "What No Bedtime Story Means: Narrative Skills at Home and School." *Language in Society* 11 (1982), 49–76.

Heijer, Johannes den. "Relations between Copts and Syrians in the Light of Recent Discoveries at Dayr as-Suryān." In *Coptic Studies on the Threshold of a New Millennium: Proceedings of the Seventh International Congress of Coptic Studies,* ed. M. Immerzeel and J. van der Vliet, 923–38. Louvain: Peeters, 2004.

Heinrichs, W., and A. Knysh. "Ramz." *EI*[2] 8 (1995), 426–30.

Heinwetter, Franz. *Würfel- und Buchstabenorakel in Griechenland und Kleinasien.* Breslau: Grasz, 1912.

Helbig, Wolfgang, with Otto Dotter. *Wandgemälde der vom Vesuv verschütteten Städte Campaniens.* Leipzig: Breitkopf und Härtel, 1868.

Heller, Scott. "The Meaning of Children in Culture Becomes a Focal Point for Scholars." *Chronicle of Higher Education* (August 7, 1998), A14–15.

Hendrickson, G. L. "Ancient Reading." *Classical Journal* 25 (1929), 182–96.

Hennecke, Edgar, ed. *Handbuch zu den neutestamentlichen Apokryphen.* Tübingen: Mohr, 1904.

———. *Neutestamentliche Apokryphen.* Tübingen: Mohr 1904.

Hennessy, Cecily. *Images of Children in Byzantium.* Farnham, U.K., and Burlington, Vt.: Ashgate, 2008.

Herder, Jenz. *Die Paralipomena Jeremiae: Studien zu Tradition und Redaktion einer Haggada des frühen Judentums.* Texte und Studien zum Antiken Judentum. Tübingen: Mohr Siebeck, 1994.

Herford, R. Travers. *Christianity in Talmud and Midrash.* London: Williams and Norgate, 1903.

Hervieux, Jacques. *The New Testament Apocrypha.* Trans. D. W. Hibberd. New York: Hawthorn, 1960.

Hill, Donald R. "Mathematics and Applied Sciences." In *Religion, Learning and Science,* ed. Young et al., 248–73.

———. "Mūsā, banū." In *EI*[2] 7 (1992), 640–41.

Hillner, J. "Monks and Children: Corporal Punishment in Late Antiquity." *European Review of History / Revue européenne d'histoire* 16.6 (2009), 773–91.

Hirschfeld, H. *New Researches into the Composition and Exegesis of the Qoran.* London: Royal Asiatic Society, 1902.

Hock, Ronald. *The Infancy Gospels of James and Thomas.* Santa Rosa, Calif.: Polebridge, 1995.

Hock, Ronald F., J. Bradley Chance, and Judith Perkins, eds. *Ancient Fiction and Early Christian Narrative.* Atlanta: Scholars, 1998.

Hofmann, R. A. *Das Leben Jesu nach den Apokryphen im Zusammenhange aus den Quellen erzählt und wissenschaftlich untersucht.* Leipzig: F. Voigt, 1851.

Holland, Louise Adams. *Janus and the Bridge.* American Academy at Rome, Papers and Monographs 21. Rome: American Academy at Rome, 1961.

Holman, Susan R. *The Hungry Are Dying: Beggars and Bishops in Roman Cappadocia.* Oxford: Oxford University Press, 2001.

———. "Sick Children and Healing Saints: Medical Treatment of the Child in Christian Antiquity." In *Children in Late Ancient Christianity,* ed. C. B. Horn and R. R. Phenix, 143–70.

Hooker, Morna D. *The Gospel According to Saint Mark*. Black's New Testament Commentaries. London: A. and C. Black; Hendrickson, 1991.

Hopfner, T. "Die Kindermedien in den griechisch-ägyptischen Zauberpapyri." In *Recueil d'études dédiées à la mémoire de N. P. Kondakov: Archéologie, histoire de l'art, études byzantines,* 65–74. Prague: Seminarium Kondakovianum, 1926.

Hopkins, Keith. "Everyday Life for the Roman Schoolboy." *History Today* 43.10 (1993), 25–30.

Horbury, William. "A Critical Examination of the Toledoth Jeshu." Ph.D. dissertation, University of Cambridge, 1970.

———. "The Depiction of Judaeo-Christians in the Toledot Yeshu." In *The Image of Judaeo-Christians in Ancient Jewish and Christian Literature,* ed. P. J. Tomson and D. Lamers-Petry, 281–86. WUNT 158. Tübingen: Mohr Siebeck, 2003.

———. "The Strasbourg Text of the *Toledot.*" In *Toledot Yeshu ("The Life Story of Jesus") Revisited,* ed. P. Schäfer, M. Meerson, and Y. Deutsch, 49–59.

———. "The Trial of Jesus in Jewish Tradition." In *The Trial of Jesus: Cambridge Studies in Honour of C. F. D. Moule,* ed. E. Bammel, 103–21. London: SCM, 1970.

Horn, Cornelia B. "Apocryphal Gospels in Arabic, or Some Complications on the Road to the Traditions about Jesus." In *Jesus in apokryphen Evangelienüberlieferungen: Beiträge zu außerkanonischen Jesusüberlieferungen aus verschiedenen Sprach- und Kulturtraditionen*, ed. J. Frey and J. Schröter, WUNT 254, 583–609. Tübingen: Mohr Siebeck, 2010.

———. "Approaches to the Study of Sick Children and Their Healing: Christian Apocryphal Acts, Gospels, and Cognate Literatures." In *Children in Late Ancient Christianity,* ed. C. B. Horn and R. R. Phenix, 171–98.

———. "Raising Martyrs and Ascetics: A Diachronic Comparison of Educational Role-Models for Early Christian Children." In *Children in Late Ancient Christianity,* ed. C. B. Horn and R. R. Phenix, 293–316.

Horn, Cornelia B., and John W. Martens. *"Let the Little Children Come to Me": Childhood and Children in Early Christianity.* Washington, D.C.: Catholic University of America Press, 2009.

Horn, Cornelia B., and Robert R. Phenix, eds. *Children in Late Ancient Christianity.* Studien und Texte zu Antike und Christentum 58. Tübingen: Mohr Siebeck, 2009.

Horner, Timothy J. *Listening to Trypho: Justin Martyr's Dialogue Reconsidered.* Louvain: Peeters, 2001.

Hornschuh, Manfred. *Studien zur Epistula Apostolorum.* PTS 5. Berlin: De Gruyter, 1965.

Horsfall, Nicholas. Review of *Strukturen der Mündlichkeit in der römischen Literatur,* ed. G. Vogt-Spira. In Rivista di Filologia 121 (1993), 81–5.

Hübner, Sabine R., and David M. Ratzan, eds. *Growing Up Fatherless in Antiquity.* Cambridge and New York: Cambridge University Press, 2009.

Hübner, Ulrich. *Spiele und Spielzeug im antiken Palästina.* Orbis Biblicus et Orientalis 121. Freiburg and Göttingen: Universitätsverlag; Vandenhoeck und Ruprecht, 1992.

Hughes, T. P. "Da'wah." In *A Dictionary of Islam,* ed. T. P. Hughes, 72–78. London: W. H. Allen, 1885, repr. 1935.

Huizenga, Johan. *Homo Ludens: A Study of the Play-Element in Culture.* London: Routledge and Kegan Paul, 1949.

Huldricius (Huldreich), J. J. *Historia Jeshuae Nazareni a Judaeis blaspheme corrupta.* Ludg. Batavorum: J. du Vivie-Severinum, 1705.

Hummel, C. *Das Kind und seine Krankheiten in der griechischen Medizin: Von Aretaios bis Johannes Akuarios (1. bis 14. Jahrhundert).* Frankfurt am Main: Peter Lang, 1999.

Hunger, H. *Katalog der griechischen Handschriften der Österreichischen Nationalbibliothek.* Volume 1. Vienna: G. Prachner, 1961.

Hunter, Richard. "Ancient Readers." In *The Cambridge Companion to the Greek and Roman Novel,* ed. T. Whitmarsh, 261–71. Cambridge: Cambridge University Press, 2007.

Huskinson, Janet. "Constructing Childhood on Roman Funerary Memorials." In *Constructions of Childhood,* ed. A. Cohen and J. Rutter, 323–38.

———. "The Decoration of Early Christian Children's Sarcophagi." In *Studia Patristica,* volume 24, ed. E. A. Livingstone, 114–15. Louvain: Peeters, 1993.

———. "Disappearing Children? Children in Roman Funerary Art of the First to the Fourth Century AD." In *Hoping for Continuity,* ed. K. Mustakallio et al., 91–103.

———. "Growing Up in Ravenna: Evidence from the Decoration of Children's Sarcophagi." In *Age and Ageing in the Roman Empire,* ed. M. Harlow and R. Laurence, 55–80.

———. "Iconography: Another Perspective." In *The Roman Family in Italy,* ed. B. Rawson and P. Weaver, 233–38.

———. *Roman Children's Sarcophagi: Their Decoration and Social Significance.* Oxford: Clarendon, 1996.

Ingen, W. van. *Figurines from Seleucia on the Tigris.* University of Michigan Humanities Series 45. Ann Arbor: University of Michigan Press, 1939.

Innemee, Karel C., and Lucas Van Rompay. "La présence des Syriens dans le Wadi al-Natrun (Égypte), à propos des découvertes récentes de peintures et de textes muraux dans l'Église de la Vierge du Couvent des Syriens." *Parole de l'Orient* 23 (1998), 167–202.

Isaacs, Haskell D. "Arabic Medical Literature." In *Religion, Learning and Science in the 'Abbasid Period,* ed. M. J. L. Young et al., 342–63.

Isbir, 'Alī Muḥammad, ed. *Risāla fī al-farq bayn al-rūḥ wa al-nafs.* Damascus: Dar al-Yanābī', 2006.

Iser, Wolfgang. *The Act of Reading: A Theory of Aesthetic Response.* Baltimore: Johns Hopkins University Press, 1980.

Iskandar, Albert Z. "An Attempted Reconstruction of the Late Alexandrian Medical Curriculum." *Medical History* 20.3 (1976), 235–58.

Jacob, Christian. *The Web of Athenaeus.* Trans. A. Papaconstantinou. Ed. S. F. Johnson. Hellenic Studies 61. Washington, D. C.: Center for Hellenic Studies, Trustees for Harvard University Press, 2013.

Jacobs, Andrew S. *Christ Circumcised: A Study in Early Christian History and Difference.* Philadelphia: University of Pennsylvania Press, 2012.

———. *Remains of the Jews: The Holy Land and Christian Empire in Late Antiquity.* Stanford: Stanford University Press, 2004.

Jacobs, Andrew S., and Rebecca Krawiec. "Fathers Know Best? Christian Families in the Age of Asceticism." *Journal of Early Christian Studies* 11.3 (2003), 257–63.

Jackson-McCabe, Matt, ed. *Jewish Christianity Reconsidered: Rethinking Ancient Groups and Texts.* Minneapolis: Fortress, 2007.

Jaeger, Werner. *Early Christianity and Greek Paideia.* Oxford: Oxford University Press, 1961.

James, Allison, and Adrian James. *Key Concepts in Childhood Studies.* Los Angeles and London: Sage, 2008.

James, Allison, and Alan Prout. *Constructing and Reconstructing Childhood: Contemporary Issues in the Sociological Study of Childhood.* London and New York: Routledge, 1997.

Janowitz, Naomi. *Icons of Power: Ritual Practices in Late Antiquity.* University Park: Pennsylvania State University Press, 2002.

Jauss, Hans Robert. *Toward an Aesthetic of Reception.* Trans. T. Bahti. Theory and History of Literature, volume 2. Minneapolis: University of Minnesota Press, 1982.

Jeffery, A. "The Mystic Letters of the Koran." *Muslim World* 14 (1924), 247–60.

Jennison, G. *Animals for Show and Pleasure in Ancient Rome.* Manchester: Manchester University Press, 1937; repr. Philadelphia: University of Pennsylvania Press, 2005.

Jerris, Randon. "Cult Lines and Hellish Mountains: The Development of Sacred Landscape in the Early Medieval Alps." *Journal of Medieval and Early Modern Studies* 32.1 (2002), 85–108.

Jervell, Jacob. "The Acts of the Apostles and the History of Early Christianity." *Studia Theologica* 37.1 (1983), 17–32.

———. "The Church of Jews and Godfearers." In *Luke-Acts and the Jewish People: Eight Critical Perspectives,* ed. J. B. Tyson, 11–20. Minneapolis: Augsburg, 1988.

———. "Das gespaltene Israel und die heidenvölker: Zur Motivierung der Heidenmission in der Apostelgeschichte." *Studia Theologica* 19 (1965), 68–96. English trans.: "The Divided People of God: The Restoration of Israel and Salvation for the Gentiles," in Jervell, *Luke and the People of God: A New Look at Luke-Acts,* 41–74.

———. "God's Faithfulness to the Faithless People: Trends in the Interpretation of Luke-Acts." *Word and World* 12 (1992), 29–36.

———. *Luke and the People of God: A New Look at Luke-Acts.* Minneapolis: Augsburg, 1983.

———. *The Unknown Paul: Essays on Luke-Acts and Early Christian History.* Minneapolis: Augsburg, 1984.

Johansen, F. "Achill bei Cheiron." In *Dragma Martino P. Nilsson,* Acta Instituti Romani Regni Sueciae series altera I, ed. K. Hannell et al., 181–205. Lund: C. Gleerup; Leipzig: O. Harassowitz, 1939.

Johnson, Luke Timothy. *Among the Gentiles: Greco-Roman Religion and Christianity.* New Haven: Yale University Press, 2009.

Johnson, William A. "The Function of the Paragraphus in Greek Literary Prose Texts." *ZPE* 100 (1994), 65–68.

———. *Readers and Reading Culture in the High Roman Empire: A Study of Elite Communities.* Classical Culture and Society. Oxford: Oxford University Press, 2010.

———. "Toward a Sociology of Reading in Classical Antiquity." *American Journal of Philology* 121.4 (2000), 593–627.

Johnson, William A., and Holt N. Parker, eds. *Ancient Literacies: The Culture of Reading in Greece and Rome.* Oxford and New York: Oxford University Press, 2009.

Johnston, Harold Whetstone. *The Private Life of the Romans*. Rev. Mary Johnston. Chicago: Scott, Foresman, 1903/1932.
Johnston, Sarah Iles. *Ancient Greek Divination*. Oxford and Malden, Mass.: Wiley-Blackwell, 2008.
———. "Charming Children: The Use of the Child in Ancient Divination." *Arethusa* 34.1 (2001), 97–117.
Jones, A. "The Mystical Letters of the Qur'an." *Studia Islamica* 16 (1962), 5–11.
Jonge, Henk J. de. "Sonship, Wisdom, Infancy: Luke ii.41–51a." *New Testament Studies* 24 (1978), 317–54.
Jordan, David R. "A Graffito from Panticapaeum." *ZPE* 30 (1978), 159–63.
———. "A Survey of Greek Defixiones Not Included in the Special Corpora." *Greek, Roman, and Byzantine Studies* 26.2 (1985), 151–97. [=SGD]
———. "Hekatika." *Glotta* 83 (1980), 62–65.
Joyal, Mark, Iain McDougall, and John C. Yardley, eds. *Greek and Roman Education: A Sourcebook*. New York: Routledge, 2009.
Juel, Donald. *Luke-Acts: The Promise of History*. Atlanta: John Knox, 1983.
Kaestli, J.-D., and P. Cherix. *L'évangile de Barthélemy d'après deux écrits apocryphes*. Apocryphes 1. Turnhout: Brepols, 1993.
Kagarow, E. G. *Griechische Fluchtafeln*. Leopoli: Societas philologa polonorum, 1929.
Kaiser, Ursula Ulrike. "Jesus als Kind: Neuere Forschungen zur Jesusüberlieferung in den apocryphen Kindheitsevangelien." In *Jesus in apokryphen Evangelienüberlieferungen*, ed. Frey and Schröter, 253–69.
———. "Die sogenannte 'Kindheitserzählung des Thomas': Überlegungen zur Darstellung Jesu als Kind, deren Intention und Rezeption." In *Infancy Stories: Stories and Intentions*, ed. C. Clivaz et al., 459–81.
Kalogeras, Nikos. "The Role of Parents and Kin in the Education of Byzantine Children." In *Hoping for Continuity*, ed. K. Mustakallio et al., 133–43.
Kalvesmaki, Joel. "Formation of the Early Christian Theology of Arithmetic: Number Symbolism in the Late Second and Early Third Century." Ph.D. dissertation, Catholic University of America, 2006.
———. "The Theology of Arithmetic." Website. http://www.kalvesmaki.com/Arithmetic/index.htm (accessed July 10, 2013).
Kambitsis, S. "Une nouvelle tablette magique d'Égypte: Musée du Louvre, Inv. E 27145, 3e/4e siècle." *BIFAO* 76 (1976), 213–23, and plates.
Kammen, Michael G. *Mystic Chords of Memory: The Transformation of Tradition in American Culture*. New York: Knopf, 1991.
Kany, Roland. *Mnemosyne als Programm: Geschichte, Erinnerung und die Andacht zum Unbedeutenden im Werk von Usener, Warburg und Benjamin*. Tübingen: Niemeyer, 1987.
Karvonen-Kannas, K. *The Seleucid and Parthian Terracotta Figurines from Babylon in the Iraq Museum, the British Museum and the Louvre*. Monografie di Mesopotamia 4. Florence: Casa editrice le lettere, 1995.
Katz, P. B. "Educating Paula: A Proposed Curriculum for Raising a 4th-Century Christian Infant." In *Constructions of Childhood*, ed. A. Cohen and J. Rutter, 115–27.

Kehily, Mary Jane. *An Introduction to Childhood Studies.* Oxford: Open University Press, 2004.

Kelly, Nicole. "The Deformed Child in Ancient Christianity." In *Children in Late Ancient Christianity,* ed. C. B. Horn and R. R. Phenix, 199–225.

Kemp, J. A. "The *Tekhne Grammatike* of Dionysius Thrax." *Historiographica Linguistica* 13.2–3 (1986), 343–63.

Kheirandish, Elaheh. "Quṣṭā ibn Lūqā al-Ba'labakkī." In *The Biographical Encyclopedia of Astronomers,* 948–49. Springer Reference. New York: Springer, 2007.

King, David A. "Astronomy." In *Religion, Learning and Science,* ed. Young et al., 274–89.

King, M. "Commemoration of Infants on Roman Funerary Inscriptions." In *The Epigraphy of Death: Studies in the History and Society of Greece and Rome,* ed. G. J. Oliver, 117–54. Liverpool: Liverpool University Press, 2000.

Kivy, Peter. *The Performance of Reading: An Essay in the Philosophy of Literature.* Oxford and Malden, Mass.: Blackwell, 2009.

Klauck, Hans-Josef. *Apocryphal Gospels: An Introduction.* Trans. B. McNeil. London and New York: T. and T. Clark, 2003.

Klausner, Joseph. *Jesus von Nazareth: Seine Zeit, sein Leben und seine Lehre.* Third ed. Jerusalem: Jewish Publishing House, 1952.

Klee, T. *Zur Geschichte der gymnischen Agone und griechischen Festen.* Leipzig and Berlin: B. G. Teubner, 1918.

Kleijwegt, Marc. *Ancient Youth: The Ambiguity of Youth and the Absence of Adolescence in Greco-Roman Society.* Dutch Monographs on Ancient History and Archaeology. Amsterdam: J. C. Gieben, 1991.

———. "Exposed, Mistreated and Marginalised: Towards a History of Female Children in Antiquity (and Beyond)." In *Quests for Humanity: The Middle Ages and the Millennium,* ed. E. A. Maré, 113–26. Pretoria: Unisa, 2002.

Klein, Anita E. *Child Life in Greek Art.* New York: Columbia University Press, 1932.

Klein, Kerwin Lee. "On the Emergence of Memory in Historical Discourse." *Representations* 69 (2000), 127–50.

Kleiner, Diana. "Women and Family Life on Roman Imperial Funerary Altars." *Latomus* 46 (July–December 1987), 545–54, and plates XIV–XV.

Klijn, A. F. J. *The* Acts of Thomas*: Introduction, Text, and Commentary.* Second rev. ed. Leiden: Brill, 2003.

———. *Jewish-Christian Gospel Tradition.* Leiden: Brill, 1992.

Klijn, A. F. J., and G. J. Reinink. *Patristic Evidence for Jewish-Christian Sects.* Leiden: Brill, 1973.

Knox, Bernard M. W. "Silent Reading in Antiquity." *Greek, Roman and Byzantine Studies* 9 (1968), 421–35.

Koffka, Kurt. *Principles of Gestalt Psychology.* New York: Harcourt, Brace, 1935.

Kohlberg, E. "al-Ṭabrisī (Ṭabarsī), Amīnal-Dīn (or Amīnal-Islām) Abū 'Alīal-Faḍl b. al-Ḥasan." In *EI*[2] 10 (1998), 40–1.

Koller, K. "Stoicheion." *Glotta* 34 (1955), 161–74.

König, Jason. *Athletics and Literature in the Roman Empire.* Cambridge: Cambridge University Press, 2005.

Konstan, David. "Friendship, Frankness and Flattery." In *Friendship, Flattery, and Frankness of Speech,* ed. J. T. Fitzgerald, 7–19.

Kortekaas, G. A. A. *Commentary on the Historia Apollonii Regis Tyri.* Leiden: Brill, 2007.

———. *Story of Apollonius, King of Tyre: A Study of Its Greek Origin and an Edition of the Two Oldest Latin Recensions.* Leiden: Brill, 2004.

Koskenniemi, E., and P. Lindqvist. "Rewritten Bible, Rewritten Stories: Methodological Aspects." In *Rewritten Bible Reconsidered,* ed. A. Laato and J. van Ruiten, 11–39. Turko: Åbo Akademi University; Winona Lake, Ind.: Eisenbrauns, 2008.

Kotsifou, Chrysi. "Papyrological Perspectives on Orphans in the World of Late Ancient Christianity." In *Children in Late Ancient Christianity,* ed. C. B. Horn and R. R. Phenix, 339–73.

Krauss, Samuel. *Das Leben Jesu nach jüdischen Quellen.* Berlin: S. Calvary, 1902.

———. "The Mount of Olives in 'Toldoth Jesu.'" *Zion* 4 (1939), 170–76 (in Hebrew).

Krauss, Samuel, and William Horbury. *The Jewish-Christian Controversy from the Earliest Times to 1789. Volume I: History.* Edited and revised by William Horbury. Tübingen: Mohr, 1995.

Krawiec, Rebecca. "'From the Womb of the Church': Monastic Families." *Journal of Early Christian Studies* 11.3 (2003), 283–307.

Kropp, Amina. *Defixiones: Ein aktuelles Corpus lateinischer Fluchtafeln.* Speyer: Kartoffeldruck Kai Broderson, 2008.

Kuhn, K. H. "Apokryphon of Jeremiah." In *Coptic Encyclopedia,* volume 1, 170–71. New York: Macmillan, 1991.

Kuhnert, E. "Feuerzauber." *Rheinisches Museum* 49 (1894), 37–54.

Kunitzsch, P. "Nuḏjūm." In *EI*[2] 8 (1995), 97–105.

Kunst, C. "Adoption und Testamentadoption in der späten Republik." *Klio* 78 (1996), 87–104.

Kurylowicz, M. "Adoption on the Evidence of the Papyri." *Journal of Juristic Papyrology* 19 (1983), 61–75.

Kyle, Donald G. *Sport and Spectacle in the Ancient World.* Oxford and Malden, Mass.: Blackwell, 2007.

L'art copte en Égypte: 2000 ans de christianisme. Paris: Institut du monde arabe et Gallimnar, 2002.

Labahn, Michael. "Scripture *Talks* Because Jesus *Talks:* The Narrative Rhetoric of Persuading and Creativity in John's Use of Scripture." In *The Fourth Gospel in First-Century Media Culture,* ed. A. Le Donne and T. Thatcher, 133–54.

Labib, Pahor. *Coptic Gnostic Papyri in the Coptic Museum at Old Cairo.* Cairo: Government, 1956.

Lacan, Jacques. "Fonction et champ de la parole et du langage en psychanalyse." *La psychanalyse* 1 (1956), 81–166. Repr. in Jacques Lacan, *Écrits,* 237–322. Paris: Seuil, 1996. English trans. Alan Seridan, "The Function and Field of Speech and Language in Psychoanalysis," in *Écrits: A Selection,* 30–113. London: Tavistock; New York: W. W. Norton, 1977.

Laes, Christian. "Childbeating in Antiquity: Some Reconsiderations." In *Hoping for Continuity,* ed. K. Mustakallio, 75–89.

———. *Children in the Roman Empire: Outsiders Within.* Cambridge: Cambridge University Press, 2011.

———. "Inscriptions from Rome and the History of Childhood." In *Age and Ageing in the Roman Empire,* ed. Mary Harlow and Ray Laurence, 25–36. Portsmouth, R.I.: Journal of Roman Archaeology, 2007.

———. "School-teachers in the Roman Empire: A Survey of the Epigraphical Evidence." *Acta Classica* 50 (2007), 109–27.

———. "When Classicists Need to Speak Up: Antiquity and Present Day Pedophilia—Pederasty." In *Aeternitas Antiquitatis,* ed. V. Sofronievski, 30–59. Skopje: Association of Classical Philologists ANTIKA and Faculty of Philosophy in Skopje, 2010.

Lalanne, S. *Une éducation grecque: Rites de passage et construction des genres dans le roman grec ancient.* Paris: Éditions La Découverte, 2006.

Lambeck, Peter. *Commentariorum de augustissima Bibliotheca Caesarea Vindobonensi liber septimus,* 8 volumes. Ed. A. F. Kollár. Vienna: M. Cosmerovius, 1665–1682.

Lamberton, Robert D., and Susan I. Rotroff. *Birds of the Athenian Agora.* Princeton: American School of Classical Studies at Athens, 1985.

Lane, Edward William. *An Arabic Lexicon.* 8 volumes. Beirut: Librairie du Liban, 1968.

Lange, N. R. M. de. *Origen and the Jews: Studies in Jewish-Christian Relations in Third-Century Palestine.* Cambridge and New York: Cambridge University Press, 1976.

Lapham, Fred. *An Introduction to the New Testament Apocrypha.* London and New York: T. and T. Clark, 2003.

Lardner, Nathaniel. *The Credibility of the Gospel History; or the Principal Facts of the New Testament confirmed by Passages of Ancient Authors, who were contemporary with our Saviour or his Apostles, or lived near their time.* London: John Chandler at the Cross-Keys in the Poultry, 1727.

———. *The Works of Nathaniel Lardner.* 10 volumes. London: William Ball, 1838.

Lattimore, R. *Themes in Greek and Latin Epitaphs.* Urbana: University of Illinois Press, 1962.

Layton, Bentley. *Gnostic Scriptures.* Garden City, N.Y.: Doubleday, 1987.

Lazenby, Francis D. "Greek and Roman Household Pets." *Classical Journal* 44.4 (Jan. 1947), 245–52, and 44.4 (Feb. 1947), 299–307.

Lazos, C. D. *Paizontas sto chrono: Archaioellênika kai Buzantina paichnidia 1700 p. Ch.–1500 m.Ch.* Athens: N.p., 2002.

Le Donne, A., and T. Thatcher, eds. *The Fourth Gospel in First-Century Media Culture.* London and New York: T. and T. Clark, 2011.

Lefkowitz, M. R. *The Lives of the Greek Poets.* Baltimore: Johns Hopkins University Press, 1981. Second ed.: Bristol: Bristol Classical, 2012.

Legásse, S. "La légende juive des Apôtres et les rapports judéo-chrétiens dans le haut Moyen Age." *Bulletin de littérature ecclésiastique* 75 (1974), 99–132.

———. "La légende juive des Apôtres et les rapports judéo-chrétiens dans le Moyen Age occidental." *Yearbook of the Ecumenical Institute for Advanced Theological Studies* (1974/1975), 121–139.

Legras, Bernard. *Éducation et culture dans le monde grec (VIIIe–Ier siècle av. J.-C.).* Paris: SEDES, 1998.

Leiman, S. Z. "The Scroll of Fasts: The Ninth of Tebeth." *Jewish Quarterly Review* 74 (1983/1984), 187–92.

Lenzer, Gertrude. "Children's Studies: Beginnings and Purposes." *The Lion and the Unicorn* 25 (2001), 181–86.

———. "Is There Sufficient Interest to Establish a Sociology of Children?" *Footnotes* 19.6 (Aug. 1991), 8.

Leroy, L., and P. Dib. "Un apocryphe carchouni sur la captivité de Babylone." *Revue de l'Orient Chrétien* 15 (1910), 398–409; 16 (1911), 128–53.

Lévi-Strauss, Claude. *Totemism*. Trans. Rodney Needham. Boston: Beacon, 1963. Originally published in French under the title *Le totémisme aujourd'hui*. Paris: Presses Universitaires de France, 1962.

Leyerle, Blake. "Appealing to Children." *Journal of Early Christian Studies* 5.2 (1997), 243–70.

———. "The Landscape as Cartography in Early Christian Pilgrimage Narratives." *Journal of the American Academy of Religion* 64.1 (1996), 119–43.

———. "Pilgrims to the Land: Early Christian Perceptions of the Galilee." In *Galilee through the Centuries: Confluence of Cultures*, ed. Eric M. Meyers, 345–57. Winona Lake, Ind.: Eisenbrauns, 1999.

Liddell, H. G., and R. Scott, eds. *A Greek-English Lexicon, with a Supplement*. Ninth ed. Oxford: Clarendon, 1968, repr. 1990.

Liebeschuetz, W. H. W. G. *Continuity and Change in Roman Religion*. Oxford: Clarendon, 1979.

Lim, Richard. "Religious Disputation and Social Disorder in Late Antiquity." *Historia: Zeitschrift für alte Geschichte* 44.2 (1995), 204–31.

Lindsay, Jack. *The Origins of Alchemy in Graeco-Roman Egypt*. London: Frederick Muller, 1970.

Lindsay, James. *Daily Life in the Medieval Islamic World*. Westport, Conn., and London: Greenwood, 1995.

Livingstone, A. "The Patter of Tiny Feet in Clay: Aspects of the Liminality of Childhood in the Ancient Near East." In *Children, Childhood and Society*, ed. S. Crawford and G. Shepherd, 15–27.

Lods, Marc. "Étude sur les sources juives de la polémique de Celsus contre les Chrétiens." *Revue d'histoire et de philosophie religieuse* 21 (1941), 1–33.

Long, A. A. *Stoic Studies*. Cambridge and New York: Cambridge University Press, 1996.

Longenecker, B. W. "A Humorous Jesus? Orality, Structure and Characterization in Luke 14:15–24, and Beyond." *Biblical Interpretation* 16 (2008), 179–204.

Lord, A. B. *The Singer of Tales*. Cambridge, Mass.: Harvard University Press, 1960.

Lory, Pierre. *La science des lettres en Islam*. Esprit de Lettre. Paris: Éditions Dervy, 2004.

Lowe, E. A. *Codices latini antiquiores: A Paleographical Guide to Latin Manuscripts Prior to the Ninth Century*. 11 volumes. Oxford: Clarendon, 1934–1966.

Luck, Georg. *Arcana Mundi: Magic and the Occult in the Greek and Roman Worlds*. Baltimore and London: Johns Hopkins University Press, 1985.

Lüdemann, Gerd. "The History of Earliest Christianity in Rome." *Journal of Higher Criticism* 2 (1995), 112–41. Original German version: "Zur Geschichte des ältesten

Christentums in Rom," *Zeitschrift für Neutestamentliche Wissenschaft* 70 (1979), 86–114.

Luhmann, Niklas. *Aufsätze und Reden*. Ed. Oliver Jahraus. Stuttgart: Reclam, 2001.

———. *Die Wissenschaft der Gesellschaft*. Frankfurt am Main: Suhrkamp, 1990.

Lüling, Gunter. *Über den Ur-Qur'ān: Ansätze zur Rekonstruktion vorislamischer christlicher Strophenlieder im Qur'ān*. Erlangen: Lüling, 1974.

Luria, A. R. *Cognitive Development: Its Cultural and Social Foundations*. Ed. M. Cole. Trans. M. Lopez-Morillas and L. Solotaroff. Cambridge, Mass.: Harvard University Press, 1976.

Lux, Ute. "Eine altchristliche Kirche in Mādeba." *Zeitschrift des Deutschen Palästina-Vereins* 83.1 (1967), 165–182 and pl. 26–40.

Luxenberg, Christoph. *The Syro-Aramaic Reading of the Qur'an: A Contribution to the Decoding of the Language of the Koran*. Berlin: Hans Schiler, 2007. Originally published in German under the title *Syro-aramäische Lesart des Koran: Ein Beitrag zur Entschlüsselung der Koransprache*. Berlin: Hans Schiler, 2000.

Lyster, William, Cornelis Hulsman, and Stephen J. Davis. *Be Thou There: The Holy Family's Journey in Egypt*. Ed. Gawdat Gabra. Cairo and New York: American University in Cairo Press, 2001.

MacCoull, L. S. B. "Child Donations and Child Saints in Coptic Egypt." *East European Quarterly* 13 (1979), 409–15.

MacDonald, Dennis R. *The Legend and the Apostle: The Battle for Paul in Story and Canon*. Philadelphia: Westminster, 1983.

MacDonald, Lee M. *The Formation of the Christian Biblical Canon*. Rev. ed. Peabody, Mass.: Hendrickson, 1995.

MacDowell, D. M. *The Law in Classical Athens*. Ithaca: Cornell University Press, 1978.

MacMullen, Ramsay. *Paganism in the Roman Empire*. New Haven: Yale University Press, 1981.

———. *The Second Church: Popular Christianity A.D. 200–400*. Atlanta: Society of Biblical Literature, 2009.

Madelung, W. "al-Kharrāz, Abū Sa'īd Aḥmad b. 'Īsā." In *EI*² 4 (1978), 1083–84.

Maier, Johann. *Jesus von Nazareth in der talmudische Überlieferung*. Darmstadt: Wissenschaftliche Buchgesellschaft, 1978.

Malbon, Elizabeth Struthers. "Disciples/Crowds/Whoever: Markan Characters and Readers." *Novum Testamentum* 28.2 (1986), 104–30.

Manser, Anselm. "Der hl. Ambrosius von Mailand über Lettern aus Zedernholz." *Archiv für Kulturgeschichte* 12 (1916), 401.

Maqāmāt al-Ḥarīrī. Illustrated by Y. al-Wasiti. 2 volumes. Facsimile edition. London: Touch@rt, 2003.

Maraval, Pierre. *Lieux saints et pèlerinages d'Orient: Histoire et géographie des origines à la conquête arabe*. Dictionnaire des lieux saints. Paris: Cerf, 1985. Second ed., 2004.

Marcus, Joel. "Jewish Christianity." In *The Cambridge History of Christianity: Origins to Constantine*, ed. M. M. Mitchell and F. M. Young, 87–102. Cambridge: Cambridge University Press, 2006.

Marcuse, Harold. "Collective Memory: Definitions." http://www.history.ucsb.edu/faculty/marcuse/classes/201/CollectiveMemoryDefinitions.htm (accessed July 11, 2013).

Maricq, R. A. "Notes philologiques." *Byzantion* 22 (1952), 360–68.

Marinescu, Constantine A., Sarah E. Cox, and Rudolf Wachter. "Paideia's Children: Childhood Education on a Group of Late Antique Mosaics." In *Constructions of Childhood,* ed. A. Cohen and J. B. Rutter, 101–14.

Markschies, Christoph. "Valentinian Gnosticism: Toward the Anatomy of a School." In *The Nag Hammadi Library after Fifty Years: Proceedings of the 1995 Society of Biblical Literature Commemoration,* ed. J. D. Turner and A. McGuire, 401–38. Leiden and New York: Brill, 1997.

———. *Valentinus Gnosticus? Untersuchungen zur valentinianischen Gnosis mit einem Kommentar zu den Fragmenten Valentins.* Tübingen: Mohr Siebeck, 1992.

Marmorstein, A. "Die Quellen des neuen Jeremia-Apocryphons." *Zeitschrift für die Neutestamentliche Wissenschaft und die Kunde der Älteren Kirche* 27.2 (1928), 327–37.

Marrou, Henri I. *Histoire de l'éducation dans l'Antiquité.* Paris: Seuil, 1948. English trans.: *A History of Education in Antiquity,* trans. G. Lamb. New York: Sheed and Ward, 1956.

Martens, John W. "'Do Not Sexually Abuse Children': The Language of Early Christian Sexual Ethics." In *Children in Late Ancient Christianity,* ed. C. B. Horn and R. R. Phenix, 227–54.

Martin, Dale B. *Inventing Superstition: From the Hippocratics to the Christians.* Cambridge, Mass.: Harvard University Press, 2004.

Martinez, David. *P.Michigan XVI: A Greek Love Charm from Egypt (P.Mich. 757).* Atlanta: Scholars, 1991.

Martyn, J. Louis. "Christ, the Elements of the Cosmos, and the Law in Galatians." In *The Social World of the First Christians: Essays in Honor of Wayne A. Meeks,* ed. L. M. White and O. L. Yarbrough, 16–39. Minneapolis: Fortress, 1995.

———. *Galatians.* The Anchor Bible. New York: Doubleday, 1997.

———. *History and Theology in the Fourth Gospel.* New York: Harper and Row, 1968. Third ed.: Louisville: Westminster/John Knox, 2003.

Masood, Ehsad. *Science and Islam: A History.* Thriplow: Icon, 2009.

Massey, Keith. "Mysterious Letters." In *The Encyclopaedia of the Qur'ān,* volume 3, 471–76. Leiden: Brill, 2003.

Mauss, Marcel. "Les techniques du corps." *Journal de psychologie normale et pathologique* 32.3–4 (1935), 271–93. Reprinted in Mauss, *Sociologie et anthropologie,* 365–85. Paris: Presses Universitaires de France, 1950. Fifth ed., 1973. English translation in Mauss, *Sociology and Psychology: Essays.* Trans. B. Brewster, 97–123. London and Boston: Routledge and Kegan Paul, 1979.

Mayall, Berry. *Towards a Sociology for Childhood: Thinking from Children's Lives.* Oxford: Open University Press, 2002.

McCartney, E. S. "Notes on Reading and Praying Audibly." *Classical Philology* 43 (1948), 184–87.

McGinn, T. "Widows, Orphans, and Social History." *Journal of Roman Archaeology* 12 (1999), 617–32.

McGuire, Anne M. "Valentinus and the *Gnostike Hairesis:* An Investigation of Valentinus' Position in the History of Gnosticism." Ph.D dissertation, Yale University, 1983.

McKenzie, Judith. *The Architecture of Alexandria and Egypt, c. 300 B.C to A.D. 700.* New Haven: Yale University Press, 2007.

McKitterick, Rosamond, ed. *The Uses of Literacy in Early Mediaeval Europe.* Cambridge: Cambridge University Press, 1990.

McKnight, Edgar V. *What Is Form Criticism?* Philadelphia: Fortress, 1969.

McNeil, Brian. "Jesus and the Alphabet." *Journal of Theological Studies* 27.1 (1976), 126–28.

McWilliam, Janette. "Children among the Dead: The Influence of Urban Life on the Commemoration of Children on Tombstone Inscriptions." In *Childhood, Class, and Kin in the Roman World,* ed. S. Dixon, 74–98.

Mead, G. R. S. *Did Jesus Live 100 B.C.?: An Enquiry into the Talmud Jesus Stories, the Toldoth Jeschu, and Some Curious Statements of Epiphanius.* London: Theosophical Publishing Society, 1903.

Meier, Friz. *Essays on Islamic Piety and Mysticism.* Leiden: Brill, 1999.

Meijer, P. A. *Stoic Theology: Proofs for the Existence of the Cosmic God and of the Traditional Gods.* Delft: Eburon, 2007.

Melugin, Roy F. "Recent Form Criticism Revisited in an Age of Reader Response." In *The Changing Face of Form Criticism for the Twenty-First Century,* ed. M. A. Sweeney and E. Ben Zvi, 46–64. Grand Rapids, Mich.: Eerdmans, 2003.

Melvin-Koushki, Matthew S. "The Quest for a Universal Science: The Occult Philosophy of Ṣā'in al-Dīn Turka Iṣfahānī (1369–1432) and Intellectual Millenarianism in Early Timurid Iran." Ph.D. dissertation, Yale University, 2012.

Merker, Gloria S. *The Sanctuary of Demeter and Kore: Terracotta Figurines of the Classical, Hellenistic, and Roman Periods.* Corinth 18.4. Princeton: American School of Classical Studies at Athens, 2000.

Mertens, Michelle, ed. *Les alchimistes grecs. Tome IV.1: Zosime de Panopolis, Mémoires authentiques.* Second ed. Ed. R. Halleux. Paris: Les Belles Lettres, 2002.

———. "Project for a New Edition of Zosimus of Panopolis." In *Alchemy Revisited: Proceedings of the International Conference on the History of Alchemy at the University of Groningen, 17–19 April 1989,* ed. Z. R. W. M. von Martels, 121–26. Leiden and New York: Brill, 1990.

Metzger, Bruce. *The Canon of the New Testament: Its Origin, Development, and Significance.* Oxford: Clarendon; New York: Oxford University Press, 1987.

———. *A Textual Commentary on the Greek New Testament.* Second ed. Stuttgart: Deutsche Bibelgesellschaft, 1992; repr. 1994.

Meyer, Arnold. "Erzählung des Thomas." In *Neutestamentliche Apokryphen,* ed. E. Hennecke, 63–67.

———. "Kindheitserzählung des Thomas." In *Handbuch zu den neutestamentlichen Apokryphen,* ed. E. Hennecke, 132–42.

Meyer, Elizabeth A. *Legitimacy and Law in the Roman World:* Tabulae *in Roman Belief and Practice.* Cambridge: Cambridge University Press, 2004.

Meyer, Marvin W., and Richard Smith, eds., *Ancient Christian Magic: Coptic Texts of Ritual Power.* San Francisco: HarperSanFrancisco, 1994; repr. Princeton: Princeton University Press, 1999.

Meyerhof, Max. "New Light on Ḥunain Ibn Isḥāq and His Period." *Isis* 8 (1926), 685–724.

———. "Les versions syriaques et arabes des écrits Galéniques." *Byzantion* 3 (1926–1927), 33–51.

Michaelis, W. *Die apocryphen Schriften zum Neuen Testament.* Sammlung Dieterich 129. Bremen: Schünemann, 1956. Third ed. 1962.

Mijallī, Nasīm. *Ḥunayn ibn Isḥāq wa ʿaṣr al-tarjama al-ʿarabiyya* (*Ḥunayn ibn Isḥāq and the Age of Arabic Translation*). Cairo: al-Majlis al-aʿlā li-l-thaqāfa, 2006.

Miller, Anne Pauline. "Studies in Early Sicilian Epigraphy: An Opisthographic Lead Tablet." Ph.D. dissertation, University of North Carolina at Chapel Hill, 1973.

Miller, Stephen G. *Ancient Greek Athletics.* New Haven: Yale University Press, 2004.

———. *Arete: Greek Sports from Ancient Sources.* Third expanded ed. Berkeley: University of California Press, 2004.

Miller, T. *The Orphans of Byzantium: Child Welfare in the Christian Empire.* Washington, D.C.: Catholic University of America Press, 2003.

Millet, Paul. "Patronage and Its Avoidance in Classical Athens." In *Patronage in Ancient Society,* ed. A. Wallace-Hadrill, 15–48. London: Routledge, 1989.

Mills, Jean, and Richard Mills. *Childhood Studies: A Reader in Perspectives of Childhood.* London: Routledge, 2000.

Mimouni, Simon Claude. *Le Judéo-christianisme ancien: Essais historiques.* Patrimoines. Paris: Cerf, 1998.

———. "Pour une definition nouvelle du judéo-christianisme ancien." *New Testament Studies* 38 (1992), 171–82.

———. "Les Vies de la Vierge: État de la question." *Apocrypha* 5 (1994), 211–48.

Mimouni, Simon Claude, and F. Stanley Jones, eds. *Le Judéo-christianisme dans tous ses états: Acts du Colloque de Jérusalem, 6–10 Juillet 1998.* Paris: Cerf, 2001.

Mingana, A. *Catalogue of the Mingana Collection of Manuscripts. Volume 1: Syriac and Garshuni Manuscripts.* Cambridge: W. Heffer and Sons, 1933.

Mingarelli, Giovanni Luigi. "De Apocrypho Thomae Evangelio . . . epistola." In *Nuova raccolta d'opuscoli scientifici e filologici,* ed. A. Calogierà, volume 12, 73–155. Venice: S. Occhi, 1764.

Mitchell, Christopher W. *The Meaning of BRK "to bless" in the Old Testament.* Atlanta: Scholars, 1987.

Miura-Stange, Anna. *Celsus und Origenes.* Giessen: A. Töpelmann, 1926.

Moore, Stephen D., and Yvonne Sherwood. "Biblical Studies 'after' Theory: Onwards Towards the Past. Part One: After 'after Theory' and Other Apocalyptic Conceits." *Biblical Interpretation* 18 (2010), 1–27.

———. "Biblical Studies 'after' Theory: Onwards Towards the Past. Part Two: The Secret Vices of the Biblical God." *Biblical Interpretation* 18.2 (2010), 87–113.

———. "Biblical Studies 'after' Theory: Onwards Towards the Past. Part Three: Theory in the First and Second Waves." *Biblical Interpretation* 18.3 (2010), 191–225.

———. *The Invention of the Biblical Scholar: A Critical Manifesto.* Minneapolis: Fortress, 2011.

Moraldi, L. *Nascita e infanzia di Gesù nei più antichi codici cristiani.* Milan: Mondadori, 1989.

———. *Vangelo arabo apocrifo dell'apostolo Giovanni da un Manoscritto della Biblioteca Ambrosiana.* Milan: Jaca, 1991.

Morenz, S. *Die Geschichte von Joseph dem Zimmermann.* TU 56. Berlin and Leipzig: Akademie, 1951.

Morgan, J. R. "Reader and Audiences in the *Aithiopika* of Heliodorus." In *Groningen Colloquia on the Novel,* ed. H. Hofmann, volume 4, 85–103. Groningen: Egbert Forsten, 1991.

Morgan, Kathryn A. "Inspiration, Recollection, and *Mimēsis* in Plato's *Phaedrus.*" In *Ancient Models of Mind: Studies in Human and Divine Rationality,* ed. D. Sedley and A. W. Nightingale, 45–64. Cambridge: Cambridge University Press, 2010.

Moricca, V. "Un nuovo testo dell 'Evangelo di Bartolomeo.'" *Revue Biblique,* n.s. 18 (=30) (1921), 481–516, and n.s. 19 (=31) (1922), 20–30.

Mounteer, C. A. "Roman Childhood, 200 B.C. to A.D. 600." *Journal of Psychohistory* 14.3 (1987), 233–56.

Mourad, Suleiman A. "From Hellenism to Christianity and Islam: The Origin of the Palm-Tree Story concerning Mary and Jesus in the Gospel of Pseudo-Matthew and the Qur'ān." *Oriens Christianus* 86 (2002), 206–16.

———. "On the Qur'ānic Stories about Mary and Jesus." *Bulletin of the Royal Institute for Inter-Faith Studies* 1.2 (1999), 13–24.

Mournet, Terence C. *Oral Tradition and Literary Dependency: Variability and Stability in the Synoptic Tradition and Q.* WUNT (2. Reihe) 195. Tübingen: Mohr Siebeck, 2005.

Müller, Iso. "Vom Baptisterium zum Taufstein: Missionierung Churrätiens." In *Churrätisches und st. gallisches Mittelalter: Festschrift für Otto P. Cavadetscher zu seinem fünfundsechzigsten Geburtstag,* ed. H. Mauer, 23–35. Sigmaringen: J. Thorbecke, 1984.

Murbach, Ernst. *The Painted Romanesque Ceiling of St. Martin in Zillis.* Ed. P. Heman. New York and Washington: Frederick A. Praeger, 1967.

Museo di Antichità Collezioni Archeologiche. *Da Roma per gioco: Giochi e giocattoli nell'antica Roma.* Rome: Electa, 2000.

Mustakallio, Katariina, Jussi Hanska, Hanna-Leena Sainio, and Ville Vuolanto, eds. *Hoping for Continuity: Childhood, Education and Death in Antiquity and the Middle Ages.* Acta Instituti Romani Finlandiae 33. Rome: Institutum Romanum Finlandiae, 2005.

Mustakallio, Katariina, and Christian Laes, eds. *Dark Side of Childhood in Late Antiquity and the Middle Ages: Unwanted, Disabled and Lost.* Oxford and Oakville, Conn.: Oxbow, 2011.

Myers, Alicia D. "Prosopopoetics and Conflict: Speech and Expectations in John 8." *Biblica* 92 (2011), 580–96.

Myss, Walter. *Kirchendecke von St. Martin in Zillis: Bildwelt als Weltbild.* Beuron: Beuroner Kunstverlag, 1965.

Najman, Hindy. "Configuring the Text in Biblical Studies." In *A Teacher for All Generations: Essays in Honor of James C. VanderKam, Volume One,* ed. E. Mason et al., 3–22. Supplements to the Journal for the Study of Judaism. Leiden: Brill, 2011.

———. "The Idea of Biblical Genre: From Discourse to Constellation." In *Prayer and Poetry in the Dead Sea Scrolls and Related Literature: Essays in Honor of Eileen Schuller on the Occasion of Her 65th Birthday,* ed. J. Penner, K. M. Penner, and C. Wassen, 307–22. Leiden: Brill, 2012.

———. "Traditionary Processes and Textual Unity in 4 Ezra." In *4 Ezra and 2 Baruch: Reconstruction after the Fall,* ed. M. Henze and G. Boccaccini, with J. M. Zurawski. Leiden: Brill, forthcoming.

Naveh, J., and S. Shaked. *Amulets and Magic Bowls: Aramaic Incantations of Late Antiquity.* Jerusalem: Hebrew University, Magnes Press; Leiden: Brill, 1985.

Nay, Marc Antoni. *St. Martin's Church in Zillis.* Berne: Society for the History of Swiss Art, 2008.

Neils, Jenifer, and John H. Oakley, eds. *Coming of Age in Ancient Greece: Images of Childhood from the Classical Past.* New Haven and London: Yale University Press, 2003.

Neusner, Jacob. "Zacchaeus/Zakkai." *Harvard Theological Review* 57 (1964), 57–9.

Newby, Gordon. *The Making of the Last Prophet: A Reconstruction of the Earliest Biography of Muhammad.* Columbia: University of South Carolina Press, 1989.

Newby, Zahra. *Greek Athletics in the Roman World: Victory and Virtue.* Oxford: Oxford University Press, 2005.

Newman, Hillel I. "The Death of Jesus in the *Toledot Yeshu* Literature." *Journal of Theological Studies* 50.1 (1999), 59–79.

Nicolas, Michel. *Études sur les évangiles apocryphes.* Paris: Michel Lévy Frères, 1866.

Nietzsche, Friedrich. "Homer and Classical Philology" (inaugural lecture delivered at Basel University, May 1869). In *The Complete Works of Friedrich Nietzsche,* volume 3, 145–70, ed. O. Levy, trans. John McFarland Kennedy. Edinburgh: Foulis, 1910.

Nijf, Onno van. "Athletics and *Paideia:* Festivals and Physical Education in the World of the Second Sophistic." In *Paideia: The World of the Second Sophistic,* ed. Barbara E. Borg, 203–28. Berlin and New York: Walter de Gruyter, 2004.

Nilsson, Martin Persson. *Geschichte der griechischen Religion.* Volume 1. Munich: Beck, 1967.

———. *The Minoan-Mycenaean Religion and Its Survival in Greek Religion.* Skrifter utg. av. Kungl. Humanistiska vetenskapssamfundet i Lund. Lund: C. W. K. Gleerup, 1950.

Noble, Samuel. "Muslim-Christian Polemic in 7th/13th Century Egypt." Ph.D. dissertation, Yale University, forthcoming.

Nöldeke, Theodor, F. Schwally, G. Bergsträsser, and O. Pretzl. *Geschichte des Qorans.* 3 volumes. Leipzig: T. Weicher, 1909–1938.

Nongbri, Brent. *Before Religion: A History of a Modern Concept.* New Haven: Yale University Press, 2012.

Nora, Pierre. "Between Memory and History: Les Lieux de Mémoire." *Representations* 26 (1989), 7–24.

———. *Les lieux de mémoire.* 3 volumes. Paris: Gallimard, 1984–1992. English trans.: *Realms of Memory: The Construction of the French Past.* 3 volumes. Trans. A. Goldhammer. New York: Columbia University Press, 1996–1998.

Norden, Eduard. *Die antike Kunstprosa.* Volume 1. Leipzig and Berlin: B. J. Teubner, 1898; fourth ed., 1923.

Norelli, Enrico. "Gesù ride: Gesù, il maestro di scuola e i passeri: Le sorprese di un testo apocrifo trascurato." In *Mysterium regni ministerium verbi (Mc 4,11; At 6,4): Scritti in onore di mons: Vittorio Fusco,* ed. Ettore Franco, Supplementi alla Rivista Biblica 38, 653–84. Bologna: EDB, 2001.

Norman, N. J. "Death and Burial of Roman Children: The Case of the Yasmina Cemetery at Carthage—Part I, Setting the Stage." *Mortality* 7.3 (2002), 302–23.

———. "Death and Burial of Roman Children: The Case of the Yasmina Cemetery at Carthage—Part II, The Archaeological Evidence." *Mortality* 8.1 (2003), 36–47.

Norton, Andrews. *The Evidences of the Genuineness of the Gospels.* Abridged ed. Boston: American Unitarian Association, 1867.

Nyberg, H. S. "Några utvecklingslinjer i Muhammads religiöse förkunnelse." *Religion och Bibel* 4 (1945), 30–40.

O'Leary, De Lacy. *How Greek Science Passed to the Arabs.* London and Boston: Routledge and Kegan Paul, 1949; repr. 1979.

Oakley, John H. "Death and the Child." In *Coming of Age in Ancient Greece,* ed. J. Neils and J. H. Oakley, 163–94.

Ogden, Daniel. "Binding Spells: Curse Tablets and Voodoo Dolls in the Greek and Roman Worlds." In *Witchcraft and Magic in Europe: Ancient Greece and Rome,* ed. Valerie Flint, Richard Gordon, Georg Luck, and Daniel Ogden, 3–90. London: Athlone, 1999.

Olick, Jeffrey K. "Collective Memory: The Two Cultures." *Sociological Theory* 17.3 (1999), 333–48.

Olick, Jeffrey, and Daniel Levy. "Collective Memory and Cultural Constraint: Holocaust Myth and Rationality in German Politics." *American Sociological Review* 62.6 (1997), 921–36.

Olrik, Axel. "Epic Laws of Folk Narrative." In *The Study of Folklore,* ed. A. Dundes, 129–41. Englewood Cliffs, N.J.: Prentice-Hall, 1965.

———. *Principles for Oral Narrative Research.* Trans. K. Wolf and J. Jensen. Bloomington: Indiana University Press, 1992.

Orfali, Bilal, ed. *In the Shadow of Arabic: The Centrality of Language to Arabic Culture: Studies Presented to Ramzi Baalbaki on the Occasion of His Sixtieth Birthday.* Leiden: Brill, 2011.

Otero, Aurelio de Santos. *Das kirchenslavische Evangelium des Thomas.* PTS 6. Berlin: De Gruyter, 1967.

Ousterhout, R., ed. *The Blessings of Pilgrimage.* Urbana and Chicago: University of Illinois Press, 1990.

Overbeck, Franz. *Kürze Erklärung der Apostelgeschichte.* Leipzig: Hirzel, 1870.

Oyen, Geert van. "Rereading the Rewriting of the Biblical Traditions in the Infancy Gospel of Thomas (*Paidika*)". In *Infancy Gospels: Stories and Identities*, ed. C. Clivaz et al., 482–505.

Paget, James Carleton. "The Definition of the Terms *Jewish Christian* and *Jewish Christianity* in the History of Research." In *Jewish Believers in Jesus*, ed. O. Skarsaune and R. Hvalvik, 22–52.

———. *Jews, Christians and Jewish Christians in Antiquity.* Tübingen: Mohr Siebeck, 2010.

Papaconstantinou, Arietta. "Child or Monk? An Unedited Story Attributed to John Moschos in Paris Coislin 257." *Bulletin of the American Society of Papyrologists* 45 (2008), 169–81.

———. "Introduction: *Homo Byzantinus* in the Making." In *Becoming Byzantine,* ed. A. Papaconstantinou and A.-M. Talbot, 1–14.

———. "Notes sur les actes de donation d'enfants au monastère de Saint-Phoibammon." *Journal of Juristic Papyrology* 32 (2002), 83–105.

———. "Theia oikonomia: Les actes thébains de donation d'enfants ou la gestion monastique de la pénurie." In *Mélanges Gilbert Dagron,* ed. V. Déroche, 511–26. Paris: Association des Amis du Centre d'histoire et civilisation de Byzance, 2002.

Papaconstantinou, Arietta, and Alice-Mary Talbot, eds. *Becoming Byzantine: Children and Childhood in Byzantium.* Washington, D.C.: Dumbarton Oaks Research Library and Collection, and Harvard University Press, 2009.

Parker, Holt N. "Books and Reading Latin Poetry." In *Ancient Literacies,* ed. W. A. Johnson and H. N. Parker, 186–231.

Parrot, A. *Malédictions et violations de tombes.* Paris: P. Geuthner, 1939.

Parry, Benita. "Problems in Current Theories of Colonial Discourse." In *Post-colonial Studies Reader,* ed. B. Ashcroft, G. Griffiths, and H. Tiffin, 36–44.

Patimo, Valeria Maria. "Una seduta deliberante nel Satyricon (101,6–103,2)." In *Il Romanzo latino: Modelli e tradizione letteraria: Atti della VII Giornata Ghisleriana di Filologia classica (Pavia, 11–12 ottobre 2007),* ed. F. Gasti, 47–60. Pavia: Collegio Ghislieri, 2009.

Paulissen, Lucie. "Jésus à l'école: L'enseignement dans l'*Évangile de l'Enfance selon Thomas." Apocrypha* 14 (2003), 153–75.

———. "Jésus enfant divin: Processus de reconnaissance dans *l'Évangile de l'Enfance selon Thomas." Revue de philosophie ancienne* 22.1 (2004), 17–28.

Paxson, James J. *The Poetics of Personification.* Cambridge: Cambridge University Press, 1994.

Pearce, J. "Infants, Cemeteries and Communities in the Roman Provinces." In *TRAC 2000: Proceedings of the Tenth Annual Theoretical Roman Archaeology Conference,* ed. G. Davies, A. Gardner, and K. Lockyear, 125–42. Oxford: Oxbow, 2001.

Pearce, Philip. "Route Maps: A Study of Travellers' Perceptions of a Section of Countryside." *Journal of Environmental Psychology* 1 (1981), 141–55.

Pease, A. S. "Auspicium." In *The Oxford Classical Dictionary,* ed. N. G. L. Hammond and H. H. Scullard, 154. Oxford: Clarendon, 1970.

Peeters, F. E. *Aristoteles Arabus: The Oriental Translations and Commentaries on the Aristotelian Corpus.* Leiden: Brill, 1968.

Peeters, Paul. *Évangiles apocryphes.* 2 volumes. Paris: A. Picard, 1914–1924.

Pelling, Christopher. "Childhood and Personality in Greek Biography." In *Characterization and Individuality in Greek Literature,* ed. C. Pelling, 213–44. Oxford: Clarendon, 1990.

Peppard, Michael. *The Son of God in the Roman World: Divine Sonship in its Social and Political Context.* New York: Oxford University Press, 2011.

Percy, William A., III. "Reconsiderations about Greek Homosexualities." In *Same-Sex Desire and Love in Greco-Roman Antiquity and in the Classical Tradition of the West,* ed. B. C. Verstraete and V. Provencal, 13–63. Binghampton, N.Y.: Harrington Park, 2005.

Perdrizet, Paul. "Une inscription d'Antioche qui reproduit un oracle d'Alexandre d'Abonotichos." *Comptes rendus de l'Académie des inscriptions et belles-lettres* 47.1 (1903), 62–66.

Perez, Gonzalo Aranda. "Joseph the Carpenter." In *The Coptic Encyclopedia,* volume 5, 1371–74. New York: Macmillan, 1991.

Perkins, Judith. *The Suffering Self: Pain and Narrative Representation in the Early Christian Era.* London and New York: Routledge, 1995.

Perrot, Charles. "Les récits d'enfance dans la Haggada antérieure au IIe siècle de notre ère." *Recherches de science religieuse* 55 (1967), 481–518.

Perry, B. E. *The Ancient Romances: A Literary-Historical Account of their Origins.* Berkeley: University of California Press, 1967.

Pervo, Richard. "The Ancient Novel Becomes Christian." In *The Novel in the Ancient World,* second ed., ed. G. Schmeling, 685–711.

———. *Profit with Delight: The Literary Genre of the Acts of the Apostles.* Philadelphia: Fortress, 1987.

Peters, G. "Offering Sons to God in the Monastery: Child Oblation, Monastic Benevolence, and the Cistercian Order in the Middle Ages." *Cistercian Studies Quarterly* 38.3 (2003), 285–95.

Pfeiffer, Charles F. *An Introduction to the Apocryphal Books of the Old and New Testament.* Grand Rapids, Mich.: Baker, 1964.

Pfitzner, Victor C. *Paul and the Agon Motif: Traditional Athletic Imagery in the Pauline Literature.* Supplements to Novum Testamentum 16. Leiden: Brill, 1967.

Pfuhl, Ernst, and Hans Möbius. *Die ostgriechischen Grabreliefs.* Mainz am Rhein: Zabern, 1977.

Philippart, G. "Fragments palimpsestes latins du Vindobonensis 563 (Ve siècle?): Évangile selon S. Matthieu, Évangile de Nicodème, Évangile de l'enfance selon Thomas." *Analecta Bollandiana* 90 (1972), 391–411.

Pichler, Karl. *Streit um das Christentum: Der Angriff des Kelsos und die Antwort des Origenes.* Regensburger Studien zur Theologie 23. Frankfurt am Main and Bern: Peter D. Lang, 1980.

Pilch, J. J. "'Beat his ribs while he is young' (Sir 30:12): A Window on the Mediterranean World." *Biblical Theology Bulletin* 23 (1993), 101–13.

Pinch, Geraldine. *Magic in Ancient Egypt.* Austin: University of Texas Press, 1995.

Pingree, D. "Banū Mūsā." In *Encyclopaedia Iranica,* volume 3.7, 716–17. London and Boston: Routledge and Kegan Paul, 1982–2011.

———. "'Ilm al-hay'a." In *EI*² 5 (1986), 1135–38.

———. "Ḳirān." In *EI*² 5 (1986), 130–31.

Pitarakis, Brigitte. "The Material Culture of Childhood in Byzantium." In *Becoming Byzantine: Children and Childhood in Byzantium,* ed. A. Papaconstantinou and A.-M. Talbot, 167–252.

Plati, Marina. *Playing in Ancient Greece . . . with Lysis and Timarete.* Athens: N. P. Goulandris Foundation-Museum of Cycladic Art, 1999.

Poeschel, Erwin. "Die Baugeschichte von St. Martin in Zillis." *Zeitschrift für schweizerische Archaeologie und Kunstgeschichte* 1.1 (1939), 21–31, and pls. 1–8.

———. *Die romanischen Deckengemälde von Zillis.* Erlenback-Zürich: Eugen Rentsch, 1941.

Poliakoff, Michael B. *Combat Sports in the Ancient World: Competition, Violence, and Culture.* New Haven: Yale University Press, 1987.

Pollard, John. *Birds in Greek Life and Myth*. London: Thames and Hudson, 1978.

Pomeroy, Sarah B. *Families in Classical and Hellenistic Greece: Representations and Realities*. Oxford: Clarendon, 1997.

Pons, Joseph. *Recherches sur les apocryphes du Nouveau Testament: Thèse historique et critique*. Montaubon: Imprimerie de Forestié, 1850.

Poplin, François. "Les jeux d'osselets antiques." In *Jeux et jouets dans l'Antiquité et au Moyen Age, Dossiers de l'Archéologie* 168 (1992), 46–47.

Pormann, Peter E., and Emilie Savage-Smith. *Medieval Islamic Medicine*. Edinburgh: Edinburgh University Press, 2007.

Pratt, Mary Louise. *Imperial Eyes: Travel Writing and Transculturation*. London: Routledge, 1992.

Preisendanz, Karl. "Die griechischen und lateinischen Zaubertafeln." *Archiv für Papyrusforschung* 9 (1930), 119–54, and 11 (1933), 153–64.

Price, Robert M. "Implied Reader Response and the Evolution of Genres: Transitional Stages Between the Ancient Novels and the Apocryphal Acts." *Hervormde Teologiese Studies* 53.4 (1997), 909–38.

Pritz, Ray. *Nazarene Jewish Christianity: From the End of the New Testament Period until Its Disappearance in the Fourth Century*. Jerusalem: Hebrew University, Magnes Press; Leiden: Brill, 1988.

Provera, Mario E., ed. *Il Vangelo arabo dell'infanzia secondo il Ms. Laurenziano orientale (n. 387)*. Jerusalem: Franciscan, 1973.

Pufall, Peter B., and Richard P. Unsworth, eds. *Rethinking Childhood*. New Brunswick, N.J.: Rutgers University Press, 2004.

Quirke, Stephen. *Egyptian Literature 1800 BC: Questions and Readings*. London: Golden House Publications, 2004.

Qvortrup, Jens, William A. Corsaro, and Michael-Sebastian Honig, eds. *The Palgrave Handbook of Childhood Studies*. Basingstoke, Hampshire: Palgrave Macmillan, 2009.

Ragep, F. Jamil. "Astronomy." In *Encyclopaedia of Islam Three*, ed. G. Krämer, D. Matrine, J. Nawas, and E. Rowson. Leiden: Brill, 2011. Brill Online. Yale University. 20 August 2012, at http://www.brillonline.nl/subscriber/uid=1850/entry?entry=ei3_COM-22652.

Rahn, Johann Rudolf. "Die biblischen Deckengemälde in der Kirche von Zillis im Kanton Graubünden." In *Mittheilungen der antiquarischen Gesellschaft in Zürich*, volume 70, 103–21. Zürich: S. Höhr, 1872.

Ramsey, W. M. *The Bearing of Recent Discovery on the Trustworthiness of the New Testament*. London and New York: Hodder and Stoughton, 1915.

Rāshid, Rushdī. *Les mathématiques infinitésimales du IXe au XIe siècle*. Volume 1. London: al-Furqān Islamic Heritage Foundation, 1993.

Rawson, Beryl. *Children and Childhood in Roman Italy*. Oxford: Oxford University Press, 2003.

———. "Death, Burial, and Commemoration of Children in Roman Italy." In *Early Christian Families in Context*, ed. D. L. Balch and C. Osiek, 277–97.

———. "Education: The Romans and Us." *Antichthon* 33 (1999), 81–98.

———. "The Future of Childhood Studies in Classics and Ancient History." In *Hoping for Continuity*, ed. K. Mustakallio et al., 1–11.

———. "Representations of Roman Children and Childhood." *Antichthon* 31 (1997), 74–95.

Rawson, Beryl, ed. *A Companion to Families in the Greek and Roman Worlds.* Chichester, U.K., and Malden, Mass.: Wiley-Blackwell, 2011.

———. *The Family in Ancient Rome: New Perspectives.* London: Croom Helm, 1986.

———. *Marriage, Divorce, and Children in Ancient Rome.* Canberra: Humanities Research Center; Oxford: Clarendon Press; New York: Oxford University Press, 1991.

Rawson, Beryl, and Paul Weaver, eds. *The Roman Family in Italy: Status, Sentiment, Space.* Canberra: Humanities Research Centre; New York and Oxford: Clarendon Press, 1997.

Rebell, Walter. *Neutestamentliche Apokryphen und apostolische Väter.* Munich: Kaiser, 1992.

Redin, M. E. K. "The Miniatures of the Apocryphal Arabic Gospel of Christ's Infancy in the Biblioteca Laurenziana in Florence" (in Russian). In *Memoirs of the Imperial Russian Archaeological Society* (*Zapiski*) 7.1.2 (1895), 55–71.

Reeder, Ellen D. "Some Hellenistic Terracottas and Sculpture in Asia Minor." In *The Coroplast's Art: Greek Terracottas of the Hellenistic World,* ed. J. P. Uhlenbrock, 81–88. College Art Gallery, The College at New Paltz, State University of New York. New Rochelle, N.Y.: Aristide D. Caratzas, 1990.

Reiner, Elchanan. "From Joshua to Jesus: The Transformation of a Biblical Story to a Local Myth: A Chapter in the Religious Life of the Galilean Jew." In *Sharing the Sacred: Religious Contacts and Conflicts in the Holy Land, First–Fifteenth Centuries CE,* ed. Arieh Kofsky and Guy G. Stroumsa, 248–69. Jerusalem: Yad Izhak Ben Zvi, 1998.

Reinhartz, Adele. "The Gospel of John: How the 'Jews' Became Part of the Plot." In *Jesus, Judaism and Christian Anti-Judaism,* ed. P. Frederiksen and A. Reinhartz, 99–116. Lousiville: Westminster/John Knox, 2002.

———. "The Johannine Community and Its Jewish Neighbors: A Reappraisal." In *"What is John?" Volume 2, Literary and Social Readings of the Fourth Gospel,* ed. F. F. Segovia, 111–38. Atlanta: Scholars, 1998.

Renard, John. *Friends of God: Islamic Images of Piety, Commitment, and Servanthood.* Berkeley: University of California Press, 2008.

Rhoads, David. "Performance Criticism: An Emerging Methodology in Second Testament Studies—Part I." *Biblical Theology Bulletin* 36 (2006), 118–33.

———. "Performance Criticism: An Emerging Methodology in Second Testament Studies—Part II." *Biblical Theology Bulletin* 36 (2006), 164–84.

Ribbeck, Otto. *Kolax: Eine ethologische Studie.* Abhandlungen der philologisch-historischen Klasse der Königlich Sächsischen Gesellschaft der Wissenschaften 9.1. Leipzig: S. Hirzel, 1884.

Riché, P. "Réflexions sur l'histoire de l'éducation dans le Haut Moyen Âge (Ve–XIe siècles." *Histoire de l'éducation* 50 (1991), 17–38. Volume title: *Éducations médiévales: L'enfance, l'école, l'Église en Occident (VIe–XVe siècles),* ed. J. Verger.

Richter, Gerhard. *Afterness: Figures of Following in Modern Thought and Aesthetics.* New York: Columbia University Press, 2011.

Richter, Tonio S. "What's in a Story? Cultural Narratology and Coptic Child Donation Documents." *Journal of Juristic Papyrology* 35 (2005), 237–64.

Ricotti, Eugenia Salza Prina. *Giochi e giocattoli.* Vita e costumi dei Romani antichi 18. Rome: Edizioni Quasar, 1995.

Riginos, A. S. *Platonica: The Anecdotes Concerning the Life and Writings of Plato.* CSCT 3, 41–49. Leiden: Brill, 1976.

Rissi, M. "'Die Juden im Johannesevangelium." *ANRW* 2.26.3 (1996) 2099–2141.

Ritner, Robert K. *The Mechanics of Ancient Egyptian Magical Practice.* Studies in Ancient Oriental Civilization, no. 54. Chicago: Oriental Institute of the University of Chicago, 1993.

Ritter, Helmut. *Ocean of the Soul: Man, the World and God in the Stories of Farīd al-Dīn 'Aṭṭār.* Trans. J. O'Kane. Leiden: Brill, 2003. Originally published in German under the title *Meer der Seele.* Leiden: Brill, 1955.

Robb, K. *Literacy and Paideia in Ancient Greece.* Oxford: Oxford University Press, 1994.

Robbins, E. I. "Nereids with Golden Distaffs: Pindar, *Nem.* 5." *Quaderni Urbinati di Cultura Classica* 54 (1987), 25–33.

Robert, L. *Études épigraphiques et philologiques.* Paris: H. Champion, 1938.

———. "Malédictions funéraires grecques." *Comptes rendus des séances: Académie des inscriptions et belles-lettres* 122.2 (1978), 241–89.

Robins, R. H. "Dionysius Thrax and the Western Grammatical Tradition." *Transactions of the Philological Society* 56.1 (1957), 67–106.

Robinson, Neal. *Christ in Islam and Christianity: The Representation of Jesus in the Qur'ān and the Classical Muslim Commentaries.* London: Macmillan, 1991.

———. "Creating Birds from Clay: A Miracle of Jesus in the Qur'ān and Classical Muslim Exegesis." *Muslim World* 79.1 (1989), 1–13.

Romiopoulou, Katerina. *Ellēnorōmaïka Glypta tou Ethnikou Archaeologikou Mouseiou.* Athens: Tameio Archaiologikon Porōn kai Apallotriōseōn Dieuthunsē Dēmosieumatōn, 1997.

Rompay, Lucas van. "De ethiopische versie van het Kindheidsevangelie volgens Thomas de Israëliet." In *L'enfant dans les civilisations orientales,* ed. A. Théodorides, P. Naster, and J. Ries, 119–32. Louvain: Peeters, 1980.

Rosén, Thomas. *The Slavonic Translation of the Apocryphal Infancy Gospel of Thomas.* Acta Universitatis Upsaliensis, Studia Slavica Upsaliensia, 39. Uppsala: Uppsala University; Stockholm: Almqvist and Wiksell International, 1997.

Rosset, François. "'False' and 'True': Infancy and Apocryphal Gospels in the Century of Voltaire." In *Infancy Gospels: Stories and Identities,* ed. C. Clivaz et al., 628–40.

Rossi, Giovanni Battista de. "Vaso fittile con simboli ed epigrafe abecedarian trovato in Caragine presso un battistero." *Bullettino di archeologia Cristiana,* ser. III, anno 6, fasc. 4 (1881), 125–46.

Rothstein, Edward. "How Childhood Has Changed! (Adults, Too)." *New York Times* (February 14, 1998), B7 and B9.

Rouwhorst, Gerard. "The Roots of the Early Christian Eucharist: Jewish Blessings or Hellenistic Symposia?" In *Jewish and Christian Liturgy and Worship: New Insights into its History and Interaction,* ed. A. Gerhards and C. Leonhard, 295–308. Jewish and Christian Perspectives 15. Leiden: Brill, 2007.

Rubenstein, Jeffrey. *Stories of the Babylonian Talmud.* Baltimore: Johns Hopkins University Press, 2010.

Rubin, D. C. *Memory in Oral Traditions: The Cognitive Psychology of Epic, Ballads, and Counting-Out Rhymes*. Oxford: Oxford University Press, 1995.

Rudloff, Diether. *Zillis: Die romanische Bilderdecke der Kirche St. Martin*. Basel: Peter Heman, 1989.

Ruoff, Ulrich, and Mathias Seifert. "Neustes zur Datierung der Bildtafeln." In Rudloff, *Zillis*, 170–71.

Russell, D. A. *Greek Declamation*. Cambridge: Cambridge University Press, 1983.

Sa'di, Lutfi M. "A Biobibliographical Study of Hunayn Ibn Is-haq al-Ibadi (Johannitius) (800–877 A.D.)." *Bulletin of the Institute of the History of Medicine* 2.7 (1934), 409–46. Reprinted in *Ḥunain Ibn Isḥāq (d. 260/873): Texts and Studies*. Ed. Fuat Sezgin. Islamic Medicine 23, 275–312. Frankfurt am Main: Institute for the History of Arabic-Islamic Science at the Johann Wolfgang Goethe University, 1996.

Sabra, A. I. "'Ilm al-ḥisāb." In *EI*[2] 3 (1971), 1138–41.

Saenger, Paul. "Silent Reading: Its Impact on Late Medieval Script and Literacy." *Viator* 13 (1982), 367–414.

———. *Spaces Between Words: The Origins of Silent Reading*. Stanford: Stanford University Press, 1997.

Salama-Carr, Myriam. *Traduction à l'époque abbasside: L'école de Ḥunayn Ibn Isḥāq et son importance pour la traduction*. Paris: Didier erudition, 1990.

Saliba, George. *A History of Arabic Astronomy: Planetary Theories during the Golden Age of Islam*. New York and London: New York University Press, 1994.

Saller, Sylvester J., and Bellarmino Bagatti. *The Town of Nebo (Khirbet al-Mekhayyat) with a Brief Survey of Other Ancient Christian Monuments in Transjordan*. Publications of the Studium Biblicum Franciscanum 7. Jerusalem: Franciscan, 1949.

Salmon, Marilyn. "Hypothesis about First-Century Judaism and the Study of Luke-Acts." Ph.D dissertation, Hebrew Union College, 1985.

Sampley, J. Paul. *Paul in the Greco-Roman World: A Handbook*. Harrisburg, Pa.: Trinity International, 2003.

Sanders, Jack T. *The Jews in Luke-Acts*. Philadelphia: Fortress, 1987.

———. *Schismatics, Sectarians, Dissidents, Deviants: The First One Hundred Years of Jewish-Christian Relations*. London: SCM, 1993.

Santos Otero, Aurelio de, ed. *Das kirchenslavische Evangelium des Thomas*. PTS 6. Berlin: De Gruyter, 1967.

Savage-Smith, Emily. "Ṭibb: 1. Medicine in the Islamic World." In *EI*[2], ed. C. E. Bosworth, volume 10, 452a–60a. Leiden: Brill, 1980–2004.

Schäfer, Peter. "Introduction." In *Toledot Yeshu (The "Life Story of Jesus") Revisited*, ed. P. Schäfer, M. Meerson, and Y. Deutsch, 1–11.

———. *Jesus in the Talmud*. Princeton: Princeton University Press, 2007.

———. *Mirror of His Beauty: Feminine Images of God from the Bible to the Early Kabbalah*. Princeton: Princeton University Press, 2002.

Schäfer, Peter, Michael Meerson, and Yaacov Deutsch, eds. *Toledot Yeshu (The "Life Story of Jesus") Revisited*. Texts and Studies in Ancient Judaism 143. Tübingen: Mohr Siebeck, 2011.

Schenkeveld, Dirk M. "Letter to the Editor." *Times Literary Supplement* (March 22, 1991), 13.

———. "Prose Usages of ἀκούειν." *Classical Quarterly* 42 (1992), 129–41.

Scherer, J. *Entretien d'Origène avec Héraclide et les évêques ses collègues sur le Père, le Fils, et l'âme.* Publications de la Société Fouad I de Papyrologie, Texts and Documents IX. Cairo: L'Institut français d'archéologie orientale, 1949.

Schindler, Alfred. *Apokryphen zum Alten und Neuen Testament.* Second ed. Zürich: Manesse, 1988.

Schlichting, Günter. *Die verschollene Toledot-Jeschu-Fassung Tam ū-mūʿād: Einleitung, Text, Übersetzung, Kommentar, Motivsynopse, Bibliographie.* WUNT 24. Tübingen: Mohr Siebeck, 1982.

Schmahl, Günther. "Lk 2,41–52 und die Kindheitserzählung des Thomas 19,1–5: Ein Vergleich." *Bibel und Leben* 15 (1974), 249–58.

Schmeling, G., ed. *The Novel in the Ancient World.* Second ed. Leiden: Brill, 2003.

Schmidt, Siegfried J. "Memory and Remembrance: A Constructivist Approach." In *A Companion to Cultural Memory Studies,* ed. A. Erll and A. Nünning, 191–201.

Schmitz, Leonhard. "Agon." In *Dictionary of Greek and Roman Biography and Mythology,* ed. William Smith, volume 1, 74. Boston: Little, Brown, 1867.

Schneemelcher, Wilhelm, ed. *New Testament Apocrypha.* 2 volumes. Trans. R. M. Wilson. Cambridge: James Clarke; Louisville: Westminster/John Knox, 1991.

Schneider, Gerhard. *Evangelia infantiae apocrypha—Apokryphe Kindheitsevangelien.* Fontes christiani 18. Freiburg im Breisgau and New York: Herder, 1995.

Schoeps, Hans Joachim. *Theologie und Geschichte des Judenchristentums.* Tübingen: Mohr Siebeck, 1949.

Scholem, Gershom Gerhard. *Origins of the Kabbalah.* Princeton: Princeton University Press, 1990.

Schonfield, Hugh J. *According to the Hebrews: A New Translation of the Jewish Life of Jesus.* London: Duckworth, 1937.

———. *Readings from the Apocryphal Gospels.* London: Thomas Nelson, 1940.

Schroeder, Caroline T. "Child Sacrifice in Egyptian Monastic Culture: From Familial Renunciation to Jephthah's Lost Daughter." *Journal of Early Christian Studies* 20.2 (2012), 269–302.

———. "Children and Early Egyptian Monasticism." In *Children in Late Ancient Christianity,* ed. C. B. Horn and R. R. Phenix, 317–38.

———. "Monastic Family Values: The Healing of Children in Late Antique Egypt." *Coptica* 10 (2011), 21–8.

———. "Queer Eye for the Ascetic Guy? Homoeroticism, Children, and the Making of Monks." *Journal of the American Academy of Religion* 77.2 (2009), 333–47.

Schweizer, Eduard. "Slaves of the Elements and Worshipers of Angels: Gal 4:3, 9 and Col 2:8, 18, 20." *Journal of Biblical Studies* 107.3 (1988), 455–68.

Schwertheim, E. *Die Inschriften von Kyzikos und Umgebung.* Volume 1. Bonn: Habelt, 1980.

Scobie, Alex. *Apuleius and Folklore.* London: Folklore Society, 1983.

Scott, E. *The Archaeology of Infancy and Infant Death.* Oxford: Archaeopress, 1999.

Seale, M. S. "The Mysterious Letters in the Qur'an." In *Akten des XXIV Internationalen Orientalisten-Kongresses: München 28. August bis 4. September 1957,* 276–79. Wiesbaden: Steiner, 1959.

Sessa, Kristina. *The Formation of Papal Authority in Late Antique Italy: Roman Bishops and the Domestic Sphere.* Cambridge: Cambridge University Press, 2012.

Setzer, Claudia. *Jewish Responses to Early Christians: History and Polemics, 30–150 C.E.* Minneapolis: Fortress, 1994.

Sezgin, Fuat. *Geschichte des arabischen Schrifttums.* 15 volumes. Leiden: Brill, 1967–2007. [=*GAS*]

Sezgin, Fuat, ed. *Ḥunain Ibn Isḥāq (d. 260/873): Texts and Studies.* Islamic Medicine 23. Frankfurt am Main: Institute for the History of Arabic-Islamic Science at the Johann Wolfgang Goethe University, 1996.

Shaked, Shaul. "The Poetics of Spells: Language and Structure in Aramaic Incantations of Late Antiquity 1: The Divorce Formula and Its Ramifications." In *Mesopotamian Magic: Textual, Historical, and Interpretive Perspectives,* ed. Tzvi Abusch and Karel van der Toorn, 173–95. Groningen: Styx, 1999.

Sheingorn, Pamela. "Reshapings of the Childhood Miracles of Jesus." In *The Christ Child in Medieval Culture: Alpha es et O!* ed. M. Dzon and T. M. Kennedy, 254–92. Toronto: University of Toronto Press, 2012.

Shiner, Whitney. *Proclaiming the Gospel: First-Century Performance of Mark.* Harrisburg, Pa.: Trinity International, 2003.

Shoemaker, Stephen J. *The Death of a Prophet: The End of Muhammad's Life and the Beginnings of Islam.* Philadelphia: University of Pennsylvania Press, 2011.

Siegert, Folker. *Der Erstenwurf des Johannes: Das ursprüngliche, judenchristliche Johannesevangelium in deutscher Übersetzung vorgestellt.* Institutum Judaicum Delitzschianum, Münsteraner Judaistische Studien 16. Münster: LIT, 2004.

———. *Synopse der vorkanonischen Jesusüberlieferungen: Zeichenquelle und Passionsbericht, die Logienquelle und der Grundbestand des Markusevangeliums in deutscher Übersetzung gegenübergestellt.* Schriften des Institutum Judaicum Delitzschianum 8.1. Göttingen: Vandenhoeck und Ruprecht, 2010.

Siker, Jeffrey S. "Gnostic Views on Jews and Christians in the Gospel of Philip." *Novum Testamentum* 31.3 (1989), 275–88.

Silberstein, Laurence J., ed. *Mapping Jewish Identities.* New York: New York University Press, 2000.

Simon, Erika. "Karren mit Bronzereliefs, 'Tensa Capitolina' (966)." In *Führer durch die öffentlichen Sammlungen klassischer Altertümer in Rom,* fourth ed., ed. W. Helbig and H. Speier, volume 2, 357–60, no. 1546. Tübingen: Ernst Wasmuth, 1963–1972.

Simon, Richard. *Nouvelles observations sur le texte et les versions du Nouveau Testament.* Volume 1. Paris: Jean Boudot, 1695. Reprinted Frankfurt am Main: Minerva, 1973.

Simonett, Christoph. "Ist Zillis die Römerstation Lapidaria?" *Bündner Monatsblatt* (1938), 321–35,

———. "Eine Schamser Landschaft in den Deckengemälden der Zilliser Decke." *Bündner Monatsblatt* (1957), 116–19.

Simonett, Jürg. "Zillis." In *Historisches Lexicon der Schweiz.* http://www.hls-dhs-dss.ch/textes/d/D1512.php (accessed July 11, 2013).

Skarsaune, Oskar, and Reidar Hvalvik, eds. *Jewish Believers in Jesus.* Peabody, Mass.: Hendrickson, 2007.

Slemon, Stephon. "Unsettling the Empire: Resistance Theory for the Second World." In *Post-colonial Studies Reader,* ed. B. Ashcroft, G. Griffiths, and H. Tiffin, 104–10.

Slusser, Michael. "Reading Silently in Antiquity." *Journal of Biblical Literature* 111 (1992), 499.

Small, Jocelyn Penny. *Wax Tablets of the Mind: Cognitive Studies of Memory and Literacy in Classical Antiquity.* London: Routledge, 1997.

Smith, D. Moody. *The Theology of the Gospel of John.* Cambridge: Cambridge University Press, 1995.

Smith, Dennis E. *From Symposium to Eucharist: The Banquet in the Early Christian World.* Minneapolis: Augsburg Fortress, 2003.

Smith, Margaret. *Studies in Early Mysticism in the Near and Middle East.* London: Sheldon; New York: Macmillan, 1931; repr. Oxford: Oneworld, 1995.

Smith, Morton. *Jesus the Magician.* New York: Harper and Row, 1978.

Sokoloff, Michael. "The Date and Provenance of the Aramaic *Toledot Yeshu* on the Basis of Aramaic Dialectology." In *Toledot Yeshu ("The Life Story of Jesus") Revisited,* ed. P. Schäfer et al., 13–26.

Solzbacher, Rudolf. *Mönche, Pilger und Sarazenen: Studien zum Frühchristentum auf der südlichen Sinaihalbinsel von den Anfängen bis zum Beginn islamischer Herrschaft.* Münsteraner Theologische Abhandlungen 3. Altenberge: Telos, 1989.

Sorabella, Jean. "Eros and the Lizard: Children, Animals, and Roman Funerary Sculpture." In *Constructions of Childhood,* ed. A. Cohen and J. Rutter, 353–70.

Souissi, M. "Ḥisāb al-ghubār." In *EI*² 3 (1971), 468–69.

———. "'Ilm al-handasa." In *EI*² Supplement (2004), 411–14.

Souter, Alexander, ed. *A Glossary of Later Latin to 600 A.D.* Oxford: Clarendon, 1949.

Speyer, W. "Fluch." *RAC* 7 (1969), 1160–1288.

Spivak, Gayatri Chakravorty. "Can the Subaltern Speak?" In *Post-colonial Studies Reader,* ed. B. Ashcroft, G. Griffiths, and H. Tiffin, 24–28.

Stanford, W. B. *The Sound of Greek.* Berkeley: University of California Press, 1967.

Stanton, Graham. *Jesus and Gospel.* Cambridge: Cambridge University Press, 2004.

Starr, Raymond. "*Lectores* and Book Reading." *Classical Journal* 86 (1990–91), 337–43.

Steenberg, M. C. "Children in Paradise: Adam and Eve as 'Infants' in Irenaeus of Lyons." *Journal of Early Christian Studies* 12.1 (2004), 1–22.

Stephens, Susan A. "Who Read the Ancient Novels?" In *The Search for the Ancient Novel,* ed. J. Tatum, 405–18.

Sternberger, Günter. *Einleitung in Talmud und Midrasch.* Eighth ed. Munich: C. H. Beck, 1992.

Stowe, C. E. *Origin and History of the Books of the Bible.* Boston: American Unitarian Association, 1867.

Stowers, Stanley K. *A Reading of Romans: Justice, Jews, and Gentiles.* New Haven: Yale University Press, 1994.

———. "Romans 7:7–25 as a Speech-in-Character (προσωποποιία)." In *Paul in His Hellenistic Context,* ed. T. Engberg-Pedersen, 180–202. Minneapolis: Fortress, 1995.

Strange, W. A. *Children in the Early Church.* Carlisle, U.K.: Paternoster, 1996; repr. Eugene, Ore.: Wipf and Stock, 2004.

Street, Brian, ed. *Cross-Cultural Approaches to Literacy.* Cambridge: Cambridge University Press, 1993.

———. "Literacy Practices and Literacy Myths." In *The Written World: Studies in Literate Thought and Action,* ed. R. Saljo, 59–72. Berlin: Springer, 1988.

Strohmaier, G. "Ḥunayn b. Isḥāḳ al-'Ibādī." In *EI*[2] 3 (1971), 578–81.

Stroumsa, Guy. "A Nameless God: Judaeo-Christian and Gnostic 'Theologies of the Name.' " In *The Image of the Judaeo-Christians in Ancient Jewish and Christian Literature,* ed. P. J. Tomson and D. Lambers-Petry, 230–43. Tübingen: Mohr Siebeck, 2003.

Strubbe, J. H. M. *Arai epitymbioi: Imprecations against Desecrators of the Grave in the Greek Epitaphs of Asia Minor: A Catalogue.* Bonn: R. Habelt, 1997.

———. "Cursed be he that moves my bones." In *Magika Hiera: Ancient Greek Magic and Religion,* ed. C. A. Faraone and D. Obbink, 33–59. New York and Oxford: Oxford University Press, 1991.

———. "Curses against Violation of the Grave in Jewish Epitaphs of Asia Minor." In *Studies of Early Jewish Epigraphy,* ed. Jan Willem Van Henten and Pieter Willem van der Horst, 70–128. Leiden: Brill, 1994.

———. "Epigrams and Consolation Decrees for Deceased Youths." *L'Antiquité classique* 67 (1998), 45–95.

Sundberg, Albert C. Jr. "Towards a Revised History of the New Testament Canon." *Studia evangelica* 4.1 (1968), 452–61.

Svenbro, Jesper. *Phrasikleia: An Anthropology of Reading in Ancient Greece.* Trans. J. Lloyd. Ithaca: Cornell University Press, 1993.

Swain, Simon. *Hellenism and Empire: Language, Classicism, and Power in the Classical World, AD 50–250.* Oxford: Clarendon, 1996.

Sweet, Waldo E. *Sport and Recreation in Ancient Greece: A Sourcebook with Translations.* New York and Oxford: Oxford University Press, 1987.

Talbert, Charles H. "Prophecies of Future Greatness: The Contribution of Greco-Roman Biographies to an Understanding of Luke 1:5–4:15." In *The Divine Helmsman: Studies on God's Control of Human Events,* ed. J. L. Crenshaw and S. Sandmel, 129–41. New York: Ktav, 1980.

———. *What Is a Gospel? The Genre of the Canonical Gospels.* Philadelphia: Fortress, 1977.

Talbot, Alice-Mary. "The Death and Commemoration of Byzantine Children." In *Becoming Byzantine,* ed. A. Papaconstantinou and A.-M. Talbot, 283–307.

Tambiah, Stanley J. "The Magical Power of Words." *Man* 3 (1968), 175–208.

Tannehill, Robert. "The Disciples in Mark: The Function of a Narrative Role." *Journal of Religion* 57 (1977), 386–405

Tate, J. C. "Christianity and the Legal Status of Abandoned Children in the Later Roman Empire." *Journal of Law and Religion* 24 (2008), 123–41.

Tatum, James, ed. *The Search for the Ancient Novel.* Baltimore: Johns Hopkins University Press, 1994.

Taylor, Joan E. *Christians and the Holy Places: The Myth of Jewish Christian Origins.* Oxford: Clarendon Press, 1993.

———. "The Phenomenon of Early Jewish Christianity: Reality or Scholarly Invention." *Vigiliae Christianae* 44 (1990), 313–34.

Taylor, Rabun. "Tiber River Bridges and the Development of the Ancient City of Rome." In *The Waters of Rome* 2 (2002), 1–20 (available online at http://www.iath.virginia.edu/rome/Journal2TaylorNew.pdf).

Temporini, H., et al., eds. *Aufstieg und Niedergang der römischen Welt: Geschichte und Kultur Roms im Spiegel der neueren Forschung.* 37 volumes. Berlin and New York: De Gruyter, 1972–1998. [=ANRW]

Terian, Abraham. *The Armenian Gospel of the Infancy.* Oxford: Oxford University Press, 2008.

Testa, Emmanuelle. "Le grotte mistiche dei Nazareni e i loro riti battesimali." *Liber Annuus* 12 (1962), 5–45.

———. *Il simbolismo dei giudeo-cristiani.* Jerusalem: Tip. dei PP. Francescani, 1962.

Thatcher, Tom. "John's Memory Theatre: A Study of Composition in Performance." In *The Fourth Gospel in First-Century Media Culture,* ed. A. Le Donne and T. Thatcher, 73–91.

Thomas, Christine M. *The Acts of Peter, Gospel Literature, and the Ancient Novel: Rewriting the Past.* Oxford and New York: Oxford University Press, 2003.

Thomas, Rosalind. "Writing, Reading, Public and Private 'Literacies': Functional Literacy and Democratic Literacy in Greece." In *Ancient Literacies,* ed. W. A. Johnson and H. N. Parker, 13–45.

Thompson, D. W. *A Glossary of Greek Birds.* London: Oxford University Press, 1936.

Thomson, D. F. S. *Catullus.* Toronto: University of Toronto Press, 1997.

Tiede, David. *Prophecy and History in Luke-Acts.* Philadelphia: Fortress, 1980.

Tischendorf, Constantine von. *De evangeliorum apocryphorum origine et usu.* The Hague: Thierry and Mensing, 1851. Reprinted in *Synopsis Evangelica.* Leipzig: H. Mendelssohn, 1854.

———. *Evangelia apocrypha.* Leipzig: Avenarius and Mendelssohn, 1853. Second ed., 1876.

Tite, Philip L. *Valentinian Ethics and Paraenetic Discourse: Determining the Social Function of Moral Exhortation in Valentinian Christianity.* Nag Hammadi and Manichaean Studies 67. Leiden and Boston: Brill, 2009.

Tolan, John Victory. *Saracens: Islam in the Medieval European Imagination.* New York: Columbia University Press, 2002.

Tollius, Jakob. [Untitled article.] In *Monatliche Unterredungen einiger guten Freunde von allerhand Büchern und andern annehmlichen Geschichten, Juli,* ed. W. E. Tentzel, 537–610. Leipzig: Johann Christian Laurers, 1697.

Tolstoi, I. I. *Grecheskie Graffiti drevnikh Severnogo Prichernomoreya.* Moscow: Akademii nauk SSSR, 1953.

Too, Y. L., ed. *Education in Greek and Roman Antiquity.* Leiden: Brill, 2001.

Török, L. *Coptic Antiquities.* Volume 1. Bibliotheca Archeologica 11. Rome: "L'ERMA" di Bretschneider, 1993.

Tottoli, Roberto. *Biblical Prophets in the Qur'ān and Muslim Literature.* Richmond, Surrey: Curzon, 2002.

Trapido, Joel. "The Language of the Theatre: I. The Greeks and Romans." *Educational Theatre Journal* 1.1 (1949), 18–26.

Trier Landesmuseum website: http://www.landesmuseum-trier.de/de/home/shop/miniatur replikate.html (accessed July 11, 2013).

Tucker, Gene M. *Form Criticism of the Old Testament*. Philadelphia: Fortress, 1971.

Turner, E. G. *Greek Manuscripts of the Ancient World*. Bulletin of the Institute for Classical Studies. London: University of London, Institute for Classical Studies, 1952. Second ed., rev. and enlarged P. J. Parsons, 1987.

Tyson, Joseph B. *Images of Judaism in Luke-Acts*. Columbia: University of South Carolina Press, 1992.

———. "Jews and Judaism in Luke-Acts: Reading as a Godfearer." *New Testament Studies* 41 (1995), 19–38.

———. *Luke, Judaism, and the Scholars: Critical Approaches to Luke-Acts*. Columbia: University of South Carolina Press, 1999.

Ullmann, Manfred. *Islamic Medicine*. Edinburgh: Edinburgh University Press, 1978.

———. *Die Natur- und Geheimwissenschaften im Islam*. Ed. B. Spuler. Leiden: Brill, 1972.

Upson-Saia, Kristi. "Holy Child or Holy Terror? Understanding Jesus' Anger in the *Infancy Gospel of Thomas*." *Church History* 82.1 (2013), 1–39.

Usener, Herbert. "Aus Julian von Halikarnass." In *Kleine Schriften*, volume 4, 316–33. Leipzig and Berlin: B. G. Teubner, 1913.

Uzzi, Jeannine D. *Children in the Visual Arts of Imperial Rome*. New York: Cambridge University Press, 2005.

Vaglieri, L. V., and G. Celentano. "Trois epîtres d'al-Kindi." *Annali, Instituto Orientale di Napoli* 34, n.s. 24 (1974), 523–62.

Vallois, R. "APAI." *Bulletin de correspondance hellénique* 38 (1914), 250–71.

Variot, Joseph. *Les Évangiles apocryphes: Histoire littéraire, forme primitive, transformations*. Paris: Berche and Tralin, 1878.

Vermeer, G. F. M. *Observations sur le vocabulaire du pélerinage chez Egérie et chez Antonin de Plaisance*. Latinitas Christianorum Primaeva 19. Nijmegen: Dekker and Van de Vegt, 1965.

Versnel, H. S. "Beyond Cursing: The Appeal to Justice in Judicial Prayers." In *Magika Hiera*, ed. C. A. Faraone and D. Obbink, 60–106.

———. "'May he not be able to sacrifice . . .': Concerning a Curious Formula in Greek and Latin Curses." *ZPE* 58 (1985), 247–69.

———. "Religious Mentality in Ancient Prayer." In *Faith, Hope and Worship: Aspects of Religious Mentality in the Ancient World*, ed. H. S. Versnel, 1–64. Leiden: Brill, 1981.

Versteegh, C. H. M. "al-Zamakhsharī, Abu'l-Ḳāsim Maḥmūd b. 'Umar." in *EI*² 11 (2001), 431–34.

Veyne, Paul. "The Roman Empire." In *A History of Private Life: I. From Pagan Rome to Byzantium*, ed. P. Veyne, 5–234. Cambridge, Mass.: Harvard University Press, 1987.

Vielhauer, Philip. *Geschichte der urchristlichen Literatur: Einleitung in das Neue Testament, die Apokryphen und die Apostolischen Väter*. Berlin and New York: De Gruyter, 1975.

View of the World from 9th Avenue. *New Yorker*, cover image. March 29, 1976.

Vikan, Gary. "Pilgrims in Magi's Clothing: The Impact of Mimesis on Early Byzantine Pilgrimage Art." In *The Blessings of Pilgrimage,* ed. R. Ousterhout, 97–107. Urbana and Chicago: University of Illinois Press, 1990.

Voicu, Sever J. "Histoire de l'enfance de Jésus." In *Écrits apocryphes chrétiens,* volume 1, ed. F. Bovon and P. Geoltrain, 191–204. Paris: Gallimard, 1997.

———. "Notes sur l'histoire du texte de l'*Histoire de l'enfance de Jésus.*" *Apocrypha* (1991), 119–32.

———. "La tradition latine des *Paidika.*" *Bulletin de l'AELAC* 14 (2004), 13–21.

———. *Vangelo arabo dell'infanzia di Gesù.* Minima di Città Nuova. Rome: Città Nuova, 2002.

———. "Verso il testo primitivo dei Παιδικὰ τοῦ κυρίου Ἰησοῦ 'Racconti dell'infanzia del Signore Gesù.' " *Apocrypha* 9 (1998), 7–85.

———. "Ways to Survival for the Infancy Apocrypha." In *Infancy Gospels: Stories and Identities,* ed. C. Clivaz et al., 401–17.

Voll-Graff, W. "Elementum." *Mnemosyne* 4 (1949), 89–115.

Voltaire (=François-Marie Arouet). *Nouveaux mélanges philosophiques, historiques, critiques, etc.* 19 volumes. Geneva: Cramer, 1770–1776.

Vössing, Konrad. *Schule und Bildung im Nordafrika der römischen Kaiserzeit.* Collection Latomus. Brussels: Société d'Études Latines de Bruxelles, 1997.

Vuolanto, Ville. "Children and Asceticism: Strategies of Continuity in the Late Fourth and Early Fifth Centuries." In *Hoping for Continuity,* ed. K. Mustakallio et al., 119–32.

———. *Children in the Ancient World and the Early Middle Ages: A Bibliography (Eighth Century BC–Eighth Century AD).* Fifth ed. (2010), available online at http://uta-fi.academia.edu/VilleVuolanto/Papers/163757 (accessed July 11, 2013).

———. "Choosing Asceticism: Children and Parents, Vows and Conflicts." In *Children in Late Ancient Christianity,* ed. C. B. Horn and R. R. Phenix, 255–92.

Wagenseilus (Wagenseil), J. C. *Tela Ignea Satanae. hoc est Arcani, & horribiles Judaeorum adversus Christum Deum, & Christianum religionem libri.* Altdorf: J. H. Schönnerstaedt, 1681.

Walker, Jeffrey. *Rhetoric and Poetics in Antiquity.* New York and Oxford: Oxford University Press, 2000.

Wallace-Hadrill, Andrew. *Houses and Society in Pompeii and Herculaneum.* Princeton: Princeton University Press, 1994.

Walzer, R. "Djālīnūs." In *EI*[2] 3 (1971), 402.

Wansbrough, John. *Quranic Studies: Sources and Methods of Scriptural Interpretation.* Oxford: Oxford University Press, 1977. Second ed.: Amherst, N.Y.: Prometheus, 2004.

Warburg, Aby. *Der Bilderatlas Mnemosyne.* Ed. M. Warnke, with C. Brink. Berlin: Akademie, 2000.

———. *Die Erneuerung der heidnischen Antike: Kulturwissenschaftliche Beiträge zur Geschichte der europäischen Renaissance.* Ed. H. Bredekamp and M. Diers. Berlin: Akademie, 1998.

Watts, D. "Infant Burials and Romano-British Christianity." *Archaeological Journal* 146 (1989), 372–83.

Watts, Edward J. *City and School in Late Antique Athens and Alexandria.* Berkeley and London: University of California Press, 2006.

Webb, Diana. *Medieval European Pilgrimage, c. 700–c. 1500.* New York: Palgrave, 2002.

Webster, Hutton. *Ancient History.* Boston: D. C. Heath, 1913.

Weinreich, O. "Heros Propylaios und Apollon Propylaios." *Athenische Mitteilungen* 38 (1913), 62–72.

Weinstock, Stefan. *Divus Julius.* Oxford: Clarendon, 1971.

Welch, A. T. "al-Ḳur'ān." In *EI*[2] 5 (1986), 412–14.

Wells, Karen. *Childhood in a Global Perspective.* Cambridge, U.K., and Malden, Mass.: Polity, 2009.

Welzer, Harald. *Das kommunikative Gedächtnis: Eine Theorie der Erinnerung.* Munich: Beck, 2002.

Werner, Shirley. "Literacy Studies in Classics: The Last Twenty Years." In *Ancient Literacies: The Culture of Reading in Greece and Rome,* ed. W. A. Johnson and H. N. Parker, 333–84.

Wesseling, Berber. "The Audience of the Ancient Novel." In *Groningen Colloquia on the Novel,* ed. H. Hofmann, volume 1, 69–79. Groningen: Egbert Forsten, 1988.

Whipple, A. O. "Role of the Nestorians as the Connecting Link between Greek and Arabic Medicine." *Annals of Medical History,* n.s. 8 (1936), 313–23.

White, L. Michael. *Building God's House in the Roman World: Architectural Adaptation among Pagans, Jews, and Christians.* Baltimore: Published for the American Schools of Oriental Research by Johns Hopkins University Press, 1990.

Whitmarsh, Tim. "Introduction." In *The Cambridge Companion to the Greek and Roman Novel,* ed. T. Whitmarsh, 1–14.

Wiedemann, Thomas. *Adults and Children in the Roman Empire.* New Haven and London: Yale University Press, 1989.

Wilcox, Judith. "The Transmission and Influence of Qusta ibn Luqa's 'On the Difference between Spirit and Soul.'" Ph.D. dissertation, City University of New York, 1985.

Wilde, Rober. *The Treatment of the Jews in the Greek Christian Writers of the First Three Centuries.* Washington, D.C.: Catholic University of America Press, 1949.

Wilken, Robert L. *The Land Called Holy: Palestine in Christian History and Thought.* New Haven: Yale University Press, 1992.

Wilkinson, Louise J., ed. *Cultural History of Childhood. Volume 2: In the Middle Ages.* Oxford and New York: Berg, 2010.

Williams, Joel F. *Other Followers of Jesus: Minor Characters as Major Figures in Mark's Gospel.* Sheffield: JSOT/Sheffield Academic, 1994.

Williams, Margaret H. "Image and Text in the Jewish Epitaphs of Late Ancient Rome." *Journal for the Study of Judaism* 42 (2011), 328–50.

Wilmart, A., and E. Tisserant. "Fragments grecs et latins de l'Évangile de Barthélemy." *Revue Biblique* 10 (1913), 161–90, and 321–68.

Wilson, Robert McLachlan. "Apokryphen, II: Apokryphen des Neuen Testaments." In *Theologische Realenzyklopädie,* volume 3, 326–62. Berlin: De Gruyter, 1978.

Wilson, Stephen. *Related Strangers: Jews and Christians 70–170 C.E.* Minneapolis: Fortress, 1995.

Wink, Walter. "The 'Elements of the Universe' in Biblical and Scientific Perspective." *Zygon* 13.3 (1978), 225–48.

Winkler, John J. *The Constraints of Desire: The Anthropology of Sex and Gender in Ancient Greece.* New York: Routledge, 1990.

Winterbottom, Michael. "Schoolroom and Courtroom." In *Rhetoric Revalued: Papers from the International Society for the History of Rhetoric,* ed. B. Vickers, Medieval and Renaissance Texts and Studies, volume 19, 59–70. Binghamton, N.Y.: Center for Medieval and Early Renaissance Studies, 1982.

Wipszycka, Ewa. "Review of Books." *Journal of Juristic Papyrology* 27 (1997), 171–72.

Wire, Antoinette. "Jesus Retold as the World's Light in Johannine Oral Prophecy." In *The Fourth Gospel in First-Century Media Culture,* ed. A. Le Donne and T. Thatcher, 121–32.

Wohleb, L. "Ein Beitrag zur Geschichte des lauten Lesens." *Philologus* 85 (1929), 111–12.

Worrell, W. H. "Qusṭā ibn Lūqā on the Use of the Celestial Globe." *Isis* 35.4 (1944), 285–93.

Wortmann, Dierk. "Neue magische Texte." *Bonner Jahrbücher des Rheinischen Landesmuseums in Bonn* 168 (1968), 56–111.

Wünsch, Richard. "The Limestone Inscriptions of Tell Sandahannah." In *Excavations in Palestine during the Years 1898–1900,* ed. F. J. Bliss and R. A. S. Macalister, 173–76. London: Committee of the Palestine Exploration Fund, 1902.

———. *Sethianische Verfluchungstafeln aus Rom.* Leipzig: B. G. Teubner, 1898.

Wyse, Dominic, ed. *Childhood Studies: An Introduction.* Oxford: Blackwell, 2004.

Young, M. J. L., J. D. Latham, and R. B. Serjeant, eds. *Religion, Learning and Science in the 'Abbasid Period.* Cambridge and New York: Cambridge University Press, 1990.

Zahn, Theodor. *Geschichte des Neutestamentlichen Kanons.* 2 volumes. Erlangen and Leipzig: Andreas Deichert, 1888–1892.

Zarcone, T., J. O. Hunwick, C. Ernst, F. de Jong, L. Massignon-[B. Radtke], and F. Aubin. "Taṣawwuf (a.)." In *EI*[2] 10 (1998), 313–32.

Zeitlin, Froma. "Religion." In *The Cambridge Companion to the Greek and Roman Novel,* ed. T. Whitmarsh, 91–108.

Zias, J. "A Roman Tomb at 'Ar'ara." *'Atiqot: English Series* 14 (1980), 63–65.

Ziebarth, Erich. *Aus dem griechischen Schulwesen: Eudemos vom Milet und Verwandtes.* Second ed. Leipzig and Berlin: B. G. Teubner, 1914.

Index